employed as work and workers moved out of the fields into the closed-in world of the carding room and the spinning mule, the power loom and the mill office. And he brings to light the sometimes violent, always impassioned, battle for the soul of the mill worker that was the direct result of these new relationships: on the one side, the exponents of the Enlightenment and Utopian Socialism; on the other, the ultimately triumphant champions of evangelical Christianity.

In his historical exploration of Rockdale, with its richness of local documents, Wallace has recovered in concrete human and technical detail the real impact of the Industrial Revolution on the individual lives and social forms of a community.

A unique and major work of scholarship from a distinguished and greatly acclaimed anthropologist.

Anthony F. C. Wallace was born in Toronto, Canada, in 1923 and did both his undergraduate and graduate work at the University of Pennsylvania (Ph.D. 1950). He has been a Professor of Anthropology at the University of Pennsylvania since 1961. Mr. Wallace also serves as a Medical Research Scientist at the Eastern Pennsylvania Psychiatric Institute. He has written four books: *King of the Delawares: Teedyuscung; Culture and Personality; Religion: An Anthropological View;* and *The Death and Rebirth of the Seneca.* He lives near Philadelphia with his wife and children.

Also by ANTHONY F. C. WALLACE

The Death and Rebirth of the Seneca (1970)

Religion: An Anthropological View (1966)

Culture and Personality (1961, 1970)

King of the Delawares: Teedyuscung, 1700–1763 (1949)

ROCKDALE

ROCKDALE

*The growth of an American village
in the early Industrial Revolution*

*An account of the coming of the machines, the
making of a new way of life in the mill hamlets,
the triumph of evangelical capitalists over
socialists and infidels, and the transformation of
the workers into Christian soldiers in a cotton-
manufacturing district in Pennsylvania in the
years before and during the Civil War* ✕

ANTHONY F. C. WALLACE

TECHNICAL DRAWINGS BY ROBERT HOWARD

Alfred A. Knopf, New York, 1978

THIS IS A BORZOI BOOK
PUBLISHED BY ALFRED A. KNOPF, INC.

Copyright © 1972, 1978 by Anthony F. C. Wallace
All rights reserved under International and Pan-American Copyright Conventions.
Published in the United States by Alfred A. Knopf, Inc., New York, and simultane-
ously in Canada by Random House of Canada Limited, Toronto. Distributed by
Random House, Inc., New York.

The appendix, "Paradigmatic Processes in Culture Change," was originally
published, in slightly different form, in the American Anthropologist,
74: 467–478, 1972.

Permissions to reproduce photographs and other illustrations are given on pages
xi–xiii.

Library of Congress Cataloging in Publication Data
Wallace, Anthony F   C   [date]   Rockdale.
Bibliography: p.   Includes index.
1. Cotton trade—Pennsylvania—Rockdale—History.
2. Rockdale, Pa.—Industries—History.
3. Rockdale, Pa.—Social conditions.
4. Rockdale, Pa.—Religious life and customs—History.   I. Title.
HD9878.R6W34   1978   974.8′14   77–20346
ISBN 0–394–42120–5

Manufactured in the United States of America

First Edition

To Monty, Dan, Sun Ai, and Sammy,
who explored the mills and streams with me

CONTENTS

Contents

Contents

Contents

PART FOUR

ROCKDALE FROM 1850 TO 1865 · THE TRANSCENDING OF A WAY OF LIFE

ILLUSTRATIONS

Illustrations

PREFACE

This book tells the story of a small American community, with a population of about two thousand souls, between the years 1825 and 1865. It is not a community with a conspicuous history; none of its residents achieved national prominence during those forty years. No famous battles were fought there; it was not particularly unique in its industry or its society. It initially attracted my interest because I lived there and was curious about the old mills and tenements that lined the creek at the bottom of the hill. But as I came to know the sources and personalities and events, this piece of local, grass-roots history became, for me, a fascinating journey into the past.

No historical or ethnographic writing can be done as a piece of "pure" description; there is always a set of more or less articulate assumptions, theories, hypotheses, methodological principles that guide the selection of sources, determine the points of emphasis, and decide the experience of closure. In this case, the requisite theoretical framework turned out to be more complex than I had expected. Minimally, I was anxious to see to what extent the concepts of the cultural anthropologist, who is used to conducting fieldwork with living informants in a small community over a one- or two-year period, could be applied to the documentary remains of a community of about the same size during a generation. At first I attempted to supplement the documentary sources with "oral history" interviews but found that, by and large, the distance into the past was too great to enable me to recover much verifiable information. This study therefore is based on written documents and drawings and on the personal observation of mill seats and buildings.

But small communities, no matter how primitive, are never really isolated, and in the case of a nineteenth-century cotton-manufacturing town, its significant environment was, literally, the entire world, for the manufacturers, and through them the workers, responded directly to economic and political events occurring in the lower Delaware Valley, in the United

States as a whole, and even in India, China, Africa, Latin America, and of course Europe. In order to understand Rockdale, it is necessary to have some grasp of the social processes going on around it—in other words, to have a theory of American, if not world, history. In this case, the significant processes were the course of the Industrial Revolution, the transformation of Enlightenment liberalism into early Utopian socialism, and the evangelical millennialist enthusiasm which, allied with Western economic and military power, was driving the industrial nations toward the conquest of the world.

And beyond this, there is an even more general theoretical frame—the notion of the way in which self-contained developments in science and technology affect the host society. The general theory of paradigmatic processes in culture change guided my initial formulation of the historiographic problem and the structure of the book. My technical paper on this topic is included as an Appendix to this book.

But what I did not really expect, and found to my considerable surprise, was the presence of "plot"—that is to say, an organized structure of conflict among the main participants in the story that required a period of time before the strategies of the sides combined toward resolution. It is this structure of conflict, among named persons about whom considerable information remains, that has made the work a poignant chronicle of struggles between well-intentioned men and women all striving toward a better age. From the diaries, memoirs, personal correspondence, letters to newspaper editors, and even business ledgers emerges a world of motives, of hopes and fears, of loves and hates, which lies just beyond our lives, but from which much of the character of our lives has been drawn.

My initial concern was whether the sources would be adequate, whether it would be possible to find enough information about one small manufacturing district to put together anything of any interest at all about its experience in the Industrial Revolution. The sources available in standard repositories turned out to be adequate for useful study, even in this microhistorical scale; in some respects, they are embarrassingly rich. For instance, concerning the major manufacturers, there exist both a published autobiography (privately printed) of the leading manufacturer, John P. Crozer, and a competent biography, based on his lost diary and containing liberal quotations from it, plus miscellaneous letters and business correspondence of his own and of his family. There is a semi-autobiographical history of Chester and vicinity by John Hill Martin, the son of William Martin, another early manufacturer, filled with local anecdote and genealogy; John Hill Martin was a devoted local family historian who joined the Historical Society of Pennsylvania and left it his own memoirs and various family papers, including his father's receipt book during the years he operated a cotton mill. There are apparently no collections of personal papers of Samuel Riddle the elder, but by some miracle business papers survive, including a daybook of 1832–35, a rent book for the tenements, and a paybook for one of the mills from 1846 to 1850. The Peale-Sellers Papers at the American Philosophical Society Library include some of the papers of Peter Hill, William Martin's partner, who married Nathan Sellers' daughter Hannah and thus acquired control of the two Chester Creek mills that Nathan bought shortly before his death. There are extensive papers of two cotton mill families preserved among the Du Pont papers at Eleutherian Mills Historical Library because of the affinal and friendship relationships among the Du Ponts, the Lammots, and the Richard S. Smiths. Some of these collections are voluminous: the correspondence of Clementina Smith, who lived in Rockdale off and on from 1832 to her death in the 1880's, includes about two thousand letters. There is a Du Pont family diary—the Tancopanican Chronicle—which records the unsuccessful courtship of Sophie du Pont by a free-thinking young cotton manufacturer, John S. Phillips. There are genealogies of the leading families. There are two local newspapers with extensive runs throughout the period preserved by the Delaware County Historical Society. There are letter-series from families of working people employed in the mills. And there are the expected standard official records: county and state archives, including tax records, wills, probate inventories; birth, baptismal, and burial records in local churches; U.S. decennial census schedules in the National Archives. And finally, there is an excellent county history by Henry Ashmead, a local resident, and several good maps from about 1810 on, including a fine real estate map of Delaware County by Joshua Ash made in 1848.

My gratitude goes out to many people and institutions who have helped me in this study. My principal debt is owing to Mr. Richmond D. Williams, Mrs. Betty-Bright Low, Mr. Robert Howard, Dr. Eugene Ferguson, Dr. Norman B. Wilkinson, Mrs. Carol B. Hallman, Mrs. Susan Danko, and other members of the staff of the Eleutherian Mills Historical Library, where many of the most valuable manuscript holdings and technological works were drawn to my attention and made available to me. I am also particularly grateful to Mr. Samuel Newsome, former president of the Delaware County Historical Society, and the staff at the library of Widener College in Chester, Pennsylvania; to Mr. J. W. Vitty of the Belfast Library and Society for Promoting Knowledge, Ireland; to Mr. Peter Parker, at the Manuscript Room of the Historical Society of Pennsylvania; to Ms. Martha Simonetti and Ms. Barbara Philpott of the Pennsylvania State Archives; to Ms. Miriam Reynolds of the Delaware County Institute of Science; to Ms.

Mary Patterson of Historic Delaware County Society; to Mr. Robert Montgomery of the Tyler Arboretum; to Dr. Whitfield Bell and Dr. Murphy Smith of the Library of the American Philosophical Society; to Ms. Helena Wright of the Merrimack Valley Textile Museum; and to Ms. Aline Bradley of the Library of the Workingmen's Institute, New Harmony, Indiana. Mr. Harold Rackley kindly showed me through the Halifax Cotton Mill of South Boston, Virginia, where cotton is still processed from the bale to finished cloth. Valued institutional support was given by the University of Pennsylvania, which provided a sabbatical year in 1972–73, by the National Science Foundation for research grant SOC 72–05293 during the years 1972–77, and by the Haas Community Fund Foundation of Philadelphia for a grant in 1970–71.

I owe special thanks to a group of research assistants and student seminar participants who contributed greatly to the project over the years, particularly Dr. Christine Lemieux, Dr. David Kasserman, Dr. Janet Robison, Mr. Robert King, Ms. Pam Crabtree, Mr. Michael Replogle, Mr. Douglas Dinsmore, Mr. Gary Dunn, Ms. Wendy Pollock, Dr. Richard Horowitz, Dr. Marshall Becker, Ms. Diane Walters, Ms. Jean Lesnick, Mr. Bertrand Masquelier, Ms. Marilyn Crill Auchincloss, Ms. Sandra Marks, Ms. JoAnn Bromberg, Dr. David Gilmore, Mr. Steven Lott, Ms. Jean Smithe, Mr. Stephen Del Sordo, and Mr. Steven Ostrakh, all of whom contributed data and ideas. Readers of chapters of the manuscript who helped the writer avoid unnecessary errors and clichés include Ms. Betty-Bright Low, Mr. Robert Howard and his father Mr. George Howard of Taylor Instrument Company, Dr. Hilda Greenwald, Dr. Eugene Ferguson, Dr. Bruce Sinclair, and Dr. Norman B. Wilkinson. Dr. Regina Flesch helped me in identifying and characterizing the fabrics produced. Mr. Walter M. Phillips of Philadelphia, Mr. Clifford Lewis III of Media, Mr. Mark Wilcox, Jr., of Ivy Mills, and Dr. Peter Sellers of Philadelphia very generously shared family records of ancestors who were residents and owners or manufacturers in early Rockdale. The Reverend Mr. David A. McQueen of Upland Baptist Church, the Reverend Mr. James F. McKendrick of Calvary Episcopal Church, the Reverend Mr. George W. Eppeheimer, Jr., of Mount Hope Methodist Church, the Reverend Mr. John W. Gilbert and Mr. George Felton of Lima Methodist Church, and the Reverend Mr. Ray Pinch of the Middletown Presbyterian Church all very kindly made available to me or to my assistant Christine Lemieux valuable materials from their church records. Mr. J. E. Rhoads of Wilmington, Delaware, provided an illuminating discussion of the philosophy of manufacturing in the older American corporation. To the present-day community of the Rockdale manufacturing district, I owe a general debt of gratitude for their patience in allowing me to wander through the various properties, taking photographs and asking questions.

Today the seven mill hamlets still remain and still bear their old names. Descendants of the first immigrant weavers from Lancashire still occupy old stone houses on English Hill, above West Branch; other working families, heirs of nineteenth-century operatives whose names appear in the old day-books and paybooks, live in houses scattered up and down the hills. Knowlton Mill was long ago washed away again, not to be rebuilt, and its place is only a grassy meadow; but the old mansion house still looms on the cliff above the stream, and a few of the stone tenements still stand in a row along the road that runs steeply up the hill to Village Green. All of the other mill structures house active businesses, although the early stone factory is often today embedded in accretions of sheds, extensions, and other improvements. At Rockdale, the old brick nail mill was torn down a few years ago, but the cotton mill still stands, now occupied by a lumber yard. The factory at Glen Riddle is used by the Sunroc Corporation, which manufactures water coolers, and when this study was begun, the old dam and race and part of the gateway system were intact. Some of these structures have been destroyed in recent years for reasons of public safety, but one of the Riddle mansions survives, still in use as a company office. West Branch, Lenni, and Parkmount were until 1972 used by the Aldon Rug Company; turbines were still in place in the wheelpits when this study commenced; all three suffered severe damage in the great flood of 1972 and the old stone factory at Parkmount was gutted by a fire in the following year. West Branch and Lenni are now occupied by, among other firms, the Westlake Plastics Corporation. Crozerville factory is intact but almost entirely surrounded by new structures of the Container Research Corporation.

Although in some cases their members have moved away, the presence of the great families is still felt in the district. All of the churches created during the evangelical movement are in good repair, with active congregations. The Willcoxes continue to occupy the tract about the grassy ruins of Ivy Mills; Darlingtons still live at Darlington Station, just north of the district. The son of Samuel Riddle, Samuel D. Riddle, maintained a home at Glen Riddle until his death in 1951; he was widely known for a breed of extraordinary thoroughbred racehorses, sired by the most famous of them all, Man O'War; and the Riddle estate has in recent years provided the community with funds for the new Riddle Memorial Hospital. John P. Crozer's family, after his death, endowed the Crozer Theological Seminary in Upland (recently removed to Baptist headquarters in Rochester, N.Y.), where generations of Baptist clergymen were trained, the most famous of course being Martin Luther King, Jr.; and further Crozer funds have gone for the support of Bucknell University, Crozer Hospital and its School of Nursing, and other institutions in the Chester area and elsewhere. The Sellers family continued to hold the lands of Parkmount and Lenni until 1908. Thus in a general way the Rockdale community continues to be affected by estates created from the profits earned by the cotton manufacturers of a century ago.

Among the many residents of Aston and Middletown who have, directly or indirectly, helped me in the course of the study, I want to acknowledge several in particular: Mr. Orville C. Morrison, president of the Sunroc Corporation, who let me wander through the ruins of the Riddles' old house and water power system; Mr. and Mrs. Robert Cropper of Lenni, Mrs. Florence Hibbert, formerly of West Branch, Mr. Merrill Fisher of Concord Road, and Mr. William Gorman of Glen Riddle, descendant of the miller of Rockdale, and his wife Nellie, all of whom gave me interesting information about life in the mill towns in the nineteenth century; Mr. E. B. Westlake, Jr., who let me see a late nineteenth-century Riddle paybook; Mr. Lou Esaph, of Middletown, who arranged for me to tour and photograph the Aldon Rug Company properties at Parkmount, West Branch, and Lenni; Mr. Thomas Ahearn, of Rockdale, who allowed me to go through the old mill at Rockdale; and my wife Betty and my sons and daughters Anthony, Daniel, Sun Ai, Samuel, Cheryl, and Joseph, who know today's town better than I. My thanks go to Mr. Angus Cameron, Ms. Bobbie Bristol, Mr. Neal Jones, Mrs. Ann Adelman, and others of the staff at Knopf for thoughtful and helpful collaboration in producing the book. Finally, I want to thank Ms. Ellen Troxler, who over the years has been able to decipher my hand and type a clean manuscript, and Ms. Vanessa Fogler and Ms. Jeanne Gallagher, who together prepared the final draft.

Anthony F. C. Wallace
Rockdale
December 1977

Part One

ROCKDALE IN 1850 &
THE CLIMAX
OF A WAY OF LIFE

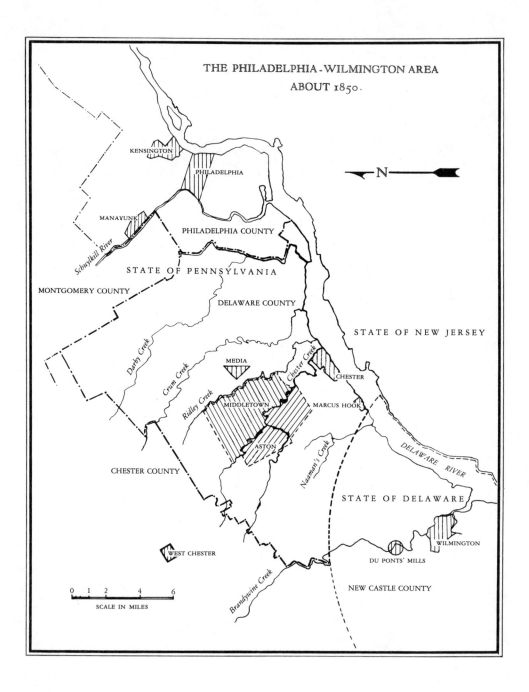

THE PHILADELPHIA-WILMINGTON AREA
ABOUT 1850.

N

KENSINGTON

PHILADELPHIA

MANAYUNK

PHILADELPHIA COUNTY

Schuylkill River

STATE OF PENNSYLVANIA

MONTGOMERY COUNTY

DELAWARE COUNTY

STATE OF NEW JERSEY

Darby Creek

Crum Creek

MEDIA

Chester Creek

CHESTER

Ridley Creek

MIDDLETOWN

MARCUS HOOK

ASTON

CHESTER COUNTY

Naaman's Creek

DELAWARE RIVER

STATE OF DELAWARE

WILMINGTON

WEST CHESTER

DU PONTS' MILLS

NEW CASTLE COUNTY

Brandywine Creek

0 1 2   4   6
SCALE IN MILES

Chapter I 𝕏

SWEET, QUIET ROCKDALE

There is a village in America called Rockdale where the people used to manufacture cotton cloth. It lies along the banks of Chester Creek in Delaware County, in southeastern Pennsylvania, between Philadelphia and Wilmington. None of the people who worked in the first cotton mills is alive anymore, but some of their children's children still live there, and the ruins of stone factories, as well as stone tenements and fine stone mansions, are yet standing. Nearby are remains of the other hamlets that made up the Rockdale manufacturing district—Lenni, Parkmount, West Branch, Crozerville, Glen Riddle, and Knowlton—where cotton yarn was spun on mules and throstles and cloth was woven on looms powered by water wheels. In the first part of the last century, in fact, all along the east coast, from Maine to the Carolinas, and inland to the Mississippi, there were manufacturing districts more or less like Rockdale, nestled along the millstreams in the hinterland of coastal and riverine ports. Now all the machines are broken up for scrap, and the northern mills are empty, and spinners and weavers work only in the great factories of the south.

As I leave my house on the outskirts of the village, drive the car along the roads twisting among the mills, tramp in the weeds by the old dams and races, stroll along the paths in the cemetery at Calvary Church, I sometimes feel that I can almost reach out and touch the people I have come to know from their letters and diaries and ledgers, that they are near, behind a thin veil of time. It was just yesterday, just down the road. And it was so far away, so long ago . . . In a certain mood of elegiacal sentimentality I can see old Rockdale glimmering through a golden haze, where the spinster Sunday School teacher Clementina Smith and her sister Harriet are still sweetly instructing the mill hands in the elements of Christian faith, and the nervous manufacturer John P. Crozer still sweats over preparing a report to the Board of Directors of the Delaware County National Bank, and John

S. Phillips, that clever mechanician, still drives his horse Mazeppa in a Byronic fury down the hills and over the bridges to court the Du Pont girls on the Brandywine, fifteen miles away.

So let us first look at Rockdale with a sentimental, even romantic eye, in the age when it had reached a kind of climax of its way of life, in the years around 1850. Later we can look more closely into the furnace of technological and social change that also was Rockdale. Rockdale at this point was enjoying the few brief years of relative equilibrium that came after decades of growth and economic uncertainty and social unrest, and just before the disaster of the Civil War.

When Sophie du Pont wrote to her friend Clementina Smith in October 1841, she mentioned with favor the contrast between "sweet quiet Rockdale" and the bustling city.[1] The quality of life in Rockdale, day by day, had a naturalness that appealed to romantic sensibility. Rocky hillsides and beech woods, farms and mills, combined wildness with cultivation in a pastoral landscape. The town was still a part of that antebellum rural north that is evoked partly by Currier and Ives pictures of cozy farms and little country mills, and partly by the Hudson River School's wilder landscapes. In both images, the elements of technology are often visible, but they are not obtrusive. Rockdale was in truth a pastoral community not far from wilderness. There was as yet no jarring sound of locomotive engines and shrieking whistles (the railroad that was to connect the Rockdale district with West Chester and Philadelphia would not be completed until 1856).[2] The mills themselves, powered only by water, whispered and grunted softly; the looms clattered behind windows closed to keep moisture in the air; even when the workers were summoned, it was by the bell in the cupola and not by a steam whistle. The machine was in the garden, to be sure, but it was a machine that had grown almost organically in its niche, like a mutant flower that was finding a congenial place among the rocks, displacing no one else and in fact contributing to the welfare of the whole.[3]

In economic matters the decade 1844–54 was for the Rockdale district an era of calm prosperity for almost everyone there. It came after nearly a generation of struggle; and it ended in an almost explosive expansion of manufacturing. But in that brief period the dream of an "American System" of manufactures, a harmony of rural and industrial interests and lifeways, nearly became reality. Industry was not harnessing power out of proportion to local resources; the falling water that turned water wheels and turbines was a non-polluting, self-renewing source of energy. The mills themselves were small, scattered along the creek at the several mill seats, and each one employed dozens rather than hundreds of workers. The system of spinning and weaving machines, and of the machine tools needed to build them and keep them in repair, after three-quarters of a century of development, was now virtually complete. And the local farmers were not incommoded by the mills; rather, the proximity of a mill enhanced the value of a farm. Advertisements of nearby farms for sale emphasized the advantage of their closeness to the mills, which were a source of alternative employment for the farmer and his family, a reservoir of laborers during slack times, and a market for produce.[4] Even the conflicts between the capitalists and the workers had been resolved in the nearly complete ascendancy of the values of evangelical reform capitalism.

Rockdale, indeed, can serve as a symbol of the early phase of the Industrial Revolution in America. Unlike England where, because of the almost universal use of steam engines for power, manufacturing was concentrated in sooty cities like Manchester, the American manufacturing districts were rural and depended upon the new country's as yet unexploited resources of water power. The Rockdale manufacturing district was almost a self-sufficient rural community, like a plantation or a commune, tied economically to world markets and financial centers by the buying of raw cotton and the selling of yarn and cloth, and linked intellectually and spiritually to the wider culture by the participation of its citizens in migration, travel, and reading. Its social structure of caste and class, its style of family life, were for the moment not seriously in question, and the deeper dilemmas inherent in its way of life were not yet fully realized by its citizens.

A TYPICAL MILL HAMLET ABOUT 1850: A SYNTHETIC RECONSTRUCTION.

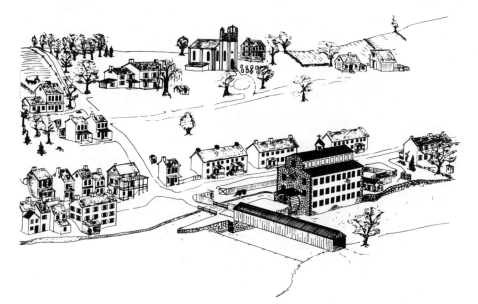

Above Left: MAN IN GIG.

Above Right: A HOT JULY DAY.

Below: FARMER WITH COWS.

Above : SWIMMING IN CHESTER CREEK.

Below: PICNIC ON NUT ROCK.

SLEEPY HOLLOW DAYS

In July and August of 1845, a young man from Lenni named Richard Griffith took his sketchbook in hand and wandered about the Rockdale district, drawing the buildings and landscapes familiar to him from youth (along with caricatures of his neighbors disguised as dogs, cats, pigs, and other assorted livestock). The sketchbook was also adorned with quotations from Shakespeare and comical illustrations of actors dressed in elaborate costume; these conceits mark him as a man of some education and worldly sophistication, perhaps now on a summer vacation at his boyhood home. (Later he was to become a cotton manufacturer on the Brandywine, but in 1845, aged twenty-six, he was apparently not yet engaged in the industry.) His views show an almost classically pastoral world: boys swimming in the creek, their clothes piled on a flat rock high above the water; a horse panting as it draws the shaded carriage up a steep hill, the driver in the seat urging "Bob" to greater effort, the ladies, on foot, heads shaded with parasols, plodding along behind to lighten the horse's burden; a picnic on top of "Nut Rock," with three bare-headed, long-haired young women and two swains, one of them on his knees before his girl (who is on her knees, too), all beneath a canopy of lofty trees; a horse (probably Bob again) trotting along the road beside a post-and-rail fence, with the same wagon behind him, captioned: "The Journey to 'Sleepy Hollow.'" (Sleepy Hollow was —and is—the name of the valley around the forks in the creek.) He even shows, in a carefully drawn sketch labeled "July 15th Lenni," made from the west side of the race, the newly reconstructed mill of Daniel Lammot. The drawing reveals a wagon pulled by three horses in line (urged on by a driver with a whip) just leaving the picker house, which is filled with unbroken cotton bales; looming above them is the typical two-story-plus-clerestory mill, with long lines of black windows, and a cupola in the middle of the roof. The mood of the drawings, where it is not simply documentary, is mildly condescending, picking out the antic foibles and rustic habits of the remote rural mill town to which he is perhaps returning after college and travels in the outside world.

But there is also an aura of prosperity about the landscape and of self-satisfaction, even of smugness, in the postures and faces of the unidentified people whom he shows. A man drives a gig, his legs encased in tight-fitting, loudly checquered pants, his chest swelling beneath a sharply cut jacket, a figure of stiff pride from the footboard up to his jutting jaw and stovepipe hat cocked forward on his brow. Huntsmen, coattails aflying, race their steeds past a farmer's well-fenced field. Ladies with parasols parade, heads demurely covered in bonnets and veiled in lace, bodies protected from neck to ankle by dresses and shawls. Four young gentlemen, one of them in a military cap, practice archery, shooting at a tripod-mounted bull's-eye target in a field. Picket-fenced stone houses with latticed porches and overarching trees stretch out along country lanes; a small barn, surmounted by weathervane, is evidently the home of pigeons returning to a pair of carefully made roosts. A bath house is seen beneath a weeping willow, sitting out in the creek at the end of a wooden quay. Workingmen, wearing low-crowned, flat-brimmed hats, perch on a wagon emerging from a covered bridge; a farmer, puffing on cigar, brings his two cows in to be milked. Even the sketch of Lenni Mill has a feeling of summer calm: in the foreground flows the smooth water in the race flanked by graceful grasses, and a large bullfrog sits on the bank, contentedly observing activities at the factory. It is all very easy, very prosperous, very pastoral; there is only one note of distress, and that is a rather stiff sketch of the great flood, captioned merely: "August 5th 1843." It shows a small tenement house inundated by swirling water, with a human figure beckoning desperately from the attic window. Clearly the world of man keeps its order; it is nature that sometimes gets out of hand. And the bath house, a very model of serenity, lies on the same page, as if it were a sequel.[1]

The leaders of the community were mostly inclined to preserve the pastoral character of the Rockdale scene and resented efforts to change it. Manufacturer Samuel Riddle was severely criticized when he cut down a beautiful grove of linden trees in front of his mansion in order to have a better view of the road.[2] Clementina Smith's mother, in describing to a friend the "view from Clemma's chamber," became almost lyrical; she was deeply moved:

> Sometimes I cannot take my eyes away—it fascinates even more than ocean scenery—there is no thought of loneliness in looking at these hills and vallies and the blue shores of Jersey, so far in the distance. This scene from Rockdale Parsonage fills me sometimes, with inexpressible enjoyment I never did enjoy any scene more, for it seems to be heavenly to me.[3]

These attitudes are, perhaps, understandable in terms of the romantic appreciation for scenes of natural beauty of the time; but even today, after much has been done to destroy the views that charmed educated residents in the 1840's, the steep forested hills, and twisting stream with grassy meadows bordering it, still conceal factories only a few hundred yards away, and allow the eye uninterrupted enjoyment of rural landscape.

There were no noisy taverns and only a small inn in the Rockdale

CHESTER CREEK.

district; the public houses were a mile or more off, the Black Bear on the Baltimore Pike and the Seven Stars at Village Green. The nights were still and dark, except when the sounds of hymn-singing at Calvary broke the stillness; the air was clear and the stars shone brightly. People were peaceful, and respectable young ladies like Clementina and Harriet walked freely, unescorted, along the dusty lanes among the fields, and in the woods in spring, gathering the wildflowers. As Clemma wrote Sophie from busy Philadelphia one May, after a brief visit to Rockdale:

> I languish now for the green fields and country quiet, and enjoyment—
> I do not know when I have felt so happy as I did last Sunday in a walk
> in the woods, to renew my acquaintance with my little friends the violets
> and anemonies.[4]

THE LORDS OF THE VALLEY

Rockdale undoubtedly drew its name from the rounded fieldstones that lie about on the surface of the ground, tumble down the steep hillsides after rain, and pave the channel of the stream. Rocky was the ground; rock was the material used for construction; and, in some sense, the men who ruled the valley were rocklike too, hard-minded competitors in business, and stern in Christian faith.

The Valley of Chester Creek

The part of the creek chosen for the business of cotton manufacturing was the three-mile stretch that descended through the most precipitous part of the fall line, where the height of the streambed above sea level dropped from about 120 feet at the upper end to no more than 30 at the lower. This steep fall of 90 feet in about three miles permitted the construction of mills at frequent intervals. By 1850, there were seven cotton mills in the three-mile stretch, with sundry machine shops and saw- and gristmills associated with them. The steepness of the gradient enabled miller and manufacturer to obtain the necessary head of water—from 10 to 20 feet—with a relatively short race and thus permitted them to economize not only on construction and maintenance costs for race and gates, but also on the cost of acquiring and maintaining the necessary acreage to contain the water right and the adjacent banks.

Chester Creek was not much different from other streams that cut their way through the fall line which runs southward like a long scar, parallel to and about ten miles inland from the Delaware River below Philadelphia. Some, like the Schuylkill, were broader; others—Cobbs Creek, Crum Creek, Darby Creek, and Ridley Creek—were perhaps smaller streams; and the Brandywine, to the south and west, ran through a less narrowly dissected terrain, which yielded a softer, more rolling landscape, and a more comfortable mixture of mill and farm.

The upper and lower reaches of the two branches of the creek were less well suited to cotton manufacturing. The only cotton mill higher up, at Trimble's on the West Branch, had reverted to the grist- and sawmill business after the failure of a cotton manufacturer in 1816. There were of course a number of grist- and sawmills, but the only other sites suitable for major manufactories were already occupied by two very old and very different enterprises—the paper mills of the Willcoxes, at Ivy Mills on the West Branch, and Old Sarum Forge, on the main branch. Both of these plantations lay at the upper edge of the fall line; the Forge in particular required the extensive forests in its surrounding area for its charcoal-fired furnaces. The fall of water above this region became much less rapid, however, and the volume slighter, as one pursued the stream across the plateau toward its headwaters near West Chester. Below the cotton district, similarly, the creek was less suitable for manufacturing. The stream completed its cut through the fall line a half-mile or so below Knowlton Mill, and thereafter flowed slowly, a broad stream wandering through widening meadows, reaching Chester four miles farther down at approximately 10 feet above sea level, after a further fall of only 20 feet.

Within the cotton district itself the landscape was craggy, not suitable for farming or grazing. The hillsides, between which the creek had for millions of years been cutting its path, dropped steeply, in some places precipitously, to the narrow floodplain through which, from mountain wall to wall, the creek meandered. The tops of the hills stood at elevations of about 200 feet above the creek, and their flanks sloped down at angles of from 30 to 45 degrees, so that across the valley from rounded crest to rounded crest stretched a space of no more than a quarter of a mile, with the creek winding a couple of hundred feet below. The flat plains, only 3 or 4 feet above the water, were made of a rich, loamy soil; being left uncultivated because of frequent flooding, they were covered with few trees, mostly with long long grasses, softly brown in winter and a rich, waving green in summer. In swampy places there were stands of cattails. The bed of the stream, except in the ponds behind the dams, was filled with sand and round pebbles of various sizes. The stream itself was most of the time no more than 50 feet wide, and a foot or two deep; clear and cold, it rushed quickly with a soft rustle over its uneven bed.

The hillsides fell so steeply that the valley had nearly the character of a rocky gorge or ravine here and there, with boulders tumbled in profusion and rough outcroppings of granite; the southern slopes remained almost perpetually in shade. The soil over the hills was filled with large rounded pebbles—fieldstones—of various weights, from the size of an egg to heavy boulders. These stones were almost universally used for construction of houses, walls, dams, and races, for they could be dug out of shallow pits by the side of the roads that clung to the hillsides and used without dressing.

In winter the hardwood forests on the hills shone with a bronze and silver sheen, as the silvery trunks of the beech and the lingering reddish brown leaves of the oaks stood out from the gray background of maple, tulip, and ash and the softer brown of the leaves on the forest floor. But in summer the gorge became a monotonous green jungle of trees and grass and weedy underbrush. The climate lay in the middle range, summer temperatures reaching the nineties, and in winter falling sometimes to zero, with rain and snow both moderately heavy. The creek thus varied in fullness not so much seasonally as occasionally in response to irregular fluctuations in rainfall and snow-melt.

It was, then, a place too rugged in terrain for farming but naturally pre-adapted for the early manufacture of cotton, with plenty of water power and an abundance of quarry and fieldstone for dams, races, houses, mills, and bridges. It was a niche prepared by time for the harmonious combination of men, machines, and nature in the pastoral phase of American manufacturing.

The Mills and the Mill Hamlets

The sites chosen by the cotton manufacturers on Chester Creek all lay within a short distance of one another. The farthest upstream, Lenni and West Branch, were only two miles as the crow flies from the lowest, Knowlton Mill; but because of the meanderings of the stream, the distance by water was about three miles. Rockdale was at the midpoint. Half a mile above Rockdale the creek forked, with the northernmost branch suffering no change of name, and the narrower and more southerly fork being called West Branch. Because the hills rose steeply from the banks, except where a narrow floodplain intervened—at most 100 yards in width—the total area of the cotton-manufacturing district was about one and a half square miles. Within this arena were concentrated the mill villages—the dams, races, mills, roads, stores, and housing—all complete and neatly separate from the farms on the plateau above.

The boundaries of the manufacturing district, the location of the mills, and the layout of the hamlets were all determined by specific limitations of terrain and technology. As we have seen, the boundaries of the district itself were set by the combined requirements that there be sufficient water power to operate the machines and that the race need not be so long that it demanded an excessively large tract of land along the stream. Within the district, the location of each mill was again decided by a combination of topographic and mechanical considerations. Each mill seat required a suitable place for a dam, a suitable stretch for a race, and a suitable spot for a mill. The ideal place for a dam was either at a natural fall or rapids or at a natural narrowing of the valley to form a gorge. At Knowlton, there was a gorge which permitted a short but relatively high dam; at the other sites, there were natural rapids which allowed shallow dams. In all cases, the

"ENGLISH HILL": TENEMENTS AT WEST BRANCH.

races were relatively short, sometimes (as at West Branch) as brief as 50 yards. Every one of the mill seats except Parkmount had been identified and used for other purposes before cotton manufacturing came in, in three cases for paper mills, in two for forges, in one as a grist- and sawmill.

The nexus of dam, headrace, wheelpit, mill, and tailrace thus defined the mill seat itself. Around the mill, other considerations determined the settlement pattern of the hamlet. First, a road had to pass by the mill in order to bring in machinery, cotton, and other supplies, and take out the mill's products. This road had to run roughly parallel to the stream as it neared the mill. The housing of the mill workers was, of necessity, in tenements constructed by the mill owner or manufacturer and located on his land, for the most part along the road that led to the mill, and as close as possible to it, for the workers had to walk back and forth to work in all kinds of weather. Neighboring farmers might board a few hands, but they simply did not have enough space for all. On the hillside above the tenements, at successively higher levels as the status of the occupant increased, were the houses and mansions of the managerial personnel, the capitalists who owned the machines, and the mill owners who owned the land. Everything was made

TENEMENTS AT PARKMOUNT.

of stone. The mills, tenements, and many of the houses were constructed of fieldstone laid in lime-and-clay mortar, reinforced with horsehair, and stuccoed yellow-brown or white. The bridges and some of the mansions, however, were made of a gray quarried stone, cut in rectangular blocks, and these houses were not stuccoed.

Looking down from the hillsides in winter (for foliage in summer concealed almost the entire scene), each hamlet across the valley presented much the same image: a road, a palisaded mill of three stories including a clerestory on the third and a bell cupola in the center, a race, a dam; on the hillside immediately behind the mill and along the road, several rows of neat stone tenements, and a few separate houses, where workers and tradesmen lived; and ascending the hill, the larger houses of the supervisory staff, with the mansions at the top, surrounded by gardens. Plumes of smoke would be ascending from the stoves in the mill and from the fireplaces and cookstoves of the houses; if one were watching at lunchtime, one might hear the bell ring the hour, and see the workers—men, women, and children—trooping home in family groups for the midday meal.

The Cotton Lords

Each hamlet was administered as almost a patriarchal domain by a mill owner or a manufacturer (often one and the same person). In the Rockdale district, only one of the mills had an absentee landlord; for all the rest, the owners and manufacturers either resided in the mansion or were represented there day by day by members of the family. In the case of the one exception, at Old Sable in Rockdale, the owner and manufacturer was a wealthy and aged Irishman who owned mills in nearby towns; he was represented locally by an English mill superintendent who lived near the mill. Thus, although there might be a considerable difference in life style and standard of living between workers and capitalists, in the normal course of events they lived next door to each other, knew the insides of one another's houses, were familiar with members of each other's family, and worked, albeit at different jobs, in the same mill.

The manufacturers were sometimes jibingly referred to by their employees, at times of labor unrest, as "cotton lords," in uncomplimentary allusion to the legendary Manchester millionaires. These English capitalists, who were often enough unfavorably described in the American press, were understood to be bloated, lecherous tyrants who brutalized their employees, worked juvenile apprentices to death, and made their money by grinding the faces of the poor. This image did not really fit the capitalists and landowners along Chester Creek, however. They were eager enough to make money. But they were not, in this generation at least, really alienated from the people who worked in their mills. Their feelings were truly hurt when, on rare occasions of labor trouble, they were accused of exploiting their employees; they believed that capitalists and factory operatives were in principle a cooperating team.

Among the eight mill owners and manufacturers, there were four men who might be called, if not the lords, at least the oligarchy of the Rockdale manufacturing district: John P. Crozer, Daniel Lammot, Jr., Richard S. Smith, and Samuel Riddle. They owned much of the land, operated the major mills, had most of the money, and—perhaps more important than anything else—controlled access to the sources of money, information, and political influence outside Rockdale itself. The most prominent of these by far was John Price Crozer, who owned two of the mills, West Branch and Crozerville. Crozer was a man of English and Huguenot descent, in his mid-fifties, and extremely wealthy. He had recently expanded his enterprises to include a new mill at Upland, downstream on the outskirts of Chester, and now lived there in a new mansion with his family and servants.

His son Samuel was in immediate charge of operations in the Rockdale district and Crozer himself took charge of the Upland development. Crozer was proud of being a self-made and largely self-educated man, a local farmboy from the county who had by toil and inflexible determination made his fortune. Crozer was a Baptist and had recently become intensely religious; he devoted much of his time to religious causes and he regarded himself as God's steward, managing his mills and mill hands and his wealth for the advancement of the community. He kept a diary in which he carefully recorded the spiritual transformation he was experiencing as the love of victory and the desire for gold were transmuted into a longing to be of service to his Savior.

Across the forks of the creek lay Lenni Mill, so named by an earlier manufacturer who associated the wild charm of the spot with its original Indian inhabitants, the Lenni Lenape, or Delaware, Indians. Lenni (and also the mill seat below it at the forks, Parkmount) was owned by Hannah, the second wife of the gentleman farmer Peter Hill. Peter Hill was a former merchant whose reputation for shady business practice and succession of bankruptcies had persuaded Hannah's father to leave his daughter the two mill seats in trust, so that Peter Hill could not sell them to cover his debts. He administered the properties for her, and the family lived in a substantial mansion from the rentals of the mill seats. Hill came of an old Quaker family in the county; his wife was a Sellers, of the famous mechanicians' clan in Philadelphia, whose members and connections included such poor but celebrated geniuses as Charles Willson Peale and whole generations of inventors, engineers, and mechanicians. But they were socially marginal in the Rockdale district, visiting little with the manufacturing families. Lenni was leased by the aging Daniel Lammot, Jr., a man of French descent in his late sixties who was connected by business and marriage to the Du Ponts along the Brandywine. The Lammots were, with their friends the Richard S. Smiths of Crozerville, the society people of the Rockdale district, the ladies spending part of the winter social season in Philadelphia and part of the summer at fashionable resorts like Cape May and Saratoga. The Lammots were very active in the religious affairs of the Church of the New Jerusalem. Peter Hill, like his father-in-law Nathan Sellers, was also a Swedenborgian, and his wife Hannah had some sympathy for her father's faith.

The Smiths were only summer residents in the Rockdale district but they were nonetheless extremely powerful in the community. Smith himself was a man of sixty, who boasted Swedish ancestry and spoke the language well (he had even served as U.S. consul in Sweden during the War of 1812). Years ago he had owned the cotton mill at the site of Old Sable Forge, and had been principally responsible for the establishment of Calvary Episcopal Church, the religious center of the community. He and his family throughout the year managed the affairs of the church, teaching in its Sunday School and parish school, selecting and providing housing for the rector, and promoting the interests of the congregation in the larger councils of the diocese, in which he was one of the leading low church evangelical laymen. His wife Elizabeth and his unmarried daughters Clementina and Harriet were constantly moving back and forth between Philadelphia, where they had a house on fashionable Clinton Street, and the old Crozer mansion which they were renting. Smith was the president of the Union Insurance Company, a post he had held since 1837, when he lost the mill during the panic; and, like their close friends the Lammots, the Smiths were connected by business and marriage with the Du Ponts.

The other major figure in the community was Samuel Riddle, who owned and operated the old Penn's Grove factory. Riddle, now in his fifties, was an Irishman who had come over from Belfast in the 1820's with only a few dollars in his pocket and had worked his way to wealth. Riddle was a nominal Presbyterian; his brother and former partner James was a "forcible," and successful, Methodist preacher who now ran his own cotton mill on the Brandywine. Samuel served as postmaster at Penn's Grove and was later to marry the daughter of a postmistress in Chester. Samuel Riddle had a salty tongue, was a genial raconteur, a cantankerous neighbor with a propensity for quarreling over fences, a conspicuous member of the Hibernian Society; having been brought up as a lad in a spinning mill on the other side of the water, he could identify with his workers. Although he was not a frequent guest in the more religious households of the community, such as the Smiths' and the Lammots', there was far less labor trouble in his mills than in those of his more religious peers.

So diverse a group would not, superficially, seem capable of much mutual understanding; yet they cooperated successfully for decades in business, politics, and local social reform and improvement. In denomination and degree of religious devotion, in social manners, in ethnic origin, in level of education, in acceptability to polite society, they were very different from one another. But they shared certain basic features which were, in their eyes, so fundamental to civilized society that they could also be regarded as necessary to a fully human identity. Foremost in this regard was fidelity-to-contract. It is difficult to overestimate the importance of this virtue in the eyes of these men. In his autobiography, written a decade later for the edification of his children—and of other people's children too, one may infer, inasmuch as he published it as a book—John P. Crozer testified in two remarkable paragraphs to the centrality of the notion of fidelity-to-contract in his scheme of things. Simple commercial honesty was, as he saw it, the moral axis around which all his human relationships 'were formed.

But a kind Heavenly Father had endowed me with some elements of power which saved me from ruin. Indomitable perseverance, and unwavering integrity, a firm resolution to do justly to others, ever ruled in my mind; and I may now, in the maturity of age and in the possession of a large fortune, recall what, in review of a long life, I believe to be strictly true—that I never knowingly or intentionally wronged any one in business. It has been the uniform tenor of my life to be upright and honest in my dealings. I may perhaps have driven hard bargains; I know I have been pretty close in my dealings; but a bargain or promise once made by me has ever been regarded sacred, and to be kept inviolable; no waver, no temptation to dishonesty, has ever assailed me, or ever crossed my mind as a suggestion.

I wish that I could make the same record as to my character and conduct, especially the thoughts of my heart in every other matter; but alas I cannot; I can think of innumerable cases, when I would be compelled to write bitter things against myself. My industry and integrity were recognized, I believe, by all with whom I had intercourse; and being careful to fulfil every pecuniary obligation or promise, I early inspired confidence. I was often much straitened for money; but, with a full knowledge of my business resources, I was careful never to make a promise to pay, without assurance in my own mind that I could comply. The people with whom I dealt early learned that I was reliable in my promises to pay, and, as a consequence, running bills were often not called for by my creditors for months after they were actually due. This was a benefit to me, and I may here recommend a similar course to every young man commencing business. Be careful never to disappoint when you promise to pay; and, if you have not the money to pay bills when due and called for, say so frankly, and at the same time say *when* you will pay, and never suffer the creditor to call beyond the second time. If it be practicable, pay a little earlier (by sending the money to him) than you had engaged to do. You will soon find your account in this course. Nothing is of so much importance to a young man commencing business as a character for integrity, industry, and promptness. The community around him will early recognize these qualities, and duly appreciate them; and they will secure a credit and willingness to do business with him, thus making amends for any want of cash capital he may be deficient in. I speak with confidence on this subject. I have witnessed it in my own case and in that of others.[1]

CROZER'S MANSION AT WEST BRANCH.

In an even more extraordinary piece of dialogue (whose alleged occurrence is significant whether or not the story is apocryphal), a Rockdale businessman once defined commercial probity as a virtue inherent in masculinity. The owner of a small coalyard, so the story goes, went to Philadelphia, all dressed up in clean overalls, to order coal. At the supplier's office the clerks paid no attention to him, a mere workingman in overalls. When at last they discovered that he wanted to buy coal, they told him that they didn't sell small lots. He explained that he wanted two or three carloads. At that they perked up, asked him his name, sat him down, and requested references. He pointed to his loins and said, "My references are here."[2]

The point of these hyperbolic testimonials on the importance of, and qualifications for, a good credit rating is that a *real man* keeps his promises, that the cornerstone of manhood is fidelity-to-contract. It was not just a Protestant ethic of hard work, punctuality, cleanliness, and other displays of godliness. And it was not an individualistic virtue; on the contrary, it was by definition a social virtue, and its significance lay in its assumption that contracts make society work and that mutual trust makes *contracts* work. These were men who really believed that social contract was the basis of human society, that manhood was a state of social responsibility, that to be a man was not just to be a virile adult male but a male credited by a community of other males with being honest in their ceaseless mutual business dealings. Thus the contract principle was at once an ego ideal and a theory of society.

But, in addition to being honest, these were men, as Crozer said of himself, of "indomitable perseverance." They wanted increase: increase in wealth, in power, in prestige; they expanded their factories, they added to their number. Bound by the rule of fidelity-to-contract once made, they were free to drive hard bargains in the negotiations leading to agreement. The contract defined the limit of mutual obligation; the participants in the game were, within bounds of legality, free to engage in shrewd practice. Thus the system was a paradox: a community of mutually trustful men, each one trying desperately to accumulate wealth and power at the possible expense of others, even as the others' sharpness, and the fluctuations of the market, constantly threatened to wash away his own accumulation. And the possibility of disaster was ever in mind, too. Only Samuel Riddle, so far as is known, had never known failure in business. A businessman's life was not conceived to be normally a smooth and steady ascent, but a perilous traversal of uneven terrain, with great peaks and valleys to be crossed before arriving at last on the green plateau of great wealth. But in this early phase of industrial capitalism, the manufacturers did not view themselves so much as competitors as colleagues, all engaged in the same profession, all matching wits against the impersonal market, with success ultimately possible for all who worked hard and made wise choices. And they were all believers in hierarchy. All had been poor and dependent upon others in their adult lives. Even in republican America, where no nobility or rigid system of classes arrogated to itself a monopoly of rank, there was visibly an order based on the exercise of power by men of capital, of political position, of judicial authority, of religious eminence. With power came the responsibility to use that position as God's steward on earth: to punish those who made mistakes or behaved wrongly, as parents punished children, and to reward the virtuous and competent. Indeed, the image of the sinner punished in his lifetime by an almighty but unpredictable Father was inscribed on the conscience of every one of these Christian leaders. At any moment the Heavenly Father might visit disaster upon any man, depriving him, in the interest of awakening in him an awareness of his ultimate need for salvation, of money, property, even family. Only at the last might the iron law of punishment be relaxed, if the Savior were willing to pardon the penitent sinner trusting in his Lord for mercy. The days of a person's dying were thus the culmination of life, for in them man and woman gave evidence of their moral condition. In his last hour, man settled his affairs on earth, providing for the payment of his debts and testifying to his hope of salvation.[3]

The psychodynamic problem, then, was to balance arrogance and trust. Intensely ambitious, striving constantly to excel others, to climb in the hierarchy, to become *more* wealthy, *more* powerful, *more* respected than other men, each believed at the same time that the world was built on trust.

A man had to trust others and be trustworthy himself, and so earn the trust of others, or he could never excel them or become a steward over them, for they would not admit him into commerce with them; and if he failed their trust, they would punish him for violating the rules. But while he strove to make others trust him, he also labored to trust in God's mercy, even though he knew that God could never have trust in him, being so miserable a sinner. One can see the structure of these capitalists' religious faith as almost a mirror image, reversed in directions, of the structure of their conception of the social contract. In the commercial world, man could rise to glory; in relation to God, he was already fallen. In the commercial world, punishment for violating the rules was certain, and trust must be mutual. In man's relation to God, the just punishment for man's untrustworthiness was ultimately withheld and man was saved from Hell if only he had trust in God and accepted Jesus as his Savior. Thus the drama of death and salvation formed, as it were, a negative image of the commercial world.

But despite the reverse symmetry in the relation between values necessary to the stability of the natural world and to the salvation of the soul, a latent dilemma remained. Can, in principle, *every* man achieve economic success? Can, in principle, *every* man's soul be saved? The noisy rhetoric of Jacksonian oratory did not answer these questions, for they fundamentally challenged not only the orthodox Protestant interpretation of Christian doctrine but also the orthodox economic assumption that there was an unredeemable class of immoral or incompetent persons who could not be trusted and whose poverty thus was made certain by the fact that they could not be admitted to the society of businessmen who were eligible for economic success.

THE SISTERHOOD

But the businessmen wrote mostly of themselves. It is in the quiet correspondence of women that the quality of life among the ruling families in Rockdale is most clearly recalled, in brief vignettes of their encounters with each other, and with their menfolk, and with the working people of the neighborhood, and in intense discussions of books and ideas and people that interested them. Out of this correspondence, and particularly the correspondence between the Smiths and the Du Ponts, emerges the outline of a network of cultivated women who constituted an intellectual society along Chester Creek and the Brandywine that played a powerful role in the polite social life of the twin communities.

If we take Clementina ("Clemma"), the daughter of Richard S. Smith, as the center, the network of women who were her constant friends and associates—with whom she talked and visited and regularly and frequently worked and corresponded—numbered fourteen. In her own family, they included her mother Elizabeth Smith, her sister Harriet ("Hattie"), and her cousin Joanna Smith. A mile up the creek, there were Anna Lammot and her stepdaughters Eleanora ("Nora") and Mary; and on the Brandywine was Mrs. Lammot's other stepdaughter Margaretta ("Meta"). Still farther up the creek above Lenni was Mrs. Willcox at Ivy Mills. On the Brandywine were the three Du Pont sisters, Sophie (Clemma's best friend), Eleuthera ("Eleu"), and Victorine ("Vic") Bauduy (Mrs. Smith's best friend). And also on the Brandywine at Kentmere were little Mary Gilpin and her sister Sarah, who had no nicknames. It was a tightly coupled network in the sense that each member knew most of the others personally and all by reputation.

They were women of parts, with one or two exceptions trained in one or another of the fashionable female academies in Philadelphia (the exceptions were educated at home by tutors and relatives), and thereafter continuously active in literary or artistic pursuits. Their education differed from the men's in paying less attention to mathematics and practically none to such disciplined fields as physics and chemistry; but the training was thorough in botany and natural history, English literature, classical and modern languages, and political and religious history; and the girls learned not merely to appreciate music and art but to play, draw, and write passable verse and essays. Furthermore, this learning was seriously valued and laid the basis for a lifelong regard for the intellectual and artistic work not only of men but of women as well. Elizabeth Smith, writing ruefully to her friend Victorine Bauduy, expressed the values clearly in praising her sister-in-law Eliza Smith:

There are few who know the worth of [her]. The capacities of her mind are really great. . . . [Has read much, was once] the best musician I have known . . . excellent French and Italien schollar. She had a great talent for painting and is ingeneous in all the tasteful employments of our sex. Everything however has been given up for the duties of the nursery & housewife.[1]

And if to a person's intellectual accomplishments were added a sincere religious concern, the possibilities of social intercourse with her were especially promising. As Clementina put it, "What is there dear Sophie more delightful than intellectual Christian society?"[2]

Ten of the members of the sisterhood were married; of these ten, two were childless; and some of the mothers employed wet-nurses for their infants at birth, or shortly after, thus freeing themselves to move about, to work, and to travel. This practice entailed the occasional inconvenience of losing some of the intimacies of motherhood; but the mothers took a practical view of the matter. Anna Lammot, on returning home from a trip, discovered that her son did not remember her at all. Although "his old associations" soon restored her to his recollection, he could not remember her name (and he evidently never did learn the name of the wet-nurse). As she put it in her usual down-to-earth style, "My title of Mamma is forgotten & he calls me nothing but 'titt-tee.' "[3] Nor were the children, boys or girls, allowed to disrupt their mothers' lives at older ages, being kept to a strict household discipline, with obedience emphasized and enforced. Boarding school at ten or eleven ended the child's residential connection for several years during the teens, except for summer vacations; after the school years, the mother was confronted with an adult child who remained pretty much under parental control as long as he or she remained in the house. It was a no-nonsense system, which functioned (and no doubt was designed) to protect the mother's role as hostess and household administrator and, increasingly, her continued intellectual development and participation in evangelical and reform activities in the community.

Like a host of others in America at this time, many of the sisterhood were ambivalent about marriage as an institution, not merely the spinsters but those already married as well. The attitude was not expressed—at least in their written correspondence—in open criticism of their own or each other's husbands. Rather, it took the form of complaints about the restrictions which the duties of housewifery and motherhood had placed (or would place) on some woman's ability to fulfill herself in an intellectual or artistic or even religious career. In writing to his daughter Margaretta shortly after her marriage to Alfred du Pont, her father simply advised her to be diligent and attentive "in the discharge of all your duties" in order to gain happiness in this world and the next. Anna was more candid. She believed strongly in the necessity of marriage, but she tended to regard the male as the dependent partner. In a series of letters to her stepdaughter, she conveyed in more or less subtle fashion this view of the potentially dominant role of the female in the marital relation. Thus in commenting on a recently announced union, she remarked in high spirits:

There is a trifling advantage on the lady's side of 10 or a dozen years—but you know your father's old maxim in choosing chickens may apply equally to all *paired* animals—"Put an old one with a young one & it will be better taken care of."

Her analysis of the character of a young clergyman was even more emphatic:

As to Mr. Ives if he does not get married soon, the best thing his friends in particular & his congregation in general can do for him is to hire him a tall strapping dry nurse—who will souse him in cold water three times a day & rub him dry with a good hard towel—He is the biggest baby extant & ought not to be tolerated in the society of even half grown ladies & gentlemen—I may venture to class myself among this last mentioned number. At least I would be glad to do so to have a writ of expulsion on him in my favour.

After Mr. Ives's marriage, he visited Anna's father's house, and she met him again there. In her opinion, marriage had not improved him:

Mr & Mrs Ives are at Papa's—They came round to spend the day about week ago, she had a relapse & was obliged to remain—He is too great a Baby to be endured among grown up people—& I have been obliged almost to make him absolutely angry before I could make him listen to reason in the management of his Wife's indisposition—The girls & Mamma can do nothing with him—but Rebecca coinciding with me, rendered him in some measure tractable—The poor girl—with a little baby to *come* & a big one *never away,* she has a poor prospect—'Tis a comfort however that the first will grow every day less of a baby, while the last is becoming more & more of one—

But as to the choice between romantic marriage and attachments to parents and siblings, she conceded—with some difficulty—that marriage probably should come first, in some cases. She discussed with her step-daughter the case of a young wife forced to choose between husband and family:

Sally Hodge goes the first of next month to Havre to meet her husband & expects to settle in France. Her youngest child was seized with convul-sions in consequence of violent screaming a few weeks ago & died in a few hours—This is shocking!—And now she goes away from all her friends & family to the end of the world for her husbands sake—This is right—but hard—He ought to be the best of husbands for she sacrifices much to him—Yet a woman would scarce feel that she sacrificed any thing if her only choice was *husband* or *family*—particularly if they were truly united & have young bonds to bind them closer—[4]

Clearly, in Anna Lammot's view, not only was marriage itself a choice, but how to conduct it was a matter of choice as well. In a marital dilemma, where divorce was not in prospect (and in most circumstances it was unthinkable), the woman might still choose to return quietly to the family in which she was born rather than remain with or join her husband. Such a possibility was no doubt vividly apparent to married women whose husbands, being forced to travel on business for prolonged periods, left them to stay with their "own" families of birth.

Within the group, Anna Lammot was regarded as the most intellectual and most accomplished. She came of a distinguished family, her father being a well-to-do merchant, and her mother the sister of the prominent Episcopal theologian John Hobart, then Bishop of New York.[5] She had been introduced to the widowed Daniel Lammot by her school friend Victorine because both enjoyed German literature and found few companions with whom to share this interest. (Anna was particularly fond of Goethe and wrote a love poem in the style of his "Ich Denke Dein.") Anna was a practiced versifier by the age of eleven, and when the young ladies from Mme Rivardi's school put together their little manuscript booklet of poetic remembrances to a departing friend, Miss Antoinette Brevost, Anna Smith's lines were more numerous than all the rest.[6] She continued to write throughout her life, in early years offering sonnets to her beloved Victorine, and later turning to verse on occasions of sorrow, as at the sickness or death of a friend or of her own children.

She took a strong interest in political affairs. On reading Mme de Staël (who like Anna appreciated German literature), she was moved to write to Victorine (who "hate[d] German") her view of what the famous writer might do for America and for her own understanding:

I wish Made de Stael would come to our country & be so good as to convince the literary world that we have some national character—It requires some helping hand as powerful as hers to raise & exhibit the genius of the Americans. She might find something here which she finds not in other countries—blessed Liberty—and the effect of this liberty on the happiness of the people would be a fine subject for her. She would indeed find no literary heroes here but we could point out to her view the Father of our country more worthy of panegyric than many whom her pen has immortalized—she would find his name entombed in the hearts of his countrymen—& behold his monument in the felicity of the people he has freed—[7]

A few years later (after eight years of marriage and the birth of three of her nine children), she launched on a public literary career, "consenting" to the printing of two pieces in a short-lived Philadelphia literary paper called *The Souvenir,* which appeared from 1827 to 1830; other contributions were published by Carey.[8] Of particular interest is an elegy on the death of George Canning, the British prime minister, published in the summer of 1828 after the statesman's sudden death, for it reveals much about Mrs. Lammot's political awareness.

The Grave of Canning

How still the scene around. Not e'en a cloud
Curtains the abbey with a passing shroud.
All, all is still, and Cynthia's silver falls
With mellow'd softness on the sacred walls.
No marble marks the spot where Canning sleeps,
A living statue pauses here, and weeps:
Affliction's semblance bends not o'er his tomb;
Affliction's self deplores his early doom.
Yes, name to England dear, the pilgrim feels,
Who trembling reads it, grief, no verse reveals;
His bosom heaves, his aching heart is dim,
The tablet quivers and the letters swim.
Farewell Freedom's martyr'd friend! Lament him, Greece!

His star arose, and in excess of light
Itself outshining, vanish'd at its height.
The dazzled world was gazing, which the spell
Broke with his broken heart, and darkness fell.
To idolize his fame, alike combine
Rank, wealth, and beauty; and with skill divine
The sculptor's chisel consecrates his fate,
To comfort England left disconsolate.
Pale widow'd Isle, methinks, she lingers lone,
While Chantry's genius bids him live in stone.
Alas! that all his mighty mind is wreck'd;
His glancing eye, and flashing intellect.

And oh! his tongue, his magic tongue, that still'd
The sound of strife, and blending, as it will'd,
The Whig and Tory with an honest zeal,
Together marshall'd for his country's weal.
Relentless Faction's pestilential breath
Can breathe no dimness over Canning's death.
With glory flush'd, and in the pride of power,

Cut off, too sensitive, ephemeral flower!
The canker care, a feverish summer cherish'd,
Just indignation nurtur'd and he perished.
Fond hope be ours, when Mercy's hallow'd breath
Winnows the seed of life, from chaff of death.
That God may bless him, and his waking eyes
Open an angel's and in Paradise.[9]

Anna Lammot was farsighted in her recognition of the importance to Americans of George Canning's career in British politics. He had been an associate of William Pitt in the House of Commons from 1793 and had taken an active part in the literary counterattack against writers of republican sentiment, contributing pieces to *The Anti-Jacobin;* later, during a stormy career as a Tory member of Parliament and public official, he served for a time as foreign secretary during the Napoleonic wars. The orphaned son of a penniless Irishman who died a year after his birth, his mother an actress of soiled reputation, he was not acknowledged as a gentleman by many of his Tory associates. He possessed a sharp and merciless tongue, which he used freely in political debate; he made many enemies, and his relations with his political rival Viscount Castlereagh led the two of them to the highly publicized duel in which Canning was wounded. After Castlereagh's suicide, Canning assumed the post of foreign secretary and leader in the House of Commons, and in this capacity managed to move England into a moderate or even liberal position among the European powers. Great Britain in effect abandoned the "holy alliance" of despotic monarchies that had been organized by Metternich and Castlereagh in the "Concert of Europe," gave diplomatic support to Greece in her struggle for independence from Turkey, and—most importantly for the United States—opposed pending Spanish efforts to reclaim her lost colonies in North and South America by recognizing the new republics and tacitly interposing the British fleet. These British actions gave powerful support to the newly enunciated American doctrine (asserted in 1823 by President Monroe) that also disallowed any Spanish effort to regain her colonies and recognized the new sister republics to the south.

Canning thus was a symbol of both liberty and conservatism in a sense not unlike Washington, whom Mrs. Lammot had lauded earlier; he represented a principle of national self-determination coupled with popular freedom from monarchical despotism. ("Popular" of course meant, for Canning—and presumably Mrs. Lammot—the middle class, the manufacturers, merchants, and professional people.) And when he died, under the stress of trying to form a Tory cabinet while his Tory political enemies refused their cooperation and resigned in droves and he was forced to derive support from the Whigs, he could be seen as a fallen hero, a martyr in the cause of liberty, without being in the least tainted by any expression of sympathy for freethinkers, Jacobins, and other radicals of the Enlightenment camp.

Anna Lammot thus was acutely responsive to the need for, and contributed her talents to the formation of, a type of social ideal that could combine patriotic American nationalism (which Canning's foreign policy then encouraged), the notion of an open class system (of which the ill-born Canning himself was a prime exemplar), and a pro-middle-class political and economic policy (which Canning, as the ally of William Pitt, and later as a member from Liverpool, had fought to preserve both from revolutionary assault and from aristocratic reaction). And Canning's were perhaps the "deeds of fame," "strange adventures," and "glorious actions" which in her premature epitaph (she lived to be eighty-two) she had lamented that her "simple life" denied her.

None of the other women in the group achieved the degree of public recognition—as well as in-group admiration—for intellectual and artistic achievement that was accorded Anna Lammot. The only one who aspired to a similar level was Mary Gilpin; but she, unfortunately for her, chose to do so not along the conventionally acceptable lines of Anna Lammot, but in a sphere that required competition with men: natural history. Intellectual interests were Mary's birthright, for her father Joshua and uncle Thomas Gilpin—papermakers and cotton manufacturers of Brandywine—were active in writing on technological and economic subjects, and Joshua was a versifier himself, particularly prolific in poems about shepherds and shepherdesses in imitation of Virgil, and a writer of works on natural history. Mary, during a walk one autumn day along the Brandywine with Sophie, revealed to her a plan to carry out research and eventually to publish a book on the natural history of the Brandywine Valley. Sophie was interested enough in natural history herself to write Clemma detailed accounts of the transformation of grubs into winged locusts. But publication was something else, and she recorded in her diary her amazement at Mary's idea:

[She] proposed to me to assist her in writing a work like the journal of a naturalist about this country. The plan was, we should each keep a journal, & read & obtain scientific information, & afterward condense our observations, lumbrations & informations, into a work like the above cited. She hinted that if we found it worthy afterwards, we might anonymously publish it! Oh dear! I was shocked at the bare idea of any words of *mine* in any way appearing in print!

Sophie politely agreed to help in secret but confided to her diary that, although she admired Mary, she could not imagine ever loving her.[10]

There are no remains to indicate that Mary ever did go on to bring together her natural history of the Brandywine. She took a long trip to England and Ireland to visit English relatives and the ancestral estate at "Kentmere." After her father's death in 1841, her home at Kentmere on the Brandywine was broken up, her mother and sister Sarah going to England, and Mary herself moving away to teach in a new school. Mary, in the opinion of Sophie, was very well qualified for a school, reading freely in Latin, French, and Italian, speaking French, and being very thoroughly educated in English literature. She was also becoming increasingly religious, residing in Bishop Lee's house and enthusiastically attending the Episcopal conventions in Philadelphia (unconventional as usual, she climbed in through a window when the entrance way was crowded). But the new teaching position ended and, without work, she fell into a depression. She recovered in the course of developing a plan for a religious school, to be conducted under Bishop Lee's auspices in Wilmington. Then this plan too fell through, despite the Lees' encouragement, because "others could not make allowances for Mary's eccentricities." Mary, in Clementina's opinion in the fall of 1845, was "not well" and ought in fact to give up teaching and go to live with her mother. Attempting next to teach Sunday School in cooperation with Sophie, Mary fell into difficulties with her former friend and began to accuse Sophie of conspiring against her.[11] Sophie blamed Mary's "unfortunate want of tact and practical knowledge of the world" for the fact that the size of her school was so far below what her "superior teaching" deserved.[12] Clementina, less closely involved, saw Mary more to be pitied than blamed. "Poor Mary!" she exlaimed in a letter to Sophie, "I do feel for her the deepest pity—her nervous state of mind makes every thing in her life sad."[13] By 1851, Mary Gilpin was accusing Bishop Lee of "persecution" because he would not let her run the parish school herself; she threatened to set up a competing school, and finally succeeded, but it, too, quickly failed.

By the spring of 1852, Mary was confined in Philadelphia in the insane asylum of the Pennsylvania Hospital, under the care of the renowned Dr. Kirkbride. For a time she was not even allowed visitors.[14] She profited from the kindness, regular discipline, good food, and physical exercise this institution (like others of the period) provided, and she was released in a few months. She then made the pilgrimage to the fashionable resort at Cape May, "so hopeful of the effect of salt air and bathing upon her health . . . poor child."[15] Thereafter she virtually disappears from the correspondence of Clementina and Sophie, except for a brief allusion in 1857 to "Mary" as a living-in patient of a Dr. Linn in New York.[16]

During the Civil War, Mary moved to the southern states, where she lived with her sister Elizabeth and brother-in-law, Matthew Maury, the eminent naval engineer and oceanographer; there she became an ardent defender of the south. After the war, she briefly adopted a pretty child from Wilmington whom she took to live in Naples; the American consul put the girl in an orphanage. Then she wandered from continent to continent and finally vanished from view. She was rediscovered in Alaska by an English-woman of rank who happened to visit a little Indian village where she found a gray-haired, wild-eyed Mary Gilpin, lying on a couch in a dilapidated hut, surrounded by a library of Greek and Latin books, all showing signs of repeated reading.[17] She eventually left Alaska for California and then took residence in Denver with her brother William Gilpin, the Governor of Colorado. But she soon departed from his house too, claiming that he held her prisoner for her money, he "contending that she had been insane for forty years and that a clergyman had written him to take her into his home because she had been living on an Indian reservation." A few months later, Mary died.[18]

The intellectual and artistic lives of the other members of the group were less public but just as serious. The correspondence of Clementina Smith and Sophie du Pont, extending over nearly half a century, from its inception was devoted in considerable part to exchanging comments and recommendations on the books the two women were reading and accounts of intellectual conversation with their mutual friends. The Smith family like others of their class (including the Crozers) was in the habit of spending an hour or two in the evening, around the fire, reading aloud to one another from the Bible, Shakespeare, and such popular writers of the day as Sir Walter Scott, Robert Browning, Washington Irving, Bayard Taylor, Hugh Walpole, Isaak Walton, and Macaulay ("he is quite beyond me . . . but . . . makes me think"). Much of Clementina's private reading—accomplished late at night or during the free hours of morning before the daily routine of housekeeping, visiting, shopping, and sewing began—was in serious religious literature and moral philosophy, such as Bishop Wilberforce's *Practical Christianity* (supplemented by a biography of Wilberforce), Abercrombie on the moral feelings, St. Thomas à Kempis's *Imitation of Christ,* various works of Matthew Arnold, Huntington's *Christian Believing and Living,* and Mrs. Jamieson and Mme Necker on the characteristics of women. She attended the lectures of Professor Agassiz on the Animal Kingdom and took a close interest in the controversy over the new Smithsonian Institution. She wrote constantly to Sophie about her reading and other intellectual and artistic experiences, particularly her music (she played the organ, piano, and harp) and painting.

And all of the women circulated their books amongst each other, or copied out long extracts for their friends' information and delectation. "Our little society," as Clementina called it, was before all else a society of people who talked about intellectual and artistic things that they had read and heard and seen and thought, whether face to face or on paper, tête-à-tête or at formally organized teas, for they planned to meet at least weekly at one or another of their houses.[19]

Chapter II ✕

A TOWN OF
MULES AND WIDOWS

For a social survey of Rockdale that includes all components of the population, one must turn to the federal census. In August of 1850, exactly five years after Richard Griffith made his sketches, enumerators trudged from door to door in the Rockdale district, interviewing the people and recording the information in the schedules sent from Washington. These schedules reveal in detail the composition of Rockdale's society at the zenith of its development.

ROCKDALE IN THE 1850 CENSUS

The 1850 census was much more thorough than those of earlier decades.[1] The enumerator was instructed to record the names of all individuals enumerated; in addition, he was to note various other facts of interest about each person: age, sex, race, country or state of birth, occupation (of adult males only); the value of real estate owned; whether the individual could read, had attended school in the past year, or had been married in the past year; and whether he was crippled or handicapped in any way, and if so, how. The information was arranged by household, with the head of the household at the top, and others below him or her (there was no reluctance to recognize females as household heads) in general order of age or status. Where two complete families occupied the same dwelling, that fact was noted, but the general assumption was that each house (for there were no apartment dwellings) was occupied by one family; other arrangements, such as the inclusion of other families or individuals as boarders, were viewed as modifications of this plan.

The enumerators—there were several for each township, each with his

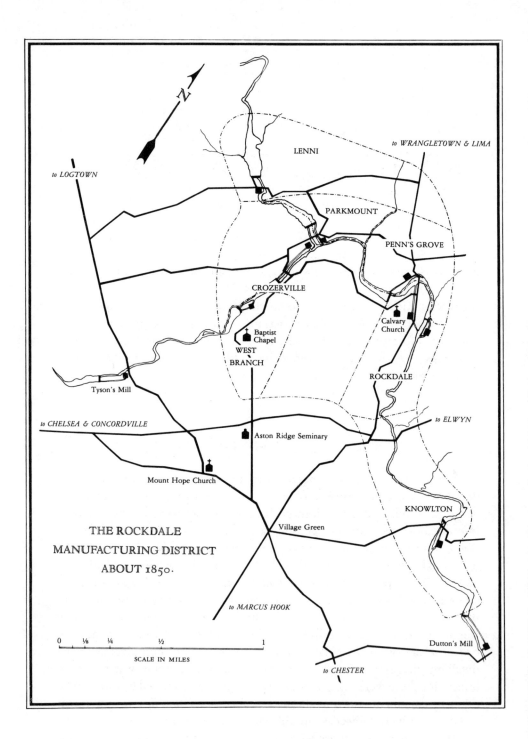

to LOGTOWN

to WRANGLETOWN & LIMA

LENNI

PARKMOUNT

PENN'S GROVE

CROZERVILLE

Calvary
Church

Baptist
Chapel

WEST
BRANCH

ROCKDALE

Tyson's Mill

to CHELSEA & CONCORDVILLE

to ELWYN

Aston Ridge Seminary

Mount Hope Church

KNOWLTON

Village Green

THE ROCKDALE
MANUFACTURING DISTRICT
ABOUT 1850.

to MARCUS HOOK

0   ⅛   ¼   ½   1

SCALE IN MILES

Dutton's Mill

to CHESTER

own jargon for occupational titles and his own ear for foreign-sounding names—did not record the addresses or even general location of the households. The final lists as they were sent to Washington consequently seemed, superficially, to present merely a random succession of the households in each township. But in fact each township schedule had a structure, for each enumerator's list remained intact as a section on the schedule. Each township list thus was a sort of collage, in which every piece represented a single field enumerator's data recorded for a particular day. This feature makes it possible to know where in the township the enumerator was at any point in the schedule. There is enough information in the property map published by Dr. Ash in 1848, in the county tax assessments, and in Samuel Riddle's paybook for Penn's Grove Mill to pinpoint the mill villages. When mill owner Peter Hill and his rentor-manufacturer Daniel Lammot were listed as neighbors, surrounded by operatives of various kinds, the enumerator was evidently in Lenni; when dozens of operative families surround Samuel Riddle's name in the list—families whose members worked for Riddle and whose names appeared in his paybook for that year—the enumerator was certainly at Penn's Grove; when the names of operatives clustered together in the census are also found together in the tax assessments as rentors from John P. Crozer at West Branch, the enumerator was obviously at West Branch. And similarly at the other mill hamlets.

From the 1850 census, therefore, emerges a reasonably complete survey of the population of the seven mill hamlets that made up the Rockdale district.

TABLE 1: *The Population of the Rockdale District by Age and Sex (1850)*

	MALE	FEMALE
80–89	2	3
70–79	8	9
60–69	27	18
50–59	70	52
40–49	84	89
30–39	102	127
20–29	161	193
10–19	277	265
0–9	281	238
	1,012	994

2,006

General Facts About the Manufacturing District

The total population of the Rockdale manufacturing district in 1850 was 2,006 persons (it thus accounted for 57 percent of the total population of the two predominantly rural townships in which it was located). These 2,006 persons were distributed among 7 hamlets whose average population was 287. There were 351 houses in the district; the average number of houses per hamlet was 50; the average number of persons per house 6. The total area of the district was almost exactly one and one-half square miles; thus the population density within the district was 1,302 per square mile. The breakdown of this population by age and sex is shown in the population pyramid in Table 1, which indicates that there were several interesting anomalies in sex and age ratios.

The most easily explained anomaly is the apparent underrepresentation of female as compared to male children under ten years of age. It is likely that, in this somewhat patriarchal society, parents and older siblings who talked to the enumerators sometimes simply failed to mention the smaller children and infants, particularly female infants, in their own or their neighbors' households.

Also readily explained is the second anomaly: the overrepresentation of both boys and girls between ten and twenty. This is almost certainly the result of a process of selective migration into the manufacturing district by families (both complete families and fatherless families) with teen-age children who could be put to work in the mills full or part time to help supplement family incomes.

More mysterious is the third anomaly: the overrepresentation of women in their twenties and thirties. There were 20 percent more women than men in their twenties, and 25 percent more women than men in their thirties: a total of fifty-seven more individual women than men in these age groups. Several factors seem to have been responsible. One was a greater tendency for unmarried adult females to remain with their families; in fact, there were thirty-seven more unmarried females than males in this age group living with parents or siblings. Another factor was a selective in-migration of broken families consisting of husbandless women and their children. Widows (as the manufacturers were wont to claim in defense of their practice of employing children) often moved into cotton-manufacturing districts for the express purpose of supporting themselves by putting their children out to work in the mills. There were fourteen such fatherless families in the Rockdale district with mothers in the twenty to thirty-nine age group. There were, on the other hand, more unattached male boarders than female of these ages. The excess of young women would seem largely to be the product of two things: a tendency for unmarried women to stay at home while their unmarried brothers moved out to seek their fortunes; and a tendency for the manufacturing district to attract widows with children of working age.

The fourth anomaly, the excess of males in their fifties and sixties, is less easy still to understand. There were far fewer unmarried widowers than widows in this age group, and even fewer old bachelors. The explanation seems to be a tendency for males to marry younger wives and, when widowed, to remarry even younger wives (this would also help to account for the slight female excess in the forty to forty-nine group and part of the female excess in the twenty to thirty-nine group).

About a quarter of the population were foreign-born: 9 percent were English, 15 percent Irish (mostly from Northern Ireland, to judge from the frequency of Scottish surnames), and 1 percent from various other countries. Although the mill owners, managers, and operatives were the core of the population, both among native- and foreign-born, there was a considerable variety of other occupational types. A number of farmers resided in the district (and the mill owners themselves usually operated a farm in connection with the mill site); there were physicians, public school teachers, clergymen, and even a musician; craftsmen plied their various trades; there were a number of shopkeepers; and there were unskilled laborers and domestic servants. Racially, the district was almost entirely white; a black man and woman worked in the inn at Lenni, and a six-person black family (the father a laborer), a single black woman, and two black teenagers lived at Knowlton, the latter in the house of mill owner Phineas Lownes (one of them—Jane Lownes—bearing his name).

But the Rockdale manufacturing district was not really a town. Administratively divided between Aston and Middletown townships, it was even more fundamentally divided among its seven constituent hamlets: West Branch, Crozerville, and Knowlton (all owned by John P. Crozer), Rockdale (owned by absentee manufacturer Bernard McCready), Lenni and Parkmount (owned by the Hills), and Penn's Grove (owned by Samuel Riddle). So let us turn to a consideration of these hamlets.

General Facts About the Mill Hamlets

The seven hamlets were in many respects very similar to one another. Each was a cluster of houses nestled around a mill, or strung out along the road that passed the mill, with a few extra structures to serve as community centers: Calvary Church at Rockdale, the Baptist chapel at West Branch, the inn at Lenni, the schoolhouses, the blacksmiths' shops (but most of the craftsmen and shopkeepers plied their trade in a room or two of their residences). The population of the hamlets ranged from 186 at Parkmount to 411 at Crozerville; the number of houses varied accordingly, from 32 to 77. The house—whether the usual two-rooms-plus-attic-plus-half-cellar stone tenement, constructed in blocks of two to four units, or the much larger farmhouses and mansions—was the natural enumeration unit, because it partitioned the population neatly into a finite number of households.

But the household was not conceived—even by the census enumerator —to be the fundamental social unit. The fundamental social unit was the simple nuclear family, composed of a mother and a father (who were assumed to be legally married, of course) and their natural children. Of the 351 houses in the district, 156 were occupied by such families living by themselves; another 96 were occupied by simple nuclear families who had taken in other people, sometimes relatives (like an aging parent or the sibling of one of the spouses or the orphaned child of a kinsman) and sometimes boarders (from individuals to whole families). If one includes all those households where the central unit was a simple nuclear family, then fully 72 percent of all the houses were occupied and headed by simple nuclear families. Most other households were composed of anticipations or remnants of the simple nuclear family: recently married couples who had not yet had children, older married couples whose children had moved away, a set of unmarried adult siblings whose parents had died, and—more common than any of the rest—one-parent families.

Most of the one-parent families were headed by women. It is not possible, in most cases, to know whether the woman was widowed, deserted, temporarily separated, or divorced. Forty-nine households in the district contained a family consisting of a woman and a child or children bearing her name. Often such female-headed families also contained several unmarried adults who remained with their mother and supported her by working in the mill. Most of the female-headed families either lived alone or helped to support themselves by taking in boarders. These forty-nine independent female-headed households amounted to 14 percent of the households in the district. Nine other independent male-headed households with motherless children, amounting to 3 percent of the total households, bring the number of households headed by a parent or parents with children to 89 percent of the total in the district. The remainder consisted largely of married couples living together (sometimes with boarders) without children. There were only six people (five white men and one black woman) listed as living alone; these, along with two female landladies and a male innkeeper, constitute the only persons in the entire district who were not living as members of a family or as boarders with a family.

The social organization of the mill hamlet was clearly based upon the nuclear family and its various modifications, no doubt in large part because, in these hamlets, most of the housing consisted of tenements rented from the mill owner, who usually let out the houses at a nominal rental to heads of households on condition that the family supply two or three hands to the mill. But this economically determined familistic structure among the mill workers was mirrored in all other segments of the community, from the mill owners down to the poorest laborers. Furthermore, in view of the tendency for adult siblings to migrate together, and for many families to remain, to acquire land in the district, and to see their children marry and move from one hamlet to another as work and housing opportunities changed, the family system involved many households in extensive sibling and affinal networks that helped to tie the whole district together into a loose consortium of related nuclear families.

If the family system was uniform and pervasive throughout the seven hamlets, so was the structure of occupation. Each hamlet had as its core the two contracting parties: the manufacturers and the operatives. The operatives were by far the most numerous occupational category in each hamlet; there were on an average thirty-six male operatives per hamlet (and about fifty women and children whose work status was not specified in the census). But there were also, on an average, ten tradesmen per hamlet—perhaps a couple of shoemakers and a tailor, a stonemason or bricklayer, a couple of carpenters, a cabinetmaker, a wheelwright or millwright, a plasterer, a watchmaker. There were about eight common laborers. And there would be about six farmers whose residences lay within the hamlet itself and who might take in as boarders an operative or a tradesman or two. In addition, there were likely to be a few educated residents as well as the mill owner's and manufacturer's family: a physician, a schoolteacher, a shopkeeper, a clerk from the mill, a musician, a colporteur (a lay missionary and distributor of religious tracts), and a clergyman. Thus in each hamlet, within the space of a few hundred yards along the road, there would be an impressive variety of social and occupational types.

This variety allowed each hamlet to a considerable extent, and the district to an even larger extent, to be a self-reliant community insofar as specialized personal services were concerned. People grew up and lived in intimate awareness of the nature of the lives and work of others; they performed services for the benefit of persons whom they knew; each was aware of his dependence upon and his responsibility for other people.

TABLE 2: *Social Composition of Mill Hamlets in the Rockdale District* (1850)

	Population	Number of Households	Households Containing a Fatherless Family	English-born	Irish-born	Mill Workers	Tradesmen	Farmers	Laborers
WEST BRANCH	192	32	2 6%	48 25%	25 13%	40 21%	0	2 1%	6 3%
CROZERVILLE	411	77	17 22%	13 3%	28 7%	36 9%	20 5%	6 1%	14 3%
LENNI	328	56	4 7%	12 4%	35 11%	30 9%	15 5%	14 4%	4 1%
PARKMOUNT	186	33	4 12%	16 9%	31 17%	26 15%	7 4%	1 1%	15 8%
PENN'S GROVE	360	62	6 10%	18 5%	93 26%	53 15%	8 2%	8 2%	13 4%
ROCKDALE	250	43	9 21%	16 6%	88 35%	28 11%	12 5%	5 2%	6 2%
KNOWLTON	279	48	7 15%	59 21%	7 3%	42 15%	6 2%	7 3%	5 2%

The Uniqueness of Each Mill Hamlet

Each hamlet took its name from the name the manufacturer gave to his mill; each also took its particular and distinguishing social characteristics from the size and composition of the work force that the mill's technology demanded. Each hamlet was unique and the sense of place was strong, so strong that even to this day, long after the spinning and weaving have ended, the people who live there will say such things as that they were born in Rockdale and grew up in Lenni, or that they married someone from West Branch, not Crozerville.

Some of the grosser statistical dimensions in which the hamlets differed were size of population, number of houses, percentage of households containing a fatherless family, percentage of population Irish-born, percentage English-born, and number of mill workers, tradesmen, farmers, and laborers. These data, arranged by hamlet, may be seen in Table 2. They show clearly that each hamlet was a unique mix of social constituents. West Branch, for instance, was small, had a disproportionately large share of English-born residents (six of the surviving tenements still stand on a bluff called "English Hill"), and was almost exclusively industrial, with no tradespeople at all, no farmers except the two that worked the mill estate itself, and very few unskilled laborers. West Branch Mill, with its two hundred looms, was specialized as a weaving mill; its yarns were made at nearby Crozerville. At West Branch, as a result of this fact, there was little call for the services of children, who were most useful as unskilled piecers and scavengers around the spinning mules and in the departments concerned with the preparation of the yarns. And the dearth of positions for children meant that few fatherless families settled there.

Crozerville, by contrast, had a high proportion of households—22 percent—containing fatherless families. This high percentage is probably related to the fact that Crozerville Mill was the spinning mill whose 7,032 spindles on mules and throstles supplied West Branch with warp and filling for its looms. Thus it provided employment opportunities for the children of widows and wives separated from their husbands, as well as children in intact families. Crozerville, the largest of the hamlets, was in a sense also the most cosmopolitan. It was the summer residence of the wealthy Smith family from Philadelphia, who rented the former Crozer mansion, and the year-round home of their friend the Reverend Mr. Charles Breck, rector of Calvary Church, and his family.[2] Crozerville also had three stores and a "huckster," two physicians, a schoolteacher in residence, ten shoemakers and a tailor (who no doubt were patronized also by the people from West

Branch), a number of small farmers, and various masons, carpenters, black-smiths, wheelwrights, drovers, and common laborers. With a high propor-tion of families of American-born farmers and tradesmen, Crozerville had a relatively low percentage of foreign-born mill operatives; and a number of its Irish were domestic servants.

Knowlton, the third of the Crozer enterprises, combined both spinning and weaving processes (60 looms, 1,548 spindles) in one factory and, accordingly, attracted a middling large number of fatherless families. Like West Branch, it was somewhat isolated and held few tradesmen, and like West Branch it seems to have favored English immigrants. Formerly managed for Crozer by an English-born weaver, Abraham Blakeley, it was now operated by Blakeley and a partner, while Crozer retained title to the land. Crozer's three hamlets together contained only sixty persons born in Ireland, amounting to only 7 percent of their total population, the lowest ratio for any set of mills owned by one person.

Lenni, owned by the Hills, who of course were large landowners in the neighborhood, and operated by Daniel Lammot, who maintained a more elegant style of living than anyone else in the district, was like Crozerville something of a social center. It boasted the mansions of the Lammots and the Hills, which were well kept and tended by professional gardeners, and a small hotel with black hostler and maid. There were numerous tradesmen. The tenements for the Lenni workers were mostly constructed across the creek some distance from the mansions, and a number of the workers boarded at the farms scattered along Lenni Road that ran through the hamlet, connecting the Rockdale district with Concordville to the west. The Lammots seem to have been slightly more nativistic than any other of the manufacturers, recruiting only 11 percent Irish- and a mere 4 percent English-born people for their settlement. Many of the Irish were domestic servants and farm workers, and one elderly Irish-born family, the McCrack-ens, were well-to-do landowners who had come over from Ireland before the War of 1812. In fact, only four Irishmen actually worked in Lammot's mill. This mill, a spinning and weaving mill, had about 2,000 mule and 2,000 throstle spindles. The number of fatherless families was low. Lenni, indeed, seems to have been designed to minimize the visibility of social problems and to maximize the charms of the pastoral life for the sophis-ticated Lammots and Hills.

The remaining three mills were all owned or operated by Irishmen and it is probably no accident that the proportion of Irish immigrants in the three hamlets associated with them was the highest in the Rockdale district. The population of Rockdale proper was 35 percent Irish-born, of Park-mount 17 percent, and of Penn's Grove 26 percent (the English-born in these hamlets amounted to only 6 percent, 9 percent, and 5 percent, respectively).

Rockdale proper, like Crozerville and Lenni, was more nearly a general village than some of the other hamlets. For more than a century it had been the site of industry, first as the home of Old Sable Forge and the nail manufactory, then of Phillips' weaving mill. The mill was now owned by Irish-born Bernard McCready and managed by English-born Thomas Blackburn. Rockdale provided housing for a number of workers at Penn's Grove factory, which was situated only a few hundred yards up Rockdale road on the other side of the covered bridge. And it served also to some degree as village center for both the Penn's Grove and Rockdale population, being the site of Calvary Church, which overlooked both hamlets from its commanding position on the hill above, and also the residence of a considerable number of tradespeople. Rockdale had a relatively large number of older males (there were fourteen men in their fifties as contrasted with only six in their thirties) and a high proportion of fatherless families (21 percent of the houses contained such a family). Both kinds of families, as at Crozerville, had no doubt been attracted by the nearby employment opportunities for children, and perhaps also by the proximity of the church, stores, and tradespeople generally. The colporteur, a twenty-six-year-old native of Ireland, was a member of one of these fatherless families; his illiterate mother, bereft of husband, was supported by him and his twenty-four-year-old brother, who worked in McCready's mill, and their sister, nineteen, who probably worked there also.

If Rockdale shone as the spiritual center of the manufacturing district, Riddle's mill at Penn's Grove was its industrial heart, with 160 looms and 4,980 spindles (both mules and throstles) in one factory. More than fifty male workers above the age of sixteen lived there, according to the census enumerators, and the payroll actually included an additional seventy women, many of them part-time workers whose occupation the enumerators did not record. Although Penn's Grove had a relatively large population—360, the largest after Crozerville—and boasted a general store and a post office, it was home to fewer tradesmen, and most of these worked for the Riddles as carpenters, plasterers, and millwrights, keeping the mill and the tenement houses in repair. Penn's Grove mostly depended on Rockdale, Lenni, and Crozerville for its shoemakers, watchmakers, tailors, seamstresses, and other practitioners of domestic crafts; it was solidly committed to work of the factory.

Parkmount was the smallest hamlet. The mill there in 1850 was being operated by an Irish carpet weaver, George Callaghan, and his son George Jr. George and Mary Callaghan were forty-four years old, had nine of their children living in their house, and provided room and board to two weavers. The Callaghans had lived for a time in Scotland, the birthplace of Mrs. Callaghan. They had emigrated to Connecticut and thence moved to Pennsylvania. They had leased Parkmount only two years before and were still working hard to make a go of it, employing their own children as piecers and scavengers at the mules. Their mill was a small one, vacated by Samuel Riddle a few years before; it housed four mules, eighteen power looms and hand looms, and worked both cotton and wool. The Callaghans wove cotton counterpanes and figured tablecloths on their power looms and woolen carpets on draw looms, which were big, complex, pre-Jacquard hand looms that required the use of drawboys to help the weaver.[3] Callaghan was making fancy goods and his mill required older, highly skilled male operatives. This may explain the curious fact that seventeen males in their thirties lived at Parkmount and only eleven in their twenties.

THE SOCIAL STATIONS

Among the residents of the Rockdale district it was recognized that there were four social levels: a highly solidified managerial class, composed of the manufacturers, mill owners, merchants, and gentlemen farmers, and their wives and children; an amorphous and embryonic middle level, probably with little clear awareness of itself as a group, composed of people who performed skilled services on a contractual basis for all classes—ministers and physicians, innkeepers, schoolteachers, small farmers, and the various mechanics, such as masons, blacksmiths, carpenters, and machinists; a large and reasonably self-conscious working class, made up predominantly of people who worked by the day for the managerial class as operatives in mills, as manual laborers, and as domestic servants; and a bottom level of indigent and degraded poor. Members of this last class of people were not visible in Rockdale, however, because, being unable to take care of themselves, they were for the most part housed in the "House of Employment" at Media, several miles away. This lowest group, physically extruded from the community and supported at public expense (with some supplemental funds from their own work in the poorhouse industries), included the insane, the mentally retarded, the chronically ill and handicapped, young orphans, some deserted wives or widows with children too young to work, and no doubt one or two who simply could not seem to manage without constant supervision. A few other members of the class of degraded poor were housed in the county prison or the Eastern State Penitentiary in Philadelphia.

The Managerial Class

Insofar as one can judge from the correspondence, property maps, and tax assessments, the families who constituted the managerial class in the Rockdale district in the 1840's were about twelve in number. Four of these households have already been mentioned as lords of the valley: the Smiths, the Lammots, the Crozers, and the Riddles. There were others, more briefly noted: Peter and Hannah Sellers Hill, who owned the mills at Lenni and Parkmount and farmed a considerable tract; George W. Hill, Peter's brother, who before his death owned Penn's Grove and farmed and operated the store there; the Willcoxes of Ivy Mills; the Sharpless family, at the iron plantation of Old Sarum Forge; the Tysons, who owned Aston Mills and other land in the township. There was Davis B. Stacey, a retired importer turned gentleman farmer, and an old and dear friend of Richard S. Smith and William Martin; the Pennells, an old and well-established family of local landowners; and the Duttons, mill owners, tanners, and inventors. This ruling group seems to have divided socially (not economically or politically) into cliques along several lines of cleavage. The Smith-Lammot-Willcox-Stacey network included "society" people, originally from the Boston, New York, and Philadelphia areas, who shared an interest in evangelical Protestant religion and came from the same general background of urban commercial families. The indigenous Quaker clans— Sharplesses, Pennells, and Duttons—kept apart socially, probably on religious grounds, and their ladies do not appear in the Smith and Lammot correspondence as participants in the sisterhood. The Hills, Crozers, and Riddles seem to have been socially alone, perhaps in part because their churches were distant (Peter Hill was a Swedenborgian and went to church at Upper Darby, the Crozers Baptists who worshipped at Marcus Hook, and the Riddles Presbyterians whose church also was located some distance away), but probably more because of personal feelings. Crozer was shy and suffered from feelings of inadequacy in social situations where he was expected to speak. Peter Hill was regarded as an unscrupulous rascal in money matters. Samuel Riddle had just lost his wife Martha, who died after giving birth to their first son, Henry, in the spring of 1850. He did not marry again until 1860, when he took as his second wife the twenty-three-year-old Lydia C. Doyle of Chester, who bore him four children, the last in 1868 (when Samuel was sixty-eight years old).[1] Riddle had a reputation, among some of the working people at least, for using broad language and telling earthy stories. In Riddle's case, too, some prejudice may conceivably have been based on the relative recency of his arrival from Ireland, but that seems unlikely to have been a major factor. The Willcox family was of Irish extraction (albeit a century and a half before), and Catholic to boot, but they were freely included in the social affairs of the Smiths and the Lammots.

The stratification of Rockdale society was physical as well as mental. The upper class lived in substantial stone houses, locally referred to as mansions, with ten or twelve rooms, always near the top of a hill overlooking the family property; the lesser classes occupied dwellings below, with the workers' tenements often almost on the edge of the stream, and immediately adjacent to the mill. (Altitude was symbolic of social elevation and thus was often invoked in names of prestigious institutions. The churches were "Calvary" and "Mount Gilead" and "Mount Hope"; Riddle's mill was "Parkmount"; the hill above Rockdale was "the Mount" and the road below it "Mount Road"; and the cluster of new tenements at West Branch, occupied by English immigrants, was dubbed "English Hill.") Each mansion had outbuildings where the horses and carriages were kept, and there might be a detached summer kitchen and a greenhouse (Phillips at least kept a

OLD MANSIONS AT LENNI HEIGHTS.

greenhouse and raised flowers through the winter, which he gave to his friends). In the 1840's, some of the mansions were being equipped with indoor toilets and had indoor pumps and facilities for bathing, and they were heated less often by open fireplaces than by iron stoves. Furnishings were comfortable: carpeted floors, upholstered chairs, beds with mattresses stuffed with cotton waste; there were pianos and harps, and tables for books and prints. Portraits and daguerreotypes ornamented walls and mantels.

One of the most distinctive features of the managerial class's culture was its cosmopolitan quality. Both men and women were accustomed to travel, or at least to the idea of travel. The women summered at the fashionable resorts at Cape May or Saratoga (the men, if they attended, suffered agonies of boredom), and in the winter they often spent part of the social season in Philadelphia or visited with friends and relatives in Boston, New York, Washington, and cities of the south. Some of the men had lived abroad (the Riddles) or had traveled abroad on business (like Richard S. Smith and Davis B. Stacey). And everyone was constantly conscious of living, not just in Rockdale, but in a nation and a world with all regions of which he or she had a concern. Every businessman followed national, international,

THE LUNGREN MANSION AT LENNI.

financial, and commercial affairs because they affected his enterprises directly, as the prices of raw cotton and cotton goods fluctuated, discount rates changed, or wars and threats of wars opened and closed markets. Every wife and daughter read books from England and France and thrilled to missionary adventures in India, China, and Africa.

Theirs was a world in which intellectual and artistic interests were part of a normal gentle life. These gentlemen farmers, merchants, and manufacturers and their ladies did not feel that they had to acquire intensive technical training in college in order to be liberally educated, well informed, and capable of managing large affairs. In fact, evangelical religion led some of them to a kind of genteel anti-scientism. In a letter "to a young man who thought that God can be better known through science than Revelation," Smith somewhat patronizingly explained that the *important* knowledge was knowledge of Scripture:

> It is evident that you understand the ground of my faith and hope to be the *Scriptures,* which I believe fully to be a revelation from God, and *without* which there is good reason to believe that man, with all the helps of science, would have a very inadequate idea of God . . . the humblest Christian can better attain through the Scriptures to a knowledge of God, and a confident hope of eternal life through Jesus Christ, than can the most learned philosopher and man of science, by any other means than through the same Scriptures. . . . When vain man attempts, as is sometimes the case, to set aside revelation by setting forth what is called some new discovery, either in natural science, or in some new system of philosophy, I remember the warning of the apostle Paul—"Beware lest any man spoil you, through philosophy or vain deceit." In reading over what I have written, it seems to me a rambling sketch of my own convictions, and I am not sure that I make myself understood; but I will sum up what I have written by saying that I hold in respect and admiration every advance in science and learning, and among Christ's most faithful followers, recognize many of the most scientific and learned men that have lived on the earth; yet I contend that God, in his revelation of himself, through the Scriptures, has given us sufficient light to *know* and serve him, and has furthermore revealed that "Eye hath not seen, nor ear heard, neither hath it entered into the heart of man to conceive the things which God hath prepared for those who love him."[2]

The members of the managerial class had a much stronger feeling of solidarity than did the members of the other classes. In addition to the women's networks, and the common commitment to an ecumenical evangelism, the group was united by a remarkable sense of economic loyalty.

Although in some abstract sense the cotton manufacturers on Chester Creek were in competition with one another, it was not the sort of competition where one man's gain was understood to require his neighbor's loss. The maxim was not "Every man for himself" in a pursuit of scarce values; to the contrary, the maxim was closer to "Sink or swim together." Everyone was expected to act in concert politically with respect to tariffs, labor relations, and the government's financial policies. Everyone was expected to be strictly honest in business dealings involving such matters as loans and discounted notes (Peter Hill's failure to abide by these norms rendered him subject to severe criticism). Everyone was expected to—and did—bring men and equipment at once to help put out a fire in anyone's mill. The contest was not so much with other manufacturers; rather, it was with a capricious environment that frequently threatened everyone with adverse economic conditions, unfriendly legislation, or hostile administrative action. This sentiment of solidarity among the members of the managerial class was not a parochial, district-by-district thing, either. It included managerial people throughout the whole region in and around Philadelphia.

Perhaps the most dramatic evidence of the strength of this feeling of mutual obligation and responsibility was the way in which the industrial and commercial insurance companies were operated. They were mutual companies in which the members bought stock and subscribed funds to be called upon when operating expenses and casualty losses required additional money. The commercial and industrial community in effect insured itself as a whole; and this meant that each manufacturer and merchant insured his "competitors" as well as himself. The boards of directors of these companies were elected from the major stockholders and subscribers. The two senior officers—the president and the secretary—were drawn from the same class. These two staff positions, which were salaried, were regarded as a kind of rotating unemployment insurance fund for failed members of the group. Among the Chester Creek managers, no less than three were at one time or another beneficiaries of the system and one other tried unsuccessfully to secure its benefits. Daniel Lammot, after his commercial failure in Philadelphia, tried (unsuccessfully) to secure appointment to the vacant post of secretary of the American Fire Insurance Company.[3] William Martin, a few difficult years after his failure in 1829, became the secretary of the Delaware County Mutual Safety Insurance Company, of which Crozer and other manufacturers were directors, and later its president.[4] John S. Phillips, after his cotton mill at Fairmount failed during the depression of the early 1840's, for a few years held the post of secretary of the Columbia Insurance Company.[5] And in 1837 Richard S. Smith, after the collapse of his merchant house in 1833, accepted the position of president of a marine insurance firm, the Union Mutual Insurance Company—and held the office until his death.[6] In assuming these positions, the officer was certain to find on the Board of Directors a number of old cronies and business associates (who had in fact been responsible for his appointment). Thus Martin's board included John P. Crozer and other Delaware County businessmen with whom he had formerly dealt as merchant, attorney, manufacturer, or state representative; Richard Smith's board included John R. Neff, the cotton importer; and John S. Phillips' board included a number of old cotton business associates and family friends: Charles du Pont, Daniel Lammot, Joseph Ripka, William Young, and Francis Gurney Smith.

The most explicit explanation of how the system worked is contained in a memorandum of Charles du Pont concerning Charles N. Buck, the president of the Columbia Insurance Company. The company was formed in 1840 shortly after Mr. Buck, a Wilmington merchant, failed in business. The early major subscribers were the Du Ponts, Lammot, and Ripka. Du Pont was very explicit in his statement in favor of continuing Mr. Buck in the presidency: "The Col. Insce. Co. was got up with the view of giving Mr. C.N. Buck the means of living."[7]

It is evident, from their use of the mutual insurance company as not only an underwriting mechanism but also a source of employment for their financially embarrassed associates, that the businessmen who made up the core of the managerial class were not simply intent on maximizing personal profit by competitive or monopolistic methods. Quite the contrary: they were committed to preserving the standard of living of all the members of a social class, often at the risk of considerable financial loss to themselves as individuals. They acted on the assumption that if they did not support one another against economic competition from outside the region, capriciously fluctuating markets, and governmental bodies apparently indifferent to their needs, they would *all* suffer. The failure of a fellow merchant or manufacturer was like the wounding of a fellow officer in combat or the illness of a fellow missionary in a heathen land—everyone rallied around to give whatever support and assistance was possible; to let him sink in adversity would only weaken, not strengthen, the survivors.

The attitudes of members of the managerial class toward the other classes, particularly the working class, can be discerned in their correspondence and memoirs. (The reciprocal attitudes of other classes are not so easy to elucidate, because their members were less often literate and less likely to leave papers to historical societies.) The managerial class was in constant and intimate contact with the other classes, employing their members to work on their farms and in their factories and to provide services of all kinds. There was a marked ambivalence evident in the expressions of class attitude. On the one hand, the managerial person definitely looked down on the members of other classes as inferior to him not merely in education, power, and wealth but also in moral strength and emotional sensibility. Even the poorer clergymen, like Mr. Huntington and Mr. Murphy, and their families, were patronizingly referred to by Clementina as "the class of people who will suffer" during hard times.[8] On the other hand, the managers were committed to the principle that individual members of the lower classes could rise and approach, even achieve, equality with their betters, not merely in the fellowship of Christ but in the pursuit of Mammon as well (and some of the managerial families were living examples of this achievement). The classes were thus fixed and permanent institutions, but individuals were not permanently fixed in any class.

The most severe expressions of class prejudice came from the pens of Clementina and Sophie and were directed at female servants and female mill hands. Sophie, for instance, once confided in her diary her surprise at seeing a working-class woman show grief over a sick child. Sophie had come on a visit of charity and found the child in the care of its Aunt Rebecca, a young woman who regularly cared for the child while the mother worked. The mother was unable to help much during the child's illness; "she did sit up once or twice—but its of no use—she only loses her rest—& she has to work." The neighbors were kind but the child would only take medicine from Aunt Rebecca, to whom fell all responsibility for its fate. When Sophie called, Rebecca was overcome with emotion; as Sophie put it, "The poor girl hid her face in her apron in an agony of tears." This seemed remarkable to Sophie, who declared in her diary, "I never saw so much feeling evinced in that class of life."[9]

Clementina too believed that women of the lower class were deficient in the finer feelings, as well as lacking in moral strength (and, if they were Irish, a prey to "Hibernianisms" and "superstitious terrors" as well). In 1857, during the illness from scarlet fever of her little nephew, which came at the time of a great snowstorm that piled drifts up against the window 5 feet deep and was followed by temperatures of twenty degrees below zero, she and Harriet had trouble with the wet-nurses. The first nurse ("Irish," for Clementina always noted the ethnic membership of servants, whether Irish, Welsh, German, or black) came down with infected breasts. The baby, after he vomited blood several times, was taken from her. The baby then lost weight and Clementina feared he would starve, for he threw up the cow's milk offered as a substitute. So he was given to a second nurse ("Welsh"), who placed her own baby with another family. Clementina nursed the Irish wet-nurse, poulticing and massaging her breasts, but regarded it as "the hardest nursing I ever did," for the nurse was "refractory" and "as you know that class of people have little self-control or patience in sickness." But now the Irish nurse, without a baby to suckle, suffered in addition from engorged breasts, and, the artificial breast pumps failing, her own baby was sent for to give her relief. After this baby had performed its service, it was sent back to *its* wet-nurse while the mother's breasts healed and she began to lose her milk. Then suddenly the Irish baby became ill and the woman and her husband rushed it back to the Smith house early in the morning through cold and muddy streets. On the doorstep the baby went into convulsions; the Smiths put it into a bath of warm water, but within a few minutes it was dead, without having reached its mother. Clementina had to tell the poor woman. The experience, she confessed to Sophie, was trying, and not least the absence of true grief:

> The passionate expression of what at first seemed like grief but proved to be rather disappointment not to have relief, mixed up with a sort of maternal instinct of pain in not having been with the child, the interment in catholic ground & endless difficulties—Marys strange and trying course, not to be entered into here, the difficulty of getting at the truth about her thro' the protestant bitterness against her among some [of] the domestics including the little new wet nurse—all these things we have had to contend with till yesterday when Mary left for another place—[10]

To what extent the conception of the lower-class person as deficient in the finer sensibilities may have been grounded in fact is difficult to judge. Certainly the view was a literary convention of the day. Clementina and Sophie read, and approved, a novel about a factory girl by the well-known English authoress Charlotte Elizabeth, whose collected evangelical fiction and poetry (with an introduction by Harriet Beecher Stowe) had been published in New York in 1847. *Helen Fleetwood* concerns an orphaned country girl who, when her foster mother is evicted by the landlord, is forced to go to the city of Manchester at the age of sixteen. Helen takes employment in the carding room of a great factory, perseveres in Christian virtue despite the coarseness of her companions and the hostility of the irreligious, and then returns to her village to die, still a maiden, of overwork, an unjust beating by a supervisor armed with an iron bar, and consumption. The work aimed to expose the hypocrisy and sham of the administration of the laws that supposedly regulated working conditions in the English factories, and to make ladies and gentlemen aware of the harsh reality that condemned the children of the poor to a living death, chained to the ceaseless machines. But the effectiveness of the plot depended upon the contrast between the pure, if simple, country girl and her evil urban proletarian fellow workers; it was almost as if the sympathy for the poor which the author sought to arouse in the reader was reserved only for the exceptional Christian poor. In a matronly and condescending way, the author described the advantages that made Helen Fleetwood more deserving of a literary memorial than most of the members of her class:

Helen Fleetwood was a girl of delicate mind, such as is often found in our sequestered villages, under the guardianship of watchful prudence, more especially when influenced by early, simple piety. There was nothing in her character unusually elevated above the class to which she belonged; but it owed something of its finer texture to the scenery of her native place, and its association with a tale of infant bereavement, of parental sorrow, that she indeed could scarcely remember, but which had often been related to her with touching pathos, though in homely phrase, by the fishermen's families around. By brooding on these, as she marked the rolling of the billows that had once ingulfed her father, she acquired a more contemplative, and perhaps a more imaginative turn of thought than most of her young companions, while a modest reluctance to make her own concerns more prominent than was suitable for so humble a person habituated her to what Mary [her friend] termed keeping her own counsel.[11]

Like Charlotte, Clemma and Sophie were willing to admit of exceptions —particularly if the exceptional person were humble and respectful. As we shall see later, Sophie once made a protégée of a little weaver named Maria Miles, who married Abraham Blakeley and eventually became a lady. Clementina also spoke highly of a young woman, Mary Elliot, who with her husband Robert was a regular member of the Calvary congregation. They were English-born, lived at Parkmount; Robert worked in one of the mills and Mary worked as a "waitress" in the Smith household and "took her meals with our girls." Mary Elliot had been a Sunday School scholar of Clementina's and in the winter of 1851, at the age of twenty-eight, became one of the teachers in the school. She wrote to Clementina in Philadelphia asking for sympathy and counsel. She also wanted advice on how to proceed with a special course of instruction for her class of girls in the proper use of the Book of Common Prayer, for she had observed that many of the girls made no use of the prayer book during services, "whether from indolence or from ignorance of its usefulness I cannot tell." She asked Sophie to recommend a book to assist her. Clementina's father at once sent Miss Elliot a copy of such a book and Clementina wrote to Sophie, who had been giving a course in the subject at the Brandywine Manufacturers' Sunday School, asking her to send a list of the lesson topics. Sophie did better than this, proceeding to copy out all of her lesson notes. On hearing of this, Mary Elliot wrote back in haste to Clementina (addressing her as "My Dear Friend"), urging her to ask Sophie not to go through with "the labor of copying her notes in order to assist me in my class." In a style both familiar and slightly stilted, she went on:

> Give my love to her as a fellow Christian and co-worker in the cause of Christ and tell her that with the very excellent books with which you have so kindly furnished me I shall be able to get along I think very well always relying on the help of God through prayer to assist me. I feel it would be imposing an unnecessary and laborious task upon her kindness to allow her to persist in her kind intentions. I shall probably be in the city next week if I am I shall come to see you.[12]

Some years later Clementina wrote Sophie praising a Mrs. Elliot, now a widow living on the Brandywine, and recommending her as the housekeeper for Victorine Bauduy.

> She is refined, and pleasant in temper and I am sure her experience and trials in life must have all tended to improve & to elevate a naturally fine character which grace has sanctified too—*All* I know of Mary Elliott is very much in her favour—and I feel sure the position must be very congenial to her feelings unless she is changed since I knew her—I dont know much of her as a housekeeper but she will certainly (after keeping house herself) know enough to be a dependance for Sister & Eleu, and she is what they most wish I believe a very nice seamstress—How glad I will be to know she is with her Sister for I do think she will be a comfort to her—She is in mind & manners much above her station too, but only shows this to her superiors by a gentle & respectful demeanour—[13]

Clearly, the members of the managerial class expected men and women of the working class to employ a style of address in their conversation and correspondence that evoked the image of equality in Christian fellowship. Clementina and Sophie expected their ex-Sunday School scholars to salute them as friends, despite the vast difference in their social positions, and dozens of letters to Sophie (and the few to Clementina that survive) from former students show an uncomfortable balance in the effort to use the language of equality while the poor grammar, uncertain handwriting, effusive politeness, and supplicant messages convey extreme dependence and fear of giving offense. No letters from workers to their employers seem to have survived; but during the 1842 strike the expressions of resentment by manufacturers against striking employees who would not take up their grievances in man-to-man discourse betray a similar standard. The managers wanted to maintain social control over the workers and at the same time they wanted to maintain the doctrine of equality before God and the law; they wanted intimacy and trust in their relationship with them and also a recognition of hierarchy.

Managerial people felt a strong sense of responsibility for the personal welfare of those workers whom they personally employed or who had been personally associated with them in church affairs. Clementina and Sophie's letters are filled with accounts of obligatory care for servants in difficulty (who are almost invariably referred to by first name with "poor" as a prefix). Thus, referring to a servant girl who died in the house of her employer, Sophie observed that it had been a difficult time for the Grimshaws, for the girl had been ill for several weeks, during which she was "entirely out of her mind." She added, "As the poor girl had no relatives in this country all the trouble & responsibility fell on them."[14] The Smiths sent a servant girl home to her family when they thought she was about to marry unwisely.[15] When "our poor little Jane" became an invalid, they kept her with them ("she has a home with us") and hired someone to do her work.[16] When the local scrap man fell ill, they arranged to get "our old friend the scrap man into the Hospital" through the help of a physician who was a cousin of Clementina's. "The poor old man builds all his hope of recovery on this, the medical treatment he will have the benefit of there."[17] The responsibility did not end with death; when "my poor Rosie" died in the almshouse in Philadelphia, Clementina tried (in vain) to persuade her minister to bury her in the churchyard instead of in the common grave ("that shocking wholesale manner practiced in those places").[18] With the Sunday School scholars, the initial assumption of managerial responsibility for a poor person's religious welfare automatically involved a mutually recognized general economic responsibility as well. Former scholars felt no compunction in writing to Sophie asking for favors: money to finance the setting up of a store, assistance to a mother in getting a letter delivered to her son who was a seaman aboard one of Commodore Du Pont's ships, advice on how to handle a difficult husband.

The concept of responsibility for those one employed or instructed might, if the person had special qualities of intelligence or character that set him apart from the mass of working people, lead to the establishment of a patron-client relationship that could endure for life. Having a patron could mean, for the workingman or woman, an opportunity to rise into the ranks of the middle class or even the managerial class. From the perspective of the managerial class, the acceptance of a working-class person as a client was a declaration that class boundaries were not impermeable; it was a means of recruiting virtuous and talented people into the society of those who ran things, and testified to the reality of America's claim to be the land of equality and opportunity for all. But we shall examine these patron-client relationships in more detail later when we look at the whole question of the social aspirations and successful careers of men and women who started out poor.

The notion of managerial responsibility for the poor—particularly the deserving poor—was also an ingredient in the ideology of the manufacturers. Crozer, writing to the liberally inclined Minshall Painter about the time that he joined the Delaware County Institute of Science, observed that he had read some articles in the *Lowell Offering* that Painter had lent him, and "if they are as they profess to be, from the pens of the female operatives it is clearly indicative of considerable intelligence amongst the females of Lowell." He went on expansively about the implications of this evidence of intellect among members of the working class (and females at that):

> I have long been sensible that there is an unjustifiable prejudice prevailing against females employed in factories—our operatives in Penn^a are in education much below that of Eastern Factories, but in virtue morality our factory girls, with here & there an exception, are unimpeachable. As an Employer my mind has often been exercised on the moral & religious improvement of the employees, we have done a little in this vicinity; yet but very little compared with what ought to be, and probably could be done.[19]

Evidently the idea of stewardship, as well as the general belief in the importance of evangelical missions among the workers, was based in part in Crozer's mind on the more general notion that the manager was in some ways responsible for the welfare of his employees, especially if they were virtuous and intelligent.

The Level of Poor Professionals, Small Farmers, Storekeepers, and Master Craftsmen

Next to the managers in the social hierarchy was a group that is difficult to characterize as a class except by exclusion from the other classes. There were a number of people, some of them living in the Rockdale district and some in the nearby crossroads centers at Village Green, Corner Ketch, and Lima, who considered themselves (and were considered by others) to be lower in rank than the managers but higher than the working people. They probably did not think of themselves as a group with common interests; it is difficult to use the term "middle-class" to denote them, for that label suggests a stable and more or less uniform life style and a considerable degree of self-awareness. Many members of this "class" were only temporarily there, being either on the way up to join the managers, or on their way down into the lower orders.

Not all professional people were of this station in life. Many were the scions of well-established families, who had chosen the ministry, the law, medicine, or the military as a respectable alternative to commerce or manufacturing or farming. Not all the brothers in a managerial family were needed to manage the family's capital ventures in the new generation. Crozer's sons, to be sure, all did go into the cotton business. But Smith's son Richard went to West Point, became an engineer, and for a time served as president of Girard College; John S. Phillips's brother was a physician; Francis Gurney Smith's son, the Thomas Mackie who married Eleuthera, was a physician; of the sons of E. I. and Victor du Pont, one—Samuel Francis—entered the Navy, and another, Henry, went to West Point. William Martin's son, John Hill Martin, also attended West Point but dropped out to become a lawyer. And Alfred Lee was the son of a well-to-do New England merchant and had independent means. These people, while remaining members of the managerial class, found careers in the professions.

But there were also poor professional people. In Rockdale, after the Reverend Mr. Lee left to become Bishop of Delaware, the rectors at Calvary Church were generally men with education but without means, who depended for their living upon the skimpy salary paid by the congregation. The situation was similar with Rockdale's physicians. Until 1841, when he left to become customs officer in the Philadelphia harbor's quarantine station (the "Lazaretto"), Rockdale was the home of the managerial-class Dr. Samuel Anderson, who lived a varied career as Navy surgeon, Army captain, sheriff, state representative, congressman, justice of the peace, president of the Delaware County Bible Society, and—incidentally—private physician. Far less conspicuous, and definitely not of the upper class, were the lesser physicians, such as Dr. Gregg of Wrangletown, Dr. Marsh of Concord, and Dr. Humphrey, the homeopathic physician of Aston. The physicians in Crozerville in 1850 were young men who boarded with the local storekeepers. And the "teachers" appear in the census as boarders and renters. There were, so far as the record shows, no military men or lawyers resident in the Rockdale district.

Apart from the professional people, there were a number of other occupational categories that fell into the level between the managing and the working class. The self-employed master craftsmen in the district whom one might wish to include in this intermediate class were quite numerous: a few tailors, a dozen shoemakers, a dressmaker, a few highly skilled masons and builders, some wheelwrights and millwrights, carpenters, plasterers, blacksmiths. There was the miller who leased and operated the gristmill at Old Sable Forge. There were several storekeepers. There were mill managers. And there were the five or six practical farmers, like the McCrackens (who were rich) and the Eachus family (who were poor), who worked for the Riddles now and then as carters and operatives, and the ten or twelve householders with half a dozen acres or so, whose properties lay within the district itself. All together, the class of poor professionals, master craftsmen, storekeepers, and farmers amounted to about 150 households.

With a few exceptions, the members of this group were self-employed. The exceptions were the ministers and the public school teachers (and probably the mill managers too), who were hired on a contract which called for an annual cycle of services in return for an annual salary; and these individuals, being better educated than the workers, certainly had a higher social status. The self-employed persons—the physicians, the storekeepers, the craftsmen, the seamstress, the miller, the farmers—sold either a service or a product to anyone with the money to buy. Cash incomes, in many cases, were probably no higher than the better paid operatives'. A few—storekeepers and farmers—had substantial real estate or other capital; the rest had only a few tools or some books and an education.

There is nothing to suggest that the members of this class, when they looked horizontally, as it were, at the others on their level who differed from them in occupation, would have thought of them all as sharing a common set of interests. The only feature they did in fact share was a view of themselves as standing below the managerial class and above the working class.[20]

The Working Class

Most of the people who lived in Rockdale belonged to the working class. They were mainly mill hands and their families; but there were three other kinds of working people: farm hands and gardeners, common laborers, and domestic servants. With only a few exceptions, working people were employed by members of the managerial class, either as hands in their mills and about their estates or as servants in their houses.

The fundamental social unit for workers, as for managers and middle-level people, was the simple nuclear family residing in its own house. To be sure, working-class families were more likely to have been broken by death or separation, and there were many unmarried men and women who had jobs in the mills and boarded with other working-class households or who were servants and lived in with well-to-do families. But the basic unit was the simple family and almost all working people lived as members of, or boarders or servants with, such a family or one of its transformations.

Economic conditions in the district made it possible for working people, and particularly the employees of the mills, to live well and save money. The functioning of the system for mill workers can best be seen by looking at circumstances of particular households for whom records have survived. Take, for instance, the family of John Blair. In August 1850, John Blair and his family were living in Rockdale in a house which they rented from Archibald McDowell (Samuel Riddle's son-in-law and the manager of Penn's Grove factory). Blair was fifty and his wife Jane forty-eight; they had five children: Ann, thirteen, Isabella, twelve, Sarah, nine, Matthew, six, and William, five; and they took in as boarders James Garrett, twenty-two, the clerk at the mill, and a young woman of twenty-four, Sarah Barlow, who was a weaver at the same mill. Sarah Barlow was English; all the rest were Irish-born. The Blairs had arrived at Penn's Grove in 1847, fresh from Ireland. During 1847, 1848, and 1849, the Blairs supplied three hands to the mill. The father, John, worked in the card room, six days a week, at $2.50 per week; in 1849 his wages were raised to $3.50 per week. The mother, Jane, worked in the card room at $2.50 per week. Their ten-year-old daughter Ann worked in the throstle room at $1 per week; her wages were raised to $2 per week after about a year. In 1849 the family could have earned, in the fifty-two weeks of the year, a maximum of $364 at the factory, but this amount was reduced by temporary layoffs and sickness to a total of $257.46 earned by the three of them during the year.

At the year's end, the father was able to obtain employment as a stonemason, which had probably been his original employment in Ireland, and his place in the mill was taken by the next daughter, Isabella, aged twelve. Young Matthew and William thus were left in the house in the care of their older sister Sarah. About 1855, the Blairs moved to Crozerville, where John worked in his trade as a stonemason; probably his family worked in the mill there. In 1860 they moved again, to a house they rented from the Riddles on "Church Hill" in Crozerville, and resumed working at Penn's Grove.

In 1850, John Blair's wife Jane worked in the card room as before. It may be worth while to look more closely at the social composition of this department of the factory. The employees who were listed in the payroll under the rubric "card room" were responsible not merely for the operation of the carding machines, which produced slivers for the spreaders, stretchers, and spinning frames in the throstle room, but also for the initial preparation of the cotton for feeding into the cards. This included the picker room, where the bales were opened and the contents mixed and beaten to remove dust and dirt, and the spreading machines, where laps (sheets of cotton wool of uniform thickness, width, and length) were carefully prepared. Proper mixing, picking, lapping, and carding were essential for the production of good-quality yarn. In March 1850, twenty-nine people worked in the card room—eight males and twenty-one females. For four of these no information remains except the presence of their names on the payroll. Of the twenty-five others, twenty had other members of their own households working in the mill, and twelve had housemates working in the card room itself (two households supplied three workers each; three supplied two).

Men dominated the card room in technical authority and were highest in pay. The boss carder, John Thompson, was paid at a rate of $48 per month (four weeks of six days each). He had held this job for six years. The four carders received from $14 to $18 per month. Three males served as laborers, probably in the picker room; one of these, the boss's fourteen-year-old son, received $6 per month, the others $8 and $10. All twenty-one of the women received $10 per month except for five, who made only $6; two of these were fourteen, one was sixteen, and there is no information about the ages of the other two.

Families, however, determined the informal social network of the department. Two of the men—the boss and one of the carders—had two other members of their households in the card room, Thompson's son and a twenty-two-year-old female boarder in his house, and the two daughters (nineteen and twenty-two) of the carder. Thompson had a daughter (fifteen) working in the throstle room as well. There were three pairs of sisters: the McDowell girls, twenty-three and twenty (they had a brother and a sister in the throstle room); the Ferguson sisters, twenty and fourteen, who came from Knowlton, where their father worked in a mill; and Hannah Massey, eighteen, and her recently married sister Ann Powell (a third sister worked as a weaver). Hannah's father owned a small farm on the hill above Crozerville.

The web of kinship was probably even more complex than the available data indicate, for census records and ledger numbers do not reveal most of the affinal connections and fail to show whether male heads of different families with the same surname were consanguineally related. Thus there were certainly brothers, sisters, cousins, and in-laws of close degree working together in the same department or in the same mill whom we cannot identify now. The statement that four out of five workers in the card room had relatives working in the same mill, or that nearly half of them had a housemate in the card room itself, is simply an understatement of the pervasiveness of kin relationships. And, of course, the workers in the card room, in addition to being tied together by kinship, were many of them close neighbors. Of the twenty-three for whom residential information is available, fifteen lived near to one another as residents of ten houses rented from among Riddle's forty-three tenements at Penn's Grove; others came from Rockdale, Knowlton, and Crozerville.

The other large departments of the factory—the throstle room and the weaving room—were similarly organized. There was a throstle-room boss who earned $24 per month and two loom bosses who earned $36 per month. Their departments were similarly composed of both males and females, with a preponderance of women: twenty to twelve in the throstle room, and twenty-nine to twenty-two in the weaving room. But there were differences in the social character of the two rooms. The throstle room was mostly occupied by young people between twelve and twenty, supervised by a few mature adults. The weavers, by contrast, were mostly men and women in their twenties and thirties, with only a few teenagers. Fifteen of the thirty-two throstle-room workers came from six households; eighteen of the fifty-one weavers came from eight households. Throstle-room workers were paid by the day and earned from $6 to $10 per month; the weavers, who were on piecework, usually producing some combination of the mill's final products (tickings, stripes, denims, and calicoes), could earn as much as $30 per month or even more, depending on skill and the time put in. The most highly specialized workers—the five mule spinners and the three warpers—earned more than any other employees except the bosses, the warpers all earning over $29 per month, and the mule spinners between $40 and $50 per month. Two of the spinners earned over $49 in the month ending March 2, 1850, making them the highest paid employees in the mill (but they, of course, had to pay their piecers and scavengers out of these earnings).

Wages were, in fact, substantial in comparison with subsistence expenses. Food cost about 15 cents per day for an active adult male requiring 3,500 calories per day; women and children required proportionately less. Rent in particular was extremely low—about 5 percent of earnings. Riddle for instance rented out to his workers a block of five stone tenements on Mount Road in Crozerville, part of an unsettled estate being administered by Edward Darlington. The block was 90 feet long, with a piazza running the entire length, and was constructed along the steep slope of Church Hill, next to where the Crozerville Methodist Church would in a few years be constructed. There was a palisade fence around the block and a dug well for the use of the families. If the houses were characteristic of the time, they were four-story structures, including a half-dug dirt-floored cellar, two main stories, and a slope-roofed attic, one room above the other, with a column of semicircular staircases rising from floor to floor on one side of the small fireplaces, and closets on the other. Cooking was probably usually done in a kitchen outside so that three rooms could serve as bedrooms. The rooms were about 15 by 15 feet in floor area and were plastered (they had been replastered a year ago, in fact).

The rental for the better of the houses was $25 per year, which amounted to $1.93 every four weeks; the other two went for $1.16 per month. Other Riddle tenements in Crozerville and Rockdale rented for about the same amount. Most of the houses and tenements in Penn's Grove itself were more expensive, generally between $2 and $4 per month, depending on size. The "old mansion," for instance, was rented out to two families who shared the $5.38 per month rental. Thompson, the card-room boss, paid $3.46 per month for a house containing himself, a wife eight months pregnant, seven children, a mother-in-law, and a boarder. House rentals ranged, to be precise, from a low of $1.15 per month to a high of $3.46 per month per household.

Rent thus claimed a very small proportion of subsistence expenses for even the lowest paid mill-working family, far less than the cost of food, which was the main expense. The Blairs, for instance, as we noted earlier, in 1849 earned $257.46 from the mill, plus about $2 per week from their male boarder and $1.25 per week from the girl, for a total of $169 in board money. This added up to a family income of $426.46 for the year. They paid in rent that year a total of $15.75; firewood for a house of that kind was about $16 per year; and food for the entire household (including the boarders) would have amounted to about $272.22. Thus the family would have had subsistence expenses of about $303.97, leaving a "profit" of $122.49. Some of this would of course be spent on shoes, clothing, household articles, and other incidentals, but it would be possible for the family to end the year with a small amount of cash savings. The card-room boss, John Thompson, paid $45 per year for his house. He himself earned $603.50 from the mill; with two of his children working, the family income from the factory was $744.24. In addition, a female weaver boarded with them; at $1.25 per week, they would take in from her another $65 for a grand total of $809.24. Samuel Duncan, the carder, and his daughters earned $430.95 from the mill, and $104 from a male boarder, for a year's income of $534.95; their rent was $30.

Boarders were somewhat less secure. Sarah Barlow, the weaver who was staying with the Blairs, earned $198.38 in 1849. Paying about $65 for board and lodging would leave her $133.38 for clothing and incidentals; she was probably able to save money. Her earnings were a little below the annual average of $198.64 for all weavers at Penn's Grove; males earned on the average slightly more than women (although at the same piece rates), averaging $237.10. A male weaver paying $104 per year for room and board would, in effect, be spending nearly half his income for bare subsistence; a woman weaver would be paying between a third and a half. But employees in the throstle room, earning $6 to $10 per month (or at most $130 per year), would have had trouble making ends meet as board-ers. And, in fact, we find that there was only one person who worked in the throstle room who may have been a boarder—a fifteen-year-old girl who lived with her sister, who was eighteen, in a household whose nuclear family actually may have been relatives. Indeed, the average age of the twenty-five throstle-room employees for whom we have ages was twenty; and if one excludes from this group the five adults over thirty, the average age of the throstle-room employees drops to fifteen. Clearly, then, only an industrious weaver, spinner, warper, senior carder, or foreman could sup-port himself or herself as a boarder; throstle-room workers and others had to be members of nuclear families.

Obviously it would be a gross error to think of the mill hands at Penn's Grove, as stereotyped views of mid-nineteenth-century cotton factory work-ers would have it, as an undifferentiated mass of exhausted, sick, and starv-ing women and children pushed about by cruel male overseers. There was a wide range of ages, of types and degrees of skill, and of income; and the women and children, being the members of families who lived in the villages around the mills and went to local churches, were not likely to be beaten and abused with impunity. Furthermore, the working people were extraordinarily mobile, and this mobility is an indication of financial ability to escape from unfavorable circumstances. Many had just recently arrived from England or Ireland and regarded places like Rockdale as temporary residences, where they consolidated their means and prepared themselves to move on to better jobs or even to homesteads in the west.

The mobility of Riddle's employees is revealed in his rent books, which show that families seldom stayed much more than a year or two in the same house. On one of the properties, for instance, which contained three houses, the average length of stay was exactly eleven months and three weeks. Some workers, of course, remained for many years and eventually bought small farms. But many more simply passed through Rockdale on their way to better (or worse) situations somewhere else.

The Riddle account books show that of the first cohort of twenty families employed at Parkmount in September 1832, eight were still employed there in January 1835 (that is to say, the attrition rate was 60 percent in two and a half years). Of the seventy-two employees listed at Penn's Grove in January 1844, only sixteen were still working there in March 1850 (an attrition rate of 78 percent in six years). Of the original twenty families working for the Riddles in 1832, members of only one were still working for Samuel Riddle in 1844 (an attrition rate of 95 percent in twelve years). Evidently there was a very high turnover—about 50 percent—in the first two years of employment, and a steady attrition at a rate of about 4 percent or 5 percent per year after that.

Not all of the workers who left Parkmount left the Rockdale district, however. Some took employment in another factory. Again looking at the 1832 cohort, it appears that in addition to the eight families who remained at Parkmount from 1832 to 1835, at least three others found work elsewhere in the Rockdale district; the attrition rate for the district as a whole was only 45 percent in these two and a half years. If we attempt to locate the 1844 cohort in the 1850 census, we find that the attrition rate for the district as a whole has gone up to 63 percent for six years. Of the 120 workers at Penn's Grove in 1850, at least 14 can be identified ten years later in the 1860 census as living in the Rockdale district; the rate now is 88 percent. These figures show that a similar, but lesser, rate of loss applied to the district as a whole; a working family had about a 10 percent chance of remaining in the Rockdale district for more than ten years.[21]

A typical case is the Morris family. Between 1829 and 1832, four brothers from Lancashire, their father, two of their brothers-in-law, and all their wives and children emigrated to America, along with a friend named John Smith. The Morris brothers were hand-loom weavers who, although still profitably employed, were discouraged about their prospects for economic and social advancement in England. The father was a carpenter and the brothers-in-law were a blacksmith and a farmer. Thomas, one of the brothers, immediately moved to Ohio with his wife and children and bought a farm; the others remained in the Philadelphia area, working at their trades. For a time they lived in the city itself; then they all moved to the Brandywine to operate power looms (except for the blacksmith, who was doing well in Philadelphia). In 1833 two of the remaining brothers, Andrew and William, and their friend John Smith moved from Brandywine to Rockdale to work at Phillips' mill as power-loom weavers. Andrew, the married brother, rented a house with a small cellar and three bedrooms for $25 per year. He worked in the mill while his wife Jane took care of the two children, one a newborn son, and also the four boarders (the unmarried brother, their friend John Smith, and two other men). Andrew and William each earned between $16 and $24 per month, and the married couple charged the boarders $2 per week. Once when the mill was stopped for five weeks to put in a new water wheel, William went to work in Manayunk; Andrew found work with a neighboring farmer at 50 cents a day and meals. In 1835, their father died at Brandywine and their mother went to live with her son-in-law the blacksmith and her daughter in Philadelphia. In 1836 brother John, his wife Ann, and their son Thomas moved from Brandywine to West Branch and all three went to work "on the power looms at mr Crosher's Mill." In October 1836, Phillips closed his mill and Andrew was thrown out of work. "He could have got plenty of work in the neighborhood but they thought it best to go to the western country. So they had a publick sale and then packed up for their jurney."

Their plan was to move out to Ohio, near brother Thomas, to buy land and set up a farm. They hired a wagon to take them to Philadelphia, where they stayed a few days visiting with mother and sister. Then they took passage by railroad and canal to Pittsburgh; this cost $21 for a family of four. Another $6.50 got them to Thomas. Andrew paid a neighbor $2 for a couple of days' looking for farmland; finding what he liked, he bought 120 acres for $150, a pig and two sows for $11.50, and hired some men to help him build a log house. The cost of the entire operation (except for food), including transporting the whole family and buying a farm, was on the order of $200. All of this had been saved out of the rent money and the earnings of one man, Andrew, a skilled power-loom weaver, in three years of work at Phillips' mill in Rockdale (he had no capital on arrival in America, for he had had to borrow money to leave England, and had not gotten himself established before settling on Chester Creek).

Next year, brother John and his wife Ann bought a $400 farm adjoining Thomas and also moved out to Ohio. The remaining components of the Morris family straggled out over the next several years. Eventually, all of them were established as farmers in eastern Ohio, except for brother William, who had become a manufacturer of jeans, which he sold from farm to farm in the summer from a peddler's wagon. The power looms on Chester Creek now were far behind them; they had been merely a means of acquiring the cash with which to buy land in the west.[22]

THE FORMS OF THE FAMILY IN A COTTON-MANUFACTURING DISTRICT

The American doctrine of family, sanctioned in religion, morality, and law, and almost universally accepted in the 1850's, held that the married pair and their children constituted the natural basis of human society. From this fundamental unit, the simple nuclear family, radiated lines of ascent and descent and affinal connection that bound each nuclear family together with others in loose aggregations of kinship. The nuclear family itself might also exist in several more or less incipient or modified forms: as a married couple whose children had not yet been born or who had died or moved away; as a surviving spouse with children; as surviving children whose parents had died. Such a family, however modified, lived together in a house. There might, however, be others who shared the house with its proprietary family: individual grandparents, uncles and aunts, cousins, nephews and nieces, grandchildren, or even more remotely connected relatives; domestic servants; and boarders who paid rent. A household thus consisted of at least one nuclear family (simple or modified) and, usually, various kinsmen, servants, or boarders.

Within the outlines of this basic pattern, several different styles of family organization were possible. In the Rockdale manufacturing district (and in other, similar manufacturing districts nearby, as on the Brandywine), two of these different styles—the workers' and the managers'—must be noted, because they functioned very differently in the economic life of the community.

Among the workers, the nuclear family was vitally necessary to the economic welfare of most adult individuals. An unmarried working-class adult of either sex could not live alone. There were no small apartments or dormitories, and even if there had been, and the person could have afforded to pay the rent, there was not enough time in view of the long working hours to keep house and cook for oneself. Thus the unmarried adult either lived with his parents and siblings (in which case he either paid rent or put his earnings into the common fund) or moved out to live as a paying boarder in the household of another nuclear family. He or she could not live indefinitely as a boarder, however. The single person was expected to marry; there was little opportunity for sexual activity outside marriage, and much risk attached to it; and, if one were eager to improve one's situation in life, it was clear that the quickest way for the working-class person to do so was to form a nuclear family partnership.

Such partnership was fundamental to the survival-and-advancement strategy of the people of the working class. Among the mill workers, the members of a nuclear family (simple or modified) constituted an effective economic partnership. Each person above infancy contributed either work or money to the unit; cash was saved and pooled as a capital fund for future travel and investment, usually in land or tools and equipment for a trade (or even manufacturing). Any combination of members might work in the factory, including husband, wife, or children, so long as there was a female at home to cook, mind the children, and take care of boarders.

The boarders were a crucially important factor in the financial plans of many working-class households, for they paid good money—$2 per week if male, $1.25 per week if female. The wife, who cooked for the boarders and did their housekeeping (which probably included laundry services), could bring in as much as $24 per month by caring for three male boarders —very likely more than the rest of the family earned at the mill. At the time of the 1850 census, between a quarter and a half of all mill workers' households were keeping boarders. The nuclear family partnership thus used the house which it rented from the mill owner as capital with which to make money.

In this working-class system it is difficult to see marriage as a means of establishing an alliance between groups. Although an extended family might—as in the case of the Morrises—travel together, it was essentially traveling as a large, dispersed nuclear family, consisting of aged parents and their married children. The in-laws came along as spouses rather than as representatives of the families of their parents. Marriage and procreation established a partnership among individuals; the nuclear family partnership was the necessary condition for the renting of capital equipment (a house) and the pooling of factory income.

The implications of the partnership family system for social attitudes within the working class at this time are interesting. A hardworking and well-disciplined family could in a few years, if not impeded by illness or unemployment, save enough money to travel west, buy land, and become farmers (where the family partnership concept was equally applicable)—or, alternatively (and far less frequently), establish credit, borrow money, and become merchants or manufacturers. The mother and teen-age children evidently were almost as productive financially as the father; and, since the partnership could remain even if the father (or mother) died or moved away, many working-class widows and widowers were heads of families and of households. As on the farm, the labor of children, even small children, was essential in household and baby-minding chores. The system did tend to reduce the amount of schooling the children received (only about half of the eligible working-class children in 1850 were listed as having attended school in the previous year). But it also probably tended to minimize the patriarchal quality of family life—a quality that only the wealthy manufacturer or merchant was able to support. In many families the wife, in addition to being a wage or rent earner, was also the partnership's business manager, collecting the family paycheck directly from the manufacturer, or from her husband and children, and formulating and administering the family budget. This situation should, theoretically, have been conducive to tension between a working father whose contribution to the partnership was not worth much more than, if as much as, that of his wife and children. And such tension in turn should have contributed to a centrifugal tendency that would, as it were, spin off discontented young unmarried men and women, to live as boarders with other working-class families, thus perpetuating that most necessary aspect of the whole system.

In the managerial class, where income was the profit of a business or a large farm owned and administered by the father, the nuclear family partnership was not economically necessary for the survival and progress of the individual. The father—the businessman—could take care of himself and his wife and children. Bachelors could live comfortably on their fathers' profits and spinsters remain at home happily with their parents and sisters. Sons might go into the family business or they might turn to one of the professions or to benevolent and charitable activities. And instead of paying boarders, the nonfamily members of the household were paid servants. Indeed, the nonpartnership aspect of the marital relationship might be most emphatically demonstrated, as in the care with which the Sellers family kept the estate of their sister, Peter Hill's wife, separate from his estate by putting it in trust.

In contrast to the working-class concept of the marital economic partnership, the managerial class thought in terms of the potential alliance implications of marriage. Nathan Sellers and James Knowles objected to their daughters' marriages to men with whom a family connection seemed economically perilous. When Sallie Knowles married John P. Crozer without her father's consent, he made it plain that no financial claims could be made on him by her new family. And when Hannah Sellers finally did receive permission to marry Peter Hill, there was thereafter a continuing financial alliance (an irritating one to the Sellers') between the two families. The Lammots and Du Ponts were intimately joined by the marriage of Lammot's daughter to E. I. du Pont's son; the business connections and friendships of the Smiths and the Du Ponts were cemented by no less than two marriages. And we shall later note the importance of affinal connections to Henry Moore, John S. Phillips, and John P. Crozer in acquiring the capital to carry out their plans for manufacturing.

Among the managerial class, furthermore, the patronymic descent group was far more important than among the workers. Such a group was formed of the successive generations of persons patrilineally descended from and bearing the name of an original male ancestor or ancestors (if they were a group of brothers) who had become established in America many years before. Living members of such patronymic descent groups considered them to be in some sense great families, and marriages were sometimes actually recognized as alliances between patronymic groups (as in the case of the Lammots and Du Ponts). One of the members would keep the genealogical records and be able to trace the family's ancestry back deep into European history. Great families often maintained contact with kinsmen in Europe and exchanged visits occasionally. To the list of such old great family names as Sharpless, Phillips, Smith, Lewis, Sellers, Gilpin, Du Pont, Dutton, and Darlington would in the next generation be added those of the managers who had become successful in this—Crozer, Lammot, Riddle. This emphasis upon a descent group identity, represented by a name and a genealogy, no doubt contributed to the members of the group a sense of being a meaningful member in an immortal corporate entity— an estimate of self far different from the identity gained as a member of a nuclear family partnership, which eventually would be dissolved by the death of its members. And it had different implications for social attitudes, too: it emphasized the value of age and of the male line, and treated women as peripheral (the daughters' children, bearing another patronym, were forever lost); indeed, in this class they were peripheral in an economic sense, being engaged in financially nonproductive tasks. Women served as the links that joined men in systems of descent and alliance, which were of course economically significant relations; but their own primary work was neither heavy housework nor factory production but rather the administration of servants, church activity, and the cultivation of artistic and literary interests.

But the working-class family style and the managerial-class family style, however different in some ways, were precise complements to one another. The managers, in order to make the profits required to support their own extended family alliances, needed a stable and contented work force, composed of nuclear family partnerships and unmarried boarders in households that provided the proper mix of males and females of various ages. They attracted such a work force by paying relatively high wages, by providing houses at very low rents, by allowing workers to raise vegetables on company land and even keep a cow or some chickens, by reducing the rents during hard times, and by helping them in many small ways with credit, banking services, and transportation. The workers, in order to save the cash needed to buy land in the west, worked hard and for the most part without complaint in the managers' mills, enduring periods of unemployment, partial employment, and reduced wages, foregoing the prospect of education for many of their children, and even allowing the evangelical women of the managerial class to find respectable and interesting work in saving their souls.

Part Two

ROCKDALE

FROM 1825 TO 1835 ❧
THE CREATING
OF A WAY OF LIFE

Chapter III 𝕏

THE ASSEMBLING OF
THE INDUSTRIALISTS

The lives of the manufacturers who came to the Rockdale district in the 1820's were, in the beginning, guided by the simple dream of wealth. Their careers had all in one way or another reached an impasse and the new venture of the day, cotton manufacturing, offered them a chance of making the fortune, and the reputation, denied them in other spheres. Despite the newness of their machines, these industrialists were conservative people who sought to preserve the gentleman's way of life in a world of shifting privilege.[1] They were not, as yet, reformers and evangelists. They were not trying to effect an industrial revolution. They were not, most of them, even very well informed about their own machinery.

But their actions were transformative. They bought up cheap the old merchant mills and common gristmills, the sawmills, paper mills, and forges that now languished along the banks of the creek, victims of economic decline. Gradual soil exhaustion, excessive lumbering, the depredations of the Hessian fly, and competition from the more efficient automated flour mills of the Brandywine were bringing ruin to the formerly prosperous wheat-producing country of southeastern Pennsylvania. The little mill hamlets that suddenly sprang up, as if conjured out of the rocky hillsides by a magician's spell, were not so much modifications of old rural communities as newly created towns. And the immigrant Irish and English operatives imported to work in the mills were to live a way of life that was still new on the earth.

It was already a region with memories of change. A hundred and forty years before, only Indians and a few Swedes lived in the valley; a trio of aboriginal survivors, an elderly man and his brother and sister, were still waiting to die in a rock shelter along Dismal Run.[2] The log cabins of the early settlers still dotted the hillsides. There were old sodden races and the ruins of dams and abutments built and abandoned so long ago that no one today knows how they began. But the importance of the new mills seemed, at first, to consist more in their contribution to national self-sufficiency than in industrial transformation. Memories and mementoes of the Battle of the Brandywine and of the War of 1812 were common reminders of the national need for independence. The British Crown was still the enemy and the Indians to the west were still the enemy within. And the new tariff of 1824, protecting the infant American industries from unfair British competition, seemed to give patriotic sanction to the daring American manufacturer.

THE FIRST ARRIVALS

In 1825, only a small group of businessmen were manufacturing cotton along Chester Creek. They were William Martin, merchant of Philadelphia, who had bought an old paper mill a few years before and had converted it to cotton spinning; John S. Phillips, a wealthy Philadelphia bachelor of uncommon mechanical aptitude, who that year took a ten-year lease on a new stone mill and installed two hundred new power looms—an extraordinary number for that day; John P. Crozer, the farmer's son, who had just acquired another old paper mill and was also converting it to cotton spinning; and the Englishman John D. Carter, who had long been a cotton spinner in the neighborhood. There were a couple of smaller cotton enterprises, soon to be replaced, of which little record remains. And several other merchants and manufacturers were on their way: James Houghton, a power-loom weaver, and John Garsed, machinist and manufacturer of power looms; the Riddle brothers, Samuel and James, cotton spinners en route from the mills of Northern Ireland; and Richard S. Smith and Daniel Lammot, prosperous Philadelphia merchants seeking fresh air and investment opportunities in the countryside close to their friends the Du Ponts along the Brandywine, the next creek over.

Some of these people would become casualties in the economic and ideological struggles of the era and would move away. The survivors—the Crozers, the Riddles, the Smiths, and the Lammots—would go on to form the nucleus of the Chester Creek manufacturing community.

It was the families of these successful evangelical industrialists who, after installing the new machines, and after defeating the freethinkers and associationists, would determine the moral character of the community. They would lead their workers through the strikes and tariff battles of the 1830's and 1840's, on into the free soil movement of the 1850's. At the last they would urge them to the carnage of the war between the states, which simultaneously—if temporarily—destroyed both the slave-labor cotton plantations of the south and the free-labor cotton-manufacturing villages of the north. And in that holocaust the struggle between the old radicalism of the Enlightenment and the newer tradition of evangelical Protestantism for control of the Industrial Revolution would for a time be resolved in a reformist, millenarian Christian capitalism.

William Martin, Jr.

William Martin was a young commission merchant in Philadelphia in 1822 to whom the Lungren family, owners of the old Lungren paper and cotton mills on Chester Creek, owed money. When the Lungrens ran into financial difficulty, Martin became one of the assignees (or receivers). In 1823 at a sheriff's sale he bought the mills, and he and his brother-in-law, Joseph W. Smith, formed a company to operate them. The Martins moved out of the city a couple of years later to live in the Lungren mansion, a new and elegant stone house, built in 1815, while William Lungren moved to the Sellers' shops at Cardington, in Upper Darby, to work as a millwright.[1] The house stood on a slope facing down the green valley, with a long prospect of the winding stream and the little clusters of houses, mills, dams, and races that sat here and there along the banks. They christened the hamlet Lenni (pronounced "Len-eye"), after the tribe of Indians—the Lenni Lenape, or Delaware—who only a century before had occupied southeastern Pennsylvania.

In 1823, just before the move, their son, John Hill Martin, was born, and it is owing to his love of his father, and his nostalgic attachment to the towns along Chester Creek where he spent his early years, that so much information remains about William Martin. John never married; during his long life as an insurance lawyer, he developed a passion for preserving records of all kinds. He made lists of the attorneys admitted to the bar of Philadelphia from the earliest times; he collected genealogical notes; he kept a diary and wrote memoirs; he finally published a semi-autobiographical history—*Chester (and its Vicinity,) Delaware County, in Pennsylvania* (Philadelphia, 1877). And he gave to the Historical Society of Pennsylvania, of which he was a member, all his historical papers, including his father's receipt book during the time when he owned the mill at Lenni.[2]

William Martin had been born in 1797 of old Delaware County families. His father, who died in the yellow fever epidemic of that year, had been a physician, trained at the University of Pennsylvania by the renowned Benjamin Rush, who it is said came to Chester to attend his former student when he learned of his illness. His mother was a daughter of old Judge Crosby, famous as a Revolutionary War hero and the last slaveowner in Delaware County. William studied law and was admitted to the bar in Chester, the county seat, in 1821. But a legal career did not appear to be as promising as a career in business, and later that year he formed a partnership with his stepuncle Peter Hill (the brother of his mother's second husband) as commission merchants in Philadelphia. Commission merchants received consignments of goods of various kinds—such as paper and cotton yarn and cloth—and held them in their warehouses for sale at the consignee's asking price. When the goods were sold, the merchant remitted the sale price minus his percentage commission; if they could not be sold, they were returned or transferred.[3] The 1822 partnership with Joseph W. Smith in the cotton mill was also a family affair. Martin had married his partner's sister, Sarah Ann, in that same year, and the partner in turn had married Martin's younger sister Ann Crosby, in a sibling exchange not unusual in those times.

The young William Martin was a fine-looking man, it was said, about 6 feet tall, with fair hair, blue eyes, and rosy cheeks, and like his father he liked to live well. He was a fancy dresser and something of a gourmet. He was a patron of Peale's natural history museum and seems to have had literary pretensions too, for he wrote poetry, of a sort, in a clear, precise, rounded hand, unusually legible in an era of spiky penmanship. The following effusion, celebrating his passion for oysters, is the only sample of verse ascribed to him that survives:

The Oyster Supper

Gently stir and rake the fire,
   Put the oysters on to roast,
"Duck Creek planted," I desire,
   They're the kind that please me most.
As the odor strikes my nose,
   My appetite much keener grows.

On the plate now see them lie,
   In the gravy plump and fat,
Finer "fish" ne'er met my eye,
   Nor "An opening rich as that";
Let me season to the taste,
   With pepper, salt, etc.,—haste.

The cloth upon the table spread,
Now knife and fork as quickly get,
With butter fresh and toasted bread
I'll have a feast unheard of yet,
While poney *brandy and segars*
Will set me up beyond the stars.[4]

As 1825 unfolded, the young Martins of Lenni appeared to be in a very prosperous condition. William's ambitions soared; he aspired to a political career, and in the fall of the next year entered the race for the state assembly on the federal Republican ticket—and won. In 1826 and 1827 he represented the county in Harrisburg, the state capital, leaving the conduct of the mill business to his brother-in-law. In the legislature he associated himself with those who were interested in the promotion of the state's system of internal improvements, particularly the canals.[5] All in all, he was a glowing young man.

John S. Phillips

Another young gentleman of promise, twenty-five-year-old John Smith Phillips, joined the ranks of the Chester Creek manufacturers in the summer of 1825. His father was a Philadelphia merchant who kept his office in the commercial quarters facing the wharves along Front Street; he also served on the Board of Directors of the Phoenix Insurance Company. The family lived alternately in a town house on Front Street and at a summer place along the Delaware above the city. John S. Phillips, the eldest of the children, had already entered the business world, as a sugar refiner in the city in partnership with Joseph S. Lovering, formerly of Wilmington, and as the partner of David Lewis, Jr., in a cotton-weaving mill in Holmesburg, an industrial suburb in north Philadelphia.[6] He was a youth with an intense interest in and aptitude for science and mechanics. In 1824 he became one of the founding members of the new Franklin Institute, along with a glittering array of the Philadelphia region's leading merchants and manufacturers —Charles and Victor du Pont, clothmakers, and Thomas Gilpin, paper manufacturer, from the Brandywine; Oliver Evans, the famous inventor and iron founder, proprietor of the Mars Iron Works; Paul Beck, Jr., the merchant and shot manufacturer; Nicholas Biddle, president of the Second Bank of the United States; George Escol Sellers, the engineer; and Joseph Siddall, manufacturer of cotton. In the same year he joined another illustrious band, the members of the older, and politically somewhat more radical,

Academy of Natural Sciences of Philadelphia. He was proposed by George Ord, famous foe of Audubon, ornithologist and editor of Alexander Wilson's *Ornithology,* and wealthy retired ropemaker, and by Benjamin Coates, a physician. Phillips' special interest, even at this early date, was conchology—a field in which he was later to publish scientific papers (and eventually to become the Academy's Curator of Conchology). From October 1824 to February 1825, Phillips attended the meetings conscientiously, along with the other regulars, Charles Lucien Bonaparte (naturalist son of Napoleon's elder brother the exiled King of Spain), John Speakman (chemist), Charles Lesueur (scientific illustrator), Thomas Say (conchologist and entomologist), Gerard Troost (chemist and geologist), and three or four others.[7]

The Academy was the scene of considerable excitement in 1824 and 1825, for these were the years of the first visits to Philadelphia of Robert Owen, the British cotton manufacturer-turned-social reformer, on his way to establish an associationist community at New Harmony, Indiana. The wealthy patron of the Academy, geologist and educator William Maclure, and his friends and fellow naturalists in that institution—particularly the conchologist and entomologist Thomas Say and Say's partner in the drug business John Speakman, the wandering botanist Rafinesque, the geologist Gerard Troost, and the artist Charles Lesueur—were captivated by Owen's visions of a new moral world. Along with hundreds of others, they were persuaded in January 1826 to make the move to the western Utopia.[8]

Phillips, despite his close association with the academicians in scientific and perhaps philosophical matters, remained behind, to emulate Owen's illustrious career in another aspect—cotton manufacturing. He was already in partnership in the cotton-weaving business in Holmesburg with his new brother-in-law, David Lewis, Jr., who had married Camilla Phillips.[9] In August 1825 the two men entered into contract with Henry Moore, the owner and manager of Old Sable Forge and Nail Works, along Chester Creek, agreeing to lease a cotton-weaving mill for ten years. Moore was to construct the mill at his own expense; it would be of stone, four stories high, 40 by 60 feet; and he was to erect tenements for the workers.[10] The mill would soon house two hundred power looms.

Phillips' motive in the move to Chester Creek was to recover the family fortunes. The firm of Phillips and Lovering had recently encountered financial trouble, and Phillips' father had endorsed his son's notes in the amount of $90,000; the father was eventually forced to pay when sometime in 1826 or 1827 the firm was unable to meet its obligations. The failure caused the entire family embarrassment; the elegant summer house, so fondly described in the memoirs of John's sister, had to be sold, and the family retired to the house on busy Front Street, only a couple of blocks from the office. Joseph, John's partner, would spend a couple of unhappy months in debtor's prison in Philadelphia.[11] At this juncture in family and partnership affairs, it was to be Lewis money and Phillips practical management that would, hopefully, recoup the loss. But to Phillips, the move out to Chester Creek was to be only a temporary exile; about 1835 he and his partner closed down operations at Old Sable Forge, removed the machinery, and set up again at Fairmount along the Schuylkill in Philadelphia.[12]

The Phillips family were principal members of Philadelphia society at a time when the city still claimed to be the greatest metropolis of the New World; they were a proud, closely knit group, who preserved family tradition. According to that tradition, the paternal grandfather, John Phillips, had settled in Philadelphia after profitably selling a cargo of slaves in the West Indies. With his profits he established a successful rope-making business and, when the Revolution came, was a staunch and prominent patriot. His son William, John's father, in later years recalled giving a drubbing to the son of General Howe when the British occupied the city and the commander chose to live in the Phillips house. William was successful in the French trade during the French Revolution; in later years, the family remained devoted admirers of Lafayette and of the refugee king, Joseph Bonaparte, who lived at that time near Philadelphia. The house at Front Street—a cavernous mansion, inhabited by the ghost of the first occupant, who fell down the grand circular stairwell in a moment of inebriation—was the scene of tea parties and balls in the early 1820's, when the Phillipses entertained their friends and their daughters made their débuts.[13]

A favored scion of distinguished stock, a youth who had never known anything but comfort and position until his recent débâcle, gangling, awkward young John S. Phillips—6 feet 3 inches tall, and thin—in 1825 was still searching for a career in which to make his mark.

John P. Crozer

Unlike William Martin and John S. Phillips, John Price Crozer was a man of little standing when he entered the cotton-manufacturing scene on Chester Creek in 1825. He came from a respectable but impecunious family of Delaware County farmers; he himself, a robustly built man of middle height, had worked the family farm unsuccessfully for ten years until 1820, when he lost the property. Since 1821 he had been struggling to maintain a sorry little cotton manufactory on Crum Creek, equipped with broken-down machines, and housed in an old mill rented from George G. Leiper, the man who had bought the farm and with whom he had briefly been partners in an unsuccessful merchant and sawmill enterprise. In 1825 at the age of thirty-two John P. Crozer had known little but hard work and failure.

But, despite the inadequacy of his machinery, Crozer had recently had some momentary success in cotton. Encouraged, in the autumn of 1824 with borrowed money he had bought the dilapidated old Mattson paper mill at West Branch, just across the forks from William Martin's place. And then, with homestead in possession, despite her father's objections he had in March 1825 married his sweetheart of five years, Sallie Knowles.

The paper mill and associated real estate cost $7,330 at sheriff's auction. Of this, $4,000 was accounted for by a mortgage (probably obtained with Leiper's help from the Delaware County National Bank, of which Leiper was a director); the balance was obtained in notes secured by his brother-in-law John Lewis's signature. (John Lewis, a prosperous gentleman farmer, had married Crozer's sister Elizabeth several years before and his mansion on the old Lewis estate at Castle Rock on the West Chester Pike had been a second home for John and his other sister Sarah.) Most of the 183 acres was rocky, wooded hillside. The mill, crowded between a steep slope and the stream, perpetually in shadow, was large enough for only two vats (for soaking the rags); nearby were a few tenements for workmen, and the two-story stone mansion house overlooking the mill, with four rooms on each floor, and various outbuildings: kitchen, barn, stable, wagon-and-gig house, smokehouse, stone springhouse, and a two-story tenant house with two rooms on each floor.

The newly married couple began housekeeping in mean circumstances. His wife brought only her clothing from home and presents from a few friends worth perhaps $50; Crozer had a few articles of furniture taken from his bachelor quarters, including bed, bedding, and some silver spoons. They spent $300 to furnish the house, with a rag carpet and windsor chairs and a mirror for the parlor, a second-hand mahogany dining table, an $8 bed, and a $5 breakfast table. They kept one female servant and boarded a number of mechanics and laborers. Mrs. Crozer did much of the housework herself while her husband worked at the mill every day till dark, and afterward at the house doing the mill's clerical and accounting work. As Crozer somewhat sharply noted in his autobiography, "The improvement in our style of living was very gradual; indeed scarcely perceptible for perhaps eight years of marriage."[14]

The objection of Sallie Crozer's father, James Knowles, was based on a parent's concern lest his daughter enter into lifelong contract with a poor man who, in Knowles's opinion, had little prospect for success. Mr. Knowles's unfavorable judgment of Crozer's prospects was not without grounds. Crozer himself, five years before, in a letter to Sallie had formally

JOHN PRICE CROZER (1793–1866).

relinquished his claims to her affection, not wishing to reduce his bride's standard of living to the level of a poor farmer. With heavy heart he had then set forth on the back of a faithful nag to seek his fortune, and a bride, in the western country. But after a tour of western Pennsylvania, Ohio, Indiana, Illinois, and Kentucky, he had returned.

The association between the Crozer and the Knowles families was an old one. Before the Revolution, Crozer's father had been a carpenter and builder; with the decline in construction brought on by the war, he had rented the Delaware County estate of the older James Knowles of Wilmington, a farm of over 150 acres. When Knowles died, it was Crozer—not the son John, Sallie's father—who was named executor, perhaps because Crozer was a principal creditor. It was no doubt in his capacity as executor that the elder Crozer collected a debt of nearly £300 on behalf of his wife's step-mother from the Knowles estate. Farming was then profitable and the elder Crozer was able to buy a farm of 173 acres in Springfield. And it was on this farm, in the fine old stone house where the celebrated painter Benjamin West had been born and first learned to draw, that John P. Crozer was born.

But the Crozer family fortunes declined drastically thereafter. The father was afflicted with rheumatoid arthritis and increasingly neglected the farm's management; the work was done by one tenant and by the sons, particularly John. The father did not believe in fertilizing the fields with either lime or manure and they grew less and less productive. At the last only the apple orchard and the small dairy of eight or nine cows were earning money. Crozer's mother was in poor health, with a sensitive stomach and a tendency to sick headaches which lasted for days. She suffered and moaned loudly and John Crozer recalled vividly, in later years, that he "would sit by the foot of the bed and weep, sometimes gushing tears and sobs, so as to excite my mother's sympathy amidst her own intense suffering."[15]

Trying to keep the farm going, and to care for an austere but increasingly inactive father and a sickly and complaining mother, Crozer as a boy had little opportunity for formal education, and attended school only up to his thirteenth year. His elder brother James, a weakly youth, was of little help on the farm and at the age of seventeen—when John was nine—he went to Philadelphia as an apprentice in a wholesale grocery house. When the father died in 1816, Crozer, now twenty-three, tried to keep the farm going. But it belonged equally to the three brothers and Crozer alone could not afford to buy it. So the family decided to sell. Even this move was a disaster. The brothers held out for $100 an acre; the only likely prospect was willing to pay $95, but they refused to lower the price, and he would not go higher. Next year (1820) they were forced to sell for $55 an acre.

In that year too another tragedy struck. The younger brother Samuel —the brilliant, talented youth of the family, who had studied medicine in Philadelphia, worked as a machinist, entertained his friends with experiments in chemistry and electricity, and studied night and day—was smitten by a religious concern. In short order he was sent by the American Colonization Society as its agent in the establishment of the first colony of repatriated slaves and free persons of color on the West Coast of Africa. The nation of Liberia was eventually to be the fruit of this venture. But young Samuel Crozer, then only twenty-three years old, died of a tropical fever, along with most of the expedition, a few weeks after arriving in Africa.

Thus to an anxious parent, the Crozers did not present the image of a family well prepared to care for a young bride of gentle birth. The couple at West Branch were not welcome at the Knowles mansion and her father did not visit them. Apart from some of Sallie's brothers and sisters, and his own sister Elizabeth and her husband John Lewis, the only friends whom the newlyweds had outside the community were—surprisingly—the family of George Gray Leiper. This was the man who had purchased the Crozer farm (at bargain price) to add to the Leiper holdings on Crum Creek, where lay the great quarries and mills of Leiperville and the family mansion "Lapidea." It was the same Leiper who had gone into partnership with Crozer in their short-lived saw- and gristmill enterprise, and it was from the same man that Crozer had rented the mill to house his rickety cotton machines. Something about Crozer must have inspired Leiper's interest, for he, his wife, and his sister Jane are remembered affectionately in Crozer's autobiography as having been among the few who stood up with them at their wedding at the Lewis house (none of the Knowleses was present). Jane Leiper's interest was particularly well remembered, as well it might be, for she was a celebrated beauty and the wife of fashionable lawyer John J. Kane of Philadelphia. Just last year she had achieved the social triumph of the season in Philadelphia, leading the ball, held in his honor, on the arm of the visiting Revolutionary hero, the Marquis de Lafayette.[16]

What Leiper, unlike Knowles, saw in Crozer was not the harassed scion of a falling family. Rather, he perceived certain moral qualities which Crozer brought into his business dealings. Poorly financed, ill-educated, and possessed of little mechanical aptitude, Crozer nevertheless (by his own confession) was a man of "untiring industry and indomitable perseverance."[17] He worked hard with his hands and in later years recalled the little, low-ceilinged card room "where I had spent so many weary and tedious hours at the cards—where I had toiled through long, anxious days and evenings—where I had figured and calculated until both mind and body were so absorbed that I could neither talk nor think of anything else."[18]

Furthermore, he insisted upon maintaining an "unwavering integrity, a firm intention to do justly to others." This, in business, meant, as he put it, that he was "careful never to make a promise to pay, without assurance in my own mind that I could comply." It was in this spirit that Crozer had acted in the summer of 1821, when he realized that the lumber business was failing, and had asked Leiper to buy him out ("I lose my summer's labor, and he to repay me, without interest, the capital I put in"). Leiper was impressed by the straightforward conduct of his partner, and the business was closed "in strict harmony and by mutual consent."[19]

Thus it must have been on the grounds of character alone (certainly not of wealth or industrial success, for the mill had barely started) and on George G. Leiper's recommendation, that in November 1825 the stockholders of the Bank of Delaware County (of which Leiper had been one of the founders, ten years before) elected John P. Crozer to the Board of Directors.[20]

John D. Carter

John D. Carter, the fourth of the cotton manufacturers who were at work on Chester Creek in 1825, was the only one of the group with extensive experience in cotton manufacturing. He was an Englishman who, having emigrated to America about 1812, shortly after his arrival took charge of an old paper mill owned by the Trimbles of Concord Township and converted it to a small cotton factory.[21] He had probably been a mill manager in England brought over for the purpose.

The Trimble cotton manufactory, as operated by Carter and his partner McKenzie, was short-lived. British manufacturers, in an almost-successful effort to destroy the American industry after the end of the war, dumped enormous quantities of cotton goods on the American auction market, driving prices for domestic products too low for any but the most resourceful to compete. Carter and McKenzie failed in 1816 in the general collapse of the American cotton-manufacturing business and their machinery was disposed of at sheriff's sale.[22]

But Carter was quickly able to recoup his fortunes. In the same year as the failure of the Trimble factory, he leased the substantial mill called Rokeby along the Brandywine,[23] and became one of the charter subscribers of the Brandywine Manufacturers' Sunday School, founded in November 1816.[24] Carter installed new spinning machinery and power looms. He was listed in the 1820 Census of Manufacturers as the proprietor of what, for that time and place, was a substantial establishment. His equipment consisted of about 2,300 spindles, 10 hand looms, and 20 power looms; he employed 79 men, women, and children, in both an old mill and a new stone one. Many, if not all, of the workers lived in the eleven tenant houses on the twenty-acre property.

In February 1822, however, Rokeby—along with all the other mills along the Brandywine—was seriously damaged by a sudden freshet. The river, choked with ice and melted snow, rose about 16 feet, and the machinery on the lower story was damaged.[25] Carter struggled on with the business but finally was forced to sell the machinery in August 1825.[26] It is a temptation to suggest that Phillips and Lewis bought Carter's power looms, for they signed their lease with Moore only five days before the publicly announced date of the Rokeby sale. But before selling Rokeby's machinery, the resourceful Mr. Carter had already acquired at sheriff's sale the Sharon Mill on nearby Squirrel Run.[27] He had difficulty, however, with his neighbor, E. I. du Pont, who had rented some of the tenant houses from the former owner to house his own workers, displaced by the freshet, and Carter was delayed in starting up his spindles.[28] Perhaps in response to the frustrations resulting from trying to re-establish the cotton business at Rokeby and Sharon after the flood, in February 1825 Carter bought the old copper-rolling mill on Chester Creek a mile below Old Sable Forge. This estate, of eight acres, with its stone mansion house, stone furnace, frame rolling mill, and thirteen tenement houses, he proceeded to convert to the cotton manufacture.[29]

A former owner of this mill was one John Hart;[30] and a Richard Hart, who was "engaged in the cotton spinning business," lived with the Carter family after the sale. The year ended for Carter and Hart on a melancholy note: the suicide of Mr. Hart. The *Upland Union*—the only local newspaper, published in Chester—rarely offered much in the way of local news. But on December 27 it published a sad account:

SUICIDE OF COTTON SPINNER

A melancholy event. On Thursday morning the 22d inst. a person by the name of *Richard Hart,* shot himself at the dwelling house of John D. Carter, Esq., in Middletown Township, Delaware County. What led to the cause of this rash deed, is not known. The following are a few of the particulars which have been stated to us. It appears that Mr. H. previous to taking his life, stated to the family that he was going to Baltimore, and between the hours of eight and nine o'clock a servant girl heard the report of a pistol, she went upstairs and found Mr. Hart, sitting on a chair and his clothes on fire, she asked him what was the matter, when he gave a groan and expired; she immediately went for Mr. Carter, and upon examination it was discovered that he had shot himself, the ball passing through his breast.

Mr. Hart had no family; he was engaged in the Cotton Spinning business and had become very much in debt.[31]

THE FIRST CASUALTIES AND REPLACEMENTS

During the six years from 1826 to 1831, the remainder of the principal manufacturers in the story, except for a few who appeared toward the end, entered the scene: Edward Darlington, lawyer and politician, who briefly owned Carter's Mill; the Garsed family, who manufactured power looms, and James Houghton, who had a weaving mill; Nathan Sellers, Peter Hill, and Daniel Lammot, who took over from William Martin at Lenni; and the Riddle brothers from Ireland. These industrial figures and their families and associates in politics and religion, and the Smith family, whom we shall look at separately, complete the cast of characters on the industrialists' side. Each of them will appear and reappear as the process of cultural transformation unfolds.

Edward Darlington

The first economic casualty among the early arrivals was the oft-bank-rupted John D. Carter, whose manufactory did not long survive the suicide of his associate Richard Hart. In April 1826, the Farm Bank of Delaware issued a summons against Carter demanding payment of $250.76.[1] In June, the cotton mill was sold at sheriff's auction.[2] In August 1826, all his goods and chattels, lands and tenements, along the Brandywine, including such machinery at Rokeby as still remained unsold, were attached by the Bank of Wilmington and Brandywine, and he was summoned to appear before the Supreme Court at Newcastle.[3] On November 14, 1826, he published a notice in the *Upland Union,* notifying them that he had applied to the court of common pleas "for the benefit of the acts of assembly . . . for the relief of insolvent debtors." A hearing was appointed for him and his creditors.[4] The consequence of this unrelenting series of financial disasters was to be his departure from the county and the state. He ultimately came to Elkton, Maryland, where in 1860 he was still in the trade of millwright.[5]

The purchasers of Carter's Mill were Edward Darlington and Thomas Clyde of Chester. Darlington was a thirty-year-old practicing attorney and Thomas Clyde was the keeper of a general store on Market Square. Neither moved out of Chester. It is not unlikely, in fact, that they kept on John D. Carter as manager of the mill until they themselves sold the place in 1829.[6] Darlington and Clyde, however, are of importance in Chester Creek affairs because of the significant role Darlington was soon to play in the legal and political system of the county as a defender of law and order and a spokesman in Congress for Anti-Masonic and industrial interests.

Edward Darlington was born in 1795 and grew up on a farm that lies along the creek just about a mile above Lenni. (The farm is still there, and occupied by the Darlington family; a small railway station has been added, and a post office named Darling which mails out, every year, thousands of Valentine cards postmarked "Darling, Pa.") His father was a member of the large Darlington clan of Chester County, and both his father and mother were devout Quakers.[7] After he graduated from the West Chester Academy,[8] Darlington taught school for a time and read law with Samuel Edwards, a prominent attorney of Chester, with whom he practiced in the county seat after he was admitted to the bar in 1821 (the same year as William Martin).[9] He was appointed deputy district attorney in 1824 and immediately achieved acclaim for his successful prosecution of a case then arousing intense public indignation. As a result of his efforts, the murderer of a defenseless Quaker shopkeeper was publicly hanged in Chester.[10] A partnership with Samuel Edwards was a passport to success in Delaware County law practice. Edwards was a Democrat, a personal friend of James Buchanan, with whom he had served in Congress, and had been one of the committee appointed to receive General Lafayette in 1824; he was a director of the Bank of Delaware County and of the Delaware County Mutual Insurance Company.[11] As his protégé, Darlington prospered rapidly and soon was looking for investment opportunities (in 1825, for instance, he was advertising in the *Upland Union* that he had $2,500 to lend).[12]

Thomas Clyde in 1826 lived at his store in Chester with his family, having just moved there from Philadelphia. His wife Henrietta's sister Arabella had married Preston Eyre, also a prosperous shopkeeper of Chester. Young Darlington was then courting Arabella Eyre's daughter Ann and they were married in April of next year.[13] Thus Darlington's partner was the husband of Ann's maternal aunt and no doubt he was addressed as "Uncle" by them both.

Peter Hill and the Sellers Family

The next of the early cohort to fail was William Martin. Martin was vulnerable because he had lost his partners. He had been bought out of the commission merchant business about 1825 (probably when Martin went to

Harrisburg) by his uncle Peter Hill. Hill applied to his father-in-law, Nathan Sellers, for a loan with which to buy out Martin's share of their partnership. Nathan approved the idea, saying to his favorite son Coleman, "Peter wishes to pay off his partner and be done with him, and it appears to me the sooner the better, if he can be wise enough to avoid other flattering connections."[14] Perhaps the elderly, plainspoken engineer was not eager to see a son-in-law associated in business with an Episcopalian gentleman-barrister; the tone is reminiscent of Mrs. Lovering's prejudicial remarks about the Phillipses—"those fine folks." And in 1827 Martin in turn bought out his brother-in-law Joseph's half share of the paper and cotton manufactory at Lenni. Thus he was left financially isolated when the panic of 1829 ruined the cotton business.

His financial needs were extensive. It was a large estate which he had bought in 1823, embracing about 206 acres on the two sides of the creek, and improved—in addition to the two stone mills and a countinghouse—by three mansions, five stone tenements, five log tenements, a barn, and a stable; livestock included six horses, fifteen cows, and a dog. All this had cost him $17,800. In addition, he had bought cotton machinery worth about $11,000. In order to obtain these sums, he had borrowed at least $8,000 from his uncle Peter Hill and $9,000 from the Contributors to the Pennsylvania Hospital. The hospital secured the loan by a mortgage on the property and Martin agreed to endorse some of Hill's notes, in effect mortgaging the rest of the property. Martin did not pay off his loans; to the hospital he simply continued to pay the 6 percent annual interest, in semi-annual installments.

Martin's ability to pay even the smallest bills ended abruptly in January 1829 when the price of cotton fell; he was unable to pay even the semi-annual interest charges on the sum owed to the hospital fund. He had no other recourse than to appeal to the Delaware County Court, who put his properties in the hands of receivers.[15]

For a businessman in such a situation, there were now several possible outcomes. If he could convince the assignees, and through them his various creditors (including the assignees), that he would in a reasonable time be able to satisfy their claims, he might be able to recover. Creditors were apt to be sympathetic if prospects were good and their own creditors not pressing, for everyone might lose if the debtor's assets were disposed of at a public auction. All that might be required, in such a case, would be a sound reputation, patient creditors, and a little time—time for the market to go up, time for the debtor to collect the sums owed him, time for friends and relations to endorse his notes or lend him money. Martin estimated that the mill property was worth about $34,500 by now; $8,000 for the two mills, $11,000 for the cotton machinery, and the rest in houses and other improvements.

But time was what one of the creditors did not have. Peter Hill had borrowed money on the security of Martin's property. With the news of Martin's failure, Hill's creditors demanded their money. Hill, unable to pay, and unable to use Martin's credit, applied to the court and demanded that sufficient of "the goods and chattels, lands and tenements" of William Martin be sold to recover the loan. Martin prepared a list of his cotton machinery, worth by his estimate $11,050, and attempted to sell it privately, but was unable to do so.[16]

Hill now turned in desperation to his wife Hannah's family, the Sellers of Upper Darby, for aid. Coleman Sellers, as the acting head of the clan, helped Hill financially "as far as [he] could afford and prudence will allow." But Hill continued importunate, and Coleman now turned to his father, the aging and unwell Nathan Sellers, for advice on how to deal with their hapless in-law. The letter is revealing:

Dear father   Apr. 2. 1829—
    In consequence of the failure of William Martin Hannah and Peter requested my advice, as it has got Peter into some difficulty. if I could have given assistance, I would not have suffered this present difficulty to have come before thee—I am not willing to make any important move without thy concurance—& have advised Peter to lay the case before thee before he proceeds any further. As far as I can understand the whole business, the difficulties arise from the want of him in getting in his debts —which are no doubt greatly abundant for the purpose, he has secured himself on Martin's property but cannot get the money until June—I have assisted them as far as I could afford, and prudence will allow and am not doubting in his ability to meet all his engagements as an honest man ought to do, I told them they should be content with a less and more sure business—which they have been indeavouring to do and I have every reason to believe they would have done but for this unfortunate failure of Martin's, with much sorrow for the necessity of given thee one moments uneasiness—

                        I remain affectionately thy Son
                        C Sellers
    I am willing to do any thing for them that thee may sanction and advise[17]

This was not the first time that Peter Hill had given his father-in-law, Nathan Sellers, cause for alarm. Nathan had, in fact, refused to permit his daughter to marry Peter Hill when he first asked for her hand in 1822. Hill had been married before; both his wife and daughter had died, and Hill himself, failing in business, had been forced to sell his interest in his wife's home, in which he held a life estate. (His wife was a granddaughter of John Morton, a signer of the Declaration of Independence; the house is now a historic landmark.) The father based the refusal on his concern that Peter Hill's "circumstances" might not enable him to support her in comfort and happiness (or in what Hill, somewhat tartly, described as "the easy affluent Style she had been accustomed to").[18] But Hill continued to court Hannah, and in July 1824 he overcame parental objections and married her. Nathan Sellers, no doubt recalling his earlier worries, now seems to have advised Hill to press the matter in court, for on Hill's application the court ordered the sale of the Martin property by the sheriff at public auction, in July.

The records do not indicate how much the machinery, the two factories, and the two hundred-acre plantation brought; but it was not enough to save either William Martin or Peter Hill. Martin lost everything, even (temporarily) his son John, who went to live with his grandfather John F. Hill (the brother of Peter Hill) in Ridley Township, where the boy remained until years later. Martin and his wife and the younger children moved to Chester, where Joseph W. Smith also resided, and made a home in a house rented for $6 per month. There Martin resumed the practice of law.[19] The Martin family tradition, as recorded years later by Martin's son John, retained a permanent sense of bitterness at the duplicity which, Martin told his son, Peter Hill had shown in the matter. John's personal journal for 1856 charged that his father failed

by *endorsing* for his *intimate* friend Peter Hill, a brother of my decd. Grandfather Jno. F. Hill. Peter Hill was, and is a rascal. And though he pretended to have failed and thus obliged father to take up the paper endorsed by him which ruined him, Peter Hill had still money enough to purchase in his wife's name the Mills & property, when they were sold, Money enough in reality to pay his debts—and what is more he ownes them now and rents them to Robt. L. Martin Esq. agent of Gen. Robt Patterson, manufacturer of Philadelphia. There is an old Mortgage debt due on this place held by an Aunt of this Peter Hill's, and Judgment now over 22 years old entered on the Bond against father—it is in reality barred by the statute, but Peter Hill with that inherent rascality of his nature, asks Father to give him $200 to satisfy it, thus admitting he really owns the Mortgage on his own property. This prevented Father from taking the Title to the Land referred to in his own name—though in reality every just debt that he ever owed has been paid in full.

John F., William and George W. Hill, his brothers, also, endorsed Peter, and were all ruined by having to pay the notes they endorsed.[20]

Apparently the Martins were not aware of the financial involvement of the Sellers family in the affair. Nor was John Hill Martin correct in his claim that Peter Hill's brothers were all "ruined," for young Martin himself lived with and was supported by one of these brothers for about seven years, and, as we shall see, George W. Hill was a well-to-do landowner in Middletown already and so remained for many years.

Peter Hill himself did not long survive Martin financially; he failed in May 1829.[21] His estate too passed into receivership, one of the assignees being his wife's brother, Coleman Sellers.[22] Nathan Sellers in the meantime moved to protect his daughter Hannah. It was he (not Peter Hill, as Martin believed) who purchased the Martin estate. He then deeded it over to his son Coleman in trust for Hannah; and Coleman gave Peter Hill his power of attorney to lease the farm and mills. Nathan died in 1830, leaving Hannah $12,000 in cash and the Lenni property safely in trust. Hannah's mother died in 1832 and Coleman in 1834; thereafter the trustee was Peter's own brother, George W. Hill. Peter Hill (fortunately for Hannah, as we shall see) never did get his hands on the property, although he realized a profit from leasing it and a few years later moved onto it as a farmer.[23]

George W. Hill was a natural choice for trustee. He and Peter in 1827 had bought the old Sharpless estate, just downstream from Lenni, which contained a variety of mills and mill seats, as well as good farms and a country store. George bought out his brother in 1829, when Peter failed, and thereafter lived happily as landlord, storekeeper, and country gentleman. This meant that the Hills and the Sellers together now controlled the mill sites along the entire stretch of creek on the Middletown side, from Lenni to Rockdale, and much of the land on the Aston side as well.[24] They proceeded to settle cotton manufacturers upon their mill seats. The first of these was Daniel Lammot.

Daniel Lammot, Jr.

In May of 1831 Coleman Sellers leased to Daniel Lammot the Lenni Cotton Factory, "the large mansion house" (the old Lungren place) with its gardens and lot, the various tenements, stables, machine shop, and so forth immediately associated with the mill, occupying in all about ten acres. The Lammot family was already in residence at the mansion and Lammot had already purchased Martin's spinning machinery and was successfully

ANNA POTTS LAMMOT (1819–75) IN 1850.

DANIEL LAMMOT, JR. (1782–1877) IN 1829.

operating the mill. The five-year lease (at an annual rent of $1,200) thus was the formalization of an existing arrangement; indeed, the lease was so precise about the exact amount of water to be drawn from the race, and the improvements needed on the water wheel, that both Lammot and Sellers were evidently writing specifications based on a year or more of actual experience.[25]

Daniel Lammot, at the age of forty-nine, was an older man than the other Chester Creek manufacturers. Like Peter Hill, he had already had a career as a merchant, first in Baltimore and then in Philadelphia; and he too had been married before and had remarried. Before moving to Lenni he had lived in the Kensington district of Philadelphia with his new wife, their little boy Daniel (age seven), and the son and three daughters of the previous marriage.

Lammot was a man with interesting connections. He had been in earlier years a partner of Paul Beck, Jr. (until 1814, when Beck retired from the firm, leaving the business to Lammot),[26] and had married Beck's daughter Susanna. Beck was a shot manufacturer and one of the most eminent of the Philadelphia importing merchants; his principal rival was Stephen Girard. The son of a young apprentice of Nuremberg who had emigrated from Germany in 1752, Beck amassed a fortune estimated at his death in 1844 to be in the neighborhood of $1.25 million. In the course of this successful financial career, however, he devoted much of his time to the improvement of Philadelphia's port facilities, serving as Warden of the Port for many years, and he was active in many philanthropies and religious causes, particularly in the support of the Episcopal Church and of the American Sunday School Union.[27]

Lammot was also connected by marriage with the Du Pont family along the Brandywine nearby, his daughter Margaretta having married Alfred Victor du Pont, the son of Eleuthère Irénée du Pont, in 1824. Lammot had been friends with the E. I. du Ponts for many years. The firm of Beck and Lammot had traded with the Du Ponts ever since the early days of their powder business, and Lammot was accustomed to visiting on the Brandywine both on business and as a family friend. After his first wife died in 1817, he met his second wife, Anna Potts Smith, through the good offices of the Du Pont family. It seems, as one of the Du Pont ladies recalled years later, that Daniel Lammot was a "grand amateur" of the German language (perhaps having acquired that taste from his association with the Becks). Victorine Bauduy had a friend from schoolgirl days who, unlike Victorine (who "hated" German), "was very much occupied at this time in reading German literature." Victorine brought them together, and Daniel and Anna were married in 1819.[28]

Lammot failed in business in 1823. For the next four years he supported himself and his family entirely from the rent of a piece of property in Baltimore which his father had purchased thirty-eight years before and which had been the subject of litigation for the past twenty.[29] His mind was "beclouded and disturbed by anxieties"; no longer actively "engaged in business,"[30] he devoted his time to the affairs of the Swedenborgian Church in Philadelphia (of which he was one of the pillars) and to vainly forming "many projects of business"—none of which amounted to anything. But in March 1825 an opportunity came to hand. The plan was for Lammot to organize a company of Philadelphia financiers, who would buy the now empty cotton-spinning mill of his friend E. I. du Pont and install Lammot as partner and superintendent. He would move himself and family to the Brandywine.[31] After some months of awkward negotiating, the plan fell through; but in the course of it, Lammot immersed himself in conversation with cotton manufacturers, sought books on the subject, and indulged in calculations of profits to be gained. What seemed at first to be "a pleasing dream" gradually began to acquire the solid shape of possibility, although, as he cautiously admitted to Du Pont, "my dear Sir, is there anything easier than to make money—on paper." In April he confided that while the plan might fall through, "I have spent several weeks in reading and thinking of mill seats and spindles, so that in any event I shall be a gainer by the amount of knowledge acquired by my reading and thinking." In June he was still studying the cotton business: "since I first began to think seriously of becoming a manufacturer, I have permitted no day to escape without gaining some knowledge."

The scheme eventually came to nothing, for the gentlemen of Philadelphia would not make Du Pont an offer for his mill that was satisfactory in his or Lammot's eyes. But Lammot was not dismayed, writing cheerfully, "Well, now I am in the market—at the disposal of the highest bidder—ready for the newest fashion, and care not how soon the change takes place."[32]

It is not clear how the finances were arranged, but in March 1828 Lammot went into business as a cotton spinner with a Mr. Robinson (perhaps the Philadelphia Swedenborgian of that name) in Kensington, the industrial suburb of Philadelphia just north of the old city, along the Delaware River. Kensington was the site of several of the textile machinery manufacturers. The family moved out in April, complaining because Kensington was "neither in the city nor out of it."[33] Daniel Lammot, however, was just happy to "get into active life again."

The competition in cotton manufacturing was intense, and, he told his daughter, "I was compelled to improve my machinery, and from my limited capital these improvements were made out of the daily produce of the Mill." He had barely gotten under way, and had accumulated little in the way of profits, when a decline in the market for cotton yarn took place in the winter of 1828–29. He went down in the same general ruin as had William Martin and Peter Hill; in fact, he was involved in the collapse of Peter Hill. Writing to his daughter on the Brandywine at the end of May, he advised her, "It is true that Peter Hill has failed." He explained that this left him in an awkward situation. Hill had borrowed about $3,000 from him, giving notes in return; in order to get cash, Lammot had had the notes discounted. But now, if the purchasers of these notes were unable to collect from Hill when they shortly fell due, they could then come back to Lammot, "and I shall be protested." Hill told Lammot that he stood "on a different footing with him from all his other creditors; and if he get time to settle his affairs, all my notes shall be paid with punctuality, and if he be compelled to make an assignment, I shall be protected." As Lammot remarked, "such may be his feelings and wishes; but in the settlement of every estate difficulties arise which had not been dreamt of."

Lammot feared having to pay off Hill's notes at that moment because his cotton business was in trouble. As he explained to his daughter,

Now, there are so many Spinners embarrassed with old debts, who from the general stagnation in trade are compelled to sacrifice their yarn to meet their engagements, that to sell at the present prices would be certain ruin to me; but to stop the mill until an improvement in business takes place, renders it necessary that I should have the means to pay my notes issued for Cotton as they fall due between this and the month of August. I had a free and confidential communication with Mr DuPont, who agreed fully with my views, and with a degree of kindness and magnanimity altogether unexpected, he made an offer of assistance which I feel most sensibly. Your Grandfather [Paul Beck, Jr.], however, is persuaded that all manufacturers must fail, and therefore refuses to give any assistance. If I cannot compass my object, but be compelled to sell my Machinery at this time, it will not command the one third of its value—indeed I do not believe any one would give much more than the price of old iron for it—such is the depressed state of Cotton spinning at this time. If I could have foreseen the present state of things, you will readily believe I would not have engaged in manufacturing. But who foresaw it, or who ever witnessed such universal commercial & manufacturing distress? It is not confined to this Country, but, from intelligence, it appears to pervade Europe, especially England & France. Such is the case and *such* is my situation. *How* it may eventuate I know not; but of this I am confident that my present embarrassment and difficulty do not arise from idleness or neglect on my part. A few days will determine the business, and whatever may be the issue, I shall have the consolation of having used my best exertions.[34]

The catastrophe happened as feared. The machinery was sold; the cotton manufactory ended its operations; and the Lammots descended into genteel poverty. Minor embarrassments followed major ones. They had to discharge the cook; and the cook, in leaving, stole half of Mrs. Lammot's favorite printed recipes. Lammot searched desperately and unsuccessfully in Philadelphia for another position. As his wife Anna described the situation to Margaretta,

Your father is occupied every day in making interest for himself among the directors & stockholders of the American Fire Insurance Company in order to obtain the office of Secretary, which Jones vacates—The salary is 2500 dollars, with a house & fuel found—His chance is *among the best* He has been told this by the President Mr. Price—It is so long since we have known such *great prosperity* as this office would secure to us that we seem to distrust the possibility of realizing it. The prospect of it however occupies *all* your father's thoughts, sleeping & waking. I remember well when I used to think all these offices were held by persons certainly not above mediocrity. They are now sought after by some of the first men of our city. But the fashion of the times passeth away & those who were highest are now prostrated.[35]

With some grumbling, the family moved again in the summer or fall of 1829, this time to Lenni.[36] Evidently Peter Hill had lived up to his word by promptly paying off enough of what he owed him to enable Lammot to buy Martin's machinery. Mrs. Lammot, who was pregnant and expecting to deliver in about three weeks, was anxious to get the transfer over before her baby was born. She did not want to travel in the fall with a young infant, even if it were only "a cold ride from Chester." And besides, she wanted to see her husband settled. As she explained it to her daughter,

I think the change elligible & every way desirable as a matter of expediency—The first wish of my heart is to see your dear & excellent father relieved of part of that anxiety which is consuming the tranquility of his life—& if by the severest economy or any other deprivation so desirable an end can be obtained, the reward would be far beyond the self-denial it would require.[37]

Unfortunately the baby was stillborn, and by the time they arrived at Lenni, the roads were so bad as to preclude a visit from their friends either in Philadelphia or on the Brandywine.[38]

So Daniel Lammot, fully separated from the familiar merchant's world of Philadelphia, isolated with his family in the little mill town of Lenni, began his second try at success in cotton spinning.

Samuel and James Riddle

The next move in the Hill and Sellers mill-seat development venture was the construction, about 1830, of a new stone factory on the main branch of the creek, just opposite the forks, on the lands held in trust for Hannah Hill. It was named Parkmount, in honor of the Irish home of the tenants, Samuel and James Riddle, and was about a quarter of a mile downstream from Lammot's mill at Lenni.

The Riddle brothers were part of a family of Scots-Irish Presbyterians from the area of Belfast. The Riddles had established themselves on Irish soil in the seventeenth century, when one of their ancestors received substantial estates as a reward for his military services in the Irish wars. Samuel and James's father, Leander, had served in the British Navy and on his retirement had become a successful cotton manufacturer. The eldest son, Samuel, born in 1800, went to school until he was fourteen, acquiring in the process what was later described, somewhat doubtfully, as "a fair English education."[39] (Samuel Riddle was not remembered, in later years, for correctness of diction so much as for his skill as a raconteur.) After quitting school, he worked for nine years in a cotton factory in Belfast, there learning the practical details of cotton manufacture. His brother James, three years his junior, followed the same course.

In 1823 Samuel, seeking "a more profitable field," set sail for the United States as an emigrant on the bark *Hope*. The *Hope* sank on the shoals off Sable Island, the famous destroyer of ships, but crew and passengers evidently were able to get ashore, and Samuel even saved his sea chest. They were picked up after a three-month stay on the island and taken to Halifax, and from there to Philadelphia, where Samuel landed with his sea chest on his back and a total of $5 Spanish in his pocket. He walked to a boarding house and immediately obtained employment in a spinning mill in Manayunk, the cotton-manufacturing district at the Falls of Schuylkill. There he became rapidly sick with "fever and ague" and had to quit. He then moved to Pleasant Mills, New Jersey, where he was able to work steadily for three years.

Evidently his letters home to Ireland were encouraging, for in 1826 the

SAMUEL RIDDLE (1800–88).

rest of the family came over: his father Leander, then about sixty, and retired from business; his brother James; and his three sisters Elizabeth, Mary Ann, and Jane (the latter two were to marry cotton spinners Archibald McDowell and Hamilton Maxwell in the Riddles' employ). In 1827, with the money they had saved, Samuel and James rented a small mill owned by George G. Leiper of Avondale, in Delaware County, Pennsylvania, and installed 2 mules of 240 spindles each. (This may have been the same mill earlier vacated by John P. Crozer.) The family moved with them and probably they all worked in the mill, which employed only ten hands.[40] When the Riddles moved in 1831 to Parkmount Mill on Chester Creek, they left Archibald McDowell behind to manage the mill at Springfield.[41]

The Riddles borrowed some of the money to purchase machinery from their neighbor in Springfield G. B. Lownes. Their financial arrangement with Coleman Sellers was apparently the same as Daniel Lammot's. They paid (directly to Peter Hill) $1,000 annual rent for the mill and the associated houses, tenements, and other structures; and they were expected to reimburse Hill for the township real estate taxes on the estate. In addition, they did business with Peter Hill for a time in his capacity as a merchant, sending him boxes of shuttle cops (yarn wound on bobbins ready for use as filling by weavers) and accepting his notes in payment for yarn sold. These transactions ended in March 1834, when one of his notes, passed on by the Riddles for cash, was protested by the next holder.[42]

The final action of the Hill brothers in locating cotton manufactories on their lands was the leasing of the old mills at Penn's Grove to new and more efficient occupants. They had leased the old woolen factory to James Houghton about 1827 shortly after they purchased the Penn's Grove tract. Houghton converted it to a cotton-weaving mill. In 1830 or 1831 John Garsed, an English machinist and weaver lately of Yorkshire, and more recently from Philadelphia, leased the old fulling mill and converted it to a manufactory of power looms. With him was his twelve-year-old son Richard, who already had four years' experience working in a cotton mill in New Hope, Bucks County, and who was later to become one of the principal manufacturers of textile machinery in the United States.[43]

With these accessions, there were now six cotton factories in the Rockdale area. Beginning downstream, the owners and managers were: Edward Darlington and Thomas Clyde, owning the spinning mill at Knowlton, and probably employing John D. Carter as manager; John S. Phillips, operating a power-loom weaving mill at Rockdale on lands owned by Henry Moore; James Houghton and John Garsed at Penn's Grove, operating a power-loom weaving mill and a manufactory of power looms, on land owned by George W. Hill; Samuel and James Riddle, running a spinning mill at

Parkmount on the Hannah S. Hill estate; Daniel Lammot, running another spinning mill at Lenni, also on the Hannah S. Hill estate; and, on the southerly branch of the creek, the spinning mill at West Branch, owned and operated by John P. Crozer.

Now came the Smith family, catalysts of community improvement, to complete the roll of major industrialists.

THE SMITH FAMILY

Richard S. Smith was a well-established Philadelphia commission merchant when at forty-four he almost inadvertently acquired ownership of Old Sable Forge, including the nail mill and Phillips and Lewis' cotton factory. Smith and his partner Joseph Haven had acted as agents for Captain Moore in the sale of his nails and had loaned him a considerable sum of money when in 1832 he became financially embarrassed. Smith and Haven took a bill of sale to his property as security, "with the condition that we should re-convey the property to him when his indebtedness should be liquidated, giving us the right of absolute possession if the debt was not paid by a time fixed." Moore then leased his own mill back from Smith and Haven for seven years. But Moore failed in business the very next year, and in May 1833 Smith (Haven having died) called in the debt and became full owner.[1]

Smith continued to rent Phillips the weaving mill and the little stone farmhouse, with its attached greenhouse, where Phillips was now cultivating rare and exotic flowers. There was some social exchange between Phillips and the Smith family living in the big frame house on the road 50 feet below him, for both families moved in the same circles of Philadelphia society. But the association was not close, and amounted mostly to an exchange of Phillips' flowers for occasional dinners; of intellectual concourse there was little, for the Smiths, although well read and well informed, were extremely devout Episcopalians, and Phillips was indifferent to organized religion. Clementina Smith's friend Sophie du Pont went so far as to refer to him as an "open Infidel," whose mill was a morally unfit environment for young Christian female operatives.

Richard and Elizabeth

The Smiths had long been uncomfortable living in Philadelphia in the summer and, believing that children were especially likely to get sick in the city in warm weather, usually sent them to friends in the country. The summer and fall of 1832—the year of the great cholera epidemic—were particularly alarming: one of their younger daughters, Eleuthera (namesake of the family's friend on the Brandywine), fell gravely ill.[2] They already knew the Rockdale community, having spent a summer there a year or so before. Now, in the spring of 1833, probably motivated in part by the desire to find safe summer quarters in the country, and in part by the prospect of being near their friends the Lammots at Lenni and the Du Ponts on the Brandywine, Richard Smith moved his family and the servants out to Rockdale. They retained, of course, their residence at 1010 Clinton Street in Philadelphia, where the family generally resided in winter, the women enjoying the social season, music and opera, and church activities, and Mr. Smith, in addition to working his usual long hours at the office, indulging his hobby of painting in oils.

Richard S. Smith was a Philadelphia gentleman. His Swedish and English forebears had played a respectable role in the life of the city and had served with distinction in the armed forces during the Revolution. He himself had played a public part during the War of 1812. Having gone to Gothenburg in Sweden as supercargo on a merchant vessel, he found himself unexpectedly advised by a pilot-boat captain of the U.S. Congress's declaration of war against England. As he received the news before the officers of British cruisers lying in harbor heard it, he hastily assembled the captains of forty American merchant vessels lying in the roads and gave them the information. Thirty-two quickly ran up the river to safety under the guns of the Swedish fortress. For saving a part of the American merchant fleet the energetic young Smith was promptly appointed vice-consul, in which capacity he busied himself trying to save other vessels and providing for the sailors discharged from the blockaded ships.[3] After the war, being fluent in Swedish and French, and having friends in England and other parts of Europe, he was successful in the commission business and became acquainted with the Du Ponts—the firm of Smith and Haven acting as Philadelphia agent for the Brandywine powder makers. His brother Francis Gurney also served as an agent of the Du Ponts. In 1824 Richard entered the insurance business, and in 1830 he was elected one of the directors, and in 1837 the president, of the Union Mutual Insurance Company; by January 1833, he had become a director of the Bank of North America.[4]

While they lived in Philadelphia, the Smiths were family friends with the Lammots. The Smith women were particularly fond of Anna, the second Mrs. Lammot, and exchanged long visits with her; they lamented the distance out to Kensington when the Lammots moved there in 1827 during Daniel Lammot's first, ill-fated foray into cotton manufacturing. They were also very good friends of the family of E. I. du Pont, with whom Smith was constantly involved in business matters. Smith greatly respected the elderly powder manufacturer and declared to Sophie, years later after her father's death, "I never loved a friend more."[5] He delighted in the stories E. I. du Pont told of his adventures during the French Revolution, particularly of the nights he spent in hiding, soaked with rain and looking "like a drowned chicken," in the Bois de Boulogne "during Robespierre's dreadful reign."[6] Members of the two families regularly exchanged house visits. And Du Pont's widowed daughter Victorine Bauduy, who managed her father's house after her mother's death, was on intimate terms with Elizabeth Smith, who referred to theirs as a "friendship which has now become necessary to my happiness."[7]

At the time of his purchase of the Rockdale property, Smith was a church-going man but not yet enthusiastic in his religious sentiments. He had been brought up in a religious way by a widowed father, who had promised his wife on her deathbed to send the children to church twice every Sunday. On his return from Sweden in 1813 he was confirmed and thereafter dutifully attended St. Peter's Episcopal Church in Philadelphia.[8] But it was the women of the family who were most warmly interested in religion. By 1829 Clementina, only fifteen years old, was teaching Sunday School at St. Peter's in the winter and at the Brandywine Manufacturers' Sunday School during her visits with the Du Ponts in the summer.[9] And it appears that the establishment of the church at Rockdale "was in large measure due to the active and untiring efforts of Mrs. Smith."[10]

Elizabeth Beach, who had married Richard Smith in 1813, had been born on Cape Ann and brought up in a palatial old house in Gloucester, Massachusetts. After her marriage she enjoyed frequent summer vacations in the northern resort. On these occasions she visited busily with old friends and relations, saw to it that the children learned to swim in the chilly water off Gloucester, and kept up her correspondence with Victorine. From wherever she was, throughout the year, she sent her friend news of illnesses and family accidents, plied her with recipes for pumpkin pudding and children's cough syrup (a heroic mixture, half paregoric, one-quarter antimony wine, and one-quarter nitre), and passed on gossip about the Lammots and other mutual friends. But mixed with the domestic information were religious bulletins, such as the latest word on the Episcopal convention in Philadelphia, and remarks about her aspirations for Clementina's spiritual growth ("pray heaven to continue her in the paths of religion and virtue"). Indeed, she was perhaps a bit possessive of Clementina's morality, reporting from New York, where they had gone for a winter round of parties, that her daughter was being very good, avoiding gaiety and display. Clementina had an admirer, a gentleman from Marseilles, with whom she talked French,

but, reported her mother proudly, she was "indifferent to all his politeness."[11]

On their arrival in Rockdale in the summer of 1833, Elizabeth Smith
and her daughter Clementina urged the paterfamilias to commence a Sunday School. As he described the event later on:

> ... the nearest Episcopal church being at Concord, five miles distant, we,
> when the weather permitted, rode over there. Being frequently pre-
> vented by the weather, we were many Sundays deprived of usual public
> worship, and my wife and daughter, having been previously connected
> with the Sunday-school at St. Peter's, Philadelphia, proposed to me to
> open a Sunday-school in the vacant room of a factory building on my
> property. This was commenced with an attendance of twenty children,
> which soon increased to one hundred.[12]

The building chosen was actually Moore's old nail mill, now vacant, and
the Sunday School met on the upper floor, sitting on benches bought at an
auction. The organization of the school was simple: Richard S. Smith served
as superintendent, and his wife and daughters were the teachers; the children were largely from the families of mill operatives in the district. The
Smiths also wanted formal Episcopal church services in addition to the
Sunday School, and they persuaded the rector of St. Paul's—the venerable
Protestant Episcopal church in Chester—who was also the lay preacher at
the Baptist church in Chester, to officiate occasionally. These services in the
nail mill were so well attended that in the summer of 1834 the bishop
licensed a young divinity student to serve as lay reader to the congregation.
Several Philadelphia clergymen also came out from time to time to conduct
services. By the fall of 1834, when the Sunday School had "the names of
140 children . . . inscribed on its roll-book," and the Sunday services were
being regularly attended, "it finally became evident that the Church had
many friends in the neighborhood and many anxious desires and prayers
were [being] offered for her prosperity and establishment therein." The
time had come to attempt the regular organization of the congregation.[13]
Later we shall look closely into the growth of Calvary Church and its
evangelical role in the Rockdale district.

Clementina and Sophie

The Smiths were actively encouraged in their missionary course by the
Du Pont women, and particularly by Sophie, Eleuthera, and Victorine.
Clementina and Sophie, of course, were best friends. When Sophie in the
summer of 1833, just after the Smiths moved out to Rockdale, married a

SOPHIE DU PONT (1810–88) IN 1831.

naval officer, her cousin Samuel Francis (Frank) from across the creek, she confessed to her dear Clemma that she had committed "treason against the Sisterhood."[14] But the marriage barely interrupted her intimacy with Clementina and actually soon was thrusting the two women closer together. For Sophie discovered herself to be in a surprisingly difficult marital situation and Clemma was her confidante.

Sophie and her husband had known and liked each other from childhood, having been brought up in the nearby mansions of their fathers, the brothers Eleuthère and Victor du Pont. Their courtship was romantic, with Sophie shyly recording in her diary a growing attachment to her handsome and amiable cousin. Usually she wrote in plain English, but on these occasions she used a simple cypher to conceal her sentiments from prying eyes. In November, after five months of marriage, she and her husband moved the few hundred yards across the creek to his family home at Louviers; the separation from Eleutherian Mills and her family there filled her with dread beforehand and regret afterward, and reminded her of the death of her mother five years before (and perhaps also of her homesickness when she was sent to school in Philadelphia ten years before, a homesickness so acute she was brought back to be educated at home). She herself expressed some bewilderment at the intensity of her distress. "Who could understand," she wrote in her diary at the time, "that my heart would be so wrung at going so little a way from my old home, & going too with such a husband, & such kind relations?"[15] A month later she was suffering such severe chest pain that she was unable to write. By February, now pregnant, she was feeling debilitated. In March she took to her bed, suffering from pain and weakness in her back, and eventually the child she carried was aborted or born dead.[16]

Sophie remained virtually bedridden, except for occasional remissions, for the next fifteen years. Her illness was diagnosed and rediagnosed as a "disease of the spine." The endless blisterings and cuppings did little to improve her condition. She became addicted to morphine, which she took regularly in order to sleep, and suffered from a generalized depression (which in later years she attributed to the fact that she "had been taking morphine a great deal & my nervous system, was greatly affected by it").[17] This depression manifested itself in part in worrying guiltily over the "wasted years" during which she should have been performing useful Christian service to others. In 1845, after a discouraging medical consultation which included a prescription of "abstinence from exercise," she concluded, "I may consider myself an invalid for life . . . unless God gives me aid I know not how to bear the burthen of life—pray for me—it is all any of my friends can now do for me."[18]

SOPHIE DU PONT CIRCA 1850.

The "contention between languor of body & energy of spirit" which Sophie recognized within herself seems to have been exacerbated at the times when she was worrying about her husband Frank's imminent departure on a new voyage. He was a naval officer when she married him, but was not ordered to sea until three years later. In the meantime she lived in dread of his leaving. In May 1834, only a couple of months after she had taken to her bed, she wrote to her friend:

Dearest Clementina, never marry a Navy officer! That is my advice to you, when you leave the Society of *Tabbies*—'Tis too dreadful to have to look forward to such long separations from one's nearest & dearest friend—[19]

She had been haunted by the thought that their first parting would be final (since the age of fourteen she had had a superstitious presentiment that she would die in 1838). Her husband's absences were, indeed, prolonged ones, and some of her acquaintances thought he should resign his commission for the sake of Sophie's health. His sea duty ran on a roughly two-year cycle, with a tour of a year to eighteen months at sea alternating with six months to a year at home. When Frank was home he was kindness itself, carrying his wife up and down stairs in his arms, on and off boats, and even into the ocean at Cape May for "sea bathing." But he was ambitious for advancement and could not linger with his wife too long. Six months after his return from his first voyage, despite his wife's presentiments of doom (or perhaps because of them), he himself applied to the department for orders to sea. Sophie deeply resented these departures and on one occasion exclaimed to Clementina, in a martyred tone, "I do not repine—I acquiesce—it is all right—but I do feel it. . . ."[20]

Actually, a few years after this, Sophie's health improved substantially and by 1850 she was again able to walk, to travel, and to visit Clementina and her other friends in Rockdale and Philadelphia, sometimes with her husband and sometimes not. She never again bore a child, however, and one may look in vain in her diary and correspondence of later years for any expression of surprise or dismay at her failure to give birth. It is as if, until some moment of acceptance of her fate, a taut body was rendered incapable of marital happiness, housewifery, and motherhood under conditions of repeated and prolonged abandonment by her beloved friend. And even after the body relaxed and the pain eased, the scars of the ordeal remained in the contours of a grim and ravaged countenance.

Clementina avoided the marital trap into which Sophie had fallen. Her sustained correspondence with Sophie began in 1834, after her friend's marriage, when she herself was nineteen years old. She had already made her appearance in society, at balls and teas and public entertainments in Philadelphia, New York, and Boston, and would continue to grace the winter social season for many years. She was used to the attentions of young swains but was already expressing disillusionment with the male part of mankind. In her first letter of the year 1834, she exclaimed: "I must really say I have given up all faith in friendships between gentlemen and ladies."[21] Although she continued to be courted by hopeful suitors for several years more, she paid little attention to their addresses. A few years later, she was claiming to have "a reputation as a member" of the society of "old maids," and by 1841—at twenty-seven—she was able to assure Sophie that she was firmly committed to a life of single blessedness.

I think I was never so safe in my life, as I am now, against all invasion. I think the *territory* proof against every attack (were there any) and [you] may believe me when I tell you, your friend *Clementina Smith* will to all appearances be *always* the same C.B.S.[22]

Clementina was correct in her opinion of herself: she never married.

Her letters do not reveal from what personal experiences and private observations Clementina derived her set aversion to marriage. But her choice of spinsterhood was explained publicly by the readily stated conviction that the marital state was, for the wife, a condition of bondage, and that only as a single woman could she have the independence she wanted. Her comments to Sophie were very blunt:

Ah Sophy well may you mourn your dependence and sigh for the unshaded state of single blessedness, when even health is so materially influenced by it. You are among the number of those infatuated beings however, who though they talk very reasonably upon those matters, would not for the world give up that state of bondage to which they have subjected themselves.[23]

She complained of her own "housewifery" in her parents' home as drudgery which interfered with reading, and labeled the ladylike activity of mantua-making a "penance" for previous enjoyments. Not for her was Sophie's "perfect resignation to circumstances." While Sophie dramatized her fate by suffering in eloquent silence, Clementina took care to protect herself by busy, even aggressive, commitment to Sunday School and missionary society duties.

There were, to be sure, disadvantages even in this course. She was subject, as long as she resided in their home, to the beck and call of both her parents. She was not allowed to visit Sophie whenever she liked but only when the complex schedule of the Smith household permitted it. Their plans had to be delayed time and again because of the necessities of waiting until after a parental vacation, or a fit of house-cleaning, or the completion of one of the semi-annual migrations between Philadelphia and Rockdale, or the need to nurse ailing relatives and to mind infant nephews and nieces, or because her parents were worried about *her* health. The frequency of these restrictions led her to occasional outbursts. Once, when she had been refused permission to visit the Brandywine because she had a cough, she complained: "indeed dearest if I could do just as I pleased, I should not be long away from you, but you see that even in a state of single *blessedness* when ladies are supposed to have their own way they are not always without restraint."[24] Her disillusionment with spinsterhood once—but only once— made her question the wisdom of her choice: "Spinsters are no more independent, than married people, if they are as much so indeed, I cannot pretend to say, what may be the effects of such a conclusion."[25]

Clementina, like the somewhat older Anna Lammot, whom she re- garded as "fascinating," wanted to involve herself somehow in the real affairs of a real world. She regretted from time to time the triviality of her efforts and felt that she was not "acting a part in the busy scene" and could only "peep at the world from out the loop hole of retreat."[26] One of the women whom she knew in the city, single like herself, desired to engage in the work of foreign missions on her own, without first marrying a male missionary; Clementina encouraged her and tried to arrange for her train- ing. But her greatest admiration was reserved for a lady missionary who had been "rescued" from her brutal husband in China by Bishop Boone and his wife, and sent back home, where she resumed her maiden name. Miss Harries (the ex-Mrs. Innes), who had a school in New York and did "missionary work" in the city, spoke before missionary groups about her adventures. Clementina heard her, met her, and was deeply impressed. "She is I think one of the most wonderful persons I ever met," she confided to Sophie.[27]

Sophie was the central person in Clementina's life; and it would be difficult to say whether her husband Frank or her friend Clemma was more important to Sophie. Theirs was a special friendship, like those of other women in the sisterhood. Friendship was a relationship that might, as Cle- mentina observed, be difficult to maintain between men and women; but in this age of romanticism, friendships between women and women, and men and men, were perhaps more freely contracted than at later times in American history. These were intense relationships, entitling the partners to exchange intimate secrets in an atmosphere of trust and the expectation of moral support. The partners thus entered into an almost romantic com- mingling of identities; indeed, among the women, the language of romance was used freely and a considerable degree of physical intimacy—embracing, kissing, sharing the same bed—was regarded as normal. In the case of women, such unions were frankly considered to compete with marriage for the partners' time, and although marital duties came first, there was recognition of the legitimacy of jealousy.

Yet there is little to suggest, in most of these friendships, that the partners engaged in any form of overt, mutually recognized, sexual congress. It is as if the friendships satisfied another need, at least among the managerial class, a need no other institution was prepared adequately to meet. To be sure, society allowed male-female friendship—but, with rare exceptions, only in the context of legitimate and fulfilled, or soon to be fulfilled, sexuality (i.e., in the affianced and marital relationship). In the correspondence and diaries of the sisterhood, husbands and wives referred to each other as friends (Sophie dubbed her husband "my dearest friend on earth"); it would seem that they did, in fact, do their best to treat each other in the warm, intimate, understanding, and respectful fashion that could properly be called friendship.

Friendship between men and women was manifestly dangerous outside courtship and marriage because it might lead to sexual relations (although marriage itself did not necessarily lead to perfect friendship). But, although it might be possible to restrict sexuality to monogamy or even deny it altogether, the need for friendship was less easily confined. This need the same-sex friendship was able to satisfy. Friendships between persons of the same sex could be cultivated with such intensity precisely because they were formally defined as (and most probably were) sexually safe. Female partners might thus innocently engage in the most extravagantly romantic rhetoric with each other, exchange intimate communications denied to their spouses, offer sonnets to each other celebrating their love, and freely fondle and caress one another both privately and in public, without either they or their friends being allowed to question the propriety of the relationship.

From the beginning of their correspondence, while they were teen-age summer visitors at each other's house, Clementina and Sophie addressed one another in terms of dearest friendship, and over the years the relationship became steadily more close. By 1835—after Sophie's marriage and the beginning of her illness—Clementina was dreaming of Sophie. Thereafter they included each other in their dreams with fair regularity and of course confided the contents to one another. At least by 1837 they were sufficiently close for Clemma to tease her friend by reporting that she had received three letters from a young gentleman in New York. "Are you not alarmed?" she inquired playfully, but quickly added the reassurance that "these were letters of business."[28] Sophie did in fact worry lest Clementina marry and be thereafter "still more beyond my reach." As Sophie confessed in her diary, a few months later,

We took a short walk in the wood together on Friday—when we returned, she played for me & sung, "Hail to the Lord's annointed." When I listen to her singing hymns; when I hear her converse, to look on her angelic countenance, I feel an admiration I cannot express. Pure & lovely being! & might *I* too, *once,* have become even such?[29]

The friendship had reached its high plateau of intimacy by the beginning of 1844, when Clementina, alluding to herself and Sophie, wrote of "the hope of an eternal union with the one ['you love' crossed out] dearest to you on earth," and urged Sophie to visit Clinton Street so that "we shall be able to be together in a room in the second story." At the end of that summer of 1844, Clementina spent some time with her friend on the Brandywine. On her return to Philadelphia she wrote Sophie a glowing letter that, in its easy transitions from romantic sentiment to religious piety to shared plans to care in a quasi-maternal way for young children of friends and relatives to news of housekeeping, testifies clearly to Clementina's sense of the fitness of their friendship in the context of church and home. The letter began:

Phil*ª* September 18*th* /44

My dearest Sophie
This day I must tell thee how many thoughts I have of thee though ever so briefly—May it be a day of blessing to your heart, beloved, and the beginning of increased and holy hopes, and joys, for the coming year. It is a day of rejoicing to my heart that God has *so blessed me,* with so precious a treasure in giving me your love and affection—so long tried and enduring—May this love and affection be more & more sanctified dearest Sophie, until the imperfect sympathy of earth shall be exchanged for heavenly intercourse—If there is one wish I would offer more fervently than another dear Sophie for your happiness it is that this year might realise to you the wish of your heart for your Husband. How much I wished for you both on Sunday that you could have listened with me to our good Bishop in the morn*ᵍ* at St Andrews afternoon at old Trinity The morn*ᵍ* sermon on the text "what shall it profit a man if he gain the whole world" &c in the afternoon "those who by patient contuance in well doing obtain glory, honour, immortality & eternal life"—The morn*ᵍ* sermon was to unconverted, afternoon more especially to careless professors—I wish I c*ᵈ* say all I w*ᵈ* of them. . . .[30]

Clementina carried her identification with Sophie's household so far that, in a sense, she identified with Sophie's marriage. She reported to her friend that she dreamed of her husband, then at sea ("he was before me so vividly & looking so well"). And, expecting Frank's imminent return a few months later, she wrote that when she thought of them together, "in that dear home, a sort of ecstasy takes possession of me in the very anticipation."[31]

The substance of their friendship was communication: they found that they could talk to each other face to face, and write to each other, and even think themselves into a state of spiritual communion when apart. Physical closeness was important because it made the communication that much more intimate. Thus Clemma could say that she wished for "a few days with you, in comfortable converse beside that *dear brown sofa—dear,* for the sake of its occupant."[32] And Sophie could make plans for a joint visit with Clemma at her sister Eleuthera's house, where "I will have a double bed in my room there so that we can occupy it together & have some cozey talks."[33] What they talked about, of course, apart from their friendship itself, was mostly conventional things (insofar as the correspondence reveals it), mainly religion, books, parties and vacations, births, marriages, illnesses, and deaths among family and friends, fancy needlework, and household chores. But it was not so much the overt informational content that mattered. The recognition of the shared attitudes, the mutual endorsement of identities, the knowledge of the other's empathy for one's own pleasures and pains were the important parts of these communications. As a result, neither could really feel alone in the world.

THE MECHANICAL KNOWLEDGE
OF THE INDUSTRIALISTS

In the early years, while their women dealt in spiritual matters, the men thought about machinery and sought out knowledgeable friends. There were important differences in the levels of mechanical information wanted by different kinds of management specialists. The mill owner and the manufacturer needed information at a relatively general level; the technical supervisor in the mill itself needed more precise data. None required the intimate knowledge of the mechanic, machinist, inventor, and practical engineer, who had to have extremely detailed tactile and visual experience, only to be acquired by working in a machine shop.

The Owner and Manufacturer:
Books, Articles, Conversation, and Travel

Many men went into the cotton manufacture after failing in another line of work or after coming into the ownership of an unfamiliar enterprise through the accidents of inheritance and financial settlement, without any prior knowledge or experience. Daniel Lammot is the best example. In an earlier section we have seen how, after he decided in 1825 to go into cotton spinning, he began a desperate search for information. A similar problem beset John P. Crozer, who had committed himself to the cotton manufacture in 1821 in an almost equally offhanded way ("I was anxious to do something, and my mind took hold of cotton spinning"). Technical ignorance nearly ruined Crozer, for he depended on others who had little more knowledge than he; "it seems to me," he observed years later,

almost a miracle that I was not crushed at the very outset. It was difficult to get any one that understood the business. There were but few in this country, at that time, who did understand it. I engaged a man named Johnson, who came well recommended, but, though industrious and honest, was incompetent. My machinery . . . was very inferior; and I an entire novice; and, what made the matter worse, yarns had become plenty in the market, and rather unsaleable, unless of very good quality. "Fearful odds" were against my success, and I now became distressingly anxious. My little all was involved, and a great deal of my brother-in-law's money. I early made up my mind that he should be protected, and every one else; that when I believed my own capital was sunk, I would go no farther; and I felt that impending ruin hung over me. My yarns would not command the full market price, while they cost me more to produce them than if the machinery had been of better construction. My mind was so thoroughly engrossed that for months and years no other subject than my business could engage or at least hold my attention. I feel, in review, that this was very sinful.[1]

What both men needed at the outset was printed literature, but there was very little available in 1821 and that little was inadequate. Lammot's principal reliance (in 1825) was on an English work, published in 1816, by a mechanician named John Sutcliffe. Sutcliffe was a millwright, a draftsman, a builder of cotton mills, a designer of atmospheric engines, and a hydraulic engineer. To his *Treatise on Canals and Reservoirs* Sutcliffe had added two sections containing "Instructions for Designing and Building a Corn Mill" and "Observations on the best Mode of Carding, Roving, Drawing, and

Spinning, all Kinds of Cotton Twist." The account of cotton manufacture occupied about 120 pages, was not illustrated, and was less a straightforward description of the machinery and its operation than a miscellany of administrative advice to a person who already understood the cards, roving frames, throstles, and mules themselves.[2]

Also available to Lammot (and to Crozer) was Abraham Rees's excellent and authoritative *Cyclopaedia,* published in London from 1802 to 1820 and republished in Philadelphia from 1810 to 1822 in forty-one volumes. The fifteen-page article on "Manufacture of Cotton" first appeared in 1812. It concentrated, however, largely on the history and economics of the industry; the actual descriptions of the several processes took up altogether only a page and a half and thus were necessarily too brief to do much more than introduce the subject. The *Cyclopaedia* also contained an eighteen-page technical article on the varieties of cotton and a history of its production; a thirty-page article on the mechanical principles involved in machinery of various kinds; and fourteen plates of excellent engravings of the machinery used in cotton manufacture, including cards, draw frames, roving cam frames, the double speeder, water-spinning frame, throstle, mule, rolling, doubling, and twisting machines, and a calico-printing machine.[3] In 1823 Richard Guest's *Compendious History of the Cotton-Manufacture* appeared in England, with its engravings (later to become famous) of eighteenth-century spinning machinery of Hargreave's, Arkwright's, and Crompton's era; Baines's history of the industry, with good illustrations of newer machinery, appeared in 1835.[4] And in 1825 John Nicholson's *Operative Mechanic and British Machinist* appeared in London; the Carey and Lea edition came out in Philadelphia in 1826. It contained a clear and concise eleven-page outline of the machine processes of cotton manufacturing, along with several excellent schematic drawings.[5] But it appeared too late to give initial guidance to either Lammot or Crozer.

The situation began to improve in the 1830's, with the anonymous publication in Glasgow of *The Theory and Practice of Cotton Spinning: or the Carding and Spinning Master's Assistant.* The first edition was published in 1832; a second edition appeared the following year, and included an account of Roberts' self-actor. The author was James Montgomery, an experienced mill manager who had not only visited many English mills but also mills in America. In his preface, he noted that

it is much to be regretted, that nothing has ever appeared on the art of cotton spinning, fitted to assist the master, manager, or artisan, in acquiring a correct and systematical knowledge of the *real* principles of the business. Almost every other important art or manufacture has its periodi-

cal, or other publication, wherein its principles are elucidated, its improvements recorded, and its difficulties explained, and to which the
artisan can apply in cases of difficulty; but the manager of a Cotton
Spinning Factory can only acquire a proper knowledge of his business,
by long experience and application in the practical department of the
manufacture, and it will depend upon the situation in which he is placed,
and the advantages he enjoys, if he ever obtain that correct knowledge
of all its details, which is essentially necessary to render him fully qualified
for managing a large establishment with satisfaction or profit to the
proprietors. Hence a treatise on this subject, in which the principles of
the art may be *unfolded,* and its details *explained* and *exemplified,* has long
been felt and acknowledged as a desideratum by the trade; to supply
which the following treatise is respectfully presented to their notice.[6]

Montgomery presented both "theory and practice combined," in a
systematic, well-illustrated work of 332 pages and 10 plates. He described
each machine, explaining its principles of operation and its function in the
total process; gave instructions on how to adjust it; and demonstrated how
to perform "the various Calculations connected with the different departments of Cotton Spinning." In 1840 Scott's *Practical Cotton Spinner and
Manufacturer* appeared; Joseph Bancroft on the Brandywine acquired a
copy of the English edition. This work went farther than Montgomery in
giving the detailed mathematical instructions of the sort Bancroft had hitherto kept in his manuscript journals. A Philadelphia edition appeared in
1851, edited by Oliver Byrne, with new material on American machines.[7]
Montgomery, Scott, and the incomparably lucid science writer Andrew Ure
with his *Philosophy of Manufactures,*[8] dominated the scene until the 1850's,
when American managers began to publish too, with Connecticut's Daniel
Snell putting out *The Manager's Assistant* in 1850 and Boston's Robert Baird
publishing (posthumously) *The American Cotton Spinner* in 1851.[9] Comparable manuals by various writers, usually experienced managers, continued to
appear year after year thereafter.

The literature available to the aspiring business manager on how to
operate a machine shop in connection with his mill was even less adequate.
The earliest general publication was the article published in Rees's *Cyclopaedia* in London in 1819, entitled "Manufacture of Ships' Blocks." It
described in some detail the system of advanced woodworking machinery
devised by Sir Samuel Bentham and Marc Isambard Brunel to manufacture
the hundred thousand pulley blocks required by the Royal Navy each year.
These machines, installed by 1808, were regarded as one of the "mechanical marvels of the time"; some of them were still in use 145 years later![10]

But the *Cyclopaedia*'s account did not address itself to the metalworking tools. In 1826 Nicholson's *Operative Mechanic and British Machinist* devoted 19 pages out of 350 to metalworking machine tools, including an account of the lathes built by the Sellers' old friends in Philadelphia, Isaiah Lukens and William Mason.[11] Not until 1841 did a general account of metalworking machine tools appear in England in the third, revised edition of Buchanan's *Practical Essays on Mill-Work and other Machinery.*[12] In the 1850's the American Oliver Byrne published a series of handbooks for the machinist and mechanic; as with the technical literature on cotton machinery, the American machine tool industry seems to have felt itself to be on a par with England's in the sixth decade of the nineteenth century.[13]

The Managers: Experience in England

At the beginning, Daniel Lammot sought an experienced technical manager for the projected mill on the Brandywine. Writing to E. I. du Pont in 1825, he touted two candidates: a "Mr. Sutton, the young man on whose judgment Mr. Beck relies," who was reputed to be well qualified as to "talents, management and economy"; and "young Bancroft," newly arrived from England and not yet established in his own mill on the Brandywine.[14] (It was this same Joseph Bancroft who eventually acquired the mill property for which Lammot was scheming.) And Crozer likewise had to turn to a supposed practical expert, the incompetent Mr. Johnson, for assistance in the technical management of his early venture in 1821. The Riddles, the Garseds, and John D. Carter—all of them British-born and bred up in cotton mills—could manage their own mills. But the less experienced Chester Creek manufacturers—Phillips, Crozer, Martin, Lammot, Darlington, and the rest—were radically dependent at the outset upon technical managers.

The manager of a cotton mill trained and supervised workers in the practical operation of their machines; he knew how to set up the machines, that is, adjust the various settings in order to have the machines produce the right weight and dimensions of lap, sliver, roving, yarn, and cloth; and he could diagnose mechanical trouble and send for the mechanic when necessary. These skills could not be acquired solely by reading even an excellent manual; they required experience in actually operating and setting the machines, experience acquired over the course of years in a number of different mills. In the early 1820's, such experience could be had in only a few places in America; for the most part, at this date, such men had to come from England. In 1821, in Delaware County, the only mill mentioned by Crozer as still operating at a profit was managed by Hugh Wagstaff—

"a practical cotton spinner from England."[15] It was a small mill, along Ridley Creek, with only 1,272 spindles (600 throstle and 672 mule) and 16 power looms; it employed 13 men, 6 women, and 40 boys and girls. Perhaps the mill's margin of success was owing to the employment primarily of children. But in 1825 the mill was purchased by James Ronaldson, who in 1827 placed Joseph Bancroft's father, John Bancroft, in charge of it.[16]

What made these English technicians so valuable, particularly in the 1820's and 1830's, was their possession of precise numerical information about machine settings and a knowledge of how to calculate such esoteric quantities as the several radii which described the form of the cam controlling the motion of the flyer on a fly frame. (The method of this calculation was copied by Joseph Bancroft from the papers of Josiah Woods. The algorithm involved six variables: the number of turns of the flyer for each turn of the front roller, the diameter of the front roller, the shrinkage of the yarn for each turn of the front roller, the diameter of the bobbin barrel, the diameter of the full bobbin, and the sum of the diameters of the cones.) Bancroft copied other machinery-setting recipes from the papers of another of his mule spinners, Evan Davies. Davies had made notes on the machine settings in the mills he had observed in England; for instance:

20's Throstle twist. Roller 55 revolutions pr minute. 1 In. diam. Rim runs 139 1/4 pr min. spindle 3920 & puts 21 1/2 turns to the Inch.[17]

Bancroft kept notes and sample calculations of his own, as well as extracts from his readings, from about 1827 to 1830, while he was getting started in his business.

Until the repeal of the laws in 1824 and 1825, England, of course, officially prohibited the emigration of persons bearing this kind of technical information; but the laws were not effectively enforced. From the 1790's onward, a constant stream of experienced supervisory personnel left England for responsible positions in American factories. By 1812, there were at least 314 alien British textile workers in the lower Delaware Valley.[18] After the repeal of the emigration laws, the stream became virtually a flood, including operatives of all levels of experience as well as managerial personnel.

Chester Creek received its share of these English immigrant technicians. Perhaps the most successful of the immigrant managers on Chester Creek was Abraham Blakeley, whom Crozer hired in 1833 to become foreman of the newly established weaving department at West Branch. Blakeley was the Lancashire weaver who had come to this country in 1828, at the age of twenty-two; thus he was twenty-seven when he was hired by Crozer. As we shall see, he married, prospered, and eventually became a prominent cotton manufacturer in Chester himself.[19] Another successful pair of manufacturers in the area (not mentioned by Crozer) were the unrelated Irishmen Dennis and Charles Kelly, who had a cotton and woolen factory in Haverford. Charles Kelly managed Penn's Grove briefly in the late 1820's.[20] And members of the British Bottomley family had been operating cotton and woolen mills along the Creek ever since 1810.[21] In fact, of the six cotton factories in the Rockdale district in 1832, three were certainly managed in whole or in part by British immigrants (the Garseds at Penn's Grove, the Riddles at Parkmount, and Blakeley in the weaving department at West Branch). Carter may have been still managing Knowlton. For the situation at Phillips' mill and at Lenni, no information is available.

ENTERING THE COTTON MANUFACTURE IN THE 1820's

In Pennsylvania, and in particular along Chester Creek, the cotton manufacture was not solidly established upon a firm basis until the 1820's. Earlier efforts did not survive the resumption of the imports of British cotton goods after the War of 1812. The enterprises along the Merrimac River in Massachusetts, established about 1815, had survived the British assault, and were already flourishing mightily, because they were founded on a somewhat different plan from those to the south: they employed a different technology, a different work force, and (of relevance to the immediate discussion) a different method of financing.

The Chester Creek system of financing cotton manufacture (and, apparently, the system in the Delaware Valley generally) had four characteristic features: (1) the mill owners and the cotton manufacturers were not normally the same people; (2) in almost every case, both owners and manufacturers assembled capital and secured themselves against failure by drawing much of their funds and assurances of support from an assemblage of both in-laws and blood kinsmen; (3) the capital committed to manufacturing was surplus money—savings and profits from other businesses—borrowed by impecunious entrepreneurs directly from individuals rather than (for the most part) from banks; (4) when the manufacturing firm was owned by more than one person, the parties were always in partnership (none of the firms was incorporated) and were usually kinsmen.

Let us look at the pattern more closely, reviewing the evidence for the nine owner/manufacturer pairs from the six mill sites (two from Knowlton, one from Rockdale, two from Penn's Grove, one from Parkmount, two from Lenni, and one from West Branch). At two of the mill seats, the mill owner and the manufacturer were the same person or persons: John D. Carter during his time at Knowlton, and after him Thomas Clyde and Edward Darlington; and John P. Crozer at West Branch. In the other six cases, the mill owner and the manufacturer were different people. (In one case, that of Peter Hill and William Martin, the parties were related by marriage, Peter Hill being the brother of Martin's stepfather.) The roles of owner and manufacturer were clearly distinct. The owner leased to the manufacturer a tract of about ten or fifteen acres, containing a mill and associated buildings for auxiliary purposes, such as machine shop, drying house, tenement houses for workers, and a mansion for the manufacturer himself. Along with the land and buildings, the owner agreed to provide power for the mill, which meant that he was responsible for the expense of maintaining a dam, head- and tailraces, gates, sluices, a water wheel and wheelpit, and shafting and gearing. The manufacturer owned the textile machinery, which he connected to the shafting in the mill, and he was responsible for buying raw cotton and selling the yarn and woven cloth; sometimes he maintained an office in Philadelphia to manage these exchange activities. The value of new machinery for a small mill like Lenni would be on the order of $10,000; when used, it might bring a third of that. The value of the mill seat and its improvements would be roughly equal to the value of the machinery, and would rent for about $100 per month.

The importance of his kindred to the manufacturer in providing the capital to acquire machinery and the mill property cannot be overemphasized. With the exception of John D. Carter, James Houghton, and John Garsed, whose financial connections are not known, every single owner and manufacturer was able to turn to nearby kinsmen for aid in assembling capital, and in every case there is evidence that he did so. At Knowlton, we have seen that in the partnership of Edward Darlington and Thomas Clyde, Darlington was the nephew. At Rockdale, the manufacturing partners Phillips and Lewis were brothers-in-law; and the owner, Henry Moore, had bought the property from *his* brother-in-law George Odiorne of Massachusetts, who was in turn related by marriage to the Willcox family of Ivy Mills, above Lenni.[1] At Penn's Grove, the owners were brothers, George and Peter Hill. At Parkmount, the owners were the Hill-and-Sellers trust, and the manufacturers were the Riddle brothers. At Lenni, the first owner-manufacturer, William Martin, had gone into business with his brother-in-law. The next owner was, again, the Hill-and-Sellers trust, and the next manufacturer was Daniel Lammot, who was backed financially by his daughter's father-in-law, E. I. du Pont. On the West Branch, owner-manufacturer

John P. Crozer had gone into business with a loan from his brother-in-law, John Lewis.

Local banks and insurance companies became important in a few years in providing capital and security against loss; but at the beginning they seem to have played little part except possibly in the case of Crozer, who became a director of the Bank of Delaware County in 1825. The Bank of Delaware County was undersubscribed, held about as much specie as it would take to build one mill, and mostly invested its funds in farms and taverns.[2] The Philadelphia banks and other lending institutions were more useful. The Riddles, and no doubt others, wrote checks on the Girard and other banks for small amounts such as workmen's wages and grocery store accounts, but the banks apparently rarely lent money to finance the ventures of the Chester Creek mill owners and manufacturers. The $10,000 or so needed to build a small mill and its associated structures, or to buy the machinery, were assembled as a patchwork of personal savings, profits from other businesses, and loans, in amounts from a couple of thousand to nine or ten thousand, secured on the property or by the endorsement of still other relatives.

There were no corporations after the model of the great, heavily financed enterprises at Waltham and Lowell in Massachusetts. These northern organizations were able to amass a starting capital of hundreds of thousands of dollars, to buy up miles of stream bank, to construct whole towns, and to engineer large systems of raceways years before the mill sites were ever leased to manufacturers. The only suggestion of such an enterprise was an ill-fated scheme of Daniel Lammot's to form a company to buy a tract on both sides of the Brandywine and to use that river's whole water power for manufacturing cotton. The gentlemen whom Lammot tried to interest in that matter included his father-in-law Paul Beck, Jr., one of the wealthiest men of Philadelphia, and his son Harvey; Guy Bryan, another wealthy merchant (as Lammot advised Du Pont, he "has *lots of money*") and president of the first fire insurance company in Philadelphia, and his son William; Joshua Lippincott (who consulted with *his* father-in-law); and a Commodore Stewart. Lammot wanted to put together a capital of $150,000 or more, buy Du Pont's vacant cotton mill (the one recently abandoned by Carter), and also the vacant mill seat across the Brandywine, and create a "large establishment." He would be the manufacturer and would hire as technical manager either young Joseph Bancroft, the cotton spinner newly arrived from England, or a protégé of Paul Beck's from New Orleans. The firm would have as many as 10,000 spindles; by contrast, Martin's single mill at Lenni at that date had only 1,584 spindles. The investors would realize 6 percent on their investments; and, according to his own hopeful calculations, Lammot would gain, even if only five thousand spindles were operating, a solid $40,000 per year after all expenses.

The plan fell through. Du Pont wanted $37,000 for his own mill, with the company to buy the seat across the Brandywine at the forthcoming sheriff's sale. But Lippincott, the central figure in the negotiations, insisted that Du Pont buy the vacant mill seat first and give it to the company along with the existing mill for the same price. When Du Pont refused this suggestion, Lippincott countered with an offer of $25,000 and the company to buy the other property. When Du Pont refused this offer too, denying that he had ever suggested such a ridiculous price, Lippincott withdrew in a huff.

Lammot next urged a corporation. A Mr. Andrews was interested in purchasing the Du Pont cotton mill and visited the Brandywine to discuss the matter. Lammot, rather casually, warned his friend:

> As to Mr. A, I presume he is fickle, and would not be a pleasant partner except under an act of Incorporation. *Entre nous,* it is said that he is an excellent judge of Cognac, and preserves his skill by constant practice. This however would not be important to a concern of 5 or more Directors; for if he but contribute his money, there will be no difficulty in employing it.[3]

Nothing came of this idea either.

In effect, it would appear that the Philadelphia area was not the place to form a corporation or even a large investment company to finance cotton manufacturing on a scale comparable to Lowell. Wealthy merchants like Beck and Bryan were not interested in putting up large sums of money on their own behalf; they were seeking safe places to invest such monies on behalf of their children, sons-in-law, and other protégés. Cotton manufacturing was only one of a number of investment possibilities for idle capital, and most of the other alternatives were probably looked upon as safer unless the associated real estate could be bought at a bargain price.[4]

Thus the mills along Chester Creek remained small, at first only amounting to one or two thousand spindles. According to Lammot's calculations, even a small one thousand-spindle mill, spinning No. 16 yarn, should make a net profit for the manufacturer of between $8,000 and $9,000 per year —a very respectable income for the period. But paper profits are only paper profits. Even Lammot, as he said (partly in humor) to Du Pont, would have been willing to give up the possibility of $40,000 per year from cotton spinning for a guarantee of $5,000 as agent. For there were many risks in the cotton manufacture: a financial panic, like the one in 1829, which set loose a chain reaction of protested notes, lawsuits, assignments, sheriff's sales, and even condemnations to debtor's prison; the inexperience of the new manufacturers, who might have trouble at first in getting and maintaining decent machinery and in hiring and retaining competent and reliable workers; and fire and flood, which could destroy only partially insured machinery, buildings, and hydraulic systems. Of the nine manufacturers, three had been involved in business failures before they came to Chester Creek, two of them (Carter and Lammot) in cotton manufacturing; and two failed within a few years of their arrival (Carter again, and Martin).

It is difficult to escape the conclusion that the pattern of low capital investment, much of it derived from private loans, including notes of indebtedness even to his cotton suppliers, made the cotton manufacturer extremely vulnerable in the early years of his venture. His loans and other financial obligations might be suddenly called in; his own creditors might suddenly be unable to pay him; the price of cotton might go up, or that of yarn and cloth down. Without much in the way of assets beyond his machinery and the notes of merchants to whom he sold or consigned cloth, he could not ride out even a brief period of business reversal. Even an experienced cotton spinner like Carter might go under, while a technically inexperienced novice like Crozer survived, because the saving factor in a financial panic was not technical expertise but a sound credit rating and loyal kinsmen.

Yet the system, in a sense, had a virtue. It selected for economic survival those manufacturers rigorously honest in business practice, sufficiently patient to start small and grow slowly, intellectually capable of recognizing (or even of inventing) useful innovations, and pragmatic enough in human relationships to be able to assemble and keep together a network of kinsmen, business associates, operatives, and representatives in the political community.

Chapter IV

THE MACHINES, THEIR OPERATIVES, AND THE FABRICS

In the spring of the auspicious year 1826 a number of manufacturers and other interested citizens met at the courthouse in Chester. Their purpose was to organize a survey of the mill seats in Delaware County. George G. Leiper, Crozer's friend, who owned the mills and quarries on Crum and Ridley creeks; William Martin, the cotton manufacturer from Lenni; and John Willcox, papermaker from Ivy Mills, were elected the survey committee. Young Willcox (he was only thirty-seven) died shortly afterward and at a second public meeting in August John P. Crozer was elected to fill his place.

The committee report was presented to the public at the second public meeting in August and was thereafter printed as a pamphlet in five hundred copies.[1] In its twenty-seven pages it described in detail the state of manufactures in the county, giving information on the water supply at each mill seat, the size and construction of buildings, the machinery in use, the number of workmen, and the productivity of the enterprise. It proceeded, from east to west, stream by stream, to list all gristmills, sawmills, oil mills (for the making of linseed oil), paper mills, iron forges, cotton and woolen "manufactories," and unimproved sites available for development. By its account, there were in the county fifty-three sawmills, thirty-eight flour mills, eleven paper mills, two powder mills, five rolling and slitting mills, fourteen woolen factories and thirteen cotton factories, and a sprinkling of other enterprises. All in all, the committee found two hundred mills and mill seats, forty-two of them as yet unimproved.

According to the survey, the five Chester Creek cotton manufacturers evidently had installed conventional equipment and were following traditional methods of operation. Their machines had been invented, in their fundamentals, in England a generation or more before. In the organization of these machines, these early manufacturers followed the principle that in the previous century the English cotton industry had followed. This principle was the physical separation of the two parts of the cotton-manufacturing process. All the machinery necessary to the *spinning* of cotton, from bale to yarn, was assembled in one manufactory. The *weaving,* whether by hand or power looms, and the finishing operations were conducted under different roofs by different entrepreneurs. Such division of the total process into two parts made it possible for an individual manufacturer to commence work with less capital and in a smaller building than if (as in the more modern fashion of Lowell) all the processes from bale to finished cloth were conducted by one manufacturer. This smallness of scale was almost a necessity, also, in a situation where the owners of mill seats were making available a dam, race, water wheel, and building which had been constructed originally for other and more limited purposes, such as papermaking or grinding grain.

THE MILLS AND MILL SEATS

Five of the mills were located on mill seats long in use. Knowlton had been a copper-rolling mill.[1] Rockdale had been developed early in the eighteenth century by the Pennell family as an iron forge—Old Sable Forge—and was still the site of a gristmill, a rolling and slitting mill, and a nail factory when Henry Moore built a cotton mill for his new tenants in 1825.[2] Penn's Grove had been the site of a grist- and sawmill and a fulling mill (to serve local hand-loom weavers of woolens) since the late eighteenth century at least, and probably (to judge from the presence of very old ruins of dams and races) from even early in that century too. Lenni had been the site of the Lungren paper factory. And West Branch had been the site of Mattson's paper factory.[3]

The Water Power:
Dams, Races, and Water Wheels

The effective machinery of the water system was a wooden wheel. These water wheels which, in their slow and ponderous revolutions, turned the gears that communicated power to the machinery in the mill, were themselves driven by the weight of water delivered to them by a more or less elaborate hydraulic system. Some were "overshot" wheels: that is to say, the water was brought over the top of the wheel in a wooden sluice, to pour down the front into wooden buckets built into the outer rim of the wheel;

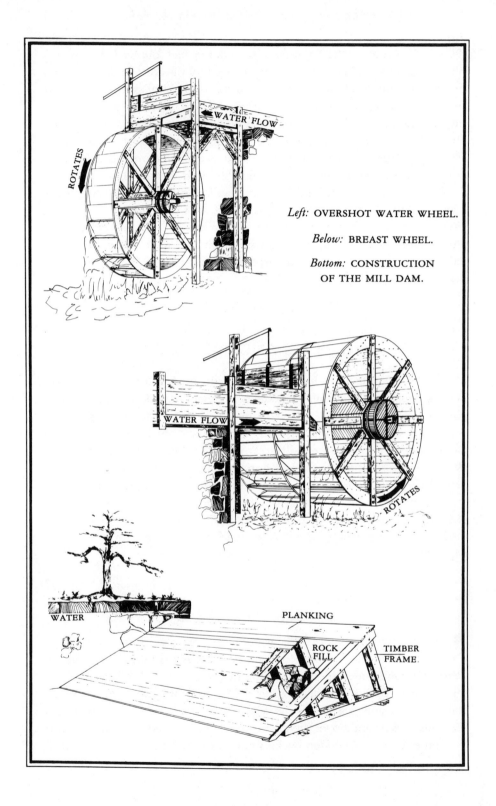

Left: OVERSHOT WATER WHEEL.

Below: BREAST WHEEL.

Bottom: CONSTRUCTION
OF THE MILL DAM.

WATER FLOW

ROTATES

WATER FLOW

ROTATES

WATER

PLANKING

ROCK
FILL

TIMBER
FRAME

others were "breast" wheels, revolving in the opposite direction, moved by water delivered to the back of the wheel at about middle height. It was the weight of the water that turned the wheel, not its impact. At the bottom, the water fell out of the buckets into the wheelpit and thence flowed out into the tailrace and so back into the stream. The wheels typically were 10 to 15 feet in diameter and 3 to 4 feet in width, and were left exposed or shielded only by flimsy sheds.

In order to drive a wheel, it was necessary to secure a vertical head of water of 10 to 15 feet, somewhere between an upstream point where the headrace cut in from the creek, and the downstream point where the tailrace returned the "used" water to the stream. The maximum theoretical horsepower derivable from the system was a function of the head and the quantity of water delivered per unit of time. An adequate head could be secured at, or beside, a waterfall, and in fact such opportunities were exploited where they occurred (as they did at Waltham, Massachusetts, for instance, or at the falls of the Passaic at Patterson, New Jersey). But along Chester Creek, and in most other situations in the Delaware Valley, the necessary head could best be obtained by digging a canal along the bank parallel to the stream, descending at a shallower angle than the stream itself. After a few hundred yards, the surface of the water in the race would be a number of feet above the surface of the water in the stream. When that vertical difference—the head—was sufficiently large to accommodate a water wheel, the wheelpit could be constructed and a mill located. The five mills cited in the 1826 survey had the following "head and fall": Knowlton, 16 feet; Rockdale, 16 feet; Penn's Grove, 21 feet; Lenni, 16 feet; and West Branch, 13 feet.[4]

The head ideally approximated (but obviously could not be greater than) the actual fall in the stream between intake of the headrace and exit of the tailrace. In order to shorten the race, and thus to reduce both the labor needed for its construction and the amount of land required for a mill seat, the universal practice was to dam the stream. The dam ensured a more constant level of water in the race because, except in flood or drought, the water would always run off at the height of the crest of the dam. Also, by the extent to which the dam raised the water level, it increased the head and provided an important reserve supply of water. Most of the dams were relatively shallow, rising no more than 4 or 5 feet above the streambed; often (as at Penn's Grove) the effective height was increased by setting heavy wooden planks into deep slots running across the crest of the dam. These shallow dams, at West Branch and Penn's Grove and perhaps at other sites, appear to have been constructed simply by piling up stones and boulders in the streambed, used wood for facing instead of concrete, and, presumably, could be built without the trouble of diverting the water into other channels. They were butted against large rocks or steep banks where a flood was least likely to carve out a new course around the dam. In cross section they generally had a relatively steep downstream side and a gently sloping upstream one. In some sites the downstream side of the dam was vertical, and constructed of cut and carefully fitted stone, sometimes with the breast coated with a smoothly rounded cement shield. The dams at Lenni and Rockdale were of this kind, and were higher, too, than any of the others. No record remains of the dam at Knowlton.

When new, the race was about 10 or 12 feet wide and nearly as deep (but silting might reduce the depth to 3 or 4 feet), with movable gates at the dam and at the pit to control the level and quantity of water being delivered to the wheel. Sometimes, if the terrain crowded the race onto a steep hillside, it would have to be constructed in part of masonry. Close to the wheelpit, wooden or metal booms and a wooden trash rack were set in the race before the final water gate, to prevent floating debris from getting into the pit to foul the wheel and clog the tailrace. The headrace might be as short as 50 yards (as at West Branch) or as long as a quarter of a mile (as at Penn's Grove).[5]

The construction of the water system, of course, required an initial outlay of considerable money, to pay a millwright to design and construct a water wheel and the auxiliary equipment in the pit, race, and dam; to pay a master mason to design and supervise the building of the race and dam;

LENNI MILL.

KNOWLTON MILL CIRCA 1920.

and to hire pick-and-shovel laborers to dig the race, quarry or find the stone, and raise the dam. Once constructed, the system could last almost indefinitely, provided breaks in the dam and race were repaired promptly, silt was removed periodically, and rotten or worn parts of the wheel and its setting were repaired. Such tasks were generally performed by local millwrights, masons, and laborers hired by the day as occasion demanded, with some help from the hired hands of the landowner, who was apt to be running a farm on the land around the mill, and from operatives, who were unemployed whenever the water wheel stopped. In any case, the water system was the financial responsibility of the landowner rather than of the manufacturer, although a manufacturer or mill manager might write the specifications, make arrangements for repair, and supervise the work.[6]

The Buildings

The arts of building dams, races, and water wheels were old and well established; but they were not standardized, nor could they be. Each water system, from dam to wheel, was a unique product, tailored to fit as well as possible the special requirements of the user and the particular potentialities and limitations of the site. Each had a special quality of its own, special problems, special possibilities for improvement.

But the early buildings were relatively standardized. They were rectangular, on an average about 40 feet wide and 55 feet long, two to four stories high, and were constructed of fieldstone laid in mortar and covered inside and out with whitewashed stucco. (The actual dimensions of the "typical" mills were: Rockdale, 41 by 61 feet, four stories; Penn's Grove, 45 by 50, two stories; Lenni, 35 by 55, three stories; and West Branch, 45 by 60, three stories. Knowlton was larger, 40 by 90.)[7] Along all walls on each floor except the top were rows of large, glass-covered windows, 5 or 6 feet high, and (because of the nature of the construction) set in softly rounded embrasures. The floor beams were massive, spanning the width of the building, set into the walls, and each supported on two posts; the floors were 3-inch-thick oak planks. The clearance from floor to beams was anywhere from 10 to 14 feet. The pitched roof was lined by a clerestory, which provided fairly even lighting to the top floor—the only room in the mill that did not require the dual lines of posts down its length. At night the rooms were lighted by oil lamps. In the original design of the buildings (except perhaps for the new building constructed for Phillips and later in the Riddles' new mill) there was no provision for heating; but Martin, and probably the other manufacturers, provided a stove for each floor.

At one end of the building was a square stairwell; all movement of personnel and small supplies had to be up and down these steps. At a place along the edge of the building where it stood next to the road a block and tackle hung from a beam near the roof, for hoisting heavy gear and bulk supplies, like bales of cotton, from carts below. Surmounting the whole, in the center of the roof, stood a cupola containing the bell that called the workers to the mill and signaled the hours of work, and also sounded the alarm in case of fire.

Well-run mills were surrounded by wooden panel fences, which enclosed the mill yard with its main mill, the mill office building, and various auxiliary frame buildings, sluices, and gates, and protected the mill from the depredations of livestock, little boys, and importunate visitors.

A system of roads and bridges was also needed for horse-drawn wagons to haul in the bales of cotton to the mill and take finished products away. The creek was too small for navigation, even if it had not been interrupted by dams, and the local Chester Creek railroad would not arrive for another thirty years. The roads were not paved, so far as we know, and they crowded in close by the mills—or the mills were built close by them—in order to facilitate the loading and unloading process. Where the mills remain today, it is evident that they were originally located at the very edge of the highway.

The Power Train:
Gears, Shafts, Pulleys, and Belts

Power was delivered into the mill by shafting geared to the water wheel. The wheel initially drove a horizontal shaft which, intersecting inside the mill with a bevel gear, transmitted its power to an upright shaft that rose the height of the building; from this, line shafts extended along under the ceiling on each floor. At this date much of the shafting was still being made of wood. From the line shafts, leather belts running on wooden pulleys transmitted power down to the machines below.[8]

There were innumerable mechanical arrangements by which this could be accomplished, but all of them required lubrication. The gudgeoned (provided with an iron-tipped bearing) wooden axle of the water wheel could be geared to the upright shaft; but the wheel could also drive, by gears, a horizontal shaft intersecting the wheel along its circumference. The upright shaft itself was apt to be made of iron; its lower tip rested in a seat lubricated by oil. The line shafting running off the gearing on the upright shaft extended along the length of the rooms, high up under the ceilings, and had to be supported in lubricated boxes or journals. The proper lubrication of all gearing and bearings was essential, not only in order to preserve as much of the power of the water wheel as possible for running the machinery, but also to protect the moving parts from wear, breakage, and overheating, which might lead to fire. Petroleum-based lubricants had not yet been invented; the lubricants available had to be compounded from animal fats and vegetable oils (such as the tallow and tar used on metal gears).

Another requirement for the power train was the coupling of sections of shafts. This had to be done by placing square-flanged collars around the ends of the shafts to be coupled, keyed to prevent slippage, and screwed or bolted together so that the axes of rotation of the two parts were in the same line. Usually the shafting, whether wooden or the increasingly common metallic, was square or octagonal in cross section. In the case of wooden shafting, there must have been a considerable degree of flexibility in the whole assembly. Nonetheless, shafting in the mills was regularly constructed to run horizontally as much as 100 feet from the upright shaft.

Leather belts were used to transmit power from the primary line shaft under the ceiling to parallel line shafts above the rows of machines, and thence to the machines on the floor below. These belts were manufactured on special order from local tanneries, particularly the Duttons' a few hundred yards away. Each belt would be 20 to 30 feet long and had to be

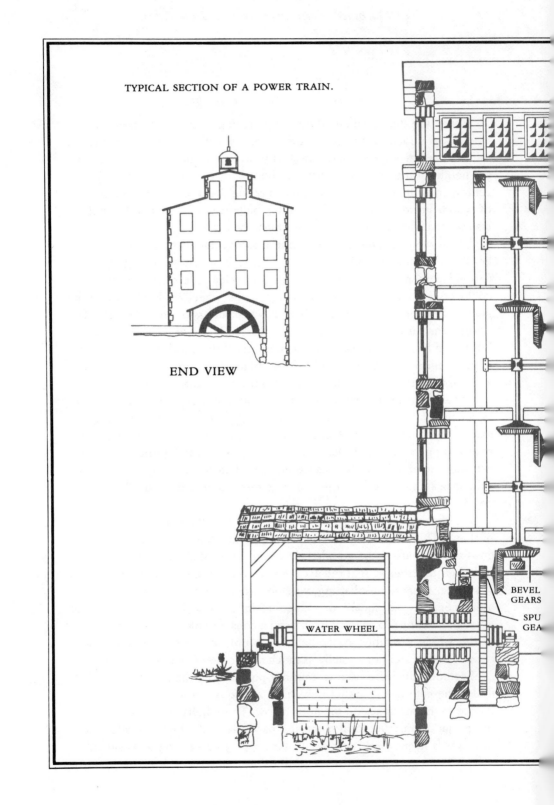

TYPICAL SECTION OF A POWER TRAIN.

END VIEW

WATER WHEEL

BEVEL GEARS

SPU GEA

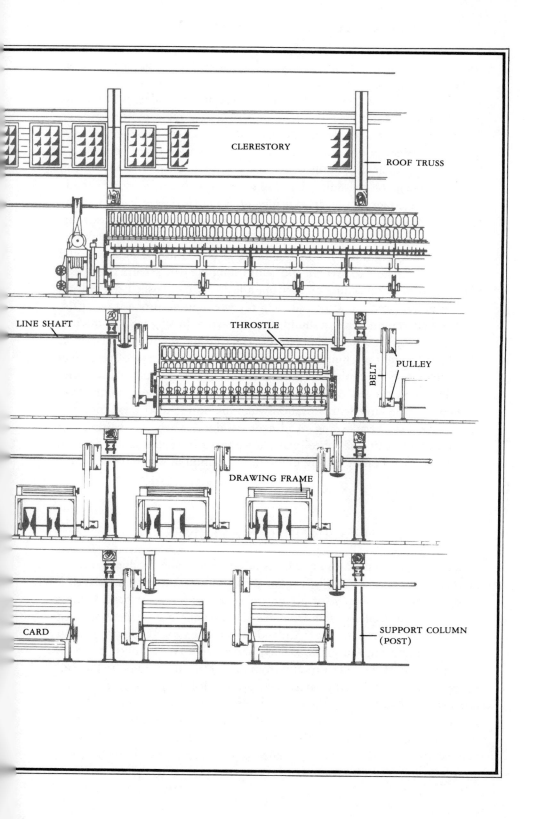

CLERESTORY

ROOF TRUSS

LINE SHAFT

THROSTLE

BELT

PULLEY

DRAWING FRAME

CARD

SUPPORT COLUMN
(POST)

constructed from 5-foot-long sections of cowhide; depending on the horse-power applied, they were from 2 inches to 2 feet in width. The sections were stitched, hooked, clamped, or glued together and the ends eventually joined so as to form an endless loop. Stretched over a pulley or drum fastened to the line shaft above, the belt ran down around a pulley fastened to the drive shaft of the machine. The effect of gearing could be achieved by varying the diameters of the connected pulleys. Once in motion, the belt resisted slippage off the pulley because to slip it would have to tilt slightly and the tilting met resistance. An ingenious clutch device known as the fast-and-loose pulley system permitted the operative to turn his own machines individually on and off. The machine drive shaft was fitted with two pulleys, closely set side by side, one of them bolted fast to the shaft, and the other loose, able to revolve without turning the drive shaft. The operative turned off his machine by shoving a lever, which pushed the belt off the fast pulley onto the loose pulley; a reverse motion turned it on again.

The mill in motion was a shuddering, creaking, hissing mass of shafting turned by the great water wheel outside. Gearing and the varying diameters of pulleys brought machine speeds up to velocities hundreds of times that of the six to twelve revolutions per minute of the wheel. Belts whirred and hummed; gears clicked; cams and cranks clanked. The whole mill must have seemed to come alive with vibration when the power train was connected at the wheel in the morning. And even at night, when the shafting and machines were still, the wheel was allowed to run at idle lest it become uneven in its motion by resting in the same position in water every night.[9]

THE SPINNING MACHINERY

The spinning mills consumed bales of raw cotton and produced, for the most part, boxes of cotton yarn—spun, dyed, and wound on "shuttle cops," or wound in warps ready for placement in power looms or hand looms.

The cotton itself all came from the slave plantations of the American south; for the most part it was Upland cotton from the piedmont plateau of Georgia and the Carolinas, a fairly short-staple cotton, eked out with small amounts of the finer product from New Orleans. It came to the mill wrapped and tied in large burlap-covered bales weighing 300 to 350 pounds. The bales were picked up at the wharf in Philadelphia or Marcus Hook by large wagons owned or hired by the manufacturer; a wagonload of cotton was ten to fifteen bales. No two bales weighed exactly the same because the cotton, after being cleaned of its seeds by the cotton gin, was

TABLE 5. Productivity of the Mills in the Rockdale District (1826–1850)

	Number of Hands	Mule Spindles	Throstle Spindles	Yarn Counts	Power Looms	Raw Cotton Consumption per Week	Cloth Production per Year in Yards
WEST BRANCH							
1826	30	648	588	15–20	none	1,100 lbs.	
1832	52	3,000 (both)		15–33	none	2,500 lbs.	
1850*	179	7,032 (both)		not given	200	not given	1,425,000
LENNI							
1826	45	936	648	18–25	none	1,200 lbs.	
1850	113	1,956	2,044	not given	not given	not given	1,000,000
PARKMOUNT							
1832	50	c. 2,500	none	8–20	none	3,400 lbs.	
1850	23	4	none	none	18	none	102,000 (diaper cloth only)
PENN'S GROVE							
1826	32	570	492	6–24	160	1,140 lbs.	
1850	114	4,980 (both)		not given	not given	not given	1,460,000
KNOWLTON							
1826	46	616	808	20	none	1,278 lbs.	
1850	46	1,548 (both)		not given	60	not given	470,000
ROCKDALE	Data too fragmentary to warrant inclusion.						

*1850 data combines West Branch and Crozerville. The 1826 data are from Leiper and Martin, 1826, p. 1821. The 1832 data (West Branch and Parkmount only) are from McLane, 1833, pp. 210–12 and 224–6, and (for Parkmount only) DCHS, Parkmount Pay Book. The 1850 data are from the NA, 1850 Census of Manufactures.

squeezed in large presses into a standard size and shape; the quality of the cotton, the design, condition, and operation of the press, and the level of humidity would cause each bale's weight to be slightly different. Each bale had to be separately weighed and numbered as soon as it was received at the mill in order to verify the weight claimed by the merchant in Philadelphia from whom it had been bought.

A series of specific operations had now to be performed on the raw cotton; each had its own location, its own machine, and its own operatives. After the bales were opened, the cotton was blended to produce a uniform staple length and was run through the picker room; then it was transferred to the carding engine; then to several preparatory spinning devices, including the double speeder, the drawing frame, the roving frame, and the stretcher; then either to the mule or to the throstle for the final spinning of usable yarn; then, for some of the yarn, to the dyehouse; and finally to the warping machine or to the machine for spooling yarn on bobbins or cops specially prepared for insertion into shuttles.[1] The number of machines of various types and the number of operatives in the Chester Creek spinning mills in the period 1826–32 and again in 1850 are summarized in Table 3.

The Picker House

In some of the mills, as a protection against fire, a separate shed attached to the main mill was used for the dust-producing initial preparation of the cotton; in others, a special room protected by iron doors and fire-resistant walls and ceiling was set aside on the ground floor. Here the bales were deposited from the wagon onto the scale, weighed, and then opened; released from the intense pressure of the packing, the loose cotton spilled out in an expanding mass of tufts and clumps. The packing rope and burlap were laid aside for sale to the nearby paper mills. The cotton from several bales (if the operation was properly done) was mixed in a large bin to form a synthetic bale or "bing." This was done in order to homogenize the raw material. Cuts from the bing were then fed into the picker (or other machines for cleaning cotton such as the willow), which clawed apart the lumps, agitated the fleece, and, by circulating air through the mass, cleaned out a large quantity of debris. Dirt, sand, grit, bits of leaves, twine, insects, seeds that had been missed by the gin, all dropped through a perforated cylinder to the bottom of the machine while the fleece moved on in the teeth of meshing gears. This machine also produced a quantity of flying dust —a highly flammable mixture of fragments of cotton and impurities—which filled the air in the picker room with itching particles. Hence work in the picker room was sometimes compared to labor in Satan's domain. After the picker, the fleece was run through the blower, which produced a long smooth sheet or "lap" of clean white cotton fleece, 2 or 3 feet wide and 1 inch thick, which could be wound on wooden drums or placed on an endless belt, for delivery to the carding engine.

The two or three male operatives who worked in the picker room, opening bales, mixing the bings, and feeding and regulating the picker, were generally young, strong, and relatively unskilled, and were paid about 40 or 50 cents per day.[2] A frequent visitor at the picker room—and perhaps this was a discouragement to those working there—was the mill manager, or a clerk representing him, who supervised and recorded the weighing of the bales of raw cotton.

The Card Room

It was universally agreed, at least by the English authorities, that the crucial stage in the preparation of cotton for spinning was the process of carding. The cotton as it left the picker room was in the form of sheets of clean batting. In this state, the individual fibers lay higgledy-piggledy in a twisted and loosely tangled mass; it was the task of the carding engine to sort them out so as to lie more or less parallel to one another. The task had to be done without breaking the fibers and had to produce a uniform, regular product; and this requirement laid upon the carding room a heavy responsibility, for cotton fibers were delicate. The finest American cotton, Sea Island cotton, had a long average fiber-length or staple, from 1 1/2 inches to 1 5/8 inches, and a very fine diameter, down to 1/2,500 of an inch; coarser cottons, of the kind used in the Chester Creek mills, were shorter by half an inch or so and could be as coarse as 1/250.

A carding engine was essentially a set of rotating, wire-toothed cylinders waist to chest high and 2 to 3 feet wide. The main cylinder seized the cotton lap, pulled it over or under other cylinders stationary or rotating at a slower pace, and delivered it to a drawing head, which transformed the thin sheet of carded cotton continuously emerging from the rollers into a loosely cohering rope or sliver (pronounced "sly-ver"). The sliver dropped in a spiral into a large tin can about 3 feet high and 18 inches in diameter.

Generally the carding machines worked in pairs, the first one to receive the lap being called the breaker card; it delivered only a carded lap to the second, or finisher, card, which produced the sliver. Each carding engine had to be of the right size and specifically adjusted to produce a sliver suitable for spinning a certain type of yarn. Usually the five or six workers in the card room, both male and female, were paid by the day; and the supervisor of the card room could earn substantial wages, on the order of

$40 to $50 per month. Each mill contained about ten cards; Martin's mill had eleven carding engines worth, by his estimate, $3,200 (nearly a third of the value of all his machinery).

The Frames for Preparing the Roving

The cotton as it issued from the carding engine looked like an endless, loosely twisted rope about as thick as one's thumb. In this form it was not ready for spinning into yarn, and it was therefore passed in sections through one or more machines that stretched and twisted it into a roving ready for one of the spinning machines. The first of these intermediate processes was "doubling," which meant the combining of slivers from two or more cans into one filament, while it was lightly twisted and considerably stretched. This operation was performed on machines called double speeders and could be repeated again and again. Doubling might commence with (as in the Riddles' mill) running twelve ends into one in the first frame, twelve into one in the second frame, and three into one in the third, yielding a doubling by a factor of 432. It then moved to a drawing frame, where the doubled and redoubled sliver was further twisted and attenuated; and thence to a roving frame, which produced a filament called a roving, wound on bobbins ready for the spinning process. For particularly careful spinners, a fourth type of machine, the stretcher, took the roving and further twisted and drew it, in a final preparation for the mule.

Essentially, all these machines were variations on a basic model, the "water frame," by which a coarse filament was made longer, stronger, and more tightly twisted. The speeders took slivers from a larger number of cans and deposited their product into a smaller number of cans; the others moved from can to can, always drawing the filament out and giving it more twist. (The number of cans required to supply the carding room and preparatory frames in a typical mill like Martin's was about two hundred.) The drawing was accomplished by passing the filament from one pair of rollers to another revolving at a higher rate of speed. From the rollers of the roving frame the sliver went down to a bobbin, on which it was wound by a flyer (whose revolutions around the bobbin imparted the necessary twist).

These preparatory doublings, drawings, and twistings took place on machines which long experience had rendered highly reliable and almost completely automatic. The room in which they functioned was serviced largely by half a dozen or so semi-skilled boys, girls, and young women. The workers carried the cans filled with slivers from the carding engines to the first of the speeders and transferred cans thereafter from machine to machine. They removed filled roving bobbins; fastened on the slivers to start a new run; pieced broken slivers; and tried to keep the floors and machinery reasonably clean. They did not regulate the speed of the machines, the pressure of the rollers and their relative speed, or do other technical manipulations; these settings were the responsibility of the overseer, probably the overseer of the carding room. They received on the order of $7 for a "month" of twenty-four days.

The Throstle

The spinning process produced "yarn"—the strong, uniform, twisted filament of hundreds of microscopically fine fibers that was the main consumer product of the mill. There were two kinds of machine used for the final spinning of cotton: the throstle and the mule. The two machines operated on different principles to accomplish the three motions of drawing (i.e., stretching), twisting, and winding onto bobbin or spindle, which are necessary in any spinning procedure. The throstle performed continuous spinning; the mule, intermittent spinning. The throstle was used largely for the manufacture of warp threads for power looms, because it made a hard, strong, coarse yarn very cheaply. The mule was the machine of choice for weft, or filling, of power looms and for all fine cotton yarn (although some of the mills used the advanced Danforth throstle, which made a relatively soft yarn).[3]

In practice, continuous spinning meant that the operations of drawing, twisting, and winding were conducted successively on a continuously moving length of roving. The roving was supplied on a large bobbin mounted

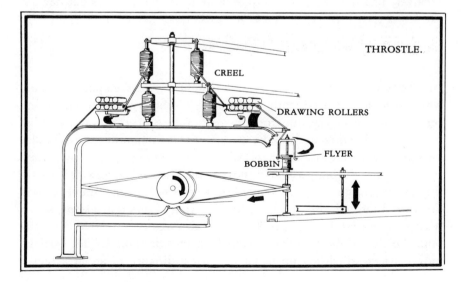

on the head of the throstle. It was drawn down through two pairs of metal rollers revolving under power. The first pair of rollers simply pulled the roving off the bobbin at a certain speed. The second pair of rollers pulled the roving out of the first pair; and because it turned at a faster speed, it pulled and stretched the roving as it passed between the two pairs. From the roller head, the thinner, attenuated roving passed down to the eye of a flyer mounted on a spindle which rotated continuously, again under power from the train, around a fixed bobbin. In order to distribute the yarn evenly on the bobbin, the flyer was made to rise and fall regularly.

A throstle was then simply a long wooden frame in which were mounted a series of such spinning units, all operating off shafts powered from the line shafting. A single throstle, like the ones in Martin's mill at Lenni, would contain about a hundred spindles and be about 50 feet long; but there was really no limit to the number of spindles which could comprise a throstle beyond the mechanical convenience of space and power supply, for each spinning unit, from supply bobbin to take-up bobbin, was a self-contained spinning entity that operated independently of the rest.

The task of the throstle operative was simple. She (for most throstle operatives were female) had simply to watch one or two throstles, stopping the machine occasionally to repair broken roving, doff the spindles of their filled bobbins, and replace the supply bobbins. This required some walking back and forth, and up and down stairs, with arms full of bobbins, some piecing of ends, and some wiping of oily parts and sweeping of cotton dust from around the machine. But basically the machine ran itself. Operatives in the throstle room therefore did not receive much more pay than the relatively unskilled labor of the picker room, about 40 cents per day.

The Mule

The supreme machine of the spinning industry was the mule. The mule was said to spin intermittently because the machinery had to be stopped regularly in order to change from one part of the process to another. What made the mule different from the throstle was the mounting of its spindles on a moving carriage which, in the 1830's, still had to be physically pushed by the spinner during parts of its movement. The roving, unwinding as in the throstle from a bobbin mounted on a creel in the main frame, passed downward through rollers which, by revolving at different speeds, somewhat attenuated it. From the rollers, the drawn roving was fed horizontally onto the tips of the spindles mounted on the carriage. As this carriage moved backward slowly on metal rails for a distance of about 4 feet 6

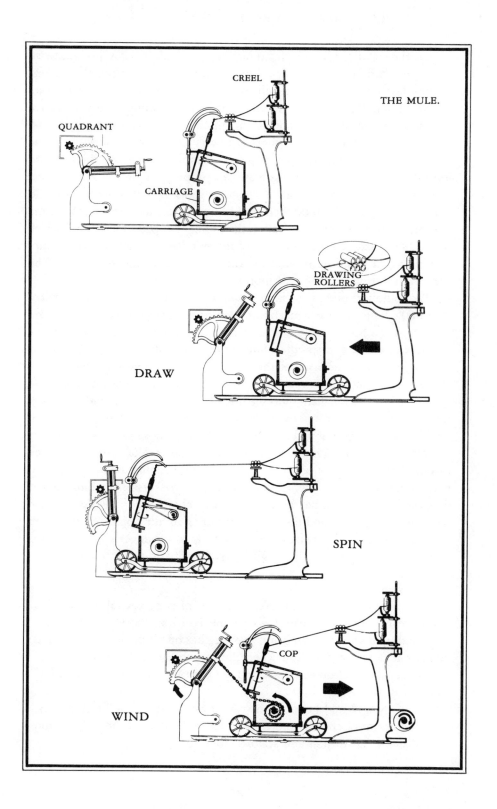

inches, the spindles rotated a fixed number of revolutions, imparting twist, while simultaneously the moving of the carriage away from the rollers, slightly faster than the rollers delivered roving, drew it out an inch or so. It was the simultaneity of the motions of drawing and twisting which gave the mule its distinctive advantage in spinning the finer yarns, for cotton roving is so constituted that if there is an unevenness in the strength of the roving, the twist will first go to the weakest (in effect the thickest and loosest) part. The mule thus made use of a property of the cotton to correct automatically any developing flaws or weak spots. A skilled operative could make finer yarns on a mule than could be made on the throstle. After the twisting terminated (automatically), the spinner tripped a faller wire, which pressed the yarn down to the base of the spindle, and started the spindles moving again while he pushed the carriage back toward the frame. The spun yarn during this forward motion was wound onto the spindle.

The mule was one of the largest and most complex mechanical devices ever made by man; larger machines, like locomotives and stationary steam engines, were power generators. The maximum size of the mules of this period was about 280 spindles. Such mules were about 60 feet long, and the size limitation was based on the physical strength required of the spinner to push, and control, the massive carriage on its inward course. The mule spinner—invariably a man—was the highest paid operative in the mill. Each spinner was assisted in operating his mule by a small team of two or even three lower paid boy or girl operatives: a piecer, whose job it was to repair the broken threads (five or six a minute) at the end of a run, when the carriage was briefly motionless; a creel attender, keeping the mule supplied with bobbins of roving (which meant carrying baskets of bobbins up and down stairs); and the scavenger, who scurried about under the sheet of yarn between the carriage and the frame, sweeping up dirt, picking up broken ends, and picking fuzzballs off the yarn. The scavenger's situation was graphically described by the English novelist Charlotte Elizabeth:

"And what is scavenging?"

"Oh, that made me laugh. You see, bits of cotton wool will stick to the thread, and they mustn't go on the reels; so there is a little girl huddled up under the frame and she snatches off all the loose wool, and throws it down so fast! and when the machine runs back, if the little scavenger did not bob and duck, and get very low, she would have a fine knock on the head."

"Poor thing!" said Helen, "she can never stretch herself out, hardly; and she is almost choked and smothered in the dust of the light cotton bits that she has to pull and scatter about her."[4]

All of the workers in the mule room were barefoot. In advanced British mills the spinner managed a pair of mules which stood parallel, back to back, so geared that while one was running out on automatic power, the spinner was free to push in the carriage of the other. But in many American mills at this date, the spinner's own muscular effort pushed the carriage in and pulled it out, and the spinner operated only one mule.

The work of the spinner required not only strength but also great skill. He had to know how to set the draw and twist adjustments on the machine so as to produce the desired thickness of yarn; he had to be able to ease the machine delicately into position during the putting-up motion. The mule spinner was not subject to an overseer; he was his own man and in charge of others; indeed, he usually was held responsible for hiring and paying his own helpers. He was paid by the piece—by the number of hanks which he produced (a hank equaled 840 yards). A good mule spinner might produce 35,000 hanks of yarn and earn $50 per month—five times as much as even the best paid operatives in the throstle room.

Warping, Balling, Spooling, and Dyeing

The final production process in the typical spinning mill was the packaging of the yarn doffed from the mule or throstle. The throstle-spun yarn, destined to be wound on the beams of power looms, was processed in a large device called a warping mill. This bulky device was essentially composed of two parts: a creel, where dozens of bobbins of yarn were mounted, enough to supply the number of threads required for the warp of a particular kind of cloth; and a large winding apparatus. The threads were assembled, before being wound on the slats of the warping mill, in a kind of gate, where they were alternately passed above and below a cord, or a rod, called a lease. This kept the warp threads in an order that could be readily reestablished when the time came for the weaver to wind them onto the supply beam of his loom. After being assembled, leased, and wound, the warp was usually packaged for transport to the weaver.

The mule-spun yarn was prepared on the mule itself in the form of cops —carefully assembled conical spirals of yarn, wound on a specially shaped spindle and removable therefrom without loss of shape. The cop was specifically designed, in shape and size, to fit into the shuttles of the weavers to whom it would be sold, and to unwind easily with the passage of the shuttle back and forth across the loom.

In addition to the warps and shuttle cops, however, the mill might have some call for yarns wound in balls or (after about 1828) on spools for household thread or for weavers who wished to make their own warps.

Such yarns were transferred to appropriate bobbins or spools on balling and spooling machines, which simply transferred the yarn from one type of bobbin to another without changing its physical quality.

Commonly, yarn was sent out to be chlorine-bleached or dyed; but some simple vegetable dyes—black from logwood, blue from indigo, yellow from sumac—were used at the mills to dye the raw stock. Indigo dye made fast color without a mordant; but most of the other dyes required a mordant and for this purpose copperas (blue-green ferrous sulfate) was used.[5]

THE WEAVING MACHINERY

The only weaving mill was that of John S. Phillips. Into his and his partner's newly constructed building, containing four stories, and measuring 41 by 60 feet in outside dimension, he had packed a total of two hundred power looms, thus creating at one stroke the largest power-loom cotton manufactory in Delaware County and perhaps in the Philadelphia area. As late as 1832, when Secretary of the Treasury Louis McLane made his famous survey of manufactures for the Congress, the nearest listed power-loom weaver in point of size was Joseph Ripka[1] of Kensington (later of Manayunk).

The weaving process was simpler so far as factory organization was concerned. There was only one basic machine to consider: the power loom itself. Undoubtedly those used by Phillips were of the so-called Scotch loom type. These looms differed from the patented Lowell looms largely in the fact that the reed or batten, which "beat up" the filling (i.e., pressed the yarn evenly against the edge of already-woven cloth after the shuttle had passed it across the warp), was actuated by a crank rather than by a combination of cam and springs. The power loom had four motions to carry out, which essentially duplicated the actions of the hand-loom weaver. First, the warp—which stretched horizontally from the beam at the back of the machine, on which the ends of yarn were wound, to the beam at the front, on which the woven cloth was taken up—had to be advanced regularly by winding the finished cloth while the warp ends were kept taut. Second, at least two heddles had to be alternately raised and lowered from a frame arching above the warp. A heddle was composed of a row of strings or wires, each with an eye through which a warp end passed. When one heddle was raised, the other was lowered, thus forming a shed or open path within the warp through which the filling was passed; after an end passed, the heddles alternated in position, enclosing the passed yarn and forming a new shed. Third, the filling had to be carried through the shed by a shuttle, a little box about a foot long with steel points at both ends. The shuttle was not so much moved by any positive control comparable to (in the days before the flying shuttle) the weaver's arm; rather, it was thrown, hard. This action was called picking; and the speed of the loom was measured in number of picks per minute. Finally, the line of yarn lying in the shed had to be pressed evenly, and as tightly as the design of the cloth required, against the line of the already-woven cloth.

The power loom was an extremely noisy machine. The shuttle was thrown through the shed by the action of a rocker arm called a picker stick, which propelled it with high velocity. It slammed hard against the side of the carriage, stopped, and as soon as the heddles shifted, was hurled back in the opposite direction. The force was sufficient to make the shuttle a dangerous projectile if it escaped from the carriage; and it was a noisy one under the best of circumstances. A room filled with power looms, in sharp contrast to spinning apartments, was so filled with the clacking of shuttles that it was impossible to hear a person speak.

Phillips crammed as many power looms as possible into his mill. Each loom measured approximately 4 feet from front to back, 6 feet from side to side, and 5 feet in height. Many of his looms were described by one of his weavers as being "double looms." This presumably meant that two looms were joined by sharing the same pulley system; they could stand closer together than two looms each separately connected to the line shafting, and thus save floor space. Record of the precise geometry of the

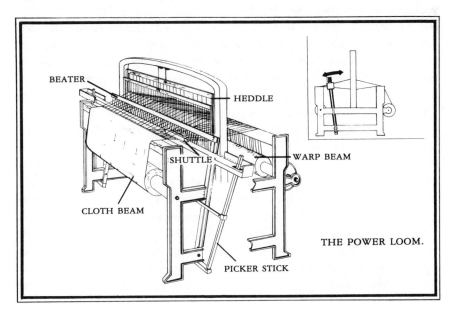

THE POWER LOOM.

arrangement of single and double looms in Phillips' mill has not survived, however.

Power looms were often served by experienced hand-loom weavers who found that they could make more money in this work than at the hand looms on which they were trained. Some of the weavers in the Rockdale mill were experienced English weavers who came to Rockdale for the money (one of whom described it, in a letter back home to England, as "an old established mill caled Philipses Mill").[2] Each weaver would handle either a pair of single looms or a pair of double looms, earning $4 to $5 per week on the former, and $5 to $6 on the latter—substantial wages, perhaps not competing with those of the mule spinners but by no means poor. Presumably there was at least one overseer, perhaps one to each floor.

The mill employed, in 1826, about 120 hands, who earned as a whole about $500 per week. This amounts to an average of a little more than $4 per week per worker. No doubt most of these operatives worked at the looms, but there were auxiliary jobs to be done: receiving and uncrating the yarn; sizing the warps (in a turbid solution of starch and tallow in water); mounting the warps on beams; setting the beams in the looms, and thread-ing each warp end through the eye of its proper string in the proper heddle, according to the prescribed weave pattern; putting each warp end through its proper slot in the reed. After a loom had woven the completed cut (about 64 yards) of cloth, the remaining warp and the beamed cloth had to be removed; the cloth had to be taken off the beam; it might then be bleached, dyed, further sized, or treated in other ways; and at last, it had to be packaged for shipment to Philadelphia.

While the loom was weaving, the weaver was necessary for only one regularly recurring task. When the cop of filling in the shuttle was ex-hausted, the weaver had to replace it with a new cop. Apart from this, he had to make sure that the machinery was operating satisfactorily and pro-ducing cloth of the desired pattern and quality. And if an end of warp or filling should break (an event which automatically stopped the machine), he had to tie the warp ends or twist together the ends of filling before weaving could continue.

It is not possible to say, from the data available on Phillips' mill, what proportion of his "hands" were male and what female. Evidently, however, the pattern here was not the same as at Lowell, with its legendary legions of young female operatives. A letter written by an English weaver named John Morris from Rockdale in 1834 identified five men who were all working in "Philipses' Mill"; his sister Jane stayed home and took care of the children and boarders. Later he noted that two male relatives and one female were "working on the power looms at Mr Croshers Mill."[3] Later on still, in the 1840's, the Riddles' paybook indicates that in the weaving department, females outnumbered males on the pay list two to one, but evidently many of the women worked only part time, so that the number of males and females actually attending looms on any one day may have been about equal. The piecework rates, 15 cents per piece (about 30 yards) of cloth, were the same for all weavers, male and female alike.[4]

Phillips' mill was a productive one. In 1826 he was weaving 30,000 yards of cotton cloth per week, worth $3,000.[5] This would represent, if the mill operated continuously throughout the year, an annual gross income on the order of $150,000.

THE MACHINE SHOPS

A typical American machine shop in the 1830's was a room containing a lathe, a workbench on which were mounted a vise and a grindstone, and a tool chest full of assorted hammers, chisels, files, and wrenches. The machinist used these tools to fashion the wood and metal parts for machinery, from the bolts and screws all the way to the massive frames, out of cast or wrought iron or steel and, sometimes, to assemble the parts. In this shop he made his own benches and lathes. Such small shops were regularly associated with textile factories. Journeymen mechanics also sometimes set up small personal shops attached to their rooms in the cities.[1]

But the independent machine shop was not really a viable business. Unlike the traditional "turner" (as the elder John Garsed had called himself in England), who used the woodworking lathe to fashion such objects as table and chair legs and who thus could serve a variety of neighborhood household needs, the machinist who worked in metal was necessarily connected not so much with households as with industries. He had to take castings, rods, or sheet metal made in a foundry, work on it in his shop, and then send the parts—or the machine—to a factory for use. This work was time-consuming and expensive. Thus, apart from the shops associated with particular factories, the bulk of machine shop practice was carried on in larger "works" employing from ten to twenty hands—and in the largest, fifty or more. These works, like the Sellers' shops in Upper Darby, Oliver Evans' Mars Works in Philadelphia, Horatio Allen's Novelty Works in New York, and the Matteawan Manufacturing Company and the West Point Foundry on the Hudson River, contained several departments: a machine shop proper, with an assemblage of lathes and other tools; a blacksmith shop, where welds could be made; a foundry, where castings were poured, and where if necessary other iron and steel products could be rolled or slit; a pattern room, where the wooden patterns for the castings were catalogued and kept; a drafting room, where plans and specifications were put on paper; and an assembly area, where the parts of large machines such as locomotives, marine and stationary steam engines were put together.

Working in a Machine Shop in the 1830's

The tools of the machinist were, in most places, very primitive. The lathe was often operated as it had been for hundreds of years, by a treadle and springpole apparatus; sometimes a hand crank was employed; in the larger shops, the lathe was belt-driven. The work was held fast in a horizontal position between the two mandrels and was rotated by a cord wrapped around one end; the cutting tool was held by the operator, with one end resting on his shoulder and the other, supported by a fixed rest, pressed against the work. Power-operated slide rests which moved along a track were still a rarity. Most of the actual finishing of metal parts other than cylindrical rollers and rods was done with a hammer, cold chisel, and a set of files, and this involved not merely the routine task of smoothing off the snags and rough edges on a casting, but also the difficult task of producing plane surfaces. (Yet incredibly accurate test planes could be achieved, always made in threes to preclude parallel concave/convex pairs, so near perfect that one surface floated on a film of air above the other and could only be removed by sliding rather than by lifting.) Milling machines were still relatively rare. It was not until 1832 in England that a really effective metal-planing machine was patented. In 1834, the Sellers brothers at Cardington Works made their own planing machine—the first such machine in Pennsylvania and the third in America.[2]

The external forms of the old guild organization were followed in a loose sort of way in the organization of these larger works. The person in charge (who might or might not be an owner) often was referred to as a "master mechanic." He might earn a substantial income, anywhere up from $100 per month. The journeyman—who owned his own chest of hand tools but not the lathes—might earn $2 to $3 per day. And the apprentice, on a three-year contract, received about 50 cents a day the first year, 66 2/3 cents the second year, and 83 1/3 the last. Apprentices usually were not legally bound, as in the old days, to a single master, but could and did move from one job to another to gain experience in the various branches of work. For instance, the artist John Rogers—later to achieve fame as the creator of "Rogers Groups," the popular table statuary of the latter half of the century—in his early years followed the machinist's trade. He served his three years apprenticeship at the Amoskeag Mills in Manchester, New Hampshire, and at Horatio Allen's Novelty Works in New York, from 1850 to 1853, learning first the use of the hand tools, then the use of powered tools, then drafting, and finally the pattern room (which housed 12,000 patterns). He served for three more years as a journeyman at Amoskeag, studying both locomotives and textile machinery; and finally went out in 1856 for a year to Hannibal, Missouri, as the master mechanic in the machine shop of the Hannibal and St. Joseph Railroad. His career as a mechanician was terminated by the panic of 1857 and he turned his talents fully to art thereafter.[3]

The work was hard and dangerous. As in the cotton mills, machinists got to work at dawn (or before) and left at dark (or after), putting in a twelve- to fourteen-hour day standing at bench or lathe. The constant handling of oily tools and iron filings quickly blackened the hands; as John Rogers complained to his father, after four days of work,

> In the first place the bells are rung at about 4 1/2 in the morning—that is to get up—at seven minutes before five they ring a second time and then we have to go into the shop and commence work. At seven we wash and go to breakfast and come back a quarter before eight—At half past twelve to dinner and back quarter past one and to tea at seven when I have felt so tired I have been to bed soon after. . . . My hands get almost black before I have been in the shop five minutes but they keep growing blacker and blacker till at last they get a regular shining polish like a new air tight stove and you may imagine what a job it is to wash them three times a day before eating. I wonder if that famous washing mixture wouldn't be good. I wish mother would try it and give her opinion. I have almost used my nail brush up for I am bound to have them clean once a day.[4]

The rooms were large, noisy with the sound of clanging hammers and scraping files, hot in the summer and cold in the winter, being poorly heated. Men arrived in relatively formal dress, with street pants, shirt, neckpiece, waistcoat, and jacket; but they stripped down to pants and shirt before standing up to the bench, where after a day's work the neophyte's ankles swelled from standing and the neck ached from bending over.

Industrial accidents were common. There was little or no personal protective equipment like goggles, and fast-moving machinery and belts were largely unshielded. George Escol Sellers recalled the time when one of the machinists at Cardington, turning a shaft in an engine lathe powered by belting, leaned over and allowed his long black silk cravat to become entangled in the carrying clog. He was nearly choked to death. A foreman of John Rogers "got his hand caught in a belt & pulled under a drum & badly hurt." Eyes were particularly vulnerable to the hot metal chips turned off by lathe and chisel: Isaiah Lukens, one of the Sellers' circle, lost an eye in this way; John Rogers got his tongue badly burned when a hot chip flew into it while he was whistling at his work, and some of his friends had permanently scarred eyeballs.[5] The most spectacular accident which Rogers recorded happened in the foundry; he reported it to his father in some awe:

We have had several accidents at the shop today. First, the main shaft in our room broke & as all speed was on it made a great disturbance. It was close to where I was at work. This afternoon the chain to the large derrick, in the foundry, broke by the weight of a tub of melted iron containing five tons of the metal & went completely over one man from head to foot & strange to say though he is pretty badly burnt yet he is not dangerously. It went over another man's face & burnt his whiskers off & that was all. They say that when iron is so hot it runs off before it burns & the reason this man was burnt so was because of his clothes.[6]

Despite the arduous nature of the work, the machinist's trade attracted in general an extremely intelligent group of young men. They were aware of the vast industrial expansion under way in the textile and transportation industries, and looked forward to educating themselves widely and generally in manual skills, technical, and even scientific knowledge as preparation for the administrative role of master mechanic or engineer, where the earnings could be substantial and the work constantly called for a creative intelligence.[7]

Machine Shops in the Rockdale District

Because of their size and weight and the consequent difficulty of transporting them (and of calling in a distant mechanic), the machines were for the most part serviced and repaired by local people. Each factory had two or three male employees who specialized in this work. The Riddles, for instance, employed a carpenter, a blacksmith, a tinsmith, and a machinist—and must have provided them with a shop of sorts. The carpenter was employed to repair the wooden parts of machines, to screw, pin, or bolt together and to varnish wooden parts of the carding engines, to cover rollers with deerskins and sheepskins, to install card clothing and fillets (wire-studded leather strips) on the cards. The tinsmith made the large cans in which the slivers were accumulated and carried in the preparation rooms. The Parkmount machine shop in the early 1830's included, at least, a small blacksmith's forge, a lathe on which the machinists could turn their own rollers for machines, a "grinder," a "cutting engine" (i.e., a milling machine), workbenches, and a supply of chisels, files, saws, and other hand tools. Other, more generalized carpenter's tools may have been kept in the barn.[8]

The Riddles' facilities were small compared with those at Penn's Grove, where the Garseds maintained a water-powered machine shop in the old woolen factory.[9] The Garsed equipment was more extensive and to them the Riddles sent some of their more difficult repairs, such as welding a broken iron shaft. Another substantial machine shop was part of the establishment at Lenni bought by William Martin in 1823. The advertisement in the *Post Boy* for December 3, 1822, contained the following specification of equipment:

> Three slide lathe and fluteing engine, turning lathes, top and fluted rollers unfinished, one cutting engine, one roving frame, seven vices, four anvils, three pairs blacksmith's bellows, stocks, dies, and taps, a quantity of cut brass wheels with blocks, spindles unfinished, fliers, lumber, iron, cast steel, a number of cast iron wheels for machinery, and a great variety of tools for machine making.[10]

No details are available on the shops at West Branch beyond Crozer's noting that his mechanics were paid almost as much in wages as the operatives for "building machinery."[11]

It is evident that each manufactory in the Rockdale district had a larger or smaller machine shop from which tools could be borrowed, repairs made to the machinery, new replacement items like card clothing be installed, and where breakable wooden items like spindles and wooden shafts could be manufactured for use in the mill. These shops also built, in part, the machines used in the mill. The manufacturer hired mechanics full or part time to operate these shops. If a particular mill did not happen to have the tools, or the skilled personnel, to handle a service-and-repair problem, the manufacturer turned first to his neighbors within the district to hire the job done. It is also noteworthy that the Garsed and Riddle shops contained machine tools of advanced design for the times: slide lathes and milling machines, both just recently invented.

Even with new machinery purchased from outside the Rockdale area, a dependence on local resources was necessary for much of the work. Mules and spinning frames purchased from distant suppliers were too large to be shipped assembled. Instead, they had to be crated in sections and put together in the factory. This reassembly could take some time. At Parkmount, the "tenth mule" arrived from Philadelphia on May 17, 1832. It was not until October that the Day Book noted that Alexander Cochrane was beginning to get the new mule ready, and in November it was recorded that it was nearly "ready for starting."[12]

The Garsed Manufactory of Power Looms

The only machines completely manufactured in the Rockdale district were the power looms produced by the Garseds. The Garseds had taken over the old woolen factory at Penn's Grove in 1830 or 1831. The history of the site, as it developed through the period up to their acquisition, is illustrative of the interplay between economic change and technological development and may be worth reviewing in some detail. A Quaker farmer, Nathan Sharpless, owned a twelve-acre tract including the old mill seat at Penn's Grove from 1791 on through 1818. (It probably had been the site of a mill from the late seventeenth century, to judge from the presence of old abandoned and forgotten dams and races in the area.) Up to 1815, the mill seat contained a three-story gristmill, sawmill, frame barn, and two houses, one of stone and the other frame. The gristmill was three stories high, in ground plan 45 by 50 feet, and contained two burr mill stones and bolting cloths for merchant work (i.e., for making the fine flours exported by Philadelphia merchants). In 1815 Sharpless constructed a "commodious" woolen spinning factory and fulling mill "with machinery complete." The property was advertised for sale in 1817 in the West Chester newspapers and was duly purchased by Isaac Sharpless and Gideon Hatton, who leased the factory and sawmill to John Hastings and the gristmill to Joseph Mancill. Sharpless, Hatton, and Hastings converted the woolen mill to a cotton factory and the associated fulling mill into a "weaver and machine maker shop." In the cotton factory they installed new machinery of the kind standard in the spinning mills of the locality: a picker, a blower, and a willowing machine for use in the picker room; 10 carding engines, with a grinding machine for the teeth; 12 drawing frames, 12 roving frames, and 1 stretcher; 4 throstles of 123 spindles each; 2 mules of 204 spindles each; 4 reels; 3 winding blocks; a yarn press; and a banding machine (for fastening crates of yarn). Becoming financially embarrassed, Hastings in 1823 sold the cotton machinery and the lease to Dennis Kelly, the Irish cotton manufacturer of Cobbs Creek; John Turner and Company seems to have taken over the machine shop.

In 1829, George W. Hill and Peter Hill jointly purchased the Penn's Grove farm and mill seat, and immediately proceeded to improve it. The old stone-and-frame building, which had been originally constructed in 1815 as a woolen factory and fulling mill, and more lately had been a cotton-spinning and -weaving factory, and "machine maker shop," they leased to John Garsed, who probably purchased the machine tools still there. This building was 60 by 30 feet, and two stories in height. Probably in view of the decline in the prosperity of the flour-milling trade (as a result of soil exhaustion and the incursions of the Hessian fly), they converted the stone gristmill into a cotton-spinning factory. This too they leased to Garsed. Garsed at first rented a house for his large family (in 1830 he had three sons and three daughters under twenty years of age; his wife died about 1835 after bearing two more children). As his profits amassed, however, he was enabled to buy first a couple of houses in Middletown, where he lived, and then a twenty-acre farm in Aston, with the necessary barn and springhouse, and a large mansion. The Hill brothers also constructed a new stone cotton-weaving mill, 96 by 42 feet, four stories high, with an attic, which they leased to James Houghton. Houghton bought a small farm with nineteen acres of land across the creek in Aston Township. He installed power looms, probably made in Garsed's shop a few yards away. The Hills quickly began to acquire more land around the site, in order to house the employees, and to add more factory buildings: a stone "drying house" (28 by 18 feet), a blacksmith shop, and a store which also housed a post office. They constructed stone and frame tenements. By 1835 the Penn's Grove site had expanded to fifty-six acres and housed twenty-two tenant families, seventeen of them in rows or "blocks" of two or four houses; by 1836 the number of families at Penn's Grove, both on and off the Hill property, was nearly forty. Garsed's three-story cotton mill had been expanded by a two-story extension 42 by 34 feet.

The Garseds probably made and sold power looms to Houghton (he installed about 150 such looms). They certainly sold power looms to the Riddles: in November 1833 the Riddles bought ten at $70 apiece; they received ten more in May 1834. They also bought eight surplus looms from John S. Phillips in the same year which may have been produced by the Garseds. Whether the Garseds had constructed the original power looms for Phillips in 1825 is doubtful; perhaps John Turner and Company, or John Hastings after his removal in 1823, had made them. Who made the looms which Crozer installed, about the same time as the Riddles, is not known.

The Garsed power-loom factory by 1840 was producing both cotton and woolen looms, probably of the "Scotch" cam-operated type, and of several qualities.[13] In that year the son Richard succeeded to his father's business, and in 1842 he began to manufacture looms which produced, in his own factory, cotton and worsted damask table and piano covers. These received a silver medal award in the exhibition of the Franklin Institute that same year for "novelty and excellence." It has been claimed that "this was probably the beginning of the manufacture of articles of this description in Pennsylvania, if not in America."[14]

In the meantime the other machine maker from Penn's Grove, John Hastings, was not far away. He and David Trainer established a weaving mill on Naaman's Creek, just above Marcus Hook in Lower Chichester Township, and there installed some sixty power looms, no doubt of Hastings's own manufacture.[15] They went out of business in 1840.[16]

John Hyde's Contract for Making Four Mules

Most of the spinning machinery used on Chester Creek had to be made by people from outside the valley. Many of them were machinists and founders in the immediate area (within a day's hauling distance), in Philadelphia, Chester, Wilmington, and along the Brandywine. Sometimes these people could be hired to take up temporary residence at the mill while they built the machinery. There is no clear example of this at Parkmount. But the records of Joseph Bancroft, who was setting up a cotton-spinning mill at Rockford on the Brandywine, fifteen miles away, simultaneously with the Riddles at Parkmount, describe the practice. A mechanic named John Hyde, of the partnership "J. and J. Hyde," agreed to make four mules of three hundred spindles each at a cost of $1.15 per spindle (i.e., $345 per mule). It was estimated that it would take Hyde and the four hands working with him six months to complete the job. Hyde would be paid $1.50 per day for each man employed at the work and $2 per day for himself while he was working. With advice from Bancroft, Hyde was to find all the materials and secure or fabricate all the patterns for the castings; the Rockford Manufacturing Company would reimburse him for the cost. He was to supply his own hand tools; the company would provide a shop equipped with certain specified pieces of water-powered equipment—three lathes, one upright drill (presumably a drill press), two grindstones, three vises, one circular saw; and various hand tools—glazers, hammers, drills, reamers, arbours, turning tools, taps, and dies. The company would also provide the services of a blacksmith. The payment was to be in installments as the work progressed, $200 by the end of the first month of work, and $140 per month thereafter, with the balance being paid in quarters at the starting of each mule. Hyde would be allowed to keep any tools not needed in the company shop when the job was over.[17]

Local Assembly of Imported Parts

The Riddles, as we have seen, bought some at least of their mules from a supplier in Philadelphia but had to assemble them in their own factory using their own mechanics. This was not the case with the spooling machine ($120) and warping mill ($50) that they bought in November 1833 from Samuel Jackson, a Philadelphia machinist. A week after they had hauled the machines to Parkmount in farmer McCracken's wagon, Jackson himself came out to set up the machinery.

In the case of some of the preparation machinery (the cards, draw frames, and so forth), the Riddles seem to have followed a third procedure: to order the necessary cast-iron sections from machinery makers in the region, to make the wooden parts in their own shop, to purchase the card clothing and other special working pieces from various Philadelphia and Wilmington suppliers, and then put together the whole machine themselves. Some of the cards they managed in this way (and some they bought complete). In October and November 1832, for instance, they bought about 1,000 lbs. of iron castings for the cards from James Flint (now a partner of the John Hyde who made the mules for Bancroft). They also paid for the use of patent patterns belonging to Parke and Tiers of Philadelphia (Parke being a "brass founder" and Tiers a "manufacturer"). Castings cost only 5 cents per pound. At the same time the Parkmount mechanics were making some of the patterns for the card parts themselves. The wire-covered card clothing and fillets they bought from Cunningham and Crawley, card clothing manufacturers of Philadelphia.

The draw frames were made in the same way. A month later they bought two cast-iron drawing frame heads from Flint, presumably making the major wooden structural parts themselves, and buying special moving parts like spindles, rollers, bobbins, and flyers from still other suppliers. The rollers for the draw frames were purchased from George Hodgson, the well-known Brandywine machinist. Each frame required two pairs of long rollers; the Riddles bought four pairs, weighing a total of nearly 150 lbs., at 35 cents per pound. The lower roller of each pair had to be fluted; the upper was covered with a soft skin. The roller coverings were bought from George Moore, a Philadelphia skin dresser. The fluting was done by Wood and Reeves. (The Hodgson firm had also earlier made rollers for two throstles for William Martin but the Martin machine shop did their own fluting.) The bobbins (634 of them) were purchased from John Crowther, a Philadelphia "turner," at a price of $6 per 100.

Exactly the same procedure was followed after they bought their twenty power looms from the Garseds in 1833. The shuttles were purchased from Jackson and Snyder. The reeds and heddles were secured from William Higham.

The Riddles, in fact, dealt with a considerable number of suppliers of machine parts and supplies, within the Philadelphia-to-Wilmington area. They bought surplus parts from other cotton manufacturers, such as Daniel Lammot, just up the stream, G. B. Lownes, near the McDowell Mill in Springfield, and William Almond, of Blockley in Philadelphia. They ordered castings from James Flint and Jonathan Bonney and Company, both probably from the Brandywine area; from Parke and Tiers of Philadelphia; and from Alfred Jenks, the former employee of the Slater enterprises who had set himself up as a cotton spinner and machine maker in Kensington. (Jenks made most of the machinery in Houghton's and Garsed's mills, except for the looms, which were Garsed's.) Their rollers they bought from Hodgson on the Brandywine. Copper steampipes for the sizing trough were installed by Benjamin O'Bryan, Philadelphia coppersmith. Carding machines and supplies were purchased from the Sellers firm of Upper Darby (the same family that had purchased Parkmount and Lenni). Chain cables and iron of various kinds came from Washington Jackson and J. S. Riddle, a firm of merchants and machinists on Front Street in Philadelphia.

The general pattern of machinery procurement followed by the Riddles is thus fairly clear. The structural frame of the machinery was made of iron, cast from patterns made by the Riddles or provided by the manufacturer, in foundries and machine shops in Wilmington, in Philadelphia, and (in the case of power looms) on Chester Creek. The card clothing, brass gears, steel rollers, bobbins and spindles, and other finely machined parts were also made in outside shops but were ordered separately by the Riddles. Many wooden parts, and parts that could be put together by the local tinsmith and blacksmith, were made on the site; and the whole machine was then assembled, tested, and adjusted by the factory's own mechanics. There were some exceptions, as in the case of the warping mill, which was set up by the supplier, but the general rule seems to have been one of local assembly.[18]

Patent Machinery from Distant Manufacturers

The Riddle Day Book for the period 1832 to 1835 reveals no instance of the purchase of machinery or parts from outside the Philadelphia-to-Wilmington area. But records from the area show that other manufacturers, at least, did turn to famous outside textile machinery manufacturers for some of their equipment. These items were shipped by water to Philadelphia, Chester, Marcus Hook, or Wilmington, and carted from there.

One of these outside manufactories which was well thought of in the Philadelphia-Wilmington area was the Savage Manufacturing Company near Baltimore. In 1825, when Daniel Lammot was making his first unsuccessful attempt to launch himself in the cotton business, he was told that it would be a good place to buy machinery. Perhaps being partial to Baltimore, his birth place, he wrote to E. I. du Pont about the matter.

If you can obtain any information respecting the "Savage Manufactory" (belonging to the Williams family of Baltimore, and situated on the Patuxent, on the Washington road, about 15 miles from Baltimore) I will thank you. I wish to know whether they manufacture Cotton machinery, and whether they have any Spindles in operation in their mills. I heard yesterday that it would be the best and largest establishment in the Country. Do not put yourself out of the way to gain the information.[19]

Joseph Bancroft bought machinery from Savage in 1832 when he was setting up his mill.[20]

Another famous machine-making locality was Patterson, New Jersey. Located in the old industrial park below the Falls of the Passaic, developed in the 1790's by Alexander Hamilton and his associates in the Society for Useful Manufactures, the Patterson mills had led a checkered career. The early ventures in textile manufacture had not been successful, but under the management of Roswell Colt, the site had attracted a considerable number of machinists, including the famous brothers George and Charles Danforth. The Patterson works produced a famous "double speeder" and William Martin's list of machinery for the mill at Lenni includes a "Patterson speeder—$100.00."[21] At a sale of machinery along Ridley Creek in 1841, also two "Patterson ring speeders" were advertised.[22]

There is no reference in Delaware County sources to machinery from the great New England manufacturers of textile machinery (although Joseph Bancroft bought some equipment from the Lowell shops and other suppliers in Massachusetts). The other great machinery supplier, however, was the Matteawan Manufacturing Company. Bancroft bought extensively from them; and in the Ridley Creek machinery sale of 1841, a "Matteawan double speeder" is mentioned.[23] Evidently, Matteawan products were being used in the area. It would appear likely that these products of distant manufactories, undoubtedly more expensive because of the shipping costs, were selected because they included patented improvements that made them essential for increased efficiency.

The famous machine-making establishments in Kensington, Patterson, Matteawan, Taunton, and Lowell represented an important and recent development on the American industrial scene: the factory which, in effect, manufactured factories, by specializing not in the production of a consumer product but in the production of machinery to make that product. These factories had an interest in making their competitors' machinery obsolete and thus added a new intensity to the pressure for technological improvement.

COMMERCIAL ASPECTS OF
COTTON MANUFACTURING

Within the mill, activities were largely confined to production, to the care of the machinery, and to the training and disciplining of the labor force. The commercial aspects of the business were conducted elsewhere. These included the keeping of records, the payment of workers and other creditors, the making of decisions about the nature of the product and about expansion or curtailment of activities, the buying of raw materials and machinery, and the selling of the product.

The Mill Office

The records of the company were preserved in a small building—sometimes a house—near to but detached from the mill. These records included a daybook (or journal) and various ledgers. The daybook was simply a large bound volume of blank paper in which, day by day, important transactions were recorded informally, in order of occurrence, by the manufacturer himself or by a clerk. Such transactions included the payment of employees and other creditors; the assumption of debts; the receipt of cotton bales; and the shipping out of boxes of yarn or cloth. But the daybook also served as a kind of business diary in which significant events of all sorts were written down: the breaking of a shaft, the repair of a gudgeon, a flood, a fire, the arrival of new families, the dismissal of an unsatisfactory operative, the construction of tenements, and so forth.

In well-kept journals prepared by clerks who knew double-entry bookkeeping, each notation carried instructions to the clerical staff as to the debit/credit status of the transaction, the account in which it was to be formally recorded (Machinery, Cotton, Employees), and the ledger number of the entry (each employee's wage record, for instance, would be recorded under his or her family's personal number). At least annually the company went through the books and prepared a statement of financial position, summarizing credits and debits.

The mill office served also as a place where petty cash business was transacted. Operatives, or members of their families, often borrowed small sums of money to buy groceries; local suppliers—general storekeepers like George Hill, millers, carters, masons—would show up requesting payment for goods and services. Although payday came around every four weeks, individual operatives might be dismissed, or leave, at any time, and they had to be paid off by cash or check. (Checks were drawn on the Delaware County Bank in Chester, on the Girard Bank in Philadelphia, and occasionally even on banks as far away as New York.)

The mill office no doubt also served as a location for discussing business; but much of the business conversations of concern to the firm were conducted elsewhere, in Philadelphia particularly, either at the offices of the firm's suppliers and customers or in the firm's own office. From the beginning, Phillips and Lewis traded in cotton cloth at their own office on Front Street; Crozer, the Riddles, and Lammot established Philadelphia offices later on.[1]

The Quality of the Product

The four spinning mills listed in the 1826 survey produced for the most part coarse yarns: "coarse," by Crozer's definition, being "No. 20, and under."[2] Cotton yarn was, and is, measured with respect to the dimension of coarseness-to-fineness by the ratio of weight to length. Although schemes differed in various parts of the world, in England and in most parts of America a standard system was employed: the "count" was given by the number of hanks which made up a pound of yarn.[3] The hank was a unit of 840 yards. Thus a pound of No. 1 yarn—a very coarse yarn—would, if laid out in a line, stretch 840 yards. Very fine yarns could be spun with counts of 300 or more; a pound of No. 300 would unwind into a single strand nearly 144 miles long!

The market determined the manufacturer's decision about yarn count. The fine mule-spun British yarns, with counts up to 300 (at least as spun by the "prince of cotton spinners," Robert Owen of New Lanark in Scotland), pre-empted the American market for fine yarns; only at the low counts could American yarns be competitive. Thus in 1826 Knowlton Mill was producing about 1,100 lbs. of No. 20 yarn per week; Penn's Grove, about 1,000 lbs. of Nos. 6 to 24; Lenni, about 1,100 lbs. of Nos. 18 to 25; and West Branch, about 1,000 lbs. of Nos. 17 to 20.[4] Yarns in this count range were suitable for the manufacture of cloths like cotton flannel, jeans, and bed tickings.

Although for economic (not technical) reasons only coarse yarns were made, this did not mean that such yarns necessarily were of poor quality. Some American manufacturers, in fact, prided themselves on the high quality of their "coarse" yarns. Quality was expressed in the strength and evenness of the strand. The better, long-stapled cottons of course produced better yarn. The common practice of spinning the waste—broken filaments with very short staple—would weaken the yarn. British mills often did this, reintroducing the sweepings into the carding process and thus into the finished product, thereby reducing the strength as well as the price of the yarn. Since about 10 percent by weight of baled cotton received in the mill was eventually lost as waste, and since the cost of raw materials was about half the manufacturer's cost, this practice could be economically significant. Other processes, too, affected the quality of the product: the efficiency of the carding, the adjustment of the drawing and twisting frames, the skill of the mule operator, the frequency of breaks in the yarn, and the deftness of the piecers. In order to be competitive with British low-count yarns, which often in periods of overproduction were dumped on the American market to be sold *below* cost, the American product had to have a reputation for quality.[5]

Buying and Selling

Much of the manufacturer's time was spent traveling between his mill on Chester Creek and the offices of the merchants from whom he bought his cotton and of the weavers to whom he sold his yarn. These people were usually located in Philadelphia. From the mill to Chester or Marcus Hook, the only means of transportation was by carriage or on horseback. From Chester or "the Hook" to Philadelphia there was, in addition to the same modes of private travel, the option of public conveyance, on water by the steam packet or on land by stagecoach (the railroad between Philadelphia and Wilmington was not completed until 1838).

There were merchants in Philadelphia who specialized in importing cotton from the south, some of it no doubt transshipped from New York but much coming directly from southern ports. Such Philadelphia firms included J. R. Neff and Company, E. N. Bridges and Company, Samuel Comley, James G. Crozier (no relative of John P. Crozer), Jackson and Riddle, Richard Pettit, W. D. Prescott, and Sloan and Relf.[6] Buying cotton involved shopping for both quality and price; purchasers would shift from one merchant to another, depending on the availability of cotton, its price and quality, and the state of the credit relationship between buyer and seller. Cotton was bought on credit, the manufacturer generally giving a note for three or four months and paying within the time period, either by check or by passing on a note (minus discount) the buyer had received from one of his customers. Cotton was sold by the name (and reputation) of the region that produced it—Upland Georgia, Mississippi, Louisiana and New Orleans, Roanoke. All of the above types, which were of middling quality, were used on Chester Creek, but Upland Georgia seems to have been preferred. The price of the cotton in Philadelphia fluctuated constantly, and over the period from 1825 to 1835 showed a gradual rise. In 1832 the price was fluctuating between 11 and 13 cents per pound; next year it rose to between 16 and 18 cents per pound. Cotton was often bought sight unseen and delivered weeks later, by ship, at Philadelphia or the Hook. When notified of its arrival, the manufacturer had to send a driver with a wagon and a team of horses to bring it from dockside to the mill. A wagonload would average about ten to fifteen bales, or 1 1/2 to 2 tons.

On his journeys to Chester, the Hook, and Philadelphia, the manufacturer also had occasion to order other materials, which similarly he had to haul in his own or a hired wagon—oil for lubrication and for the lamps that lighted the mill on winter mornings and evenings; coal to burn in the stoves; mordants and dyestuffs; sheet iron and tin; leather belts for the shafting; and, of course, the machinery.

The products of the mill were sold to three kinds of market. In the case of spinning mills, yarn was sold to power-loom factories; to merchant houses who took goods on commission, or bought them outright; and to a miscellany of small local buyers—storekeepers, individual employees, and neighbors. The weaving mill, of course, produced gray goods ready for bleaching, dyeing, or printing. The spinning mills produced several types of product. Shuttle cops, in the count range of No. 8 to No. 24, were sold primarily to other manufacturers who operated weaving mills. They were packed in numbered wooden boxes, weighing when full anywhere from 150 to 200 lbs. each, and were carted in the company's wagon to the purchaser. The yarn in cops was sold by the pound: "Angola" cops (about No. 8) in 1832 sold for 45 cents per pound; lower-quality "Canton Flannel" cops (about No. 15) brought only 20 to 22 cents. In general, the higher counts of yarn, within the 8 to 24 range, might bring a few cents more in price but the major variable was quality. Some boxes of cops (in the same count range) were sold to commission merchants, who retailed them to hand-loom weavers in Philadelphia. A very small quantity of "balled yarn" was also produced for retail sale.

Finished cloth from the weaving mills was counted by the "piece." A piece of cloth (i.e., the quantity woven from a single warp) would be about 28 to 30 yards in length. The cloth was packed either in cases, about thirty pieces per case, or in bales of about forty pieces. The cloth was sold by the yard, however, not by the piece. In 1834 "printing cloth" from the Riddles sold for 6 cents per yard; Canton flannel for 13 cents per yard.

The third major product was cotton laps. The cotton lap was a sheet of thick cotton batting, perhaps a yard wide and several yards long. It was an intermediate product of a spinning mill, being initially produced by the machine called the spreader, immediately after the raw cotton had come through the picker, and then refined at the special card called the lap card. Laps were originally designed as a standardized, carefully weighed quantity of cotton—usually 8 ounces—which could be fed evenly into the carding machine to yield a more uniform sliver. But there was a considerable domestic market for laps, which could be used as the filling for patchwork, and for other purposes as "cotton wool." Laps sold for about 10 cents a piece and a spinning mill would consign hundreds of them per month to commission merchants, local general stores, employees and neighbors.

Even the by-products of the mill were sold. Some clean waste was sold off to employees and neighbors; but most of the waste (much of it very dirty waste from the picker room and some of it oily floor sweepings) was sold to nearby paper mills, along with the ropes and bales in which the raw cotton was delivered, to be used in the manufacture of rag paper (wood pulp was not yet used to make paper). Some was sold to manufacturers of carpet filling. And some was also sold to nearby machine shops, for use as wipers for oily parts and to clean up metal filings, and later to fill up journal boxes on railroad cars. The bagging sold at about 1 1/2 cents per pound; ropes brought 1 1/4 cents; waste brought 1/2 to 1 cent per pound. The quantities were considerable: the Riddles sold at least 5 tons of waste per year to two nearby paper mills, and smaller quantities to a variety of local enterprises and individuals.

The various commercial transactions were handled for the most part by an exchange of four-month notes: the manufacturer would take personal three- to six-month notes in exchange for his wares, and would give notes in payment for his raw materials. Because the manufacturer's debtors and creditors were in turn buying and selling by exchanging notes, the system was one of intricate financial interdependence. James Houghton sold much of his cloth to Henry Farnum and Company. He accepted their notes, and when he bought yarn from the Riddles, he passed them on (allowing a discount of about 2 or 3 percent) to the Riddles, who either turned them in to the local bank for cash (minus the bank's discount) or passed them on to a cotton merchant. If they got into the hands of a bank, the bank collected from the original debtor. A typical example of note passing occurred in January 1834, when the Riddles paid Henry Sloan $378.96 on their bill for a load of cotton with a note they had accepted from Peter Hill, to whom they had consigned yarn. Peter Hill had received the note from Moses Redpath, who had originally received it from Robert Cumming. Inasmuch as Peter Hill was not commonly looked upon as a good risk in financial matters, the Riddles had secured an endorsement from Peter's brother George, the local storekeeper, with whom they kept an account for groceries.

Thus the note-exchange process permitted complicated financial transactions to be completed "in the city" with a minimum use of cash (paper money or specie). Complementing the use of commercial paper, some bills were also paid by checks on the Delaware County Bank in Chester and the Girard Bank in Philadelphia. And in the local community, a barter system operated on a small scale to supplement the exchange of paper. The paper mills, for instance, to whom waste was sold, paid part of their bills with reams of paper.

The principal outlay of cash, in fact, was in the payment of the workers. On payday every fourth week, the mills brought in a few hundred dollars in cash from the Delaware County Bank. Petty cash was also available in the mill office at all times to lend to employees or their families as an advance on wages. But some of the workers preferred to leave some part of their money on the books, uncollected, until such time as the family moved, or some substantial new expense required its use.[7]

The Shift to Complete Process Factories

The first generation of factories—those built before 1832—were modeled after the English practice, in that each mill conducted *either* spinning or weaving; none did both. And the Riddles even excluded throstle spinning, concentrating exclusively on their ten mules to produce filling (and small quantities of warp).

This procedure was perhaps efficient in its simplicity, but it minimized the potential profit of both the spinning mills and the power-loom factories by introducing a packaging and transportation cost, a discount cost, and a profit margin between the spinner and the weaver. A spinner, if he added power looms, could sell to himself the necessary yarn cheaper than he could sell it to a weaver; consequently, he could sell the cloth cheaper than the specialized weaver could. Furthermore, if the spinner had both throstles and mules, he could manufacture all the kinds of warp and filling he required.

The first major shift in the manufacturing process along Chester Creek was more an economic or managerial than a technological one. It was the installation of power looms in mills hitherto exclusively devoted to spinning, and the elimination of businesses exclusively devoted to weaving.

The Riddles began the shift in November 1833 when they bought their first ten power looms from John Garsed. It is not entirely clear when John P. Crozer came to the same decision. When he answered Secretary of the Treasury Louis McLane's questionnaire in April 1832, he made it clear that all he made was "Cotton yarn, No. 15 to 33. . . . There are power looms in the neighborhood which consume part of the yarn; the balance is sold in Philadelphia to hand loom weavers."[8] But by March 1834, the English weaver William Morris who worked in Phillips' mill wrote home, "There is 4 powerloom mills in this neighborhood, 2 more starting, 2 of them containing about 150 looms each."[9] The two large ones were Phillips's and Houghton's. One already in motion, on a small scale, was at Parkmount. This leaves three other sites for the introduction of power looms in 1834; and the only possible locations were Lenni, West Branch, and Knowlton. Evidently by the end of 1834 *all* of the spinning mills had added power looms. By 1836 three members of the Morris family were "worcking on the power looms at Mr Crosher's Mill."[10] By May 1837, when Crozer testified to the Senate Committee, he had looms in his main mill and had added "a small weaving factory, employing twenty-seven persons; only three or four young children employed in the latter."[11]

The exclusive power-loom factories lingered for a few years. But Lewis and Phillips' lease was not renewed in 1835 (in part, as we shall see, for reasons other than economic) and their place at Rockdale was taken by a complete process manufacturer, Bernard McCready. And both James Houghton and the Garseds were displaced in 1842 when the Hills sold Penn's Grove to Samuel Riddle. Thus in the decade between 1832 and 1842, the old system of partial process mills was entirely replaced by complete process mills, which took baled cotton in and sent out cloth.

WORKING IN PARKMOUNT MILL IN 1832

Construction of the factory on the Hills' unimproved mill seat at the forks was begun in 1831. The work was done to the specifications of the brothers Samuel and James Riddle. The Hills invested $7,000 in the dam, race, and water wheel, and $10,000 more in the mill building.[1] The building was made of a local green stone (serpentine), 132 feet long and 58 feet wide, two stories and an attic, and was set along a sloping hillside on the north side of the main branch of the creek, just above the forks.[2] The dam was about 5 feet high, and a relatively short race, perhaps 100 yards long,

Top: COTTON PLANTATION

Bottom: WILLOWING

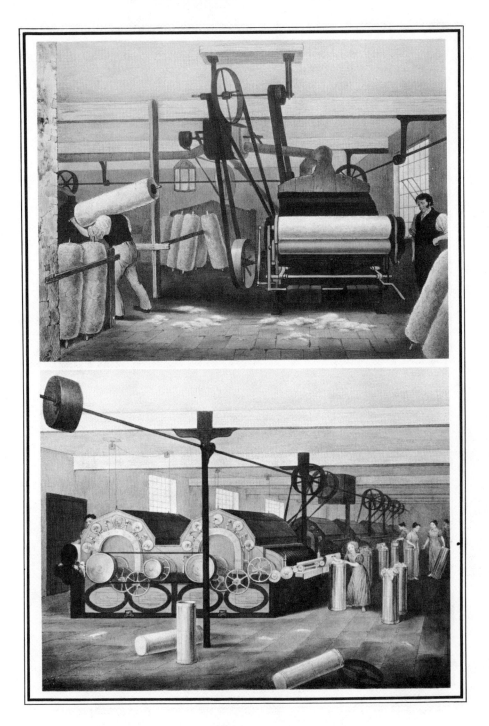

Top: LAP FRAME

Bottom: CARDING

Top: BOBBIN AND DRAWING FRAMES

Bottom: SPINNING

Top: BLEACHING

Bottom: WARPING AND WINDING

(168)

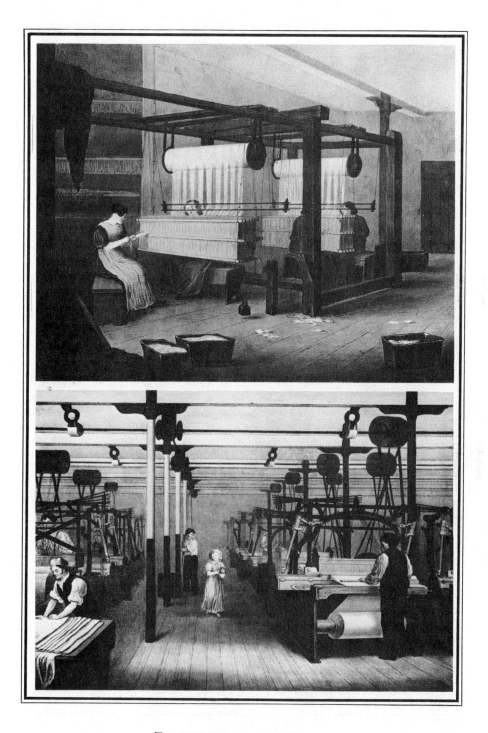

Top: REEDING, OR DRAWING IN

Bottom: WEAVING

Top: DYEING

Bottom: PRINTING

ran along the hillside to the water wheel. The wheel was a breast wheel, at the upstream end of the mill, and was roofed over with boards. The road curved around the mill and crossed over the race by the picker house to the covered bridge that led across the creek to John B. Ducket's paper mill.

The Riddles owned the machinery, which cost them about $16,000. They started out with a highly specialized operation, buying no throstles at all, investing instead in ten mules, a larger number than the other local mills. This gave them between 2,500 and 3,000 spindles. The mules were probably located in the attic, which provided a large floor space, well lighted by the conventional clerestory windows, and unencumbered by the lines of supporting pillars needed on the floors below. The floor below probably housed the card room, containing a spreader and at least two large carding engines—a breaker, or lap, card and a finisher card. In the adjoining room on the same floor were probably located the double speeder and the six drawing frames. The warping mill was probably on the same well-lighted floor. The machine shop, the packing and shipping room, and the storage areas for machinery, lumber, metal, cotton bales, and dyestuffs were probably on the ground floor. The picker room and the dyehouse very likely were in attached buildings. Nearby were the barn and the mill office.[3]

The Riddles' mill was unique among the local spinning mills in its exclusive use of mules for spinning and in its roomy floors. Although they put the wheel in operation late in 1831, the business of manufacturing began a few months later. The journal of "Parkmount factory" opens with the notation: "Day Book commenced on the first of February one thousand eight [hundred] and thirty two." But the Riddles were not content to leave their manufacturing methods constant. From that first day on, the daybook records a constant sequence of modifications and improvements: the building of new tenements, the purchase and setting up of new machinery, the adjusting of the old machines to make better yarn, the covering of the water wheel, eventually the purchase of power looms (in 1834). Later we shall discuss in detail the nature and implications of these technological changes.

The December 12, 1832, Cohort of Workers

The first regular payday was December 12, 1832. Before that time—no doubt because the mill was still establishing itself and the Riddles were spending almost all their cash on the purchase of machinery and materials—the workers were paid only small sums "on account" and were buying their groceries on the mill's credit. They were living, of course, in tenement houses owned by the mill and credit was also being extended for their rent.

Let us look at this first cohort of workers at Parkmount—the workers present on December 12, 1832—in some detail. The first observation, one whose importance cannot be overemphasized, is that the factory treated the domestic household, not the individual, as the unit of production. Usually the household consisted of a nuclear family, including husband, wife, their children, and perhaps attached relatives. But it might also consist of a one-parent family, or a man and his sisters, or various other household combinations. Occasionally, the "household" consisted of only a single male boarding with a worker family or at a nearby farm. Such situations often were temporary, occurring when a man took a job, leaving his wife and children behind to catch up with him later when circumstances (including the availability of a house near the factory) permitted. These household units were treated as economic units. The wages of all the workers in the household were paid to the effective head of the household (male or female), and all the members were assigned the same ledger number. When a new head of household rented one of the mill houses, he sometimes even signed an agreement to make available for work in the mill a specified number of "hands." The rent book contains seven such contracts in 1853 and 1854. For example, the following is the agreement signed by Joseph Wright:

Octr 1—1853   I have rented to Joseph Wright the house lately occupied by Alexander Crozier on the following Conditions. Joseph Wright Agrees to keep 2 Hands working in the factory at all times While he occupies the House, (sickness of the Hands excepting) and that he will give 2 weeks notice of his intentions to leave the house and of the hands to quit work (under all Circumstances) if required and at the expiration of the 2 weeks notice to give up peaceable possession of the House or forfeit the lying times of the hands or in case of removal the hands will forfeit without a regular notice being given. [signed] Joseph Wright[4]

At the time of the first payday on December 12, 1832, there were twenty household units providing hands to the mill. It is worth introducing them by name:

JESSE ALEXANDER and family, consisting at least of Alexander, his wife Margaret, and his two sisters. Jesse Alexander began work as a carder in April; his family joined him and moved into "the new house" in May 1832. His two sisters also worked in the mill and they had as a boarder still another worker, Neill Cairns. The Alexanders left the regular employ of the Riddles in April 1833 but remained in the neighborhood at least until November, when Jesse Alexander was paid $40 "for repairing the Dearborn" (a type of light wagon). For work in the mill during this period they received at least $189.32.

RICHARD BATES and family, including Bates and his wife, both in their twenties, and their three sons, two of them infants and one between seven and twelve. The nature of his work in the mill is not disclosed in the daybook. His son, from his age, must have been a piecer or scavenger. Presumably Bates occupied a house, for he paid road taxes and owned a cow. The Bates family arrived from Lower Darby (a township adjacent to Philadelphia) in the summer of 1832 and left in May 1833. During this period they earned at least $253.23. The Bates seem to have been a troublesome household, for the daybook notes in October that Bates's cow "went out of the pasture" and in December the son was fired "for smoking a Cigar in the mill."

FRANCIS BONNER and family, including at least himself and his wife; whether or not they had children is not known. Bonner arrived in September and worked briefly in the mule room as a creel attender; before the month was out he had his own mule and was spinning flannel. His family joined him late in November. They remained at least until January 1835, when the daybook closed, but were no longer in the neighborhood when the decennial census was taken in 1840. From September 1832 to September 1833 the Bonners earned at least $250.24.

NEILL CAIRNS, single, boarded with the Alexanders. It is not clear what he did in the mill. He remained from May 1832 to April 1833 and during these eleven months earned at least $160.88. He could read and subscribed to a newspaper.

ALEXANDER COCHRANE, a man in his sixties, and his family, consisting of his wife (in her fifties) and three grown children (ages seventeen to thirty-two, the youngest a son John, and two girls) arrived from Chester in October 1832, in the wagon usually used for hauling cotton bales. He was an experienced mule spinner and was initially assigned to getting the new mule ready. In the first year of work, the family earned at least $180.65. They remained through 1834.

WILLIAM COCHRANE, age about thirty and probably a son of Alexander, and his family, consisting of his wife, a brother of working age, a working sister named Sarah, plus another sister or sister-in-law and three male children under five years of age. William Cochrane was a mechanic who specialized in fine carpentry, such as making wooden patterns for the castings of carding engine parts. He also did general carpentry, making the boxes for shipping shuttle cops, and maintaining and repairing the barn, the sluice gates, and the mill building itself. At least two of his family also worked in the mill. The William Cochranes earned, from November 1832 through October 1833, at least $414.95.

JAMES CROOKS arrived in December 1832. His wife Mary, and their son James Jr., who was about five years old, came on in the following summer, occupying one of the tenement houses. Crooks, who was between twenty-two and thirty-two years of age, was a warper and his wife sometimes worked at balling yarn. They were a stable family who worked steadily for the Riddles until 1849. They bought books, purchased a cow from the Riddles (at a cost of $19), and produced babies. By 1840 the household consisted of eight persons, three of them engaged in "manufacturing": James and his wife Mary, his teen-age son James, another son under five, three daughters, one under five, and two (Jane and Isabella) in their teens. One of the grandmothers, a woman in her sixties, also lived with them. During the first year, December 1832 through November 1833, the family earned at least $217.32.

RUTH ANN FREDD, a widow (or abandoned wife) of about fifty, and her five children arrived in February 1832 and occupied one of the tenement houses. The children included little Mary, aged somewhere between seven and twelve; Elizabeth, between twelve and seventeen; William, between seventeen and twenty-two; James, in his twenties; and John, age unknown. All of the children worked in the mill, as did Mrs. Fredd; James, apparently, was also a hand-loom weaver who manufactured cloth at home. But Mrs. Fredd collected the wages for the whole family and carried out the various little financial negotiations with the mill that included borrowing petty cash, purchasing firewood, and securing orders on local millers and storekeepers for barrels of flour and other foodstuffs. Between February 1832 and February 1833 the family earned at least $148.33 in wages plus unknown amounts from boarders. They remained in the area into the 1840's and worked for the Riddles at least through January 1835.

JOHN GAUN worked for the Riddles only occasionally in the period May 1832 to February 1833. There is no information about what work he did or about his household. He earned only $3.50 and disappeared from the record after February 1833. By 1835 a "Jno. Gawny" was working in Bancroft's spinning mill on the Brandywine.

JOHN McDADE was apparently a single man of about thirty who arrived from Marcus Hook in July 1832. His mother Rachel was at the time the only McDade in Delaware County. She seems to have been a widow between fifty and sixty years of age, and had three sons between seventeen and thirty-two, of whom John was probably one. John learned about mules by working his way up from a piecer to creel attender; he began operating a mule in September. His sisters joined him in January or February. But in March he was "turned off" for fighting with Neill

Cairns; the Riddles evidently considered him to be at fault. He did not leave the area immediately, however, for he reappears in the 1840 census with a wife and three children, the eldest younger than ten. The McDades earned at least $184.20 during their time of employment.

ARCHIBALD McDOWELL, age twenty-four, was if not already, then soon to become, a brother-in-law of the Riddles, marrying their sister Mary, age twenty-two. He arrived in the United States about 1831 and may have been living and working at the factory in Springfield before moving to Parkmount. McDowell worked as a mule spinner for the Riddles from September through January. By next March 1833, Mc-Dowell had entered into a partnership with Joseph Gibbons, the owner of the land on which the Springfield factory was located, and the family moved back to Springfield. The Riddles continued to keep an account with them, ordering their cotton and selling their yarn. The McDowells eventually moved back into the area, and McDowell worked again for the Riddles as a highly paid spinner; by 1850 he had become the superintendent of the Glen Riddle factory.

SAMUEL McMULLEN was a mule spinner who began to work in July 1832 and continued through January 1835. There is no mention of his having a wife and children; he may have been one of the sons of a well-established local family across the creek in Aston Township headed by James McMullen. James McMullen first appeared as a head of household in the census lists in 1810; in 1830 he was between forty and fifty years old and had a son between fifteen and twenty. James was mentioned in the daybook as a purchaser of a piece of Canton flannel. The last mention of James McMullen in the census records was in 1840; he then still had in his household a son aged between twenty and thirty. From July 23, 1832, to July 28, 1833, Samuel McMullen earned at least $281.28.

HUGH McMUNN, age twenty-five, mule spinner and later carding superintendent, arrived at Parkmount directly from Ireland in December 1832; his family, including wife Elizabeth (also twenty-five) and four children (Mary, five; Eliza, three; John, one; and Archibald, a newborn infant), emigrated in the spring of the following year, no doubt after the birth of the new baby, and moved into one of the company houses. He worked for the Riddles until 1844, and returned to Penn's Grove in 1850, along with wife and children. He purchased books and subscribed to a newspaper. From December 1832 to December 1833 he earned at least $191.33.

JOHN McNAMEE, age twenty-five, was a blacksmith who worked full time for the Riddles from November 1832 until about January 1834. He was unmarried. From December 1832 through November 1833 he earned at least $160.94. In 1850 he was practicing his trade in the industrial suburb of Kensington and was married.

HENRY McNEILL, mule spinner, arrived with his family at Parkmount about November 1832 and left on May 27, 1833. He did not move far, only to Lenni, where he entered the employment of Daniel Lammot. Based on the information contained in the 1840 census, he was in his middle twenties to early thirties in 1832, with a wife in her twenties, a son between seven and twelve; an older man, between fifty-two and sixty-two, lived in the household. At least three of the family worked. Later on, the McNeills returned to work for the Riddles at Penn's Grove. Between December 1832 and June 1833, at their final reckoning, the family earned $220.74—a substantial income for six months.

HENRY McVEY arrived in August 1832 and in September began to operate a mule. His family seems to have joined him in December, when they began to rent one of the tenement houses. They left in January 1834. From August 1832 through July 1833 McVey earned $208.31.

HAMILTON MAXWELL, in his twenties, was another of the Riddles' brothers-in-law. A Scots-Irishman too, from the Belfast area, he was soon to be married to Jane Riddle, twenty-five, and came over to the Springfield factory from Ireland in 1829 or 1830 with his mother Mary Maxwell. They seem to have had no children. Hamilton Maxwell was an expert carder and on occasion the Riddles lent his services to the McDowell and Gibbons factory for a day or two. He worked at Parkmount from August 1832 at least until January 1835 but disappears from the local records after that. His wife Jane died in 1836. From August 1832 through July 1833 he earned (from the Riddles) at least $156.

ISABELLA MOORE was the daughter of a Mrs. Moore who collected her child's petty wages. Apparently she worked only occasionally from April 1832 to May 1833. This may have been the family identified in the Middletown census of 1830 headed by Mary Moore, a woman then in her fifties, who lived with two males, fifteen to twenty and twenty to thirty, and two females, fifteen to twenty and twenty to thirty, presumably sons and daughters and perhaps sons and daughters-in-law.

WILLIAM SHAW, originally from Baltimore, began to work as a mule spinner for the Riddles in July 1832 at the age of twenty-one. There was a Mrs. Shaw who worked as a weaver at Houghton's; and "William Shaw and girl" were paid together on two occasions. The composition of the Shaw household is not clear; there was a house (road taxes were paid); perhaps Mrs. Shaw was his mother, and presumably the "girl" was a member of the household, for joint payment of wages invariably implied household unity. Shaw left the Riddles in May 1833 to go to work for

John P. Crozer. His wages for the eleven months amounted to at least $176.38. He later moved to Manayunk, and in 1837 testified on working conditions in cotton mills during the Pennsylvania Senate's investigation of child labor.

JAMES WIER was a man in his early forties who already lived in Aston Township, with three of his children—a daughter Maria (aged twelve to fifteen), a son (seven to twelve), and another son (under seven). His wife, in her early thirties, in 1830 resided with the rest of the children (William, aged ten to fifteen, Lydia, aged five to ten, and a son under five) in Christiana Hundred along the Brandywine. In September 1833 the family was reunited, moving into "the Log House," and they remained at least through January 1835.[5]

It is clear, from the characteristics of the households just described, that they mostly were simple nuclear families composed of husband, wife, and children. The married couples were usually young, in their twenties or early thirties. Occasionally the household consisted of a woman (or a man) supporting herself (or himself) and children without the aid of a spouse through the collective labor of parent and children. Bachelor males tended to be boarders in other households. Usually the husband was the principal wage earner, with additional smaller sums being earned by the children and sometimes also by the wife.

The Organization of Work in the Factory

Ten of the male wage earners were mule spinners. With the exception of John McDade and William Shaw, they were all married men. Each of them operated a single mule. Each had at least two and probably three helpers: a creel attender, who replaced exhausted bobbins of roving and probably doffed filled cops; a piecer, who mended broken threads and cleaned up around the mule; and a scavenger under the sheet of yarn. These helpers could be either boys or girls and were often the children of the spinners themselves or of their co-workers. The spinner was treated as a subcontractor (and in census returns, even as late as 1850, might be referred to as a "cotton manufacturer"), paying his creel attender and piecer out of his own wages. As Samuel Riddle said, "The mule spinners are paid by the quantity they do, and they employ their own help."[6] Although the spinners did not own their own mules, they traditionally took a proprietary interest in them. A mule spinner seems to have learned his skills at first by serving as a creel attender on someone else's mule for a month or so; at least the Parkmount Day Book shows several spinners beginning work as spinners' helpers. The spinner was theoretically paid by the number of hanks he produced. But the number of hanks was not measured directly; rather, it was calculated by taking the product of the number of pounds of cotton spun and the yarn count. Thus 700 lbs. of No. 15 was calculated to produce 10,580 hanks of yarn. The spinner was paid between 2 1/2 and 3 cents per pound of cotton spun, getting more for the finer counts. Using the equipment installed in 1832, an average spinner could spin something like four bales of cotton (at 350 lbs. per bale) into No. 15 yarn per month.[7]

The other identifiable male job specifications were the carding master, the mechanic, the blacksmith, and the carpenter. The mill office clerk, not identified, probably was also male. There may have been a man in charge of the drawing and stretching frames. The mill superintendent was probably one of the Riddle brothers. These positions (not counting a superintendent) would account for the "16 men, from 8 to 10 dollars per week," that the Riddles reported employing in the questionnaire printed in the McLane report in 1832. They also reported employing "20 young women, 2 dollars per week, and fourteen at 4 to 5 dollars per month." The young women worked for the most part in the carding room and around the draw frames; but some worked as helpers at the mules. The "fourteen at 4 to 5 dollars per month" would be the creel attenders and piecers at the mules, who might be children of twelve or less, and workers in the picker room.

Because of the smallness and intimacy of the group, who not only worked but also lived cheek by jowl, the participants in the system probably thought of its organization less in terms of a "table of organization" than as a system of rules, enforced by discipline, that would ensure the continuous, uninterrupted performance of the various interdependent parts of the manufacturing process. In the Riddles' mill, these rules were not printed and posted (although Samuel Riddle, in his testimony to a Pennsylvania Senate investigating subcommittee, averred that they should be) but were normally told to an employee when he was hired, and thereafter communicated by example and by informal word-of-mouth transmission among the workers. From Riddle's testimony, and from the Parkmount Day Book, the Parkmount factory "rules" can be readily deduced. It may be worth noting that Riddle and other manufacturers used the word "rule" to indicate both a standard operating procedure in a descriptive sense ("This is a pretty general rule," "It is not a regular rule") and also as a requirement enforced by discipline, having the nature of a contract ("We have not required the hands to sign the rules; at some they do; I believe it the best way").

1 A week's work is seventy-two hours. The mill starts at five o'clock in the morning in the summer, stops half an hour for breakfast and three-quarters of an hour for dinner (both eaten at home), and closes at seven. In winter, the mill starts at six-thirty and ends at eight-thirty, with the same time off for meals. Time is signaled by the bell.

2 Workers are paid every four weeks in cash money.

3 Two weeks' notice is required of intention to leave employment and to vacate rented housing; workers will continue to work as usual during this period.

4 Fighting, swearing, obscene language, and undue familiarity between the sexes are not allowed.

5 Workers will be clean and suitably dressed for their work.

6 Two weeks' wages will be kept back until the worker's account is settled at the termination of employment.

7 There will be no tobacco smoking or possession of alcoholic beverages within the mill.

8 Work shall meet standards of quality set by the manufacturer.

These rules were enforced by threats of dismissal or suspension, of docking and withholding wages, and of blacklisting—punishments that were imposed on non-complying workers. Thus the Riddles fired John McDade for fighting with Neill Cairns, and the Bates boy for smoking a cigar in the mill. They also "turned off" Robert McMullen in August 1832 "for making bad work." John P. Crozer testified to the standards of sexual morality required, saying of his young women weavers, "departures from chastity are not common. Females of loose character, if known, or *even suspected* as such, would be immediately dismissed from my factory, and I think could not get employment in any of the neighboring factories."[8]

Actual records of docking wages for tardiness, or of permanently withholding the two weeks (or more) back wages as punishment for tardiness or for not giving notice, do not appear in the Riddle Day Book. Samuel Riddle testified:

We have no punishment, but putting persons who offend away. We keep two weeks' wages back. We have always paid back wages when persons left us without giving two weeks' notice, after holding it a little while; a great many, in such cases, retain it. It is a rule that those employed shall give two weeks' notice of their intention to quit. Very often, this is notified to persons employed; sometimes it is not; it is generally mentioned when an engagement is made.[9]

Blacklisting also is not mentioned in the Riddles' account books but it was implied in Crozer's remarks about unchaste female employees.

Perhaps the most difficult and controversial aspect of discipline had to do with children. In the first place, the young piecers, creel attenders, and scavengers were not technically the manufacturer's employees at all; their discipline was the responsibility of the mule spinner who hired them. Riddle, in recalling his youth in Ireland ("I have been working in a cotton factory since I can recollect. . . . I was not more than nine years old when I was put into a factory, and have been raised in one"), observed, "There was a great deal of whipping there, we have not here." Crozer, speaking in a similar vein in 1837, said, "when factories were first established in this vicinity, severe whipping was often practised, but it was found not to be the best mode of management, and has been, in a great degree, abandoned." Riddle even claimed that if the children who worked for the mule spinners "were oppressed in any way, they would tell me, of course." Certainly the children not working for spinners were disciplined by foremen and carding masters. But probably the most effective measure in maintaining both the general level of efficiency, cleanliness, and propriety and a not-too-severe mode of discipline for "the little ones" (as Riddle called them) was the informal culture of the workers. It must be remembered that all of the people who worked in the mill lived within easy walking distance, and most in the sixteen tenement houses located within 100 yards of the mill. The spinner's team, the carding masters' assistants, the young hands in the preparation room, were, if not their own children, then the children of neighbors who also worked in the same mill. Real brutality, made visible by bruises, welts, tears, and headaches, would not only offend the abused child's parents but also interfere with the work, for an injured or panic-stricken child would not be able to do good work. And a large proportion of the piecers were, the daybook makes plain, not the children of the spinners. The record shows, for instance, that Joseph Pedrick pieced for Francis Bonner, Mary Fredd pieced for Richard Bates and later for Sarah Cochrane (in the card room), Sarah McDade pieced for James McBride, Lydia Wier and later Joseph Pedrick for Hugh McMunn, Charles McNamee for David Crummer, and so on. One may suspect that, at least by the 1830's, the manufacturer and his agents must have avoided, as much as possible, involving themselves in any direct way with the physical discipline of "the little ones," leaving that arena to the community of workers. This meant, as other witnesses in the Philadelphia area testified, discipline by ridicule and "taunting," occasionally supplemented as required by cuffs, slaps, kicks, and ear-boxings.

Physical Working Conditions

As Crozer testified, many of the mills had not been designed as cotton factories. The ceilings were too low, the rooms were too small, and as a result the operatives were crowded together in narrow quarters with inadequate ventilation. None of the mills on Chester Creek employed exhaust fans, although they were known in the Philadelphia area, and on cool or windy days the windows were kept shut. In two places, the picker room and the card room, the problem of ventilation was particularly severe. The air was filled so thick with "flyings" that breathing was difficult and workers developed a constant cough. In an effort to prevent the escape of the dust the machines were boxed in, but this was not particularly effective. Furthermore, windows in these rooms could not be opened because the breeze would blow around even more of the fibers. As Crozer remarked,

> In the extreme heat of summer, the spinning mills, particularly the card rooms, are rather oppressive, when a free passage of air cannot be admitted, which is the case, if there is any wind—but in modern built factories, with high stories, a free circulation is always preserved; no other means employed to ventilate, but by the windows.[10]

Even in winter the room temperature was kept reasonably high (in the seventies if possible) by using stoves, because the cotton required warmth.

The language used by Crozer to describe the mill in the summer was mild compared with the vivid rhetoric of a Pittsburgh physician. He testified:

> The factories are ill ventilated; their atmosphere is constantly impregnated, and highly surcharged with the most offensive effluvia—arising from the persons of the inmates, and the rancid oils applied to the machinery.
>
> The temperature of their atmosphere is generally high, approaching a medium of from sixty to seventy degrees in winter, and rising to eighty and even ninety degrees in summer. Their atmosphere is constantly filled with floating particles of cotton; the finer the yarns to be spun, the higher the temperature must be. Cotton yarns cannot be spun in any atmosphere other than this. The cotton wool, when impregnated with the oil used to diminish friction in the machinery, and in the usual temperature of the rooms, emits a most offensive fetor. This fetor, acted on by the azote and hydrogen abounding in the rooms, gives an atmosphere which none but those accustomed to it can respire without nausea.
>
> In the rooms where the cotton wool undergoes the first process of

carding and breaking, the atmosphere is one floating mass of cotton particles, which none but those accustomed to it, can breathe, for an hour together, without being nearly suffocated.

No doubt this odoriferous effect was intensified in some mills (not the Riddles') by the provision of loosely partitioned water closets on the working floors (usually but not always separate for males and females). Other observers noted that new employees experienced "a little nausea at first and their appetite for food is lessened."[11]

Another factor significantly affecting the comfort and ease of the work was the quality of the early stages of preparation. American factories generally devoted less attention to the carding and preparation of the roving than did English factories. The result was an inordinately high frequency of breakage, starting with the sliver emanating from the finisher card, continuing with the various drawing and stretching frames, and culminating in the throstle and mule rooms. An experienced spinner reported that in English factories, where one piecer attended two mules, the child walked twenty-five miles per day. With only one mule to attend in America, the distance theoretically would be halved; but this advantage was more than overbalanced by the effects of poor quality in the preparation of the rovings. An experienced English carder, employed by Joseph Ripka of Manayunk, testified: "I consider the work of piecers, here, at the mule, greater than in England, although here the children attend but one mule; the reason is, that the work in England is much better prepared, and requires less piecing."[12] Thus, ideally, a child might sit a large part of the day, if the work were well prepared; but in general it was not possible, and the child, like the other workers, had to stand and walk for the full twelve to fourteen hours per day.

The effect of the long hours of constant physical labor, attending the continuously operating machines, was fatiguing enough for adults. Some spinners, being piece workers, preferred to work less. A Scottish spinner, for instance, testified, "I consider a great evil in the business the length of time we have to labor; I consider eight hours labor per day, as much as I can bear, in justice to myself; I work by the piece." The effect on children was striking, particularly upon first entering the mill. The ankles tended to swell, the appetite to decline. William Shaw, erstwhile Parkmount employee and afterward one of Crozer's workers, testified succinctly in 1837 about the effect on children of conditions in the factories he had known:

The children are tired when they leave the factory; has known them to sleep in corners and other places, before leaving the factory from fatigue.

The younger children are generally very much fatigued, particularly those under twelve years of age; has not heard frequent complaints of pain; more of being worried; has known the children to go to sleep on arriving home, *before* taking supper; has known great difficulty in keeping children awake at their work; has known them to be struck, to keep them awake.[13]

THE PRODUCT: THE FABRICS OF CHESTER CREEK

The final product of the mills on Chester Creek was woven cloth, packed in wooden boxes and shipped to Philadelphia for sale by commission merchants. All of this cloth, with the exception of a small amount of carpeting woven on draw looms (later replaced by Jacquards), was made on power looms, most of them Garsed's. These looms had an approximately 40-inch beam and produced "cuts" of cloth approximately 64 yards long. It was all relatively "coarse" stuff, made from the short-staple Upland cotton, which could only be spun in the lower counts (up to 42), and woven in plain and twill weaves. The yarns commonly used were 10 to 20 count, and the closeness of the weaves was on the order of forty-five to sixty warp ends and forty-five to sixty picks to the inch. Whatever the technical capabilities of the machines and the workers, they were only able to compete profitably with British manufacturers in the coarse lines (fabrics made from yarns of

PRINTED CALICO FROM BUSTLETON MILL, PHILADELPHIA, CIRCA 1825.

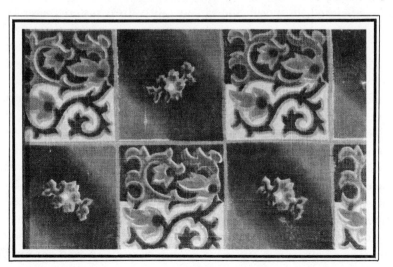

count 20 and below). In 1832, the Riddles complained: "We have to spin and weave the coarse and less profitable article."[1] In 1845, when John P. Crozer was asked whether it would be practicable to get up an exhibition of Delaware County cotton manufactures, he replied in an almost apologetic way:

> The manufacture of cottons & woolens in this county though considerable in amount does not comprise any great variety of styles nor of a kind fitted to make much display but I presume most of the manufacturers might be induced to exhibit samples, and some of them would take some care in getting up these samples or specimens,—[2]

The only relatively fancy cloths of which record remains were a quantity of soft but finely woven "diaper" cloth, manufactured by the Callaghans, who took over Parkmount in the 1840's, and Garsed's "damask" table-cloth, woven on his own special patent power loom—but the Garseds moved to Philadelphia in the 1840's, and the Callaghans' output was relatively small (about 100,000 yards of diaper cloth per year, selling at 16 cents per yard).

The fabrics produced by the other six mills were destined to be tailored into workclothes, flannel underwear and night clothes, ticking, and table-cloths. Of the over 5 million yards of goods produced on Chester Creek in 1850, about 1 million were plain-woven gray goods or printing cloths, mostly called calicoes and muslins. They were undoubtedly gray goods as they left the mill (i.e., neither bleached, dyed, or otherwise finished), and in construction ranged from about forty-five by forty-five up to sixty by sixty threads per square inch. Their ultimate use could range from grain bags, if left unfinished, to muslin sheets and calico dress material after being finished by bleaching, dyeing, or calendering in a Philadelphia factory. The rest of the fabrics were mill-finished, with some mill-dyed yarns used in the warp or filling, and in the case of some fabrics like the Chambray used for workshirts, sized in a solution of starch. Chambray was a plain weave; but by far the majority of the approximately 4 million yards of mill-finished goods were twills. Twills, with their fine herringbone construction, were the preferred weave for the ticking, Canton flannel, drills, denims, and stripes, for they could be compacted more easily into a strong, heavy-duty fabric, with construction on the order of sixty-five by sixty-five, than could the square-woven printing cloths. Although twill weaves required looms fitted with more than the two harnesses sufficient for plain weave, the number of harnesses (usually only three, four, or five) was well within the lobe-number capacity of the cam shafts that raised and lowered the harnesses. The manufacturer's price for tickings was 9 or 10 cents per yard; for

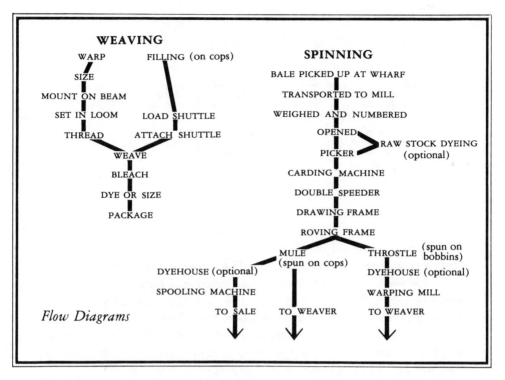

WEAVING

WARP   FILLING (on cops)

SIZE

MOUNT ON BEAM

SET IN LOOM   LOAD SHUTTLE

THREAD   ATTACH SHUTTLE

WEAVE

BLEACH

DYE OR SIZE

PACKAGE

SPINNING

BALE PICKED UP AT WHARF

TRANSPORTED TO MILL

WEIGHED AND NUMBERED

OPENED

PICKER   RAW STOCK DYEING (optional)

CARDING MACHINE

DOUBLE SPEEDER

DRAWING FRAME

ROVING FRAME

MULE (spun on cops)   THROSTLE (spun on bobbins)

DYEHOUSE (optional)   DYEHOUSE (optional)

SPOOLING MACHINE   WARPING MILL

TO SALE   TO WEAVER   TO WEAVER

Flow Diagrams

denims and Canton flannels, 7 or 8 cents per yard; for calico, only 3 cents.

Although the fabrics were "coarse," in the technical sense, this did not mean that they were of poor quality in their lines. From the 1840's on, the Chester Creek manufacturers exhibited at the annual fall fair at the Franklin Institute, at the Delaware County Institute of Science's fair, and on occasion at the national fairs in Washington, D.C., and were not unsuccessful. Daniel Lammot, who produced mostly fine-quality ticking, in 1846 exhibited at the National Fair in Washington, D.C., and his ticking earned special mention; in 1851 he won a gold medal for bed ticking at the Franklin Institute. In 1856 Samuel Riddle received mention at the Franklin Institute's fair for his Canton flannel—"fair merchantable goods." Crozer and others of the Rockdale district's manufacturers exhibited at the Delaware County autumn fair and their goods received favorable notice.

The fabrics were plain, serviceable goods, which passed into the market to be finished and cut up into workclothes, uniforms, underwear, bedding, tablecloths, and other humble articles. Gray, or striped in blue and brown (the dyes were indigo and logwood, bay, and sumac, with copperas as mordant), they were used and no doubt when worn out were for the most part sold as rags for the paper mills. No identifiable fragments have survived into the twentieth century.[3]

Chapter V ❧

THE INVENTORS OF
THE MACHINES

The machines installed in the mills in the 1820's were regarded by few observers as permanent equipment. The knowledgeable manufacturers knew that their mules and throstles were becoming obsolete even as they were being bolted into place and that they would have to be replaced long before they wore out. For textile machinery was still evolving at a rapid rate. In 1837, after their surveys of cotton manufacturing in the state, a committee of the Pennsylvania Senate reported that, because of continual innovation, the useful life of cotton machinery was less than a decade.

> Ten years ago, it was generally supposed, that few improvements in machinery could take place. The machinery of that day, is now useless; and another period of ten years, may make the same difference; manufacturers are subject, in this particular, to a heavy tax. He who advances with the times, must incur the cost of continual improvement; he who lags behind, must lose in the cost of his productions.[1]

It was not until the 1850's that spinning machinery reached a relatively stable plateau in the curve of progress so that, once installed, a card, a throstle, or a mule could be expected, with decent care and minor improvements, to continue working at a profitable level of efficiency for thirty or forty years. And it was not until the 1890's that the power loom reached a comparable degree of completeness.

Each major improvement in the technology, wherever made, eventually put pressure on virtually every textile manufacturer in the world, because each improvement made it possible to make a product more cheaply, or of better quality, or both. Many innovations were, of course, found to be far less important than their sponsors claimed; but some of the minor inventions were effective in special applications, and even the inventions that were to prove useless contributed to a general climate of technological drivenness. The awareness of a constant progress of technology forced every manufacturer to be alert at all times to the degree of obsolescence of his machinery and to be prepared to buy new equipment in order to stay in the technological race.

Crozer was acutely conscious of the significance of technological advances for his own business. He complained in his autobiography that the poor quality of his first machinery—bought used from "a little mill on the Brandywine" for $4,000—was nearly fatal to his enterprise at the start. Not only was it badly made, it was also "badly planned."[2] But he and his mechanics worked with it and he added newer and better machines as well. By 1832 he reported that the cost to him of spinning yarn had decreased over the past seven years entirely as a result of technological progress. "The improvements continually making in machinery has lessened, in a greater or less degree, the cost of spinning in each successive year." But he noted, too, that each year about two-fifths of his profits were spent in buying new machinery.[3] Daniel Lammot remarked also, in connection with his short-lived cotton-spinning venture in Kensington in 1829, the imperative nature of technological change: "In order to work to advantage, I was compelled to improve my machinery, and from my limited capital these improvements were made out of the daily produce of the mill."[4] These necessary expenses for mechanical improvements contributed to his financial embarrassment in that year. Although the Riddles did not explicitly note in their daybook the need for continual upgrading of machinery, there are frequent entries indicating that they were aware of, and keeping up with, technological progress. By October 1832 they had had a spreader installed, and were having trouble with it, finding it difficult to weigh the laps in a reliable way. The spreading machine was described in Montgomery's 1833 Glasgow edition of *The Theory and Practice of Cotton Spinning* as "a recent invention," which had become so popular in Scotland that "there are few Spinning factories in this country where it has not been adopted."[5] Montgomery also discussed the very same difficulty in its use that the Riddles had met with —an irregularity in the weight of the laps if great care were not taken. And concern about the quality of the machinery was expressed by the working people, no doubt because it affected the ease of the work, the productivity of the mill, and the mill's competitive position in the market; the last would in turn affect earnings and job stability. Thus, in writing home to his brother in England a series of answers to questions about prospects for immigration, William Morris reported, among other good features of Phillips' mill, "Our machinery is good. . . ."[6]

Everyone, in fact, in the Chester Creek manufacturing district was thinking about machinery: how to operate it, how to arrange it, how to adjust it, how to maintain and repair it, how to improve it, how to construct it. There were local inventors, local machinists and mechanics, local machinery manufacturers. And outside was an immediately significant American and European industrial community, filled with people manufacturing and improving textile machinery, not only in nearby centers like Wilmington and Philadelphia, but in Patterson, New Jersey; at Matteawan along the Hudson River; in New England; and, of course, in the great textile districts of England, Scotland, and France. What was happening in these places, in the way of invention, affected Chester Creek directly and almost immediately because it affected the price and quality of competing yarns and fabrics.

THE MAIN SEQUENCE OF INVENTIONS

The stream of inventions transforming the cotton manufacture were made almost exclusively in the three countries of England, France, and the United States; and by the 1830's, these inventions were no longer likely to be the work of talented amateurs. In the eighteenth century, a motley group of English and American inventors had produced the great initial inventions: a clergyman, a barber, a vacationing college graduate, and a cottage weaver, among others. Now the situation was different. By the 1820's the significant improvements for the most part were being made in the great machine shops, by professional engineer-machinists whose attention was directed to the solution of classic problems in textile machinery and to the perfection of machine types according to well-established principles. Invention had become a competitive activity in research and development, requiring considerable capital for the support of the inventor, the production of prototypes, the patenting of the product (if possible) in at least three countries, and its marketing and installation in an actual factory.

In America there were seven great centers of innovation in textile machinery: the shops at Saco, Maine; the Lowell machine shops in Lowell, Massachusetts; the Mason and the Whitin machine shops in Taunton, Massachusetts; the various shops in and around Providence, Rhode Island; the shops of the Amoskeag Manufacturing Company in Manchester, New Hampshire; the Matteawan Manufacturing Company, along the Hudson; and the complex of shops at Patterson, New Jersey. The important inventors, men like Paul Moody, the Danforth brothers, John Thorpe, Gilbert Brewster, William B. Leonard, and William Mason, allowed themselves to be employed in these centers because only here could be found the money, the machine tools, the machinists, and the ambition needed to support successful major inventions. But many individual contributions also came from more isolated inventors in machine shops in places like Wilmington, Philadelphia, and even Rockdale.

Although the intensity of work toward particular inventions was determined in large part by the inventors' perceptions of what the market demanded, the possibility of success and the nature of the solutions were determined by a more abstract principle: the implications inherent in the technological paradigm itself. In a sense, the inventor's improvements were prefigured in the possibilities inherent in the machine or in the form of interaction between the machine and the operative. The goal of invention was to increase productivity and decrease cost. The means were three: first, to replicate, in wood and metal and leather, some action of a human operative; second, to perform this action faster than the operative (or than another machine); third, to render the machine less subject to failure and easier to readjust, repair, or replace if and when it did fail. The main principles along which a solution could be sought often were well known and even traditional. Typically, many efforts would be made before one or two successful solutions cast other partial solutions into obsolescence and swept the field. But once such successful solutions were found, it became necessary for virtually all manufacturers to acquire them in order to remain in the price competition.

Hence came the sense of technological pressure even in small places like the Chester Creek manufacturing district. There were no great machine shops there to produce major innovations (although, as we shall see, there were inventors on a smaller scale). Technological progress appeared to the manufacturer, no less than to the operative, as a continuous threat to his economic survival. The manufacturer had to improve his old machines or buy new machines in order to increase productivity and reduce labor cost per unit of production; the operative had to prepare himself for the day when a less skilled person (a young woman, or a child perhaps) could take over his job at an improved machine, or even to see the machine operate by itself, almost like an automaton.

The Self-Acting Mule

A classic example of—and a major event in—the innovative process was the development of the self-acting mule, which was adopted in the Chester Creek area in the early 1840's. Because of the economic importance of this invention, and the social consequences resulting from the changes it made in the role of the mule spinner, we shall go into the history of this invention in some detail.[1]

The mule in its simplest form had been invented in England in the previous century by a young weaver named Samuel Crompton. Crompton was unmarried and lived with his mother and crippled father in an ancient manor house, Hall i' th' Wood, near Bolton in Lancashire. Bolton was a major textile district and Crompton had worked in the area since childhood, first at the spinning wheel, then at the jenny, and finally at the hand loom. He had acquired some formal education by going to school at night and was aware of the development of Arkwright's water frame.

As a hand-loom weaver, Crompton was acutely conscious of a serious shortcoming of both the jenny and the water frame: neither could produce the fine yarn (from the 40's on up) in the quantity that was needed to make the more expensive cloths like muslin. These yarns had still to be imported from India. The limitation of the water frame was the dragging action of the flyer which, as it pulled the attenuated roving around the bobbin, tended to break all but the coarse hard yarns suitable for warp. The jenny, although it could spin fine soft yarns for the filling, was relatively slow and laborious. Crompton's goal was to invent a machine that could quickly and easily manufacture soft yarns in the high numbers. Beginning at age twenty-one, he spent the years from 1774 to 1779 perfecting the device to accomplish this task. He worked entirely alone and made all the parts himself except for some brass gearing.

The mule jenny, or mule, as a concept was a combination of certain parts of Arkwright's water frame (patented in 1769) and Hargreave's spinning jenny (invented in 1767 and patented later). There are three essential actions which any spinning machine must perform: the draw, by which the loose roving is attenuated or drawn out (usually 1 inch of roving being stretched to between 9 and 10 inches of yarn); the twist, by which the attenuated roving is twisted, the amount of twist determining in part the fineness and the hardness of the yarn (for No. 20, made from No. 2 roving, for example, the twist would be on the order of twenty-three turns to the inch); and the winding on, by which the spun yarn is wound onto a spindle or bobbin to form a removable yarn package. The simultaneity of twisting and stretching was the great virtue of the mule. It is a mechanical property of cotton yarn that, when stretched and twisted simultaneously, the stretch goes first to the loose, fat, weak sections. Drawing out these loose spots allowed more twist to be added to them and produced a finer, more even, and stronger yarn.

For the draw, the mule employed pairs of drafting rollers, as did the water frame. The roving ran from a bobbin, entered the first pair of metal rollers, where it was pinched between the leather-covered top roller and the fluted, polished bottom roller, and passed on to the second, similar pair of rollers. But the second rollers were rotating more rapidly than the first, and this drew the roving out lengthwise. From the front rollers, the roving passed to spindles, rotating rapidly (in the early mules, at about 1,700 revolutions per minute). The spindles were slanted, as in the spinning wheel and jenny, so that the yarn ran off the continuously rotating rounded end, thus acquiring twist as on the spinning wheel. As the drawn roving issued from the front rollers, the carriage bearing the spindles retreated for anywhere from 54 to 60 inches, gaining slightly—1 or 2 inches—on the rate of supply from the rollers, and thus further stretching the yarn. At the end of the draw the rollers stopped, clamping the roving tightly. The spindles however continued to rotate, now at double speed, imparting more twist up to the number of revolutions required by the count being made. The carriage might next retreat another 6 inches or so, the spindles still spinning. This slow second stretch, supplemental to the draw, was of great importance to the quality of the finer yarns (but was not necessary to the low counts). The movement of the carriage then stopped and the spindles were rotated briefly backward to free the yarn from the tips (the "backing-off" motion). Next, the yarn was pushed into position for winding by dropping a wire onto the yarn, thus pressing it down onto the cop being formed. Finally, the winding on was accomplished by the spinner pushing the carriage with his knee back toward the rollers while the yarn wound on the rotating spindles. The winding on was the critical operation for the spinner; the best contemporary description of how the spinner accomplished this task is that of Andrew Ure in 1835:

The spinner having seized the faller-rod with his left hand, gives the faller-wire such a depression as to bear down all the threads before it to a level with the bottom of the cop, or conical coil, of yarn formed, or to be formed, round the spindles. While his left hand is thus nicely applied, under the control of an experienced eye, his right hand slowly turns the handle of the pulley in communication with the spindles, so as to give them a forwards rotation, and his knee pushes the carriage before it at the precise rate requisite to supply yarn as the spindles wind it on. Three simultaneous movements must be here very delicately and dexterously performed by the mule-spinner; first, the regulation of the faller, or guide-wire, continually varying in obliquity; secondly, the rotation of the spindles, perhaps 1,000 in number, at a measured speed; and thirdly, the pushing in of the carriage at such a rate precisely as to supply yarn no faster than the spindles take it up. In fine spinning upon a mule . . . where nearly 1,000 threads were spun at once of almost invisible tenuity; the skill and tact required in the operator deserve no little admiration, and are well entitled to a most liberal recompense. In the process of winding-on, so as not to break the threads, and in coiling them into the shapely conoid, called a cop, the talents of the spinner are peculiarly displayed. As the carriage approaches to its primary position, near to the roller-beam, he allows the faller-wire to rise slowly to its natural elevation, whereby the threads once more coil slantingly up to the tip of the spindle, and are thus ready to co-operate in the twisting and extension of another stretch of the mule. Having pushed the carriage home, the spinner immediately sets the mule again in gear with the driving-shaft, by transferring the strap from the loose to the fast steam-pulley, and thus commences the same beautiful train of operations. It is during the few instants after the carriage starts that the lively little piecers are seen skipping from point to point to mend the broken threads. Whenever it has receded a foot or two from the delivering rollers, the possibility of piecing the yarn being at an end, the children have an interval for repose or recreation, which, in fine spinning at least, is three times longer than the period of employment. The spinner likewise has nothing to do till after the completion of the fresh range of threads, when he once more *backs off* the slanting coil, and winds on the "stretch."[2]

The mechanical structure that Crompton built to perform these actions involved three main parts: a fixed frame or head, which included the creel (the rack of roving bobbins) and the drafting rollers; a movable carriage, bearing the spindles, which rolled back and forth on wheels in tracks laid on the floor; and a power train, which as Crompton developed it amounted to a man turning a handle on a fly wheel (the "fly") mounted at one end of the machine, thereby turning a combination of belts, gears, and drums that ultimately turned the rollers and spindles and moved the carriage back and forth. The number of spindles in Crompton's first mule was only forty-eight; but there was no limit in principle, since any number of segments of bobbin-rollers-and-spindle could be set up side by side on a longer or shorter frame and carriage. The limit on size was imposed partly by the need for a completely rigid, correctly aligned machine and partly—and just as importantly—by the limitations of the mule spinner's strength and skill.

Crompton at first used his mule to make fine yarns to weave on his own loom. He did not have enough money to patent his idea (and in fact the principle of the mule was never patented). As his skill increased, Crompton was able to make and sell his fine yarns at enormous prices, ranging from 14 shillings per pound for No. 40 to £2.10s. per pound for No. 80. But he was unable for long to keep his machine a secret and was finally induced to reveal it for the small sum of £70. Mules were soon being produced in great numbers. By 1780 the British cotton trade had increased fivefold, in considerable part because British weavers could now produce fine muslins cheaper than imported Indian fabrics. The machine so swept the British spinning industry that thirty years later there were 4.5 million mule spindles at work in England and Scotland and only 500,000 spindles in jennies and water frames combined.

Improvements were made quickly and for the most part were, like the mule itself, not patentable. By the 1790's, water and steam power were being applied to the movement of the carriage and of the spindles during the draw. The size was increased to several hundred spindles. The limit, however, was about three hundred spindles, because one strong man could turn no more than about three hundred spindles during the winding-on motion, and the winding-on motion still remained manual. The fly was moved from the end to near the center of the machine because that position gave better balance to the movement, and (in England) the machines were operated in pairs facing each other so that one spinner could manage the winding alternately on each machine while the draw (being a simple but slower operation) proceeded mechanically. By 1800, however, the course of improvement of the mule had reached a plateau, for the winding-on action remained a task for the spinner himself to control.

At this plateau, the mule as it was managed in England was an extremely productive device. The cycle time, from the first wind on a bare spindle to the last on the completed cop of No. 80, was about twenty hours; for No. 20, it would be nearer ten hours. During this time, the machine performed about 2,400 draws—roughly 2 draws per minute, for the high English counts, and 4 to 5 per minute for the coarser yarns being spun in America.[3] (This difference accounts for the fact that in American mule rooms the spinner could mind only one mule, the draw being too quick to permit him to turn around and wind on another machine.) The completed cop was a package of yarn about 5 inches in length and 1 1/2 inches in width, with a conical shape at both ends. A cop of No. 20 contained about three hanks, weighed a couple of ounces, and took a day to make; but inasmuch as each machine had on the order of three hundred spindles, its production per day was about three hundred cops, weighing about 45 lbs. in all.

The goal of inventors, from Crompton's time on, was to make the mule completely automatic so as to reduce to a minimum the manufacturer's dependence on the highly skilled, highly paid, and often independent-minded adult male spinners. A number of unsuccessful automatic mules were introduced, one as early as 1790; but it was not until the brilliant English mechanician Richard Roberts, of the firm of Sharp and Roberts of Manchester, turned his attention to the problem that a fully effective solution came. The story is told that Roberts was solicited to undertake the task of developing an effective self-actor by a delegation of manufacturers intent on breaking the spinners' strike in 1824. However that may be, Roberts did solve the problem. It took him five years, two patents, and an outlay of £12,000 by his firm.

The problem in completing the automation of the mule lay in the winding-on action; and the solution was, in a sense, predetermined by the requirement that the mule produce the coreless yarn package which slipped off the spindle when it was complete, called a cop, rather than a spool wound on a bobbin which had to be removed with the yarn. The cop was the most ancient of the package forms, going back to the earliest spinning wheels and before that to the distaff and spindle. It was perfectly adapted to installation in a shuttle, for it unwound without snarling in either direction at high speeds. But its changing size and geometry during the ten to twenty hours of its formation precluded any simple mechanical coupling of spindles to a source of power so as to draw in the carriage and wind on at a constant speed. A substitute had to be developed for the spinner's left hand on the faller wire guiding the yarn up and down the spindle, and for his knee and right hand varying the speed of the spindles, the tension in the yarn, and the distance that the carriage ran in, so that the carriage arrived at its stopping point after winding on exactly the amount of the draw. If it arrived too soon, the yarn remaining in front of the rollers would snarl into lumps that would not stretch out on the next draw. If it arrived too late, all the ends would break at once in the spinning disaster called the "sawney."

Roberts first solved the guide wire problem in his 1825 patent by adding a counter-faller to press the yarn up from the bottom a few inches in from where the faller pressed it down, and by attaching the faller itself by rods to a doubly inclined plane or "copping rail," which moved the wire and thus the yarn up and down on the winding surface of the cop. The whole rail also moved slowly downward on inclined planes as the cycle continued, to move the whole winding action farther and farther up the spindle (see the illustrations on pages 141 and 167).

The other problem was to vary the winding speed of the spindles in direct proportion to the inward speed of the carriage and in inverse proportion to the diameter of the cop at the point of winding on. Roberts solution was so ingenious, and so perfect, that it excited universal admiration in his day and enjoys continued acclaim even in this. It was to drive the spindles during the run in by the unwinding of a chain wrapped around a drum geared to the shaft that drove the spindles. One end of the chain was fixed to the drum, the other to a movable nut mounted on a screw shaft that was attached to a "quadrant arm." The quadrant arm was a quarter wheel, which rotated a fixed distance during the run in of the carriage and at a speed exactly proportional to the speed of the carriage. As the arm moved through its quarter rotation, it pulled the chain off the drum at a varying speed directly communicated to the spindles. Further variation was accomplished by setting the nut so as to be closer or farther from the drum, thus also varying the speed of the spindles by varying the length of chain drawn during the run in. The nut had to be reset frequently during the first part of the cycle while the base of the cop was being built up.

Roberts' achievement provided the breakthrough to real automation of the mule at a level comparable to that of the throstle. Although the spinner at first was required to remain in attendance to reset the quadrant nut as required, this job could be taught simply and even itself be made automatic —so automatic that eventually, in British factories, the spinner could be transformed into an overseer of a dozen or more mules, supervising the work of piecers and creel attenders and making sure that the machinery was operating correctly. Only three years after its introduction, the experienced Scottish manufacturer James Montgomery, in a book widely read in America, enthused:

> The self-acting mule described above, is necessarily complex; but, perhaps, it is one of the most beautiful specimens of mechanical combination that is to be found; exhibiting a rare degree of original invention, highly creditable to the ingenuity and perseverance of the inventor; whilst, at the same time, it furnishes an illustrious example of the wonderful perfection to which machinery has attained in our manufacturing processes.[4]

By 1865, as a result of the continuing success of the self-acting mule, there were 44 million spindles in operation in Great Britain.

Although the patent was announced and the English machines came into production in the early 1830's, Americans do not seem to have hastened to secure them. It was not until 1840 that the self-actor came to America. In 1838 Sharp and Roberts sold one of their self-actors, and the American patent rights, to a partnership including the owner of the Globe Mills of Fall River, Massachusetts. The mule itself was delivered in the spring of 1840. Davol & Durfee immediately began manufacturing the Roberts self-actor, and (in the opinion of the cotton historian William Bagness) "soon revolutionized cotton spinning in America." The labor cost of spinning low-count yarns went down from about 11 cents to (eventually) 3 1/2 cents per hundred hanks. About the same time the experienced American mechanic William Mason—a counterpart of England's Roberts—patented his own self-acting mule and began producing it in his own machine works. It was similar in design to Roberts' but lacked the quadrant arm, replacing that action by other devices. About 1841 the strenuous, if illegal, efforts of Mr. Leonard of Matteawan to secure a model of a third type of self-actor, the Scottish mule, were crowned with success and a few shops produced some of Mr. Smith's self-actors. Mason and Davol & Durfee both produced excellent machinery and shared the American market for years, although other manufacturers later entered the mule-manufacturing business. But the Roberts and Mason mules manifestly outperformed the less effective Scottish mule and its production was discontinued.[5]

The self-acting mule was adopted on Chester Creek and in the Brandywine area about 1842. It was an expensive machine. John Bancroft purchased a "self act[g] Mule" on December 31, 1842, at a cost of $4,439.09.[6] It would appear that this represented the total cost of a new mule fitted with the self-actor mechanism; but the mechanism could be purchased separately, along with a new head-stock, for about a fifth of the cost of a new machine. Riddle seems to have been using self-actors in his new mill at Penn's Grove in 1844, for in January of that year he was paying only five mule spinners (out of a total work force of seventy-four). They were producing from 35,000 to 45,000 hanks every four weeks, at a piece rate of 10 cents per 100 hanks. Ten years before, his ten mule spinners working ten mules at Parkmount were producing 10,000 to 20,000 hanks in the same period at a piece rate (for No. 15) of 11 cents per 100 hanks. It seems likely that Riddle simply moved his mules, replaced the head-stocks with the self-actor mechanism, and got along with half as many spinners (each minding two mules) at 10 percent lower piece rates. This is assuming the yarn counts remained the same; if the counts were raised, the piece rates would be more than 10 percent lower.[7]

Improvements in the Throstle

The economic goal in introducing the self-acting mule was to reduce production costs by increasing the speed and reliability of the machine, thereby allowing a reduction in the piece rates; because the machines worked so nearly automatically, the number of skilled spinners necessary to mind a given number of spindles was simultaneously reduced. The case of the throstle was different. It had already been perfected to the point where relatively unskilled hands, usually young women, could mind these highly automatic machines. The reduction of cost in the throstle room was to be sought principally by improvements in its most vulnerable part: the bobbin and flyer. The traditional flyer, as introduced by the Arkwright generation of water frames, was little different from that invented by Leonardo da Vinci and still commonly used on household spinning wheels. Operating at the high speeds made possible by water power, the flyer tended to wobble and vibrate; minor imbalances, presenting no problem at speeds below four thousand rpm, at higher speeds caused injury and breakage to the yarn and even damage to the flyer itself. The higher speeds were necessary to the spinning of finer yarns.

The throstle inventions were made in America because in England the mule had virtually absorbed the spinning industry. The traditional practice was to fix the flyer to the top of the spindle; flyer and spindle rotated together, pulling the yarn around a more slowly rotating bobbin. The first improvement was the "dead spindle," used at Waltham and Lowell from about 1813. Here the spindle was fixed and was used merely as a pivot on which the flyer turned, the flyer itself being welded to a power pulley that rotated around the spindle. Speeds up to nearly five thousand rpm could be reached with the dead spindle. The next major improvement was the invention of cap and ring spinning about 1828. Both inventions proposed to solve the problem of flyer vibration by making the bobbin the actively rotating, twist-imparting element. In the cap frame (which ultimately proved to be less successful in cotton spinning), the yarn was guided onto the bobbin by the edge of a fixed cap, around which it was dragged by the rotation of the bobbin. The ring frame employed a similar principle, but less cumbersomely, the rotating bobbin pulling the yarn through a guide or eyelet ("traveler"), which also was pulled around the bobbin on a ring —or, in some models, with the ring itself moving.

Ring spinning made possible speeds in the neighborhood of seven thousand rpm, and eventually, after the 1850's, it replaced all other forms on the spinning frame; but initially the "Danforth throstle" was very popular. It was probably in widespread use on Chester Creek by 1850 when the Delaware County Institute of Science awarded a prize to Lownes and Blakely, of Knowlton, for "one box of Danforth throstle bobbins, filled with yarn."[8] Samuel Crozer was one of the judges, and Abraham Blakeley was one of the Crozers' former employees. Alfred Jenks of Bridesburg, in Philadelphia, was manufacturing "ring frame throstles" in 1853.[9] Some time after he left Rockdale, Richard Garsed invented an improved spindle and bobbin arrangement for the ring frame. He did this at a time when concerted efforts were being made to improve the ring spindle, by a number of inventors, so as to enable it to be run at high speeds with less power. The purpose of these efforts was to make it possible to spin a soft filling yarn at as low a cost as on the mule.[10] The problem was eventually solved and the mule thereby doomed to ultimate extinction in the twentieth century. By 1905, the ring frame had nearly taken over the field in America, there being then 17.9 million ring spindles to only 5.2 million mule spindles.[11]

*Richard Garsed and Improvements
in the Power Loom*

Rockdale's only contributor to the main sequence of inventions was Richard Garsed, the young son of John Garsed, manufacturer of power looms.[12] He had been thoroughly steeped in a family tradition of mechanical arts. His father had been a joiner by trade in England before emigrating to the United States. He himself began to work as an operative in a mill in New Hope, Bucks County, in 1827 at the age of eight, and after the family moved to Chester Creek, he continued to work in his father's power-loom factory. In 1837, at the age of eighteen, he began to experiment with increasing the speed of the Garsed looms. At first they ran slowly, at 80 picks (i.e., crossings of the shuttle) per minute; by 1840, when he took over the management of the business, they were running at 140 picks per minute. The means by which this was accomplished have not been recorded and he took out no patent for these improvements.

Garsed also set himself to solve one of the main problems with power looms as they existed in the 1830's: their inability to weave figured fabrics, like damask, automatically. The difficulty had to do with the fact that, for anything except simple weaves, a relatively large number of heddle harnesses was required. Each harness was attached to a rod (called a treadle), which rode on a cam attached to a rotating shaft under the loom. This system of revolving cams replaced the foot treadles of the old hand loom. Because the warps could not be raised more than 6 or 7 inches high to make the shed (the space between the warp ends through which the shuttle passed), the lobes of the cams could not be more than 6 or 7 inches in their maximum extension, and had to be rounded gradually enough to give a reasonably smooth action to the heddles. This posed no problem for the plain, over-and-under weaves used for muslins and calicoes, for which the shed was formed by two harnesses only. Nor did simple twills—such as Canton flannels, denims, and tickings—require an elaborate harness system, three or four being sufficient. Very simple satins could also be made with four harnesses. But, because of the geometry of the cams, four or five harnesses was the limit. Shedding required that only one cam—and thereby one harness—be raised at a time; and, with the necessary dimensions, there was space for only three or at the most four cam lobes to be introduced before a given lobe came into raised position again. Adding more cams would simply mean that the shed would become too narrow for safe passage of the shuttle.

By 1842, Richard Garsed had solved the problem and exhibited at the annual fair at the Franklin Institute a sample of "cotton and worsted damask table covers." The judges were impressed by the "novelty and excellence" of the Garsed damask, "a new article in our manufactures, which promises successful competition with the imported." The Garseds were awarded a silver medal. They exhibited "marseilles toilet covers" (a heavily figured fabric with an embossed effect) in 1844 and received an honorable mention, and in fact continued to receive awards for various fabrics up until 1850.[13]

The contribution of Richard Garsed to the development of the power loom thus lies in that part of the power-loom paradigm which may be called the "cam-and-harness" action. But the cam-and-harness action is only one way of forming a shed; there is also a type of action in which a harness containing a fixed set of heddles is not used at all, each heddle being pulled by a separate cord or wire, as in the old hand-operated draw and Jacquard looms and the newer dobby loom. Eventually the dobby and Jacquard principles proved to be the most practical for complex weaves, because they could be used not only for relatively simple damasks but also for elaborate tapestries. Dobby looms could manage fifty or more harnesses; the Jacquard program of punched cards could manage thousands of combinations of warp threads. Garsed's inventions, and others in the cam-and-harness tradition, thus were an interim solution, to become obsolete when the dobby and Jacquard-programmed looms came into extensive use in American weaving mills.

The patent for his first cam-and-harness invention Garsed received in July 1846. His solution to the multiple cam problem was to take an old mechanical principle—the production of a reciprocating action by means of a grooved cylinder—and combine it with the motion of a rotating cam. Instead of requiring as many cams as there were harnesses, Garsed's device used only one cam. On either side of the cam extended a cylindrical hub. The cam and cylinder were both carefully grooved around the circumference and each circumferential groove connected with the adjacent groove by a diagonal. There was one less groove than the total number of harnesses on the hubs plus one on the cam. As many treadles as there were harnesses rode in the grooves, one riding at all times on the cam lobe. As the cam shaft rotated, the cam and cylinder slid back and forth on the shaft, the lobe of the cam raising each harness in order as its treadle passed over the cam. In principle, half a dozen or more harnesses could be easily controlled in this way, because the treadle of inactive harnesses simply rode out the rotation of the shaft on the cylindrical hub.

Garsed claimed that this shedding process worked at a higher speed than those relying on an ordinary cam system (and certainly it worked faster than shifting cams by hand or using the hand loom).[14] Garsed's biographer maintains that the scroll-cam, patented in 1846, "greatly simplified the power loom, and was almost universally adopted on the sliding cam loom."[15] Garsed went on (after leaving Rockdale) to invent an even more complex shedding system, for which he received a patent in 1849.[16]

In other ways the power loom was being improved during this period. The Draper self-acting rotary temple (to keep the selvage of the finished cloth from pulling in as it was wound on the beam) was in common use by the 1830's, effecting an increase of loom productivity of about 15 percent. (The saving lay in eliminating the labor time required for the weaver to adjust the old temples by hand.) Automatic stop actions, which detected faults such as broken warp or filling yarn, or a shuttle being caught in the shed as the harness changed, were developed in the 1830's and 1840's, greatly reducing the amount of time required to supervise the looms and permitting economies on labor. One major desideratum was not achieved, however, until the Northrop loom was perfected in the 1890's. This was a fully automatic cop-and-bobbin changing action, which would permit filling in the shuttle without stopping the loom. In the 1830's, a weaver had to put new cops into shuttles anywhere from five hundred to a thousand times per day. In order to save time, the weaver pulled the leader of filling through the eyelet near the end of the shuttle by "sucking in." In the process, he inevitably inhaled a certain amount of dust and lint. Improvements in shuttle design, and eventually the fully automatic Northrop loom, saved both time and the weaver's health.[17]

THE LESSER INVENTORS OF CHESTER CREEK

Although Richard Garsed was the only member of the Chester Creek community in this period to contribute to the main sequence of inventions, he was not the only inventor. The lower Delaware Valley—like most other parts of the country—was buzzing with news of mechanical progress. Much was being done, particularly in nearby Chester County, in the way of improvements in agriculture: new methods of fertilizing the fields, new crops, new breeds of livestock, new plows, mowing machines, threshers, and reapers. Interest in machinery was almost universal; mechanical progress appeared almost as an agency of millennium. Invention was usually a matter of making a small improvement on a machine already in widespread use. Some such improvements were patented; but often they were not patented at all because they were regarded, by their originators, as processes for use in their own shops or factories rather than as new objects for sale or lease. Some improvements involved no new gadgetry at all and were simply a rearrangement or recombination of the old (as in the shift to complete process manufacturing), or an alteration of a procedure (as by repeating a step), or an experiment in changing the conditions of the process (such as temperature, time, pressure, or tension). Thus the history of patents is less than the history of invention and far less than the history of mechanical progress. What is significant is the constant and intense concern with improving mechanical processes at all levels, from the unpatentable empirical discovery of a better schedule for oiling spindles to the highly patentable main sequence invention of the self-acting mule.

Of particular interest to us are five figures: John S. Phillips, who invented and patented an industrial filter; the Riddle brothers, who seem to have devised a new method for sizing warps; J. Dutton, cousin or brother of Thomas Dutton the tanner, who made the industrial belts for the Riddles' (and probably for other manufacturers') machinery; the family of Henry Moore, who held a patent on a nail-making machine; and Nathan Sellers, manufacturer of wire card teeth.

John S. Phillips and His Filter for Turbid Liquors

In 1828 Phillips received a patent for "an improvement in the construction of filters, for separating the impurities from turbid liquors." The invention was noticed in the *Journal* of the Franklin Institute, but unfortunately Phillips had advised the editor that he was planning to make some additions which would be the subject of a future patent; further description was deferred until the future patent should be granted, "when the whole shall be particularly noticed."[1] Apparently he never took out another patent on his filter, and so the *Journal of the Franklin Institute* never printed an account of the whole thing as was its custom. With the Patent Office fire in 1836, the official record was destroyed. Phillips never bothered to reconstruct the patent and no other record seems to have survived.

Although it is conceivable that the Phillips filter was intended to remove lumps and other impurities from the thick starch solution (a "turbid liquor") used for sizing warp yarn, it is more likely that it applied to sugar manufacturing, in which he was still engaged in 1828 with Joseph S. Lovering. He probably did not bother to perfect the device after the business—and the friendship—ended. As described in 1833 in Benjamin Silliman's *Manual on the Cultivation of the Sugar Cane, and the Fabrication and Refinement of Sugar,* the new method of refining by steam, then being practiced by

Joseph Lovering and his new partner Merritt Canby in their Philadelphia factory, depended critically upon the filtering process. The filter, noted Silliman, had been patented in 1828, and its construction and function were described in general terms:

> The syrup . . . is raised to a slight simmer and the first scum removed; when it is let into the filter, which is situated in the next story below and directly under the clearing cistern. The external part of the filter is a strong box; it contains a great number of filtering frames, which are covered with a kind of Russia duck, or cotton cloth. The frames are arranged vertically; they are made of tinned copper, crimped, so as to present vertical grooves on each side against the canvass, which is made into flat bags, with a hem about an inch broad and one-eighth of an inch thick, all around the mouth of each bag, and a frame is put into each bag to distend it. The distended bags being put into the filtering box, with their mouths downwards, and all the hems pressed tightly together, the fluid percolates from the outside of the bag to the inside, trickles down the grooves, and runs off by a cock. The pans prevent the turbid liquor from running down outside of the frames, and, at the same time, serve to keep the bags at a small distance from each other. . . . The syrup, at an elevated temperature, and aided by hydrostatic pressure, traverses the filter, whence it flows perfectly clear and bright to the receiving cistern.[2]

It would seem that after the dissolution of the partnership, Lovering continued to use the process he and Phillips had developed together. At that time, only three other sugar refineries were using this process, one in Philadelphia, one in New York, and the third in New Orleans. All the rest employed blood and eggs—in large quantities—to precipitate impurities, a process less effective than the steam, filter, and vacuum system, and possessing the added disadvantage of filling the neighborhood with the stench of rotten eggs and putrefying blood. In all likelihood, at least in the beginning, Phillips also manufactured the cotton cloth used in the filters.

Lovering's refinery was given high praise by Silliman, who was one of the most eminent American chemists of the day. Lovering, of course, went on to wealth as a maker of superior sugar in his anthracite-fired steam refinery in Philadelphia, and to fame as the practical chemist who, by devising a method of processing it, made sorghum a major source of refined sugar.

The Riddles and Their Sizing Trough

One of the classic problems of the weaving process was presented by the need to "size" or "dress" the warp threads in order to lubricate and toughen them. The old-fashioned method, used by hand-loom weavers for centuries, was to brush a soupy mixture of oil and starch made from flour onto the warp after it had been wound onto the take-up beam. This operation required halting the actual weaving while the size was applied by hand; and, worse than that, the weaver had to wait for the warp to dry before he could pass the shuttle again. With the advent of power looms early in the nineteenth century, both in England and America, the demand for increased productivity led to the invention of devices to spin the warp yarn on a special warping frame (a variety of throstle), which built it upon a beam rather than a bobbin, in order to eliminate the time spent on the warping mill. The need to reduce the time the weaver spent dressing the warp led to the development of mechanical dressers that automatically applied sizing before the warp went into the loom. Radcliffe's dresser of 1803, for instance, applied sizing to a temporary beam as it came from the warping frame, dried it by fans or (after 1832) on hot cylinders, and wound it on a back beam ready to be inserted into the loom. Warping frames and dressers, however, were expensive (the Lowell products, for instance, sold for about $600 and $1,000 respectively).

When the Riddles set up their weaving operation in 1833 and 1834, they could not take advantage of all this new technology. Their mules could not spin warp yarn onto beams, only onto cops, which then had to be rewound onto beams. Nor did they invest in one of the expensive dressers. Instead, they employed a method of their own which was never patented but which anticipated by several years the English invention of the tape-sizing machine or slasher. The Riddles assembled the system themselves; like so many of the "improvements" of the period, it was an unpatentable new process rather than a patentable new gadget.[3]

The Riddle system was to rewind their warp yarn from mule-spun cops onto a beam by use of a warping mill. The ends were then drawn, in parallel, through a trough filled with hot size, heated by steam-filled copper pipes in the bottom. The steam was produced in a copper boiler over a furnace burning anthracite coal (hauled from Norristown, on the Schuylkill River). The boiler arrived in November 1833 (purchased from James Houghton); not until July of next year were the copper pipes installed in the trough. It is not clear how the sized warp was dried; very likely it was put through rollers to squeeze out excess size and then passed over steam-heated plates or cylinders as it was wound on the loom back beam.

Whether the Riddles themselves developed the system or found it in use, perhaps in Houghton's and Garsed's mills, is not likely to be known. But it doubtless was effective in accomplishing its purpose—to size the warp in a particularly smooth and effective way, by drawing warp yarn through hot size (which was much less lumpy than cold size), and then packaging the warp so that it reached the weaver completely sized and dry, ready for uninterrupted use.[4]

The Duttons and the "New Planet"

The Duttons were an old Quaker family. They had arrived with William Penn in 1682 and, according to tradition, had trudged up the Indian trail from Chester to occupy their five hundred-acre farm along the creek. Their tract now lay just over the hill from Rockdale and was the site of the tannery, operated by Thomas Dutton, which made the leather driving belts for the mills in the neighborhood. A generation before, a branch of the family had purchased the Forest Dale mills, just below Knowlton, where the road (now known as Dutton's Mill Road) crossed the creek. This branch of the family were country millers, operating a grist- and sawmill for local people.

In the 1830's, the proprietors of these two establishments were, respectively, Thomas Dutton at the tannery and Jonathan Dutton at Forest Dale mills. Thomas Dutton, born in 1769, was already an elderly man, thrice-married, corpulent, with an interesting history. He told tales of the time when the British Army under Lord Cornwallis camped at Village Green after defeating the Americans at the Battle of Brandywine. He described how the British hung two of their own soldiers who had plundered local houses and molested young women; they remained hanging from the limbs of an apple tree on a farm in Aston after the Army moved away. Dutton even remembered hearing the cannon salute at the signing of the Declaration of Independence in Philadelphia when he was seven years old. Young Dutton built the tannery in 1790 and followed the trade until 1808, when he moved with his family to the Quaker mission of the Seneca Indians at Tunessassa, at the edge of the Seneca reservation, just across the Pennsylvania line in New York State. There he remained as manager for four years, during the time when the Quakers and the prophet Handsome Lake and his half brother, the old Chief Cornplanter, revitalized the decaying Indian culture by introducing a new religion and modern agricultural methods. After that, for four years he directed the Delaware County Poorhouse. On returning to Aston after the death of his first wife and his remarriage, he took up his tanning business again. He achieved some local notoriety as an innovator for establishing a stationary steam engine at his works, made by William Parrish in Philadelphia—the first, it is alleged, in Delaware County.

Jonathan Dutton was a cousin of Thomas and at this time the miller of Forest Dale. This Dutton was an inventor—one might almost say an indiscriminate inventor, for he experimented constantly with all sorts of new processes and machines, and sometimes even patented his devices. Of immediate relevance, for instance, to the needs of his cousin and the local industries was his "Clasp to Unite Belting." A problem with leather industrial belts was, and is, that they have to be made up of sections of cowhide. The usable portion of a hide is only about 5 feet long and 4 or 5 feet wide, from the back and sides of the animal. Any belt longer than 5 feet therefore has to be made up of 5-foot (or less) sections; and the sections must be firmly joined. Dutton's description of his clasp gives some insight into the methods then in use:

> This clasp, for uniting any kind of belting, on wheels or pulleys, for propelling different kinds of machinery, is a very economical plan for tightening the slack of belts, &c. as it is strong, durable, and makes a smooth splice, and is done in one-tenth of the time that a thong splice can be made, and is also 50 per cent. better than that or a buckle. It consists of two plates of iron or brass, 1/2 or 3/4 of an inch wide, with their edges made circular, so as to fit the face of the pulleys, and connected together with three or four screws or whatever number is necessary; the taped plate which the screws connect in should be rather thicker than that under their heads, to allow a sufficiency of thread in it for strength.
>
> To make the connection, the belt being the right length, lay the flesh sides of the ends together, as a shoemaker holds his work to close it,— lay a plate on, mark and make the holes through,—then put both plates on and screw them together,—then open it and hammer the seam inside. . . .[5]

In 1848, Dutton gathered together the accounts of his various inventions, both patented and unpatented, and published a description of them in a twenty-eight-page pamphlet entitled *The New Planet, Containing a Degree of Novelty: Being an Effort Toward the Pleasure, Comfort and Convenience of all Citizens.* He introduced the work with a little philosophical essay which breathes, in simple language, the climate of enthusiasm for invention of the time:

The subject of this small treatise is interesting, directly, to almost every person, as it is calculated to cast some reflection on new theory, or lead to new ideas, in this rapid progressing age of improvement,—when the apparel with which we are clad, the vehicles in which we ride, the seats on which we repose, the publications which we read, the music which soothes and delights us, the articles which furnish our dwellings, the implements of husbandry, the vessels which float upon the ocean, the artificial channels for the transportation of the productions of the soil from one part of the country to supply the wants of another, all have incorporated within them the inventor's skill, and have attained their present degree of perfection through his labor; and man, whatever may be his occupation, scarcely moves during the livelong day, or performs a single act during the whole of his routine of business or pleasure, without having constant occasion to thank departed inventors for the convenience, facilities, and comfort afforded by their mechanism.

With respect to our primary and most elegant pieces of mechanism, however incomprehensible they may appear to the inexperienced, they are, in the eye of the practical man, mere elegant modifications and combinations of a few simple principles.[6]

The body of the work gave descriptions and drawings of no less than sixteen novelties: an ornamental fountain (covered by a design patent); a patented method for cooling and freezing water by means of the alternate compression and expansion of air; a plan for cutting ice by means of a steam-powered rotary saw mounted on a steam-powered sled; a machine for kneading dough ("This is meant to do away with the practice among bakers of kneading the dough with their hands—even the bare feet have been represented to have been used"); a portable chain pump; a pressure fountain pump; a method of preventing ice from forming on sidewalks by means of steampipes under the pavement; a sportsman's boat with secret (underwater) oars ("a very successful contrivance for getting within shooting distance of wild geese, black duck, or any kind of water fowl"); the belting clasp noticed earlier; a machine for shelling corn; a mincing machine for the sausage maker; a system for manufacturing ice in an icehouse by spraying water in fine drops against the walls; a similar method for making ice in the open field; a substitute for the water wheel, in the form of an endless chain carrying buckets; a vertically shafted windmill with collapsing vanes (a re-invention of the old Persian windmill); and a proposal to provide locomotive engines with boxes of sand to scatter on the rails and so prevent the wheels from slipping in snow or ice.

Of all these devices, the refrigeration equipment and the endless-chain water power would seem to have been potentially the most significant. The cooler and ice-making machine, while perhaps not widely used, was based on the same thermodynamic principles as the refrigerators of a century later; the hydraulically efficient chain wheel, being designed to make possible the use of small streams as well as large, and obviating the need for big, expensive wheels and large wheelpits to accommodate them, probably was never widely used. The idea had been current for years, however (in fact, patents for overshot strap or chain water wheels dated back to 1809), and the 1831 edition of Jacob Bigelow's *Elements of Technology* contained a description of the chain wheel and a drawing virtually identical with Dutton's.[7] Furthermore, the hydraulic turbine—compact, cheap, easy to install, and efficient for applications, like driving cotton machinery, where horsepower requirements were known and constant—was being introduced from France during the 1840's and would soon be installed in the mills on Chester Creek.[8]

Thomas Odiorne, Henry Moore, and Their Old Sable Works

The Henry Moore from whom Phillips and Lewis leased their cotton factory in 1825 was the owner of an old forge built in the previous century by the Pennells. Moore had acquired it from one Thomas Odiorne of New Hampshire. It was Odiorne who had bought it from the Pennells and named it Old Sable Forge, after the family foundry of the same name in New England. The Moores and the Odiornes were intricately connected by a maze of cousinships and marriages, and were further related by marriage to the Willcox brothers of Ivy Mills, who had wedded a pair of sisters whose mother was an Odiorne.

The Odiorne family had a variety of industrial interests. Thomas had gone into cotton manufacturing as early as 1791 in Exeter, New Hampshire.[9] Later, in 1814, he owned the Old Sable Forge which supplied the nails used in building the Boston Manufacturing Company's factory at Waltham;[10] about the same time, he had an interest in a foundry on French Creek in Pennsylvania (not far from West Chester).[11] The acquisition of a foundry on Chester Creek was therefore only one chapter in the history of an expanding family business. Thomas Odiorne bought the mill in 1808 and sold it to his cousin and brother-in-law (Captain Moore had married Thomas's sister Ann) in 1815. Moore held it until 1832.

The Odiornes were an educated family—"Boston people of that cultured kind," as Mary Willcox's biographer put it.[12] The brothers George (1764–1846) and Thomas (1769–1851) were the active leaders of the clan in the early 1800's. George left school at the age of eighteen and began his career as a merchant in Exeter; in 1799 he moved to Boston with his brothers to establish a dry-goods importing firm and spent two years in England as the company's agent; between 1805 and 1809 he was the cashier of a Boston bank. Thomas acquired a more extensive formal education, graduating from Dartmouth in 1791 and going into the book business. He took advantage of this connection to publish some volumes of his own poetry that celebrated the progress of mankind. In 1792, for instance, he produced *The Progress of Refinement,* which asserted a divinely planned coordination of man's development in science, in the fine arts, and in virtue.[13]

In 1806, the three brothers bought a mill seat at Malden, Massachusetts, and erected a nail factory. Shortly thereafter they bought, for $10,000, the rights to the patented nail-cutting and -heading machine of one Jesse Read, and began to manufacture cut nails automatically. As Read patented successive improvements on his nail-making apparatus over the next twenty years, the brothers bought them up one by one; finally, in 1829, Thomas Odiorne himself took a patent on "nail machine feeding machinery."[14] Although there was some temporary sales resistance from conservative carpenters, and the nail mill at first lost money, it eventually became successful.[15] It was probably in order to control their supply of nail rods, which were generally made from Pennsylvania iron, that the Odiornes acquired the forges on Chester Creek and French Creek. By 1815, the manufacture of machine-made "cut-nails" was an "enormous industry," for the manufacturers could make such nails far faster and far cheaper than the old wrought-iron nails, which had to be individually hand-fashioned.[16]

Jesse Read and the Odiornes were not the first Americans in the cut-nail business. One of the oldest patents had been taken by Jacob Perkins in 1795; and he and others before and after, both in England and America, were busy making improvements from 1790 on into the 1850's. Perkins was forced out of his partnership in the nail factory at Amesbury, Massachusetts; his place was taken by Paul Moody, later to become famous as the mechanical genius of Waltham and Lowell. The Odiornes and their nail factory at Malden, and Moody and the Amesbury works, eventually came into conflict over the issue of patent infringement. Thomas Odiorne sued Amesbury in 1819, alleging infringement of Read's patent; the suit was dismissed on the grounds that Jacob Perkins' patent already covered the process.[17]

By 1820, when the census takers recorded American manufactures, the Old Sable Works on Chester Creek—a rolling and slitting mill and nail factory—was consuming 150 to 200 tons of bar iron per year and employing ten men. The principal product was nails, with some hoop and sheet iron, sold in part to neighboring enterprises (the Riddles would buy their nails from Moore). The nails were made on five "patent Saving-Labour nail machines . . . which cut & head nails at one operation."[18]

Old Sable probably bought bar iron from Sharpless's Old Sarum Forge, up the creek a few miles, or from the ironworks on French Creek. The Old Sable Forge reheated the iron, rolled it out into broad sheets 1/2 to 1/4 inch thick, and then slit these sheets into long strips as wide as the nails were long. The nail machine received the red-hot strips, cut them into the roughly tapering form of the finished nail, and formed a flattened head. Some human skill was still required, as an early description of a nail factory near Patterson, New Jersey, reveals:

> The human portion of the machine holds in his hands a staff or stick, one end of which rests in a prop behind him for the sake of steadiness, and upon the other end is a clamp with which the plate is held. As the action of the cutter is not reciprocal, it is necessary that the plate should be turned at each cut; and as the machine moves rather rapidly, this is a delicate operation which the feeder only acquires after considerable practice. The end of the plate being square the first clip from each is an abortion, and this accounts for the fact of so many of these misshapen nails being found in each cask.
>
> When the plate is cut up the feeder throws his clamp over a spur which projects from the side of the machine, pries it open, throws the remnant aside to be reheated with the rest of the scraps, seizes another plate with a pair of pincers, fixes it in his clamp, and goes on as before.
>
> The machines are gauged to cut different-sized nails, and their speed decreases in the same ratio as the size of the nail increases. Thus the machine which cuts a "twenty-penny" moves at about one-eighth the speed of another which is cutting "eight-pennies."[19]

Although the Odiornes' nail patents were based on the work of others, Thomas Odiorne did take out two unrelated patents of his own, both in 1835, one for a ship's pump, and the other for a steam whistle to signal the alarm "when the water is low and perilous in a steam boiler."[20] The boiler alarm could conceivably have been of value in his own enterprises, if any of them made use of stationary steam engines to power the forge machinery. But the main power was still water in 1832 when, before the date of the invention, Henry Moore sold the forge on Chester Creek to Richard S. Smith and Old Sable's fires went out forever.

Nathan Sellers and the Making of Card Teeth

Nathan Sellers, even before the Revolution, is said to have been the first American to enter the business of wire drawing and wire working; during the war he was released from military service because these skills were needed in the making of paper currency and other essential paper products. He used fine brass wire to make flat woven molds, which he supplied to the Willcoxes at Ivy Mills and the Gilpins on the Brandywine. These molds were employed to scoop up a film of rag pulp from the surface of the vat; the water would drain out through the spaces in the molds. Later he went into the business of making card teeth for carding cloths and fillets. Card teeth were made of fine iron wire about 3/32 of an inch in diameter. The Sellers firm would make the wire teeth, bend them, and then send them out to a veritable army of thousands of women and children who set them in leather. (Later he took on as partner John Brandt, the Lancaster mechanic, who had invented a machine for setting card teeth automatically.)

Sellers' wire came from the Old Sable Forge as a secondary product of the earlier, pre-Odiorne nail-making process. In the old process, the slitting rollers produced long, thin rods, which could be cut into wire nails, or slit rods reworked into wire. The first task in making wire from slit rods was to transform the cross section from square to circular; next, the wire was drawn through a die to reduce the cross section and elongate it; and finally the drawn wire was coiled by hand and annealed (reheated in an oxygen-free container).

Before the Revolution, Sellers attempted unsuccessfully to mechanize the first part of the process at Pennell's forge on Chester Creek (which then produced old-fashioned wrought-iron hand-finished spike nails). As his grandson recalled:

> Grandfather induced the proprietor of this slitting mill to erect a furnace for reheating these rods and to have some grooves turned in his plate rolls, thinking that by passing two or three times through these grooves would give a good round wire rod; but it was not a success, the slit rods were rough and irregular on their corners; on passing through the rolls corner pins were driven into the rods not perfectly welded, so that the wire drawn from them was full of flaws.[21]

So they reverted to the older blacksmith's process of pounding the repeatedly heated rods into cylindrical form with a water-powered triphammer, using a semicircular die as a bedplate, and cracking off the scale by hand. The hot wire was then drawn through a die with the desired cross section, lengthening it as well as making it finer. And finally, the coils of wire were annealed in a special process developed by Sellers. The annealing, which was necessary to make the wire more malleable and ductile (and thus less subject to breakage while being formed and set as teeth in card clothing), required heating to a high temperature and then gradual cooling. Annealing in the open furnace permitted extensive oxidation of the surface of the wire; the resulting scale was conventionally removed in a bath of sulfuric acid. But this damaged the wire and made it brittle again. Sellers' solution was to heat and gradually cool the coils of wire in sealed earthenware or iron pots, so tightly packed with wire and wet clay that all air was excluded. The wire thus annealed came out of the pots as bright and shiny as when first drawn. Sellers invented the annealing process before 1780. He never patented it and he even communicated it to an English firm which, after the unsuccessful experiment at Pennell's forge, was supplying him with wire for card teeth. The English firm successfully kept the secret until the turn of the century when the retort method of annealing was reinvented in France and reintroduced into England.

Sellers also devised other improvements for his wire business, such as a machine for weaving the faces of wire molds. But for the most part the improvements were intended not as patentable inventions, a source of income in themselves, but—as in the case of Crompton and his mule—as labor-saving devices for use in Nathan Sellers' own business.[22]

THE INTERNATIONAL FRATERNITY OF MECHANICIANS

The production machines—the machines that transformed raw materials into consumer products, that generated power, that propelled bullets—were made by a small group of highly skilled men then termed "mechanicians." They designed these machines and often themselves worked with forge and lathe, and hammer, cold chisel, and file, to make the mules and looms, the steam engines, the firearms parts, and all the other machinery that made up the Industrial Revolution. These men were also the inventors and users of machine tools—the machines that made machines.

The presence of a substantial cadre of mechanicians in England, France, and the United States was probably a main reason for the rapidity of the spread of manufacturing in those countries. The production machines themselves did not move easily across oceans until the latter part of the nineteenth century. Thus, although Great Britain was the source of most of the basic *ideas* for textile machinery, few if any of her machines were actually being imported into America. Whether English or American in concept, American machines were made in America in American machine shops, largely by American-born machinists. To be sure, there were emigrant English machinists and they were an important source of mechanical information as well as manpower. Such men as the Hodgson brothers, the Brandywine machinists who made throstle rollers for the Chester Creek manufacturers, and James Wagstaff (probably a relative of Hugh Wagstaff, the cotton spinner), also of Brandywine, who made spindles, were however probably not bringing over uniquely British machine tool designs.[1] For America already had a well-established machinists' trade, which was attracting many extremely talented men and even young gentlemen.

The machinist's practice in the early nineteenth century merged imperceptibly into that of the blacksmith, the iron master, the machine maker, the engineer, the draftsman, the artist, the inventor, and the natural scientist. Established and successful manufacturers and merchants—men of good family—were quite willing to commit their sons as apprentices in machine shops. The trade was an old one and had a sense of community, which encouraged the transmission of technological information by methods of demonstration and practice, as well as by the immigration of experienced operatives and the travel of American machinists abroad.

Although some successful mechanicians were manufacturers, the culture of the machinist was fundamentally different from that of the manufacturer: the machinist thought with his hands and eyes, and when he wished to learn or communicate he made a drawing or a model; the manufacturer and manager thought with his larynx, as it were, and when he wished to learn or communicate, did so with words, in conversation or in writing. The machinist had dirty hands from working with tools; the manager had cramped hands from writing.

In contrast to the British machine shops, where the workers, "according to the English plan of division of labor, were only perfect on a single branch," the American shops emphasized the acquisition of general technical skills and the perfection of machinery. George Escol Sellers, in his visit to England in 1832, was constantly amazed at the technological backwardness of the British machinist trades (even in their most advanced forms, as in the famous Maudslay Works). In England there was a strict specialization of labor, some "men working a lifetime with hammer and cold chisel," others devoting themselves to the lathe, and all (with the exception of planers) working with relatively clumsy tools. Observed Sellers:

As a boy I had worked on a Maudslay single mandrel ungeared lathe, with one of his slide rests that had been imported as something extraordinary, the lathe being driven by a great wheel with a man at [a] handcrank. I have the impression that this slide rest started both Tyler and Lukens to designing their improved one, which, for solidity and firmness, so increased the amount of work that the Maudslay rest was laid aside and the lathe transferred to the pattern shop as a light-running wood lathe long before I went to England. Therefore I was much surprised at finding that class of tools without any improvement in daily use.

I had been accustomed to see in our American shops, although many of their lathes had wooden shears with light cast-iron guide shears bolted on them, the rests or tool carriers traversed by chain or pinion in rack, with heavy suspended weight to hold them firm on the guide shears, turning off shavings of more than double the depth and feed of anything I saw in the Maudslay Works. It did appear to me that tools were not keeping up with the requirements of the times, but I noticed under construction a heavy double shear lathe, and two planers in use. This was evidence that the proprietors were looking towards saving manual labor. I thought if they could see the festoons of great wrought-iron shavings from the lathes of Rush and Muhlenburg, of Bush Hill, Philadelphia, or of Kemble's West Point Works, New York, as hung in their offices, it would spur them on in that direction. . . .

When I took in my hand their heavy, short, stubby cold chisels, their short, clumsy, broad-faced, short handled hand hammers, I felt it would be impossible for me to handle such tools with any prospect of approximating their results; I would as soon expect to reach them with the stone cutter's round wooden mallet. The evolution in form and make of such tools had in America far outstripped England.[2]

Another notable feature of the American shops was the heterogeneity of workers. In the Sellers' shops one might meet, work side by side with, and learn from, a veritable social potpourri: German princes traveling incognito to learn the mechanician's art, gentlemen's sons, college professors, professional artists, English artisans with literary tastes, third-generation American mechanics. American workmen tended to be respectable, literate, independent, jealous of seniority and privilege, and ready to fight foreigners: John Morton Poole at Matteawan recounted how an English master mechanic was beaten up by the man he replaced, and the youthful George Escol Sellers learned with dismay of the plot to abuse his friend Henri Mogeme, the wandering German mechanic of noble blood.[3]

The career of George Escol Sellers' young drafting teacher, John

Henry Hopkins, illustrates the quality of men who entered the mechanicians' fraternity in this period. Born in Dublin in 1792, he had emigrated to America with his parents and lived for a while in Bordentown, New Jersey, with the French émigrés who concentrated there. He was taught by his mother, a professional teacher, to paint and draw and play the cello; he colored the engraved plates for Wilson's *Birds of America*.[4] On his arrival in Philadelphia, he supported himself in part by teaching mechanical drawing to a class of young, aspiring machinists, including the five-year-old George Escol, and by playing the cello. He also served a mechanic's apprenticeship in the Mars Works of Oliver Evans and for a time lived with the Evans family, studying broadly in mineralogy and chemistry. In 1813 he moved from Philadelphia to manage an iron furnace in the Ligonier Valley. Then he moved to Pittsburgh, studied law, and became one of that city's leading attorneys. But, now converted from deism to Christianity, he abandoned law for the Episcopal ministry, and eventually became the first Bishop of Vermont. In this post he gained notoriety as a defender of slavery although his actual position on the subject, articulately presented in sermons, tracts, and books, was merely that the Bible did not explicitly prohibit slavery.[5]

The Philadelphia Mechanicians

The master mechanics who made the production machines for other men to use in England and America were, in the early decades of the nineteenth century, a small group of a few hundred men, all of whom knew each other by sight or reputation. As a recent mechanician remarked in his *History of Machine Tools*, "over the years those interested formed a closely knit federation."[6] Each locality had its own network, but the networks overlapped as apprentices traveled to gain experience and the journeymen and masters to gain fame and fortune.

In the Philadelphia area, in the 1820's and 1830's, there were a number of well-known machine makers who employed others in their shops and gave leadership to the trade; there were also plenty of lesser figures. In general, even the more prominent proprietors of the specialized machine shops did not make the great fortunes of the successful merchants, nor were they or their families usually members of "society." As the son of Coleman Sellers—one of the most famous mechanicians of the day—said of his father:

As to Fathers social position in Phila. it was all he wanted. Neither he nor Mother made any pretentions to the St. Peter's set or the codfish aristocracy that had better been called. High wines sugar rum and molasses with a spice of African blood.[7]

They were respected by the gentlemen merchants but were not part of their social world.

In Philadelphia, and its surburban industrial suburbs to the north, some names were long distinguished. In Bridesburg, Alfred Jenks maintained his great shops for making textile machines; later, Richard Garsed would be prominent there also. Oliver Evans, the early inventor of automatic flour-milling machinery and of high-pressure steam engines for river steamboats, had his foundry and shops, the Mars Works, on Spring Garden Street; after his death in 1819, it was continued by his sons-in-law, James Rush and John P. D. Muhlenburg. On Market Street between Fifth and Sixth was the store and paper mold and card manufactory of Nathan Sellers; his son Coleman, and John Brandt of Lancaster, built the shops at Cardington, on the Sellers estate in Upper Darby, where they manufactured machine-set card clothing and built locomotives. Matthias Baldwin's locomotive shops were also downtown near the Sellers' Market Street factory. Patrick Lyon manufactured his famous line of fire engines; and Jacob Perkins worked in partnership with Thomas Gilpin to develop an automatic watermark-impressing roller before his departure for London in 1819. Joseph Saxton—later to work for Alexander Dallas Bache, first president of the American Association for the Advancement of Science, in the Coastal Survey, and to become an associate of Joseph Henry, of the Smithsonian Institution—was then working for Isaiah Lukens. Franklin Peale was employed by the U.S. Mint, designing improvements in the machines used for coinage,[8] and collaborating with Matthias Baldwin in the development of steam locomotives.

After the death of Benjamin Franklin, the public relations manager and in a sense the public symbol of the fraternity, until his own death in 1827, was undoubtedly the aged Charles Willson Peale. Peale as a youth had studied in London under Benjamin West. Remembered by later generations as the principal portrait artist of the Revolution, he painted one of the most popular likenesses of George Washington. Peale was the very prototype of the eighteenth-century intellectual. He operated, for a time, a small cotton factory at Belfield, in north Philadelphia; he made numerous mechanical inventions; and he established his famous Museum of Natural History, for many years located in Independence Hall, as a kind of public educational institute. There he displayed such interesting objects as stuffed animals and birds, shown in their natural habitat in well-painted and appropriately furnished settings, and the newest mechanical inventions (such as Oliver Evans' steam engine and Baldwin's locomotive). There distinguished mechanician-scientists gave lectures on chemistry and electricity, aided by laboratory demonstrations and illustrated by lantern slides. Peale represented to the full the Enlightenment's profound faith in man's ability to solve his problems, and to secure happiness for himself and others, by the observation of nature and the application of reason alike to mechanics, to husbandry, and to social relations.[9]

The interconnections of this technological community were multifarious, for the men were intimately involved with one another in business, and the women were related by marriage and by the business associations of their husbands. Coleman Sellers—Hannah Hill's brother—had married Charles Willson Peale's daughter Sophonisba in 1805 and had been (briefly) a partner with Jacob Perkins in the manufacture of fire engines. Sellers and Perkins dissolved their partnership when Sellers objected to Perkins' unsuccessful effort to outdo Pat Lyon's celebrated fire engine — an effort that impaled a child onlooker's foot on a steel spike. Perkins then teamed up with Thomas P. Jones, a lecturer at the Franklin Institute and editor of its *Journal* from 1826 until his death in 1848, and Commissioner of Patents in 1828 and 1829. Some institutions were magnets for mechanically inclined people because of their need for advanced technology. The U.S. Mint, for example, was a center of collaborative enterprise. The directors included the Drs. Robert Patterson, *père et fils,* of the University of Pennsylvania; among the first coiners were Adam Eckfeldt, the inventor of Pat Lyon's fire engine design, and Franklin Peale, erstwhile manager of his father's Museum.

The kaleidoscopic quality of this flux of business relationships was simplified by the intimacy of the men in their personal contacts. They visited each other's shop constantly to exchange information, to stand silently watching a new machine or a new process, to speculate about the future of mechanism. By and large, they knew each other's business and did not hesitate to show each other inventions in embryo, trusting their peers to honor their priority and the economic advantage it might mean. Their patents were often not taken out until years after the invention had become widely known in the fraternity; patents once taken were sometimes not announced or enforced, the patentee trusting his customers to honor his interest without reminder. To be sure, there were patent-infringement suits, like those levied by the embittered Oliver Evans, yet many of these were directed not against fellow mechanicians but rather against exploitive manufacturers.

The Network Outside Philadelphia

The mechanicians traveled frequently, partly on business to discuss new construction and partly just to gain information. Travel was a mode of education for mechanicians as well as merchants. The mechanicians of the Brandywine Valley, which was in its own right a center of machine shops of all kinds, were in constant contact with their brethren in Philadelphia. Charles Willson Peale sent his sons Titian and Franklin to serve apprenticeships with the Hodgson brothers. George Escol Sellers recalled in his later years riding out to Delaware County about 1818 (when he was a boy of ten) with his father Coleman Sellers and Oliver Evans. Evans was then sixty-four and within a year or two of his death; but he talked vigorously about the future course of technological progress. On another occasion about the same time, George Escol and his father visited Thomas Gilpin and Lawrence Greatrake, Gilpin's technical manager, and spent the evening with them and E. I. du Pont from the powder mills.

The pattern of traveling to learn is also illustrated by the peregrinations of John Morton Poole and his brother-in-law Edward Bancroft of Wilmington. Initially financed by a loan of $100 from Charles du Pont, they wandered in a leisurely way through the 1830's from one machine shop to another, stopping for a couple of years to work at Matteawan, returning to the Brandywine, then spending two or three more years in the shops at Providence, Rhode Island, and finally going on to Boston and Lowell (where letters of introduction provided by Du Pont made possible their first commissions). Poole returned to work as a foreman (at $60 per month) in the locomotive shop of Charles and George Escol Sellers at Cardington in Upper Darby, before finally going on to establish the Poole machine shops in Wilmington.[10]

The mechanicians also often made a pilgrimage to England, still the fountainhead of mechanical innovation, in order to acquire technical sophistication (and, sometimes, to steal industrial secrets and entice away English mechanics). The visits to England of Francis Lowell, who there gained knowledge of the working principle of the power loom, and of Joshua and Thomas Gilpin, who studied textile and papermaking machinery, were well known in their day. Lowell's trip resulted in the patent Waltham loom and the great industrial growth at Lowell; Gilpin patented his imitation of John Dickinson's endless papermaking machine (the first introduction of continuous papermaking in America).

But many trips were undertaken less in the spirit of espionage than of a genuine desire to learn about English machines and processes that were not regarded as secret and to tell the Englishmen about American progress. These visits seem to have been understood in that light and were carried on even during the War of 1812 (Joshua Gilpin was in England and traveled freely gathering technical information all during the conflict). Many of the Philadelphia mechanicians who worked as civil engineers during the period of canal and railroad construction before 1840 visited England, including Erskine Hazard, Samuel Kneass, Solomon Roberts, and William Strickland. In the winter of 1832–33 George Escol Sellers traveled in England to learn about English papermaking machinery from Bryan Donkin and John Dickinson; but he also visited the shops of the late Henry Maudslay—celebrated as the inventor of the first workable slide rest for the engine-powered lathe; Sharp and Roberts' shops at Manchester; the Royal Mint; and the tunnel under the Thames then being constructed by Marc Isambard Brunel. And he found time to visit his old friend Jacob Perkins' "Adelaide Gallery" (or "National Gallery of Practical Science"), where he found a display of remarkable machinery invented by Perkins and his old Philadelphia friend Joseph Saxton. Saxton had in fact just invented the first practical commutator for an "electric magnetic motor" and an electric generator. Soon after Sellers' return, Isaiah Lukens built an electric generator for Peale's Museum.[11]

The inter-state and international character of the mechanicians' fraternity was also maintained by migration in search of opportunity. After the lifting of British restrictions in the 1820's, a steady stream of English and French mechanicians of greater or lesser degree came to America; of the hundreds of these immigrants in the Philadelphia area, among the best known were the Hodgson brothers and the Greatrake family on the Brandywine. The Du Ponts imported French mechanics while they were setting up their cotton and powder mills. And within the country, as opportunities opened one after the other in the growing frontier cities in the west and burgeoning south, mechanics from the east coast traveled to construct railroads, locomotives, steamboats, mints, and textile factories.

The mechanicians' fraternity, then, was consciously international, indifferent (insofar as technology was concerned) to national boundaries and to international conflict, committed to facilitating technological progress by a continuous, free exchange of information among themselves. They talked constantly to one another of ideas for improving processes and were eager to show the uninformed the value of a more advanced procedure.[12]

The Size of the Fraternity

It would be interesting to develop a census of the fraternity in order to measure its size and other social characteristics. Although this task would go far beyond the needs of the present study, some notion of an order-of-magnitude kind is worth having. The materials provided by the mechanicians of the Sellers family, who were among the leaders in the group, give an intimation of the number of mechanicians—the creative, innovative master mechanics working in metal—in the English-speaking world. In the period 1820 to 1840, something like three to four hundred such men were working. The whole group, including journeymen and apprentices, totaled probably no more than six thousand persons, if one estimates (generously) an average of twenty journeymen and apprentices for every master.[13]

The memoirs and recollections of George Escol Sellers even provide a minimal list of names for the members of the network whom the Sellers family of this period counted as kin, as teachers, as business associates, or as friendly acquaintances. Although the Sellers network included some people from the worlds of politics and commerce, its male members were primarily people who worked with their hands as mechanicians, artists, scientists, and naturalists. Taken all together they made up a substantial portion of the leadership of the technological community of the lower Delaware in the early nineteenth century; as the century wore on, many of them contributed largely to America's industrial and scientific development. Many names in the fraternity are missing, but their absence does not necessarily imply lack of acquaintance, for George Escol Sellers was writing in his eighties and was being deliberately selective. His roll call is impressive, nonetheless, numbering perhaps 100 men in America and England whose names are well enough known even 150 years later to justify inclusion in the national biographical dictionaries, and another 50 who were at least significant figures in their own communities during their lifetimes. Sellers' description makes it plain that nearly all the several hundred master mechanicians of the English-speaking world knew each other by name and reputation, and that each man probably had met and talked with most of his peers on one occasion or another or had corresponded in writing. The mechanicians' fraternity of England and America was a tightly woven network of men, who shared a common awareness of the state of the art, the problems to be solved, and the progress each man was making. The fraternity can only be compared to the practitioners of a discipline like physics or mathematics, or of a school of art or a theological tradition. It was, in Thomas Kuhn's sense, a paradigmatic community.[14]

THE SELLERS FAMILY

One way to understand how the fraternity of mechanicians was organized and how it functioned is to study its families. We have already observed how, for the small beginning cotton manufacturer, an assemblage of kinfolk was indispensable as a source of capital. A similar importance must be attached to the role of kinship in the organization of the mechanicians, at least on a local level. In addition to family's importance in capital formation, when and if the mechanic expanded his enterprise from the level of a craftsman's shop to a machine manufactory, family also served to recruit young people into the trade, to provide a setting for education even more effective than the apprentice system (which in itself was a quasi-kinship system anyway, even in a legal sense), to channel new technical information, and generally to reinforce the solidarity of the class of mechanicians by binding them together in loosely overlapping networks of marriage and descent.

The Sellers family, already met in various capacities in the Rockdale district, provides a classic example of this reinforcing and uniting role. Geographically centered in Upper Darby, their kin network extended throughout the lower Delaware Valley; their business connections extended throughout the United States and Great Britain; and their technical contributions to mechanics, engineering, and science, both during and after this period, were widely recognized as important. In this discussion, however, we shall be concerned not so much with recording their triumphs of invention as with delineating the way in which the Sellers family connection interpenetrated a large sector of the mechanical community.

The Network of Blood Relations

Inasmuch as the mechanicians were exclusively men, it is best to look at the Sellers family first as a system of descent in the male line. The patronymic descent group provided the structure of educational opportunity and career identification that was basic to the role of the family.

Samuel (1655–1732), the first of the Sellers family to come to Pennsylvania, arrived in 1682 along with the earliest Quaker settlers and acquired the original Sellers estate on Cobbs Creek in Darby. He was a weaver and so was his son Samuel Jr. (1690–1773), who invented a machine for twisting worsted yarn (a mixture of cotton and wool) and built Sellers Hall. His son John (1728–1804) was the first of the great Sellers mechanicians. He developed the water power of the Sellers estate to run a complex of sawmill, gristmill, and tilt mill. He developed a method of weaving, not the traditional worsteds, but wire, to make sieves for sifting grain. He was a friend of Franklin and along with him one of the original members of the American Philosophical Society. He was also a surveyor, and in 1769 contributed his skills to the Society's celebrated observations on the transit of Venus, which established Philadelphia as a place of learning in the eyes of many European *savants*. He represented the growing radicalism of the intellectuals of Philadelphia: a revolutionary patriot, he was disowned by the Friends.

Among John Sellers' children, Nathan, David, and John are of particular interest in this connection. John remained on the Sellers place as the miller. Nathan (1751–1830) and David (1757–1813) teamed up as partners in 1798 and on Cobbs Creek started the first cotton mill in Delaware County (it burned in 1815). The brothers meantime had moved to Philadelphia, where they established their shop to make wire for card teeth and paper molds, and where they made the cards and the paper molds, and did other kinds of machine shop work.

Nathan's children included Hannah, who married Peter Hill and moved to Chester Creek, and on whose behalf Nathan purchased Lenni Mill and the mill seat at Parkmount. One of Nathan's sons was Coleman (1781–1834). After David died in 1813, and Nathan retired to Millbourne in 1817, Coleman and his cousins James and David carried on the business in Philadelphia. James invented a new kind of riveted leather hose for fire engines. In 1828 Coleman and his cousins divided the family machinery business. James and David maintained the old Philadelphia wire works. Coleman took as partners his own sons George Escol (1808–1897) and Coleman Jr. (1827–1907), and moved out to a new factory site that they called Cardington, in Upper Darby, where they manufactured everything from carding and papermaking machinery to locomotives. George Escol, who later published an intimate and revealing memoir, *Early Engineering Reminiscences (1815–1840)*, went on after his father's death in 1834 to become a machinery manufacturer in the western states; the young Coleman became a famous engineer who, among other things, in 1860 invented the first stereoscopic movie camera and in the 1890's designed and installed the Niagara Falls hydroelectric plant.

But perhaps the most famous Sellers mechanician of them all was descended from Nathan and David's brother John, the miller at Upper Darby. This John's son, also named John (1789–1878), built up the establishment at Millbourne into one of the most productive merchant flour mills in the country by constantly adding new machinery. And *his* son William became one of the pre-eminent mechanical engineers of the nineteenth century. In 1853 he organized, with his brother John, a factory that manufactured machine tools, thus moving effectively the mechanician's practice to a second level. (During the earlier period, the machine shops that turned out the parts for production machines made their own lathes and other machine tools. A few machinists in England and America in the 1820's and 1830's were building small numbers of lathes for the trade. Sellers' factory manufactured machine tools of many kinds, in large numbers, for other machine shops.) He was granted over ninety U.S. patents for various inventions. He organized the plant which supplied—at no profit—most of the structural steel for the Roeblings' Brooklyn Bridge. He proposed a system of screw threads which became the U.S. standard. He became president of the Franklin Institute, a trustee of the University of Pennsylvania, and a member of the National Academy of Sciences.[1]

Even so brief a review as this suggests that more was at work in the Sellers mechanical tradition than the simple inheritance of talent. There is an evident accumulation of expertise, an intensification of focus in the four generations from John (of transit-of-Venus fame) to Coleman Jr. and William. The process by which this trans-generational growth was accomplished was one of careful personal tutoring of the young sons of each generation by their grandfathers, fathers, uncles, and older brothers. The clearest account of the practical combination of family identification and education is afforded by the George Escol Sellers memoirs of his own, his brother Coleman's, and his father's boyhoods in Philadelphia in the late eighteenth and early nineteenth centuries. George Escol was not bound out as an apprentice but was with his father almost constantly, in the shop and on other occasions of interest:

I was standing with my father on the curb looking at the fire, when Philip Garrett rushed up in a great state of excitement, seized my father by his arm, and said: "Coleman, if thee can dam the stairways and hatchways of the upper floors of those two warehouses (pointing), and I can get a foot of water on the floors, we can stop the fire at that fire wall, but if we let it work down the walls will fall, the whole block will go, and there is no knowing how much more." My father turned me over to some one to see me safe home, and left with Mr. Garrett. I learned afterward that my father, with board partitions that he tore down, succeeded with them and gunny bags in damming both stair and hatchways, making small crevices tight by having large quantities of bran thrown on the floors. The roofs were on fire and would soon fall in. Lines were formed for carrying up water by the bucketfull.

Instead of going home as directed, I for hours had my place in the empty bucket line. While this was going on Garrett was having section after section of hose attached to both the Philadelphia and the Diligent engines, only to burst before the water reached the upper floors. Fortunately the Resolution Company had a number of new sections of hose which were pressed into the service, and were attached next the engines where the pressure would be greatest. The floors were flooded, the attics and roofs fell into the water, and spreading fire was stayed. The success of this expedient was so complete that it turned the attention of all firemen in the direction of securing more reliable hose. . . .[2]

Young George Escol, and presumably Coleman Jr. as well, were present in the shop on occasions when the famous and near-famous mechanics of the day stopped in to talk and tinker, and as we have seen, he went along with his father to meet the aged Oliver Evans, the Gilpin brothers, and the Du Ponts along the Brandywine. He watched inventions being made, was present at their trial, and saw them discarded when they failed. He heard the mechanicians who visited his father's shop converse about machinery. "Old Blind Hawkins," for instance, who had lost his sight during an epidemic while he was serving as supercargo on a slave-ship in his youth, would visit and expound his ideas for the use of high-pressure steam to operate steam engines and rapid-firing steam guns. These ideas were later developed by another of the visitors, Jacob Perkins, when he went to London. A list of the men whom George met and listened to in conversation with his father would include all the famous mechanics of Philadelphia and many others from towns all up and down the east coast.

But it was not only a father and son relationship. He spent summers in the country with his paternal grandfather Nathan at Cardington, and with his maternal grandfather Charles Willson Peale near Germantown, absorbing a sense of the traditions of both family and the trade. George Escol's father Coleman had likewise spent summers with *his* grandfather John Sellers, the first of the great inventors of the clan.

George had the highest esteem for his father and his grandfather. He wrote in his later years of his intense youthful admiration of his father, who was

a very fine horse man, and I recollect when I thought him the best rider with a single exception, that I had ever seen. He sat as if he and his horse was of one flesh. . . .

My earliest recollection of Father was that I thought him the most wonderful man that ever lived. He had the knack of explaining everything to a boy's comprehension and often in very few words. He was free with his pencil in making clear and accurate sketches of what he wanted to illustrate. When what puzzled us at school and we were called stupid by the teacher all we had to do was to go to Father with our troubles to be set right. He went to the bottom of everything left nothing to chance.[3]

In the old house in Philadelphia, his father had a small machine shop in the garret which he shared with his sons and in which he gave them their initial instructions in machine tools.

The garret [was] all in one, had dormers front and rear and one window in the centre in the west wall. It was by this window that Father had his file bench and turning lathe. On the front side of the great chimney stack was our boys carpenter bench. Father's bench was on the other side the chimney, both sitting crossway of the garret. It was in this garret that both Charles and myself got our first lessons in handling tools. We were always encouraged to try, no matter what failures we met with. One day father came up and found me with my little jack plaine trying to plaine a pine board about 6 or more feet long. He stood a moment looking at me, then said, "Escol if you would begin at the stop end it would be easier and make smoother work. It is easier to plane down than up hill," but said I, "Father the board is dirty and would dull my plane, I am trying to get under the dirt. What do you mean by planing down hill?" He said, "The front end of your plane is held up by the rough board and you have to set the bit deeper than if you take a short shaving off of the stop end, then the front of the plaine is below what you want to cut and the bit need not be set so deep and the work will be smoother. Try it." And I did, and I tell this as evidence of his always giving a reason and his reasoning and illustrations a lesson.[4]

George was also proud of his grandfather Nathan, of whom he wrote (although slightly patronizingly):

We all know that he was a skillful worker in wood and wire and not bad in metal for the time in which he lived and with the poor tools and appliances at his command. When I think of what he accomplished he appears to me to be as great if not greater inventive mechanic, everything considered, as the grandest of the present time.[5]

These recollections, written in 1894, three-quarters of a century after the events, were warmed perhaps by nostalgia. But they show clearly enough a pattern of family training which was based on the assumption that the father's craft was good enough for his sons to follow and that the son should become, in effect, his father's apprentice in very early childhood. This meant a close, personal association in which the father deliberately included the child in his work, showing him how to use the tools, keeping him around the shop, and carrying him along on business travels. In this way was laid the basis for a deep, if somewhat competitive, identification, as the son sought first to become like his father and then to excel him if possible in their shared and chosen craft.

The Network of In-Laws

Connections by marriage were as important as descent for economic purposes, for they provided added sources of partnership and capital, opportunities for education and recommendation, and a forum for the exchange of ideas. After children were born, of course, they were the source of consanguineal alliances as well. They offered an additional set of connections to tie together the loose fraternal assemblage of mechanicians.

One important affinal connection of this kind was formed between the John Sellers line of Millbourne and the Pooles of Wilmington, Delaware. John Sellers was a successful miller but he did not contribute much personally to the family's tradition of mechanical invention. In 1817, at the age of twenty-seven, shortly after undertaking the management of the new mill his father had built for him, he married Elizabeth Poole, the eldest daughter of William Poole, a Brandywine miller (and friend of Oliver Evans). Elizabeth Poole was a strong and intelligent woman, who "had been the congenial companion of a very intellectual father," and (in the opinion of the county historian, who knew them well) "brought into her husband's home a wisdom beyond her years."[6] One of their eleven children, William, born in 1824, was apprenticed at the age of fourteen to John Morton Poole, his maternal uncle, when Poole started up a machine shop in the basement at Joseph Bancroft's mill. This John Morton Poole, who had been born in 1812, had served his mechanical apprenticeship at the Matteawan Manufacturing Company and had studied science and mechanical drawing at the Franklin Institute in Philadelphia. He had been partners briefly with Edward Bancroft (the brother of Joseph), who had worked at Cardington for several years for Coleman Sellers and Sons, and his sister Sarah was married to Joseph Bancroft.

William Sellers stayed with his uncle for seven years as a machinist's apprentice. He then took charge of the machine shop at Edward Bancroft's mill on Ridley Creek. In a few years he moved to Philadelphia to set up his own plant for the manufacture of machine tools; there he was joined in partnership by Bancroft. In 1853 William's brother John joined the firm as partner. The firm of William Sellers and Company, as indicated earlier, pioneered the design and manufacture of machine tools.[7]

An affinal connection of equal importance was formed with the Pooles in 1805 when Nathan Sellers' son Coleman married Charles Willson Peale's daughter Sophonisba. This alliance brought the two families into a close consortium. Charles Willson Peale was then principally devoted to the development of his famous Museum, which he hoped would become a "School of Nature" at the heart of a national university. To the Museum, as lecturers and laboratory workers, he attracted most of the scientists, artists, and mechanicians of Philadelphia. Of Peale's numerous progeny, two—Franklin and Titian—had at the suggestion of E. I. du Pont been apprenticed in 1813 to the Hodgson brothers in their machine shop on the Brandywine.[8] After a year, with an introduction from Coleman Sellers, Franklin went for another year's experience to work at William Young's cotton mill at Rockland. This was to be their preparation for taking part in managing the Peale family's little cotton factory at Belfield near Germantown. But, like so many others, the Peales' cotton factory did not survive the renewal of British imports after the end of the War of 1812, and the three mechanically trained brothers—Franklin, Titian, and Charles Linnaeus—went on to other things. Franklin, however, returned to mechanics, working for Coleman Sellers for a time, and later serving as an employee of the U.S. Mint, where he invented a steam press and eventually (in 1840) became Chief Coiner. It was Franklin also who, a temporary victim of religious enthusiasm, married the daughter of the Gilpins' mechanical expert, Thomas Greatrake. The Greatrakes were Quakers and the young woman was a "Quaker Preacher" of extreme religious zeal. After their daughter was born, Eliza became psychotic, running away from home and threatening to kill the child. She was placed in the Philadelphia Hospital for a time and the marriage was annulled; eventually she was returned to her parents.[9] Another of the Peales, Raphaelle's son Edmund, lived with the family of Coleman Sellers and worked for a time in his factory.[10] And George Escol remembered in later years his own summer visits to Belfield, to stay with his grandfather Charles Willson Peale, where he recalled hearing a discussion of Redheffer's famous—and fraudulent—perpetual motion machine.[11]

Evidently, then, the Sellers' connections by marriage with both the Pooles and the Peales were routes by which young people were recruited into mechanical pursuits, trained, and placed in positions of employment. They bound together three important mechanicians' families of Philadelphia and Wilmington.

THE FRANKLIN INSTITUTE

Although the mechanicians' work in its informal organization and its function was not unlike a scientific field, in other important respects it differed markedly from any of the academic disciplines. For one thing, they lacked a publication in which issues of importance to the profession could be debated and new information of general concern be communicated. They also lacked a formal method of proof that went beyond the claims of experience and authority to be comparable to the experimental method of science or the logical methods of mathematics or theology. They had no way of conclusively demonstrating the validity of a technical proposition, such as "Overshot wheels are more efficient than breast wheels." And, finally, they did not have a system of formal education, which could standardize mechanical training and relate it to useful information in the sciences; all that remained of formality in the mechanics' education was the lingering remnant of the apprentice system.

Up to this time, mechanicians had perhaps not felt such a disciplinary apparatus to be necessary. It was notoriously difficult anyway to talk or write about machinery without recourse to drawings or even three-dimensional demonstration. "Proof" of correctness or error often seemed self-evident to the eye—a thing either worked or it didn't. The apprentice system—limited, in America, by the need for generalization—was an effective one in a largely nonliterary field of knowledge; and the physical sciences had little to offer the mechanician beyond the opportunity for training and employment as instrument maker. Indeed, up to this point in history, science probably owed more to technology than technology did to science.

But technological problems were beginning to arise that required a more "scientific"—that is, methodical and systematic—approach. The increasing demand for power was stimulating a deluge of improvements and inventions in water wheels, turbines, and steam engines. Questions about the relative efficiency of the many different designs were not easily answered; and the increasingly obvious dangers of imperfectly understood mechanisms, such as steam engine boilers, which had a distressing propensity for explosion, particularly on passenger-carrying steamboats, could no longer be dismissed. Mechanicians themselves were realizing, furthermore, that they were wasting a lot of time reinventing each other's discoveries and —worse yet—rediscovering each other's mistakes. Oliver Evans, for instance, in 1818 complained to Coleman Sellers, while they were on their way to install some flour-milling equipment in Delaware County, about the need for published records in technology:

Mr. Evans had much to say on the difficulties inventive mechanics labored under for want of published records of what had preceded them, and for works of reference to help the beginner. In speaking of his own experience, he said that everything he had undertaken he had been obliged to start at the very foundation; often going over ground that others had exhausted and abandoned, leaving no record. He considered the greatest difficulty beginners had to encounter was want of reliable knowledge of what had been done.

Even at that early day Mr. Evans suggested and urged the formation of a Mechanical Bureau that should collect and publish all new inventions, combined with reliable treatises on sound mechanical principles, as the greatest help to beginners. He did not believe it could at that time be made self-sustaining, but it would be to the interest of mechanics, manufacturers and merchants to subscribe to its support.[1]

Evans on the same occasion also remarked on the need for a school to teach mechanical drawing. This was not felt only as a technical requirement. It was believed by some that "theory" (i.e., science) and "practice" (i.e., mechanics) should be taught together in order to render practice more consistent and theory more realistic. Furthermore, both in England and in the United States there was a widespread feeling that mechanicians, who were assuming an increasing importance in the economic life of their countries, ought to be more broadly educated so that they could assume a role of nearer social equality with the liberally educated merchants and financiers who dominated society.[2] In England and Scotland, institutes for the education of young mechanics and operatives had been popular from the turn of the century and libraries already existed there; in Philadelphia and Boston, where young mechanics could read, clubs were often formed (and as often dissolved) where books were discussed and issues of the day debated.

And then, overshadowing all of this, there was the problem of proof. Every profession needs to have conventional standards for judging the merit of the productions of its practitioners. Sometimes the citation of authority will do, but this was not the tradition among the mechanicians, who tended to be more or less irreverent toward the pretensions of the great. The elegant proofs of mathematics, based on the laws of logic, hardly seemed applicable. The prevailing criterion for the merit of a mechanical "statement" was experience: whether the thing worked, whether it created more problems than it solved, how much trouble it was to manufacture, how prone to break down, and so forth. These criteria, however, were difficult to apply systematically and were liable to provoke unresolvable arguments, like the acrimonious contention between Oliver Evans and Benjamin Latrobe over the potential usefulness of high-pressure steam engines in propelling boats and wagons. Furthermore, the criteria were crudely empirical and not based on an analysis of the significant variables at work in the system. When such variables became too numerous, the complexity of the problem exceeded intuitive comprehension and required recourse to some system of experiment, some protocol for recording results, some means of publishing the findings.

The Founding of the Franklin Institute

The Franklin Institute of Philadelphia was organized in 1824 for the purpose of solving, or at least contributing to the resolution of, all these problems.[3] The "leading spirits" in organizing it were the master mechanicians of Philadelphia, the mechanic-manufacturers: Matthias Baldwin, then running "a general jobbing machine shop"; Samuel V. Merrick and John Agnew, who were partners in a foundry in Southwark and manufactured fire engines; Henry and Steven P. Morris, makers of iron and brass forgings, particularly umbrella frames; James Sellers and Abraham Pennock, inventors and manufacturers of riveted leather fire engine hose; James Rush and John P. D. Muhlenburg, sons-in-law of Oliver Evans, and owners of the Bush Hill ironworks; Professor Robert M. Patterson, Professor of Mathematics at the University of Pennsylvania, and later director of the U.S. Mint; and Franklin Peale, then working for Coleman Sellers.

Bestirring themselves with vigor, these gentlemen succeeded in mobilizing the support of the entire mechanical community of the Philadelphia-to-Wilmington region, gaining subscriptions for membership from the Du Ponts and the Gilpins along the Brandywine, from James Ronaldson the cotton manufacturer of Darby, from Philadelphians Charles and George Escol Sellers, Oliver Evans the iron founder's son, himself an iron founder, William Lippincott, the cotton manufacturer with whom Daniel Lammot would be involved next year, John S. Phillips the sugar refiner, and many others, including even some men who were principally merchants and financiers like Nicholas Biddle and Paul Beck, Jr., Lammot's first father-in-law.[4]

The Board of Managers went to work at once to implement solutions to the problems of the mechanical community. Ad hoc committees were appointed to examine and evaluate new inventions; John S. Phillips, selected for his knowledge of chemistry, was a member of the first committee, along with the well-known mechanicians David N. Mason and Isaiah Lukens. After careful tests at Frankford Arsenal, they published a report recommending the new percussion caps for use in firing rifles and cannon.[5] A mechanics' high school was begun, with a well-qualified academic faculty, to teach philosophy, mechanics, chemistry, mathematics, and architectural and mechanical drawing. A standing committee was formed to examine and report on newly patented inventions and an exhibit was held for domestic manufactures, with prizes for quality and novelty; both of these activities continued for many years. And a new hall was constructed to house the growing organization. In 1826, the *Franklin Journal and American Mechanics' Magazine* was launched under the editorship of Thomas P. Jones. (In 1828 the name was changed to *Journal of the Franklin Institute.*) Jones, an Englishman by birth, had been editor of the *American Mechanics' Magazine,* founded in New York the year before. Jones moved to Washington in 1828 to become the superintendent of the U.S. Patent Office, but he continued to edit the *Journal* from Washington until his death in 1848.

The mechanics' school slowly foundered; the committee structure and the *Journal* gradually became the principal agencies by which the purposes of the Franklin Institute were carried out. The problem with the school, apparently, was the difficulty of actually joining the technological and scientific subjects. To be sure, the mechanical and thermodynamic principles by which machines moved and bridges stayed in one place were those expounded in Newton's physics; the geometry of mechanism was no different from that of Euclid. But many of these principles were, in simplified language, matters of common knowledge; it was not always clear to the mechanic what advantage the more abstruse theoretical formulations of science gave him in solving practical problems. Take, for instance, the highly publicized claim of the Edinburgh mathematician and physicist Dr. John Robison that James Watt had based his improvement of the steam engine upon the doctrine of "latent heat" expounded in courses of lectures he had attended at the University of Edinburgh. Although Robison and Watt were indeed close friends, Watt was obliged to deny the connection (although he politely conceded the general value of science). The knowledge on which he depended in making the improved steam engine with external condenser was in large part folk knowledge; thus, said Watt, "It was known very long before my time, that steam was condensed by coming into contact with cold bodies and that it communicated heat to them. Witness the common still, &c. &c." Furthermore, he had conducted a series of experiments of his own on the Newcomen engine which led to the practical improvements. Dr. Joseph Black and his theory of latent heat had been useful only in explaining "how so much cold water could be heated so much by so small a quantity in the form of steam." Watt went on to explain:

But this theory, though useful in determining the quantity of injection necessary where the quantity of water evaporated by the boiler, and used by the cylinder, was known, and in determining, by the quantity and heat of the hot water emitted by Newcomen's engines, the quantity of steam required to work them, did not lead to the improvements I afterwards made in the engine. These improvements proceeded upon the old-established fact, that steam was condensed by the contact of cold bodies, and the later known one, that water boiled in vacuo at heats below 100°, and consequently that a vacuum could not be obtained unless the cylinder and its contents were cooled every stroke to below that heat. These, and the degree of knowledge I possessed of the elasticities of steam at various heats, were the principal things it was *necessary* for me to consider in contriving the new engine.[6]

Ignorance of such elementary principles could of course be crippling to a mechanic's program of invention, as George Escol Sellers remarked in discussing his friends John Brandt and Jacob Perkins. Brandt had had no formal education in geometry; "he did not understand the simplest drawings. He said he was often mortified by not being able to understand sketches." All his drawings had to be made full size; he could not understand them reduced to scale. As Sellers recalled it,

It was by mere accident that I discovered his mental difficulty. All his thinking was, if I may so express it, *full size*. The trouble was in reducing to a given scale and carrying both in his mind at the same time. Up to the point of this discovery it would take pages to describe the various devices I resorted to, but now all was plain sailing. By working with him on full-size drawings, it was not long before he understood them and became quite proficient.[7]

But the real question was not whether all mechanics needed to know how to read scale drawings and to calculate proportions, or to have an elementary knowledge of the condensing power of cold water and the expanding power of steam; it was rather whether this level of need required a long series of abstract academic lectures on the major branches of science and mathematics.

The standing committee on exhibitions, from the fall of 1824 onward for half a century, annually organized a public exhibit where American manufacturers could display their products, particularly those notable for novelty and quality. Premiums, advertised in advance throughout the country, were awarded in the fall and the names of the winners were published in the *Journal*. Among the categories of prominence, of course, were cotton yarns and cloth and the machines used in manufacturing them. Entries were submitted from all parts of the United States, and the Philadelphian, Chester Creek, and Brandywine manufacturers submitted their samples. In 1825, for instance, the firm of Lewis, Phillips, and Company, then of Holmesburg, won the silver medal for "the best piece of blue Nankeen made in the United States, in imitation of the Chinese."[8] J. Garsed and Company, then of Frankford, submitted eighteen rolls of gray shoe thread; although it did not receive a medal, it was commended for being "well made and strong." In 1827, Robert Beatty, a toolmaker of Village Green (and briefly later the lessee of Knowlton Mill), received a silver medal for his edged tools, which "sustained the high character they have always borne" as superior to foreign. The Garsed brothers received awards through the 1840's for their power-loom-woven "cotton and worsted damask table covers," their "Marseilles . . . toilet covers," and other fabrics. It was not until the 1850's that Daniel Lammot and Samuel Riddle began to exhibit; Lammot received a gold medal in 1851 for bed tickings, and Samuel Riddle honorable mention in 1856 for his Canton flannels, rated as "fair merchantable goods." Crozer never seems to have exhibited at the Franklin Institute.[9]

Another regular feature of the *Journal* was its report of British and American inventions. This was undoubtedly a great boon to inventors and manufacturers alike. The Patent Office issued annual lists of inventions, giving the name assigned to the device by the inventor, but neither describing nor evaluating it. The *Journal* published a description of what its committee on inventions considered to be the most significant, often quoting directly from the patent specifications, and sometimes essaying an evaluation of an invention's utility compared with others in its class.

And there were formal articles: summary descriptions of the state of the art in some branch of technology; outlines of the principles of a discipline of science; exhortations to mechanicians to make use of the accumulating contributions of science.

The Franklin Institute undoubtedly had an important effect upon the mechanicians' practice. By stimulating national pride in American manufactures, by providing the mechanicians themselves with news of the state of the mechanical arts and the sciences, by communicating in the pages of its *Journal* an awareness of the need for scientific method, the Institute facilitated the pace of mechanical progress. But the failure of the mechanics' schools, which were patronized more by the general public than by young mechanics, was perhaps an omen of an effect its own success was slowly helping to bring about: the splitting of the mechanicians' fraternity into two, unequal, classes—the class of the practical artisan-mechanic, with limited education; and the class of the engineer and the architect, who employed scientific knowledge to solve fundamental problems of design.

The Committee on Water Power

Five years after its birth, the Institute began to function as a research organization, carrying out applied scientific investigations on behalf of the industrial community. The first of these enterprises was launched in 1829, when a "committee of inquiry" was formed to "fix by actual experiments . . . the value of water, as a moving power, and the relative effects produced by it upon wheels of different construction."[10] Within a few years, two more committees were formed: a Committee on Weights and Measures, and a Committee on the Explosion of Steam Boilers. The last was also the most highly publicized and its work resulted in federal safety legislation as early as 1838—the first such federal regulatory action, in fact, in the national experience.[11] But of more immediate relevance to the cotton manufacturers on Chester Creek was the work of the Committee on Water Power.

The Committee was composed of many of the leading mechanicians of Philadelphia, including some of the men who had founded the Institute a few years before. The chairman was Samuel V. Merrick, the iron founder; the first members were Benjamin Reeves, nail manufacturer; Isaiah Lukens, machinist; Rufus Tyler, machinist; and Andrew Young, brass founder. They were soon joined by Matthias Baldwin, machinery manufacturer; John Agnew, Merrick's partner; James Espy, mathematics instructor at the Franklin Institute; James Rush, iron founder; Frederick Graff, superintendent of the Philadelphia Water Works; William H. Keating, chemist; and at the last moment Alexander Dallas Bache, the professional scientist who was to head the scientific activities of the Institute for many years. This blue-ribbon panel announced their plan and solicited subscriptions, and letters with reports and suggestions, from all over the United States. Money and information came from local manufacturers, of course, but also from such other interested concerns as the Schuylkill Navigation Company, the Society for Useful Manufactures at Patterson, the New England Society for Promoting Mechanical Arts, and Warren Colburn, engineer at Lowell. The City Council of Philadelphia granted the Committee the right to use the water power at the dam connected with the Fairmount Water Works; the firm of Rush and Muhlenburg constructed the building to contain the experimental apparatus.

The Committee first analyzed the nature of the problem. Their approach was essentially a Baconian, inductive one, depending less upon *a priori* theory than upon systematic collection and tabulation of quantitative data. They described this empiricist approach succinctly in their report:

There is perhaps no subject connected with the extensive branch of mechanics, for which theory has done so little as for that which considers the effect of water upon wheels; the different theories advanced are at variance with each other, and with practice, so that the candid theorist confesses that the circumstances, attending the action, are of so complicated a nature as to baffle his powers of investigation. Experiment, then, can alone guide to results worthy of confidence.

The experimental inquiries in relation to water-wheels which have, deservedly, attracted most attention, are those of Smeaton. The means of a single individual could not be competent to prosecute such a subject upon the scale required to make the results entirely practical, and we find the ingenuity of Smeaton labouring against the difficulties incident to the contracted dimensions of the apparatus which he was obliged to employ, and arranging with great skill and resource the best means to render serviceable the working models which were used in his experiments.

The experiments of Bossut, which rank next in extent to those of Smeaton, were comparatively few, and were principally made upon the undershot wheel.

It would not be profitable to enumerate the isolated experiments made in different countries upon this subject, since the sum of the information which they convey is extremely small. Of late years this branch of inquiry has been but little prosecuted, and the committee are not aware that any experiments, except a few in France, having in view a particular form of wheel, have been made, which tend to throw light upon the subject of their labours.

Such was the progress made in this subject when the Institute undertook it, with a view to obtain such results as should afford to the millwright a sure and safe guide in his practice, and thus contribute essentially to the promotion of one of the most important of the Mechanic Arts.[12]

The problem was indeed a complex one, in view of the number of variables that could have an effect on the usable power produced by water wheels. These variables included the volume of water turning the wheel; the head (the distance from the mouth of the sluice above the wheel to the floor of the wheelpit); the size and shape of the gate releasing the water; the type of wheel (overshot, pitchback, breast, or undershot), the diameter of the wheel, the number of buckets, its mass and angular velocity; the materials of which it was made; friction, lubrication, and so on. Apparatus had to be designed so that these variables could either be kept constant (so as to simplify the analysis) or be carefully and precisely varied according to plan. The Committee's analysis of the problem was pragmatic but in its way elegant too; the central problem of measurement, of course, was to compare power applied (energy expended) with work accomplished by any particular wheel arrangement.

One of the most important questions which arose for the discussion of the committee, was the measure of power expended, and of effect produced, to be adopted in their investigations. They finally determined upon one which, while strictly correct in principle, was at the same time, from its simplicity and ease of application, well adapted to their purposes, viz. for the measure of the power applied, the weight of water expended multiplied by the height of the head, (kept invariable,) above the bottom of the wheel; and for that of the effect, the weight raised multiplied by the distance through which it was raised. In order that this measure of effect may be accurate, the friction and inertia of the machine must be considered. The friction was carefully ascertained by experiment and the proper allowance made for it, as will appear in the course of this report. Any resistance from inertia was avoided by causing the wheel, and of course the weight raised by it, to move, before beginning an experiment, with a velocity which would remain constant during its progress.[13]

The apparatus, consisting essentially of a variable water-delivery system, a work-measuring device, and a set of water wheels, was built by the fine machinist Phillip Garrett and completed by the spring of 1830. The 123 planned experiments, involving 1,381 trials, each one repeated at least once to ensure reliability, were immediately begun. The research had to be interrupted in December 1830, with a few of the experiments still to be done; these were probably completed in the spring of 1831.

The result of these labors was a massive body of tabulations which, in effect, rated each combination for its efficiency. Efficiency was measured as the ratio of power expended to effect produced. Power expended was measured simply by the weight of the water, multiplied by the distance (head) through which it moved, necessary to lift a constant mass a certain distance. The "effect" was the sum of the weight of this mass, and the quantity of friction overcome in raising it, multiplied by the distance it was raised. Efficiencies ranged from lows of about 60 percent, for some combinations, to highs of nearly 90 percent for others.

By July 1831 the Committee was ready to give practical answers to practical questions of the kind hundreds of millers and manufacturers were asking.[14] Questions and answers were drafted to give a quick response to standard letters of inquiry. They may be summarized as follows:

Q: What is the advantage of the overshot over the breast wheel?
A: About 4 to 3.

Q: What is the optimum ratio of the diameter of the wheel to the head of water in the pit?
A: The power of the water comes from gravity not from impulse; hence the diameter of the wheel should be the maximum possible fraction of the head.

Q: What is the proper head?
A: Take care to ensure an adequate supply at all seasons.

Q: What is the optimum number of revolutions per minute?
A: It varies directly with the head.

Q: Where is the best working point for gearing, belts, etc.?
A: There is no rule; it depends on convenience at the particular installation.

Q: What is the optimum depth of the back water under the wheel?
A: No clear answer can be made but the committee recommends low heads and the "pitchback overshot" wheel, whose direction of rotation tends to free the wheel of water.

Q: What is the optimum depth of shrouding on the buckets?
A: That which minimizes the loss of fall.

But, having completed their research, and having publicly promised to publish the results, the Committee on Water Power now faced a frustrating problem of communication. The results were crudely empirical, in the sense that they could not be expressed in a concise set of mathematical equations. The whole mass of data would have to be presented so that the practical millwright could find the optimum type of wheel for his particular setting somewhere in the tables reporting the 123 experiments. The report never was published in a single volume; instead (an unfortunate decision), it was published in installments in the *Journal of the Franklin Institute.* The first installment appeared in March 1831; additional parts came out in 1832 and 1841. The early chapters created an international sensation. The British Association for the Advancement of Science was told by a distinguished speaker, the engineer George Rennie, that the Committee's researches "eclipse everything that has yet been effected on this subject," and the London *Mechanics Magazine* praised it as an example of the value of "organized and cooperative" inquiry.[15] But the last sections, apparently, never were published. By the 1850's, the new and more efficient turbines, and the versatile steam engines, were combining to drive out the water wheel from just those sophisticated establishments whose managers would earlier have wanted to read the Franklin Institute's study. The water wheel research was a landmark in the application of scientific method to technology. But its value to the community of mechanicians was drastically reduced by the difficulty the researchers had in communicating their findings to an eagerly waiting public.

THINKING ABOUT MACHINERY

The work of the mechanician was, in large part, intellectual work. This was true in spite of the fact that he dealt with tangible objects and physical processes, not with symbols, and that some of what he did was done with dirty hands. The thinking of the mechanician in designing, building, and repairing tools and machinery had to be primarily visual and tactile, however, and this set it apart from those intellectual traditions that depended upon language, whether spoken or written. The product of the mechanician's thinking was a physical object, which virtually had to be seen to be understood; descriptions of machines, even in technical language, are notoriously ambiguous and extremely difficult to write, even with the aid of drawings and models.

As with the work of those who think in words, schools of thought or traditions flourished among the mechanicians too, embracing a preference for a particular kind of solution to a type of mechanical problem, or a devotion to a particular expertise. Some of these traditions could be subsumed under the relics of the ancient craft guild system. There were turners, tinsmiths, masons, millwrights, brass founders, and so forth. The master in each of these crafts was the custodian of highly specialized skills, which he passed on to the coming generation of apprentices, teaching largely by demonstration and example. But the other kind of tradition depended upon the collaborative working out, by generations of mechanics, of the potentialities hidden yet implicit in a certain principle of mechanism, and the solving of the problems each successive improvement called forth. Their situation was not unlike that of scientists in the normal development of what has been called a paradigm.[1] When a basic innovation was introduced, it was embodied in an actual machine; the machine, and copies of it, rather than verbal descriptions, communicated the paradigm. But with each machine came problems to eliminate and improvements to add, all within the ambit of the original conception. Thus the mule of Crompton—a synthesis of the jenny and the water frame—constituted a paradigm for mechanicians to work on for the next 150 years. Machines were not "invented" in complete and finished form; rather, they were the product of generations of collective effort. The paradigms themselves often were never patented, and if they were, the patent was rarely left valid and uninfringed for long; what was patentable was not the paradigm but an improvement.

The kind of thinking involved in designing machine systems was unlike that of linguistic or mathematical thinking in its emphasis on sequence as opposed to classification. To the linguistic and mathematical thinker (for mathematics is merely very formal language), the grammar that embodies the rules of sequence is a given; what is crucial is the choice of the correct word or phrase, denoting a class of concepts, and the collection of attributes appropriate to describe the thing in mind. To the mechanical thinker, the grammar of the machine or mechanical system is the successive transformations of power—in quantity, kind, and direction—as it is transmitted from the power source (such as falling water or expanding steam), through the revolutions of the wheel, along shafts, through gears and belts, into the intricate little moving parts, the rollers and spindles and whirling threads, of the machine itself. The shapes and movements of all these hundreds of parts, sequentially understood, are a long yet elegantly simple moving image in three-dimensional space. In this mode of cognition, language is auxiliary—often so lagging an auxiliary that the parts and positions of a machine have no specific name, only a generic one, and if referred to in words, have to be described by such circumlocutions as "the 137th spindle from the left," "the lowest step of the cam," or "the upper right hand bolt on the governor housing."

The complexity of thought required to understand mechanical systems would seem in no way inferior to what is required for the trains of reasoning in mathematics or the common language. Thinking visually and tactilely has an inherent disadvantage, however, in comparison with thinking in language. Those who think in words—on subjects which are thought about effectively in words—can think a sentence and then utter it for others to hear. If one visualizes a piece of machinery, however, and wishes to communicate that vision to others, there is an immediate problem. Speech (and writing) will provide only a garbled and incomplete translation of the visual image. One must make the thing—or a model, or at the least a drawing—in order to ensure that one's companion has approximately the same visual experience as oneself.

In the Western world, an effect of this special problem in communicating technological information has tended to be the growing isolation of those who think in mental pictures. Theologians, humanists, even scientists can converse freely because the thinking is done with the same system of symbols as those used in communication. Indeed, it has become conventional to assume that thought itself is merely a kind of internal speech and to disregard almost completely those kinds of cognitive processes that are conducted without language, as though they were somehow more primitive, and less worthy of intellectual attention. Those who think about machinery have tended to undervalue their own accomplishments, or to deny that the process is intellectual at all, and to belittle "intellectuals" in turn.

This process was already evident, and efforts were under way to combat it, in the 1830's. The flourishing of mechanics' institutes, mechanics' literary associations, mechanics' magazines and newspapers, all filled with traditional humanistic verbiage, must be seen as efforts to bridge the gap between the two cognitive styles. Daniel Lammot could and did write fluent pages on the problem of determining the relation between the truth of good and the good of truth in Swedenborgian theology; but he had difficulty finding out how cotton machinery worked. The mechanics who founded the Franklin Institute understood the working of machinery; they had little patience with philosophical arguments that could not be settled by recourse to experiment. Science appealed to both sides as a suitable means for closing the gap, for it was couched in some of the most elegant linguistic formulations developed by man—the symbol system of mathematics—and yet referred itself to nature by means of experiments which required tangible apparatus and visible measurements. The result of bringing together the mechanician and the scientist was productive: it produced scientific engineers and clever experimental scientists. But it also split off the lower range of the mechanicians, to remain as mere "mechanics," artisans, and craftsmen fundamentally alienated from the engineer and the architect, who design machines but leave it to the mechanics to build and maintain them.

The problem of the relationship between science and technology has remained. In the 1830's, the inventive mechanician needed to have some knowledge of basic physical principles and, increasingly, an awareness of the rigorous requirements of the experimental method of proof. Yet, although he thus profited from some scientific training, his improvements in machines and industrial process seem to have been suggested less by new scientific discoveries calling for application than by interesting old technological problems calling more urgently for solution because of economic pressures. And as often as not—perhaps more often than not—the solution was suggested by other innovations within the mechanicians' tradition rather than by advances in science. The problem is still being argued 150 years later.

Part Three

ROCKDALE
FROM 1835 TO 1850
THE STRUGGLE
FOR CONTROL
OF A WAY OF LIFE

Chapter VI

THE ENLIGHTENMENT'S LAST CAMPAIGN

The way of life in Rockdale at any given time, as in any cotton-manufacturing district, was in some respects imposed on everyone, from mill owner to operative, by the technology itself. Location, settlement pattern, work organization, and household structure were at the beginning not so much forced by a selfish managerial class upon an unwilling working class as developed as the most immediate mutually convenient solutions to the problem of powering and operating the machines.

But other aspects of the quality of life were usually determined unilaterally by the manufacturer, and this was the case in Rockdale too. Because he controlled the machinery, the manufacturer could set wages and hours for the operatives on a take-it-or-leave-it basis, could decide whether to operate his factory full time, part time, or not at all, and could freely exercise his right to replace workers with new labor-saving machinery. Some manufacturers, like John P. Crozer, claimed these privileges as a moral right. The manufacturer's goal was to employ his machinery to make as much money as possible for himself and his partners, or for his corporation; the operatives were incidental to this process, and their financial profit, or even general welfare, was not conceived to be a primary economic purpose of the enterprise.

A clear conflict of interest between operatives and manufacturers was thus built into the whole system of cotton manufacturing from the beginning. But not only were the operatives in the mills themselves in economic competition with the factory enterprise. Traditional craftsmen—hand-loom weavers, carders, spinners, and other artisans who worked in the cottage textile trades—were threatened with unemployment; and, as the factories spread, thousands were in fact left to choose between the poorhouse and the cotton mill. Furthermore, some of the early urban industrial centers, the most conspicuous of which was Manchester, grew helter-skelter and as a consequence of the private decisions of dozens of industrial capitalists and landowners. These urban conglomerations of mills and tenements, far more than planned company towns like Lowell and New Lanark, displayed social pathologies plain for all to see, in the shape of high rates of industrial accidents and industrial diseases, squalid housing, smoke-filled air and polluted rivers, inadequate sanitation, malnutrition and starvation, drunkenness and prostitution. These conditions were, of course, deplored by all observers. But who was responsible? The more self-righteous manufacturers, and their clerical apologists like Bishop Potter of Chester, were prone to blame the poor for their own poverty, claiming it to be a result of immorality and neglect of Christian principle. Angry workmen blamed the manufacturers for throwing people out of work by bringing in new machines, for reducing wages and closing the mills when the market fell, and for forcing the workers, particularly women and children, to spend long hours under poor conditions. But behind the question of immediate blame was the larger issue: Who *should* control the machines of the Industrial Revolution?

The manufacturers, and economists generally, were not in a position to give much more of an answer to this question than to point out that the person who owns the machine obviously has the right to turn it on and off and determine the conditions of its use. The employment of semi-automatic machinery on this large scale had not really been conceptualized as yet in philosophical or economic terms. Classical economic treatises, like Adam Smith's *Wealth of Nations* (1776), could not foresee the new social and economic problems soon to be posed by industrialization. The problems of concern had to do with wages and rents and commerce, not industrial production; and the theoretical task was conceived to be the forging of a rational alternative to a state-controlled mercantilism. The traditional European capitalist was a merchant, not a manufacturer, anyway. He might be a landowner, an owner of buildings, an owner of money, an owner of raw materials, commodities, and manufactured goods. But he was not a manufacturer himself. Manufacturers were traditionally people who made things by hand—artisans, tradesmen, craftsmen, mechanicians—and many of them owned their own tools and machines. The traditional spinners and weavers, in the slowly dying cottage textile industries, owned their own spinning wheels and looms and were manufacturers; in relation to them, the role of the merchant-capitalist was to distribute raw materials, collect finished products, and place goods upon the market.

It was, furthermore, common in this period for certain large, technologically sophisticated enterprises to be the monopoly of the state. In the United States, the federal government operated a postal service, mint, navy yards, and arsenals; the states built and managed turnpikes, canals, railroads, harbors, icebreakers, towboats, and breakwaters and, in the case of Pennsylvania, proposed to use the profits to support government without taxes. Religious communities, practicing a kind of primitive communism, successfully operated factories employing the most modern machines. Crozer himself had visited Father Rapp's establishment at New Harmony. Public enterprise was accepted as being in the public interest.

Thus, despite the rapid investment of private capital in the new machines in England and in America, it was by no means a settled economic principle in either country that large-scale manufacturing, and other technological enterprises that exceeded the capacities of handicraft industries, should necessarily be regarded as exclusively the province of private capital, along with banks and merchant houses and great estates. By hindsight, it may appear that because large-scale manufacturing required great capital investment, far beyond the capacities of inventors and mechanicians, the existing sources of private capital would necessarily take control. But in the late eighteenth and early nineteenth centuries, before industrial capitalism became the dominant economic institution, there were many thoughtful people who still saw alternative ways of using the new machinery. Much of the social conflict in England and America in the early nineteenth century can be regarded as a struggle—a brief struggle, to be sure—for control of the machinery of the Industrial Revolution.

The most immediately available line of answers to the question of who should control the machinery was provided by articulate men and women who had been brought up in the intellectual tradition of the Enlightenment. The common principles of that extensive intellectual movement had been laid down in the late seventeenth century and the first three quarters of the eighteenth; by 1825, these principles had been proclaimed for so long, and by spokesmen with such varying degrees of talent, that to some they seemed archaic intellectual conventions when they were not self-evident truths; to others they appeared as a tattered collation of infidel abominations. It was a complex tradition, with its own national and theoretical varieties, and it is not possible here to do more than summarize those commonly accepted ideas that were most relevant to the social issues raised by the rise of industry. In brief, the Enlightenment taught an orderly universe, the adequacy of reason to solve man's problems, the necessity of learning from nature and experience rather than from books, the innate goodness of man, the essential equality of man, a universal natural religion devoid of priests, revelation, and superstition, and the progressive improvement of civilization without divine intervention. In America the creed was given various theological phrasings by the left-leaning religious sects and factions, such as the Hicksite Quakers, the Unitarians, and the Universalists, and by nonsectarian Deists; it was articulated in the economic and political theses of the more radical members of the mechanicians' community, who as craftsmen supported the Workingmen's movement, and by a number of philosophical economists.

The application of these general principles to the problems posed by industrialization was to be the work of a generation of romantic, freethinking radicals who tried—and failed—to wrest control of the machines away from the private owner and place it in the hands of the community. This radical movement had its adherents in Rockdale.

THE FREETHINKERS OF CHESTER CREEK

To play with the ideas of the Enlightenment, and particularly to practice free thought—that is, to question the established wisdom openly—was one of the traditional perquisites of the educated. It did not imply abandonment of one's place in society. On Chester Creek, it was the literate people— gentlemen farmers, merchants, manufacturers, lawyers, doctors, clergymen, mechanics—who in the 1820's were reading and debating the ideas of the early Utopian socialists. At the county seat itself, the infant Chester Debating Society in January 1826 considered the subject: "Will Robert Owen's system as explained by himself contribute to the happiness of mankind?" The secretary of that Society, John K. Zeilin, who announced the topic, was hardly a radical freethinker. He was twenty-three years old, deputy prothonotary, and clerk of the town council. At the moment he was reading law under Edward Darlington, and would later become well known in the county as an attorney, occupant of various appointive offices, and colonel of the militia. In politics he, like his mentor Darlington, moved from the Democratic Republican side in the 1820's to the Whigs in the 1840's.[1] But right now, free thought was still respectable, and at the jubilee celebration of the Fourth of July in Chester in 1826, toasts were raised to such symbols of liberty as the Marquis de Lafayette, Simon Bolivar, and— by John K. Zeilin—to Missolonghi and the grave of Byron.[2]

The Democratic Republican newspaper, the *Upland Union,* similarly, while in no sense an organ of free thought, gave space and consideration to more or less liberal positions, printing bulletins on the progress of the New Harmony settlement, publishing Robert Southey's "Complaints of the Poor" in the poetry column and notices of feminist Mary Wollstonecraft Shelley's new book, *The Last Man.* All this, of course, was to be found amidst material of very different tenor: editorials on the female virtues and on the need to be ever aware of approaching death, reports of the activities of the major political parties, church announcements. Perhaps the *Upland Union's* policy might be summarized as one of attempting to appeal to the full spectrum of respectable educated opinion and interest—and this, in 1826, included the freethinkers.

Among the owners and manufacturers in the Rockdale district, however, there seems to have been at this period only one man who could be regarded as a freethinker in any sense. This was John S. Phillips, the manager of the power-loom factory by Old Sable Forge. And among the nearby gentry, the best-known free enquirer was the gentleman farmer Minshall Painter.

John S. Phillips, the "open Infidel"

There is no evidence to suggest that Phillips was an active follower of Robert Owen or Fanny Wright, or that he had any interest in the Valley Forge Commune (of which more later), which was founded on Owenite principles. It would seem that he was a freethinker in the generic sense: an adherent of no creed, whether religious or political, but dedicated rather to the application of intellect—and particularly his own very considerable powers—to the answering of questions of interest to mankind. Before his removal to Rockdale, it will be recalled, he had joined both the Franklin Institute and the Academy of Natural Sciences. He had a particular interest in one of the specialties of Thomas Say—conchology, or the study of molluscs by the collection and examination of their shells—and after he returned to the city he continued this interest as the Curator of Conchology at the Academy. During his early membership in the Academy, he regularly attended the weekly meetings, where he met and conversed with both the liberal naturalists Say, Bonaparte, Troost, and Lesueur, and also the more conservative faction, including his own sponsor George Ord, who was strongly opposed to the political tendencies of his colleagues. Phillips' attendance temporarily ceased, however, early in 1825, about the time when his plans for the Rockdale cotton factory were getting under way.

Upon his arrival at Rockdale, Phillips rented a small stone house from Moore, on the hill overlooking the forge and factory. He lived alone, except perhaps for a housekeeper, and seems to have devoted himself intensively to mechanical interests, including the new sugar-liquor filter which he patented, and to the problems of power-loom machinery. There were not, in 1825, many intellectual companions for him in the neighborhood. Crozer, who lived a couple of miles down the road, was preoccupied with the problems of his own machinery. He had some interest in communal experiments, having visited New Harmony on his western tour, during Father Rapp's occupancy, before he sold it to Owen. But Crozer was a shy man, country-educated, and not comfortable with worldly intellectuals from Philadelphia.

Phillips' prospects for intellectual companionship improved in 1829 when the Lammots arrived at Lenni. One of the family was a young man of about twenty-one, Ferdinand Fairfax Lammot, and despite the difference in age (Phillips was nine years older) they became fast friends, riding about the countryside together and oftentimes spending the night with Ferdinand's sister Meta, now Mrs. Alfred du Pont, at Nemours on the Brandywine. Although the Lammots were Swedenborgians, and thus adherents of a complex theology designed to counteract deism, they too challenged conventional religious wisdom. In any case, the young men seem to have been able to understand one another well.

By the fall of 1830, Phillips was becoming a frequent visitor to the Brandywine, sometimes with Ferdinand, sometimes with his brother Clifford or his sisters Camilla, Eveline, or Elizabeth, but most often alone on a gig drawn by his horse Wildfire. His visits were all the more frequent because he was often in Wilmington on business and spent many weekends at the spa at Yellow Springs to the north. An overbearingly talkative man, insistent on expressing his own thoughts, he was not sensitive to the needs of others for food, rest, and privacy, and he drove the Brandywine ladies to distraction by his attentions. He was, furthermore, looking for a wife, now that his cotton business was successful, and had his eye most particularly on the twenty-year-old Sophie Madeleine du Pont (although his eccentricities kept everyone in doubt as to his actual intention). The Du Pont girls kept a sardonic diary of the visitors to the house, often including a disparaging quip about any male who displeased them. John S. Phillips for three years occupied a conspicuous place in this diary and its entries reveal a good deal about his interests. He liked to read the Romantic poets, reciting Burns's poetry aloud from memory, and naming his new horse (after Wildfire went blind) Mazeppa, no doubt in honor of Lord Byron. He adored the opera, especially *The Hunchback.* His favorite song was "How Shall He His Pain Discover?" and he liked to entertain the ladies with ghost stories on cold winter evenings. He grew quantities of exotic flowers—*Datura,* roses, *Thunbergia alatta,* heliotrope, dahlias—in his greenhouse and presented them to the ladies in arrangements of his own design. He invented mechanical devices for smoking and watering his plants, and new procedures for curing them when ill. He planned to grow grapes by the thousands under glass. He designed and manufactured fireworks; he lec-

JOHN S. PHILLIPS (1799–1876).

tured people on phrenology and the mechanical principles of power looms. He made outlandish clothing for himself: huge India rubber boots, a woven nose-mask for the cold, a gray suit that looked like a coat of armor. And, of course, he was forever advising the ladies on their own proper skills: knitting, sewing, and cooking.

The image provided by the diary, thus, is of an awkward "giant" (as Eleuthera described him), a big bearish man, enthusiastic and overbearing in manner, indiscriminate in his interests. They called him "the Knight of Rockdale" and (in allusion to another tilter after windmills) "Val de Peñas." Indifferent to religion and no attender of churches, he nonetheless tried to please a group of highly evangelical young ladies by bringing them tracts for their Sunday School. Little is recorded of his social views from the diary, except for what can be inferred from his taste for Romantic poetry. He talked, as one of them said, of everything: "Of dogs & horses, love & marriage, death & heaven, politics & domestic economy &c &c &c." It is only in the correspondence of Sophie du Pont that an intimation of a more sinister kind appears—the allusion to the "mill of an open Infidel" who can only have been Phillips. Phillips himself seems to have had a wry awareness of the awkward contrast in his character between the manufacturer and the intellectual. Among his favorite works was *Warreniana*, a mildly satirical volume that celebrated the poetic advertisements written by a fictitious manufacturer, Robert Warren, for his "immortal" brand of boot blacking. Warren, "egotistical" and "unfortunate in love," was saluted in this memorial by a series of poems in the style of the English poets, particularly Byron and the Lake poets, that invariably concluded with a request that the reader buy Warren's shoe polish. Phillips thought it very funny.

Phillips was a bore to the ladies in his social group—and, as it turned out, he never married. But, as we have already seen, the fault lay not entirely in his character. Really to interest the Smith sisters, the Brandywine ladies, and the Lammot girls would have required more than light conversation and considerate manners. They were looking for men whom they could convert to evangelical Christianity; men like Phillips "the Knight of Rockdale," freethinkers with a loudly romantic flair, would-be Byronic heroes, were not good candidates for Heaven.[3]

Minshall and Jacob Painter
and the Delaware County Institute of Science

About a mile north of Wrangletown lay the farm of the bachelor brothers Minshall and Jacob Painter, the last scions of a Quaker family long resident in the area. Although they still kept to the use of "thee" and "thou" in family correspondence, they were Deists—avowed infidels and rationalists. Their faith was that science—the study of nature in the largest sense—would lead both to personal serenity and to human progress. They approached the world of learning with a kind of innocent, wide-eyed eclecticism. In the style of the early naturalists, they imported live exotic plants and built up a botanical collection which became known, after the estate passed into the hands of a brother-in-law, as the Tyler Arboretum. They kept a cabinet of minerals, observed the heavens through a large telescope, set up their own printing press, tinkered with early photography. They subscribed to horticultural and technological journals and put together a library that makes a fair sampling of early nineteenth-century titles in geography and natural history. They were interested in the cause of women's rights (and particularly in Fanny Wright), in Utopian socialism, and in the workingmen's movement. And for a time they were involved in political anti-Masonry, taking the populist interpretation that Freemasonry was nothing but a cloak for nepotism.

They had no use for religion. Minshall, the more articulate of the two brothers, once wrote to his sister:

> I will not permit myself to be chatechised but openly profess to be infidel to the popular religions they being neither what nature inculcates nor good sense allows. . . . If we knew when a man was born we might almost unerringly foretell his religious faith, but infidelity is that peaceable state where dogmatical nonsense is preached no more tho' the leprous taint of slander is on the name. Credulity is great and ignorance is her prophet. . . . Modern orthodox religion [is viewed by the infidel] as picture gallerys and fossil museums dug out of ancient literature and now strangely associated.[4]

And Jacob Painter was equally critical of organized religion:

> Old forms of religion like old forms of government must submit to the revolutionary effects of time. Antiquated views and rites yield slowly and obstinately. It has been concluded that there must be a creed, terrible in its effects to the disobedient—laws must be cruel—religion must be stern —and ceremonies must be strict, and instead of promoting a good feeling, the whole becomes a thing of formulas.[5]

Despite their unorthodox religious views, the Painters were fully accepted as members of the Philadelphia area's community of mechanicians and natural philosophers. In the gatherings of this group, disputation about religion and politics was regarded as bad manners, and infidel and evangelical cooperated comfortably in projects for the advancement of systematic knowledge. Out of the informal gatherings of Delaware County's intellectuals there grew, in 1833, the organization known as the Delaware County Institute of Science. One of the five founding members was Minshall Painter, who acted as secretary for thirty-six years; among the others were George Smith, M.D., who served as president until 1882, and who as a Pennsylvania legislator was in the 1830's working with Thaddeus Stevens for the passage of the public school law (actually passed in 1834); and John Cassin, who would become internationally renowned as an authority on ornithology. Within a few years William Martin, Edward Darlington, and John P. Crozer had joined; Daniel Lammot, the Riddles, the Hills, John Garsed, and James Houghton did not join but did subscribe to the building fund for the hall, which was constructed near the future site of Media, the new county seat, in 1837, on a lot donated by Minshall Painter.

The Institute was consciously modeled after the Franklin Institute (minus that Institute's initial concern with mechanics' education). It attracted the attention of the leading mechanicians of the area. One of its sponsors was James Ronaldson, the cotton manufacturer who had been a prime mover in the founding of the Franklin Institute; and Dr. Robert Patterson, then director of the U.S. Mint, gave the address at the opening ceremonies for the Institute's building. Its program of monthly lectures attracted much attention, for controversial topics were confronted, such as the question of an alleged native inferiority of the African race. Its library included works on all sides of important subjects: in the field of education, for instance, it contained both Pestalozzian Joseph Neef's progressive *Sketch of a Plan and Method of Education* (1808) and Joseph Lancaster's popular rote-learning program *The British System of Education* (1812). In the natural sciences it had *The Bridgewater Treatises on the Power, Wisdom, and Goodness of God as Manifested in the Creation* (a series of texts in popular science) and also technical journals like Silliman's *Annals of Science* and the *Journal of the Franklin Institute*.

Further, the Institute undertook significant research and development activities. It inaugurated an agricultural development program, distributing seeds and cuttings of "all the most important grains, plants, and fruits suitable to our soil and climate." One of the members, Dr. Joshua Ash, produced a detailed property map of the county in 1848, showing natural features, roads, all major towns, factories, and township and property lines; the president, Dr. Smith, prepared a geological survey and went on to complete a history of the county (although its publication was delayed until after the onset of the Civil War). In 1846, and for ten years thereafter, the Institute held a competitive fair in the autumn, awarding prizes to Delaware County producers in various fields of endeavor: to cotton manufacturers for their cloths, to mechanicians for edge tools and machinery, to ladies for their needlework and painting, to farmers for their corn and vegetables and livestock, even to professional men for improvements in medical and scientific equipment.[6]

In all of this, the Institute served as an open marketplace for ideas, not only on technical and scientific subjects but on controversial social issues as well. In such a setting, criteria of religious orthodoxy were out of place and the only goal was knowledge. As Minshall Painter put it, "Truth we want be it ever so terrible . . ."

Such a point of view was a legacy of the Enlightenment that was difficult for even the most hardened evangelical professors to put aside. John P. Crozer was an increasingly zealous Christian, but he found the Institute's scientific positivism compatible with his own Christian understanding. He was closely involved with the Institute's affairs until he moved to Upland, and in the 1840's was for a time its corresponding secretary. After reading Buckland's *Bridgewater Treatise* on geology and paleontology, which contained much evidence from the fossil record about the antiquity of Creation and the succession of life forms leading up to man, he was moved to write in his diary a liberal testimonial of mingled scientific and religious faith:

The yet not fully understood science of geology may interfere with the literal sense of the first chapter of Genesis, but can never overthrow the Christian theory; and it is satisfactory to find eminent geologists—those who have adopted the opinion that the world has existed many thousand ages—fully and unequivocally believing in the truths of revelation.

When I was a child, and first learned the philosophy of the rainbow in the heavens, I was disappointed, grieved, and wished I might be misinformed. I had always been struck with the beautiful sublimity of the Scripture account of the rainbow, and had received the impression that it was sent as a special messenger from God on each occasion of its appearance; and when I saw it accounted for as an ordinary arrangement of nature, it seemed to detract from the high dictation, "I do set my bow in the clouds." Thus it was with me when geologists assumed the position that the world, instead of being the Almighty's work in six of our days, was clearly many thousands or millions of years in becoming what it now is. I felt confounded, but further reflection makes me think differently; and if geologists establish their position, and agree among themselves—which as yet they are far from doing—I shall find no difficulty in the least with my religious sentiments. God is yet the Creator of all, and Moses was his prophet; man is a fallen creature, and Jesus Christ came into the world to save sinners. These truths remain unaffected by geological discoveries, and will ever remain amid the wreck of matter and the crash of worlds.[7]

It was Minshall Painter who nominated Crozer for membership in the Institute. The two men had had a brief prior correspondence, on the subjects of the need for savings banks for working-class people and the intelligence of the mill girls of Lowell. After Crozer joined, the correspondence continued on Institute subjects for at least several years. Crozer addressed his infidel colleague as "Esteemed Friend," and was almost certainly influenced in a liberal direction by Minshall Painter's evident good will and by his exposure to the positivistic philosophy of the English naturalists. Whether Crozer ever influenced Painter is less sure. Some years later, still an unreconstructed and even dogmatic infidel who had no use for the idea of God and afterlife, he expressed his irritation at the patronizing attitude of some evangelicals he knew:

go where you will the *presumptious man of god* is flaunting his religion and asking a part of your substance to support it, lauding those who side with him and hurling damnation on his opposers. It is common to hear it said infidels who are honest and intelligent, are Christians at heart and it is no consequence they deny it religious professors will have it so.[8]

The Workers

Little information remains about the political views of the workers in the Rockdale district in the period from 1825 to about 1832. There were no strikes and no local chapter of a Workingmen's Party. There were, however, many freethinkers among the working people. Writing in retrospect, the mill owner Richard S. Smith, who came to Rockdale in 1833, recorded:

Infidelity stalked boldly among the people; the disciples of Paine held public meetings to inculcate his doctrines, and on one occasion when a Presbyterian clergyman gave notice that he should preach on the evidences of Christianity, he was interrupted by some of those who attended for the purpose with a volume of Paine's works in their hands.[9]

Yet there survives no direct evidence of informed political interest in early Utopian socialism among the workers of the Rockdale district. One weaver, a member of an English immigrant family, the Morrises, who worked at Phillips' and Crozer's mills from 1832 to 1834, expressed fervent satisfaction in one of his letters home: ". . . to think that we are in a free country, free from the oppressive tyrants of King, Priests and Lords." And the same man, writing in 1841 after he had moved to Ohio, wrote to his brother in

England: "I have been informed that you have gained some steps of reform in England and also that there is a new society there called Sochilestes [socialists] which have increased very fast and got very numerous. Please to let us know if there is many of them about you. . . ."[10] But the evident unfamiliarity of weaver Morris with the word "Socialists," and his failure to mention any analogous society in America, suggests that Fanny Wright, Robert Owen, and the Utopian socialists generally had not been a common topic of conversation among the operatives in the Rockdale mills during his sojourn there in the early 1830's.

One is left with the impression that despite the presence among the workers of some anti-clerical freethinkers who read Thomas Paine and liked to heckle preachers, there was little organized radical political thought among the rank-and-file operatives. There would be a number of reasons for the confinement of such views to a few literate mechanics and experienced mule spinners (of whom altogether there cannot have been more than about fifty at this date). One was the illiteracy of many of the population; a number had come from England, Scotland, and Ireland, where schooling was not yet universal, and the state of Pennsylvania did not provide free public schools until late in the 1830's. Many of the workers who put their receipts for wages in William Martin's receipt book in the 1820's could not sign their names and had to make their mark.[11] Women and children, who constituted about half the work force, could not vote and were expected to be politically passive. A few men were conservative Catholics, Methodists, Baptists, Presbyterians, Episcopalians, and Quakers, and would be unlikely to identify with disciples of Paine and Volney. And some of those who might have been interested were probably intimidated by the general opposition to such views on the part of their employers (Phillips, who had hired William Morris, perhaps excepted). Furthermore, because the roles of mule and throstle spinners were new and did not have behind them an ancient, medieval guild, the spinners on Chester Creek, as in Philadelphia, had no union which could join, or be inspired by the example of, the Mechanics' Union of Trade Associations and its socialist leader William Heighton.

The workingmen (other than mechanics) on Chester Creek were in an ideological limbo, as it were, separated by barriers of geography, illiteracy, sex, age, and novelty of profession from the sources of radical thought in the cities.

The Hecklers

And finally, there were local rowdies who made up a kind of infidel rabble. The best example of their anti-religious terrorism is preserved in the history of the Lima Methodist Church (as later recorded by William Fox, an early member of the congregation), at the time when James Riddle was preaching in the early 1830's. The house in which devotional services were held stood near the Porcupine Tavern and not far from the Black Horse Tavern; the neighborhood, about a mile north of Rockdale, was called Wrangletown. The tavern people, as Fox recalled later, were "very wicked, drinking, swearing & dancing," and did not take kindly to the presence of evangelists turning their "world upside down." The confrontation between evangelical Christianity and its enemies was sometimes violent:

the rabble would come and swear we should not hold Meeting that they would tear the house down upon us, and would try to pull out the Logs and throw stones at the door and burst it open; and hold dogs by the ears to make them howl and [illegible] to throw brimstone down the chimney and smoke us to death, often fasten us in, when we would have to put one out of the window to open the door.

One man came and took the Bible from the preacher and said it was not the word of God and broke up the Meeting; We tried to hold Class Meeting at nights but this they would not allow for they would come with such force that they would break the Meeting up for that night. One night they struck Wm Fox on the head 3 or 4 times and cut his head, we then applied to the Law for that man and put him to jail and he had to pay 100 dols so that put a stop to their carrying on and the little church had peace for some time.[12]

THE CONTEXT OF POST-REVOLUTIONARY RADICALISM IN THE LOWER DELAWARE VALLEY

The few freethinkers of Chester Creek were by no means isolated from sympathetic colleagues, however, and the educated class, whether religious or infidel, were constantly exposed to radical social doctrines. The Phila-delphia-Wilmington area which surrounded Chester Creek was, during the years of the American Revolution and in the two generations that followed, the center of radical social thought in America. As the commercial, industrial, and (for a time) political center of the state and the country, Philadelphia in particular attracted to itself all varieties of opinion. Here, in the citadel of freedom, the home of the religiously tolerant Quakers and the forum of the great radical mechanicians Benjamin Franklin and Thomas Paine, belief in the principles of the Enlightenment survived in public life long after it had been politically eclipsed in both France and England. The European Enlightenment never really took intellectual root in New England, preoccupied from the first by the challenge of establishing (or disestablishing) a rigorously Calvinist commonwealth. It flourished in Virginia, despite the presence of slavery (repugnant to men of advanced mind), but as the northern cotton-manufacturing industry stimulated the plantation economy, the need to justify slavery increasingly diverted the attention of southern intellectuals. It was in the City of Brotherly Love, and in the lower Delaware Valley region of which that city was the center, from Wilmington to Trenton—and increasingly during the 1820's in New York City—that the goals of the Enlightenment continued to motivate a significant body of citizens.

Because the Philadelphia area provided the intellectual environment of the educated members of the Chester Creek community, we shall now look carefully at the radical tradition of thought in the region in the early nineteenth century. Both Christians and infidels among them had friends among the freethinkers, read newspapers reporting and editorializing on free thought and Utopian socialism, knew cousins and nephews who attended progressive schools, listened to political speeches extolling the communal way of life. The families of conservative manufacturers and mill owners in the Rockdale district might indeed feel themselves to be besieged by a surrounding army of infidels.

The Pennsylvania Constitution of 1776

The Commonwealth of Pennsylvania itself had been created in a kind of radical *coup d'état* by the left-wing Patriotic movement, which in 1776 produced a revolution within a revolution. Led mostly by mechanicians—Benjamin Franklin, printer; David Rittenhouse, surveyor; Thomas Paine, bridge-builder; Christopher Marshall, druggist; and George Clymer, merchant—the radicals seized the opportunity provided by a widely based popular clamor for separation from England to press for leveling social reforms. At a hastily assembled constitutional convention in 1776, a state constitution was framed which fundamentally challenged the old economic and social structure of the commonwealth; it was put into effect before the promised referendum could be held. It has been termed the most radical charter for government yet adopted in the English-speaking world, being more egalitarian in its franchise provisions than anything produced in even the most extremely republican stages of the French Revolution. Coleman Sellers's father-in-law, Charles Willson Peale, was an ardent partisan of this constitution.

The constitution began with a preamble on the nature of man, following in general the precepts of John Locke, to the effect that man was a creature of his experience and thus of his society. It went on to a declaration of rights. This bill of rights established almost complete religious liberty by making all free persons who professed belief in God and the Bible eligible to vote and hold office. This meant that all Protestant sects were on an equal footing; beyond that, that Roman Catholics could vote and hold office; some believed it even opened the franchise and officeholding to Jews (for the Jewish bible was, in effect, the Christian Old Testament). The constitution also eliminated all property qualifications, not only for the right to vote but for the right to hold office as well; the franchise was extended to all free men who had reached their twenty-first year, had resided in the state for one year, and had paid some tax (or—a concession to the wealthy—who were the sons of freeholders). Thus not only were the white working poor enfranchised; even free blacks were eligible to vote and hold office. Judges were to be elected for a fixed period on fixed salaries; there was to be a unicameral legislature (reducing the power of the wealthy class, which traditionally was exercised in the upper house) with broad administrative as well as legislative powers; the traditional high authority of a usually conservative president and council were greatly weakened; and a Council of Censors was appointed to protect and amend the constitution. Various specific reforms were incorporated, too, to meet popular complaints, such as a prohibition on the imprisonment of bankrupt persons for debt, and a provision for universal education at county expense.

This constitution was so revolutionary in its implications that the social conflict it aroused seriously hampered the commonwealth's ability to wage war against the British. Conservative religious leaders, like Henry Melchior Muhlenberg, voiced fears of a government by "Jews, Turks, Spinozists, Deists, perverted naturalists."[1] And on the economic front, as one constitutional historian has summarized it, it was a class struggle between an incipient middle class of tradesmen and mechanicians and a well-established aristocracy of landowners and bankers.[2]

The political forces supporting the constitution of 1776 centered in the cities of Philadelphia and to a lesser extent in Lancaster and Pittsburgh; it had the support of the "New Light" Presbyterians, and thus of many of the Scots-Irish in the western counties. The well-to-do rural agricultural areas, particularly in Delaware and Chester counties, were staunchly in favor of replacing it by a less restrictive document, and at length the anti-constitutionalists were able to assemble a new convention, which in 1790 produced a new charter for the state. This document turned the state back to a system of government that maintained more nearly the traditional separation of powers among the executive, legislative, and judicial branches. The executive was restored to strength, the legislature returned to bicameral form, and the judiciary were virtually tenured for life; their removal required impeachment. In many ways it was a copy of the federal Constitution of the same year; and not coincidentally, for Pennsylvania's experience was debated in the federal convention. But the 1790 constitution could hardly be called reactionary: there was still universal manhood suffrage for taxpaying freemen; the right to the franchise and office was open to all who believed in one God and a future state of rewards and punishments; and all children were to be educated, if necessary in public schools.

The disillusioned adherents of the earlier constitution, as the years of Federalist power slipped by, coalesced as "Republicans" around the figure of that arch symbol of Enlightenment man, Thomas Jefferson; hard-line patriots, they cherished an enduring sympathy for France, a festering suspicion of England, and a fear of any step toward a system of centralized federal power as being merely a means for gradually returning the people to the monarchical and mercantilist shackles from which the Revolution had freed them.[3]

Revolution's Legacy: Jeffersonian Republicans, Freethinkers, and New Lights

The spectrum of post-revolutionary ideology, ranging from the most conservative Federalists at one end to the most radical Democratic Republicans at the other, included more shades of opinion than could be represented in party politics. Parties, indeed, were apt to be condemned as mere instruments of political expediency, and after the temporary triumph of the Federalists in the 1790's in establishing workable organs of state and national government, a single Republican "party" seemed to accommodate most shades of social thought. Under the aegis of Thomas Jefferson, a leftward-leaning rhetoric returned increasingly to favor in the first two decades of the new century.

The principles commended by this rhetoric, which have been called Jeffersonian, were most popularly expressed in the writings of Thomas Paine and Constantin François de Volney. Paine had been the literary firebrand of the American Revolution; his calls to revolt had been predicated upon the notion, enshrined in the Declaration of Independence, that all men are created equal, that all have certain inalienable rights, and that governmental interference with these rights justified—indeed, required— a people's rebellion. Paine was condemned to death *in absentia* in England; moving to Paris in support of the French Revolution, he was imprisoned there. In 1797 he wrote *The Age of Reason,* an Enlightenment tract heavy with anti-clerical sentiments. When Jefferson entered the White House in 1801, he wrote cordially to Paine in France, inviting him to return to the United States on an American warship as the guest of the nation. Although he was constantly harassed by the Federalist and religious press, Paine lived out his life in New Jersey and New York, promoting deism as the "Republican Religion" and conversing with his friends (including men like Charles Willson Peale and Robert Fulton) among the Republican mechanicians of the new country.

Volney, a scholarly Frenchman, for a time the administrator of an experimental agricultural community in Corsica, and an actor in the French Revolution also, in 1791 had published his *Les ruines; ou, méditation sur les révolutions des empires,* and in 1793 a popular little "catechism" deriving morality from the laws of nature. Volney's *Les ruines* was quickly translated into English and in that language became widely known as *Volney's Ruins.* It was a popularization of common eighteenth-century theories of cultural evolution and historical criticisms of religion. Acknowledging only an otiose deity, Volney roundly condemned all existing religions as priestly impostures motivated by greed and facilitated by ignorance. He saw the origin of civilization as an event that had occurred in Egypt, where, he asserted, "A race of men now rejected from society for their *sable skin and frizzled hair,* founded on the study of the laws of nature, those civil and religious systems which still govern the universe."[4] In effect, Volney argued that the social contract, potentially so ennobling to all when founded on natural law, had been broken by greedy men who had used, and still used, palaces and temples to take the riches of the earth to themselves and plunge the balance of mankind into misery and despair by means of their false superstitions and despicable religious justifications.

In the 1790's, Volney was as impressive to the young freethinkers as was Paine. Jefferson was very much pleased with *Les ruines* and corresponded with Volney; and when in 1798 the aging Pierre du Pont de Nemours came to New York as the appointed French consul, Volney accompanied him. Du Pont was rejected, however, and Volney returned to France. But Jefferson, reading Volney's *Les ruines,* translated the first twenty of its twenty-four chapters and sent them to Volney, by hand of a mutual friend, William Maclure, for his approval. (Eventually the American poet Joel

Barlow completed the translation, and Jefferson's draft was burned at his request.) Paine made use of Volney's book in writing his own tract, *The Age of Reason.*[5]

The "Jeffersonian" position (if it can be treated in such typological terms) was essentially a middle ground between the extremes. "Jeffersonians" believed in a God but not in ritualistic, priestly, theologically involved religions, and were apt to be Unitarians, Universalists, or Quakers, denying both the bureaucracy of Catholicism and the cosmic élitism of the Calvinist tradition. They believed (rhetorically) in freedom and equality, but in fact were apt to be slaveowners and to regard Negroes and American Indians as inferior races doomed to extinction if they remained in contact with the more advanced European stocks. They conceived of an America (to use Leo Marx's felicitous phrase) "of the middle landscape," comfortably enjoying the virtues and delights of the rural life, yet taking up the advantages of the mechanician's ingenuity; they would exchange American (and especially southern and western) farm products for European (and to some extent northeastern U.S.) manufactured goods.[6] They indulged themselves in literature, natural history, and mechanical experiments, and were apt to sympathize more easily with the philosophy of the French Revolution than with that of the pragmatic English constitutional monarchy.

But pervading the Jeffersonian tradition was a position on the matter of civil government. The Jeffersonians disapproved of, feared, and saw no need for a strong, centralized, hierarchical administrative apparatus. They sought minimal expenditures, minimal debts, minimal taxes, minimal tariffs, minimal governmental regulation, minimal banking, minimal chartered monopolies. In an America of plantations and hamlets, diversified in economy and only lightly dependent on a few seaports for foreign trade, there would be no need for standing armies, legions of depraved urban poor, swollen bureaucracies. The people would rule directly. Everyone would be a kind of country gentleman, on some level on the scale from yeoman to master of Monticello; and even if he were much of the time occupied by commerce, by a profession, or by a mechanic's trade, he would still be able to retire to his house and garden, to read and write pastoral odes, or papers in natural history, or letters to a circle of thoughtful friends.

In an America for a generation, from 1800 to 1824, presided over (one can hardly say administered) by Jeffersonians, free thought in the Enlightenment style flourished. There was a large segment of the press that served as a forum for Republican freethinkers. Some of the newspapers, like the Philadelphia *Aurora,* were in effect party organs, which translated into immediate political application the general principles of republicanism. The *Aurora* had been edited at first by Benjamin Franklin Bache—a grandson of the American philosopher—and then, after his death, by a fiery immigrant Irishman, William Duane, who married his widow. Duane, a friend of Tom Paine, quickly became one of the leading political figures in the party and, as editor of the *Aurora*, one of the principal propagandists of Republican principles. Another Republican editor was John Binns, a pro-Irish Englishman who had been a close associate of William Godwin and other English radicals. He was tried in England for treason in 1798, but acquitted; he came to America in 1801, to live in Northumberland County near Thomas Cooper, the English radical, and Joseph Priestley, the exiled chemist and fellow Unitarian, who also had been a victim of the repressive English reaction to the French attempt to translate Enlightenment principles into political realities.

Until his death in 1809, Paine tried heroically to make Reason the "Republican Religion." Most Enlightenment intellectuals would find nothing offensive in the bland contention that man could know God by the use of reason, and know by the same means the duties that God expected of him, and thereby be able to live happily in this world and the next. But such a generalized belief, coupled with an antipathy toward organized religions, would not entirely satisfy those who valued the ceremonial fellowship of co-religionists or the leadership of a recognized ministry. For such liberals as these, the three plain creeds—the Society of Friends, the Unitarians, and the Universalists—offered the congregational structure of religious denomination without demanding much more than simple Reason in the way of ritual or theology. The Quakers, and particularly the followers of Elias Hicks, were devoted to social equality (including the abolition of slavery); the Unitarians, who had grown out of the liberal movement in the Congregational and Presbyterian churches, denied the doctrine of the Trinity and even the divinity of Christ; the Universalists asserted that all men were eligible for salvation. In these denominations, as in all of the period, there was a wide range of political and social beliefs; the most radical of them all, politically, were probably the "New Light" or "Blue Light" Quakers, who advocated immediate emancipation of slaves, and equal rights for women, and regarded the grave and respectable officers of the conventional Friends' meetings as a stiff, authoritarian, repressive lay priesthood.

The ideological ambience of Jeffersonian post-revolutionary Pennsylvania was thus one in which many of the beliefs and values of the previous century's Enlightenment were widely held by respectable people in all social classes. Even the more conventionally devout, and more aristocratic, Federalists were for the most part accustomed to recognizing all but the more extreme exponents of these views as respectable colleagues and fellow citizens. Deists were no longer impelled to write anti-clerical literature and were willing to accept quiet church-goers as practitioners of natural religion. In these matters, for many Pennsylvanians, a live-and-let-live philosophy would seem to have been the most comfortable. And in political matters, too, the issues were (in regard to the national offices) less and less a struggle of Federalists and Republicans, and more and more a matter of factional dispute among adherents to an all-embracing, inchoate populism.

The superficial vulnerability of the Jeffersonian Republicans lay in their indifference, if not antipathy, to the traditional religious organizations. The more orthodox Protestant groups, from the days of the Revolution onward, maintained a kind of guerrilla warfare, characterized chiefly by intermittent hit-and-run tactics against infidels and freethinkers like Tom Paine. This guerrilla warfare, as we shall see, eventually in the 1820's turned into an organized onslaught of awesome proportions. But the Jeffersonians had an inner weakness which would only become crucial as the pressure of increasing population and technological improvement mounted. They believed, fundamentally, that men were accountable not to their superiors but to their peers; they could not tolerate a principle of subordination. They placed a kind of blind faith in the reasonableness of men; they expected that cooperation would occur naturally, without constraint, as soon as artificial restraints of property, class, government, and religion were removed, and spontaneous associations could arise. And thus they did not think very seriously about the problems of designing efficient bureaucratic management; they rejected the very concept of one "managing" another as unmoral.

French Educators in the Enlightenment Tradition

The "rich Scotchman" William Maclure who had been Jefferson's messenger to Volney was at the center of a rather specialized contingent of émigré French naturalists and educators in the Philadelphia area (including one who taught school for a time in the Rockdale district), whose pedagogy was founded on the theories of Jean Jacques Rousseau and the practice of Pestalozzi and Von Fellenberg. Maclure himself had been born in Scotland in 1763; he came to America on commercial business frequently after the Revolution, and in 1796 he was naturalized as a United States citizen. He was a tall, heavy-set man, quiet and polite in conversation, a bit shy, and inflexible in his opinions. Having accumulated a private fortune by the age of thirty, he was retired from business and was devoting himself to the intellectual interests and the philanthropies which his great wealth allowed him to indulge. He was elected to the American Philosophical Society in 1799 and in 1812 helped to found the Academy of Natural Sciences, of which he was president from 1817 until his death in 1840. He personally carried out the first geological survey of the United States and became president of the American Geological Society; he came to be known as the "Father of American geology." He knew France from his mercantile days, was a devotee of the rational principles of the early Revolution, and traveled extensively on the continent attempting to settle American claims against the new régimes. In the course of these activities, he acquired a collection of some 25,000 books and pamphlets on the French Revolution, which he presented to the Academy of Natural Sciences in 1821 (and which is now kept as a special collection by the University of Pennsylvania). In politics he was a Jeffersonian Republican-turned-socialist, who believed that the salvation of the world depended upon improving the education of youth. In 1821 he had founded an experimental educational community near Alicante in Spain; the community had been disbanded and the lands returned to a monastery as a result of the conservative revolution in 1823, and he was now back in Philadelphia.[7]

Maclure had first encountered the Pestalozzian system of education in 1805 when, in the company of Napoleon Bonaparte, Minister Talleyrand, and the American ambassador, he visited the experimental school of Joseph Neef in Paris, where Neef was attempting to demonstrate the value of the Swiss innovator's new method of education in an asylum devoted to war orphans. Although a committee of inquiry eventually reported favorably to the First Consul on the Pestalozzian method as an effective means for educating the poor, the immediate reaction of Napoleon and Talleyrand was cool. Maclure took advantage of the educator's disappointment to invite him to bring Pestalozzi's method to America, promising to pay his and his bride's expenses and guaranteeing him three years' salary at $500 per year. Neef, disillusioned by the circumstances of the orphanage and the inflexibility of the French bureaucracy, agreed.

Joseph Neef was an Alsatian, a big, burly, bearded ex-soldier of Napoleon's, with a *basso profundo* voice and a penchant for loading his language with military oaths. He had been wounded in battle in 1796 and still carried a musket ball lodged in his skull above the palate (where it was to remain for the rest of his life, the cause of constant headaches). He was an independent-minded and ingenious man, now thirty-six, who had acquired a good Jesuit education and was familiar with the philosophical works of the Enlightenment, including the writings of Condillac—the purveyor of a Lockean philosophy of learning not ill adapted to rationalizing the Pestalozzian point of view. During his convalescence he read the early works of Pestalozzi. Inspired, he went to meet Johann Pestalozzi in Switzerland and was at once employed by him as a teacher of gymnastics and various elementary subjects.

The Pestalozzian theory of education could not have been more dramatically at odds with conventional theories of education in the Western world. Pestalozzi had been inspired by reading Rousseau's old pedagogical fantasies, *La Nouvelle Héloïse* and *Émile,* and he had resolved to implement the principles which they—and the whole thrust of Enlightenment humanism—implied. Rote-learning from books, and the kinds of false conceits that books taught, were eschewed as an inadequate, indeed a perilous base, on which to set the early education of a healthy, courageous, happy, and creative human being. Men should live according to the laws of nature, and nature herself should be the teacher, both the extrinsic nature that surrounded the child and the child's own nature within. The teacher was not to be an authority but rather a kind of friendly Socratic elucidator, who put the child in the way of knowledge and, depending on his natural curiosity and enjoyment of learning, encouraged him to *discover,* in himself and the world, the elementary principles on which all knowledge was based. The child learned the mental reckoning of numbers, arithmetic, and geometry by manipulating objects; morality and ethics from inner contemplation; geography, geology, biology, astronomy, and the other natural sciences in excursions and observations. The child was never to be punished; but his natural sociability would readily inspire him to follow his teacher in the disciplined marches, gymnastic exercises, use of firearms, and military drill which Pestalozzian educators believed were necessary to a free people.

Neef came to Philadelphia in 1806 and first set himself to learn English. No doubt as an exercise in the language, as well as for the sake of advertising the method and the new school, he began shortly to write a book in English—*Sketch of a Plan and Method of Education*—which he published at his own expense (or more likely Maclure's) in Philadelphia in 1808. This work was remarkable not only for its value as a pedagogical treatise but also for its simplicity and clarity. In the preface, Neef set forth the philosophy of his plan for saving America from the fate of Europe by means of education:

There lives in Europe, beneath the foot of the Alps, an old man whose name is Pestalozzi, a man as respectable for the goodness of his heart as for the soundness of his head. This man, endowed by nature, or rather nature's god, with the felicity of an observing mind, was forcibly struck by the vices, follies, and extravagancies of the superior ranks, and the ignorance, superstition, and debasement of the inferior ranks of society. He perceived that from these impure sources flowed all the miseries that afflicted his unhappy fellow creatures. Being no disciple of Zeno, the woes of his brethren naturally imparted their anguish to his sensitive heart. The host of calamities, under which he saw his fellow men groaning, deeply grieved his feeling soul, and the gulf of evils, into which he viewed mankind plunged, called forth the most cordial and sincere compassion. Tears fell from his mourning eyes but they were manly tears. Far from being disheartened by such a sad spectacle, he had the courage to enquire into the causes of human misery; he went even a step farther and endeavored to find out a wholesome remedy, calculated to destroy at their very source those evils which inundate the world.

Considering that man is born neither good nor bad, but that the disposition to become either good or bad is intimately interwoven with his organization, he became soon convinced that our education is the only cause of our becoming either good, useful, intelligent, rational, moral and virtuous beings, or wicked, noxious, ignorant, senseless, superstitious, and therefore miserable creatures. His mind was necessarily directed toward investigating the established systems of education; and after a mature examination thereof, he conceived that, without a radical reformation of the prevailing methods, it would be perfectly useless to expect any better results. This reformation became now the subject of his meditations. After having sufficiently digested these most important ideas, he began to communicate his thoughts to the world. In a plain but striking way he unfolded his plan of reformation and displayed the happy consequences to which it would lead. His book was read; his sagacity was admired; his benevolent counsels were applauded—and forgotten: But he did not despond. The same object was exposed to view over and over again, in all the forms and shapes of which it was susceptible; and yet was the desired reformation still to be begun and executed. Determined not to depart this life without at least seeing his theory tried, he resolved, in his old age, of making a full experiment of it himself. He therefore established a school. Other men, animated by his philanthropical enthusiasm, joined him; and thus began a work which will render Pestalozzi's name as dear and venerable to posterity as the deeds of many of his contemporaries will render them execrable to future generations.[8]

In 1809 Neef opened his boys' school on a hill above the Falls of Schuylkill, in the old mansion on the estate of the late Reverend William Smith, first provost of the University of Pennsylvania. The school rapidly acquired both pupils and reputation. His neighbor at the Falls, Oliver Evans, sent his son Oliver Jr. to Neef; other prominent Philadelphia families sent their young scions, including the son and stepson of William Duane, leading Republican politician and editor of the *Aurora,* and still other children were sent from places as far away as Savannah, Louisville, and Boston; in all, he taught about a hundred boys during the four years the school remained at the Falls. Visitors described in vivid terms the boys on excursions into the surrounding woods, which they were allowed to penetrate to the distance of half a mile, and Neef's whistle to bring them back:

Mr. Neef had a method of putting his two fingers in his mouth and producing a tremendous loud whistle. The boys would be scattered around the neighborhood, but when they heard the whistle, you could see them running from all directions to a common center.

It was his custom when roaming around the country with his boys to encourage them to hunt for anything singular or curious in the way of a plant, flower, mineral, etc. When they found anything that excited their curiosity, they would take it to him, and he would on the spot make it the subject of a lecture with his boys gathered around him. . . . [9]

And politician William Duane was still sufficiently impressed, fifteen years later, to write an enthusiastic testimonial for his sons' former teacher, whom he recommended as the man to direct the public school system of the State of Kentucky:

There is only one system of Education in existence fit for a country that is free, or for a people to whom intellectual knowledge is essential in an age where knowledge is power and ignorance is weakness. And perhaps you may be surprised to learn, that there is only one man in this country, and that one man is in Kentucky, who is powerfully qualified to teach and to enable others to teach it. But such is the fact, and I shall not hesitate to name him to you, and to give you my ideas of his system; as I know it; I can warrant the perfection of its practice. There is living near Frankfort, a German of the name of Joseph Neef. He was a coadjutor of Pestalozzi of Switzerland. He was offered very rich temptations to go to Russia; he preferred coming to the United States, and he was mistaken. He is the most disinterested man I ever saw, and most capable. No science to him difficult or strange, because his method is such that he can analyze them all. In short, his system is expressed by the word analytic; for as all knowledge consists of the comprehension of facts, and the ideas of which that knowledge is composed, he is a teacher of facts. . . .

Locke and Condillac have given the outline; but it was Pestalozzi of Switzerland who realized it (the system) in modern times; and it is now spreading silently over Germany, and has been introduced into France, Spain, Russia, and England. There are, and were, of the schools, in England and in Ireland, eleven. I am possessed of several of the elementary books, translated into English, from the German, published in Dublin, and have 20 volumes in German published in those countries. But Mr. Neef requires no book; nor does any one who acquires his method.[10]

Maclure in the meantime had brought over as an assistant teacher a frenetic, arrogant, half-trained physician and experimenter with Pestalozzian methods whom he had met in Paris, one Phiquepal d'Arusmont. Phiquepal's vanity left an indelible impression on anyone who knew him. Maclure, later on, was to say, "He is a dangerous man who can influence so many men. . . . He is, I think, the vainest man I ever knew and when the Vanity is disappointed, he will go to bedlam." Robert Dale Owen was of a similar opinion: "A wrongheaded genius whose extravagance, willfulness, and inordinate self conceit destroyed his usefulness." But Neef, dependent upon Maclure for support, was unable to get rid of Phiquepal. In 1813 the two men left Philadelphia to set up their school in Village Green, just half a mile from Chester Creek; Maclure apparently had hopes of adding a farm to the school, for he believed in combining manual education with the Pestalozzian method, after the manner of Von Fellenberg at Hofwyl. Some of the pupils accompanied Neef and Phiquepal in the move; and others were added, notably David Farragut, later admiral and Civil War hero. Farragut, then under the guardianship of Commodore Porter of Chester (a controversial sailor who surrendered his ship to the British during the War of 1812 and was, with Midshipman Farragut, released on parole), remembered Neef warmly all his life:

> I accompanied my friend Captain Porter to Chester, where I was put to school at a queer old individual named Neif [sic]. His method of instruction was simple to the extreme; he had no books, but taught orally on such subjects as he desired us to understand. The scholars took notes, and were afterward examined on these lectures. In the afternoon it was customary for us to take long walks, accompanied by our instructor. On these occasions Mr. Neif would make collections of minerals and plants, and talk to us about mineralogy and botany. The course of studies was not very regular, but we certainly had an opportunity of gaining a great deal of useful information and worldly knowledge. We were taught to swim and climb and were drilled like soldiers, branches of instruction to be accounted for probably by the fact that the old gentleman had been one of Napoleon's celebrated guards. I do not regret the time passed at his school, for it has been of service to me all my life.[11]

But the school at Village Green gradually dwindled, fewer and fewer boys attending (perhaps on account of the financial exigencies of the war) until Neef and Phiquepal had only twelve pupils. At this point, in 1815, Neef abandoned Village Green and moved—with Josiah Warren, one of his pupils, as his assistant—to a new school in Kentucky, which also failed, and then out to a backwoods farm. Phiquepal went back to Paris in disgust.[12]

But Maclure was not disheartened. He successfully established his manual labor schools in Georgia and tried to reopen the Pestalozzian school in Philadelphia with a new teacher from France. This venture also failing in 1820, he persuaded Phiquepal to open a Pestalozzian school in Maclure's house in Paris. Here Phiquepal trained the remarkable Mme Marie Duclos Fretageot, who was soon to found Maclure's second Pestalozzian school in Philadelphia.

Mme Fretageot was a vivacious woman of thirty-seven who needed to work. She was the sole support of a young son and of an invalid husband, a French officer who had managed to survive the long retreat from Moscow but who had been both mentally and physically ruined. In 1821 Maclure sent Mme Fretageot and her son to Philadelphia, with money to pay for school supplies; accompanying her as teaching assistant, also at Maclure's expense, came the young naturalist and artist Charles Lesueur. In the fall she opened a boarding school for girls in a rented house on Filbert Street. The physician to the school was Dr. William Price, next-door neighbor to Coleman Sellers, and a successful Philadelphia physician. The son of the superintendent of the Friends' School at West Town, not far from Chester Creek, Price had a close interest in educational reform, and was enchanted by the enthusiastic French schoolmistress. She taught him about the new methods of education and gave him books about Robert Owen's new views of society. Gradually they came to share romantic plans for a life in the same household, devoted to Pestalozzian educational projects and the realization of Robert Owen's new moral world.[13]

Among the pupils who attended Mme Fretageot's school was a young lady named Gabrielle ("Ella") du Pont. Gabrielle was the offspring of an unfortunate marriage between Amelie, daughter of Victor du Pont, and a rascally Englishman who had been recommended to Victor as an experienced woolen mill manager, alias William Clifford. Clifford, to the great if temporary satisfaction of Amelie's parents, married the plain-looking but virtuous and intelligent young woman after he had been managing the mill for a year. But a year and a half after the wedding, with Gabrielle already born, the family learned from an English workman that Clifford had a wife, a child, and another name in England. Clifford left the banks of the Brandywine and Victor arranged for both Amelie and her daughter to use

her maiden name of Du Pont.[14] The ten-year-old Gabrielle was sent to
Mme Fretageot's school in the fall of 1823; from her letters, it is clear that
she formed a strong attachment to the place. Mme Fretageot was a strict
headmistress, who provided an education that seems to have emphasized
more the sciences and practical arts than the classics. The girls studied
drawing (with M. Lesueur, who became a summer visitor to the Brandywine), music, English composition, French, arithmetic (with Phiquepal),
botany, and geography; they were taken on excursions to Peale's Museum
and to the zoo, where they were allowed to ride on a real live elephant's
trunk. Also they all were taken to Quaker religious services on Sundays,
probably at the Hicksite meetinghouse; Ella, unimpressed, alluded in her
casual spelling style to "the foolish Redicules quacer Meeting I am allways
tierd when I am there."[15] She formed some friendships which survived the
break-up of the school two years later, particularly with the Sistaire sisters,
Frances, Lucy, and Sarah. After two years with Mme Fretageot, Ella wrote
her cousin Sophie, who was attending Mrs. Grimshaw's establishment, that
Mme Fretageot's school was "as good as all the Mrs. Grimshaws in the
world."[16]

All in all, it would appear that the Maclure-sponsored Pestalozzian
schools of Philadelphia, by the quality of the education they offered, were
able to attract substantial respect and patronage. They were to become one
of the channels through which Owenite news and propaganda were fed into
the city.

The Academy of Natural Sciences of Philadelphia

At the meeting of September 28, 1824, John S. Phillips—not yet
removed to Rockdale—was nominated to the Academy of Natural Sciences
of Philadelphia by Dr. Benjamin Coates, a physician, and George Ord, a
wealthy ropemaker. He was immediately elected—and also allowed a con-
tinuation of the loan of two books on conchology which he had borrowed
from the Academy Library. For several months thereafter Phillips was one
of the most active of the eighty or so members of the Academy, attending
the weekly meetings with the eight to ten regulars, borrowing books, and
conversing with the eminent naturalists and mechanicians who belonged to
the institution.

The Academy had been formed in 1812 by seven idealistic young
professional men who believed in science and the "rational disposal of
leisure moments." Their founding minutes observed that

In this large city young gentlemen generally have few modes of social recreation when their daily business is over except frequenting theaters at considerable expense, taverns, gaming houses, dancing rooms or places of a more degrading atmosphere, where they can gain no improvement but are sure to acquire habits injurious to the spirit of a good citizen.

The Academy's rooms were to provide "a literary lounge and points of reunion . . . where younger men may improve in company with men of travel and information, and where every respectable individual . . . may read the American and foreign journals . . . without exposure to the intrusion of improper elements." Banned from the conversation of these young gentlemen would be the disturbing topics of religion or partisan politics; instead, science, which like natural religion "allows and promotes the good of all without limitations of Sect, Party, or of Nation," would be their sole topic; they would devote their attention to "the progress of science, the facts discovered, the efforts, the developments, the expansion, the illucidation, the lightening penetrations, the gleanings, the irradiations of the human mind throughout the world."[17] The kind of science the founders had in mind was what might best be called descriptive natural history: a mixture of botany and zoology (emphasizing the Linnaean classification of new species), geology and mineralogy, and chemistry. Thus their interests were more specific than those of the already aged and prestigious American Philosophical Society and less practical than those of the yet-to-be-created Franklin Institute.

After its founding, the Academy proceeded to add new members, one of the first being William Maclure. Among the early recruits were the leading mechanicians of the city, including John S. Phillips, Titian Peale, Stephen Long, William H. Keating, Robert M. Patterson, Thomas P. Jones, Isaiah Lukens, and William Kneass, all of whom would in 1824 help to found the Franklin Institute. Many eminent and highly respected Philadelphia businessmen were also added in the early years, including Nicholas Biddle, soon to be president of the Second Bank of the United States; Roberts Vaux, the Quaker philanthropist and educational reformer; John Vaughan, wealthy merchant and long-time secretary of the American Philosophical Society; and John P. Wetherill, successful chemist and one-time pupil of Joseph Neef's at the Falls of Schuylkill. The institution also took on more extensive functions as its membership grew. A technical *Journal* was begun in 1817, the library was expanded, and the collections of specimens for study—thousands of minerals, fossils, insects, shells, fish, reptiles, birds, and plants—were rapidly expanded. The Academy became an internationally known center for scientific research and publication.

In this development, among the most aggressive intellectual entrepreneurs were a small set of Enlightenment radicals, mostly Pennsylvania
Hicksite Quakers and Bonapartist exiles from Europe. Four of the seven
founders were of this group. Their president from 1812 until 1817 (when
he moved temporarily to Baltimore and Maclure took over the office) was
Dr. Gerard Troost, the Dutch geologist and pharmacist from Amsterdam
who in 1807 had volunteered to serve Napoleon. Louis Bonaparte, King
of Holland, sent him to Java as a mineralogist; the expedition was inter-
cepted by the British and Troost eventually found himself in Philadelphia.
Troost was a noted Freemason and in religion a promulgator of the anti-
Calvinist Arminian heresy. Dr. Camillus Macmahon Mann, a physician, was
a pro-French refugee from the Irish rebellion of 1798 (which had been
instigated and supported, albeit ineffectually, by the French Revolutionary
régime). John Speakman and Thomas Say were deistic Quakers and partners in an apothecary shop that failed. Speakman moved, temporarily, to
Pittsburgh, where he became a principal figure in the notorious "Pittsburgh
Society of Deists" (whose fate will be considered in a later section); he
claimed that "lack of knowledge of the laws of nature is the source of all
social evils." Thomas Say was a nephew of the well-known naturalist William Bartram. After his father set him up in business with Speakman, the
young apothecary endorsed the notes of a brother who was soon afterward
bankrupted by *his* partner's embezzlement. Say lost everything he owned
and turned his face away from business, devoting himself to science, living
in poverty, and depending on the patronage of wealthy friends, particularly
Joseph Gilliams, dentist and co-founder of the Academy, and William Maclure. Despite the technical inadequacy of his education in the Friends'
School at West Town, Say carried on an astonishing program of scientific
studies. He taught himself to read in Latin, German, and French. He
collected specimens of insects and molluscs with Maclure, George Ord, and
Titian Peale in Florida in 1816 and in the west in 1819 when he accompanied Stephen Long's exploring expedition. Back in Philadelphia, as a
curator of the Academy he lived with his collections in the hall of the
institution, allegedly subsisting on 6 cents per day for food and sleeping
under the skeleton of a horse.[18] Say lived up to the hoary myth of "mad
scientist in his laboratory"; but he also published forty-four scientific papers
by 1825.

Later recruits on the radical side included Charles Lucien Bonaparte,
son of Napoleon's brother the ex-King of Spain, who lived with his famous
$10,000 mistress on an estate in New Jersey nearby and, with Say's help,
was writing papers and a book on ornithology; Charles Lesueur, artist-
naturalist, protégé of Maclure and Mme Fretageot, and one of the few

surviving members of the disastrous French scientific expedition to Australia of 1800 (with François Peron he brought back 100,000 specimens, including 2,500 new species), who was now writing with Ord's help some forty-one papers for the Academy's *Journal;* and Reuben Haines, Hicksite Quaker, brew-master and farmer of Germantown, who was for twenty years the recording secretary of the Academy.

Although in 1824 the truly radical group within the Academy's membership probably amounted to no more than a dozen persons, they were among the most active in the institution's affairs, publishing most of the scientific papers and occupying many of the offices (including the presidency and the secretaryship). They maintained close working ties with the faculty of Peale's Museum, with the American Philosophical Society, and with the Franklin Institute. They had access to many of the leading merchants, mechanicians, and professional men of the city. They were in a position to keep alive and vigorous, and in favorable public view, the Enlightenment tradition of social criticism and Utopian rationalism.[19]

The Associationists in Philadelphia and Wilmington

Word of exciting new English speculations on the means of curing the evils of society began to reach the lower Delaware Valley and the Rockdale district early in the 1820's. In the year 1820, a friend was writing to Coleman Sellers about "Robert Owen's plan laid before the Parliament of Great Britain for employing the poor and the labouring classes who have no employment and improving their morals, also for educating and training their children to virtue and usefulness."[20] Mme Fretageot possessed a French translation of Macnab's description of Robert Owen's new views of society and lent it to her friend Dr. Price in 1822. In the next year, a New York chemist and schoolteacher, John Griscom, published an account of his visit to Owen's community at New Lanark.[21] And William Maclure, who visited New Lanark in 1824 and said that the three or four days he spent there were "the most pleasant of my life," in a letter to Mme Fretageot (perhaps unconscious of the irony) compared New Lanark to the admirable new Philadelphia jail:

I never saw so many men, women and children with happy contented countenances, nor so orderly, cheerful and sober a society without any coertion or physical constraint. It is on a par with the moral experiment in the new jail of Philadelphia, with the advantage of being executed by one philanthropic individual free from the caprice of municipal regulations.[22]

Owen's own major works were already before the public in English editions and were being discussed in the widely read English and Scottish reviews. The first—*A New View of Society; or, Essays on the American Principle of the Formation of the Human Character, and the Application of the Principle to Practice* —was opened for sale in 1817, after private circulation by the author to the principal men and governments on earth; and the second—*Report to the County of Lanark of a plan for relieving public distress, and removing discontent, by giving permanent, productive employment to the poor and working classes, under arrangements which will essentially improve their character and ameliorate their condition, diminish the expences of production and consumption, and create markets co-extensive with production*—appeared in 1821. The Philadelphia *Aurora,* the Republican party organ, had been publishing pieces of Owen's writing from 1818 on. And numerous visitors from England, the continent, and America had for years been making the pilgrimage to New Lanark to observe the remarkably efficient and productive factories of "The Prince of Cotton Spinners," surrounded by the neat tenements of pleasant, orderly workers and their families, and the remarkable schools; almost to a man, they returned praising Owen's solution to the problem of humane industrial management and his proposals to reform society by means of "association."

Owen's arguments were well timed. The notion of "association" as an alternative to the traditional capitalistic order of society was being made respectable in the revivals of Christian communalism, currently practiced with visible economic success in America at New Harmony, Indiana, where the followers of Father Rapp had gathered, and in the several Shaker communities. In England several small experimental communities were already forming, inspired by Owen's writings and by economist John Gray's *Lecture on Human Happiness* (itself influenced by Owen); in Spain, Maclure was launching his ill-fated educational commune.

The first communal plan in Pennsylvania was probably the one revealed by John Speakman of the Academy of Natural Sciences. Temporarily residing in Pittsburgh, and a member of the Society of Deists there, in about 1823 he wrote to his friend Thomas Say in Philadelphia about his experiences, and concluded the letter with the unveiling of a truly Utopian scheme for the creation of an associationist community, which would be a "heaven" for scientists:

it is the intention of some of us as soon as we can acquire the necessary funds to purchase and improve some insolated spot, and there form a community something like the Harmonites and Shakers, who we see have arrived at the height of prosperity although governed by phantoms, and would it be slandering common sense to suppose, that a number of rational beings could not do as well, in a community so organized that the interest of each individual depended upon the prosperity of the whole. But our object is not riches, rather a school for ourselves and children as it is particularly intended that the knowledge of nature shall be the polar star or grand object to which all our exertions shall tend. A combination of talents (unrestricted) we hope will be as productive as the combination of labours and our happyness will be necessarily in proportion as we acquire knowledge, for man cannot err but from ignorance or disease. Their is no learned or scientific men among us; but as I said before our grand object will be to make our community a heaven for men of that description. We also hope to give our fellow plebians a practical proof that the whole train of parasites who are sucking their best blood are not only not necessary but that they are in reality the principal cause of all the disorders in society.[23]

The plan went forward during 1823 under the unfortunate title of "the community of wealth." Thomas Say wrote to Maclure about the project and Maclure wrote back casting cold water on the idea. Mme Fretageot heard of the plan in March 1824 and, as she said, "laughed much" when she learned where it stood. There had been at first a "great number" but now only two or three remained interested. Mme Fretageot, ever mindful of the power of sex to prompt association, merrily advised Mr. Say that "they would never put such project in execution if they cannot have some ladies among them."[24] (Mme Fretageot's flirtatious ways were something of a disadvantage in certain quarters of the Academy, however. Say's friend and biographer George Ord was later to refer to her, on the news of her death in Mexico during the cholera epidemic of 1832, in unusually uncharitable terms as a "brazen strumpet." But he took a dim view of the "whims and follies" of associationists generally.)[25]

PREACHING THE NEW MORAL WORLD

The high-water mark of post-revolutionary efforts to improve the world by the earnest application of Enlightenment principles came in the years 1824 and 1825, when an aged hero, the Marquis de Lafayette, and two young reformers, Fanny Wright and Robert Owen, landed almost simultaneously on America's shores. The associationists of the lower Delaware Valley were galvanized into action; the people generally were caught up in the dialogue of social reform.

Lafayette and Fanny Wright

The Marquis de Lafayette was, of course, revered by all as a comrade-in-arms of the American soldiers who had fought for America's freedom. But he was also known as a political activist in the cause of liberal social ideals that flowed generally out of the French Enlightenment tradition. Fanny Wright was a popular British writer, an admirer of America, which she saw as the land of freedom, equality, and progress, where the rights of women, of slaves, of the working poor, could be advanced by legislation and educational reform and by the establishment of Utopian communities. Robert Owen had developed his ideas for social reform out of practical considerations involved in the planning of New Lanark, the optimal company town. He believed that man was, for good or ill, the product of social institutions, and that these institutions could be rationally designed so as to produce a healthy, happy, wholesome, creative people. The key was the establishment of rural communes similar to New Lanark.

The Marquis de Lafayette arrived first, in August of 1824, as the guest of a grateful nation. He was popularly remembered as the young warrior who had come to Washington's aid in the dark days of the American Revolution; he was almost continuously fêted, wined, dined, interviewed, waited upon, paraded, and otherwise celebrated by Americans of all parties for a solid year. He was entertained lavishly in Philadelphia in September and October, and his hostess at the grand ball was, as we noted earlier, the Crozers' friend Jane Leiper Kane. He took the time to visit Mme Fretageot and Phiquepal's school. From Philadelphia he descended to Chester, where after a midnight celebration in the brightly illuminated village, he was entertained at the house of Colonel Joseph Anderson, an old companion-in-arms (also recently a Republican congressman and a friend of William Martin). The Marquis had visited Chester once before, nearly fifty years ago, having stayed there the night before the Battle of Brandywine, and returning there to have the wound in his leg dressed after the defeat. From Chester, the Marquis went on to Wilmington, staying with another old friend, Victor du Pont, and taking time to attend his son's wedding.[1]

On and on the Marquis's tour went, endlessly triumphal, crisscrossing the country back and forth from his headquarters in Washington. He visited Philadelphia again, in July of next year, and again stayed with Victor du Pont on the Brandywine, where he had a private business matter to settle between the Du Ponts and their relatives in France. It was a time of celebration, almost the half-centennial of the Revolution, in which everyone joined to honor the plainly dressed, slightly gruff old soldier for deeds of glory in the country's dawn.

There were those, however, who were less than pleased with the Marquis's concurrent political conduct. A believer in Enlightenment values, and an ardent Freemason, he had been one of the movers in the early days of the French Revolution. And after the Revolution's demise, during the Bonapartist and Bourbon accessions, he remained a conspirator on behalf of all sorts of liberal, even revolutionary causes in France (including the bomb-planting Carbonari, a terrorist group), and a personal patron of the new generation of radical believers in liberty, equality, and paternity. In 1821 he read a book praising America as the land of freedom, written by a young Scotswoman, Frances Wright, and at once wrote to her, inviting her to visit him in his medieval château at La Grange, forty miles from Paris. Fanny Wright, fresh from her visit to utilitarian philosopher Jeremy Bentham, visited the Marquis with her sister Camilla in the summer of 1821, and they in turn were frequently visited by him in their apartment in Paris. There Fanny took as her lover one of the Carbonari conspirators, General Pepe, who was soon to fight in Spain and Greece, and finally in Italy, against the resurgent despotisms in Europe. After Pepe's removal from the scene, Fanny's companionship with the aging and widowed Marquis became so close that scandalous stories began to circulate. They talked of marriage and of adoption, but his sisters intervened.

It was in the midst of this platonic liaison, uncertainly and by turns romantic and respectfully filial in its content, that the Marquis's voyage to America was planned. Fanny and her sister hoped to make the trip as members of the official party, but they were persuaded to travel separately. And so, mile after mile, the Wright sisters followed the official procession, sometimes waiting in rented rooms for secret midnight visits from the general after the day's speechmaking and dining were ended, and sometimes, in congenial company, joining the party of Fanny's "Paternal Friend." Such an occasion was afforded by the Marquis's visit to the aged Jefferson at Monticello, where the two women were invited to spend some time—"the invitation which they value most in both hemispheres."[2]

The Advance on New Harmony

It was in the midst of this atmosphere of revolutionary nostalgia and reformist anticipation that Robert Owen descended on the United States in November 1825, literally like a god from a machine, to recruit associationists to form his first Utopian socialist community—the "Community of Equality"—at New Harmony, Indiana. With his son William and his aide-de-camp Captain Duncan MacDonald, he made a triumphal social tour of New York, Philadelphia, and Washington, D.C., lecturing on his new view of society and displaying his scale model of the Utopian community of the future (eventually to be deposited in the U.S. Patent Office). In Philadelphia he visited the Franklin Institute, the Athenaeum, the American Philosophical Society; an affable and chatty man, on numerous social occasions he met and charmed the mechanicians, the scientists, the intellectuals, and their wives and daughters. He visited Mme Fretageot at her school and captivated her at once. She described their meeting in an enthusiastic letter to her old friend William Maclure:

> . . . I have had the visit of Mr. Owen. When he entered in my house I took his hands saying: there is the man I desired so much to converse with! And you are, said he, the woman that I wish to see. We are old acquaintances and in the mean time he gave me a kiss of friendship that I returned heartily. We talked about one hour and half, but we could not talk freely. I was surrounded by some visitors and our conversation was but on general subjects. He told me he will in his return have a private conversation with me. He thinks it will be in April next.
>
> You have no idea what pleasure I felt when I was talking by the side of a man whose actions and principles are so much in harmony with mine. When he said that children must be taken just when born in order to write in those blanck paper but what is correct, I felt an encrease of desire to arrive at that periode of my life where as much by my economy and the help of some friends I shall be able to put in practice that project of taking little babies who will be absolutely mine. Next Spring I will be in company with those two me[n] for whom I have the greatest esteem: You and Him . . .[3]

Owen bore an introduction to, among others, Coleman Sellers from the Sellers' London correspondent, and Sellers in turn introduced Owen to his friends at a gathering which young George Escol (who was not especially taken by Owen) recalled somewhat wryly in his reminiscences:

> Father to introduce Owen who he felt bound to show some attention to, gave a party mostly to gentlemen in the old square parlour. If I could recall and name all the male guests it would give a good idea of Fathers social standing, but I shall only name those who were *roped in by Owens silver* tongue, it could not have been by his personal[ity], to a Phrenologist or Physiognomist his narrow high back sloping forehead would give no indication of his great brain power.

Dr. Wm. Price and wife
P. M. Price
Thomas Say, the Naturalist
Dr. Fraist—chemist then head of Farr & Kenzies afterward Powers &
Whiteman
Charles Longstreth
Sarah Turner
Mr. McCluer, a rich Scotchman

. . . It was in the square parlor that I first became acquainted with Rob.
Dale Owen, David Dale [Owen] and the sister afterwards Mrs. Fontleroy
wife of the Civil Engineer. David [*sic*—Sellers undoubtedly meant Richard Owen], the youngest son, I did not become acquainted with, but with
Robert and David a life long friendship existed.[4]

The affinity between the Owen party and the intelligentsia of the Philadelphia area was grounded in part in a common interest in machinery of
all kinds. But it went beyond this. They were all products of a British social
system that encouraged men of unusual mechanical aptitude to rise above
the traditional restraints of class and guild. Free to accumulate capital, to
patent useful inventions and to reap the profits, to acquire manners and
education, and if sufficiently successful even to mingle in gentle company,
the English and American mechanicians formed an élite cadre dedicated to
the rule of reason and the improvement of mankind. England and America
owed their accelerating industrial pre-eminence over other nations in large
part to the freedom of innovation they granted their mechanicians. But
freedom to think rationally about technological improvements could not
easily be separated from freedom to think rationally (more or less) about
social improvements also. Thus the fraternity of mechanicians included a
vital part of what remained of the radicalism of the Enlightenment.

Sweeping on with an entourage of followers to New Harmony, Indiana
(accompanied part of the way by the notorious John Dunn Hunter, the
"white savage," on his way to set up a Utopian interracial Indian-white
community in Texas), Owen concluded the purchase of the ten-year-old
religious community of the Rappites, who were moving back to Pennsylvania. The town and surrounding plantations, including some buildings
located on a little over thirty square miles, cost him $150,000. Leaving one
son and Captain MacDonald to receive the quickly assembling mélange of
would-be members of the new community, Owen returned to the east and
began again, in a somewhat more leisurely manner, to propagandize among
the élite of America. He visited Jefferson, Madison, Monroe, and Jackson.
He was received by President Adams and delivered two discourses "on a

New System of Society" in the hall of the House of Representatives, before the President, the cabinet, and the members of Congress. These speeches received wide public attention. He ceaselessly endeavored to mobilize all of the disparate enlightened reformers around his standard, arguing that "the more good means are reunited the effects are powerful, but when scattered they do little or no effect."[5] He served, indeed, as a kind of seed-crystal, around whom arranged themselves in regular form a remarkable number of Enlightenment Utopians, for in each of the towns that he visited he was received by the local Free Thinker's Society, converted a number of the local radicals to his plan, and encouraged a few families to pull up stakes and move west.

It was not, however, until a year later that Owen was able to bring together his great Philadelphia contingent in the "Boatload of Knowledge" that floated unsteadily down the ice-filled Ohio River in January 1826. The forty persons who made up the party included Owen, MacDonald, and Robert Dale Owen; William Maclure and his scientific library; a contingent from the Academy of Natural Sciences: Dr. Gerard Troost, Thomas Say, John Speakman, and Charles Lesueur; the two Pestalozzian teachers from Philadelphia, Mme Fretageot and Phiquepal d'Arusmont, along with a number of their pupils, including the son of one of Lafayette's Carbonari associates, and several of the girls from Mme Fretageot's school, among them the Sistaire sisters, favorite friends of Gabrielle du Pont; and Dr. Price and his family, who were planning to join in the teaching experiments. On the way they visited Joseph Neef near Louisville and contracted with him to come to New Harmony in the spring to teach in the schools. And by summer, Fanny Wright was there on a visit from her experimental plantation at Nashoba, Tennessee, where she and her sister planned to educate and eventually to free a small group of Negro slaves. With the arrival of Fanny Wright, it appeared that Owen had managed to put together the best library, the best school, the best institute of natural science, and the best assembly of liberal intellectuals in the United States. In that same summer of 1826 on the Fourth of July—the fiftieth anniversary of the United States —Owen was encouraged to proclaim his "Declaration of Mental Independence." As, fifty years before, the American colonies had emancipated themselves from political tyranny, so now the New Harmonites declared themselves free of the principal social evils that afflicted mankind: "PRIVATE, OR INDIVIDUAL PROPERTY—absurd and irrational SYSTEMS OF RELIGION—and MARRIAGE, founded on individual property combined with some one of these irrational systems of religion."[6]

But even at the hour of celebration, disaster was fast overtaking the Enlightenment's last campaign. Within a year John Dunn Hunter, who had been inspired by Owen to create his Red and White Republic of Fredonia, would be lying dead in a shallow creek in Texas, shot in the back by hired Indian assassins.[7] Fanny Wright, prostrated with fever, would be on her way back to England with her new friend Robert Dale Owen to recuperate from the frustrations of Nashoba, now being characterized in the public press as "one great brothel."[8] And in the spring of 1827 Maclure and Owen would have parted on ill terms, Owen selling his interest to Maclure and returning to England, and Maclure making preparations to move forever to Mexico. Although there remained at New Harmony, under the leadership of Owen's sons, many of the original settlers in a loose federation of communities, and although in after years the town nourished a remarkable concentration of natural science research, the great communitarian Utopia, which was to serve as the model for reforming the world, had failed.[9]

News of the trouble at New Harmony was on its way back to the Philadelphia area long before the public collapse of 1827. The people of the Brandywine received word from a quixotic, impecunious Parisian friend of Victor du Pont's, one Gabriel Rey, who was visiting America to recoup his fortunes, and who had walked and floated out to New Harmony in the spring of 1826, hoping to become a member of the Society there. He carried with him friendly letters of introduction to her old teacher Mme Fretageot from Gabrielle du Pont and her grandfather. Gabrielle expressed a wish to see her "dear Madame" and the Sistaire sisters, and wished "that Harmony is not so far from here for I would love to have the pleasure of going there to see you. And we have heard tell so much good of the settlement of Mr. Owen that we have a great curiousity to see it."[10] Victor was equally cordial, asking to be remembered to his acquaintances Phiquepal and Lesueur, and recommending Rey warmly as one who had been recommended from France by members of a family closely connected with Lafayette:

M. Rey whose first goal was to betake himself to Arkansas to establish there, having [read] all the publications of Mr. Owen has become enthusiastic about a plan which tends so evidently to ameliorate and to realize the great goal of all societies, and which should, under a government free and exempt from prejudices like ours, succeed better than anywhere else. The object of M. Rey in visiting the establishement at Harmony is to settle there and become a member of it, if they judge that his knowledge and talents of several kinds can be useful.[11]

Mme Fretageot wrote back in a letter to be delivered by William Owen, who wanted to visit the Du Pont powder factory and the Gilpin paper mill, and who would bring the Du Ponts up on events at New Harmony. But she conveyed some doubt about the acceptability of M. Rey, who was keeping everyone in the dark about the nature of the skills he could bring to the service of the community.

Rey for his part was extremely critical. In a long letter completed on April 14, after he had left, he described in picaresque detail his ten days in New Harmony. He arrived in a broken-down steamboat at supper time on April 5 and went at once to Mme Fretageot's house to present himself and his letters from the Du Ponts. Seeking to please, he addressed her as

the patroness of the Society. She replies to me that she was not even a member of it, that she would be whenever she wished, but that up to now she had not had any reason to want it . . . *that what it is that is responsible for the fact,* she tells me whispering as if for fear of being indiscreet, *that the Society is not getting along very well at this moment, is that there are more heads than arms.* . . .

Rey went to bed supperless, spent a sleepless night on a hard, short, creaking bed, and got up at dawn to walk around New Harmony. On his peregrination he came upon a mired horse, groaning and apparently *in extremis;* the horse was still lying there helpless when he left nine days later. Eventually M. Rey was admitted as a probationer but he left anyway, disillusioned by what he had seen.

As Mme Fretageot had said, there were too many heads and not enough arms. No one seemed to be really in charge. Rey spoke to Robert Owen and his son, to William Maclure, to Phiquepal, to Mme Fretageot, and found that they were not even members of the Society (perhaps not wishing to risk all their capital in so uncertain a venture). And certain community services, like laundry and shoemaking, were not being performed at all because they were considered degrading. "The great equality which they publicise, has the result that if no one wants to take up certain jobs, no one dares or is able to require anyone to do them." Phiquepal made his own shoes and did his own washing; Mme Fretageot was able to persuade her schoolgirls to wash her linen but had to do her own ironing. A new constitution was just being announced but already two groups had separated themselves from the main body

because, being workers, they did not care any longer to take responsibility for a large number of women and children and parasites, or to support various expenses of which they did not appreciate the utility, such as the $30 in candles per month to enable the pantalooners to dance, or for the daily reports made in the evening at the Chancellery, on the conduct and work of everyone, and on the plans for the administration in general;

divided into 8 departments presided over by 8 prefects or chiefs: 1st science, 2nd teaching . . . agriculture, commerce, etc.

The farms were not producing enough even to feed the population, let alone produce a salable surplus. And, although full membership required a substantial endowment of the community, no profits were promised (these being devoted to founding new societies) and the individual could not sell his interest if he decided to leave. Indeed, Rey now regarded himself as a dupe, along with the rest, for having entered the community at all:

> There is perhaps not one who does not regret having come: but when they find themselves without money enough to leave, are not even with their family, and there are some who have even taken children from their parents, since it does not cost more at New-Hny. Thus they stay only because they cannot do anything else (without the obliging, the persuasive foresight of Mme. Du P. I would find myself in the same situation) but some pray that things worsen to the point they will be forced to clear out.[12]

New Harmony was only a small town of 750 people; but among the principalities of mind it was an empire, and the crash of its falling was heard throughout the Western world. By the nascent evangelical Christians, in particular, the New Harmony experiment was seen as "designed to revolutionize, not to improve, but to break up, the existing condition of society." Its failure was to be hailed happily by John P. Crozer: "This is another instance of the folly of men in their efforts to establish communities repudiating or failing to recognize the Christian religion as the basis of society and good government."[13]

But the failure of New Harmony did not discourage the prophets of associationism. Even before the model communes at New Harmony and Nashoba collapsed, their founders had taken to the road to preach the Utopian socialist gospel to the American people. The *New Harmony Gazette* (and its sequel, the New York *Free Inquirer*) and other free-thought presses circulated news, theoretical essays, and propaganda. Owenite clubs were founded in many cities and fledgling communes formed in country places. For about a decade Fanny Wright, Robert Owen and his sons, and the anarchist Josiah Warren kept America in a stir, from St. Louis to New York, and from Niagara Falls to New Orleans.

Robert Dale Owen and Fanny Wright made public addresses repeatedly in both Philadelphia and Wilmington in the later 1820's and early 1830's. In Philadelphia a newspaper was established in 1828, the *Mechanic's Free Press,* which, along with the usual miscellany of news, sentimental poetry, and advertisements, published extensive political and economic discussion on cooperative and socialist lines. In Wilmington, the *Delaware Free Press* appeared in 1830, dedicated to providing a forum for the Hicksite Friends of the Brandywine area and for the views of Robert Owen, Frances Wright, Thomas Paine, William Maclure, Johann Pestalozzi, and their colleagues. The effect of all this talking and writing on the people of the lower Delaware Valley was complex: it mobilized some to defend received religion; it inspired others to question, to experiment with "association," and to organize the first workingmen's political movement. These social developments were perhaps more important, even if relatively inconspicuous, than the glamorous disaster on the Wabash.

The Valley Forge Commune

There were many people who listened with enthusiasm to Robert Owen during his Philadelphia visits in 1824 and 1825 but for one reason or another were not free to follow him to New Harmony.

Thomas Gilpin, for instance, the paper and cotton manufacturer from the Brandywine, and uncle of Sophie's friend Mary Gilpin, met Owen in Philadelphia in 1824 and "expressed a great desire to see Mr. Owen's plans introduced."[14] In a small way, Gilpin was already emulating Owen, for he had built around the paper mill a very pretty little industrial community which, like New Lanark, excited admiring comment from its many visitors. A bachelor, he lived part of the year in Philadelphia and part in a cottage adjoining the mill, where he had a greenhouse, an icehouse, and a garden with lemon trees and various fruits and vegetables; his elder brother Joshua lived nearby with his family in the mansion of Kentmere. Gilpin's cottage and the greenhouse and icehouse were always open for the refreshment of the many summer visitors who walked out from Wilmington to admire the Brandywine scenery and the Gilpins' endless papermaking machine; the workers and their families were allowed to keep their produce cool in the icehouse. "As a manufacturing district," recalled a literary commentator of the day who had been brought up in Wilmington, "it was long proverbial for the neatness and orderly conduct of its population." The paper mills themselves were said to be a marvel of neatness and order. The various departments were located in different structures. In the mote-picking room, for instance, thirty women sat at high stools at a long table set along the wall below the windows, each wearing a clean, ironed apron, picking flaws out of the wet paper. "Not a cobweb marred these white walls, nor was dust allowed to soil the floors." Outside, the thirty or so families who supplied the ninety hands employed in the mill lived in model industrial housing:

"Tier upon tier of stone cottages, yellow-dashed and well ventilated, rise up before you on these hills, shaded by forest trees, each having a yard nicely paled and ornamented with shrubs and vines, climbing to the roofs, mingling taste with comfort."[15] Like Owen, Gilpin went to great pains to educate the workers' children, building a schoolhouse for sixty pupils and employing a full-time schoolmaster; in the winter there was a night school for adults.[16]

Another friend and admirer of Owen was the secretary of the Academy of Natural Sciences, Reuben Haines of Germantown. Like Gilpin (who was an old school mate) an anti-slavery Quaker of the Hicksite faction, he was a gentleman farmer and brewer of Germantown. He was a particular friend of the émigré Bonapartes, of the Peales, of the Sellers, of Audubon, and of the radical members of the Academy who joined Owen in New Harmony. His special concern was education and he was in the midst of planning an infant school in Germantown when Owen arrived in 1824.[17] Haines first met Owen, however, on his second visit to Philadelphia, in the fall of 1825, had him out to Wyck, the family mansion, for dinner, and accompanied him on a recruiting trip to New York a few days later.[18]

Haines was to be the prime mover in the formation of the Delaware Valley's first and only experiment with Owenite socialism. But apparently the earliest stirrings were made in Wilmington. The day after dining with Haines, Owen went off to Wilmington with Dr. Price and a Mr. Gause "to see the society formed there."[19] This was very likely the same group who in 1824 had "formed themselves into a sort of society for the purpose of promoting his plan of association." They had invited Owen to meet with them but he had been unable to find time then.[20] Now seemingly inspired by Owen's presence, the group consolidated its plans. On December 22, 1825, fifteen members of the Friendly Association for Mutual Interests met and subscribed $28,000 to get things started.[21] On January 19, 1826, they formulated a constitution, which in March was printed as an appendix to the Philadelphia edition of Owenite economist John Gray's *Lecture on Human Happiness*.

The preamble to the constitution, after first declaring that the great first principles of human action should be love for "The Great First Cause and Creator of All Things" and for "our fellow-creatures," went on to condemn the present unhappy condition of mankind. Man today was "the enemy of man"; only "a new and *entirely different* plan" could give hope for a better state, in which man's natural rights, "which have been taken from us by human policy," could be realized again. The new plan, as laid out in the constitution, envisaged the accumulation, by the subscription of $10 shares and the donation to the common fund of all of the members' private property except furniture, of a capital stock of up to half a million dollars. With this fund the Association would purchase real estate and establish buildings for the community at Valley Forge on the Schuylkill River. There, the constitution declared,

> . . . we will commence erecting a commodious establishment for the accommodation of visitors and travellers; also, permanent buildings for commercial, manufacturing, mechanical, scientific, religious, and other purposes; and, as soon as necessary arrangements can be made, we will commence and complete the building of a village for the permanent and *equal* accommodation of all the Members, on a plan similar to that presented by *Robert Owen*.

The actual organization of the community, however, was left rather vague, except for the specification of the shareholders' financial rights and obligations. There was to be initially a board of twelve town managers, including both men and women, plus a clerk and treasurer, "to transact the affairs of the Company." The distilling, vending, and excessive use of ardent spirits was discouraged, and all members must be "MORAL, SOBER, and INDUSTRIOUS." Free medical and nursing care would be available to the sick and injured; a communal kitchen, laundry, clothing and furniture warehouse, and heating plant, all built and operated on "scientific principles," would relieve the female part of the Company "of domestic labor and permit them equally to enjoy the pleasures of social intercourse, and the acquisition of knowledge." All children, including children of deceased members, would be educated by a method combining practice and theory. All members were expected to engage in useful work "according to their age, experience, and capacity." But the solution of the problem of *ensuring* the adequate performance of technically and economically necessary tasks was left rather vague. Members, "if inexperienced in that which is requisite," were expected to "apply diligently to acquire the knowledge of some useful occupation or employment." Even this might not ensure the success of business enterprises, so the hiring of specialized labor was authorized: "If at any time there should not be a sufficient number of persons in the Company, fully competent to the management of the different branches of industry, the Company shall engage the assistance of skilful practical men from general society." And if enough funds were not subscribed at the outset, the Company was authorized to go into debt in the purchase of the Valley Forge estate.[22]

The names of the organizers were not printed with the constitution which they signed, but it is clear that Reuben Haines of Germantown was one and John T. Gause of Wilmington another. John Rogers, Philadelphia hardware merchant and the owner of some mills at Valley Forge near the Association's property, was the president; one James Jones, "the only wealthy person among them" and the principal shareholder, was the treasurer. William Maclure subscribed $5,000 (but his subscription was never taken up). And in the summer of 1826 the Prices, discontented with New Harmony, returned at Haines's urging to join the Valley Forge community.[23] Other members are said to have included the Philadelphia Hicksite Quaker Abel Knight; Constantin Rafinesque, the widely traveled botanist; and the eccentric "high priest" of the associationists, E. Postlethwaite Page, who dressed himself entirely in green "as a rebuke to the devotees of fashion."[24] (Duncan MacDonald with Robert Dale Owen met Page first in New York where, preceded by a green calling card, he announced himself as "the page of Nature." After listening to Page claim that he was in constant receipt of revelations from nature, and that he had in olden times been King David's page, MacDonald asked Owen uncomfortably, "Are we *all* crazy, do you think, Robert? Have we been poking into great subjects and thinking of a world's reform, until our brains are addled, and we are fit inmates of a lunatic asylum?")[25] All in all, about three hundred people (perhaps fifty families) settled at Valley Forge—only about a quarter of the number anticipated by the organizers.[26]

The estate upon which the community was established was a pair of old iron-manufacturing plantations about fifteen miles above Philadelphia. It was a well-chosen site, strategically located on the semi-navigable Schuylkill River and canal down which anthracite was being carried to Philadelphia, and already established as an industrial and farming community. One part of the estate, including Washington's old headquarters, the forge itself, and a rolling and slitting mill, was purchased from a private owner in Germantown for $17,000. The other, of several thousand acres, including a rifle armory and the old cotton mill of Hugh Wagstaff, who had recently died, was contributed by John Rogers in return for stock scrip with a face value of $65,000. Thus the community possessed a valuable industrial establishment which should, under its own operation or by lease, have been able to earn a substantial profit. It had been inspected the year before by Haines, Troost, Lesueur, Thomas Say, and William Maclure, and Maclure had recorded in his diary the active state of the enterprises:

stoped at the Phenix Iron works passed Mr. Rogers cotton mill 1500 spindles & 24 power looms spins to No 30 all iron frames and well made the Iron works welding scraps made up into bundles which they rais to a white heat in a reverbatory furnace with Virginia coal and after it has passed thro the Cylanders brings it to a red heat in a furnace with anthracite have not yet applied with success the anthracite to smelting iron or making bars supposed that they have not yet applied a sufficient blast nothing but the common bellows. . . .[27]

The farmland, laid out among softly rolling hills, was fertile and well watered. The Valley Forge community probably had, economically, more prospects of success than New Harmony and was commensurate in scale.[28]

The community was launched in the spring with a fanfare of publicity even in newspapers of generally conservative editorial sympathies. It was the subject of a long and friendly notice in the *Gazette of the United States,* which saw it as affording full evidence "for judging of the adaptation of Mr. Owen's system to the views, policy, habits and education of our citizens." This account was republished in the Federalist *Village Record* of West Chester.[29] Of course the *New Harmony Gazette* and other associationist papers gave it their congratulations. And at Kendall, Ohio, a copy of the Valley Forge Constitution was used as the basis for the formation of still another Owenite community under the same name: "The Friendly Association for Mutual Interests." The Kendall community's constitution, dated March 17, 1826, copied the Valley Forge community's preamble verbatim, with a few added phrases condemning economic competition. The text itself followed the Valley Forge version very closely, although there was less careful specification of financial arrangements, and the other articles were somewhat reordered. There is no indication of any overlap in membership.[30]

But despite good will and extensive resources, the Valley Forge commune failed, almost simultaneously with New Harmony. (The Kendall community survived until 1828.) The course of events is not clear but by July 1826—which cannot have been more than three or four months after families moved to the site in substantial numbers—William Maclure was writing in alarm to Mme Fretageot. He had received a copy of the Valley Forge Constitution and was appalled; it "seems to retain no feature of the cooperative system but the money making. . . . I do not know what to think of it." His financial agent in Philadelphia advised him "that he is afraid they will not succeed." By September, he reported, "The Valley Forge is broken up into separate communities and many of the old number in whom I had confidence when I subscribed to their community left it and the whole tottally changed so that Im exhonerated from all claims to my subscription."[31]

The break-up evidently was precipitated by the withdrawal from membership of the principal stockholders and their demand that they be paid in cash for their contributions. This was impossible, so John Rogers and James Jones took their reimbursement in kind, Rogers receiving all the combined estate except Washington's headquarters, which fell to Jones, who moved out from Germantown and lived there until his death about 1840.[32]

It was later to be claimed that Presbyterian religious opposition in the community drove the Friendly Association out; but this is unlikely. Many, if not most, of the associationists were members of the Society of Friends, albeit of the more radical Hicksite persuasion, and were not likely to be persecuted by Presbyterian vigilantes. The reason for the collapse of the community, in Maclure's opinion, was a faulty perception of the principles of cooperation. The doom of the Valley Forge community, he felt, was written into its constitution:

> an article gives no interest for 5 years to any of the members that may put in money but 5 p c to all thus a trifle that will induce all the members to put anything they hold in a false name. Beginning with [illegible] all the profits are to be divided equally the 5th year and every year afterward ... the division of profits puts all into the individual scramble I fear there is not a sufficient number of adults on the continent who comprehend the system to form a community we must take time and not give money without securing the end we wish to accomplish for the only means we have of forwarding the system is by our money preaching goes to the wind and is lost in the forests I'm convinced that a few thousand dollars some years hence will do 10 times more good than at present of all the spurs to industry money is the most inaffectual[33]

The disillusioned associationists, however, blamed John Rogers—"a deceitful, speculative person," wrote the daughter of Abel Knight—rather than any deficiency in the constitution or the principle of "communism," as she called it. The community sent out a "Macedonian cry for help" in the persons of Abel Knight and his wife, who visited the Shaker settlement at New Lebanon, New York, in the summer of 1827. The Shakers sent down missionaries in the fall and the upshot of it all was that a good many of the dispossessed Valley Forge families were converted to Shakerism and removed to New Lebanon, about ten families joining in the summer of 1828 and a number of others later.[34] Still others no doubt found homes in various religious communities and some must have remained in the area. By 1828 the Valley Forge commune was no more.

Craft Unions and the Workingmen's Party

The ideas of Owen and of the socialist followers of the English economist David Ricardo were brought forcefully to the attention of the skilled workers of Philadelphia by a number of articulate social philosophers in the workingmen's movement. One of the most influential was a young English-born shoemaker named William Heighton of Southwark, who signed his writings "Unlettered Mechanic." Heighton had, in point of fact, acquired sufficient learning to read John Gray's *Lecture on Human Happiness* (which had earlier been an inspiration to the Valley Forge associationists) and he was a forceful writer himself. Some of Gray's ideas in turn came from Robert Owen, but he had been most deeply impressed by William Thompson (an erstwhile secretary of the utilitarian Jeremy Bentham), who had written a book entitled *Distribution of Wealth* (published in London in 1824) about inequalities in society. Both Gray and Thompson, and Heighton after them, argued for the Ricardian socialist view that it was labor that gave value to commodities and manufactured products and that the laborer was entitled to receive *all* the value of his labor. The inequalities and miseries of society stemmed from the fact that in actual practice the producer received only a fraction of the value he added to the product by his labor, the balance being usurped by the capitalist, who charged rent and interest and paid minimal wages, keeping the difference to himself as "profit." A more equitable system would require purchase by the exchange of labor time alone.

Heighton in 1827, in his initial "Address to the Members of Trade Societies, and to the Working Classes Generally," suggested a plan by which laborers could improve their condition and ultimately effect this end. He proposed to secure new legislation to restrict the introduction of new "labor-saving machinery" (which was used by manufacturers to get rid of dissatisfied workers) and to curtail bank charters, corporations, and monopolies. This new legislation was to be secured by the workingmen themselves *nominating and electing their own candidates.* He was not proposing, then, the creation of new exemplary communities, like New Harmony and Valley Forge (both, he probably knew, already failed); rather, he was proposing a seizure of legislative power in existing communities by organized political action. Owen, who read Heighton's address during a visit to Philadelphia in June 1827, commended it in his lecture at the Franklin Institute as important reading for "every producer in America" and as containing more wisdom than "all the writings on political economy I have met with." He had it republished in England in 1827 and again in 1833.

But Heighton's "Address" was only the starting point. He went on to found three preparatory organizations: a Mechanics' Union of Trade Associations, to provide economic and legal aid to strikers; a Mechanics' Free Library; and a newspaper, published by the library, of which he served as editor—the *Mechanic's Free Press.* With these tools, Heighton was prepared to create a political party. The Mechanics' Union was a source of funds, an organizational structure, and rallying point; and the newspaper was a medium of communication, not only of socialist philosophy but also of news of local economic conditions, strikes, meetings, petitions, and political information.

In format, the four-page *Mechanic's Free Press* was similar to other weekly newspapers of the time. It provided bits of poetry, fiction, editorials, foreign news, local news, announcements, and advertisements. It reprinted Gray's *Lecture on Human Happiness* and regularly ran news of Robert Owen, William Maclure, and Frances Wright. It announced that Neef's book on the Pestalozzian system of education was for sale (agent Reuben Haines), and reprinted essays by Robert Burns and poetry by Lord Byron. It gave space to Hicksite Quakers, advertised the *Universalist Review,* and ran announcements of Masonic publications. It opposed the enforcement of the Christian Sabbath blue laws, particularly those closing taverns on Sunday. And it called for subscribers to new communalistic ventures, including a housing cooperative entitled "The Associated Friends for Mutual Interest," which proposed to buy houses for subscribers at 50 cents per week; a successful "Labor for Labor Association," which modeled itself after Josiah Warren's "time store" in Cincinnati, where labor time was exchanged for goods; and several producers' cooperatives which dispensed with the services of the wholesaler.

But all this was preparatory to the major political effort. In the summer of 1828, public political meetings were held (regularly interrupted by hecklers from the pro-Jackson organization), which led eventually to the nomination of candidates on the ticket of the Workingmen's Party for all thirty-nine of the municipal and county offices. Most of the candidates were also on either the Adams or Jackson tickets, but eight were put up exclusively by the Workingmen's Party. None of the Workingmen's exclusive candidates won in 1828, for they polled on the order of 300 to 500 votes each, as against 3,500 for the typical Adams candidate and 4,500 for the Jacksonite. In 1830 the Workingmen did better, however, actually electing six of their own exclusive candidates to city and county offices. But the party's strength declined in 1831 and it never fielded candidates again. The Mechanics Union itself had already met for the last time, in 1829, and the *Mechanic's Free Press* ceased publication in 1831.

The reasons for the quick demise of the Workingmen's Party are complex. It was inspired by a social philosophy that required, not just local improvements in wages, hours, and working conditions, but fundamental changes in major social institutions. Its platform called for universal free public education, limitation of the powers of banks, a mechanics lien law, restriction of monopolies, abolition of imprisonment for debt, repeal of the militia laws, and curtailment of the introduction of labor-saving machinery. Some of these positions, to be sure, were already being, or were soon to be, seized by the Democrats or by the nascent conservative parties like Clay's National Republicans and the Anti-Masons; but others were condemned as abominations of infidel "workeyism." Furthermore, it was a third party challenging the local remnants of the old Federalists as well as the ascendant Democrats under Jackson; a political nuisance, threatening to take the balance of power in closely contested elections, it was harassed from all sides.

But the workingmen's movement, as it was being organized by Heighton and his associates, had an internal vulnerability as well. It was essentially a federation of the old skilled trade organizations, which in an earlier age had functioned as guilds, admitting masters as well as journeymen, and serving as much or more to regulate the quality of work and to provide death benefits as to control prices and wages. In this newer age, these ancient associations were being called upon not only to continue their functions but to add more: to serve as an efficient mechanism of economic conflict over wages and hours by the use of the strike; to raise the social level of the mechanic by means of education; and to transform society as a whole in accordance with a radical (conventionally radical, to be sure) secular social philosophy. Thus oriented, the movement could only call upon the resources of the *nonreligious* members of the traditional handicrafts unions —the carpenters, cordwainers, hand-loom weavers, housepainters, printers, pharmacists, and so on. Most of these craftsmen were middle class in aspiration and, with their religious fellows, eschewed the thousands of unskilled Irish and black laborers; they had no use either for the women and children employed in the mills. The mule spinners, who might have been recognized as practitioners of a skilled trade, had not organized themselves into a handicraft union that would fit into the overall trade union structure.

With the demise of the Workingmen's Party in Philadelphia, and of its associated organs, the craft unions restricted themselves to the narrower issues of wages and hours. In this arena they were successful. In 1835 a general strike by the handicraft unions brought masters to recognize the ten-hour day generally for the skilled trades in Philadelphia. But the political price was high. The craft unions abandoned the political field to the representatives of capital. And they failed to establish effective ties with the textile mill workers, who therefore remained unorganized and whose employers were still able to impose the twelve- to fourteen-hour day.[35]

THE THEORY OF COMMUNAL INDUSTRIALISM

The various political and intellectual traditions which have been brought together here under the banner of the Enlightenment were, of course, diverse. But they did share certain general beliefs that can be understood as applications of the principles of Enlightenment philosophy to societies undergoing industrialization. The Enlightenment proper, clearly, while it included an avid interest in mechanism on the part of its philosophers, and while it foresaw continuing improvements in the condition of mankind as the result of advances in science and technology, was not aware of any "Industrial Revolution." Diderot's *Encyclopédie,* for instance, devoted much space to technology but the English inventions in cotton manufacturing came too late to be represented. Thus what is labeled the "theory of communal industrialism" was derived from, but was not part of, the classic Enlightenment tradition, and had other roots as well, particularly that aspect which emphasized the small rural commune as the primary economic institution.

The idea that a balanced agricultural-industrial economy was possible in a nation of small rural communes was reasonable at this time in American history. Southern cotton plantations and northern iron plantations, both raising much of their own food, providing for the educational and spiritual needs of their residents, and producing a crop or product for exchange, showed the economic feasibility of the arrangement. So also did the well-established tradition of Christian Utopian communities like the Shakers and the Economists, which successfully combined industry, agriculture, and trade. Company towns like New Lanark and Lowell, with their carefully planned integration of technology, social structure, and education, developed as corporate communities in rural areas. The social and ideological innovations proposed in the theory of communal industrialism would, the idealistic reformers argued, simply improve on these models, leading to greater material prosperity and to a more wholesome social life. It was not until relatively inexpensive and efficient steam engines were available in quantity in the 1850's that the idea of the rural commune lost its manifest reasonableness. No longer dependent on the water wheel and turbine, the reliable steam-driven factory could now be placed along a railroad beside a harbor, within a great city, with associated savings in transportation costs, and with such accessibility to the seat of commerce that the wilderness lost its plausibility as a site for industry.

The essential tenets of the theory of communal industrialism would seem to be contained in eight points:

1 Mutual agreement and cooperation, rather than selfish competition, are the basic principles upon which to found the institutions of a good human society.

2 Man is a product of learning in a physical and social environment; the community can produce good, or depraved, men and women, depending upon the education of children and the social conditions of adults.

3 Reason and experiment, not revealed religion, are man's only proper guide.

4 Rank, social class, and the bonds of matrimony are unimportant as a principle of social organization and in a good society can be dispensed with.

5 Local economic decisions, as well as political decisions at all levels, should be made by democratic procedures.

6 Real estate and machines should be owned and controlled by the community, not by individual proprietors.

7 Small rural communities, combining in a balanced way both agricultural and industrial pursuits, are the natural context of human economic, educational, and social institutions.

8 Such communities can be largely self-supporting insofar as food, fuel, and other necessities are concerned, but should also engage in specialized production and trade in a national and international system of exchange.

But it was not only the triumph of steam over water power that doomed the rural industrial commune (as it did also the privately owned country cotton mills). There was a kind of romanticism in the attitudes of the radical reformers. In their passage through the wars of liberation, the ideals of the Enlightenment had gradually assumed a heroic posture. The American Revolution, the French Revolution, the struggles for freedom in Spain, Italy, and Greece, and the Romantic movement in art and literature had given the cool wisdom of illuminism a ruddy, dawn-streaked, romantic fervor. It seemed that the transformation of the world was now about to happen. Their eyes fixed on new horizons, the romantic radicals failed to perceive certain fundamental contradictions in their position. Great rationalists, they failed, like Robert Owen at New Harmony, to recognize that the organization of work in a free Utopian community must be at least as rationally designed as in a capitalist's factory or plantation, and that the efficiency of workers must be ensured by an equally effective system of inducements and discipline. Great proponents of equality, they assumed that an intellectual élite, standing above the democratic process, should make the fundamental decisions. Great opponents of concentrated wealth, they allowed their social experiments to depend upon private fortunes not merely for their capital but their operating budgets. Severe critics of the institution of marriage, they chose to overlook the importance of the nuclear family to the financial plans of working people. Thus, although some of their opponents might concede them to be right in certain particulars, such as their demands for free public education, for freedom for slaves, for increased rights for women, for the reform of the militia, and for a mechanics lien law, these opponents could also point to the fact that not one secular communal society had been able to succeed. And the failures could be attributed, not to specific reform sentiments that looked reasonable to almost anyone, not even to the advocacy of communal as opposed to private property, but to the two major social positions of romantic radicalism: its opposition to marriage and—worst of all—to organized religion.

Religion, in fact, was the wheel on which the theory of communal industrialism would be broken.

Chapter VII ℣

THE EVANGELICAL
COUNTERATTACK

In the 1790's, as the new republic was settling down to a national life, some of its Christian citizens, alarmed by the progress of "infidelity," began to seek a revival of religion. They believed that the violent excesses of the French Revolution were a direct result of the infidel philosophy of the Enlightenment. And they began to realize that many of their comrades-in-arms, in their own American Revolution, had been infidels and devotees of the same Enlightenment, and that thousands of their friends and neighbors, personally respectable and patriotic though they might be, were tainted by these beliefs.

The first phase of this second Great Awakening was not as spectacularly successful in converting infidel artisans and merchants in the cities, and gentlemen on plantations, as it was in exciting religious hysteria in remote and lonely settlements along the western frontier. But during the second decade of the century the evangelical movement began to reformulate its ideology. The harsher dogmas of Calvinism, codified in the Hopkinsian doctrine that the damned should be converted and taught to take pleasure in the prospect of eternal suffering at the hands of God, were being softened to offer a likelihood of salvation to all who would be saved. Large organizations, ecumenical in spirit, drew upon the vast financial resources of successful businessmen; the American Bible Society, the American Tract Society, the American Sunday School Union, and many other Christian and benevolent societies applied sound business methods to the task of reforming America.

Prominent in these affairs, and an extreme example of the evangelical type, was Philadelphia's young, wealthy Presbyterian evangelist, the Reverend Dr. Ezra Stiles Ely. Born in New England in 1786, he had graduated from Yale and early in the century had spent a year saving souls in New York City's hospital and almshouse. As a product of that year's work he published a remarkable book on his evangelical experiences with prostitutes, the destitute and dying, and the insane. After publishing also a refutation of Hopkinsism, he was called to the Pine Street Church in Philadelphia, where he quickly became a leader in the evangelical movement. Handsome, curly-haired, and aggressive, he was a charismatic leader. He was one of the founders of the American Sunday School Union; he launched the campaign to stop the federal government from breaking the Sabbath by transporting the mails on Sunday; he was the secretary of the Board of Trustees of new Jefferson University and personally paid the cost of the first building.[1] On the Fourth of July, 1827, Dr. Ely delivered a sermon (later published) in the Seventh Presbyterian Church in Philadelphia which signaled to the wise that the evangelical movement had entered a new phase: a counterattack against the infidels by direct political action. It was to stir violent controversy and, in its literal sense, was neither correctly understood by his opponents nor implemented by his followers. Under the title "The Duty of Christian Freemen to Elect Christian Rulers," the sermon declared that the United States was a Christian nation and that "all our rulers ought in their official stations to serve the Lord Jesus Christ." God did not want "Deists." "I propose, fellow-citizens, a new sort of union, or, if you please, *a Christian party in politics,*" cried Dr. Ely. Christians should be politically active and should go to the polls, using their franchise to exclude infidels and immoralists (such as slanderers, seducers, and drunkards) from public office. His spirit was ecumenical: he admitted Presbyterians, Congregationalists, Baptists, Methodists, and Episcopalians to the fold; Catholics were not mentioned, and Jews and Mohammedans were excluded.

Although he stated explicitly that he did not wish any religious test to be prescribed by the Constitution for the inauguration of public officials, he was at once accused—and not only by infidels—of advocating a union of Church and State. His American Sunday School Union, currently applying for articles of incorporation from the State of Pennsylvania, was condemned as part of a scheme to fill the nation with Sunday School scholars, who would in ten or twenty years elect one another to fill every public office in the land. The Sunday Schools were seen by worried liberals as "dictators to the consciences" of millions, as exercising a power of censorship over the reading matter of the people, as a secret Christian army preparing to conquer the republic from within.[2]

Although Ely's call was shouted down, it expressed a widely felt mood of evangelical determination to go on the offensive against infidelity and to convert America into a truly Christian commonwealth. The lot of the publicly avowed unbeliever would be a hard one, for he was obstructing God's work. And the true Christian would have to do more than preoccupy himself with the evidences of his own salvation; he would have to work hard to save the unbeliever.

CALVARY CHURCH IN ROCKDALE

In the Rockdale district the leaders of the evangelical response to the threat of infidelity were Richard Somers Smith, his wife Elizabeth Beach Smith, and their daughters Clementina and Harriet. As their young friend John Hill Martin said of them later in his history, the story of their Christian work shows "what good one man and three women can accomplish in a country neighborhood."[1] The Smiths guided the revival of religion in the little cotton hamlets and inspired other community leaders to make substantial contributions to the evangelical cause. The Lammots, the Crozers, the Willcoxes, the Darlingtons, and the Riddles were influenced by their example; each in his own way served the cause of Christ among the working people, whether directly by way of religion, or indirectly through politics or knowledge of political economy. And ultimately as a group they were able to impose a Christian moral dominion over the Rockdale district.

The Organizing of Calvary Church

The decision to organize the parish was made during a time of growing economic distress both for the Smiths and for the operatives in the Rockdale district. A brief economic recession swept the country in early 1834, caused (so the Smiths and the Du Ponts believed) by an inevitable tightening of credit as the Second Bank of the United States fought bravely back against the tyrant Andrew Jackson's veto of its charter and his reckless removal of the federal deposits. Discount rates on new loans were as high as 19 percent; the value of cotton yarn was falling.[2] Clementina wrote to Sophie from Philadelphia in January complaining of the depression and reporting that there was "a great deal of misery among the lower classes in this city."[3] And by February Sophie was responding with exclamations of dismay at "the dreadful consequences of distress that fill every part of our land . . . this change over its once flourishing and happy population!"[4] In March the Riddles' Parkmount Mill was closed for a week "owing to the business being so dull," and the price of yarn was down, No. 15 from 24 to 22 1/2 cents per pound and No. 20 from 26 to 23.[5] But John Phillips' mill apparently was unaffected by the general decline in commerce, for in March

RICHARD S. SMITH (1789–1884).

one of his weavers, William Morris, wrote home to England reporting cheerfully that he and three other men were boarding with his brother Andrew and "all working" in "an old established mill called Philipses Mill."[6] And Crozer was not affected by the decline until 1835, when the death and total insolvency of his chief customer for yarns cost him nearly $6,500, about half of his assets in finished goods.[7]

Merchants, perhaps, were more sensitive to the shrinking of credit than were the manufacturers. In any case, in January 1834 Smith's commission house failed, and in April he lost his membership on the Board of Directors of the Bank of North America.[8] Although he "bore it perfectly . . . the Christian in adversity,"[9] he must have been profoundly distressed. His financial difficulties continued to deepen and soon the Rockdale property itself was in jeopardy. In February 1836 it was put up for sale by the sheriff. No doubt by prearrangement, it was purchased by a nephew (his brother's son), who reconveyed it to his uncle five months later, after the difficulty was settled.[10]

Despite these distractions, the Smith family proceeded resolutely with their evangelical plans. In November 1834 a meeting was held in the nail mill for the purpose of organizing a congregation. A constitution was adopted as prescribed by the Episcopal canons and the name Calvary (suggested by the then Bishop Onderdonk) was given to the new church. Smith became one of the two wardens and young Ferdinand Lammot served as a vestryman. Soon after, the Reverend Mr. Marmaduke Hirst, the rector at nearby St. John's in Concord, was appointed "missionary" by the Society for the Advancement of Christianity in Pennsylvania. The designation of this church as a mission—meaning that it was not financially self-supporting —survived for more than a hundred years.

The next step was to construct a church building. Now for the first time substantial sums of money were required; and at this juncture Smith was in no position to make a large contribution. Nevertheless, in July 1836—just about the time when he resumed possession of his own property—the vestry met and decided to purchase a lot offered to the church by a neighbor for $100. At this same meeting, a building committee was elected, including Smith. Five days later the committee reported that they had agreed with a local man to do the carpenter's work for $250 on the building, which was to be 45 by 30 feet, two stories in height, with a tower 10 feet square, and a basement with two finished rooms. It had been designed "in the Gothic style" by Smith's friend, the architect—now Bishop of Vermont—John Henry Hopkins. In August, the cornerstone was laid by Bishop Onderdonk; at the end of the service an offering was taken amounting to $27.78. By winter the shell was completed and a basement school room, with accommodations for 250, was plastered and furnished; and in this school room, on Christmas Eve in 1836, the first service was held in Calvary Church before a crowded congregation. Thereafter divine service was held in the basement at least once every Sunday. As Smith proudly reported (in partial justification of a request for more funds): "The attendance is seldom less than 100 persons, and although accommodations are prepared for 250 persons, it sometimes happens that there are not seats for all who attend."[11]

It is plain in the records that the young church constantly suffered from want of money. Many of the parishioners were hard-pressed mill workers, and the Smiths, the principal organizers, were able to provide more in the way of time and influence than hard cash. Even in 1838 the upper part of the building, intended for divine worship, was still unfinished; thus, no pew-rents, the normal source of an Episcopal church's income, could be collected. As Smith put it in his request:

> . . . it is now the anxious desire of the Congregation to raise the necessary funds to complete it; and by means of the pew-rents to offer a more adequate compensation to their Rector; the mode of raising funds by voluntary contributions being too uncertain. . . .
>
> The embarassments which have affected every branch of industry, having borne peculiarly hard upon the operatives of the manufacturing districts, the Congregation of Calvary Church are not able to raise among themselves the means necessary to complete the building, for which purpose about $1000 will be required. They appeal therefore to the pious members of the Episcopal Church for aid to enable them to establish the good work which has been commenced.[12]

The problems in completing the building were matched by the difficulties of providing adequately for a rector. For a year, the Reverend Mr. Hirst survived on a salary of $200 per annum, "which was raised by contribution in sums averaging $3.00 each." He resigned, however, in June 1838, and was replaced in September by the Reverend Mr. Alfred Lee, who fortunately for Calvary Church was a man with a private income from stocks and bonds. Lee, his salary advanced to $300 per annum, donated the entire amount over the next three years to pay for putting in the pews and generally completing the church edifice (although a bell was not installed in the tower until 1859).[13]

In all of his activities on behalf of Calvary Church, Smith had the backing and support of important figures in the Protestant Episcopal Church. His elder brother James was a prominent Philadelphia attorney and a zealous evangelical layman—counsel for the Bank of North America, a member of the Common Council of Philadelphia, a trustee of the University of Pennsylvania, a vestryman at St. Peter's Church (of which the Richard S. Smiths were communicants), and founder of the Society for the Advancement of Christianity in Pennsylvania. He was a prominent committee man in state and national Episcopal organizations, and thus was in a position to give his brother Richard advice and support in his efforts to establish Calvary Church.

But probably the most important of Richard Smith's advisers was John Henry Hopkins, Bishop of Vermont. He was in the habit of staying with the Smiths, in Philadelphia or at Rockdale, whenever business brought him to the Philadelphia area. A former architect who specialized in churches in the Gothic style, Hopkins provided without charge the plans for Calvary Church. He preached from the pulpit of the church and no doubt his many books and pamphlets, presenting a high church approach to evangelical religion, were read and circulated among the congregation.

Hopkins could present forceful advice on the danger of foreign and domestic radicalism to a working-class congregation. As we noted earlier, he had been brought to America at an early age by parents fleeing from Dublin about the time of the pro-French Irish rebellion of 1798. He had been an apprentice to free-thinking Oliver Evans at the Mars Works and had lived with the Evans family. He had taught George Escol Sellers mechanical drawing.[14] He had managed an ironworks in western Pennsylvania. He grew up among the French émigrés who congregated around Bordentown, New Jersey, and after moving to Philadelphia he got to know a crowd of refugee foreigners—French, Scottish, Irish, Spanish, German. They were "irreligious, infidel, and loose on many subjects of morality." His youthful reading was "Paine, Volney, Hume, Mirabeau, Voltaire, and Rousseau," and it was only gradually that he was weaned away from deism by reading tracts attacking Tom Paine and his ilk by Hannah More and other early evangelical authors. He was at first attracted by the Quakers and the Swedenborgians; after he moved to Pittsburgh in his twenties he joined the Episcopal Church.[15]

Thus Hopkins could stand before the working people of Rockdale not only as the bishop who was Smith's houseguest and as the architect who had designed their church, but also as a former workingman himself—a former Deist, a draftsman, an iron master's apprentice, and for a time an iron master himself. A vigorous defender of Christianity against infidelity, he also was a living example of spiritual growth in a man of working-class origins who had moved from youthful skepticism to mature Christian faith. As Smith and Hopkins walked side by side along the winding roads of Rockdale, they demonstrated for all to see the Christian fellowship of the worker and the capitalist.

The Congregation

By 1841, when Lee was called away to Wilmington to serve as the first Bishop of Delaware, the organization of Calvary Church was complete, with a rector and a vestry (even though this was technically a mission), two wardens (one of them Smith), and a loyal congregation.

The congregation in the initial period from 1834 through 1844 included on the average members of at least seventy-five or eighty households. There were nineteen contributors from fifteen families to the original building fund at Easter in 1838. They paid amounts ranging from $2 from working people to $10 from Richard S. Smith. This fee entitled the donor to the right to worship and "all of the privileges of the Church & of the burial ground." Bishop Onderdonk, at the time of the dedication of the new church in July 1838, confirmed a class of twenty-five new members, and he confirmed two more classes in 1839, together amounting to thirty-four persons. Some of those confirmed had already contributed to the building fund; and there were several families with more than one member undergoing confirmation. There were a number of baptisms and marriages in this early period too, many of them involving persons who neither contributed nor were confirmed in Rockdale; and among the first wardens and vestrymen were some persons who were not mentioned as contributors and who were not confirmed at Rockdale. By the end of Lee's ministry, he and his predecessor had confirmed a total of 135 new members of the church and he listed 77 communicants.

Clearly the congregation included a core of persons who were already confirmed Episcopalians. Some of these, like the Smiths, were well-established members of the Church when they moved to the Rockdale district; others were old residents of Aston and Middletown townships, who had been accustomed to worship (weather and the roads permitting) at St. John's in Concord and St. Paul's in Chester, both five miles or so away, and now found it more convenient to attend Calvary. This old-resident group certainly included Isaac C. Derrick, Smith's co-warden, a prosperous farmer and head of a large family who lived at Village Green. The already confirmed Episcopalians, both new residents (about eighteen families) and old (about seven families), would be entitled to present their children for baptism, to be married in the church, and to be buried in the churchyard without further ado. Thus some of the new confirmations were simply young adults from families in which the parents were already confirmed. Parents in about twenty-five families joined confirmation classes and were brought into the church in 1838 and 1839. And there were certainly a considerable number of other families—one might estimate about twenty-five—who had a connection with the church that did not include full membership, such as attending Sunday services, sending children to the Sunday School, presenting children for baptism with a regular member as sponsor, being married to a regular member, and perhaps even being buried in the church cemetery. Some of these persons were members of other denominations who found it difficult to travel the distances required to worship elsewhere. Many of the unaffiliated, as time went on, no doubt were confirmed, and probably the size of the confirmed congregation grew to include members of as many as a hundred families. But the population's mobility was so high that as one family joined, another left the district, and an accurate measure of the congregation's size would have been difficult to accomplish even then.

The social composition of the congregation seems essentially to have involved two classes: a group whom one can call the local gentry and a group of mill operatives and domestic servants. There seem to have been relatively few ordinary farmers and mechanics. The gentry were the substantial farmers, like Warden Derrick, and a set of mill owners and manufacturers: the Richard S. Smith family; the families of Joshua and John Garsed of Penn's Grove; the family of James Houghton, also of Penn's Grove; and young Daniel, Ferdinand, Eleanora, and Eugenia Lammot (who did not follow closely their parents' Swedenborgian preferences). The working people included the Pattersons, who worked as domestic servants for the Smiths, and a large number of operatives' families. Many of these were English- or Irish-born and a number were widows' households.

Let us take for example Elizabeth Standring (age sixty-two years in 1840) as head of a fatherless household that included a boy fifteen to twenty, a woman twenty to thirty, and a girl fifteen to twenty. From 1844 to 1846, Riddle's mill employed an Elizabeth Standring (probably a daughter) as a weaver; the same mill also employed a James Standring (listed under the same ledger number and probably her son) until December 1844. James Standring and his sisters moved out of the Rockdale district before 1850, for no one by the name of Standring was listed there in the census of that year.

Another case of a Christian widow's household is that of English-born Elizabeth Taylor. In 1836, when she was fifty-one, she and her husband Joshua presented their six-year-old son Joseph for baptism by Rector Hirst. Joshua died (or left) in the next year or two. In 1838 Elizabeth contributed in her own name to the building fund; she was confirmed in 1839; and her teen-age daughters Mary and Hannah were baptized the next year. In 1850, at sixty-five, she was living with Hannah, a weaver, and her son James, also

CALVARY CHURCH.

a weaver, in Middletown. Evidently James and Elizabeth both moved, for neither was buried in Calvary churchyard.

And still another instance is presented by John and Rachel Cardwell, aged thirty-two and twenty-three, both of them Irish-born and recently married, who in 1840 presented their newborn daughter, Sarah, for baptism. Ten years later, John Cardwell was working as a weaver at Penn's Grove and his family had expanded by the addition of four more children. None of this family of Cardwells was buried at Calvary; they probably moved out of the district in the 1850's.

Because of the frequency of removals from the district, the uncertain vicissitudes of records, and the ambiguities of names, it is not possible to learn much about most of the other working-class families who were associated with Calvary Church in the early years. But from these few examples, and others about whom census or employment data survive, it is clear that most of the people in the congregation were from working-class households, with the mother living and working at home and husband or children working as operatives in the local cotton mills. It was these people who filled the pews at worship service and whose children came to the Sunday School in the basement, who made up the bulk of the confirmation classes, and who called upon the rector for the sacraments. It was the manufacturers and landowners who served as wardens, as vestrymen, and as representatives to the diocesan convention in Philadelphia.[16]

The Message from Calvary

In addition to performing the sacraments, a Protestant Episcopal rector had another duty: he was expected to deliver at least one sermon every Sunday, or to arrange for a "supply." The balance of his emphasis between ritual and preaching determined whether the minister was high church or low church. The Reverend Mr. Lee was a low church man. A slender, scholarly young man of thirty-one, he had graduated from Harvard Phi Beta Kappa and was near the top of his class. He had practiced law for several years before entering a theological seminary, and had been ordained only a few months before. He had been recommended to the Smiths by the Reverend Dr. Clemson, the rector of the church in Chester, who had met him while Lee was traveling for his health, and in September 1838 Lee had visited the Smiths in Rockdale. There he met and was approved by Bishop Hopkins. Upon accepting the ministry at Rockdale, the young rector, with his wife, two children, and two domestics, being unable to find a comfortable house in the neighborhood, was invited to live with the Smiths. As Smith expressed it in later years, the two households made "a most happy family circle," and "the love and affection then commenced" continued for the rest of their lives.

In the years after he left Rockdale to become the Bishop of Delaware, Lee became a prolific author of works on Christian subjects; well versed in Greek and Hebrew, he assisted in the preparation of the revised version of the New Testament which was issued in 1881. He prepared his sermons carefully—a severe trial for him, for his eyes were weak and sore, and he depended upon Mrs. Lee to read to him and act as his amanuensis. Many were to be printed later, some by his former congregation at Rockdale. But, although they were elegant in composition and erudite in their allusions to scientific knowledge and to classical literature, their rhetoric was evangelical. He was at all times conscious that his duty was preaching sinners to repentance and salvation. He held before the congregation the nature of sin—infidelity, the envy of others' prosperity, the frequenting of taverns, gambling houses, and haunts of vice—and its awful consequences—eternal torment. He pictured the satisfaction of repentance, of placing one's faith not in the world but in the love of God, and of confidently awaiting, at life's end, translation into a realm of eternal and peaceful joy. And not only this; God would reward His servants in this life as well:

The Lord honors his young servants by giving them favor in the sight of men, attracting them to love, confidence and esteem.

. . . They who seek first the honor that cometh from God, who act upon convictions of right and duty, who pursue the straight-forward course of virtue and obedience to God, inspire the confidence and command the respect of society. They are trusted and beloved. They are honored in prosperity. They are befriended and assisted in adversity. Even those who oppose and dislike religion are constrained to admire it when fairly and consistently presented in the daily life.[17]

Lee was ever aware that he was actively opposed by enemies of religion. In his "Farewell Discourse" to the Calvary congregation in September 1841, he not only adjured his flock to be consistent in Christian conduct, as he had taught them "publicly, and from house to house." He also warned them not to believe "the slanders so often spread abroad by the enemies of religion." He deplored the fact that "these who call themselves Christians [are] broken into sects and parties almost innumerable," and noted that "the infidel and scoffer seize upon the inconsistencies of Christians, as a matter of railing accusation against the gospel."[18]

The new rector was, in fact, attempting to launch a revival of religion in the Rockdale district by a type of preaching and personal counsel which created intense anxiety. It was very effective. One Sunday afternoon Mr. Lee preached from the text to be found in Acts, Chapter XVI, verses 30 and 31: "Sirs, what must I do to be saved? And they said, Believe on the Lord Jesus Christ and thou shalt be saved, and thy house." Lee went on in a solemn way to represent "the unwillingness of the human heart to receive this doctrine and rely upon it." After church the people sang "Jesus Saviour of my Soul," and "many of the congregation appeared to be much impressed." Next Sunday, Clementina reported to Sophie, "Mr. Lee preached the most admirable discourse I have heard from him." She went on to describe with pious satisfaction the spreading of religious fervor in the congregation:

Coming out of church I saw a young person very much affected so much so she could not repress her tears, she told me the cause of her grief was that she was so great a sinner she did not know what would become of her. There are many in this frame of mind among the congregation. I know how much you will rejoice with holy joy to hear of repenting sinners.[19]

By the spring of 1841, Clementina and Sophie were congratulating one another on the success of the Rockdale mission. Clementina exulted:

The state of things & the spiritual state of the people at Rockdale, is most encouraging—I never heard anything like it, except in Baxter's charge at Kidderminster where I believe he preached to a congregation of renewed people.[20]

And Sophie confided to Clementina that Ferdinand Lammot had told her "that the congregation was already too large for the church, & that they spoke of adding to the building."[21] It was, indeed, in large part because of Lee's reputation for evangelical success in a difficult working-class mission that he was, in 1841, elected Bishop of Delaware, with headquarters in Wilmington.[22]

After Lee's departure, his successors were supervised by Bishop Alonzo Potter of Chester, a learned clergyman who had a close interest in congregations of laboring people. Potter had been Professor of Moral Philosophy at Union College in New York and was the author of *The Principles of Science,* a popular book first published in 1841, aimed at tradesmen and apprentices. In this work he celebrated the recent progress of industry and the dignity of labor; he compared the hierarchical organization of the cotton mill to the Great Chain of Being. Potter was a perennial favorite speaker at mechanics' institutes and had lectured to the operatives at Lowell.[23]

But Lee's zealous ministry and Potter's interest in the spiritual advancement of workers were only half the story of the revival at Rockdale. The other half was the Sunday School which the Smith ladies administered and taught. Clementina and Harriet, and their mother, launched the operation on a Saturday afternoon in October 1833 with a magic lantern exhibition in the old nail factory; "the children & parents were highly gratified." Clementina busied herself with the administrative problems of collecting books and tracts and arranging for teachers. The school gained about twenty regular attenders during the summer but it lapsed during the winter when the Smiths went back to the city. They returned in the spring, redoubling their efforts, and by 1836 the school seems to have been fully established, with about 120 scholars; in 1838, there were 150 scholars, 15 teachers, and a library of 300 volumes.[24] Clementina complained to Sophie that forty-two of them "were commited to my attention in the Infant School, which I concluded was no desirable undertaking." Indeed, with major responsibility for the Sunday School falling to her, and with her duties as church organist requiring her to practice as well as perform, Clementina felt herself to be overworked.

The school was organized into three classes: an infant school, a boys' school, and a girls' school. Later on there would be classes for young adults as well, but of that more later. The general model for the school was, of course, the Brandywine Manufacturers' Sunday School, which had been organized and led by Victorine Bauduy since 1816. Clementina during her summers with Sophie along the Brandywine had served as a teacher in this school. It was nonsectarian, accepting children whose parents were Catholics, Episcopalians, Presbyterians, or in fact of any religious persuasion (including outright indifference). There the ladies instructed the young in the elementary skills of reading, writing, and arithmetic, and taught them some of the basic principles of Christian belief and practice.[25] Although the Calvary Sunday School was conducted under the auspices of the Protestant Episcopal Church, there is every reason to think that it too was relatively nonsectarian in its approach, in accordance with the ecumenical nature of Lee's views and the anti-sectarian philosophy of the community's leadership. Probably, however, it was more openly religious in its style than the Brandywine, for the Pennsylvania law of 1836 providing free public education for all children enabled the Sunday Schools to concentrate on religious subjects.

Some of the children who attended the Calvary School were former scholars from the Brandywine. This was so with the Miles family; it is worth recording their case in some detail, for it illustrates the profound moral impact which the intimate relationship between the Du Pont and the Smith ladies and their charges had on some of the growing young people in the community.

Mrs. Sarah Miles, a widow and a Methodist, appears in the record book of the Brandywine Manufacturers' Sunday School in 1829, when she is recorded as having entered her three children, Maria, age fifteen; Sarah, age ten; and William Sampler, age seven. In October 1831 the family removed to the Rockdale district. Mrs. Miles was in very poor health, suffering from consumption, and Maria worked in a mill to support the family. One of the Du Ponts, on visiting the Lammots at Lenni in preparation for a wedding, looked up the Miles family and found that Maria wanted to talk to her former teacher Sophie. So a meeting was arranged for nine o'clock in the morning a few weeks later. Sophie put a very careful account of the occasion in her diary:

Accordingly after breakfast I was called out of the parlour, & told a girl wanted me—I found my poor Maria, seated in the kitchen, terrified & shrinking from the noisy bustling assembly of servants. To talk to her there was impossible. I first asked her to come upstairs. Her timidity made her fear to do so, which instantly perceiving, I led her out into the yard, where we conversed some time. Maria's humility, the piety she evinced, her tearful eyes, & simple expressions of affection for me, touched me deeply. I could not help contrasting the scene, the conversation, the *feelings* it inspired, with those of the gay houses the night before, & I deeply felt that for my self, happiness was more to be found in the humble hope of having directed or encouraged a fellow being in the way of peace; than in all the laughter, & dresses & noise & folly the world calls gaiety. . . . Maria was sad—she said her mothers health was bad—she said she wished extremely I would have come to see her mother—I wished it too—I gave her my little hymn book, she was much gratified—she opened her bag to put it in, observing at the same time "This is the bag you gave me, I have kept as well as I could" & in truth, she has kept it as well as I could, it looks like new—I spoke to her of our eternal interests, I reminded her, tho' here we might meet no more, yet we had the same Home in view, where we would be in a little while—She wept so much she could scarcely say goodbye, but pressed my hand warmly, & so we parted—I love to think of this visit.[26]

A year later, after spending a day in Rockdale, Clementina told Sophie that Mrs. Miles was now gravely ill, and so the two women went to visit. Again Sophie, deeply moved by the experience, recorded the event in detail in her diary:

She is evidently in a consumption, & was confined to her bed since many weeks—she spoke of her illness & its probably fatal result with the calm resignation & hope of a Christian. But one thing troubled her, she said: it was, to leave her girls in a place so unsuitable to their moral welfare, without guide or protector—She said she had greatly desired to see me that she might request me to be a friend to her Maria, after death had removed her last parent. She thought that she should leave them in such easy circumstances, that they being industrious girls, could get their own living very well. She hoped that they would have saved enough to be able to learn a trade & be set up in it. But then, who would give them advice? Who would direct their minds beyond this world's gain, to the attainment of treasures for eternity. Who would counsel them to follow in the narrow way that leadeth to everlasting life?—She said that she knew I had been a true friend to Maria & given her the best of advice when she was my scholar—All she asked was, that if Maria came to me when she was gone, I would give her the same counsel & instructions I gave then. I promised her that I would, as far as it might be in my power—And I gave Maria *then* such advice as my brief time allowed—I was much touched &, I trust, benefitted, by the mother's converse—I thanked my God who had made me the instrument of giving some comfort to her last hours by the knowledge there was *one* who would care for her Maria's *soul*—& I prayed that I might be of use to the poor Girl. But I found *her* changed from the meek, drooping, yet frank & affectionate girl I used to instruct. There was a certain carelessness about her, & sometimes a smile rather sneering altho' she appeared really rejoiced to see me, & tho' she wept much when I spoke of her Mother's illness—still, when I dwelt on religious subjects, the aspect of her face was changed from that reverential interest it used to wear—This pained me, for I knew she worked in the mill of one who was an open Infidel & whose workmen were very worthless! Poor Girl, I trust she may yet be saved from the dangers that surround her, & be a true disciple of our blessed Lord—[27]

The "open Infidel" in whose mill Maria worked was, as we noted earlier, John S. Phillips.

In order to save Maria, after her mother's death a year or so later, Sophie decided that she and her sister Sarah should learn the milliner's trade. She was able, "after a good deal of difficulty," to get them a good situation in Wilmington, with board and room with a respectable family. But after learning the trade they went back to Rockdale to work in the mills anyway, "as they made more money." Although Maria was not listed as being connected with Calvary Church, Sophie reported with satisfaction that her conduct remained "always highly satisfactory" and "she continued pious." Sarah, however, "attended long the Sunday School at Rockdale," where she gave evidence of being really interested in religion.[28]

Another family of Brandywine scholars who moved to Rockdale were the Millers. In 1830 Henry Miller, a forty-five-year-old German-born Presbyterian, a weaver by trade, and his thirty-five-year-old wife Margery entered their daughter Sarah, age eight, in the Brandywine Manufacturers' Sunday School. Eight years later the family moved to Rockdale and Sarah carried with her a card of recommendation to Calvary Sunday School. In 1839 the Millers had their new son Bartholomew baptized and in the same year Sarah and another daughter, Hannah, were confirmed. Hannah and Sarah worked as weavers at Penn's Grove in the 1840's. In 1850 the family was still residing in the neighborhood, the father now retired and living with his wife and five of his children, including Sarah, who was thirty-four and still unmarried. They seem to have been supported by their twenty-six-year-old wheelwright son.[29]

The school had its ups and downs, for Elizabeth Smith, Clementina, and Harriet were frequently away, spending the winter in the city and part of the summer vacationing. Sometimes it was not possible to recruit sufficient teachers and for a while the boys' department was closed for want of an instructor. But nonetheless the operation was a great success, and Clementina and Harriet continued to help the school until their deaths in 1884 and 1905.

Calvary Sunday School's importance to the community was made conspicuous in its triumphant management of the Rockdale district's Fourth of July celebration in 1837. Ordinarily, in this period, the Fourth of July was a day of disorderly political picnics; innumerable long-winded toasts were drunk to the heroes of the Revolution and of subsequent transactions, including such figures of infidelity as Byron, the martyr of Missolonghi; the saloons were open and the roads were crowded with rowdy men and women. The Smiths and the rest of Calvary's congregation made the Fourth of July of 1837 an occasion of a different sort. No less than six hundred Sunday School scholars and their teachers assembled for a religious celebration; about the same number of spectators were present.

In fact, virtually the entire population of the district must have gathered together in the open air to honor the nation's birthday. Clementina, writing to Sophie a month later, was still ecstatic over the sight of the community "uniting in a rational and proper celebration of the day." She said, "It was the happiest day I ever passed."[30]

Evangelical Womanhood

Clementina and Sophie were not the only members of the Rockdale sisterhood to take an active interest in religion; religion became almost a profession for some of them. The sisterhood were not feminists; their correspondence is bare of favorable mention of Fanny Wright and other early advocates of women's liberation. They did not, at least in writing, advocate female suffrage, or liberalization of the divorce laws, or restrictions of a husband's right to administer his wife's property, or female entry into the all-male professions. But they did press enthusiastically into the one niche in the occupational structure that was opening its doors wide to women. This niche was Christian evangelism, an enormous business which not merely permitted, but actively encouraged, the participation of women. The evangelical movement across the nation recruited thousands of women to work as Sunday School teachers, benevolent association organizers and fund raisers, musicians, tract distributors, visitors to prisons and almshouses, and home visitors in the domestic missionary field; as fund raisers for foreign missionary societies; and even as co-workers with their husbands in accessible foreign areas (which by the 1840's included parts of Europe, India, China, and Oceania). Although men generally directed all of these operations, they were genuine team efforts in which the female members played specialized and therefore indispensable roles. Nowhere else in American society (except in the mills themselves) could women be accepted by male associates as intellectual and moral equals.

The reasons for this acceptance of women in the evangelical movement were complex. It was not that in these settings men stood aside and turned "morality" over to the women, on the ground that by some constitutional predisposition women were the proper custodians of social virtue. The evangelical clergy claimed moral authority not only over the male laity but over women as well; the lay leaders at least conceded no superiority to women. It was rather that middle-class women were an indispensable source of educated hands to the work. Largely excluded from the professional and commercial worlds, bored by "housewifery" and "the nursery" (where most of the chores were done by servants and nurses anyway), they could dedicate twenty or so hours per week to the day-to-day work of evangelism, freeing the clergy for the more special tasks—administration, preaching, administering the sacraments, writing sermons and books, counseling—for which they had been trained. The work of conversion and reform yielded immediate rewards. It was done with real people in real communities and it had visible consequences in social change. It was done in company with real colleagues, male and female, with whom strategy and tactics, triumphs and defeats could be discussed face to face. In the evangelical movement, women were making a commitment to change the world.

There was, inevitably, a certain sexual tension inherent in this situation. Infidels and heathen men might not respect the female visitor's claim of chastity; how she would protect her virtue, without driving away the object of her benevolence, was a topic of considerable interest to the evangelical woman. The story which Clementina's ideal, Miss Harries, told in Boston, and which Clementina wrote out for Sophie's edification, revolved around precisely this dilemma, and is worth quoting here because Clementina regarded Miss Harries as an avatar of womanly perfection in the Lord's work, and her life's history as a kind of female *Pilgrim's Progress:*

Her ac't of the visit of a chief of the island of Balet where she was in the house alone, at midnight (for no earthly friend was near to care for her protection) was evidence how our Heavenly Father provides for the care of his weakest ones—in the tact and ability she displayed. She heard a knock at the door in the middle of the night, a night she said of deep depression and hardly knew what to do, in her loneliness but she felt as the knocking continued she must open the door, and instantly a rough grissly looking native, with only a girdle to cover his nakedness sprang in—She received him with a smile and apparent pleasure and much formal politeness addressing him in his own language—He had a bowl of buffaloe milk he said he had brought to the white woman hearing they were fond of it, but the evident motive was curiousity to see her—She then set herself to work to entertain him, though all the time very much alarmed particularly when he asked if all her skin was as white as her face —she put a bold face on the matter & instantly drew up her sleeve to assure him it was, and in some of the accounts she gave him of our country customs, that of churning with sheep he rolled over & over on the floor & roared with laughter—I can give you but a trifling idea of all that lovely lady said & hope I shall remember much to tell you, when we meet dearest. (When we meet!!!) What a privilege it is on our earthly pilgrimage to meet such persons so highly gifted, so humble and so tried.[31]

Temptation presented itself also in the interactions between male and female workers in the movement, particularly as they involved the clergyman and his female congregation and staff. Scandalous rumors were constantly afloat, implicating this or that minister and a female member of his flock. Bishop Onderdonk of New York was publicly convicted of adultery with one of his parishioners by an ecclesiastical court; and the Reverend Dr. Tyng advised all young men in the ministry to be as circumspect as possible and never to enter into even the most spiritual of discussions with a woman alone. Perhaps tensions of this kind were among those that Clementina meant when she replied, in a long and emotional letter, to Sophie's anguished report that she had been condemned to abstinence and invalidism by a new physician's diagnosis in 1845:

My portion as you know has not been without trial of its kind and it is only each individual heart that knoweth its own bitterness. I have had trials of sin and temptation which you have never known (I believe) and no words could express the gulf of my heart as I find myself yielding to them—It almost overthrows my hope of adoption many times and makes me fear that mine is only the hypocrite—My many privileges rise up as fearful witnesses against me, and I cannot say that I have "My heart sprinkled from an evil conscience"—I cannot say this to any but you beloved or my dear Hattie, but do pray very earnestly for me dear Sophie not for comfort, but that I may be enabled to overcome and inherit a portion in Christ at last. I only want a steady single eye and a heart filled with the *one* purpose to do God's will—You told me to tell you of myself & I did not mean to do so when I began but you see that I have, instead of comforting you, (which I so long to do) poured out the sorrows of my own heart—[32]

The problem posed for the evangelical layman by the practical need to work in intimate comradeship with attractive women was perhaps more difficult than that of the clergyman, who was expected to maintain a certain reserve in the conduct of his religious duties. Those members of the male population who considered themselves to be by birth, breeding, and occupation "gentlemen" (and who were so considered by others) were often still guided, in their relations with women, by a moral standard and a set of beliefs about sexuality that had prevailed in England during the seventeenth and eighteenth centuries. In this view, women were not the inherently pure, gentle, but fragile vessels that a later generation believed them to be. To the contrary, they were as apt as men to be lusty, deceitful, and even violent; a good and intelligent woman was to be admired and respected for having achieved her character by much the same application of energy and determination as it required in a man. A gentleman, in turn, was expected to honor his female relations and women of character; but he was allowed, or even expected, to indulge his natural appetites with women of a lower category, whose status did not require respect for their sexual virtue. Such accessible females might be ostensibly virtuous but lonely wives and widows, or intelligent and educated courtesans, or servant girls, or whores, and the escalations of male gallantry and female response provided a more or less standardized gambit for distinguishing between the truly virtuous women and the ones who in varying degrees of readiness would surrender to temptation. The traditional gentleman thus could legitimately be something of a sexual sportsman in his spare time; womanizing was a kind of recreation, sharply distinct from the man's work, but taken seriously to the extent that here, as in other sports, the pursuit, and evidences of success in the hunt, involved masculine vanity and honor.

Although America was supposedly a simpler and more virtuous nation, where the amatory adventures of decadent aristocrats did not characterize the republican gentleman's life ("gentleman" here ideally being defined by such meritorious qualities as fairness, hospitality, and generosity rather than by birth, breeding, and occupation), the traditional sportsman's ideal was in fact very much alive. And, inevitably enough, it was more alive among infidels and populist politicians than among Christians and sober manufacturers. (The failure of the Enlightenment tradition to rationalize any real equality of the sexes was perhaps one of its major weaknesses in the ideological combat of the early nineteenth century.) A classic illustration of the public survival of the sporting gentleman image during this period is the widely rumored career of the beautiful Italian courtesan Amerigo Vespucci. This "black-eyed, well-formed Italian lady," allegedly a descendant of the Amerigo Vespucci for whom the continent was named, had come to the

United States in 1838 in hope of a congressional grant of public lands in appreciation of her ancestor's role in the country's history. She circulated interesting accounts of herself: that she (like Fanny Wright) had been the mistress of a revolutionary officer who fell in one of the battles to free Europe in the 1830's, that she had dressed as a man, that she had even fought in the same engagements. She bore a saber scar on her hand to prove it all true. The Biddle family introduced her to Philadelphia society and she was escorted about the city by the great Whig banker Nicholas Biddle. But Biddle's interest was friendly, fascinated—and platonic. Vespucci soon tired of Philadelphia and went on to Washington, where she met the Democratic President's son, "Prince" John Van Buren, one of the leaders of the more radical wing of the New York Democrats, and became his mistress. John Van Buren was a gentleman of the sporting type. Putting her up in the final hand of a high-stakes poker game, he lost her to a wealthy upstate New Yorker, who took her off as his "fancy woman" and kept her in "utter loneliness," so it was said, in his remote mansion at Ogdensburg, New York, along the St. Lawrence River.[33]

Against the model of the sporting gentleman, the evangelicals were in the process of creating a new image: that of the "Christian gentleman." Both sexes contributed to the formulation of this ideal. The Christian gentleman would be, of course, a *converted* Christian, fully sensible of his need for salvation and for justification by faith. But he would also be vigorous, hardworking, and successful in a professional, commercial, or manufacturing career; a contributor to missionary and reform causes; intelligent, well informed, and articulate. In his personal relations he would be trustworthy, humble, sincere, lively and amusing on social occasions yet fundamentally serious and concerned. In his dealings with women, he would regard the fair sex as man's complement, of a softer constitution but one of equal value, deserving always of respect, even in the case of those whom lowly birth, or financial disaster, or seduction by a philanderer had brought low. He would avoid consorting with prostitutes and other loose women before marriage and would be faithful to his wife after.

Evangelical women placed great pressure on their male friends and relatives to conform to this ideal. Sophie and Clementina pressed Samuel Francis Du Pont mercilessly, during the 1840's, until early in 1844 Sophie reported that he was having a religious awakening. Clemma responded (in italics): *"It is unmingled joy."*[34] After one visit to the Brandywine, Clementina said of her departure that it would be a relief to Sophie's husband to be able to "smoke his segar in peace."[35] But she dismissed their fears of offending him; a higher duty stood before them: "Our conduct and our conversations *ought* to condemn the worldly minded around us, and if it *does,* we cannot hold the place we desire in their estimation, we want to make our religion amiable, forgetting the impossibility of this."[36]

At last he surrendered and in April 1849 was confirmed by Bishop Lee in Wilmington. Although Sophie was not present, at the bishop's command ("the excitement might have disabled her for the whole summer"), her victory was an enduring one. Samuel Francis Du Pont became an evangelical worker, too, supporting foreign missions and requiring Christian services on board his ships.

The women of the Chester Creek-Brandywine sisterhood pressed Christianity on others as well, sometimes with success and sometimes without. Sophie's sister Eleuthera contributed to the conversion of their brother Alexis. Alexis became an ardent evangelical, and he and Victorine nearly precipitated a family feud by insisting on the construction of a church on Du Pont company grounds. (Alfred du Pont, a nonsectarian of deistical leanings, clung angrily to the old family policy that forbade the promulgation of *sectarian* religion on their business property.) Those who persistently refused to submit to conversion, and who defied the ideal of the Christian gentleman in other ways, were subjected to heavy sanctions indeed: they were silently excluded from the list of men eligible to marry members of the group (and thus excluded from reproductive and educational participation as well). Clementina, for instance, dismissed a potential male admirer airily as "a Unitarian, and apparently indifferent to religion, not a man of cultivated mind."[37]

But the courtships of John S. Phillips provide the best case in point. At first, in their view, arrogant and inconsiderate, boastful and excessively gallant (unlike the *"good* humble Mr. Lee"), then sickly, depressed, and contrite, he was made a figure of fun in the private communications of the sisterhood, as "Val de Peñas," the Knight of Rockdale. As word of his rejections spread, his addresses, already deemed painfully boring, became demeaning as well, and one after another the objects of his attention— Sophie, Eleanora Lammot, Joanna Smith, Clementina, and Harriet—turned him away with pity. The fate of Phillips testifies to the power of evangelical womanhood, in the 1830's and 1840's, to control the system of marriage in well-to-do Christian families. Phillips was a gentleman; but he was not, in their opinion, a truly *Christian* gentleman.

THE BENEVOLENT WORK
OF OTHER MANUFACTURERS

Although Calvary Church was the leading religious institution in the Rockdale district, ministering to Protestants generally, members of other denominations contributed along their own lines to the evangelical effort. There were Baptists, Methodists, Presbyterians, Swedenborgians, and Catholics in the district, and the manufacturers attempted, in one way or another, to provide for their needs.

John P. Crozer and the Baptist Sunday School

John P. Crozer was a Baptist who had been converted in his youth by the Reverend Dr. William Staughton. Staughton was, like so many of the influential evangelical leaders, a man of education and intellectual accomplishment as well as a spellbinding preacher. He had been a minor published poet in his early years; he had earned his Doctor of Divinity at Princeton; he edited an edition of Virgil and prepared a Greek dictionary. From 1823 to 1827 he was Chaplain of the U.S. Senate; before he died in 1829 he had been president of two colleges. It was an image of the *educated* Christian that Staughton projected; and Crozer, who was not well schooled himself, believed profoundly in a Christian education.[1]

So also did his wife. She had been brought up along Ridley Creek, not far from the mill, and although nominally an Episcopalian had for several years before her marriage been a member of a small informal congregation of Baptists there. She "often raised the hymns in public worship" and taught in the Sunday School, which, as she told her sons, "was under the Robert Raikes plan, that is, it was intended to teach the ignorant to read and write, with a religious influence." (It was Raikes's ideas that also had inspired the Du Ponts to found the Brandywine Manufacturers' Sunday School and thus indirectly the school at Rockdale.)[2]

When the Crozers arrived at West Branch in 1825, there was no school closer than Village Green and all schools were private "pay-schools." In order to induce his workers to remain during periods of unemployment, Crozer found that an effective tactic was to pay out of his own pocket their children's school fees. But these schools provided a purely secular education. Nor were there frequent opportunities for religious worship in the neighborhood, either for the mill workers or the Crozers. As Crozer recalled it years later: "We went to places of worship irregularly. There was no stated preaching near except at Mount Hope (Methodist), one and a half miles distant; and alas! we were not under a strong religious influence. I look back on this part of our life with grief."[3] It was not until some years had gone by, and the cotton factory was beginning to bring them a more comfortable income, that the Crozers began to think seriously again of church and school.

The first renewed conscientious church attendance by the Crozers was at the tiny Baptist church in Marcus Hook, five or six miles away on the banks of the Delaware. This church was only 25 feet square. Crozer's son Samuel recalled the place with mixed feelings:

> It was old and dried up, as it appeared to me. There were few young people in attendance, and the singing was execrable, but there were some very good old people in the congregation, which was small. . . . Rev. Joseph Walker preached there for many years and without salary. He had, I think, no theological training, but received a collegiate education. Perhaps no man ever lived who felt more strongly "woe is me if I preach not the gospel." Originally a country merchant, he conducted his business with success, and then felt called on to preach, continuing the two employments. Finally he abandoned the store, and devoted his life to God's service. He would preach morning and evening at Marcus Hook, and ride five miles to West Branch in the afternoon, and preach in the building erected by my father. I also remember that Mr. Richard S. Smith, an Episcopal gentleman, had a room cleaned up in an old nail factory at Rockdale, and Mr. Walker preached there. This grew into the Episcopal church at that place. He had an intimate acquaintance with the Bible, and was one of the salt of the earth.[4]

By about 1832, the Crozers began to think of establishing a Sunday School. They encouraged a young Presbyterian clergyman, then located in the neighborhood as an assistant to the aging pastor, to stay in the area and revitalize an old and decaying Presbyterian church called Mount Gilead or the Blue Church, which had originally been constructed to serve the needs of the Scots-Irish workmen at Old Sarum Forge a few miles to the north. It was located in a neighborhood called Logtown, not far from West Branch, and its Irish-born pastor was famous for his strong sermons on the subject of temperance. The Crozers, as nominal Baptists, were committed to temperance by church doctrine anyway, and Crozer found himself drawn to Presbyterianism. He took an interest in denominational politics in Philadelphia and became active in the affairs of the Middletown Presbyterian Church, of which Mount Gilead was an outpost. Middletown Presbyterian was one of the oldest churches in the countryside, having been founded in 1720, and its present building dated back to 1766. In 1842

Crozer gave an address at Middletown Presbyterian and spoke warmly of the ancient edifice and its builders:

> This ancient edifice, truly venerable in appearance, was erected by godly men, who have for three-quarters of a century slept in death. This is one of the oldest places of worship in the whole country and its substantial and venerable walls testify that the yeomanry by whom they were erected were willing to honor God with their substance, and in that day when farm-houses were of the plainest and simplest kind, they were willing to pay for a large and commodious edifice, and dedicate it to the worship of Almighty God.[5]

Crozer's remarks were made at a time when the Presbytery of Philadelphia was (in his words) making "some attempt to impress life into these decaying churches." And, in truth, both churches were sadly in need of inspiration, for in 1835 the Crozers' friends the Landises left Mount Gilead, and in 1839 its pastor was trampled to death by his horse. "Mount Gilead," Crozer wrote his friend, "looks very desolate I fear that it is destined to remain in its present forlorn state." Early in 1842 Middletown Presbyterian lost its minister too and for the next four years was to be dependent upon "supplies."[6]

With the departure of the Landises, Crozer seems to have determined to take matters into his own hands at West Branch. In 1836 he built a commodious chapel, 60 by 40 feet in plan, to house a Sunday School and to provide a place where visiting clergymen, such as the pastor from Marcus Hook, could occasionally preach. The Smiths were delighted to hear of the new school at West Branch, "where it is very much needed," and they responded gladly when Crozer invited them to march their scholars the two miles along Mount Road to West Branch for a ceremonial opening in February 1837. The core of the occasion was a lecture on the subject of Sunday Schools. As Clementina described it:

> . . . we assembled 90 children and walked over in procession to the chapel. The children sang the 110th hymn very sweetly & were very suitably addressed by a Mr. Chaugis from Delaware. I trust the example of our school will induce some to follow it and Mr. Crozer will succeed in his undertaking.[7]

Crozer assumed the responsibility of superintendent of the new Sunday School, and probably Mrs. Crozer, already experienced in Sunday School work, served as one of the teachers. It used the standard publications of the American Sunday School Union (of which Crozer was later to become a member of the board), which started the children off with a primer and spelling book, carried them forward with first-, second-, and third-class readers, and gradually exposed them to readings from the testaments. Samuel Crozer years after recalled the method of teaching Bible verses to little children:

> Tickets were likewise given us for committal to memory of God's word. When I was a child, we received one ticket for each seven verses recited, and when they accumulated to three hundred and sixty, a Bible was presented. I remember also I received my Bible. I am of the opinion that memorizing God's word was more prevalent in olden times than at present.[8]

It is difficult to estimate the success of Crozer's school. A few months after its opening, in testifying before a Pennsylvania Senate committee investigating the employment of children in manufactories, he strongly emphasized the value of the combination of religious and secular instruction, and (although modestly omitting his own name) drew attention to the usefulness of his own enterprise at West Branch:

> Considerable attention is now given to Sabbath School instruction, at the factories of Chester creek, and its influence promises to be extensive upon the whole; the religious, moral, and social condition of the factories there, is advancing, particularly amongst the young women and children, including the boys under fifteen years of age.
>
> The common school system is adopted in our township, and the school directors are desirous to make it efficient; two of the schools are located near the factories. An owner of one of the factories, built at his own expense, a house for Sabbath schools, and occasionally, a place of worship, or lecture room, the basement story of which, he has given free of rent to the school directors of the district, in order to give the children in his employ, increased opportunity of education, by bringing the school to their residence.[9]

When the Crozers moved in 1839 to a house near a new factory at Crozerville, they apparently brought their Sunday School with them, conducting it in their own home. The original chapel became in effect one of the public schools and its religious functions were eclipsed; certainly no regularly organized Baptist congregation developed in West Branch, although as late as 1848 "West Branch Chapel" still was to be found in Ash's map of Delaware County, at the site of the Crozer's former mansion. After the closing of West Branch Chapel, the Crozers rented pews and worshipped at Calvary Church.

Crozer's other contributions to the religious and moral development of the district consisted of serving on committees of the local chapters of larger benevolent societies. He was, as early as 1829, a member of the Board of Managers of the Delaware County Bible Society, whose goal it was to place a copy of the Scriptures in every dwelling in the county. In this work he was associated with the various clergymen and county court officers who were active in evangelical and reform causes. The Bible Society, finding only about three hundred families destitute of the Bible, placed a copy in each household and went out of business in 1830. But the same men now organized themselves into the Delaware County Tract Society, which distributed the nonsectarian Christian classics published by the American Tract Society. In 1838, when the Aston Township Committee of the Temperance Reform Association of Delaware County was organized with two hundred members, Crozer and Alfred Lee were two of the founders. The Society met on occasion at Calvary Church, to hear addresses on missionary topics and to collect money (at a meeting in June 1841, for instance, the collection at Calvary amounted to $63.36).[10]

James Riddle and the Methodists

The Riddle brothers were not united in their religious affiliations. Samuel was a nominal Presbyterian, as befitted a Scots-Irishman; but he was not noted for zealousness in the faith at this period of his life, and the Presbyterian churches at Middletown and Mount Gilead were in a languishing condition anyway. His younger brother James, however, had been converted to Methodism as a young man before leaving Ireland, and on his arrival on Chester Creek he associated himself with old Mount Hope Church. He was the more scholarly of the two, devoting his spare time in his early years to "reading and religious exercises," and amassing a substantial library.[11]

Mount Hope was one of the oldest congregations in Delaware County, dating back to 1807, when Aaron Mattson, the paper manufacturer, donated land on Aston Ridge for a cemetery and a strictly Methodist meetinghouse. Before this, the local Methodists had met at Mattson's house on the hill overlooking West Branch (the same house later to be the Crozers' home). The congregation had been formed when the district was primarily agricultural; thus it included, in addition to the patron Mattson, the McCrackens (a prosperous English farming family who among other things did hauling for the Riddles) and a number of local millers, lumber dealers, and substantial farmers.[12]

Shortly after the Riddles arrived in 1832, the church at Mount Hope was the scene of a revival led by the itinerant English revivalist James

Caughey. As a result of his inspirational sermon, Methodism enjoyed a marked revival in the Rockdale district.[13] The congregation at Mount Hope expanded so much that a new church, across the creek in Middletown, was organized, and in 1838 Mount Hope itself was enlarged. James Riddle became the lay preacher of the new Lima Methodist Church, although he retained his original membership at Mount Hope. He was relieved by ordained ministers from the Chester Circuit in 1835.[14]

About 1839 James married a Quaker lady and at the same time moved to the Leiper estate at Avondale, on Crum Creek, where he operated a cotton mill in partnership. In 1844 he purchased the old Gilpin estates on the Brandywine and the family removed to Kentmere. But, until he built a Methodist chapel along the Brandywine, he retained his membership at Mount Hope Methodist Church, and served on the board of the Delaware County Tract Society. He apparently was ordained after the removal and bore the title "Reverend." The family genealogist recorded:

> He has been heard to say he had two calls: one to preach the gospel, and the other to manufacture cotton goods; and he was one of the few who proved successful in both. He occupied a very leading position among the local preachers of his denomination, and was president of their National Convention in 1864. Being a natural and forcible speaker, his pulpit and platform efforts were received with great favor. Not forgetting in the tide of business the calls of duty, he provided well for the moral and religious welfare of his tenants.[15]

The Society of Friends

The mill owners and manufacturers who were members of evangelical denominations—Smith, Garsed, Houghton, Crozer, and James Riddle— were the leaders in building new religious institutions in the community. Those who belonged to denominations that were not evangelical—at least not at this point in their history—were less active.

There were numbers of Quakers in the district, for many of the original settlers had been members of the Society of Friends, and their descendants still lived on the large farms and plantations in the area. There were monthly meetings at Chichester, to the south, and at Concord and Middletown, to the north. But few if any of the workers in the mills were Quakers, either local or migrant. And anyway the Society of Friends was rent by the bitter internal struggles of the Hicksite schism, which left little energy for missionary efforts. Indeed, perhaps the last Quaker missions from Delaware County had been to the Seneca Indians in northwestern New York and

Pennsylvania, where in a little settlement called Tunessassa Quaker families had lived since 1798, teaching the Indians the practical arts of agriculture, raising cattle, and keeping up a family farm in the white man's style.[16] Thomas Dutton, the tanner who supplied the belts for the local cotton factories, had managed the farm at Tunessassa from 1808 to 1813; after that he took charge of the county poorhouse for four years before returning to his tanning business.[17] Edward Darlington, the owner of the mill at Knowlton from 1829 to 1832, was a Quaker, but he was more concerned with law and politics than religious enthusiasm.

Daniel Lammot, the New Church, and Fourierism

Daniel Lammot, Jr., at Lenni, was still a Swedenborgian, although he and his family worshipped at Calvary Church, as well as at the newly built Church of the New Jerusalem on Darby Creek, near the Sellers estates.[18] Probably so also was Dr. Gideon Humphrey, the homeopathic practitioner of Village Green whom the Lammots and occasionally the Smiths called upon (and who sometimes treated the Riddles' employees when they were sick or injured).[19] The Swedenborgian faith, which had so excited Lammot when he lived in Philadelphia, was millennialist in philosophy, holding that the millennial age had already begun. But it was not evangelical in practice. It was very much an élitist religion, offering experimental church services and promulgating new and unusual Christian doctrines of a generally Unitarian character, which required extensive study and which were difficult for simple Bible-reading working-class people to understand. Furthermore the "New Church," still establishing itself in America and in the throes of angry factional disputes over church governance, was in danger of being subverted by the socialist doctrines of Robert Owen and Fanny Wright. Thus the immediate task for conservative Swedenborgians like Lammot was not to bring the working people to Christ but to keep the radicals from taking over the New Church while its bickering factions looked away from the Temple.

Lammot had been especially busy in 1824 and 1825 when radical propagandists swept through Philadelphia. "New Light" Quakers had preached before his congregation, denying the divinity of Christ. His minister, the Reverend Mr. Maskell W. Carl, and another, the Reverend Mr. Roche, listened to Owen lecture in 1824. Roche was so much impressed that he tried to start a community in Bucks County. Lammot regarded Roche's enthusiasm for socialist experiments as naïve and confided to a friend:

I fear Mr. Roches plan of establishing a New Church commonwealth will lead to the injury of his friends. Knowing but little I shall not say much on the subject: yet it is not difficult to see that with $50,000 very little could be done in the establishment of the different manufactures contemplated—the erection of the necessary dwellings & other improvements & the purchase of land whereon to commence the Commonwealth. I understand that Mr. Owen expended 10,000 pounds sterling on his New Lanark establishment.[20]

This same friend, speaking of another vulnerable Swedenborgian, said that "a Mr. S." worshipped an idol—and that idol was Fanny Wright. Lammot approved of the evaluation.[21] The Mr. S. in question was David Simmons, a gentleman farmer of Bucks County, who actually offered his farm as the site for the community, claiming $10,000 thereby as his investment. But Roche and Simmons could not recruit enough people to complete the capital fund and the plan was abandoned.

Once out on Chester Creek, Lammot's concern over the state of the New Church continued. In 1840 he brought out the Philadelphia minister Robert de Charms to christen the infants and to administer the New Jerusalem sacraments to the grown-up children, including "even Ferdinand."[22] In 1843 he felt obliged to take a stand against Fourierism (though he had not read any of the works of Fourier) because so many in the New Church, particularly in New York City, were discussing the possibility of establishing Fourierist phalanxes. (New York was a center of dissemination of Fourierist doctrines, largely purged of their free-love content, through the writings of Charles Brisbane in Horace Greeley's New York *Tribune.*) The dalliance of Swedenborgians with the idea of religious community was not new. In England in the 1790's, as Lammot recalled, there had been a plan to establish a Utopian settlement on the West Coast of Africa, at Cape Masurado, close to where the Colonization Society had later attempted to plant its colony. But the plan fell through.

Lammot gave the subject of associations careful thought and concluded that, Owenite or Fourierist, they were neither practical nor spiritually desirable. His position was clear and articulate and, coming from a leading layman, no doubt influential. A few of the phalanxes that were organized on Fourierist lines had a substantial number of New Church adherents; but the movement within the church never fully matured as an official commitment:

The question presented to my mind on this subject has been what is the object of association? Is it to supply our wants our comforts or indulgences with less labour and more certainty or is it to help us forward in our regeneration? If it be for temporal purposes it must be viewed in that light, and its feasibility considered. What capitalist would place his money out of his reach and control without the prospect of gain commensurate with the risk of thus placing his funds? Out of church, I apprehend the scheme would not receive much favor, and in the church there are but few capitalists, and these few so far as I can judge would not submit their judgement and means to the management of persons who have not given evidence of capacity to ensure equal or greater success in the accumulation of capital. Success is the criterion by which capacity for business is judged.

That greater economy can be observed by a well regulated association than by families generally I admit; but why? because families have some love to gratify such as handsome habitations, furniture and clothing or luxurious indulgences and display in society, and to obtain this, every opposing consideration is forced to yield. All this is human nature, and for a season it may remain latent in an association, but will in time manifest itself and then the supposed grievance will be magnified by the consideration that restraints are imposed and liberty curtailed for in addition to the laws of the country, the laws of the association must be observed. All this will beget discontent, and will work out the distruction of the association. Very few of us consider any expenditure extravagant which lends to our gratification and any restraint upon such gratification will be felt as oppressive. . . . I may yet add that there are and ever will be grades in society and every parent desires to select associates for himself and family. Such selection cannot be made in an association and hence will arise dissatisfaction.[23]

MORAL ORDER IN THE MILLS

The ambience of religious revivalism in the manufacturing district did not suffuse the factories themselves with the spirit of Christian love. To be sure, in the mills certain realistic requirements of factory discipline, such as punctuality, subordination, and sobriety, could be rationalized in terms of traditional Protestant ethical conceptions. But they could also be rationalized in terms of technological necessity. The relationship between the evangelical propaganda to which the manufacturers subjected the workers on Sundays, and the actual regimen of work during the rest of the week, was complex, for the manufacturers were moved to maximize profit and minimize the expense of management as well as to promote Christian conduct.

A curious customary mixture of moralities in the factories was developing, with some management actions and attitudes clearly aiming at the moral improvement of workers and others indicating indifference. These mixed messages pertained to the presence—and sometimes the absence—of work rules.

Work Rules in Cotton Factories

Beyond those rules of thumb that operatives had to learn and practice in order to run the machines efficiently and safely, every factory had a set of rules of a more general kind, some of them vaguely moral and some explicitly so. Sometimes these rules were printed; often, printed or in long hand, they were posted in the factories; frequently (although not at Riddle's mill) new hands were required to sign them.[1] Violation of these rules was enforced by a system of punishments.

Some of the rules were safety regulations of an obviously necessary kind. At Parkmount—and no doubt in every establishment in the industry—there was a fixed rule against smoking inside the mill. Oil and cotton dust were all about; in some places they made an explosive mixture, which could be ignited by sparks from a pipe or cigar. Violation of this rule was grounds for discharge. Fighting in the mill could also lead to discharge, for it could result in lost time, inattention, and damage to machinery and goods. Coming to work drunk would be grounds for dismissal.[2]

Other rules dealt with the organization of work. Punctuality had a peculiar importance in these early mills, far beyond what has become customary in later times when each machine is moved by its own electric motor, and this importance had nothing really to do with the Protestant ethic (although that ethic could be used to rationalize it). As we showed earlier, in mills of this era, whether powered by water or steam, each machine in the plant was driven by a belt attached to a line shaft running off the main shaft which was connected to the water wheel. Once the main shaft was connected to the prime mover, every shaft and every belt in the building began to turn. Although each machine could be disconnected from the shafting by moving a hand clutch, which shifted the belt to the loose pulley, the entire factory was designed mechanically to run under a full load of machinery. Furthermore, at the big mules and carding engines, where several people were required to service one machine, the absence of one little boy or girl piecer might immobilize not only the machine but also the mule spinner and another helper. And, since the machines were designed to run in line, so that cotton was moving continuously through the plant from one machine to another, the absence of workers to tend any machine could stop the entire factory by interrupting the supply of materials at one point and piling up excessive quantities at the next.

Rules about punctuality therefore were rigid. Tardiness was punished by docking wages or, if repeated, by dismissal—even in the case of the small children. Working conditions in the mills of two of the Chester Creek manufacturers were described in the 1837 Pennsylvania Senate investigation, and the witnesses (including Riddle and Crozer and William Shaw, one of their past employees) all agreed on the severity of the punctuality requirements. William Shaw, who worked two years for the Riddles and then for Crozer, reported:

> I have known work to commence as early as twenty minutes past four o'clock, in the summer season, and to work as late as half an hour before eight, P.M.; an hour and a-half allowed for breakfast and dinner, when the hands all leave to go to dinner—children and all; the ringing of the bell was the notice to begin, and docking wages the penalty; the foreman rings the bell and stops the machinery. In the cities, the engineer rings the bell and stops the machinery.
>
> The period of labor is not uniform; in some cases, from sun to sun. It is most common to work as long as they can see; in the winter they work until eight o'clock, receiving an hour and a-half for meals; an hour and a-half is the entire time allowed for going, eating and returning; and that time is often shortened by the ringing of the bell too soon.
>
> Punishment, by whipping, is frequent; they are sometimes sent home and docked for not attending punctually; never knew both punishments to be inflicted; generally the children are attentive, and punishments are not frequent.

Riddle felt that the factory regimen in Northern Ireland, when he worked there as a youth, was more strict than in the Chester Creek factories: "Children suffered very much under that system. They got to adhere to their regular hours, pretty much. The time was still severe on them. There was a great deal of whipping there, we have not here." And Crozer noted that the children, if they were to be employed at all, had to work under the same discipline as adults: ". . . the work of children cannot be shortened, without also abridging that of adults, as the labor of one is connected with that of the other, being part of a system, which, if broken in upon, destroys a connecting link in the chain of operations.[3]

A related work rule mentioned by the Chester Creek witnesses was that children should be constantly attentive and not sleep in the mill (even if not at the moment actively employed). Violations of such rules were punished in a variety of ways: notifying the parent, sending home, docking wages, pulling ears, slapping, whipping, and outright dismissal.

Not even mentioned, but implicit throughout the testimony, was the assumption that the orders of managers to overseers, overseers to spinners and weavers, spinners to piecers and scavengers, and in general orders from bosses to operatives, were to be obeyed promptly and efficiently. Also unmentioned was the assumption that there were some limits to the power of the manager to discipline workers. In 1833 there had been a precedent-setting case in the nearby Montgomery County's Court of Quarter Sessions. An overseer in the cotton factory of Bernard McCready had been indicted on the charge of beating one of the young operatives under his direction, a lad of fourteen. The jury found him guilty, fined him $1, and assessed him the costs of prosecution. *Hazard's Register* intoned:

> By this trial a principle has been established for the government of those "clock-work institutions," which will deprive certain petty tyrants of much of their usurped authority, and secure to the operatives a degree of protection under the laws of our country, which will tend to render their situation less onerous, because they will feel themselves more secure from oppression. The march of free principles is onward, and the time is fast approaching when the rights of the working-man shall be respected, and his person be protected from wrong and outrage.[4]

But for less obviously work-related moralities, the practice differed from factory to factory. Thus, speaking of cleanliness, one of the traditional Protestant virtues, William Shaw declared that "no attention is paid by the manufacturer, or others in the factory, to the personal cleanliness of the children." Robert Craig, the manager at John S. Phillips' mill at Fairmount in Philadelphia, reported, "No attention is bestowed by the managers or proprietors, to the personal or bodily cleanliness of the children." But Crozer said that the children in his mill were "generally cleanly." Another object of varying concern on the part of manufacturers was the possibility of undue intimacy between the sexes. No manufacturer attempted to segregate the sexes by room or even by type of machine, except for putting males at the more strenuous or more skilled jobs. But there was concern about the provision of water closets. The Senate committee regularly asked about sanitary conveniences. Shaw observed: "No particular attention is paid to morals; the boys and girls are not kept separate in the factories; they have different water closets, generally separated only by a partition. . . ." Craig also noted that "the water closets of the boys and girls are separate." The Riddles went a little further, separating workers by age as well as sex: "The boys and girls at our mill have different water closets; the boys and girls in different parts of the yard; the men and women the same house, but a partition between them." Crozer did not mention the subject of toilets in his testimony.

Still more various was the attitude toward profane and obscene language. Although the one was deemed wrong because blasphemous, and the other because it implied—or might lead to—loose sexual conduct, the mills varied in their concern. Crozer was emphatic: "no improper conduct or conversation is allowed in well conducted factories—at least there is not in mine." But Samuel Riddle was indifferent to the whole question, putting it on a "Boys will be boys" level: "I do not think that boys in factories are more in the habit of using profane and obscene language, than those out of doors; when a number of boys get together out of doors, they always do these things. I think that the girls do not use such language." Shaw's experience was that the typical manufacturer did not care: "No particular attention is paid to morals . . . obscene language is frequently used, not often by females; profane language is frequently used; care is seldom taken to prevent these things; if their work is done, it is all that is required. . . ." And Craig contradicted himself, declaring in one passage that "no attention is paid to the morals of the children in the factory; they are neither advised nor reprimanded, unless they neglect their work," yet in another place testifying that children were dismissed for using bad language: "Profane and obscene language is too frequent in the absence of the superintendent, and happens between boys and girls, and is injurious to the morals in a great degree; no other means to prevent it is resorted to other than dismissal when the superintendent hears them at it."[5]

Crozer, indeed, as might have been expected, was the most moralistic of the local manufacturers whose factories were the subject of testimony. He had, he said, a policy of dismissing any female employee who had a doubtful reputation:

> The young women employed, are possessed of a proper self-respect, and departures from chastity are not common. Females of loose character, if known, or *even suspected* as such, would be immediately dismissed from my factory, and I think could not get employment in any of the neighboring factories.[6]

None of the written regulations survive from any of the Rockdale mills, but the "Rules and Regulations of the Matteawan Company" in 1846 have been preserved. Matteawan, as we noted earlier, was one of the most successful of the cotton manufactories, and a center of machine-making. When it was visited by Robert Owen in 1824, the proprietor had made a point of his high moral expectations, informing Owen's party, when they praised the appearance of the workers, "that when a girl did not shew a disposition to be clean & neat in her dress they turned her off."[7] The rules in 1846 had not been relaxed; their severity certainly exceeded that of the Rockdale district (perhaps as a result of the hard Calvinist convictions of the proprietors, who were members of the Dutch Reform Church):

No person will be admitted into the yard during working hours, except on business, without permission of an agent. At all other times, the watchmen will be invested with full control.

The work bell will be rung three minutes, and tolled five minutes; at the expiration of which, every person is expected to be at their work, and every entrance closed, except through the office, which will at all times be open during the working hours of the factory.

No person employed in the manufacturing departments can be permitted to leave their work without permission from their overseer. All others employed in and about the factory are requested to give notice to the agent or superintendent, if they wish to be absent from their work.

No talking can be permitted among the hands in any of the working departments, except on subjects relating to their work.

No spirituous liquors, smoking, or any kind of amusements, will be allowed in the workshops or yards.

Those who take jobs will be considered as overseers of the persons employed by them, and subject to these rules.

Should there exist among any of the persons employed, an idea of oppression on the part of the company, they are requested to make the same known in honorable manner, that such grievances, if really existing, may be promptly considered.

To convince the enemies of domestic manufactures that such establishments are not "sinks of vice and immorality," but, on the contrary, nurseries of morality, industry, and intelligence, a strictly moral conduct is required of every one. Self-respect, it is presumed, will induce every one to be as constant in attendance on some place of divine worship as circumstances will permit. Intemperance, or any gross impropriety of conduct, will cause an immediate discharge of the individual.

The agent and other members of the company are desirous of cultivating the most friendly feeling with the workmen in the establishment, believing they are to rise or fall together. Therefore, to promote the interest and harmony of all, it is necessary there should be a strict observance of these rules and regulations.[8]

Creating an Ethical System for the Workers

It is clear, from the consideration of work rules, that the manufacturers, whether ardent evangelicals or stubborn infidels, all gave to the requirements of technology and economics the first priority in designing factory discipline. They were willing, in fact, to require the workers to behave in ways, and to labor under conditions, that they themselves, and the community generally, conventionally regarded as conducive to immorality. They recognized that the system of long hours prevented the children who worked in factories from getting any education at all—even though the spirit of the Revolution, and the rhetoric of Jacksonian democracy, favored educating all the young people of the commonwealth. Illiteracy, by rendering religious instruction more difficult and Bible-reading impossible, was in itself an obstacle to the moral improvement of the working class. Both Riddle and Crozer therefore testified in favor of prohibiting the labor of children under twelve in cotton factories, in order to free the early years for basic education and to protect the very young from the immoral influences of factory life. And both Riddle and Crozer favored an overall reduction in hours of labor. But they were not willing to introduce these reforms into their own factories, and opposed unilateral legislation by the Pennsylvania legislature on the subject, because, they said, they feared that manufacturers in other states, lacking such laws, would have a competitive advantage and would drive the Pennsylvania manufactories out of business. The demands of conventional morality, when they conflicted with the iron laws of technology and economics, regularly were accorded second place.

Samuel Riddle was eloquent and direct on the problem of balancing economic interest against child welfare:

I think that it would be better to prohibit the employment of children under twelve years of age; the children under that age, would then have a better chance of going to school. I don't think it would increase the wages of labor; I don't think it would make any difference in this respect. The parents of children employed in factories, would be generally opposed to it, I think. A great many widow women have no other way of support, and they would want to get their children into factories at an earlier age. There are too many fathers who are themselves idle, and live by the work of their little children; they would be opposed to it. If children over twelve only, went into factories, the time of labor as now practised, would not make any odds. No system could be established about factories by which children could be required to be schooled a portion of time; when children are employed, the men could not do the work the little ones does; we can't dispense with the work of children in factories. I believe the manufacturer would be better if the hours were shortened—if they were shortened all over the U. States; otherwise I would fear the competition of other States. The children might be instructed under such a system, by night schools.

I should think that it would be good, that boys should not be employed until they were twelve, and until they can read and write. I think it would be better all round; it would not increase the wages of labor; it would be good for the rising generation, and better for the factory. Generally, the children in factories are not able to read and write; they would be inclined to learn, if they had the opportunity. It would be preferable to have girls put on the same footing, but as to age of employment we do not consider it so important.

A system, such as I suggest, would operate very hardly on the poor people, unless you gave it time, by providing that it should commence a year or two as the public schools have been commenced.

. . . I think that a length of labor of sixty-six hours a week in Pennsylvania alone, would effect us so that we could not compete with other States. We pay higher for wages here than they do at the Eastward, and when times are bad, they can under-sell us, so that we have to stop.[9]

Crozer was also eloquent, but somewhat more defensive than Riddle, blaming the resistance to reform even more explicitly on the parents:

The adults employed in manufactories, have, within the last few years, expressed much anxiety to shorten the hours of labor, and have made application for this purpose, to their employers; no direct grant has been made, but the time has been somewhat shortened generally; the parents of children employed, have not, I think, taken an active part on this subject, probably from the fear, that a corresponding reduction of wages would follow; I think many employers might oppose abridging the hours of work, because it would then be necessary to increase the fixed capital of buildings and machinery, to obtain the same amount of work—but the strongest objections arise from the apprehension that a change in the time of work, unless it was of general application throughout the United States, would give other States an advantage over us.

Education is much neglected about manufactories; a large portion of the families employed, are those of indigent widows, who require the work of their children for support, or of idle, intemperate fathers, who do little or nothing themselves towards supporting their families: and these, especially the latter, have but little inclination to school their children, and it is frequently the case, when employers encourage the schooling of the children, the parents object and postpone, with the complaint of being "unable, *for the present,* to lose the labor of the child"; employers have not always encouraged education; small operatives have often been scarce, and employers were therefore, desirous to retain the children in the factories; this difficulty has mostly disappeared on Chester creek, and perhaps in other places as small children have become more abundant.

I think legislative action, for the protection and education of factory children, desirable—yet, I am constrained to say, the necessity of the case arises more from the conduct of parents, than that of employers.[10]

The manufacturers evidently were experiencing a moral dilemma. They were committed, at least as responsible citizens if not also as evangelical religionists, to the moral and mental improvement of the people, and especially of the children, who were connected with their mills. But successful management of a factory in a competitive market economy in their opinion required them to tolerate, or even create, noxious working conditions for their employees: denial of educational opportunity, exposure to profane and obscene language, promiscuous association of the sexes and of different age groups in intimate working arrangements.

The solution was to urge reform, not in the mill but in the institutions of the community, and particularly in the educational system. The Pennsylvania Senate investigating committee in 1838 reported a bill which provided that no children under ten would be permitted to work in factories; that children over ten who did work in factories, but could not read, write, or keep accounts, should be sent to school three months in every year of employment; and that children under sixteen should not be allowed to work more than ten hours per day.[11] But the bill did not pass; in fact it was never brought to a vote.

The manufacturers relied on the community to resolve the problem: on the parents to bring up their children properly; on the Sunday School to educate them and give them elementary religious instruction and moral guidance; on the newly created system of public schools (instituted in 1836 as a result of the Commonwealth law of that year) to provide free education to all children; and on the Sunday School teachers and clergy to instruct both children and adults in Christian duty.

The clergy responded to this charge in a complementary way. Instead of demanding of the manufacturers that they reform their factories, they demanded of the workers that they recast their own thinking along lines that would render factory reform unnecessary. Ministers across the land prepared tracts for presentation to working-class people that would detach them from any lingering remnants of infidel philosophy and provide them instead with a set of Christian ethical principles. These would enable them, among other things, to cooperate successfully with the existing capitalist economic system and with the factory system that was growing up within it.

Alonzo Potter, the Smiths' friend and after 1841 the Bishop of Pennsylvania, wrote such a tract. It was first published about 1838 as a review in one of the periodicals, when Potter was Professor of Moral Philosophy at Union College, and republished in 1841 as an appendix to a book entitled *Political Economy* which bore Potter's name on the title page. The basic treatise on political economy contained in this book was actually an acknowledged republication of the first ten chapters of Scrope's *Political Economy* (published in England in 1833), with fairly extensive editorial changes by Potter. Potter's appended seventy-page essay, entitled "The Condition of Labouring Men in the United States," is however worthy of close attention not only because Potter was to become an influential Church leader, but because as the Smiths' friend, and as the bishop personally responsible for the Rockdale mission, he visited the community on many occasions, spending at least one day annually to confirm new members, and on these and other occasions he addressed the people from the pulpit of Calvary Church. We can be sure that the view of the workers expressed in this essay was communicated to the people of the Rockdale district both directly by the bishop and indirectly by the rectors and Sunday School teachers.

Potter's essay was a warning to the nation against what he regarded as the wave of political demagoguery, feeding on working-class disaffection, that in his view was associated with the party of Andrew Jackson. He explicitly compared the present age to turbulent periods of the past, from the French Revolution back to classical times, and repeatedly associated trade unions with such labels as Jacobinism and Terrorism and such names as Marat and Robespierre. He painstakingly exposed the shallowness of the "something for nothing" philosophy of the workingmen who clamored against the unequal distribution of property. He compared them to the "champions of equality" in Revolutionary France and demonstrated that, although *extreme* distinctions of wealth and property were politically undesirable, a degree of inequality was unavoidable. A "community of goods," as proposed by Robert Owen and Saint-Simon, would merely produce an "equality of servitude" under a dictatorial master like Owen himself at New Lanark. Only a society based firmly on the principle of private property would permit both true liberty and a reasonable distribution of wealth.

Having established the moral principles on which a good society must be based, he went on in more detail—and this discussion was the major part of the work—to show that "combinations of working men," with their fearful power to strike against employers and to coerce into obedience their own members and other workers as well, were inherently undesirable. Although not referring to the Masonic order in so many words, he compared the evils of trade unionism to the evils of Freemasonry:

We hold that the power lodged with associations is safe from great and dangerous abuse only when their objects are clearly avowed and their proceedings substantially public; when their composition is so far promiscuous as to secure them from a clannish spirit and an anti-social policy; and when the influence on which they rely is of a purely moral nature, appealing to something higher than fear. Allow them the use of violence, or even of intimidation, and they will soon usurp the place of law, and erect themselves into the most intolerable of all tyrannies. Suffer them to imbody but the members of one profession or class, and those but of one sex, and they will evince an exclusiveness and identity of feeling, and be liable to ebullitions of passion, which will render them always troublesome, finally, permit them to proceed in secret, and for purposes not fully known or explained, and the temptation to convert them into instruments of oppression for political or religious ends will be nearly irresistable.

And he flatly accused the trades union movement of being foreign in origin and tending to socialism, atheism, and sedition:

However desirable it may be to ameliorate the outward condition of men and to enlighten their understandings, it must be admitted to be inconceivably more desirable to raise the tone of their deportment and moral sentiments. In increasing their physical and intellectual resources merely, we may but increase their misery, and the mischief which they will inflict on their families of the public. No body of men is more dangerous than one raised in influence above the mass of those engaged in similar pursuits, and constantly busied in inspiring jealousy and promoting agitation. That such is the case with these Unions we do not affirm. But it is worthy of notice, that their leaders are generally from abroad, and that their doctrines respecting labour and capital are often propagated in close connexion with tenets by Mr. Owen respecting Politics and Religion. Now we know something of the style and spirit of the literature which thrives amid such tenets. The Halls of Science established under the auspices of Mr. Owen push their researches into the realms of atheism and sedition. They have little taste for anything farther. So with Trades' Unions. They convene their members to hear of "equal rights," "rapacious capitalists," "grinding employers." But we are informed of no libraries that they have established; of no lectures that they have instituted; nor, indeed, of any measures for the diffusion of useful knowledge, which were not already prevalent and of easy access.[12]

Potter's views on unions were extreme. Probably not even the Rockdale manufacturers were prepared to go as far as he in condemning unionism. But in his intellectual polarization of Enlightenment and evangelical approaches to problems of economics, he correctly formulated the dialectic out of which the synthesis of the next decades would evolve.

THE RISE OF POLITICAL ANTI-MASONRY

Ever since the 1790's, there had been chronic harassment of political radicals in America on the grounds of religion. Sometimes, within a community, the harassment was subtle and covert, amounting to no more than some degree of social isolation (as in Phillips' case) or a refusal to take a "good and intelligent" infidel as more than a crypto-Christian (as with Minshall Painter). But often the harassment involved was more harsh. Personal attack, both physical and literary, was a technique used more or less openly by the more militant Christians throughout the first two decades of the century to suppress the freethinkers and Deists who questioned fundamental Christian beliefs and touted radical social doctrines. Sometimes the violence involved prominent freethinkers: Tom Paine, formerly hailed as the heroic pamphleteer of American freedom, was now made a symbol of degraded atheism in the torrents of abuse that flowed over him from the religious press; mobs hurled rocks and imprecations at Fanny Wright and forced her to cancel appearances when she passed through Pennsylvania; Abner Kneeland, erstwhile Philadelphia Universalist clergyman and chaplain to the Masonic lodge, was convicted of blasphemy in New England and served sixty days in jail. But usually the violence was more discreetly managed and was applied to more vulnerable targets. In either manner, it created—or continued—a tradition of Christian terrorism against followers of the Enlightenment tradition that must be recognized as part of the ambience in which the ideological conflict of the age was being fought.[1] Two cases, involving persons on the edge of the network that centered in Rockdale, are worth citing as illustrations of the phenomenon: the harassment of John Speakman, John S. Phillips' associate at the Academy of Natural Sciences of Philadelphia, when Speakman was a member of the "Pittsburgh Society of Deists"; and the brutal treatment of the widely read and outspoken journalistic critic of evangelical Christianity, Anne Royall.

It was in the midst of this feverish Christian response to the threat of infidelity that a political movement arose, quasi-terrorist in some of its aspects, dedicated to the exclusion of members of the Masonic order from the public life of the nation. This movement must indeed be regarded, as Lee Benson and others have suggested, as the political shock force of the Protestant evangelical movement, responsive to the call of the Reverend Ezra Stiles Ely of Philadelphia for "a Christian party in politics." The Anti-Masonic members of the legislature in Albany stated defensively in 1829:

> Anti-masons proscribe and persecute no man. The charge is founded upon the fact that anti-masons resolve *not to elevate to office* those who ADHERE to the masonic fraternity. This is neither proscription nor persecution. No individual has a right to demand the suffrage of another. The bestowment of it is exclusively the right of him who possesses it. To withhold from an individual what he has no right to demand and no claim to possess until it is freely given, is no *persecution*. To annihilate the institution of Freemasonry, or render it harmless, anti-masons have formed the resolution to *withhold* their suffrages from those who adhere to the order.[2]

But the apparatus of terrorism was still there: spectacular trials, legislative investigations, and pressuring of witnesses to testify under the threat of being jailed for contempt of court.

John Speakman
and the Pittsburgh Society of Deists

During his brief sojourn in Pittsburgh in the early 1820's, John Speakman was a member of a group known as the Pittsburgh Society of Deists. It was an informally organized colloquium, which met in the home of a tradesman. Upwards of two hundred people would assemble on Sunday evenings to hear religionists and freethinkers debate such issues as the authenticity of the Scriptures and the divinity of Jesus. Writing to his friend Thomas Say later on, Speakman described how one after another the zealous defenders of the faith, Methodist and Presbyterian, were laid low by the powerful arguments of their free-thinking opponents. At last the ministers of Pittsburgh laid aside "all their petty broils of rivalship, and united as a band of brothers, prophesying and doling out the dreadful consequences to all those who undertook to judge the scriptures according to the dictates of their fallen natures." Six of the principal participants were accused before a magistrate of "speaking loosely of Jesus Christ and of the scriptures of truth," and one was charged with conspiracy. At jury trials in the mayor's court, conducted with questionable fairness and relying upon perjured witnesses, the man at whose house the meetings were held was convicted (although an appeal to the State Supreme Court later reversed the conviction)[3] and fined $10 and costs. Another victim, although found not guilty, was assessed court costs; he went to jail rather than pay. The leader's shop, next to his house, was mysteriously set afire and burned down. The Deists' meetings ceased.

It was in response to this sequence of events that Speakman developed his early plan for a Utopian community of scientists, to be founded in some remote place, far from the clutches of the Holy Alliance—"that all devouring monster whose voracity increases in proportion to the number of its victims."[4]

Anne Royall and the "blue-skinned Presbyterians"

The aging widow of long-dead Major Royall, a Virginia gentleman of deistical views who had served the republic during the Revolution, Anne Royall in the 1820's and 1830's was a traveling newspaper woman who wrote "black books" about her travels, full of personal anecdote and social criticism. She repeatedly passed through the Philadelphia-Wilmington area. In a material sense, she lived poorly on her subscriptions and fees; her delight came from exposing corruption in high places and from cutting through the pretensions of popular fads, such as anti-Masonry and the evangelical crusade, to reveal the hypocrisy within. Although she was not a follower of Owen, she wrote up a friendly interview with him, and published a favorable notice of Joseph Neef and his Pestalozzian School ("I should rejoice to see a school of this description in every county, town, and city of the Union"). She chose to defend the Masonic order, which had helped her financially during the writing of her "black books," at the very time when the tide of anti-Masonic feeling was running high. And she tilted constantly at the "blue-skinned Presbyterians" ("May all their throats be cut") and other fanatical religionists who were creating the evangelical alliance. The American Sunday School Union, the American Bible Society, the American Tract Society all came under her displeasure. She labeled as "treason" Ely's proposal for a Christian party in politics.

But the response was brutal and effective. She was accused in print of having been a prostitute. She was regularly snubbed by the pious. When she sought an interview and a subscription from the Reverend Dr. Ezra

Stiles Ely, she was refused; she memorialized the moment in her usual mocking way:

> I was informed that his house stood back from the street, in a square, and on his gate I would see a silver plate with "Rev. Dr. Stiles Ely" on it in large letters. I found the gate, and the silver plate—the big letters—the big house—and the BIG man. The big door was open. The doctor appeared, but I briefly repeated my business. He turned off short and said he was engaged.

She was horsewhipped in Pittsburgh and run out of town by a mob of students in Virginia. In 1827 she visited Burlington, Vermont, and was thrown out of a store and down a 10-foot flight of steps by a zealously religious storekeeper. She suffered a broken leg, a dislocated ankle, and a sprained knee, and was for a time severely hampered in her movements. In 1829, living in Washington, D.C., her house was stoned and windows broken by a Sunday School class meeting in an engine house next door; the parents, led by an elder of the First Presbyterian Church, kept her awake at night, praying beneath her broken windows for her salvation. The parents were succeeded by mobs of children, black and white, employed "to shower the house with stones, yell, and blow horns." A few weeks later she was accused before a grand jury by the same elder and his son, his daughter, and his daughter-in-law, and by several federal officials, including the recently dismissed Librarian of Congress (to whom she had complained about the presence of the books and pamphlets of the American Sunday School Union scattered over the reading tables), the House Sergeant-at-arms, and the Senate office clerk. There were three charges: that she was "an evil-disposed person"; a common scold and slanderer; and a disturber of the peace and happiness of her peaceful and honest neighbors. At a nationally celebrated trial she was convicted, fined $10 (which she did not have), and required to post a $100 bond to guarantee that she would keep the peace for a year (i.e., that she would not write). Two newspaper reporters, concerned over the freedom of the press, paid the fine and put up security for her good conduct.

Anne Royall was not silenced; she went on attacking the evangelicals in her "black books" and giving favorable notices of liberals and even radicals. But there were fewer and fewer journalists and local free enquirers who were willing to risk poverty, beatings, insults, and harassment by the courts in following her example.[5]

Edward Darlington and the Anti-Masonic Party

The seed around which political Anti-Masonry crystallized, in the supersaturated solution of ideological controversy that was filling the nation in the 1820's, was the reported murder in 1826 of William Morgan of Batavia, New York. Allegedly, he had been abducted and executed by the Masons for having, contrary to his oath, planned to reveal the secrets of the order in a published book. Allegedly, also, a conspiracy of Masons in the courts and legislature was protecting the murderers and impeding the investigation. By 1828 mass meetings were being organized in New York, Massachusetts, Pennsylvania, and other northern states; petitions were being drafted and forwarded to legislatures; newspapers were being established (one, *The Anti-Masonic Register,* on Chester Creek) to promulgate Anti-Masonic doctrine and to serve as the vehicle for ticket formation and party organization. Eventually, Pennsylvania elected an Anti-Masonic governor and legislature; the former governor, and other witnesses, were subpoenaed to testify before a legislative committee to reveal the crimes of Masonry. It was not until the Buckshot War of 1838 (when rioting Democrats drove the Anti-Masons out of the Assembly) that the tide of Anti-Masonic fervor really began to subside from the commonwealth.

One of the manufacturers of Chester Creek was prominently involved in political Anti-Masonry: Edward Darlington. In politics he had begun his career as a Democrat in a part of Pennsylvania traditionally dominated by one of the few surviving Federalist constituencies in the nation. In 1830, running for Congress as an Anti-Mason from Delaware County, he was defeated by the candidate of the Chester County Anti-Masons. In 1832 and 1834, however, he was elected to Congress on the Anti-Masonic ticket itself and in 1836 was returned as a Whig. Thus the Chester Creek manufacturing district was, from 1833 to 1839, represented in the House of Representatives in Washington by an anti-Jackson man who, for the first four years, was actively affiliated with the Anti-Masonic Party. Although there is no reason to suppose that Darlington was not genuinely opposed to the Masonic order, his political activity and his correspondence do not actually concern themselves with the issue of Freemasonry. He was the close friend, legal representative, and partner of the Chester Creek manufacturers and he represented their interests in Congress. He was a friend of Henry Carey, the leading American economist. He opposed Jackson's veto of the recharter bill for the Second Bank of the United States; he opposed the withdrawal of funds; he supported the tariff to protect the cotton industry; he opposed the expansion of slavery into the new states and territories of the Union; he opposed slavery in the District of Columbia and favored the plan of the American Colonization Society to ship freed blacks back to Africa; in his most vehement political stand, he opposed prohibiting the introduction of anti-slavery petitions to the House of Representatives. He was, in short, the very epitome of the proto-Republican as he appeared in the days before that party was able to mobilize the numerous but scattered proponents of the protective tariff, benevolent Christian capitalism, and free soil into a national political consensus.[6]

The Odiornes and the Meaning of Anti-Masonry

The conduct in office of such respectable Anti-Masons as Edward Darlington (and there were many like him) does not suggest in any way a paranoid, fanatical, extremist type of politics. There were, to be sure, political inquisitions on the state level of suspected or admitted Masonic evil-doers; many lodges closed temporarily. But it would appear that, fundamentally, the Anti-Masonic activities of the decade 1828–38 simply provided an organizational mold within which to form a party composed of many of those who—whether they considered themselves to be former Federalists, anti-Jackson Democrats, pro-Clay National Republicans, or Whigs—shared a belief in America as a Christian capitalist nation, dedicated to manufacturing and progress and populated by free men, all of whom would have sufficient education, religious training, and income for personal success, and who would therefore be able to view the social classes as complementary rather than antagonistic.

But this ideological position was being *consciously* formed as an answer to the very popular deistic and atheistic socialist doctrines of Robert and Robert Dale Owen, Fanny Wright, Thomas Paine, and in general the deistic *philosophes* who had rationalized the Revolution in France. The Anti-Masons also opposed the Democrats, including not only the liberal "locofoco" faction but also Jackson and Van Buren and their bank and tariff policies. Furthermore, the Anti-Masonic Party developed very shortly after —and in obvious opposition to—the Workingmen's parties of Philadelphia, New York (the Owen-Wright faction), and Boston. One might indeed suggest that it was Anti-Masonic rhetoric which forced upon "The Democracy"—an old, entrenched, and in its own way very conservative political machine—the image of liberalism. The Enlightenment policies of Thomas Jefferson lived on, in reality, more fully in the Workingmen's Party than in the Jacksonian Democratic Party, despite the presence in that party of some old-line liberal politicians.

From the perspective of ideological combat, then, let us look more closely at the doctrines of anti-Masonry. They were, to begin with, not new but already a generation old and were formed, not in western New York in response to the murder of William Morgan, but in England, France, and Germany in response to the French Revolution. The doctrines of anti-Masonry were expounded in some detail in a little work compiled by James C. Odiorne (who was the cousin and brother-in-law of George Moore, nail-maker of Chester Creek until 1832, and cousin also of the Odiorne sisters of Ivy Mills who had married the wealthy, politically active, and conservative Willcox brothers).

Odiorne's *Opinions on Speculative Masonry* was published in Boston in 1830. Much of the content was conventional rhetoric, condemning the order as an élitist group held together by secret oaths and obscene and blasphemous rituals requiring the Mason to give higher loyalty to his order than to God, Church, or State. This was the superficial populist objection to Freemasonry, the first level of analysis of the institution. It appealed to a wide body of public opinion.

But there was a second level, and this harked back to the hue and cry against Freemasonry which had developed in England during the 1790's, when the British establishment was undertaking to discredit the French Revolution. The argument on this level was formulated by Dr. William Robison, the distinguished physicist of the University of Edinburgh, in 1794. Robison claimed that an ancient conspiracy existed, which aimed to overthrow all organized religion and to destroy all legitimate governments; in recent years it had worked through a peculiar secret organization, the Illuminati of Bavaria, which had infiltrated the Masonic order to infect French public opinion with the infidel views of the *philosophes*. The Masonic order thus was held to be directly responsible for launching the Revolution in France and for fomenting popular disaffection in England, Ireland, and even the United States. Robison was the supreme authority for Anti-Masonic intellectuals. The organizational aspect of his view was expressed succinctly in Albany on May 5, 1829, in an address by the "Republican Anti-Masonic Members of the Legislature of New York, to their Constituents":

The institution in this country receives with passive obedience, whatever is transmitted from the *foreign* seat of its empire. Here it has formed a confederacy embracing the whole extent of our republic. All our territory is parcelled out, and a branch of the institution established in every section. It has its meetings in the darkness of night and security of secrecy, for towns, counties, states, and the whole Union. The institution is prepared to act throughout the land, with concert, energy and decision, and to receive its impulse from *foreign command.* Its immense resources enable it to attempt the greatest objects. Nothing is too lofty for its ambition or beyond its means of accomplishment. In Europe the institution has been made the cloak of innumerable crimes. In its dark conclaves plots, stratagems, and treason have been designed against governments and religion, and the institutions of civil society, and put in a train of successful execution, while its infatuated votaries were unconscious of the object of the master spirits that impelled them to action. What has been attempted in other countries *may* be expected in our own. The organization of the institution here, fits it for the purposes of treason. Its extended confederacy furnishes the opportunity for the widest communication. The masonic cipher gives the instrument of safe correspondence, and its secrecy enforced by horrid obligations and appalling penalties, affords the assurance of security. The question then is presented to the American people whether they will sacrifice DEMOCRACY or annihilate the institution of *Freemasonry,* which threatens its existence.[7]

The Reverend Moses Tacher of Massachusetts expressed the ideological issues in another succinct discussion in Odiorne's volume of illuminism as a kind of acephalous social movement:

You inquire "what evidence I have, that masonry leads directly to infidelity?" and, if "it is pretended that masonry and the system of illuminism are mutually coupled together?" If you had said *systems* of illuminism, I think you would have given a more just representation of the subject. Illuminism, I conceive to be *one;* but its *systems* are many. Illuminism is a popular name for infidel Philosophy, comprising all its doctrines, and shades of doctrine, from Deism, to Atheism and complete skepticism. The *systems* of this philosophy are exceedingly various, and so artfully either contrived or *adopted,* as to "deceive, if it were possible, the very elect." I speak of systems belonging to illuminism, as either contrived or *adopted;* because this infidel philosophy has indeed contrived some, and *adopted* others, already fitted for its reception. Of some of these systems you have given the names: as, the "Society of Carbonari" in Germany, the "United Irishmen," and the "Ribbon-men," in Ireland, &c. You justly observe, that "distinctions like these are of little consequence where one grand object is in view." Yet I think, you have fallen into a mistake, and confounded the *systems* of illuminism with illuminism itself. Illuminism, I grant, is the same, in every place, and in every country; whether it is called "Philosophy," "Reason," "Liberty and Equality," or "infidelity." Its systems, however, are not only as various, but as *distinct* as its *names;* and exactly adapted to answer its own purposes, though suited to the different nations. By systems, I here mean, those different combinations and societies, organized and governed in very different ways, professing to promote entirely different objects; but whose grand and ultimate design *has always centred* in infidelity. Now, I ask, What system was adopted by the illuminees of France in order to "crush the Wretch," and to accomplish their designs against religion and government? To trace all their plans, and develop all their schemes of wickedness, would require more time, talents and learning, than can be commanded by me, or perhaps by *you*. The following, however, are among some of the measures which they adopted: To hold secret correspondence, to circulate infidel tracts, control and corrupt the press, and to superintend the instruction of children and youth. Some of their bolder steps, were, to publish their Encyclopedia, seize upon the Royal Academy, and bring it entirely under their corrupting influence. . . .[8]

It is clear enough, then, that Anti-Masonry attacked precisely the views of the liberal-to-radical range being so energetically promulgated in the 1820's by the Marquis de Lafayette, Robert Owen, Fanny Wright, and the Workingmen's Party of Philadelphia. These views, based in considerable part on the philosophy of the Enlightenment (illuminism), proposed, in effect, to take control of the Industrial Revolution away from capital and put it in the hands of workers. Anti-Masonry now defined them as the corrupt doctrine of an ancient, worldwide conspiracy, which aimed to annihilate Christianity, topple existing governments, abolish private property, and violate the sanctity of marriage.

But there is an even deeper level of analysis than this. Anti-Masonry appealed to the dormant yet by no means forgotten tradition of witch-fear in European culture. The testimony at English trials of accused witches, and the records of the Inquisition, clearly show that their accusers believed witches to be members of an ancient, secret, and powerful organization, with its own hierarchy, its own mythology, and its own orgiastic rituals. This tradition was invoked by the Anti-Masonic scholars Dr. Robison and the abbé Barruel, upon whom the Anti-Masonic agitators who chose the second level of analysis all depended for their information. Dr. Robison virtually accused the Bavarian Illuminati (the corruptors of French Masonic lodges) of practicing old-fashioned witchcraft (although he himself did not believe that witches had supernatural powers). Thus, in revealing the contents of the papers found during a police raid on the house of one of the Illuminati, he noted plans to organize a sisterhood of sacred prostitutes (to "procure us both much information and money") and a series of infernal recipes or secret poisons, aphrodisiacs, and abortifacients:

There are, in the same hand-writing, Description of a strong box, which if forced open, shall blow up and destroy its contents—Several receipts for procuring abortions—A composition which blinds or kills when spurted in the face—A sheet, containing a receipt for sympathetic ink—Tea for procuring abortion—A method for filling a bed-chamber with pestilential vapours—How to take off impressions of seals, so as to use them afterwards as seals—A collection of some hundreds of such impressions, with a list of their owners, princes, nobles, clergymen, merchants, &c. —A receipt *ad excitandum furorem uterinum,*—A manuscript intitled, "Better than Horus." It was afterwards printed and distributed at Leipzig fair, and is an attack and bitter satire on all religion.[9]

And the abbé Barruel charged that the Masons were the perpetuators of the ancient Manichaean heresy.[10] In effect, they raised the specter of an ancient pagan cult, its members despising God and the Christian virtues, dedicated to the use of love magic and abortion medicine in its pursuit of sexual license, and prepared to murder its enemies if threatened. This is indeed the image of the witch cult of Western Europe, cast upon the screen of political events in the Atlantic community less than a hundred years after the last witchcraft execution in England, and not much longer in America.

The conclusion is inescapable that political Anti-Masonry in America in the decade 1828–38 must be understood, ideologically, as an aspect of the evangelical Protestant crusade against infidelity. It singled out, as the symbol of the hated tradition of the Enlightenment, the institution of Freemasonry, and cast itself in the role of savior of the republic from an international conspiracy. It was, in effect, the "Christian party in politics" for which the more zealous evangelicals were calling. Its intellectual origins in the immediate past lay in the conservative polemical literature that opposed the French Revolution, particularly Dr. Robison's book *Proofs of a Conspiracy;* but more deeply it drew emotional form from the traditional European fear of a pagan underground of witches and worshippers of Satan.

Although the movement passed quickly as an organized political force, it was able to gather together a variety of respectable men dissatisfied with the policies of the Democratic Party of the day. These men—inconspicuous men like Chester Creek's Edward Darlington and also conspicuous figures like the redoubtable Thaddeus Stevens—worked together to hammer out an economic and political policy that emphasized capitalist industrialization, free soil, universal free education, and the complementary rather than competing interests of the social classes. They thus contributed importantly to the development of an articulate Christian capitalist philosophical alternative to the still influential spokesmen of illuminism. And they contributed to the branding of an indelible impression in one part of the American political consciousness that somewhere, somehow, beyond America's shores there exists a Satanic empire whose minions are ever at work to destroy the republic and take over the world.

DEFEATING THE INFIDELS ON CHESTER CREEK

Despite the rhetoric of Jacksonian democracy and its apparent benevolence toward the common man, America in the 1820's and 1830's was drifting to the right. The thousands, perhaps hundreds of thousands, of respectable Deists and social liberals were less and less free to express their views publicly. A tighter order in society was in the making, and its signs —the rise of machine politics and modern party organization; the expansion of slavery in the south and the progressive denial to free blacks in the north of access to former economic and political privileges; the growth of powerful evangelical religious organizations and benevolent societies—were visible everywhere. On Chester Creek, the mill owners chose an Anti-Mason to represent their views in Congress. Calvary Church hammered the few infidels and radicals among the manufacturers, mechanics, and operatives into silence. Pennsylvania's new constitution of 1837 *withdrew* the franchise from free blacks.

Smith's assessment of the success of Calvary Church in changing the moral tone of the Rockdale district was enthusiastic as early as April 1838:

> . . . much of good has been done and the cause of religion and piety advanced by the establishment of the Church and School in the neighborhood. The population being Manufacturers and a large proportion of them young persons, no one who is not familiar with the privations that neighborhood suffered for want of religious instruction, can imagine the change that has been effected by the opportunities thus offered and by the establishment of the means of grace among them. The nearest place of worship heretofore was two miles distant. The children roamed at large on the Lord's Day trespassing on their neighbors, and that sacred day was more than any other marked by noise and turbulence, intemperance and profanity. Infidelity stalked boldly among the people; the disciples of Paine held public meetings to inculcate his doctrines, and on one occasion when a Presbyterian clergyman gave notice that he should preach on the evidences of Christianity, he was interrupted by some of those who attended for the purpose with a volume of Paine's works in

their hands. These persons, no longer finding countenance for such opinions, have either left the neighborhood, or no longer advance them, and the improvement in the morals and deportment of the people is so evident to persons who, altho' themselves indifferent to religious truths, are yet interested in the establishment of order, that a voluntary testimony has been given in favor of the Church as the means by which this great change has been produced.[1]

Clementina's friend Sophie, who when she first heard of plans for a Sunday School wrote to say, "from what you have told me of the people in your neighborhood, I know of no place where the benefits of a Sabbath School instruction are more needed," by 1839 was congratulating her friend that "the cause of the Lord [was] thus prospering." And in 1842 she was reporting to "Clemma" the "most cheering account of Rockdale" she had heard from another friend.[2]

The leaders of Calvary Church clearly had in mind the link between infidelity—the lack of faith in Christ—and the social philosophy of the Enlightenment. In inviting Lee to accept the call to Calvary Church, Smith drew explicit attention to the peculiar spiritual needs of the locality. "Rockdale," he said, "is not a regular village but a manufacturing establishment . . ." And he went on to explain:

A large proportion of the congregation consists of operatives in the Factories many of whom are young persons of 17 to 25 years of age brought up in the Sunday School—& of the impression made among these you may judge by the fact that 25 persons chiefly of this class were confirmed in the Church by the Bishop at his annual visitation on Sunday last—[3]

And again, reporting a few years later in the wake of the turnout of 1842, he pointedly noted the incompatibility between striking and Christian conduct:

And should some of those to whom their beloved pastor dispensed the visible signs and tokens in the Holy Sacrament have violated the covenant of which they were the pledges; should they during the season of angry strife and excitement which a year after convulsed our manufacturing establishments, have forgotten the commandment delivered unto them, and departed from "that conversation which becometh the Gospel of Christ," we are not without hope that some even of these have discovered the "root of bitterness" which lay undiscovered in their hearts until this temptation caused it to spring up; and having by God's grace succeeded in eradicating it, may hereafter produce good fruit, as evidence of the sincerity of the profession made at our altar.[4]

There is no reason to accuse Smith or Lee of consciously conspiring to use the Church as a tool to control the workers in order to increase or protect their own personal financial profit. Smith probably suffered a loss by the departure of the "Infidel" Phillips, who maintained a large establishment and must have paid substantial rent; for a number of years, Smith was able to rent Old Sable Works only as a grist- and sawmill. Neither Smith nor Lee personally managed or owned, even in part, any of the mills that were struck. The issue was a much larger one and involved competing world views—views of the nature of man and the cosmos that challenged at every point the doctrines of the Enlightenment. Where the Enlightenment taught a vague deism and an assured afterlife, the evangelicals taught a Christian Trinity and the risk of hellfire. Where the Enlightenment taught the adequacy of reason, the evangelicals taught the need for faith and revelation. Where the Enlightenment taught that man is by nature good and that flawed societies have made him bad, the evangelicals taught that he is by nature sinful and the faults of society cannot be cured until he accepts his need for salvation. Where the Enlightenment taught that children should learn from the school of nature, the evangelicals taught that they should study from the Bible. Where the Enlightenment taught that all men were equal, the evangelicals taught that there were mutually dependent social classes. Where the Enlightenment taught that social life is based on negotiable contract, the evangelicals taught that it is based on government and law.

On an ideological level, then, the conflict was dialectical—a stable, structured system of opposites. The initial strategy of the evangelicals was not to produce an intellectual synthesis but to deny categorically any validity to the "infidel" position and to convert or suppress the infidel himself. In this campaign they were moderately successful: few dared to assert an infidel, Enlightenment philosophy on Chester Creek after 1838; and only the more militant, nationally famous freethinkers were likely to be heard at public lectures or to be read. But on Chester Creek and elsewhere, private opinion was more varied than public behavior would indicate, and even the silenced infidels subtly contributed to the eventual formation of a synthetic social strategy in the next decades.

Chapter VIII

THE EMERGENCE OF
CHRISTIAN
INDUSTRIALISM

The conflicting ideological systems of illuminism and evangelism were, like systems of theology or science, pure paradigms that admitted little in the way of compromise. They could be cherished or abandoned but they could not in their main arguments be changed: the number of their proponents might wax or wane but the basic propositions were immutable.

Yet the attention of ideological disputants may wander, may turn to the practical issues of the day, to the realities of technological and economic change. This is what happened to Chester Creek, and to other American communities, in the ideological struggle between the free enquirers and the evangelicals. Even as Bishop Potter was fulminating against combinations, and the aging Robert Owen was still roundly condemning priestcraft, the lawyers and judges and practical politicians, the manufacturers and economists, were putting together the outlines of a creed that was neither illuminism nor evangelism but a little bit of both, with ad hoc principles thrown in as needed solutions to practical problems.

The proffered solution was ingeniously simple: it offered the promise of earthly prosperity to all who worked, and spiritual prosperity to all who had faith. To be sure, the infidel would have to accept his need for Christian salvation, and the manufacturer would have to concede the right of a union of workers to improve their economic condition. But a smooth "Harmony of Interests" (as the economist Henry Carey put it), rather than conflict, was really the natural state of society; and if everyone realized it and cooperated, everyone's interests would prosper.

But the full working out of this scheme of salvation was not realized on Chester Creek until after a period of hard times, of depression, and of labor conflict, culminating in an appalling natural catastrophe: the great flood of 1843.

THE RECESSION OF 1834 TO 1842

Hard times came to the capitalists and workers in the cotton industry well in advance of the national panic of 1837; but the panic never was for them the economic disaster it became to other segments of the economy. There was a brief drop in yarn prices in the winter and spring of 1834, as the nation's economy sagged after Jackson vetoed the bill to recharter the Second Bank of the United States and withdrew the federal deposits from the embattled institution. Parkmount Mill closed for a week because business was slow and other mills closed temporarily or went on part-time schedules. In April, Crozer, writing to his congressman, Edward Darlington, enclosed a census of underemployment and unemployment in the Rockdale mills which vividly displayed the uncertainty of the cotton business in this period:[1]

Lewis and Phillips	130 hands	half-time
James Houghton	120 hands	less than half-time
S. and J. Riddle	30 hands	two-thirds time
J. P. Crozer	90 hands	one-third time
Daniel Lammot		full time

But within a few weeks the Riddles were back to normal in yarn and in addition had commenced their weaving operation, making chambray, twill, and Canton flannel. By the end of the year 1834, an inflationary process was under way, the price of raw cotton rising and the price of yarn going up correspondingly; No. 20, for instance, recovering from its low of 23 cents per pound in the spring to 29 cents by Christmas.[2]

Crozer's only difficulty during this period of general economic uncertainty came early in 1835, when his chief customer for yarn, John Steel of Frankford, died insolvent owing Crozer $6,500—"nearly half of what I was worth," as he recorded in his autobiography. "The shock was tremendous and nearly drove me distracted." But Crozer, with his usual ability to rebound from "ruinous loss," went to work harder than ever:

For some days I felt so cast down that I could not attend to my factory business, could not stay in the factory; but in a week or ten days my native energy triumphed. I had much ado to meet my engagements, to "keep my head above water"; but all went right and I redoubled my diligence. Hitherto I had spun yarn only; I now decided to weave also. Powerlooms had now become general. I borrowed money to buy twenty looms. All subsequent extensions, in both weaving and spinning, were out of profits. I was very successful in weaving, and in all my business from this date.[3]

Indeed, Crozer profited from the difficulties of others. In the very year of Steel's insolvency, he was able to purchase Knowlton Mill from the man who had acquired it from Darlington. In 1837 John B. Ducket, the paper-maker who operated a small mill in the forks of the creek, opposite Park-mount, fell into financial difficulty, and in 1838 the Bank of Delaware County foreclosed the mortgage and took title to the property.[4] Crozer was a stockholder and, as the bank's official history declared, "a director of the Bank of Delaware County from 1825 to 1862, except with intermissions as required by the laws of those times . . . a dominant figure in the history of the institution."[5] Although he did not take title from the bank until 1843, Crozer took physical possession of Ducket's property in the fall of 1839. As he recorded the event in his autobiography:

> Our residence was at West Branch until the year 1839. All our children but the two youngest were born there. We had purchased Crozerville property and built a factory there, tearing away the old paper-mill, and putting up some tenements, but had not decided to remove. The dwell-ing-house there was better than that at West Branch, but there were some objections which made us hesitate. In the month of November, 1839, however, we removed, with the expectation of this being our permanent home. We had often thought of a city life in the future, but had made no definite plan about it.[6]

Evidently one of the economic functions of the panic was to facilitate a kind of economic selection, stronger enterprises gobbling up defaulting ones cheaply with the assistance of sheriff's sales and bank foreclo-sures.

Although no financial records of the Riddles remain for the period 1835–43, there is no reason to suppose that they were in serious difficulty during the recession. In 1837, Samuel Riddle declared, "We are now working but three days in the week, some have stopped altogether."[7] But he was sufficiently solvent in 1843, after his brother James split the partner-ship, to purchase the entire George W. Hill estate.

Among the mills which did stop was Phillips'. But his decision to end his enterprise at Old Sable was not the result of financial reverses, for business was generally good in 1836. Perhaps he was prompted by his disappointments in love; perhaps by the pressure of opinion in the Calvary congregation (the church's front door opened almost directly onto his front yard, 50 feet away) against his "Infidel" views. In any case, he left, and with his brother-in-law invested instead in a mill at Fairmount. The workers left unemployed were quickly taken up at other factories in the neighborhood. As the brother of one of his former employees succinctly put it, "It seems that his employer was a wealthy man and thought he could make more by some other kind of speculation. So he stopped the greater part of his machinery. B[rother] Andrew was thrown out of employment." But by the next year things were different. Writing in June to his brother in England, William Morris gave an account of the recession on Chester Creek and its causes:

> . . . times have been very dull for six or seven weeks past. Some cotton mills have stopped, some runing half time and some full time and their is a great many manufactorers and mechanicks out of employment. This pressure of the times is oweing to the bad regulations of the currency for since the United States Bank has been put down from being a national bank, it gave rise to many petty banks. These encouraged a high run of speculation and everything demanded high price but the foreign merchants demanded payment in hard money which [strained?] the banks and then the merchants and speculaters began to fail which [led to a] great stagnation. . . .[8]

Actually, only two of the factories in the Rockdale district remained "standing" during most of the recession. One of these was the Knowlton cotton factory. This factory had burned to the ground in 1834 before Crozer purchased it. Crozer continued to rent the tilt mill to the manufacturer of edge tools from whom he bought it and a year or two later rebuilt the stone cotton mill; but this probably did not get into operation at once, given the general dullness of business. The only cotton manufacturer who seems to have failed outright was James Houghton, who closed his weaving mill about 1837 or 1838. Houghton died a few years later owing a sum to commission merchant Henry Farnum sufficiently large for Farnum to be appointed by the court as administrator of his estate.[9] Burt and Kerlin, who leased the Phillips mill from Richard S. Smith, failed in the spring of 1843, but their failure may have been in part the result of labor trouble.[10]

Daniel Lammot is the one manufacturer whose experience in the depression is recorded in any detail. In his correspondence with his son-in-law Alfred du Pont for the period 1836 through 1842 there is a clear record of his difficulties and of the expedients by which he managed to survive. He entered the period of recession under the handicap of a large loan from his other son-in-law Thomas Hounsfield, on the order of $30,000, which he had spent enlarging his works to accommodate a weaving department. Hounsfield decided to leave the area and, despite his prior verbal assurances that it was a "permanent loan" for seven years, now demanded his money. With some difficulty, Lammot managed to get his friends to make credit arrangements to satisfy Hounsfield with notes for shorter periods—up to eighteen months.

Lammot had labor trouble in 1836 and was forced to raise wages. And he was never able to count on the "tricky" Peter Hill, his landlord, to be cooperative in emergencies like breaches in the race or broken headgates. By May 1837 he was under the necessity of borrowing still more money, "on the ground that sales cannot now be effected, but that it is still desirable to keep the mill running." He turned repeatedly to the better capitalized Du Ponts, who were customers for some of his yarns, for aid in the form of direct loans and credit assurances. The crisis for Lammot and Son was reached in July 1837, at a time of year when sales were low anyway. Waln and Leaming, the commission merchants to whom they consigned most of their principal product (fine printing cloths), told Lammot (and other customers) that henceforth they would "refuse to advance on any goods until sales are made." Since the Lammots depended on these cash advances to pay off their notes as they came due, and thereby to renew their credit for the purchase of more bales of cotton (paid for with still other short-term notes), they were on the brink of having to stop their mill for want of cotton. It was little comfort to be told by commission merchants to hold on to the printing cloths until January, when the "low prices of Goods at auction" would rise again, as they always did, as the printers began to make new goods for spring and the ice-choked harbors kept out competing supplies from New England.

The Du Ponts came to the rescue, working out a deal with Lammot to manufacture fine cloth for them, at so much per pound, out of raw cotton furnished for the purpose. The house of Francis Gurney Smith in Philadelphia, the agents of the Du Ponts, forwarded the cotton bales to Marcus Hook and Chester, whence the Lammots had them hauled to Lenni, re-weighed them (saving the Du Ponts from 5 to 15 lbs. per bale), and worked them into printing cloth. The cloth was then baled and sent back to Smith's for sale at Du Pont's risk. (A bale of fine printing cloth contained on an average 1,235 yards, weighed about 195 lbs., and sold for about 8 to 8 1/2 cents per yard.) Between August, when the arrangements began, and November, when the job was completed, Lammot's mill had received thirty-five bales of cotton and sent out sixty-five bales of finished cloth. The total cost to E. I. du Pont de Nemours and Company was estimated by Lammot at about 7 1/4 cents per yard of printed cloth; for a total of 80,122 3/4 yards, this amounted to about $5,800. Of this, Lammot charged $3,640 (most of which no doubt was manufacturing cost). The rest of the cost to the Du Ponts was for buying the cotton and commission fees. At a price of 8 cents per yard, the Du Ponts would make a net profit of about $600.

Lammot's enterprise limped along through the depression and he never did extricate himself from the maze of notes in which he was enmeshed. In 1838 he shifted to the manufacture of coarser cloths, after hearing that the Boston firms were unable to sell their fine cloths but could not meet the demand for coarse. By 1842 he was in trouble again, the mill stopped, and Peter Hill (himself as usual in financial distress) demanded payment of rent. Once again he turned to Alfred:

> Remington still urges us to start, promis^d to advance as formerly, and stating his conviction that Tickings must rise in the spring as the stock is not heavy and many manufacturers of them have failed. Common prints are said to be scarce in the market, and printing cloth must advance next month. But we are not yet started and not entitled to advance, and know not where to apply for relief but to yourself and we do it reluctantly because you have already advanced us so largely. Yet if you can advance or lend us your note at 4 ms, for about $900 we can have it discounted at the Bank of N. America.[11]

THE STRIKES OF 1836 AND 1842

The workers in the Rockdale district had been quiet during the labor disturbances that agitated Philadelphia in the late 1820's and early 1830's, probably because there were few members of trades unions in the Rockdale district (except for the mechanics). Cotton mill operatives, even though they might be termed "spinners" and "weavers" in tax and census lists, did not proceed from formal apprenticeship to the status of journeyman; often they were merely called "laborers," and mostly did not belong to the unions of cotton spinners and weavers. There was not even any vigorous opposition when mills closed or went on part-time work in 1834. But in 1836, as prices rose again and the mills' business quickened, there were turnouts, the strikers demanding raises in pay or shorter hours at the same pay. They were acting in unison, if not in concert, with striking craftsmen in Philadelphia.

The Strike in 1836

The confrontation began in February, when operatives employed in the Chester Creek manufactories met at the Seven Stars Tavern in Village Green to organize a "Trades Union" (also referred to as the "Chester Creek Trade Association") in opposition to "the long-hour system enforced by employers on hands in cotton mills against their will." One of the organizers was William Shaw, who worked at West Branch. Crozer fired him at once; and immediately Crozer's hands turned out briefly in protest.[1] Shaw was a young but experienced mule spinner (he was twenty-five), who had been born in Baltimore and had come north eight years before to work in the mills. He had spent two years with Samuel Riddle (he and "his girl" were one of the cohort of families who started out with Riddle in the new mill at Parkmount) and the last three years with Crozer. His particular objection was the over-working of children in the mills. After being discharged, he went to Philadelphia to work in a mill in Fairmount, and while there he helped to organize the petition to the Pennsylvania legislature that resulted in the Senate investigation of 1837. Shaw was the first witness interviewed by the committee and we reviewed some of his testimony in the last chapter; we shall look at his testimony in detail again later.[2]

Negotiations between the workers and the employers continued without result until May, then the disturbances began. The dispute dragged on all through the summer. The rhetoric used by the operatives was radical (as the Smiths painfully observed during their efforts to establish Calvary Church); the methods may have been violent. In January, the mill at West Branch burned out; at the end of June, Crozer's barn burned down.[3] Lammot's factory was struck in May and June, and his surviving account provides most of the detail of the tactics of the two sides. On May 18, writing to Alfred, he reported that the anticipated turnout had occurred after he fired two of the troublemakers and was preparing to replace them with new hands:

> As I apprehended, I found the mill in an uproar on my return home. My spinners were out and the other hands ready to rebel. Ferdinand will start immediately for Norristown, where there is a suitable family anxious for a place. I have now two spinners at work, but the discharged hands are prowling about, doing nothing the law can lay hold on, but keeping the hands so uneasy, that I am confident, if I were to leave home for one hour, there would be another uproar and turn out. The hands that are threatened and driven from their work dare not tell me, for they believe

their lives would be endangered by giving testimony against each other. The matter is a manifest conspiracy, but I have not testimony to pursue it, otherwise I would have the Sheriff at work very quickly.[4]

Two weeks later, the mule spinners were still out on strike and the ringleaders were still fomenting trouble. Lammot attempted to appease the weavers by raising their piece rates; the rest of the factory then turned out, demanding that their wages be raised too.

I have been extremely anxious to get over to see you all, but for the last two weeks, I have had a very anxious and perplexing time. My Mule spinners turned out 2 weeks ago, and when they found I had discharged the two ring leaders, they became turbulent, and excited almost an insurrection amongst the other hands. The morning I started to town, the hands were quiet. I had not been absent an hour before the weavers turned out. Ferd. remonstrated with them for waiting until I had left home, and then turning out. They returned to work and continued until I returned, and then turned out again. I advanced the price of their weaving, and then the rest of the hands turned out. These had to turn in as they came out, and the discharged spinners kept up the fomentation by geering them for returning to work, calling them nobs. Until to day I have not felt easy for half an hour; but how it will be on Monday I cannot say, but expect further excitement. At this time the disturbance is peculiarly unfortunate for we are short of hands in every department. This long story will account for my not visiting you sooner.[5]

The strike, coming at a well-chosen time when the demand for cotton yarn and cloths was high, seems to have been at least partially successful. And although the "Trades Union" itself did not survive the strike for long, hostility toward the manufacturers remained. Writing to Minshall Painter a few years later, Crozer deplored the suspicions that workers still entertained against their employers:

The work people cannot be convinced that employers have not some interested & selfish motive in view in all their plans. This prejudice had its origin in the unfortunate "Trades Union" which embodied, a few years ago, all our work people nearby—and although the Society is, I believe, quite broken up its injurious influence exists, and is likely to exist for a long time to come in a greater or less degree.[6]

A reciprocal prejudice, of course, was held by the employers. Crozer's and Lammot's language was guarded, but their attitude of perplexity and resentment at the distrust in which they were held, and their readiness to take punitive action against ringleaders, were plain.

The whole matter came in for a public airing next year in the Senate's abortive investigation of the working conditions of children employed in cotton mills. Crozer and Riddle both testified, more or less blandly, that they would like to see the hours of child labor reduced nationally, not just in Pennsylvania. The more extreme positions were taken by William Shaw, the discharged ringleader from West Branch, on the operatives' side, who testified first, and by Joseph Ripka, the principal manufacturer in Manayunk, who testified last. Shaw was forthright in condemning the manufacturers for the overworking of children and the neglect of their educational needs:

> The greatest evils known are, first, the number of hours of labor, and the number of children employed. . . . The proportion of children varies in different establishments; has known more than one-fourth to be children under twelve years of age: under twenty years, would include in many cases, three-fourths; not many are apprenticed; they are usually hired to employers by parents and guardians. The hours vary in different establishments; in some I have worked fourteen and a-half hours. . . . The labor of the children is in some cases excessive—in others it is not. The children are employed at spinning and carding. The question of excessive labor is more upon the kind of work; carding is the hardest work; their work is regulated by the operation of the machinery, at carding; and they must stand during the whole time; considers twelve or fourteen hours labor excessive at either branch for a child. I have known children of nine years of age to be employed at spinning; at carding, as young as ten years. . . . I think no attention is paid to education during the time they are employed in factories, except what they receive from Sabbath schools, and some few at night schools, when they are in an unfit condition to learn; the children attend Sabbath school with great reluctance; many will not attend in consequence of the confinement of the week.

But Joseph Ripka saw the matter in a completely different light, claiming that the only reason for labor strife was the evil "Trades' Union" and that he employed children mostly as an act of charity:

> If any evil exists in the factory system, it is the principles of the Trades' Union, which has been introduced amongst the laboring classes in general; it has been imparted to this country by English and Irish men within a few years, and has the tendency to destroy the good feeling which has, heretofore, existed between the employer and the workman in this coun-

try, and the leaders are men, either of low character or designing politicians. To show that the principle is a bad one, the leaders are always trying to keep the working people in an excitement, to have them always ready for a turn-out, they lay contribution on the working classes, and expend the money amongst themselves, by going about from place to place to make speeches, and encourage them to turn out. When labor is plenty, the workingmen will get good wages and find plenty employment without the aid of the Trades' Union, and in hard times, the Trades' Union cannot keep up wages or find employment for the working classes. If they could do it, why don't they do it at the present time. . . .

I employ twenty-five children under twelve years of age, and they are pressed on me by widows, or by mothers of dissipated husbands; and when I do employ them, it is for mere charity than any thing else. Children, under twelve years of age, are of no profit to the employers in cotton factories, it is the age when they ought to be educated, and I have always been against to employ them. . . .

The labor for children is not excessive.

The children do not appear tired when they leave work.[7]

The general economic decline, beginning with the financial panic of 1837, placed the unions in a poor position to call for strike actions against employers who reduced wages or otherwise failed to meet the expectations of operatives. Some of the manufacturers kept their mills operating more to provide wages than to produce cotton goods, for although the yarn and cloth might be unsalable now, it would probably be sold later, and if starving operatives left the district to find work elsewhere, the manufacturer would be hard-pressed to find new, trained operatives at a time when all the mills would again be seeking them. Besides, providing work was a matter of Christian charity in an age when there was no source of public relief but the poorhouse, which separated husbands and wives and children, and exposed the respectable poor to the influence of the immoral, the improvident, and the insane.

The Strike in 1842

The mills on Chester Creek kept limping along in an off-again on-again fashion through the depression; but a nadir of some sort was reached in the spring of 1842, when, in an effort to keep their mills running and their books showing some sort of profit (or at least a lesser rate of loss), the manufacturers imposed a third 15 percent reduction in wages. The blow was softened, in Crozer's case at least, by a reduction in the rent charged for company houses; but since rents were already very low, amounting to only about 5 percent of a family's earnings, such an economy was not significantly compensatory at all. And so the workers struck again. This time the outcome was less favorable for them.

The precipitating event was the announced intention of the manufacturers to reduce the piece rates for weavers a further 10 to 15 percent depending on the employer's circumstances, beginning Monday March 21. This reduction had been agreed upon by all the manufacturers as a result of a meeting amongst themselves. It was the third such percentage reduction since the relatively prosperous year of 1840 and meant, in effect, that the rates had gone down almost 50 percent in two years. But the reduction itself might not have been enough to precipitate a strike. Some of the manufacturers went to the trouble of talking the matter over with their employees in advance, explaining that the fall in the selling price of the cloths required this temporary measure and that rates would go up again as soon as economic conditions justified it. Samuel Riddle specifically showed his employees this courtesy; in the ensuing disturbance his mill was not struck; and he did not testify as a witness against the strikers at the trial. Other manufacturers were prevented in part by circumstance: Lammot's mill was idle for repairs but scheduled to open on Monday the 28th, and he posted the new rates on the gates in the workers' absence. Crozer posted his "military notice" as he always did. Garsed and Pierce never made any announcement at all; they simply deducted 12 1/2 percent from the paychecks on the payday at the middle of April. Whether Burt and Kerlin announced the reduction is not clear, but as a precaution against trouble they had erected a watchtower. With their mill at Old Sable already surrounded (as was typical of the day) by a wooden panel fence, the addition of a watchtower must have made the place look like a fortress. Some of the manufacturers —notably Garsed and Pierce—also were already in the practice of paying in orders on the local store (which might be the company store) and in notes due, which could only be redeemed (if at all) at banks in town. Crozer, by contrast, always paid in cash.

The first meeting of the strikers was held after work on Saturday afternoon, March 19, at Brown's general store, which was located on Mount Road in Crozerville. Mark Wild, a young foreign-born weaver at Lammot's Lenni Mill, spoke to a crowd of disgruntled male weavers from the porch of the store, introducing the main speaker, and urging the group not to commit violence and to act only in ways that were within the law. The main speaker was Hiram McConnell, also an immigrant (probably from Northern Ireland), a retired worker from outside Delaware County who was living on his savings "earned long ago"[8] and devoting his time to organizing cotton mill operatives in Delaware County, New Jersey, and perhaps elsewhere. He was, in fact, a professional labor organizer who expected trouble and carried a pistol for self-defense. (While he was serving as chairman of the Chester Creek committee, McConnell also served as a delegate to a committee of strikers in New Jersey and even organized a march of armed men from Rockdale to Darby to protest conditions at Charles Kelly's mill there.) The business of the meeting at Brown's store was to make plans for a turnout at Burt and Kerlin's weaving mill.

The turnout at Burt and Kerlin's took place as planned on Monday about nine o'clock when the mill stopped to allow the hands to take breakfast. A core of strikers left the mill. Then a crowd of men, as many as one hundred, surrounded the gates of the mill and called to those remaining inside to come out. Some of the leaders entered the mill and terrorized the female operatives, seizing them by the arms and attempting to drag them out. The mill resumed working, with a reduced number of operatives, while the strikers outside kept up their shouting, and small groups of frightened workers gradually trickled out through the gates. Threats were made to duck or drown in Chester Creek any "nobstick" (one who continued to work—in later jargon, a scab). The mill closed at dinnertime. And next day a burly striker did in fact duck a "nobstick," one James Broadbent, in full view of an assembled crowd. Broadbent was thrown into the millpond from the breast of the dam and his head was held under water for a while; then as he made his escape, he was beaten and knocked into the race. His persecutor laughed and said, "That'll wash the bugger's sins away." It was these events at Burt and Kerlin's—the plan to duck nobsticks, the shouted threats, the actual ducking—which formed the basis for the later trial of the strike organizers on charges of conspiracy and riot.

At the end of the week, on Saturday afternoon again, the strikers held another meeting, this time to formalize their organization and to turn the force of the strike against the next manufacturer. This meeting was attended by women as well as men, and again Wild and McConnell, the principal organizers, spoke first, followed by others. At this meeting, the usual parliamentary procedure at public meetings was employed: a chairman and other officers were chosen, resolutions were passed, and a committee was then elected to conduct the business resolved upon at the meeting. The resolutions were reduced to writing. Although no copy has survived, the testimony of witnesses who were present shows that there were demands that the manufacturers reverse the piece rate reduction for weavers and that they cease the despised practice of paying wages in the form of orders on storekeepers. Hiram McConnell, as experienced labor leader, became chairman of the committee. McConnell then turned the crowd's attention to the issues concerning Lammot's mill at Lenni. It was to be struck on Monday morning, when it was scheduled to be reopened; nobsticks were as usual threatened with ducking or worse. On Monday morning, in due course, the strikers presented themselves at Lammot's mill. The mill's operatives streamed out and the machinery stopped.

The next mill to be closed was Garsed and Pierce's weaving mill at Penn's Grove. In addition to the main general charges, Garsed and Pierce were accused of paying their workers less per piece than Crozer paid. By now, McConnell had at his disposal a small army of striking men and women, whom he kept busy at meetings every day or so where he and others harangued them. On Thursday March 31, the workers formed themselves on Church Hill and marched across the Rockdale bridge toward Garsed's mill. The workers ran to the windows and the aged Joshua Garsed and his sons personally guarded the gates as the column of strikers, two abreast, approached up the hill. The men marched in front, some of them banging on kettles; then came a small fife-and-drum corps; a squad of women took the rear. The usual process occurred: the sympathizers quit at once and the rest of the operatives, their resolve to stay gradually worn down by anxiety, straggled out after them.

Crozer's mills were struck about three weeks later. Crozer, of course, was operating three mills by this time: the original factory at West Branch and the two new mills at Crozerville and Knowlton, the latter specialized as a weaving mill. This case was complicated by the fact that while his weavers were on strike demanding merely a return to former rates, his mule spinners were out demanding an increase. Crozer's factories were infested by columns of marching, shouting, fife-and-drum-playing men and women.

By the end of the month of April, all the mills along the creek were at a standstill except Samuel Riddle's at Parkmount. Efforts to persuade the strikers to return to work had been unavailing, for the 20 to 30 percent who wished to return at the former rates were intimidated by their more violent fellows. But the employers had no intention of giving in. John P. Crozer's views were probably representative of the rest. He had recently begun to keep a diary, and in it he recorded his feelings about the strike. Comparing it to the events of 1836, he said:

In the present disagreement there is more of deep determination and greater indications of violence than formerly. But as the issue is fairly joined, I cannot for a moment think of yielding. . . . I do not know if all the employers will be firm, but for myself I have not the most remote idea of yielding, and shall rather never start than be compelled to yield.

After forty days had gone by, some of his mule spinners requested an interview with him, which he granted. He was unbending:

> I had a good deal of conversation with them, perfectly calm on both sides, and we parted in a friendly manner. I am inclined to think that the interview was sought under the hope or expectation that I would propose some compromise. I, however, thought best, in reply to a question asked me as to the probability of the mill starting, to say, positively, that the mill would never start except upon my terms.

His resolution was fortified by his awareness that the strike was in fact a benefit to the employers, permitting them to stop the mills entirely at a time when continued operation would merely take money out of the employer's pocket and put it in the hands of the operatives. As he noted in his diary: "In a pecuniary view the cessation of work will not, I think, be any injury to me or to any of the employers. With all of us, goods, if sold now, must be sold at a sacrifice, and none of us could continue working without making sales. We are therefore prepared for a long suspension."[9]

But Burt and Kerlin seem to have panicked. Perhaps they feared damage to their persons and property; perhaps they took a moralistic view. In any case, unable to open their mill on Monday April 25, five weeks after they had been struck, they summoned the sheriff "to quell the riot and violence, which was said to exist in this place." Mark Wild and Hiram McConnell were not arrested at this time. As McConnell described it: "Myself and a few others endeavored to explain the matter to the Sheriff and those with him, and it is due to the Sheriff to say, his conduct and the conduct of those with him was highly commendable, and instead of taking us prisoners, they went away our friends." Failing to persuade the sheriff that a riot was in progress, John Burt made a written offer to the strikers the same day. The committee rejected it and Hiram McConnell now took his case to the people at large, publishing a long exposition of the issues in the *Upland Union* for May 3. Burt and Kerlin's curious offer is worth quoting:

> The proposition is, that if the hands will agree to work and take goods at the price they brought last fall, they shall be paid the old price, after deducting the price of fall cotton; otherwise, if the hands agree to work at the deduction and work up the stock now on hand, and if goods will not allow the advanced price, stop the mill entirely.

The strike dragged on. There were now roughly four hundred people out of work in the Rockdale district. In order to provide food for the strikers and their families, the committee set up a store which accepted the provisions donated in substantial quantity by sympathetic neighbors and farmers; these, and other supplies purchased by the committee, were distributed to those who needed assistance.[10] But such expedients were hardly adequate. Crozer's diary makes it plain that he was prepared to see hunger motivate the workers to return on his terms: "Some of the families around us are beginning to need the necessaries of life, which we would, under different circumstances, supply with a liberal hand. We have to do something for a few of them, but feel it due to ourselves to be sparing, in consequence of the cause of their distress."[11]

Toward the middle of May, the employers resolved to act firmly to end the struggle in such a way as to discourage a repetition. Eighteen of the strikers, including Hiram McConnell and Mark Wild, were arrested on charges of conspiracy and riot. The case was brought to trial very quickly —within a couple of weeks of the arrest—in Chester in the Delaware County Court of Sessions, Judge Thomas S. Bell presiding. Judge Bell, now in his forty-third year, had been an attorney in West Chester and a delegate to the State Constitutional Convention. He bore a reputation for learning, for courtesy, and for severity. As a local historian later put it, "on one occasion . . . he aroused considerable feeling in sentencing a child ten years of age to a protracted term of imprisonment for stealing a small sum of money."[12] The public prosecutor was the prominent Chester attorney and politician Samuel Edwards under whom Edward Darlington had read law. Edwards had served in Congress and was a close friend of James Buchanan; he was reported to be one of the most influential background advisers in the Democratic national machine. He held the sinecure of Inspector of Customs at the port of Chester, was a director of the Delaware County National Bank (as were both Kerlin and Crozer), and counsel for the Philadelphia, Wilmington, and Baltimore Railroad. The attorneys for the defendants, Joseph S. Lewis of West Chester and William D. Kelly of Philadelphia, were competent lawyers but were from outside the community that supplied both prosecutor and the jury. The issues involved were sufficiently important for Philadelphia readers to take an interest. And so the *Public Ledger* sent a correspondent to cover the trial, who dutifully recorded a partial transcript of the testimony in the five-day hearing.

It was a colorful trial. Some, but not all, of the manufacturers testified against the strikers: John P. Crozer, John Pierce, John and Richard Garsed, and John Burt. Daniel Lammot and Samuel Riddle did not testify, nor did any of the accused testify in their own defense. Most of the witnesses were workers, some of whom had been opposed to the strike (including the man who had been ducked in the creek) and some of whom had taken part. Five of the witnesses were women.

After five days of testimony, the jury was charged by Judge Bell. They retired briefly and returned with a verdict of not guilty of both charges for fifteen of the defendants. Hiram McConnell, Mark Wild, and Major Rowe were found innocent of riot but guilty of conspiracy, and sentenced to pay fines of $35, $30, and $30, respectively. Hiram McConnell was in addition required to pay the cost of prosecution on the charge of riot, which amounted to more than $1,000. Unwilling (and perhaps unable) to pay, they were committed to the old Chester jail, where they were visited by the friendly editor of the *Upland Union*. He said he found them

> now living with our Sheriff, happy as the King in his princely palace, and declare their present situation a kingdom compared with the prison of cotton tyrants. They have been prepared with feather beds, chairs, table and stationary, and our good citizens are constantly loading them with the comforts of human bliss. The former companions and friends of these benevolent men are still holding meetings on Church Hill, in the vicinity of Rockdale, and I understand that several factory ladies are delivering public addresses to hundreds in attendence.[13]

But the conviction really did signal the end of the strike. One by one, the mills reopened as the weavers agreed to work at the reduced rates; Crozer's mule spinners came back on Crozer's terms. Governor Porter, hearing of the hard feelings being engendered by the protracted dispute, remitted the fines, and the sheriff released Wild and Rowe; shortly after that, a subscription paid for the costs of prosecution, and Hiram McConnell was freed. He left the district. By the Fourth of July the mills were limping along again, at reduced rates, operating part time, sometimes stopped for extended periods.[14]

The Meaning of the Strikes

Throughout the decade from 1828 to 1837, while the craft unions were successfully organizing, the workers in the mechanized textile factories lagged behind. During the boom year of 1835, after a series of strikes, most of the craft unions of Philadelphia even won the ten-hour day for their journeymen, including Kensington's thousands of hand-loom weavers. But the ten-hour day did not apply, even in a legal sense, to the operatives in the city's cotton mills. The men and women who tended the power looms in Manayunk, Blockley, and Fairmount still put in their twelve to fourteen hours, and so did the weavers on Chester Creek. So too did the mule spinners, with their piecers and scavengers, as did the young women who tended the throstles and drawing frames, and the lads who worked in the card and picker rooms.

The cotton mill workers had no craft unions in America (in contrast to England, where the mule spinners at least were organized in a trade union). The traditional crafts themselves were old, hundreds or even thousands of years old; and their trade associations, formed in medieval times to control standards of training (through the apprentice-journeyman-master system) and quality, and to provide benefits for unfortunate members and their families, were also old. The journeymen usually hired out at daily wages or on piecework to a master craftsman, but often they owned their own hand tools and sometimes even worked in their own homes; thus they could be, in a sense, small capitalists. When the hand-loom weavers struck, the master weavers (who were really capitalist cloth merchants and manufacturers, some of them employing hundreds of weavers) could not replace them with strikebreakers because the strikers owned much of the machinery. A clear career line was laid out in the trades, from an apprenticeship unpaid (or even paying) of three to seven years in the shop of a master tradesman, to a journeyman working for daily wages or at piecework, in his own home or a master's shop, to the master tradesman, who might become in effect a wealthy merchant-contractor.

Among the factory skills, mule spinning came closest, perhaps, to a craft but it was a craft learned informally, and often quickly, by a youth who first familiarized himself with the machine by working for a few weeks as a piecer, and then, under the instruction of the experienced spinner, by trying out the machine himself. The mule spinner was the employer of his piecers and scavengers; but they were certainly not apprentices. And he did not own the mule he operated; the mule, which was far too large ever to be accommodated in an ordinary private dwelling, was the property of the manufacturer, who paid the spinner by the hank of yarn. Similarly with the power looms: they were the property of the manufacturer and were assembled in a factory, where men and women supervised them. Experienced hand-loom weavers, like the Morrises, sometimes took jobs operating "the power looms," in order to make more money, but their craft skill was not needed and inexperienced young women (ineligible by sex for membership in the weavers' union) could be, and were, taught to operate them successfully. Still less could the skills involved in tending the throstles and draw frames and carding machines and pickers and blowers be compared to traditional crafts. All of these jobs were new, less than a hundred years old in England, and less than fifty years old in America, and they were jobs, not occupations. Although they required some skill (as does even "unskilled" labor), they could not be defined as crafts because the entire social context in which the job was done was different from the craft context.

Thus from the first in the cotton districts, not only on Chester Creek but in the Philadelphia mill neighborhoods as well, the problem of labor organization differed from that in the already organized urban-based trade districts. The organization was an ad hoc strikers' group rather than a union that endured between strikes. Furthermore, the cotton weavers' approach, both in 1836 and 1842, was to organize factory by factory (or district by district) rather than by craft, and the organizations were named after the district rather than after a skill. One job specialty (invariably either mule spinners or weavers) might take the lead; but the action was against the factory as a whole (or a group of factories) and the technique was to turn out *all* the workers, not just the mule spinners or weavers. The strategy of organization was more comparable to what later came to be called "industrial" unions than to "craft" unions. These differences explain in part why the operatives in cotton mills seem to have been marching to a different drummer. During the flurry of strikes by the painters, trimmers, glass cutters, white smiths, saddlers, cordwainers, and other crafts in Philadelphia in 1835 demanding the ten-hour day, the operatives on Chester Creek were quiet. In 1836, the same trade unions in Philadelphia struck for higher wages; this time the operatives on Chester Creek struck too, for higher pay or shorter hours. But the strike in 1842, although not an isolated one, and led by a professional outside organizer, seems to have been fought out on strictly local issues at a time when some trades organizations were turning their attention to national unions and Fourierist socialism.[15]

An examination of the records of the 1842 strike (the names of only a few strikers survive from 1836) shows that it was led by substantial members of the community.[16] Of the eighteen men brought to trial, thirteen (including a "boss weaver" and a beamer) were weavers or connected with the weaving department; one was a machinist; the occupations of four cannot be determined. Most (ten) were single but there were about five married men in the group. Their incomes ranged from $100 to $200 per year (according to tax assessments, which were apt to underestimate). At least seven were church members, and probably more, because the early membership records of the Methodist and Presbyterian churches have not survived. And eleven continued to live in the Rockdale district for at least two years after the strike.

Mark Wild—the local co-leader with McConnell, and the advocate of law and order—was perhaps typical of the better established leadership. His name does not appear in the 1840 census, which means that he and his wife Sarah probably arrived in Rockdale in 1841. He was an English-born weaver who in 1842, according to the tax assessor, was earning at the rate of about $200 per year. He and his wife were baptized at Calvary by Bishop Onderdonk in the same year. He remained in the district after the strike, still working as a weaver—and saving money. In 1847, when he was employed by Samuel Riddle at Penn's Grove, he purchased a residential building lot from the Houghton estate. As late as 1856 he was still working as a weaver for Crozer.

Other members of the trial group were established members of the community. John Radcliff, the machinist, had been a resident of Aston Township before the 1840 census. In 1840 he was a man of between forty and fifty, with a wife about the same age; four children lived with them, the eldest a girl between fifteen and twenty. He owned his own house and two and a half acres of land. He and his wife were members of Calvary Church and like Wild remained in the area after the strike. John Gore, one of the men who ducked Broadbent, was more representative perhaps of the younger men. He was a weaver, twenty-three years old, and he remained after the strike—in fact, he lived in Aston Township all his life and was buried in Mount Hope Cemetery in 1895. Joseph Talbot, the other man who helped to duck Broadbent, was also a weaver and single. He had paid taxes in Aston since 1829; he left in 1842 after the strike.

The leaders of the 1842 strike were evidently for the most part a nontransient group, interested in putting down roots in the community. Their demands were essentially conservative: they objected to a pay cut and to certain practices, specifically the failure to consult with them beforehand about the reduction, and the payment of wages not in cash but in store orders.

The public rhetoric, both verbal and dramatic, seems to have been commanded by Hiram McConnell. But even McConnell's rhetoric was curiously unradical. Although he roundly condemned the despotic manufacturers, he threatened only to bring the people's wrath down upon them by supporting the political fortunes of the Democratic Party and by opposing the Whig tariff: ". . . if after the pains the whigs have taken to show their real character, the people ever trust them again, it shall not be till my humble voice had been heard by every ear and resounded in every grove throughout this union." And his invective, while colorful, was not radical in the Paine sense. He did not condemn the clergy; he did not attack the institutions of society; he did not even attack the class system, but only the injustices perpetuated by those who exploited it:

While ambition, jealously [*sic*], cupidity and the blind love of innovation keep up a deplorable struggle among the people—some misguided by false promises of an expiring faction that has been laboring to overthrow the sovereignty of the people and establish an aristocracy; others influenced by needy circumstances and dependent on the few for employment, to gain the necessaries of life, the majority of the citizens of these free states are miserably brutalized, to languish out their days in incessant drudgery, by those of opulence and tyranny. The lordly manufacturer, speculator and adventurer dispise the people and believe themselves born to reign over them and drive them to and fro over the land as beasts of the field. They seek to decieve the ignorant by night and by day, mentally, moral [*sic*] and politically, when myself and others having suffered from their faithlessness, dared to withstand their tyrannical and oppressive measures, and expose their craft, they combinedly entered into a malicious prosecution, raked up all their tools and menials who had to swear at their bidding against a number of humble and industrious operatives, and were wanton enough, so far as regards myself, to try to villify [*sic*] my character. . . .

The public organs of the two political parties of Delaware County responded, of course, very differently to the strike and to the populist declamations of Hiram McConnell. The *Upland Union,* ever-watchful sentinel of the locally outnumbered Democrats, at first took the strike as an opportunity to vilify the opposite party. In March and April the *Union* attempted to portray the strike as the working people's revenge against the Whigs for having misled them into voting for William Henry Harrison in 1840:

The Tippecanoe and Tyler too editor of the Delaware County Republican stated in his last paper, that there had been a strike among the workmen on Chester Creek, and that he was not aware of the cause. So far as we have been informed on the subject it appears, that the deluded operatives, misled by log cabin parades, the idle display of flags and banners, inscribed with a reduction of wages, and the direct and positive declarations of their Tip & Ty leaders, that their wages were at that time too low and that rather than reduce them, they would quit business and that a change of administration only, was wanting, to ensure higher wages and better times. The change has been had and the golden dreams of the deceived workmen have resulted in two reductions of their wages each time 15 per cent, and in the unholy attempt to reduce them 15 per cent more. Under this gross violation of promises and professions the present strike has been produced, and the sympathy of the whole community is on the side of the workmen, who have been deluded by political knavery and humbug. Another political crusade is about commencing and instead of log cabin and hard cider, protective tariff home league, American Industry, etc. are the political catchwords of the same party, let the producers guard against the election of wooden whiggery in all time to come.

But the paper eventually withdrew this charge, inviting as it did the countercharge of the *Delaware County Republican* that the Democrats were trying to take partisan advantage from a community misfortune.

The *Republican*'s editor fancied himself a master of political satire and he took the turnout as an opportunity to portray the striking operatives as a passel of silly revolutionary followers of the outmoded associationist creed of Robert Owen. In May the *Republican* ran a letter to the editor describing a visit to "the Thermopylae of America, where the few resist the many and where oppression such as was never before heard of had driven hundreds of half-starved operatives to collect en masse and demand their natural rights." He went on (tongue in cheek) to describe the resolutions which were, he alleged, "unanimously adopted" at a meeting of the striking workers:

> RESOLVED, That a great revolution is about to take place of which we are the thrice honored instruments, a revolution that will teach men the strength of weakness, the riches of poverty, and the omnipotence of despair.
>
> RESOLVED, That the eyes of the world are upon us; that the starving millions of Europe are at this moment urging us onward.
>
> RESOLVED, That our names and the name of Alexander M'Keever [editor of the *Upland Union*], our great, talented, and immaculate mouthpiece will descend to posterity adorned with such honors as the heroes of the paltry revolution of 76 never dreamed of.[17]

And on July 8, long after the strikers had been convicted, the *Republican* still was harping on the same theme. On that date it published a hoax in the form of another letter to the editor from "A Hater of Oppression" (the style suggests the author was the same as before). The letter proposed the establishment of a "Chester Benevolent Factory," a cooperative enterprise to be owned by the workers, and to be housed in the courthouses and jails of Chester—"the hateful establishment of a bygone and barbarous age." The factory's "Rules and Regulations" were to be as follows:

RULE 1 No stockholder shall be permitted to hold more than _____ shares of stock at fifty dollars per share.

RULE 2 Every operative employed shall have the privilege of subscribing for five shares of stock without obligation to pay for the same. The fact of his being a workman is to be considered equivalent to money paid.

RULE 3. No person shall be employed in this factory who cannot bring satisfactory evidence that he or she has been distinguished either in *this* or some other country, by opposition to the employer; or, in other words, to tyranny and oppression.

RULE 4. The workmen shall always have the privilege of keeping one or more persons to regulate matters with the foreman or manager, whose business it shall be to dictate to said foreman how and where the hands are to be placed in the factory—what new workmen shall be employed; what amount and kind of work shall be done, and all other things conducive to the comfort of the work people.

RULE 5. No person shall be discharged from this factory without his or her consent. A contrary course evidently conflicts with proper liberty, and is one of the greatest evils in factories generally.

RULE 6. No reduction of wages shall at any time take place, without the workmen themselves request it to be done; they are certainly the best judges as to what is reasonable and proper.[18]

But the windy political rhetoric of Hiram McConnell, the *Upland Union,* and the *Delaware County Republican* fails to convey the more visceral sentiments of the local participants in the conflict. The manufacturers expressed resentment at the operatives' lack of trust; the clergymen deplored their falling away from grace. In his diary, Crozer recorded some personal discomfort at the alienation of his employees:

It would be gratifying to me to see the laboring classes have plenty of work at a fair compensation, but this can never be unless employers are prosperous. This is so plain that it is to me a subject of surprise that work people so generally rejoice in the embarrassments and downfall of their employers.[19]

But in a public letter to the *Republican* he was even more defensive than in his privately recorded thoughts. In the open forum, Crozer went to some pains to defend his "right to conduct my own business in accordance with my own judgment," and to justify his actions:

The unfortunate Chester creek excitement has for some time past occupied a full share of interest in the county. The tendency of these disturbances to destroy peace and good order in a community is so evident, that whatever difference of opinion may exist as to the cause from which they originated, all good citizens must unite in deploring such occurrences. But it is gratifying that quiet is again restored, and though there may be remains of disaffection—a rankling and smothered feeling of resentment in the breasts of some—it is hoped that such feelings will subside without unnecessary proscription on the part of employers, or deep rooted hatred on the part of the employed. . . .

Much has also been said of the lordly and aristocratic conduct of the employers, and especially as applied to myself; particular charges have not been made I believe, and therefore I can only reply in general terms —nearly the whole of a life, not now short, has been spent in the bosom of this my native country. I am consequently, known to very many of its inhabitants; they are therefore competent to judge how far the epithets, aristocrat, lordly oppressor and tyrant will apply.[20]

Probably Crozer felt more pain at the rupture with his working people than did some of the other manufacturers. A man at once shy, ambitious, and devout, he repeatedly acknowledged—to his diary—that he had trouble balancing his intense drive toward worldly success with his need for assurances of salvation. His general solution of the dilemma was to believe, and claim, that he acted as God's steward, responsibly administering his profits for the general welfare. Public accusations by his own employees that he was doing no such thing, that he was a "cotton lord" motivated solely by self-interest, were disturbing and spurred him to vigorous efforts to convince others that he was indeed righteous as well as successful.

The professional evangelicals of the district—and particularly the clergymen and the Sunday School teachers—saw the strike as a setback in the battle against the infidels. Church and Sunday School attendance fell away (no doubt because strikers did not like to be told that they were morally wrong in striking). Even pillars of the congregation, like Mark Wild, had lamentably assumed roles of leadership in the turnout. Clementina, when she came out to Rockdale after the strike, found "much that is saddening in this place now." Among the saddening things was the bitterness of some of the working people, and particularly of strikers against nobsticks. Sarah Miles, the sister of Maria, had joined the turnout (Maria, now married to Crozer's foreman, "took no part in the 'turnout' or the improper conduct"). Sarah would not even speak to the members of other families who did not join the strike. Clementina, on visiting one family on some errand of mercy, asked if they knew the Mileses. "The Mother of the family said they did,

with much emotion, that since the 'turn out' Sarah . . . whom she loved as a daughter would not speak to them, because this poor woman's daughter had persisted in going to the mill." Clementina went on to generalize about the disregard of religion among the striking workers:

There is much to grieve and distress the heart of christians here, in the thought that many have made shipwreck of their faith and have gone far astray from the promises they professed to love—It would seem as if the Spirit of Evil had been abroad among this people, and the evil speaking lying, and slandering we hear of is really heart sickening—But I hope and believe there are some who are returning to a sense of their duty, some who mourn bitterly, who have been insensibly led into a course for which their hearts now condemn them, and to such I believe their experience in error will be a salutary lesson. I feel assured dear Sophie these poor deluded people have had an interest in your sympathy, and prayers, remember them still dearest, and him who ministers in the midst of them —The Sunday School, was really desolate the first Sunday we were here, but the children as well as the people are returning to their former habits, and have Many of them appeared in the school again.[21]

But perhaps in the end the most significant public appraisal of the strike was contained in Judge Bell's widely published charge to the jury (which in effect gave the rationale for the jury's subsequent conviction of the three conspirators). Judge Bell carefully reviewed the English common law, and British and American precedents, bearing on the nature of the crime of conspiracy. He pointed out that it was not criminal for two or more persons to combine or confederate to perform a lawful act. But if the combination sought an unlawful end, or planned and encouraged the use of unlawful means—such as violence against persons, destruction of property, or the threat of such acts—to attain even a lawful end, then it was a criminal conspiracy within the meaning of the law. Certainly it was a lawful act to refuse to work at certain wages, or to combine to request or attempt to persuade an employer to raise wages or to restore them after they had been reduced. But if the evidence showed that the combination of strikers advocated or planned the use of force (such as ducking nobsticks) in the pursuit of such legal aims, then, whether or not the force was ever used, they, or some of them, were guilty of conspiracy. If force was in fact used, then conviction on the charge of riot was also justified. The jury decided that the evidence against the defendants for their actual use of illegal force (i.e., the ducking of James Broadbent) was in some manner inadequate, but that the threats constituted a conspiracy. And thus the three men were convicted.[22]

The significance of the judge's charge lay in the fact that it declared that a combination of workers *peacefully* turning out on a wage-and-working conditions issue, and *peacefully* attempting to persuade fellow workers, and employers, of the justness of their cause, was not illegal. The jury's verdict might be argued with on the grounds of evidence; the conviction of the three leaders might leave a residuum of gall. Yet the judge's charge represented a moral victory not for the manufacturers but for the workers.

THE GREAT FLOOD

No sooner had the strike been settled than workers and capitalists were assailed by a disaster affecting both: the great flood in 1843. The problem of flash floods (or "freshets," as they were called in that day) was a perennial one along millstreams. Every now and then, high water would damage dams, races, headgates, and the machinery and materials in the lower stories in the mills. But with the increasing industrialization of the county, freshets were becoming an ever more serious threat, partly because of the increasing magnitude of capital investment, and partly because the environment itself was changing as a result of human action. The progressive denuding of once forest-covered hills, the building of drains and culverts, and the construction of roads and covered areas all helped rain and melt-water to flow more rapidly into the streams. And the dozens of dams and bridges added a special danger. Always built *above* the mill and most of its associated housing, when a dam broke it released a sudden burst of water upon the structures below it, structures already weakened by the rising stream. Bridges had the same effect because, as floodwaters rose, they created artificial dams by trapping large and small trees, floating debris, and silt and stones. Eventually, when the bridge fell, the effect upon structures below it was much the same as in the breaking of a dam. The potentiality was building for a catastrophe of unanticipated proportions along Chester Creek.

There had been some warning. In January 1839, there was an unusual warm spell accompanied by rain. The streams rose fairly rapidly and eventually reached a high-water mark as much as 18 feet above normal. Clogged with floating ice, in addition to the usual wooden debris, this freshet destroyed a number of bridges and swept away the breasts of many dams. The stone spans at Rockdale and Penn's Grove were demolished and many factories were damaged. At Knowlton, newly acquired by Crozer, the loss amounted to $5,000.[1]

On August 5, 1843—a Saturday, the day before Lammas, the ancient harvest festival, when St. Peter's imprisonment and release were to be celebrated at Calvary—there occurred the greatest flood in the memory of the inhabitants of Delaware County.[2] It was preceded by a northeasterly storm that deposited up to an inch of rain over all of the lower Delaware Valley. Late in the afternoon, primarily over northern Delaware County, the northeaster was followed by three hours of wildly stormy weather. The sky was so dark that it was difficult to read a newspaper; observers thought that the irregular movement of low-flying clouds must be the result of some extraordinary atmospheric commotion like the collision of two separate storm systems. A tornado tore down a swath of fences and trees in Concord and Bethel. Small gales struck from varying quarters. There was heavy and continuous thunder and lightning; barns were burning on the horizon. And rain fell in great sheets and lines and gobs of translucent water, sometimes reducing visibility to 50 yards or so, sometimes strangely permitting distant scenes to be perceived unobscured. Within three hours, on the upper waters of Chester Creek, there fell approximately 16 inches of rain. Crozer, immobilized (he was still recuperating from the midwinter spill from a sleigh in which his thigh had been broken), observed the scene from three to six o'clock in the afternoon from his residence on the hill above Crozerville factory:

About 3 o'clock under an unusually dark sky, rain commenced falling in torrents, accompanied with vivid lightning, and almost continuous peals of thunder. The lightning was more vivid than ever before witnessed by him in the day time, nor had he ever before heard so much loud thunder at one time. The heavy rain terminated a few minutes before 6 o'clock. Crozerville lies in a basin surrounded by steep acclivities. In every direction from these hills, sheets of water poured down, and mingling with the swollen current below, presented, together with the rapid succession of forked lightning, a scene of awful sublimity.[3]

By about 4:30, long before the end of the cloudburst, the creek had escaped its banks. At about 4:45 the creek began suddenly to rise at a rate of approximately 1 foot per minute, to an added height of about 8 feet as it moved downstream during the next hour. This sudden rise would take the form of a sloping wall of water 5 to 10 feet high, thundering along at about twenty miles per hour, carrying with it as battering rams a tumbling mass of trees, furniture, and parts of buildings. Between six and seven o'clock the waters reached their maximum height: at West Branch factory, they were 23 feet above normal; at Lenni Mill, 18 feet; and at Knowlton, where the flats narrowed and the stream flowed be-

tween two high, steep banks, the flood reached its highest level at 33 feet.

All of the dams and bridges in the Rockdale district were severely damaged and most of them were washed out. At West Branch, the dam gave way at 4:45 P.M. and its ten acres of impounded water descended suddenly upon the stone warehouse; by five o'clock, the warehouse began to disintegrate and soon fell, sending up clouds of dust from the crushed mortar. Soon after that the water wheel, mill gearing, dyehouse, and size house floated off. Then the northern wing of the factory collapsed into the torrent, with its eighty power looms and other machinery; the center building lost a corner. At Knowlton, Crozer's newly constructed weaving factory, three stories high, 76 by 36 feet—"beautiful . . . and filled with power looms, all new, and of the best construction"—was swept away to its foundations. The onlookers were romantically impressed by a peculiar circumstance of the disaster: "When the large factory went down, the roof remained entire while in view of those who witnessed its fall, the undulations of the current being sufficient to cause the factory bell in the cupola to toll the knell of its own sad catastrophe."[4]

At Lenni on the East Branch, the damage was less severe than at West Branch or at Knowlton, but even here the loss was considerable: the dam, race, stone office building, smith shop, and log tenement swept away, the county bridge just below the mill almost totally destroyed, a large quantity of cotton and finished goods and yarns ruined. Recalling the episode years later, Lammot's memory of the freshet was that "it washed away my office and all its contents—all my books, papers &c, including all my N[ew] C[hurch] correspondence, &c."[5] Crozer's office was also destroyed. The loss of an office was particularly serious because duplicate sets of books, receipts, orders, and other papers were not kept, so the amount owed by the mill owner's debtors, and his debts to his creditors, could not be positively determined; the manufacturer had to depend on the good faith of those with whom he did business.

Along with the collapse of the mill structures, the operatives' tenements on low ground were also washed away; it was in these structures that all the loss of life occurred in the Rockdale district. Most occupants were able to escape before their houses were destroyed, but some waited until their homes were surrounded by the flood. Six persons were killed when a set of four stone tenement houses near Penn's Grove factory collapsed. Their owner was an elderly, retired English cotton worker, John Rhodes, who lived in one of the houses and rented out the others. He refused to leave the safety of his dwelling until the suddenly rising waters made escape impossible. He was drowned, along with his two unmarried daughters and a granddaughter who was visiting with them at the time. An adjacent house,

occupied by a young married woman with a nursing child, also collapsed and the mother and daughter disappeared; their bodies were not found for some time. In addition to the six who died, there were dozens of homeless people in the Rockdale district whose houses were washed away or so damaged and filled with mud as to be unfit for habitation. And all the workers lost the vegetable gardens which they were accustomed to plant on the fertile bottom lands by the edge of the stream. Most of the ten or twelve ruined houses had been occupied by workers, the owners and managers ordinarily placing their mansions on higher ground; the only mill owner whose residence suffered was Samuel Riddle, and that building did not collapse.

One of the first things done after the flood was the organization of a county-wide relief committee, which collected over $3,000 and made cash grants to 131 families (including 404 children). In addition to this, well-to-do local families extended aid on a personal basis to individuals whom they knew. Inasmuch as most of the houses were rented from employers at rates of $1.25 to $2.50 per month, and the average grant per family was about $25, it seems that the committee was able to grant money sufficient to provide rent and food for several months for each family. Much furniture, clothing, and household utensils were lost in addition. But there was plenty of work in reconstruction for households with able-bodied adult males. And though the twenty-one households headed by widow women were likely to suffer because they included no one able to take part in the heavy work of reconstruction, this social category was so explicitly an object of special recognition in the factory towns, and so emphatically singled out for identification in the report of the flood written by Crozer and his colleagues, that the special needs of widows and their children were probably met by charitable neighbors.

The damages and financial losses in the Rockdale district were listed in contemporary records as follows:

LENNI MILL (owned by Hannah Hill and occupied by
Daniel Lammot and Son)—$3,000 for Lammot,
$2,000 for Hill
Dam and race swept away
Office destroyed
Goods and yarns swept away
County bridge ruined

WEST BRANCH MILL (John P. Crozer)—about $20,000
Dam and race swept away
Road between West Branch and Crozerville washed away

Warehouse, containing goods and yarns, swept away
Stone dry house and office swept away
Size house swept away
North wing of factory, containing 80 power looms, swept away
Center building damaged and machinery injured
Water wheel and mill gearing swept away

CROZERVILLE MILL (John P. Crozer)—about $5,000
Dam and race nearly destroyed
Cotton house with 30 bales of cotton swept away
Spinning machinery on lower story injured
Bridge carried away

PARKMOUNT MILL (owned by Hannah Hill but unoccupied)—$1500
Dam injured
Forebay of mill swept out
Water-wheel thrown out of position

PENN'S GROVE MILL (Samuel Riddle)—$3,000
Dam and race swept away
"Old Mill" carried away
Machinery in cotton factory much damaged
Riddle residence damaged
2 houses (owned by George Peterson) destroyed $700
4 houses (owned by John Rhodes) destroyed $1200
1 house (owned by E. Churchman) destroyed
County bridge destroyed

OLD SABLE MILL and Estate (owned by Richard S. Smith)—$3,000
2 dams destroyed
4 stone dwellings (unoccupied) destroyed

KNOWLTON MILL (John P. Crozer)—about $20,000
New stone mill, 76 × 36, filled with new power looms,
with much stock in woven goods, swept away
Old frame mill occupied by James Dixon swept away $1,000

Crozer's factories suffered so much more than those of his fellow manufacturers because of their particular sites. West Branch and Knowlton were both located on very low ground, below very short races, at points in the stream where there were natural rapids and where the hillsides were steep and very close together (at Knowlton the gorge was only about 100 feet wide). Crozer noted that "other mills suffered much less than ours," and for a while seems to have regarded his calamity as a divine dispensation to which he must resign himself. As he set down his thoughts in a letter to his sister, a few days after the flood (while still "water-locked" in his residence):

My loss of property is very great, probably little, if any, short of fifty thousand dollars; and I feel, of course, and feel deeply, for this is human nature; but I trust and believe I meet it with the resignation of a Christian and the firmness of a man somewhat accustomed to vicissitudes; and, moreover, though I have witnessed the result of years of diligent application to business pass away in a few hours, yet I have a considerable fortune left, sufficient with the economy which we have hitherto practised, to maintain my family genteelly.

But even as he was resigning himself to a lowered standard of living and a less extensive business, Crozer was taking steps to restore his enterprises to their former state of prosperity. Three days after the flood he had more than eighty people at work, "cleaning machinery, hunting for goods, washing and drying them, and a part digging a channel for the creek" (its old channel being filled with rocks, the stream had taken over the tailrace of Crozerville Mill as its new course). A month later, Crozerville Mill was in full operation, and his men were at work rebuilding West Branch—a complex operation, involving cutting a new road into the hillside, reconstructing the dam and race, relocating the creek, and constructing new buildings. Thirty looms had been salvaged from the waters of Chester Creek, some of them as far as a mile downstream, and he had ordered forty new ones. Crozer expected to see West Branch back at work in October. But as for Knowlton, Crozer gave up; and this meant that all the workers' families left the hamlet. In his diary he recorded, in his typically defensive way, his sorrow at the abandonment of the village:

There is something impressive in the sudden breaking-up, like that of Knowlton; and the scattering for ever of a little community of workpeople, with whom I had pleasant intercourse, saddened my heart almost or quite as much as the loss of so valuable an estate. I really feel an interest in my people, an affectionate interest, but I suppose few or none of them think so, or are aware of it.

Within about a year, all of the factories were re-equipped and at work again with the exception of Knowlton and still-unoccupied Parkmount. The unsightly mud deposits on the flats at Crozerville and at other points in the stream were covered with green grass and weeds; the bits and pieces of machinery still lying scattered about in the underbrush were rusting and rotting; the eye was becoming accustomed to the new course of the stream. The ruin of the first construction work on the Chester Creek Railroad to connect Rockdale with Chester and West Chester was abandoned. (The railroad was not actually put through until a decade later, although it had been incorporated in 1836, with Crozer, Smith, Lammot, and Samuel Riddle as commissioners.) Crozer's valedictory summation was almost casual:

My loss was greater than I supposed when I wrote to you last. But great as it is, I am not a poor man by any means. And though it was trying, extremely so, to have the earnings of years pass away in a few hours, I feel now pretty much the same as though it were not gone. The loss need occasion no change in our mode of living, not even in our little deeds of charity, and can only be felt in the amount we might have to leave our children. Your sister bears this, as indeed she does every sudden visitation, with becoming firmness and resignation.

And he added later in his diary: "by-and-by all will no doubt appear right and easy."[6]

THE REDEFINITION OF THE COTTON MILL OPERATIVE

The 1842 strike won for the cotton mill operatives a clear recognition from the court that, like the workers in traditional trades, they had a right to organize a union and to strike (just as the employers had the right to fire them and hire strikebreakers). But the changing position of the operative was in fact, as a result of the working of three other processes, moving him even further away from the status of the skilled craftsman. These three processes may be called leveling, depoliticizing, and the favoring of managerial over manual skills.

Leveling: The Self-Acting Mule
and the Decline of Labor Specialization

In the earlier years, the cotton mill typically contained a highly diversified group of people doing a variety of tasks requiring different degrees and kinds of skill: males and females; children, youths, and adults; the small and dexterous and the big and burly; the unskilled laborer, the highly skilled carder, mule spinner, and weaver, and the inventive mechanician; part-timers and full-timers; the low-paid scavengers and piecers, earning $1 or $1.50 for a full six-day week, and the well-paid mule spinner, earning $30 or $40 per month. But a number of technological and social processes were at work to reduce the amount of variation in some of these categories. To be sure, the conscious goal of the manufacturers and the operatives was not to homogenize the work force; yet this was an effect of their actions.

One of the leveling factors was the introduction of new machinery that was more nearly automatic, or faster, or less prone to break yarn, or less likely to break down and require repair. A most significant innovation of this sort was the self-acting mule, which (as we saw in Chapter V) was introduced into his mills by Samuel Riddle prior to 1844, probably at the time when he moved from Parkmount to Penn's Grove. Bancroft on the Brandywine bought a self-actor about the same time and almost certainly Riddle's fellow manufacturers in Rockdale were also investing in self-actors. The self-actor worked faster, broke fewer threads, held more spindles, self-cleaned much of the fly, and did not need a spinner to push in the carriage during winding on. Although a spinner had to mind the self-actor, tuning it and repairing the bands, and although it still needed the service of piecing, a single spinner could now manage two mules back to back, each of which was substantially larger than the single mule he operated before, and do it with only two piecers to take care of both piecing and cleaning. In Riddle's case, between 1834 and 1844 the number of mule spinners was reduced from ten to five but the number of hanks produced per month quadrupled. Thus he was able to reduce the piece rate, and increase the total monthly wage for the mule spinner without increasing the amount of labor the spinner had to perform.

The effect, however, was a leveling. The mule spinner did not have to be as skilled as he once was; he approximated more closely the passive machine-minders who worked in the spinning and weaving rooms. And in terms of potential labor organization, it reduced the number of mule spinners to so small (but so highly paid) a fraction that their potential utility as strike leaders was probably actually reduced. There is a tradition, in fact, that the self-acting mule was deliberately perfected by Richard Roberts in the 1820's in England for manufacturers aiming to break the power of the mule spinners' union, which was constantly inconveniencing the manufacturers by turnouts for higher wages. When in 1835 the *Journal of the Franklin Institute* brought Roberts' mule to the attention of American mechanicians, the editor listed its advantages:

It produces a considerably greater quantity of yarn, of more uniform twist, and less liable to break, and it winds on the cop more evenly and closely, so that the yarn is more desirable for the weaver. . . . One of the recommendations of this machine to the spinners, is, that it renders them independent of the working spinners, whose combinations and stoppages of work have often been extremely annoying to the masters.[1]

But even the self-actor required a spinner to supervise it; and strikes were factory-wide turnouts, anyway, so it is doubtful that the new mules were introduced in America with anti-union sentiments as the principal motive. The primary effect was to reduce the cost per hank of spun yarn to the manufacturer; and, by improving quality, to increase the value of the product. The reduction in number of mule spinners was a secondary consequence. But halving the number of mule spinners was not all; the self-actor was so clean and broke so few ends that the scavengers, who were the youngest children working in the mill, could be dispensed with. Thus even without any laws against child labor, the advance of technology reduced the need for it. The self-acting mule, in sum, cut in half the number of most highly skilled adult operatives and least skilled child helpers in any mill into which it was introduced.

By 1835 the Scottish mathematician and popularizer of technological development, Andrew Ure, was able to generalize about this leveling process. The situation now, he declared, was far different from what it had been when Adam Smith wrote his "immortal elements of economics." At that time, automatic machinery being little known, Smith was led to regard "the division of labour as the grand principle of manufacturing improvement." But now, as a result of the continuing improvements in machinery, the differentiation of labor by skill and strength was outmoded:

In fact, the division, or rather adaptation of labour to the different talents of men, is little thought of in factory employment. On the contrary, wherever a process requires peculiar dexterity and steadiness of hand, it is withdrawn as soon as possible from the *cunning* workman, who is prone to irregularities of many kinds, and it is placed in charge of a peculiar mechanism, so self-regulating, that a child may superintend it. . . .

The grand object therefore of the modern manufacturer is, through the union of capital and science, to reduce the task of his work-people to the exercise of vigilance and dexterity,—faculties, when concentrated to one process, speedily brought to perfection in the young. In the infancy of mechanical engineering, a machine-factory displayed the division of labour in manifold gradations—the file, the drill, the lathe, having each its different workmen in the order of skill: but the dexterous hands of the filer and driller are now superseded by the planing, the key-groove cutting [i.e., milling], and the drilling-machines; and those of the iron and brass turners, by the self-acting slide-lathe. . . .

An eminent mechanician in Manchester told me that he does not choose to make any steam-engines at present, because with his existing means, he would need to resort to the old principle of the division of labour, so fruitful of jealousies and strikes among workmen; but he intends to prosecute that branch of business whenever he has prepared suitable arrangements on the equalization of labour, or automatic plan.[2]

The tendency in the 1830's and 1840's, then, was for the cotton mill machinery to become progressively more specialized and intricate, while the cotton mill operative became progressively more standardized and indifferently skilled.

The Depoliticizing of Labor

Another process that was tending to alienate the operative from the artisan was the general depoliticizing of labor. Political activity provided a basis for association among trades and specialties that transcended differences in the particulars of each group's economic problems. Driving labor from the political arena would reduce solidarity among the groups. This end had already been achieved in part by the conservative press's successful association of the "workeyism" of the 1828–32 period with Robert Owen, Fanny Wright, and Tom Paine. Although there had been indeed many radicals in the Workingmen's Party then, there had also been many who were essentially middle class in aspiration—not only mechanicians, physicians, and other professionals, but many ordinary craftsmen as well. The workingmen's popular front had proposed to achieve certain broad social reforms by sending liberal representatives to Congress and the state legislatures. The charge of "infidelity" split the workingmen's movement and silenced many of its advocates of reform.

Into this breach the evangelicals and conservatives moved with alacrity, simply taking over from the radicals certain of their own issues, particularly the establishment of a free public school system, the dismantling of the militia system, the abolition of imprisonment for debt, and the passage of a mechanics lien law. Again, it is not likely that many of the capitalists consciously plotted to eviscerate the labor movement politically by stealing its best reform issues and pursuing them piecemeal. (This degree of Machiavellian foresight might have been possible for an iron founder like Thaddeus Stevens, who was able so adroitly to develop popular political issues which coincided with the pursuit of private interest that despite his economic conduct he became known as "The Great Commoner." But not many manufacturers were as ruthless as Stevens in the pursuit of power.) Rather, these reforms, long advocated by workingmen's groups, were simply swept up in the swelling tide of the Christian social reform movement, along with temperance, prison reform, the rehabilitation of prostitutes, and the building of special hospitals for the insane. Thus the liberal newspapers and workingmen's organizations were deprived of exclusive advocacy, as it were, of their most readily salable issues, and were left in an exposed position to argue the most controversial ones: religion, the licensed monopolies (such as the Second Bank of the United States), tax reform, electoral reform.

Working together, the evangelicals, capitalists, and workers managed to put through the Pennsylvania legislature in the period from 1831 to 1854 a series of reform bills. In 1831, 1834, and 1836, a series of laws was passed which created a system of free (but not compulsory) public schools. In 1833, imprisonment for small debts was abolished. The old law establishing the compulsory militia system was repealed in 1849. And in 1854, a mechanics lien law was passed after a generation of earnest pleading. Each of these legislative reforms was of primary benefit to poor working people, and each benefited them twofold: in relieving them of some aspect of the social stigma of economic inadequacy, and in providing practical economic aid.

Before the public school laws were passed, there had indeed been a provision, written into the state constitution in 1790 and implemented by appropriate legislation (the so-called Pauper Law) in 1809, that children whose parents could not afford to send them to the private schools in their neighborhood were entitled to public aid. This aid took the form of tuition payments by the county directly to the teachers. But in order to determine eligibility, applicant parents had to declare their indigence to the township tax assessor; the name was recorded in the tax records; and the children going to school at the expense of local taxpayers were branded with the stigma of poverty among their peers. The Sunday Schools were a less invidious alternative but they operated irregularly and required submission to some sort of religious discipline.

Let us look at the system in Aston Township in 1829. In that year a total of nineteen children from ten households were listed as applying and being eligible for schooling at county expense. Two of the households were headed by widows (one of them was the Hannah Lower who with her family joined Calvary Church when it was founded). Three of the poor parents were weavers who later came to work power looms for Samuel Riddle. The children, eight boys and eleven girls, ranged in age from five to eleven. Of these only one boy and seven girls actually attended school in that year. These "parents of poor children" eligible for county aid were by no means poor in the sense of the poorhouse poor. The families were headed either by respectable widows or by men who worked in trades; they earned at a rate (if regularly employed) of up to $250 a year and one man even owned a cow. But the children's tuition was just too much. Further-more, if working-class people earning up to $250 per year were eligible, it is certain that many working-class families who were eligible were not applying, some of them no doubt wanting their children to earn money in the mills rather than go to school at their parents' or the county's expense, and some also presumably not wanting the social stigma of a public disclosure of poverty.[3]

The new laws of 1831–36 proposed to change all this, and a number of the manufacturers were active in their support of the reform. William Martin—now a prosperous attorney and secretary of an insurance company —took the lead in organizing a petition in favor of the act of 1834 (which its opponents threatened to repeal). In Aston, Richard S. Smith was in 1836 elected a member of the first school board of Aston Township, and he offered the Rockdale school (which stood on his property) to the board rent-free. Crozer offered his chapel as a schoolhouse. John Garsed became a school director in 1840. In Middletown, Peter Hill sold the board a half-acre lot near Parkmount Mill and a schoolhouse was erected on it in 1837. In 1844 Samuel Riddle was elected a school director.[4]

Another emotionally freighted reform—but one that all classes joined in demanding—was the abolition of imprisonment for debt. Both rich and poor were vulnerable to the archaic procedures which permitted the court, on petition of a creditor, to incarcerate a debtor under noxious prison conditions for an indefinite period, until the debt was paid or the creditor satisfied. Patrick Lyon, the eminent mechanician, had been unjustly imprisoned for debt years before in Philadelphia and had written an impassioned account of his experience; for years petitioners had bombarded the legislature demanding an end to the practice, especially as it bore so harshly on the poor, who did not have wealthy relatives and friends to buy their freedom and who consequently might languish for months for want of a few dollars. Shocking accounts were printed in the liberal press of the abuses to which the poor, particularly moneyless widows, were subjected in debtors' prisons. At last in 1833 the state legislature passed an act "to abolish imprisonment for small debts." Other legislative enactments followed.

The next of the grosser social inequities to be legislated away was that provision of the state militia law of 1792 which required militia service of all white males between the ages of eighteen and forty-five. Certain occupations were exempted (federal officers, mail stage drivers, ferrymen on post roads, postmasters, clergymen, schoolteachers, ships' pilots, judges, sheriffs, and jailers). On the first and second Mondays in May, every year, the state's militiamen were required to drill in company and battalion under their elected officers (election to officership in the militia was a widely used step toward political office). Discipline was theoretically the same as in the regular Army and absence without leave was subject to fine or imprisonment.

The militia requirement was a severe burden to the workingman. He was required to give up two days' pay every year, he had to furnish his own uniform and equipment; and if he was unable to afford the cost, he was subject to fine and ultimately imprisonment. The well-to-do could avoid the whole problem by paying the fine or by organizing their own volunteer companies separately and, after seven years' service in these, becoming exempt from the state system. The inequity was so obvious that absentees were frequently not reported and fines not collected; militia day itself became a day of drinking as much as of marching. At last this system too was abolished, the law being repealed in 1849. No one was really sorry to see it go; and for those who were, the local volunteer companies were still available.

The mechanics lien law was perhaps of more actual importance to artisans than to the factory operatives, but it did apply to the machinists, blacksmiths, masons, and carpenters who worked about a mill. The issue was an economic one. When a building contractor became insolvent while a building was under construction, the mechanic—a mere "wage earner" —who had put in time working on the structure was often left unpaid while "privileged creditors" like banks, moneylenders, tavernkeepers, and merchants were allowed by the court to recover their debts from the remaining assets of the debtor. The mechanics wanted the status of privileged creditor too. The legislature put off action on the measure until 1854, when it passed a law which "gave mechanics first preference, up to one hundred dollars, in the property assignment of insolvent corporations."

Management Skills as the Pathway to Success

In the trades, an indispensable ingredient of success was skill, manifested in manual dexterity, felicity of design, quickness of operation, avoidance of fatigue. The journeyman had to be more skilled than the young apprentice; and the master had to be able to demand a high level of skill both from the apprentices who learned from him and from the journeymen who worked for him. But such a progression of skills did not occur in the cotton mill, except perhaps in the transformation of the young piecer into the adult mule spinner; and this pathway was open to fewer and fewer piecers, as the self-actor made their work less and less necessary. A mule spinner, once installed before his mule (or between his two self-actors), could move to no higher status by skill alone and might, indeed, stand between the very same two mules for all the forty years of his working life, tuning and adjusting them until they spun (so he fancied) like no other two mules in the world.[5]

The way to success was by the development—or the happy possession —of managerial skills. There were essentially three intermediate management positions to which an ordinary operative in a small mill might aspire: carder, spinning-room overseer, and boss weaver. The carder was responsible for the preparation of the cotton for spinning: the picker room, the carding machines, and the drawing and roving frames. Once the bobbins of roving were delivered to the mule or throstle room, the spinning-room overseer was responsible; he performed quality-control checks on the number and strength of the yarns being spun, communicated instructions as to changes in count or degree of twist, and recorded the number of hanks spun by each mule. The boss weaver, similarly, was responsible for overseeing the setting up of the looms, for the receipt of shuttle cops and warp beams, for quality control, and for the recording of the yards of cloth woven by each loom.

These jobs required the overseer not only to know the operatives' work in a technical sense, and have the ability to assess the quality of its product, but also to be able to manage a group of men, women, and children so as to maximize their productivity for the mill. The skills of management were skills in social relationships: being able to command when necessary, to persuade, to mollify, to cajole; to mediate between the human needs of the operatives below him and the economic demands of the directors and owners above him; to coordinate his schedule and organization with that of the overseers adjacent to him in the process. The overseers thus were paid more, much more, sometimes even (as in Riddle's mill) in proportion to the productivity of their department. In January 1844, for instance, the power-loom department at Penn's Grove employed thirty-four people (eighteen men and sixteen women), whose wages amounted to $387.20 (an average per weaver of a little more than $11). For overlooking the looms the overseer received $96.80, calculated at the rate of 25 percent of the weavers' total wages. Since the weavers were paid on a piecework basis, the boss weaver was being paid according to the productivity of his department. The throstle room seems to have had three or four overseers, who like the spinners were paid per diem wages, but at a rate about four times as high as the ordinary machine-minders (one man received $28 per month, and Archibald McDowell—the Riddles' brother-in-law—$24 per month). The five mule spinners, however, seem not to have required an overseer. Six years later, in January 1850, there were still only five mule spinners and still no mule-room supervisor. But there was a carding master (at $48 per month), a throstle-room overseer (at $24 per month), and a man responsible for "overlooking looms" (at $64.50 per month).[6]

It was the policy of at least some of the manufacturers and mill owners (and specifically Crozer and the Smiths) to cultivate and advance this class of foremen or overseers. Abraham Blakeley, an erstwhile Lancashire operative, was Crozer's loom overseer from 1833 to 1846, when he went into business as a manufacturer himself, renting the rebuilt Knowlton Mill from his former employer.[7] He was superintendent at the Sunday School in the little chapel at Knowlton.[8] Hayes P. Griffith, the "loom boss" at the weaving mill owned by Richard S. Smith, was a member of the Calvary congregation and a personal favorite of Clementina; as a a boy he had lived with the Smiths and served them as a waiter.[9] Indeed, the path to worldly success for an aspiring operative would seem to lead from the machine to the overseer's little office to the door of the nearest church or Sunday School.

But such a process of advancement effectively removed from the ranks of the machine-minders many of their natural leaders, the very men who might have organized effective unions and led strikes. Together with the processes of leveling and direct depoliticization, it worked to redefine the cotton mill operative as a semi-skilled laborer, not a craftsman, politically passive, with conventional social views and a limited capacity to organize in opposition to the owners and managers of the mills.

WORKERS AS OBJECTS OF PITY:
THE TEN HOURS LAW

When the struggle between management and labor began in the 1820's, the cotton mill workers, despite their anomalous position in the roster of trades, had generally had a high opinion of themselves as a radical reforming element in society. By the mid-forties, despite a practical improvement in their material conditions, the textile workers had become objects of public sympathy and of the religious reformer's condescending concern. They were now for the most part children, and, as Clementina once put it, "poor girls that work on the looms."[1] The mode of passage and enforcement of the ten hours law symbolizes the transformation.

One of the standing complaints of cotton factory workers was the long working day, on the order of fourteen hours, including about an hour for meals. The Pennsylvania Senate committee's investigation in 1837 had included testimony from operators and manufacturers alike alleging that the protracted hours of work were injurious to the health of children and left them so tired that they could not pay attention in night school or sometimes even in Sunday School. Poor factory children could not of course take advantage at all of the free public schools, which thus, in effect, were reserved for the children of more affluent parents. The turnouts in 1835 and 1836 in Philadelphia had won the journeymen of that city a ten hours agreement with the master tradesmen; but nothing had happened to benefit the operatives as a result of either their own strikes in 1836 and 1842 or the Pennsylvania Senate investigation of 1837.

In 1846, the operatives of Philadelphia, inspired by a brief strike of the factory girls at Pittsburgh in support of a ten hours law, formed their own "Ten Hours Association." They wrote an address to "The Working Classes of the Country," which urged it as beneficial to employers and employees alike that the ten hours system be universally adopted. The address was printed in the *Upland Union.* It described the evil consequences of the long hours in graphic terms:

We see the laborer in the morning approach his toil with a dread of its long protraction and excess, that even a sound night's slumber, and long continued habit have failed to wear away. We see him as the day declines with wearied limbs, and gloomy thoughts, and cheerless spirits, casting upon the setting sun a lingering and heart-sick glance, or after it is gone from view, listening in despondency to hear, through the clattering of machinery, the hour of his delivery from toil. We see him unable to fulfill towards his family the offices and duties of his station, because his weary-ing labors have substituted petulance and gloom for the feelings of affec-tion; and languor and indifference for the power of instruction. We see him producing wealth by perpetual exertion, yet living a life of unceasing anxiety and want. We see him subjected to continual privations, inconve-nience and suffering, and cut off from the ordinary sources of gratification and enjoyment. We see him in ignorance, servility and degradation, and deprived of the time, the taste, the energy, necessary for his elevation and improvement. We see him losing all interest in matters of general impor-tance, and degenerating into a mere machine, with intelligence to guide him in his labor, and compensation enough to keep him in profitable working order and economical repair.

Invoking the welfare of mankind, the spirit of the age, and the evidence of progress in justification, the paper called upon the nation to fix a date for "the general change."

A second, related, complaint was that children of tender years ought not to be employed at all. Although many widows were supported by their children's wages, and although the nimble little fingers of the young were supposedly uniquely qualified for handling delicate yarns, there was a persistent argument in favor of keeping younger children out of the factories. The considerations advanced in support of restrictions on the age of labor included the hazard to health, the threat to morals, and the need for education. These arguments also had been expressed by witnesses before the Senate committee in 1837 but had seen no result.

Precedent existed for government intervention. England had had legislation on the books since 1802 that aimed to protect the health and morals of factory children. In 1834 a new Act of Parliament provided that no person under the age of eighteen was permitted to work at night or to labor more than twelve hours per day or for more than a total of sixty-nine hours per week. In 1840 President Van Buren by executive order had put federal employees on a ten-hour basis. And in 1847 the New Hampshire legislature became the first in the nation to pass a law specifying that ten hours was a legal day's work (although its effectiveness was reduced by a clause permitting special contracts which extended that limit).

The passing of the New Hampshire law served as a signal to Pennsylvanians to renew their demand for a statute defining the length of the working day in textile factories (i.e., the length of time that an employer could *require* an employee to remain at work). In the summer of 1847, editorials began to appear in papers of both Whig and Democratic persuasion, urging the state legislature to take up the matter in its fall sessions. The editor of the *Upland Union* in July urged the passage of a ten hours law in plain terms:

> The Parliament of Great Britain has passed a law enforcing the ten hour system in all manufacturing establishments. This is a highly meritorious act, and will add much to the mental and physical comfort of the men, women and children whose necessities compel them to labor for the support of themselves and others. The State governments here should move early in the adoption of this salutary measure, which gives to the closely defined manufacturer time to revive his physical energies and improve his mind, thus qualifying him to perform more work than when exhausted by long confinement. The adoption of their system even by factory owners, with good moral regulations and facilities for mental improvement will increase the interest and comfort of employers and employed.

In the fall, the mechanics and operatives of Philadelphia held a mass meeting to agitate the question. The keynote address was delivered by a gentleman who claimed to have risen from the ranks of labor. He advanced the main arguments in favor of a ten hours law and advised the workers how to proceed. "You propose," he observed, "to change, in some degree, the position which exists between the employers and employed." It behooved them to act not rashly and hastily but with the caution and deliberation that belong to "a thinking class," to "avoid all unnecessary excitement," and never to "assume personal hostility to your employers." Capitalists and workers were alike creatures of Providence and equally deserving of respect: "It is perfect folly to make war upon either capital or employers as such; for no man would be a laborer could he be an employer, and perhaps it is the duty—certainly it is the right of every operative—to look forward to the time when he will be an employer."

But, caught "in the vortex of speculation and competition," the capitalist, "in the unlimited control of enterprise and capital," could not help but forget the rights of labor now and then. Thus he could not be relied on to correct the evil himself. As a result, "the people" were overworked, and "energies, health, faculties, are enervated, if not destroyed." Furthermore, the employment of children and the long hours both tended to interfere with home life. It was this threat to the *home* that particularly justified the operatives' petition: "if anything can be dearer than *home*—upon this . . . depends, almost entirely, the health, the virtue, and the intellect of these *now* 'little ones,' who are hereafter to constitute the Republic." But the operatives could not accomplish the relaxation of factory discipline by themselves. Action by the government was necessary and proper, he argued, because the government had the general right to correct evils in society.

The operatives of Delaware County, like their brothers and sisters in Philadelphia, organized to press the cause. At a meeting toward the end of October at Odd Fellows Hall in Village Green, attended by delegates from all over the county, a resolution urging the legislature to pass a ten hours law was voted unanimously. The argument was based partly on the need to protect the health of the workers, partly on the need of operatives for more free time, and partly on the need to curb overproduction. Long hours were "depriving the operatives of all opportunity for the cultivation of their minds, and unfitting them for mixing socially with the intelligent of other pursuits, as well as for the enjoyment of those literary treasures so liberally bestowed by an enlightened press. . . ." Long hours were also blamed for business cycles:

In a commercial point of view, the evils of the present system are not less clearly seen, in seasons of prosperity, enabling the more grasping to run their mills even for longer than usual time—generally against the wishes or inclination of the operatives, to the disadvantage of their more moderate brethren; thus, in a short time, causing a glut in the market—breaking up manufactories—throwing workmen out of employment—breaking up families and scattering them helpless and dependent upon the community —increasing misery, crime, and pauperism, throughout the land, adding a vast amount to the local taxes, and over-burthening all other pursuits.

And the operatives demanded to be included in the bright Utopian future that lay ahead in America's destiny:

> With a population of over twenty millions and an increase which if continued will, in fifty years, swell the number to one hundred millions of human beings, with our vessels floating on every river in this vast land, our railroads running through and almost encircling it, our ships on every ocean, with their sails spread to the wind, carrying our products of industry to every clime, who can fail to be impressed with the conviction that a higher and nobler destiny awaits us than that of being employed fourteen hours a day in obtaining the means of subsistence?[2]

A central executive committee was established, with two representatives from each mill, and a committee of correspondence was set up to coordinate with groups in other counties. A petition was prepared, which was sent to the Delaware County representatives in the Assembly and Senate in Harrisburg. But the senator refused to present it to the Senate and the operatives had to collect the signatures all over again. It was finally presented by a sympathetic senator from Lehigh. The committee met every week for the next several months, developing further petitions and lobbying measures, and providing statements to be reprinted in the newspapers. There was no strike. Passage of the law was achieved in March 1848.[3]

The Pennsylvania Ten Hours Law provided that ten hours in any one day, in all cotton, woolen, and other textile factories (and paper mills), was "a legal day's labor." No minor or adult could be required to work more than ten hours in one day or more than sixty hours in one week; no child under twelve was to be hired. The penalty for each infraction was a $50 "fine." But there were two flaws: the fine had to be recovered by suit "in like manner as debts of like amount are now recovered by law"; and minors between the ages of fourteen and twenty-one could be employed any number of hours "by special contract with their parents or guardians."[4] The law was to take effect on July 4, 1848.

The response of employers varied from place to place. In Philadelphia City and County (including the large concentrations at Manayunk and Kensington) the law was being observed even before the Fourth of July.[5]

In Pittsburgh, where the norm was twelve hours, the manufacturers resolved not to comply with the law and proposed to work out twelve-hour "special contracts" with their employees. Two thousand operatives who refused to agree to twelve-hour contracts were laid off. At the end of the month there was a "riot" when the unemployed workers attempted to close the twelve-hour mills. But at the end of August a settlement was reached: the manufacturers agreed to the ten-hour day and the workers who were paid by the day accepted a 16 percent pay cut.[6] In Delaware County, however, the law was simply ignored for five years by a band of manufacturers who claimed that the new law would place them in an unfavorable competitive position in relation to other states and who considered it to be an unconstitutional interference with the right of employers to hire whoever they wished on whatever terms were mutually agreeable.

What the county historian, Henry Ashmead, called "this little speck of nullification in the hitherto loyal county of Delaware" was carefully planned. The manufacturers let it be known in advance that they had determined to close their factories for several weeks after the Fourth of July, giving as an excuse the claim that they had large stocks of unsold goods on hand and, in the presence of a low market, wanted to wait until prices rose. Many of the operatives who had been active in working for the passage of the law, realizing what was in store for them, "withdrew and sought other means to secure a livelihood." After the lockout (which presumably exhausted many of the workers' savings) the mill resumed on the old system. A few refused to return and in effect went on strike. They too eventually either had to find other types of employment or move away.

And so, as far as the mills on Chester Creek were concerned, things went along in the old way, in placid defiance of the law, for five years. But it was embarrassing to evangelical manufacturers to be patently in violation of the law while zealously urging obedience to the law upon their employees. Furthermore, they were unable to argue that the new law put them at a competitive disadvantage to other Pennsylvania manufacturers, for the other counties were in compliance, and Delaware County factories were, in that matter, taking unfair advantage of their fellow manufacturers. But of course the other states in the Union did not all have a ten hours law— and Massachusetts in particular did not. So "some of the more conscientious of the manufacturers" made the astonishing proposal to the operatives that if they, the operatives, could persuade the New England manufacturers voluntarily to go on the ten-hour basis, then the Delaware County factories would obey the laws of their own state! Even more astonishingly, a delegation of Pennsylvania operatives did go up to Boston and attempt to persuade the mill owners of Waltham and Lowell. They met with indifferent success and returned to present the results to their own manufacturers.

By now public opinion was beginning to turn against the obstinate defiance of law by the richest and most powerful men in the county. A mass meeting was held at the old courthouse in Chester and a resolution passed, urging that "a trial should be made of the effects of the new law." John P. Crozer also now changed his position and urged his fellow employers to comply with the statute.

And so, in 1853, the law of 1848 was actually put into effect in Delaware County. The effects turned out to be much as the operatives had argued. Production did not in fact decline; it rose. After a few years Crozer testified enthusiastically for it, pointing out that in the end both sides had gained: the workers had greater access to opportunities for moral and intellectual improvement; and the manufacturers "got more work done per hour, or at a less rate of expense, than ever before."[7]

With the resolution of the ten-hours controversy, a generation of peace between capital and labor began in Rockdale and the other mill towns of Delaware County. The most obviously noxious aspects of the cotton factory system—the use of the labor of very young children and the excessively long hours—had been reformed; and the workers had for the most part accepted a position of unorganized passivity. In an era of benevolence toward the disadvantaged, with improvements being made in the treatment of the insane, the mentally retarded, the imprisoned, and the indigent, both well and ailing, the cotton mill operatives had come under the protecting shield of reform. But in the process they had abandoned their political ambitions, their organized unions, even their confidence in the effectiveness of the strike. The cotton factory workers had, as a class, become powerless.

THE THEORY OF CHRISTIAN CAPITALISM

The Chester Creek manufacturers, like many of their peers, were subscribers to a developing economic philosophy that may be called "the theory of Christian capitalism." It grew more out of the need to rationalize what was already happening in places like Rockdale than out of existing traditions in political and economic theory. It was formed in part to provide an intellectually satisfying response to Utopian socialists and to southern advocates of free trade; but it also served to reassure the capitalist and worker alike that the British economic system, their principal competitor, was fatally oppressive to workers, to colonial populations, and to developing nations, and that the gloomy English economists, led by Malthus and

Ricardo, were supporting its evils by wrong-headedly claiming that these evils were the inevitable checks and balances. It was a point of view that connected strictly economic variables—rents and wages, capital investment and prices, and so forth—to other dimensions of society, including the general welfare, historical process, and a system of Christian religious values.

A principal local codifier of this body of thought was Henry C. Carey, son of Matthew Carey, the Philadelphia publisher and protectionist pamphleteer. Henry Carey had spent the first forty years of his life working in the successful publishing business of Carey and Lea, then the largest in America. When he retired with a substantial fortune, he began to study political economy, and in 1835 published the first of his eight books and three thousand pamphlets. Carey was something of a system-builder, who tried to develop first a unified science of economics, then a unified social science, and finally a unified body of laws that would bring together the physical, social, mental, and moral sciences in one grand formulation. In this large scheme he was not successful; but his economic theories were very widely read in Europe as well as in the United States. He vigorously denounced the British economists' prescription of free trade and *laissez faire* as the solution to all economic problems and became the most articulate exponent of the economic argument for the protective tariff. Like David Ricardo, he regarded labor as the source of all economic value, and considered that capital and labor were the active and passive partners in an indissoluble marriage in which both must prosper or decline together. Carey was widely consulted by practical men who could look upon the retired successful businessman, with his tendency to strong language and his enthusiasm for their pragmatic view, as one of themselves. Among the Chester Creek manufacturers, he was on visiting terms at least with the Darlingtons, the Smiths, the Sellers family; General Robert Patterson, who bought Lenni Mill when the Lammots moved to the Brandywine, was one of his closest friends.

In 1850 the first edition of Carey's central work on protectionism appeared, with the evocative title *The Harmony of Interests, Agricultural, Manufacturing, and Commercial.* It contained essays previously published by Carey in a periodical, *The Plough, the Loom, and the Anvil,* which he had established a few years before. The book's theme was the basic complementarity of the sectors of the American economy, all of which—and social life in general —would be advanced in unison by the protective tariff. The tone of the book was violently anti-Britain: anti her free trade policy and her economists of despair, Malthus and Ricardo. It was also Utopian, almost but not quite millenarian, in a chauvinistic sort of way, looking forward to a time when the Union should embrace the globe and bring all nations together under the flag of the United States in a Christian empire governed by the holy doctrine, "Do unto others as ye would that others should do unto you." In contrast to the exploitive and militaristic "English system," he described a system of world economy which, he said, "we may be proud to call the American system, for it is the only one ever devised the tendency of which was that of ELEVATING while EQUALIZING the condition of man throughout the world." He went on, in the book's climactic final paragraphs, to describe the American destiny:

> To raise the value of labour throughout the world, we need only to raise the value of our own. To raise the value of land throughout the world, it is needed only that we adopt measures that shall raise the value of our own. To diffuse intelligence and to promote the cause of morality throughout the world, we are required only to pursue the course that shall diffuse education throughout our own land, and shall enable every man more readily to acquire property, and with it respect for the rights of property. To improve the political condition of man throughout the world, it is needed that we ourselves should remain at peace, avoid taxation for the maintenance of fleets and armies, and become rich and prosperous. To raise the condition of woman throughout the world, it is required of us only that we pursue that course that enables men to remain at home and marry, that they may surround themselves with happy children and grand-children. To substitute true Christianity for the detestable system known as the Malthusian, it is needed that we prove to the world that it is population that makes the food come from the rich soils, and that food tends to increase more rapidly than population, thus vindicating the policy of God to man. Doing these things, the addition to our population by immigration will speedily rise to millions, and with each and every year the desire for that perfect freedom of trade which results from incorporation within the Union, will be seen to spread and to increase in its intensity, leading gradually to the establishment of an empire the most extensive and magnificent the world has yet seen, based upon the principles of maintaining peace itself, and strong enough to insist upon the maintenance of peace by others, yet carried on without the aid of fleets, or armies, or taxes, the sales of public lands alone sufficing to pay the expense of government. . . .[1]

Probably not all of the manufacturers were as sanguine as Carey about the elevating and equalizing effect of the American economy on other nations. But all subscribed with him to certain basic themes which together make up a coherent theory of Christian capitalism that could be opposed to socialist philosophies. (Indeed, Carey's economics was adopted as an alternative to Marx's by at least one marginal German social theorist, Karl Eugen Dühring, and thus indirectly was influential enough to force Engels to elucidate the Marxist position on the class struggle more clearly in the "anti-Dühring" pamphlet so as to contradict Carey's Utopian "harmony-of-interests" philosophy.)[2] The basic elements of the idealistic theory of Christian capitalism would seem to be the following propositions:

1. Capitalistic enterprise is the supreme creative act, in no wise antithetical to the spirit or the letter of Christian doctrine, and beneficial to the whole community when conducted according to principles of financial probity.

2. The stewardship of wealth on behalf of the community for purposes of social reform and Christian benevolence, not the mere maximization of private profit, is the proper central economic motive of the capitalist.

3. The economic system, like other systems in nature, when functioning properly is governed by an equilibrium principle or "harmony of interests," so that agriculture and manufacturing, capital and labor, are all interdependent and will prosper or suffer together.

4. Government is responsible for allowing the economic system to function in a naturally harmonious way by protecting it from destructive foreign intervention by means of a protective tariff.

5. Although hierarchical relations are necessary in society, between parents and children, between employer and employees, and between the social classes, all men are entitled to earn such advancement in this hierarchy as their natural endowments, moral qualities, and perseverance individually entitle them to.

6. Under such a system economic progress is inevitable and will be unchecked by the Malthusian restraints on population because the productivity of a healthy economic system will always grow faster than the population itself.

7. Economic growth will inevitably be accompanied not only by an improvement in the material standard of living but also by an elevation of the people socially, morally, and spiritually, tending ultimately to a truly Christian commonwealth.

Clearly this theory was more hortatory than descriptive. But, when one examines the lives of the manufacturers, it clearly also was an ideology that gave the manufacturers effective criteria for making decisions. And, for a time at least, the American economic system seemed to be working in just about the way that the theory of Christian capitalism said it should.[3]

Part Four

ROCKDALE FROM 1850 TO 1865 ⚔ THE TRANSCENDING OF A WAY OF LIFE

Chapter IX

MARCHING
TO
MILLENNIUM

Beneath the smooth surface of American prosperity in the years before the Civil War, a vast turbulence was stirring. The northern manufacturers and their workers, in dozens of districts more or less like Rockdale, had created for themselves a comfortable and progressive way of life. After the labor troubles of the 1830's and early 1840's, a settlement had been achieved between the manufacturers and the workers and they had closed ranks in support of the "American System." The continued welfare of this system, they claimed, depended upon a protective tariff and a state-subsidized transportation system for the manufacturers, and for the workers cheap land in the west which could be bought with savings out of wages. But as the decades wore on, the delicate political compromises with the south, the supplier of cotton for the mills, began to break down. These compromises had been worked out in the belief that an awareness of the true harmony of interests would increasingly prevail. Sectional conflict between the manufacturing north and the agricultural south became ever more moralistic in its rhetoric. Eventually evangelical enthusiasm joined forces with economic and political self-interest to form a new Republican Party. And almost simultaneously, the millennialist interpretation of history that was latent in American ideology burst forth in militant glory. To the evangelical, millenarian, Republican manufacturer and worker in towns like Rockdale, the Civil War was not fought merely to preserve the Union from disruption, or even to abolish slavery; far more important than that, it was the first major clash in the war that was predicted in the Book of Revelation. It was the beginning of the greatest and final war, the beginning of the war for the conquest of the world for Christ.

THE ECONOMIC TAKE-OFF

As the depression began to ease in the mid-1840's, and the protective tariff was restored after a decade of lowered rates, the manufacturers and the workers on Chester Creek experienced a dramatic increase in their opportunities. Manufacturers expanded their operations, improved their factories, introduced new machinery; some of the workers invested their savings in machinery and went into manufacturing on their own. Small, precarious enterprises were rapidly transformed into large, secure institutions with plenty of capital available for continuing expansion. The decade from the mid-forties to the mid-fifties was the era of economic take-off for the cotton industry on Chester Creek.

Men of Enterprise and the Chester Project

With the general prosperity of the county and the presence of surplus capital available for investment, in 1845 a number of citizens began to consider whether the old town of Chester might not be revitalized. Chester Borough, which lay immediately around the little fishing harbor, was in many respects a dying town, long ago eclipsed as a port by Philadelphia and Wilmington (and, indeed, even by nearby Marcus Hook), and it had recently been deprived of its status as the county seat in favor of the more centrally located Media. It had long since ceased to grow and in 1840 had a population of only 740 souls, not many more than it had possessed a century before. The surrounding land in Chester Township was occupied by farmers in easy circumstances, who, as the town's historian said, "would not sell a foot of ground at any price, and who looked upon those who would build a city here as visionary men, who would run themselves in debt, and ultimately fail."[1] John Broomall, a business partner of John P. Crozer's, described the borough as it was in 1840:

For a century and a half nothing but its Court house distinguished it from Marcus Hook, its neighboring fishing town. Long since the commencement of the present century, its inhabitants consisted of three or four tavern keepers, a doctor, a few dozen fishermen, two country storekeepers and a custom house-officer, whose arduous duties consisted of signing a receipt for his small salary four times a year.[2]

And Samuel Crozer, who moved into the township with his father a couple of years later, described the place in wry terms:

Chester in the Year 1847 had but about nine hundred and fifty inhabitants, and it was a very old and dried up town. It was stated that only one building had been erected in the town in fifty years, and that one was so long in completion that it had an old appearance before it was finished.[3]

Nevertheless, the township had obvious advantages as a site for industry. The seven-year-old Philadelphia, Wilmington, and Baltimore Railroad ran through it, and there was plenty of land (if only the farmers could be persuaded to sell) where mill workers, merchants, tradesmen, and manufacturers could reside and on which factories, schools, churches, stores, and other institutions could be built. Although water could not provide the power for more than a limited number of mills, the new generation of reliable stationary steam engines could be used instead. With almost all of the promising mill seats taken up in the Rockdale district and in the other manufacturing centers along the Delaware County fall line, the only reasonable place for economic expansion was at a convenient transportation center like Chester.

There were four men who, acting in loose concert, achieved the revitalization of Chester. The first to act was John P. Crozer. Now extremely prosperous from his mills at West Branch, Crozerville, and Knowlton (in his diary he stated matter-of-factly, "I have a large fortune"), he was looking for opportunities to invest his profits. He was attracted to Chester Township because he was growing tired of the long carriage and sleigh ride between Crozerville and the train station at Chester, where he boarded "the cars" that took him and the other manufacturers to Philadelphia at least once a week to conduct business. And he had just had the harrowing experience of a thigh broken by a spill from the sleigh one night on his way home. When part of the Flower estate, including the old seat of Chester Mills, with sixty-six acres and the venerable Caleb Pusey House (built in 1683 and one of the most ancient structures in the commonwealth), came on the market in 1844, Crozer bought it, with some misgivings, for $13,-500. He at once set about constructing a cotton factory (five stories, 138 by 50 feet), dozens of surrounding tenement houses, and a mansion on the hillside overlooking the new town, which he named Upland (after the old Swedish name for the area). By 1847, when the Crozers moved into their new mansion, there were forty-six tenement houses on flats below them. The mill was an innovative one, for an eighty-horsepower steam engine had been attached to supplement the water power (which was supplied by a precariously long race extending a mile upstream through other men's properties to a remote dam). It had 11 self-acting mules with 3,864 spindles, 7 or 8 throstles with another 2,000 or so spindles, and 150 power looms. In 1849 the enterprise was incorporated and the commissioners were old friends: George Leiper, Edward Darlington, Samuel Edwards, Daniel Lammot, and John Broomall.[4]

The confidence in the township's future displayed by so successful a businessman and banker as John P. Crozer no doubt inspired the other three principal leaders in the restoration of Chester. Thirty-year-old John M. Broomall, prominent and prosperous Quaker defense attorney, now perceived the advantage of investing in the riverfront properties between Chester and Marcus Hook. After prolonged negotiations, in the course of which Edward Darlington acted as counsel (and Darlington had also been involved as trustee of the Flower estate during its transfer to Crozer), in 1849 Broomall was able to purchase a fifty-acre farm on the west side of Chester Creek with Crozer as his partner. In the next several years he and Crozer bought up a string of riverfront farms, almost to the boundaries of Marcus Hook. Broomall and Crozer planned their South Ward real estate development venture carefully, laying out wide streets, building houses and factories and selling the improvements at cost to those without capital, and taking up to 75 percent mortgages on the land itself (it was on the sale of the land that they planned to realize their profits). They were very successful, and in 1855 Broomall was able to buy out Crozer's interest. Broomall also started the restoration of the old Market Square in Chester itself, buying the burned-out store and dwelling of Preston Eyre (Darlington's father-in-law) and eventually embellishing the site with "fine stores of ample dimensions." As the first official city directory put it a few years later, "from this date others multiplied, and a stimulus seemed to have been given to building and trade." And by the same directory of 1859 it was reported that Broomall and Crozer's South Ward development had prospered exceedingly:

Upon this purchase there have been built forty-four brick dwellings, two cotton factories, five cotton and wollen [*sic*] factories, one bleaching and finishing factory, one dyeing factory, one oil mill, one steam saw and planing mill, one sash and door factory, one large seminary, numerous shops, coal and wood yards, three ship yards, and six hundred and ten feet of wharfing, besides other improvements.[5]

The third of the Chester project's entrepreneurs, John Larkin, Jr., had been approached by Broomall with an offer of partnership during the negotiations for the first South Ward farm, but he turned it down. (No hard feelings were involved, evidently, for Broomall a few years later married Larkin's daughter.) Larkin soon after completed the purchase of eighty-three acres of land in the North Ward, including the site of the old racetrack now used as grazing meadows. Like Broomall and Crozer, Larkin laid out and graded the streets and maintained them without township assistance, constructed houses, stores, foundries, shops, and mills, and either sold or leased the properties. By 1881, when he sold the last remaining building lot out of the eighty-three acres, Larkin had built over five hundred houses and places of business (including several large cotton mills).

The fourth of the entrepreneurs was a cotton manufacturer named James Campbell. Campbell was an English weaver, now forty-four, who had emigrated to the United States as a young man. He worked first as loom boss for John S. Phillips at Rockdale and then became manager of James Houghton's factory at Penn's Grove. When Houghton failed in 1837 and removed to New Jersey to re-establish himself in business again, he urged Campbell to go with him. But Campbell declined, no doubt in part because he had married John Garsed's eldest daughter Angelina and they wanted to remain near her family. Angelina's father, who had six new power looms on his hands that insolvent customers had refused to accept, gave his son-in-law the machines and set him up as a manufacturer in one of the vacant buildings at Penn's Grove. He was industrious and successful, even in the midst of the depression, and George G. Leiper (who had earlier helped Crozer to get started in business) now proposed to build a cotton factory at Leiperville on Ridley Creek if Campbell would lease the property. The agreement was made.

Campbell was very successful at Ridley and accumulated "considerable capital." Now, in the early months of 1850, he looked at the central part of Chester and saw the possibility of converting some of the old structures there to manufacturing purposes. In January, when the public buildings were put up for sale after the removal of the county seat to Media, he purchased the old county jail and workhouse. The jail was "a miserable old rat-trap, nearly all the bars of the windows rusted off . . . it could only retain those inmates who were too indolent to make an effort to escape." In March he bought also an old bowling alley adjacent. These buildings he quickly renovated to receive a steam engine and a hundred power looms; in a few years, he had enlarged this factory out to the prison yard walls, and installed Jacquard looms for weaving fancy quilting fabrics. The astonished inhabitants of the borough celebrated the arrival of modern industry with extravagant rhetoric. The *Delaware County Republican* hailed the establishment of Pioneer Mills as a historic event: "In this mill will be the first looms ever set in motion on the spot first occupied as the capital of Pennsylvania, and Mr. Campbell will be the Columbus in manufacturing in Chester." When the machinery was set in motion, a small crowd of Chester's citizens were present. They broke into a cheer and spontaneously sang "Hail Columbia."

Campbell went on to purchase other properties in the borough for cotton weaving and was regarded as the man who made the borough of Chester "into a manufacturing town."

By the eve of the Civil War, the one-time county seat of Chester, with its little fishing village and surrounding township, had indeed been transformed into a major manufacturing center, with an extensive cotton industry, iron foundries, machine shops, furniture factories, and shipyards. Although the persons principally responsible for launching this local economic revolution made money in the process, their motives cannot be regarded as solely economic in the limited sense. The sense of Christian stewardship, and perhaps even a sort of primary creative urge, must have played a part too. Or at least the town liked to think so. When Crozer, for instance, asked, for his share in the South Ward development, only his original investment and 6 percent interest, he was leaving to Broomall a sizable profit. The lands which had been sold by 1855 had brought almost twice what the partners had put in; Crozer could thus have asked for easily double the amount of profit he actually received. When he was reminded of this, he replied "that he had gone into the enterprise not to make money, but to aid in the development of Chester, and that he was quite content that the profits should go to Mr. Broomall, who had done the chief part of the work."[6] Larkin, Broomall, and Campbell also seem to have been motivated as much by a desire to be known by the honorific title of "enterprising men" (to use Broomall's own phrase) as to make a fortune. "Enterprising men" would be praised as those "who made the place what it is." In Crozer's language, they could demonstrate that they had been "good stewards," using their God-given talent for making money in such a way that it benefited the whole community. Broomall's memorialists noted that he always managed his property development program on terms of a liberal character, and although after half a century the company that held the remaining lots eventually sank under a burden of debts abandoned to him by his associates, Broomall left the field with a good name and the gratitude of the community for having created the South Ward. "He battled royally under the load and would have succeeded in carrying it through to a successful conclusion if it had not been for the contraction of values under the slowly gathering financial storm which broke upon the country in 1893."[7]

John Campbell, likewise, lost the Pioneer Mills during the panic of 1857. His eulogist Henry Ashmead, a fellow resident of Chester and county historian, wrote a commendatory account of Campbell's misfortune:

Campbell was very successful, accumulating considerable capital, which he subsequently lost in his effort to develop the borough of Chester into a manufacturing town. His object was attained, hundreds have profited by his endeavours, but in the panic of 1857, when many of the commission-houses with whom he dealt suspended, it embarrassed him, and finally caused his failure. So great had been the struggles to prevent this result that his health broke under the strain, and after several years of almost unintermitting illness, during which his indomitable energy never forsook him, he died, May 14, 1862.[8]

Campbell was not, however, really crushed by the events of 1857, for he continued to operate other mills and continued to serve, along with other men of enterprise, on the town council.[9]

John Larkin's career was uniformly successful. He spent over thirty years developing the North Ward; it was not until 1881 that he sold the last vacant building lot. During much of this time he was a prominent member of the town council and in 1866 he was elected the first mayor of the newly incorporated city. Yet his biographer Ashmead felt obliged to describe him too as a true steward, a man of enterprise struggling to help the people, and suffering mightily in the process.

In the present North Ward, Mr. Larkin, in spite of great opposition, carried out his designs fully. It is related that although he laid out the streets in that part of the town, and dedicated them to the public, the borough authorities refused to keep the highways in repair, and at his own expense he maintained a force of men at work upon them. On one occasion, when a member of the Town Council complained that the streets in the old part of the borough were neglected, contrasting them with those of Larkin-town, which were neat and well kept, and declaring that the public moneys should not all be expended in one locality, another member informed the speaker that Chester had never contributed a dollar for that purpose, and that Mr. Larkin had personally paid for all the highways made, as well as maintaining them in repair. Not only did he do this, but he constantly built houses, stores, foundries, shops, and mills, in conformity with a rule he had adopted at the beginning of his enterprise that every dollar he received from the sale of lands or buildings should be expended in further improvements, and hence, for any person desiring to start in business, he would erect the required structure, and lease it to him or them, with the privilege of purchasing the property at its cost price within ten years. Mr. Larkin has built over five hundred houses and places of business, several being large cotton-mills. In 1881 he sold the last vacant building-lot remaining out of the original eighty-three acres he had bought as an unimproved tract, thirty-one years before.[10]

It is plain that the entrepreneurs who directed the Chester project were not motivated solely by the prospect of personal financial gain. They lived in the communities that they were building; they served the community in public office; they were prepared to accept long delays in realizing limited profits; and in some cases they sacrificed health and wealth together after making substantial contributions to the community's economic progress.

The Rise of Workingmen to Wealth
in the Rockdale District

There was no such dramatic a program of capital investment in the already established Rockdale manufacturing district as there was at Chester; but there was a noticeable expansion of some of the old mills. Daniel Lammot's new mill, of course, had already been built in 1838; his daughter Margaretta du Pont, on visiting it, exclaimed, "I could never imagine a cotton mill to be in such order and cleanliness."[11] Samuel Riddle substantially enlarged the Penn's Grove mill in 1845. Bernard McCready, the Norristown manufacturer, upon purchasing the Old Sable property from Richard S. Smith in 1845, erected a new spinning mill to complement Phillips and Lewis' old weaving mill. And, about 1851, after the death of Peter Hill, Daniel Lammot finally removed his manufacturing operation to another mill on the Brandywine, where so many relatives and friends lived, leaving the mill at Lenni to be leased to the growing textile empire of General Robert S. Patterson.

More significant of the changing times, perhaps, was the fact that in this decade of general prosperity, more and more working people were crossing class lines to become merchants and manufacturers. This was not a new phenomenon, of course. John P. Crozer was not born in poverty; but his father had been a carpenter and an unsuccessful farmer, whose son's wealth and prominence were earned by years of hard work. Similarly the Riddles, although they came of gentle stock in Northern Ireland, had arrived in the United States with no more than a few dollars, and had succeeded in cotton manufacturing by dint of strenuous exertions of their own. And we have already met James Campbell, the Callaghans, the Morrises, Mark Wild, and Archibald McDowell, who by dint of steady application, frugality, and saving ways—and the kindly intervention of friends and kinsmen—had accumulated enough capital to move up from the operative's level to that of the farmer or manufacturer. But let us now look more closely at the cases of two Rockdale operatives, Abraham Blakeley and John B. Rhodes, who rose to degrees of wealth that approached even the Riddles' and the Crozers'.

Abraham Blakeley was a Lancashire weaver who had emigrated to the United States in 1828 at the age of twenty-two. After employment as a weaver in Germantown and Pottsville, in 1833 he came to West Branch as Crozer's weaving foreman. In 1836 he married an Irish woman, who died in about a year, leaving him with an infant son. In 1838 he married Maria Miles, the protégée of Sophie du Pont. He worked diligently for Crozer, saved his money, and in 1846 formed a partnership with Phineas Lownes to manufacture cotton at Knowlton, buying the machinery and leasing the factory from Crozer. The business flourished. In 1853 Blakeley sold his interest and next year removed to a new three-story brick mill, 100 by 45 feet, erected for him by John Larkin in the North Ward development. In this move he again had the assistance of a partner (perhaps Larkin himself) but in 1857 he was able to buy out this gentleman's interest. He now embarked on the manufacture of work cloth—tickings, denims, and stripes —entirely on his own. The business prospered and grew until eventually "Blakeley and Sons" of Arasapha Mills were employing 200 hands in half a dozen buildings with 8,500 spindles and 276 looms, all powered by a Corliss steam engine. Finally he purchased Bishop Potter's mansion and moved into it with his family.

Blakeley followed the classic line of career development. First he was a capable weaver, then a loom boss, then a partner in a small leased factory, and ultimately the owner of a large establishment. When he entered upon manufacturing at Knowlton, he took on the superintendence of the Baptist Sunday School there. Upon his removal to Chester as a successful business-man, he shifted his allegiance to the Methodist Episcopal Church, becoming a leading lay worker, trustee, and steward. In politics he was a Whig and then a Republican, and he served for many years on the Chester City Council. He produced nine children and cared for his wife's sister, Sarah Miles, who was not married and lived with the Blakeleys. A few years before his death in 1886, he received the standard encomium from the city's historian due to a man of enterprise: "Mr. Blakeley has since his residence in Chester been among its most enterprising and public-spirited citizens, and has contributed largely to the building up of its trade and its importance as a manufacturing center."[12]

Maria Miles was, at the time of her marriage, to use her own phrase, a "poor desolate orphan," who recalled with gratitude the instruction she had been given by the benevolent Sophie du Pont and Victorine Bauduy at the Brandywine Manufacturers' Sunday School and the training in sewing and tailoring she and her sister had acquired with their help. Sophie and Clementina kept in touch with the Miles girls, both before and after Maria's marriage, and Maria, and later her daughter Sophia du Pont Blakeley, continued the correspondence. The changing style of the letters reflects the strains involved in the social transformation from a destitute orphan working in a weaving factory to the respected wife of one of Chester's leading citizens.

Maria's first letter to "My dear teacher" was written in 1835 when she was twenty years old. The hand was childish and unformed, the spelling uncertain, punctuation completely absent, and she signed herself "your old hooler Maria Miles." The burden of the message was the gratitude of the "poor desolate orphans" ("we shall never be abel to repay you") and their acceptance of Sophie's plans to send Sarah out to learn "the tayloring trade." The tone was almost obsequious: "you can do what you think best for us."[13] Another letter in 1836 expressed similar dependency and an almost masochistic acceptance of misfortune: "i think on my dear mother often but i have found tis good for me to bear my father rod afflication makes me learn his law. . . ."[14] After that there was a long lapse in the correspondence until she and her husband were established in the business at Knowlton. Then the letters to her "Dear Friend" resumed, now written in a firm and more sharply slanted hand, with almost perfect English grammar and spelling. The Lammots figured as mutual friends; Sophie du Pont was sending presents to her namesake, who was about four years old. And along with family news, a more formal kind of ceremonial religious compliment made its appearance in Maria's communications:

> above all I do feel very thankful that you still keep remembering me at a throne of grace—I often think of you in my prayers and hope to see you again soon but if not permitted to see your friendly face in this World I will try by God's assistance to meet you in our Father's kingdom where parting will be no more—[15]

Thereafter through the years of the Civil War she and Sophie exchanged letters, gifts, prayers, and religious sentiments. Maria was determined to raise her children "in the fear of the Lord." Gradually Maria's hand became stronger and the tone more egalitarian. The last letter, in 1862, assumed the idiom of equality that characterized Clementina's correspondence. Maria had found a "suitable girl" to work in Sophie's household, who was "over forty, and very respectable and pious." If Sophie wanted to take her, then either sister Sarah, or namesake Sophie, or Maria herself "will come down with her to see you," and "the family join in sending their love to yourself and sister."[16]

The second case is that of John B. Rhodes, who was born in Rockdale in 1829. His grandfather had come to the United States in 1827 (to be drowned, with two of his daughters, in the flood of 1843) and his father had arrived the year after. The father worked in Phillips' weaving mill and young John commenced working there too at the tender age of six, "with a view" (as his biographer expressed it) "to becoming proficient in that branch of industry." Working in the various departments of the weaving mill, and going to school at night, he gradually acquired both money and knowledge. In 1850, as soon as he attained his majority, he married a local girl (Bishop Potter performed the ceremony) and in the same year became a storekeeper in Crozerville, where his father (although still an operative) had purchased a piece of property. The store prospered, and in 1864 John and his brother Samuel bought Aston Mills (about a mile up the creek from West Branch) and converted it into a cotton and woolen weaving factory. Eventually the Rhodes firm was to acquire both Knowlton and West Branch from the Crozers.

As with the other self-made men in the district, John B. Rhodes did not restrict himself to business associations. He was active in the affairs of the Oddfellows Benevolent Lodge, No. 40, of Aston (founded in 1831 by his father and others prepared to defy the general anti-secret society sentiment of the Anti-Masons). In politics he was, after the war, a Democrat, and he was a delegate to the party's national convention in 1876. Throughout his early years he was active in the affairs of Calvary Church (although later on he joined the Methodists). Indeed, he and Thomas Blackburn, an operative at Rockdale, achieved lasting, if humorous, notoriety in the annals of Calvary Church for having at their own expense installed an old second-hand church clock in the tower. The clock's bell tolled the hour "with commendable exactness" for several months. But then something went wrong:

> . . . one Sunday morning, just as the Rector announced his text, the clock began to strike. It continued to strike until it had tolled off a hundred and gave every evidence that it would strike a thousand. Mr. Rhodes, who was in the congregation, could stand it no longer. Rising from his pew he ran through the church up into the steeple and stopped the untruthful timepiece, bringing to an end its existence, once and for all.[17]

The pattern of success for such working people in Rockdale, including others who were mentioned earlier, is a consistent one. They were highly skilled operatives, who worked hard, saved their money, invested the capital in a farm or business (often with the help of relatives or of a benevolent established merchant or manufacturer), and earned the trust of the community by probity in financial dealings, conspicuous activity in the church, and performing public service when asked. It would be impossible to estimate what proportions of any cohort of young operatives, entering work in the mill in any one year, would eventually succeed as landowners, merchants, or manufacturers in later years. Few, of course, could achieve as high a level of success as the Crozers, the Campbells, the Riddles, the Blakelys, and the Rhodeses. But the high visibility of these few self-made men gave reality to the claim of Christian capitalism that America was an open society where any man of talent, ambition, and good will could make money and contribute to the development of the community. Many more must have succeeded in a lesser way, for the scale of industry and commerce was still small enough to permit a workingman to enter the ranks of the capitalists with no more money than what he and his wife had saved from wages and boarders' rent.

THE POLITICS OF THE MANUFACTURING INTEREST

One issue upon which almost all manufacturers had agreed, from the beginning of the republic, was the need for a protective tariff. It was the continuing dispute between northern cotton manufacturers and southern cotton growers about this tariff which, in various permutations and escalations, for many years maintained the polarization of the states that eventually made the war inevitable.

The Protective Tariff

In Delaware County, the tariff issue was, along with anti-Masonry, the central political theme of the 1820's and early 1830's. The people of the Rockdale manufacturing district were principal figures in the effort to ensure that Congress established and maintained a high tariff on imported cotton goods in order to protect their yarns and fabrics from British competition. The manufacturers bitterly recalled the years after the War of 1812 when the British had attempted to stifle the American textile industry. British goods were dumped on American docks in huge quantities, to be sold at auction at prices so low that American factories could not compete. Hundreds of businesses were ruined. As a result demands were of course made for a more adequately protective schedule of import duties. But merchants and farmers, who profited most in a situation where they could sell American agricultural products and raw materials to England with minimum duties and could purchase English manufactured goods cheaply in return, resisted raising American duties on English goods. After years of controversy, Congress finally passed (with the prodding of Pennsylvania senators and representatives) the significant tariff act of 1824. Henry Clay, in the debates about the issue, coined the phrase "American System" to denote a national policy combining protective tariffs and internal improvements with due concern for the interests of merchants and farmers. It was in 1825, the year after the establishment of the first meaningful protective tariff, that John P. Crozer and John S. Phillips and his brother-in-law commenced their manufacturing of cotton on Chester Creek, thus establishing the Rockdale manufacturing district.

Conflict in Congress over the protective tariff remained at a feverish pitch for the next generation, southern planters and many northern farmers and merchants favoring a low protective tariff, or even a tariff for revenue only, and the manufacturers of textiles, iron, and other products threatened by European competition demanding high protective walls. Although the protective tariff had its ups and downs during the years before the Civil War (when a high protective tariff was again imposed), the rates on cottons mostly fluctuated between about 20 and 30 percent *ad valorem.* This level of protection was adequate to prevent the British from dumping huge quantities of cheap, low-quality goods on the market and in effect restricted importers to the better quality goods, made from mulespun yarns of higher count than were usually produced in American mills. But variations, or threatened variations, even within this range were sufficient to arouse intense political activity.

In the Rockdale district and along the Brandywine, the cotton manufacturers, and as many workers as they could manage to carry with them, were staunch partisans of Henry Clay and his "American System." Clay was an occasional visitor to both the Brandywine and Chester Creek, and one of the mills on the Brandywine was named for him. In December 1833, when agitation over the tariff was at its height, the friends of Henry Clay at Chester learned that their man was making a brief visit to Philadelphia on his way to Washington. At once a committee was appointed "to wait on him, and request him to visit the Borough of Chester, on his way to the seat of Government, to afford themselves and their fellow citizens of Delaware County, an opportunity of personally paying their respects to him, as a testimony of their sense of his private worth and public usefulness." The ten-man invitation committee, which included William Martin and one of Peter Hill's brothers, was successful, and Henry Clay visited Chester, to enjoy a reception organized by a local arrangements committee of thirty that included most of the Chester Creek manufacturers, among them James Willcox, Dennis Kelly, John P. Crozer, Daniel Lammot, and John S. Phillips. Clay, upon alighting from the steamboat, was received at a public house by, as the normally Democratic *Upland Union* noted, "a large assemblage of the citizens of this county, without distinctions of party," and he remained long enough to shake hands with all and partake of the refreshments.[1]

The absence of the Riddles on the occasion of Clay's visit was not evidence of any reluctance on their part to express themselves in favor of the tariff. When in 1832 Secretary of the Treasury Louis McLane (an erstwhile Brandywine cotton manufacturer) made a survey of the nation's manufacturing establishments for the purpose of providing Congress with evidence of the need for a protective tariff, the Riddles wrote a vigorous response to local commissioners agents Matthew Carey and C. C. Biddle:

CHESTER CREEK, March 28, 1832.
GENTLEMEN: Although we believe that some of the queries proposed in the letter which we have received from you, are very improper, inasmuch as they have a direct tendency to expose to public view a person's private affairs; and further, it is easily discovered they have proceeded from a source unfriendly to the manufacturers' interest; yet we hasten to answer them, in consideration of their being sent you, gentlemen, who are well known to have been the long tried friends of our country's best interest. We would, therefore, deem it highly improper to pass by your communication without noticing it. But we would wish to mention a few thoughts that crossed our minds whilst reading these queries that have emanated from the Treasury Department. If we can gather any thing from the apparent bearing of them, the design is, first, to ascertain the least possible profit the manufacturer can, by any means, carry on with. Secondly, to find out the least possible wages the working class can live upon; and thus by measuring out and dividing a bare subsistence to each class connected with manufacturing, the protective duties could be lowered; the system of tyranny that disgraces the factories in England could be introduced; children would have to do the work that young women does now; young women would have to do the work that men does now; and bye and bye petitions would be carried into Congress (similar to the one Mr. Saddler took into the House of Commons a few months ago) "stating the cruelties practised on children in the factories." Gentlemen, the tariff cannot be lowered, unless the working class is reduced to the same state of degradation, poverty, and wretchedness, as they are in England; then, and only then, can the American manufacturer enter into the lists of competition with his foreign rival, or else there can be no manufacturing establishment carried on. Reduce the tariff, and at once you stop every cotton manufactory in our State. . . . Reduce the tariff and unfurl the banner of "free trade," and then we'll have a beggared starving population, without a sufficiency to procure the necessaries of existence; and

then we may lay on poor rates, build poor houses, erect penitentiaries, get an armed police, additional constables—standing army—erect gallowses, &c.; all this will follow in the train of the contemplated reductions in the protection of American industry. The spirit of every noble-minded citizen revolts at the idea of sacrificing our working population to the idol of foreign policy, or taking the bread out of the mouths of their children, and giving it to the supporters and menials of aristocratic tyranny. Gentlemen, you'll pardon us for obtruding these remarks upon your time.

> With much deference, we respectfully
> remain your obedient servants,
> SAMUEL & JAMES RIDDLE

To Messrs. MATHEW CAREY, CLEMENT C. BIDDLE

In response to the question, "Would reducing the tariff on cotton to 12.5% cause you to abandon your business or manufacture at reduced prices?" the Riddles replied:

29th. Most assuredly it would not only cause but force me to abandon my machinery, which would be valueless, as well as my business. Who would take the lease of my mill off my hands? Who would pay a $1,000 a year for a place that had to be abandoned? Who would consume the farmers' productions, &c?

"If you had to abandon your business," they were asked, "how would you employ your capital?" They replied:

30th. What capital would we have to employ in another business, when it is invested in machinery, water power, buildings, &c? These would be rendered valueless at once. Capital as well as business would be destroyed, and every individual who owned machinery would be ruined. They might take them to England, and try to sell them there, for they would be of no value in America; or, I might say rather in the free States; perhaps the experiment might be tried to work them with the slave population, in order to keep pace with the improvements of England in cheapening labor and grinding the faces of the poor.

And, asked whether they could turn to a more profitable pursuit if the tariff were reduced, they answered sarcastically:

31st. If we were forced to abandon our business, and consequently our establishments, although there is many businesses as profitable as ours at present, how could we engage in any? We might go with the Indians beyond the Mississippi.

Crozer, who also replied to the same questionnaire, was more temperate, contenting himself with the matter-of-fact observation that if the tariff were reduced to 12 1/2 percent, he would be compelled to abandon his business, his machinery would be of no value (because no one else would be able to manufacture cotton), and "I think there are few pursuits so uninviting as cotton spinning would then become."[2]

Between elections, the conventional way for political advocates to attempt to influence Congress was to present petitions, and this was the course which the Rockdale manufacturers took in concert with others of Delaware County. The years 1832 and 1833, while President Jackson was trying (ultimately successfully) to persuade Congress to reduce the tariffs to a level commensurate with the Treasury's needs for revenue, were a time of intense petitioning. The method employed by the proponents of a position was to call a public meeting at a house or inn, and elect a chairman (or a president and vice-presidents), a secretary, and a committee to draft the resolution. The resolution, quickly composed (more likely prepared in advance), would then pass unanimously and in succeeding days might be carried about the county to collect signatures. Finally, the petition would be carried to Washington to the district's representative, who would submit it to Congress. Tariff petitions were regularly bi-partisan, the request of signatories acting as individuals rather than as representatives of a Democratic, Federalist, Whig, or Anti-Masonic party.

Two pro-tariff petitions were submitted to Congress from Delaware County, the first in June 1832 and the second in February 1833. Daniel Lammot was a member of the first committee on resolutions, along with George W. Hill, Dr. George Smith, and Preston Eyre. The secretaries, who would transmit the resolutions to Congress, were James Willcox and Samuel Edwards.[3] The petition respectfully drew the attention of Congress to the present prosperity of the country under the benevolent protection of the tariff, and urged defeat of the bill currently before Congress that proposed a reduction in the rates—a move "calculated to spread ruin and disaster amongst us."[4] At the second tariff meeting, Daniel Lammot was chairman and George W. Hill secretary; the committee to prepare resolutions consisted of John S. Phillips, John P. Crozer, George G. Leiper, and two other businessmen. This petition, in addition to urging the retention of the moderate import duties provided in the act of 1832, pointedly attacked southern opposition to the very principle of the protective tariff and the imminent danger of abandoning the tariff altogether:

This law, passed after long debate and great deliberation, and not yet in operation, is to be superseded by one of obvious hostility to the best interests of our country. And what is the cause of this ruinous measure now urged upon Congress? Is the violent clamor of South Carolina sufficient cause? Have any facts been adduced to prove that the South is oppressed by the operation of the tariff? It is, however, demanded that the principle of protection be abandoned. The principle of protection had been too distinctly given in the constitution, and affirmed by legislation, for the last forty years, to admit of any doubt or cavil at this time. A sense of justice will at all times cause us to respect the rights of others; but, in doing so, we ask that our rights should be respected also.

The complaining States have lately been clamorous against the tariff as oppressive, unjust, and unequal; the catalogue of opprobious epithets has been exhausted against the manufacturers, a class of citizens called to their present pursuits by the voice of the nation, encouraged to perseverance by every administration from that of Washington to the present; and now, after a lapse of many years, and after investments amounting to more than two hundred millions of dollars, they are to be sacrificed, and for what? To silence the arrogant demands of South Carolina. . . .[5]

The offensive bill was nonetheless passed, reducing the *ad valorem* rates on cottons and woolens to a level below that of 1816.

The tariff issue was powerful enough even to distract the mind of a rejected suitor. When in January 1832 John S. Phillips, after a prolonged series of courting visits to Sophie on the Brandywine, at last "popped the question" (as Eleuthera put it) through Sophie's father, he was refused by Sophie—and the topic of conversation between Phillips and her father then shifted to the tariff! The scene was described in an amusing letter by Eleuthera to her sister Victorine:

> . . . After he had sat there some time Mr P. told him that he must be aware that for the last 18 months he had been attached to his daughter that he had not spoken before because he was not in circumstances to marry and that now he was in a situation when he could make a wife happy & comfortable. He then began to give Papa a description of his fortune which Papa interrupted by assuring him that was of no consequence that he never had influenced his children and they were perfectly free to choose for themselves. Mr P still persisting in going on Papa told him Mr P am I to understand that you wish me to communicate yr intention to my daughter "Yes Sir said Mr P.—Papa & he then talked on other matters. . . . [After dinner] Papa with g' delicacy said "Mr P. I thought best after what you told me this morning to go and see my daughter, She bade me say that she was grateful for the proof of esteem you have given her but that she cannot return the sentiments of attachment you

have for her—Papa paused—he gave a grunt—a dead pause ensued—
"Mr Phillips said Papa I hope that this will not make any difference in
our friendship"—not a word did he say—When Papa saw this he took
up a newspaper and read a few minutes then addressed the knight on
the subject of the tariff on which they talked as if nothing had occured we
soon returned and talked about the roads yr letters &c till Wildfire coming
to the door. . . . He took his leave. . . .

And Eleuthera added, "In all this affair what shocks Sophy most is the
grunt."[6]

The Second Bank of the United States
and the Delaware County Memorial

Equal, for a time, to the tariff in the intensity of emotion it aroused, but
shorter-lived as an issue, was the controversy surrounding Congress's refusal to recharter the Second Bank of the United States, and the Jackson
administration's withdrawal of federal deposits from its vaults. The manufacturers were for the most part in support of the Bank, which seemed to
them to serve as a brake on cycles of irresponsible speculation, and then
depreciation, and thus as some sort of guard against financial panics. In the
early months of 1834, as business generally declined under burden of a
widespread anxiety about the federal bank policy, the Chester Creek manufacturers wrote desperate letters to Edward Darlington, their representative
in Congress, who regularly sent them alarming news from the seat of
government. Samuel and James Riddle expressed themselves, as was their
style, in hyperbolic, even apocalyptic, imagery:

. . . never was a period in the history of our country when it could be
said with more truth "we are in the midst of a revolution" than the
present period. The Demon of the storm is up furiously draging onward
the Revolutionary cart driven by the Spirit of Party the fierce, revengeful,
implacable, unmerciful, unreasonable, Spirit of Party crushing beneath its
angry wheels our Country's boast—our Country's Glory. What makes
her loved at home and never abroad. The good of the people is no longer
the rallying point for which everything of less importance is sacrifice.
High handed measures of vindictive revenge against anti-Partisans seems
to be the order of the day, and upon the altar of this Molock must be
sacrificed the Peace, the happiness, the industry of the people to gratify
the unholy ungovernable vengeance of this incensed *Deity.* . . .[7]

Crozer, less given to dramatic language, merely alluded to "the unhappy experiment of our infatuated president," and sent Darlington a census of unemployment in the Rockdale mills.[8]

In March 1834, "a very large and highly respectable" group of citizens of Delaware County assembled, without distinction of party, to consider "the propriety of the measures adopted by the Executive of the United States in relation to the removal of the deposites [*sic*] of the public money from the Bank of the United States." The usual names of manufacturers occurred among the lists of officers and committee members: John P. Crozer, William Martin, Daniel Lammot, George Escol Sellers. The proceedings drew attention to the financial distress already affecting the county and predicted (correctly) "that still greater and lasting evils are in store for the people." This new memorial pointed out that all classes of persons suffered:

> . . . that the citizens of Delaware county are engaged in trade, agriculture, and manufactures; that, independent of all other capital employed in their various pursuits, there is in the county upwards of $1,500,000 invested in manufactures, producing annually a manufactured property to the value of $2,000,000 and upwards, giving employ to about fifteen hundred people, the whole of which business, in consequence of the present state of the currency and alarm, is on the very brink of total prostration; a number of the manufactories have already stopped, and the hands without employ or the means of support; agricultural produce daily depreciating, and the country swarming with laborers seeking employ.

The petition asked for the rechartering of the Bank and the return of the Treasury deposits, and objected to the tyrannical, vindictive, unconstitutional actions of the chief executive. It also took time to reprove the President for his ignorance of elementary economic principles: *"Resolved,* That the doctrine entertained and expressed by General Jackson, that all who trade on borrowed capital ought to fail, is unworthy and unbecoming a Chief Magistrate of an enlightened, business, and enterprising people."

This time the petition was submitted to Congress with about 2,500 signatures from across the county. The same familiar names appeared again: James Houghton, John S. Phillips, John Garsed, Nathan Sellers, Charles Kelly, Samuel and James Riddle, John P. Crozer, Daniel Lammot. And next to the names of the manufacturers were set the names of their senior male employees, the mule spinners, machinists, loom bosses, and carding masters. Although a pro-Jackson petition was also produced on the same day, it carried few signatures and was evidently the work largely of the Democratic Party faithful. It is clear that the vast majority of the male workers in the Delaware County mills favored the recharter of the Second Bank on the basis of the immediately felt economic distress that followed the removal of the deposits.

*To the Senate
and House of Representatives
of the United States:*

The memorial of the undersigned, citizens of the county of Delaware, in Pennsylvania,

RESPECTFULLY SHOWETH:

That your memorialists are *farmers, manufacturers, mechanics, merchants,* and *laborers.* That they have heretofore prospered in their several pursuits, and from the sound and healthy state of business amongst them, they had reason to expect continued prosperity. But, in the midst of these expectations, they have suddenly experienced a distressing reverse; a few months ago every branch of trade was active; now, many of our mechanics are without employment, our manufactories some of them closed entirely, others partially suspended operations, and many of them preparing to wind up their business, should Congress do nothing to relieve them. Our merchants unable to collect their bills; the price of agricultural products rapidly declining; a great reduction in wages, and the certainty of many hundreds being left without employment. Thus, in a few short months, your memorialists have passed from a condition of enviable prosperity, to one of distress and threatening ruin.

The number of signatures amounted to about 15 percent of the total population of the county, about 30 percent of the male population of the county, and probably 60 or 70 percent of the adult male population. The Delaware County Memorial was formally presented to Congress by Edward Darlington; it was the first time the county's representative had spoken from the floor of the House.[9]

The methods of some of the manufacturers in securing this appearance of consensus were somewhat exploitive. The Riddles paid their mule spinners $6 apiece (a week's wages) to attend the meeting and sign their names.[10] Others were less gentle in their usages. Six years later, in the depths of the depression that the manufacturers blamed on Jackson's tariff, banking, and hard money policies, and in a presidential election year, the Democratic *Upland Union* charged the manufacturers in the Rockdale district with refusing to hire any but anti-Jackson men. It was a scathing column:

TYRANNY—PROSCRIPTION. A laboring man of this county having heard that a wealthy manufacturer on Chester Creek, wanted to employ hands in his business, offered his services to him. The federalist and manufacturer commenced with the usual cant phrases of hard times: the "government is ruining the manufacturers, paralyzing business, breaking the banks, in favor of a gold and silver currency," &c &c, and we can't afford to hire labor. Very well said the laborer, you do not wish to hire me, so good by. Stop, stop said the manufacturer, we want a hand or two, but what are your politics? We want no hands about us but what are opposed to the Government. The laborer indignant at this insulting attack upon his feelings & principles, the blood boiling in his veins, rose and said, "Sir, I have always voted the democratic ticket, and intend to do so again—so good by to you."

The paper thundered warnings of retribution to come at the polls to this manufacturer ("an unfeeling slave to the old doctrines of Federalism")— a retribution that would fall on all the manufacturers as a result of their "violence and proscription to American citizens." A few months later, the same paper accused the manufacturers on Chester Creek of practicing "white slavery" by forcing their workers to vote against the Democratic ticket. An anecdote was told of "an extensive manufacturer and a bank director" (who could have been none other than John P. Crozer) who "exulted in the declaration that all his hands were against Van Buren except one, and that he should also vote against him in the election. Only think of the humiliating position of a man pretending to some character, who would make such a boast?" Another manufacturer, alleged to have been in his cups at the time, was said to have approved Crozer's boast, and to have given it as his own opinion that workers should be fired if they refused to vote according to their master's will.

Finally in July (as election time neared) the *Union* took direct aim at "The Manufacturers" in an editorial explaining that the Democrats were pro-tariff but anti-Bank (because the Bank was setting itself above the government). And again a certain manufacturer and bank director was arraigned (no doubt Crozer once more):

Shortly before the governor's election, he told his hands with apparent disinterestedness that, "I know you are free men, and have a right to vote for whom you please, but unless you vote as I do, our business will be injured and I will have to discharge you."

The *Union* demanded legislative investigation of such practices.[11]

The Transformation of Issues and the Conservation of Sides:
Tariff, Free Soil, and Slavery

In the 1820's and 1830's, while the northern manufacturers were struggling on weekdays against southern planters about the tariff and against Democrats about the Bank, they were also, in their evangelical mode, on Sundays combating the infidels and Utopian socialists, who were likewise in favor of free trade (because it promised lower prices to the workers) and against monopolies (like the Second Bank of the United States). Evangelical capitalism thus found itself fighting at the side of a motley band of allies against a confusing array of enemies, and experimenting with a variety of political vehicles, before, in the 1850's, a viable Republican Party was able to enlist broad popular support for a national policy congenial to the manufacturing interest. The Federalists, the anti-Jackson Democrats, the Anti-Masons, the National Republicans, and the Whigs all for a time gave expression to the manufacturers' values. But the values of a dominant national party had to represent more than the transparent self-interest of the manufacturer in having a good transportation system, a protective tariff, a stable currency, and a dependable work force. In order to achieve national support, the manufacturers' values had to be anchored in a social issue of paramount national concern. That issue was the politicization of the moral struggle between north and south over the extension (or contraction) of slavery.

The northern cotton manufacturer at the beginning of the century had been able to ignore the moral paradox implicit in his business. He deplored on principle, either as an evangelical Christian or a free-enquiring radical, the system of slavery. But that did not mean that he was an abolitionist or that he liked blacks, whether free or slave. He knew that the bales of raw cotton he took into his mill were produced by southern black slaves and that their price would be higher, and his profits lower, if they were to be produced by white farm labor paid at northern rates. Furthermore, the southern plantation was a major customer for his own product, which was used (in different qualities, of course) to clothe both slaves and masters. The cotton-manufacturing industry in the north, employing relatively highly paid white operatives, was inextricably bound in a reciprocal trade relationship (via intermediary merchant houses) with the slave-operated cotton plantations in the south. The expansion of the northern industry required, and resulted in, the expansion of the cotton plantation system and the extension of slavery. Thus it was emotionally necessary to dissociate the moral issue of slavery from the economic realities of manufacturing cotton.

The initial conflict in this economic compact had to do not with slavery but with the tariff on foreign imports. The plantation owner saw himself as having little to gain from a protective tariff to protect the northern customers for his cotton, for he could dispose of his cotton to English and other foreign markets (and even if rarely done, construct cotton factories run by slave labor himself). The tariff simply raised his costs and invited retaliation against his own export. The long years of debate over the tariff resulted in a series of compromises that permitted both sections to prosper. But the acrimony of the arguments had established, by the early 1830's, an awareness of tension, a choosing of sides on the basis of regional interests, that promised to make other issues more difficult to resolve. And, one may suspect, both sides also had increasingly to deal with a sense of moral dissonance. The southern planter, Christian or Deist, needed to justify slavery; the northern manufacturer, evangelical or Unitarian, needed to justify his ignoring of slavery.

The arrival of increasing thousands of immigrants in America, many of whom served for a time as operatives in cotton mills and then moved on to buy farms and businesses in the west, added a new ingredient to the situation. As the lands in the midwestern states were purchased from the Indian tribes who inhabited them or were acquired by conquest from Mexico, thousands of working people spent their savings to buy land. Workers in cotton mills did not feel chained to their machines for a lifetime of drudgery; they could put up with hard working conditions because they knew that they could, if all went well, move west in a few years as homesteaders on virgin land. The only condition that could block the movement was the pre-emption of large areas for cotton plantations and farms operated by slave labor. Small farmers could not compete with slaveowners in the same markets. Northern opposition to the south thus took on an added economic dimension. Not only were the manufacturers constrained to resist southern demands for lower tariffs; their workers, however they felt about the tariff, wanted to move into states and territories where the soil was free. The struggle over the constitutions of new states, slave or free, was not merely a matter of ensuring balance in the voting power of the sections in Congress. The availability of free soil was functionally necessary to the manufacturing interest because it contributed to the maintenance of a highly productive factory labor force with high morale. Thus the initial transformation of the tariff issue was into a regional issue that involved free soil as well as productive tariffs. By espousing free soil as part of their program, the manufacturers were in fact (whether intentionally or not) bringing to their side politically large numbers of working people whose dream it was to save money from factory wages in order to buy a western farm.

With northern manufacturers and workers solidly aligned on the tariff and free soil issues, with the south as common enemy, all that was needed to cement the alliance was a sense of moral outrage at the south. This was encouraged by the various movements that aimed at improving the status of blacks and reversing the history of slavery. From the highly conservative contributors to the American Colonization Society to the radical Garrisonian abolitionists, there came into existence a spectrum of organizations which had as a common theme the righting of the wrongs done to black slaves by southern planters. Such a moral theme could assure the northern cotton manufacturer and his operatives that they were not responsible for the evils of slavery (even though they indirectly profited from it). And it would provide a common target of displaced resentment (using the south as scapegoat) in a situation of potential labor conflict.

The transformation of political issues from the 1820's to the 1850's, insofar as they were experienced by the cotton manufacturers and their workers, was from disagreement with the south over the tariff, and resentment of the extremely belligerent style of southern rhetoric, to political struggles with the south over free soil, to moral condemnation of the south for the sin of slavery. The functional advantages of this transformation were obvious: it consolidated the workers and the manufacturers in a political and economic alliance and contributed to two decades of relative labor peace. The disadvantage was not foreseen: the continuing escalation of an increasingly moralistic conflict between the regions that placed in jeopardy the whole "American System."

The Manufacturer-Politicians

The manufacturers to a man considered that it was their responsibility to influence events at the seats of government. There were three levels of political activity open to them. The minimal level involved voting, influencing the votes of others (by gentle persuasion or threats), organizing petition meetings, and signing petitions. All of the manufacturers were active on this level. The next step was to engage in political party activities, such as serving as a delegate or a member of a committee, and to accept township and county administrative positions (such as on the school board). At least nine of the cotton manufacturers were active on this level during much of their lives; of these William Martin, Edward Darlington, and James and Samuel Riddle were most prominent. And three of these last four were also, at one time or another, prominent on the third level as candidates for, or holders of, elective office at the state or national level.

Samuel Riddle represents the second level. His political profile was relatively inconspicuous (although one of his biographers inaccurately claimed that he was so busy in promoting the high tariff that he had "presided over all the tariff meetings in Delaware county since the commencement of the agitation").[12] He was appointed U.S. postmaster at Penn's Grove in 1842 (later marrying the daughter of a postmistress from Chester) and retained the post until his death in 1887. From 1844 to 1848 he served as one of the elected directors of the public schools for Middletown Township. (Six others of the manufacturers were elected to the school boards of the two townships.) In 1849 he joined the Hibernian Society, a quasi-political ethnic organization which worked to improve the condition of Irish immigrants, attended its meetings regularly, and for a time served on its committee on finances. (He probably also helped to organize the local chapter of the Society which eventually, in 1892, built a brick hall for its meetings at Rockdale, just across the street from Calvary Church.) And he was active enough in conservative politics to serve as a delegate to the 1856 Whig state convention in Harrisburg, along with his friend Edward Darlington.[13] Samuel Riddle's brother James did not become active politically until he moved to the Brandywine; he was an unsuccessful candidate on the Republican ticket for governor of the State of Delaware.[14]

William Martin had a more illustrious career in politics. He started out as a Federalist, spending the 1827–28 term in the House of Representatives in Harrisburg; thereafter he was prominent in county politics as a chief burgess of the Borough of Chester and an organizer of tariff and bank petitions; after his removal to Philadelphia as director of the Delaware Mutual Insurance Company, he was active in public school affairs, for a time serving as president of the Philadelphia School Board. During Martin's term in the state legislature, the two leading questions were the program of internal improvements by canal and railroad, and a system of free public schools for the children of the state—particularly the children in cotton-manufacturing districts. Martin was, as his voting record shows, a consistent supporter of the extension of the canal system and he voted in favor of issuing a charter for the proposed new Pennsylvania Railroad. He voted regularly in favor of acts to encourage Pennsylvania agriculture and manufactures.[15] The event of which he was most proud, however, was his association with Thaddeus Stevens in introducing a bill to establish "the public school system" in Pennsylvania. According to Martin's son, Stevens asked Martin to prepare such a bill. Martin accordingly drew up "An Act to provide for the education of children employed in manufactories; and also to ascertain the extent and increase of said manufactories in this commonwealth." It was introduced as Bill No. 80 by Thaddeus Stevens. After prolonged debate and agonized opposition by representatives from other manufacturing districts, the bill passed the House, but so late in the session that the Senate did not act on it and it failed to become law. It is said to have served, however, as the basis for the successful act of 1834 establishing a public school system in the State of Pennsylvania.[16]

By all odds the most consistent and successful political career among the early manufacturing group was that of Edward Darlington. We have already noticed some of his activities in the political arena at the time of the furor against Freemasonry. But his career, although not a notable one in political histories of the state, exhibits clearly the transformation of issues, and the evolution of political philosophy, of the economic group whom he represented in a series of elective and appointive offices.

Basically Edward Darlington was a Delaware County Court House lawyer. He read law under Samuel Edwards, a respected Democrat who had himself served terms in both the state and national legislatures. Although Edwards did not hold elective office thereafter, he was, along with the Leiper brothers, one of the Democratic Party leaders in the county, and he was a personal friend of James Buchanan, with whom he had served in the House. Edwards served, like William Martin, as chief burgess of the city for a couple of years, and from 1838 to 1842 he held the sinecure position of Inspector of Customs at the port of Chester (an ancient sinecure indeed, for Chester's international trade had been largely pre-empted by Philadelphia a century before).[17] With Edwards as his mentor and associate in legal practice, Darlington entered county politics as a Democratic Party worker, and by 1825 was serving as secretary at party assemblages. But by 1828 his position had shifted to the right and he participated in a political rally of anti-Jacksonians at Valley Forge in July 1828, where toasts were raised to such heroes of conservatism as Henry Clay ("The intrepid champion of his country's rights, and inflexible advocate of American industry"), Matthew Carey ("Although the friends of Jackson have burnt his effigy, his works have survived the conflagration"), and Darlington's cousin Dr. William Darlington ("The early and efficient advocate of the American system and the policy of Internal Improvement").[18] By 1830 he had joined the crusade against Freemasonry and ran for Congress on a combined Anti-Masonic and Federalist ticket. And, of course, he was elected to Congress in 1832 and 1834 as an Anti-Mason; in 1838, after Pennsylvania Anti-Masonry had received its cruel defeat in the "Buckshot War," when its members were chased by a mob from the chamber and refused the seats necessary to organize the legislature, he was returned as a Whig. Although apparently he did not run again for legislative office and went back to the full-time practice of law, Darlington remained active in the Whig politics of the county and the state until at least 1857, retaining his by now ingrained antipathy to the "loco-foco" wing of the Democratic Party. He was elected district attorney of Delaware County and served in that office from 1851 to 1854. And, of course, he eventually joined the new Republican Party as the Whig organization quietly disintegrated in the years immediately preceding the Civil War.[19]

The evolution of Darlington's political philosophy can be discerned clearly in changing party affiliations. Starting out as a typical Pennsylvania Democrat, favoring the grand old party of Thomas Jefferson but committed to Clay's "American System" of protected manufactures and state-managed internal improvements, he became an anti-Jackson Democrat when he perceived the American System to be threatened by the leadership of his own party. When the revelations of the Masonic conspiracy appeared, and the dangerously liberal tendency of the loco-foco Democrats became even more evident, he joined the Anti-Masonic Party and was sent to Congress. There, anti-Masonry was not a principal object of legislative concern but the American System was, and Darlington voted consistently in favor of the Second Bank of the United States, in favor of high tariffs, in favor of internal improvements, in favor of rules to ensure the safety of boilers on steamboats, and in favor of the encouragement of invention and exploration.[20] He signed a petition in favor of temperance along with other congressional and executive leaders.[21] He corresponded and visited with Henry Carey, Matthew's son and principle economic philosopher of the American System.[22] In these conservative views, he seems to have been consistent and even harsh, joining Thaddeus Stevens and the more radical wing of the Anti-Masonic Party in 1835 in their refusal to endorse Harrison as the party's presidential candidate, and relishing such gossip as the news that some of John Bancroft's relatives in England "say Jackson is the very man they wanted to be President, and if they can only get America into their clutches again, she will have a harder struggle to get free."[23]

But a new dimension was added to Darlington's concerns when he went to Washington: the problem of slavery. He voted consistently with the minority who wanted to outlaw slavery in the District of Columbia, who recognized the right of slaves to petition Congress for the redress of grievances, and who opposed the automatic tabling of all resolutions from citizens opposing slavery. In some of these votes, he was in a highly conspicuous minority: he was one of only eighteen congressmen to vote against a resolution declaring that slaves do not have the right to petition Congress (there were 162 votes in favor). And although he generally voted in favor of national defense measures (such as appropriations bills for fortifications), he would not favor the early annexation of Texas when it appeared that it was certain to become a slave-state. But there was a point at which he would compromise. When a resolution was offered declaring that the United States government has no authority with respect to slavery, he failed to join the six who voted against it; he simply abstained.[24]

John M. Broomall, Crozer's partner in the development of the South Ward, completed the process of political transformation in the manufacturing districts of Delaware County that was begun by Edward Darlington. Like Darlington, he was a birthright Quaker, and after the schism of 1828–29, he was raised in a radical Hicksite household in Chichester Township. Like Darlington, he studied law under Samuel Edwards and began practice in Chester in 1840. He was a trial lawyer and practiced what in later years would be termed "criminal law." It was said that he was engaged for the defense in all the homicide cases in Delaware County for a period of about fifty years after his admission to the bar and that no client of his was ever convicted on a first-degree murder charge. Opposed to capital punishment, and generally disposed in favor of the unfortunate, he prosecuted, so to speak, his defense by shrewd appeals to emotion and by ruthless assaults upon the credibility of prosecution witnesses. As his memorialist observed:

He had the power of conveying some prominent favorable feature of his case to a jury throughout the trial, even in spite of the rules of evidence, and he was looked upon as an uncurable competitor in a case. His cases were won by selecting beforehand some particularly strong point and by keeping it continually in view. He would use all the other facts in the case as ancillary to the dominant idea.

These aptitudes for public debate were natural qualifications for a political career. By 1850 he was leading the radical Whig faction in the county in a revolt against the hegemony of the Eyres. He was an effective stump speaker and was soon elected to the state House of Representatives. For a time his career as a Whig fell into eclipse because he refused to join the secret order of the Know-Nothing Party, being opposed on principle (like Darlington and Thaddeus Stevens) to secret societies of any kind. But in 1856, when the Republican Party was forming in Pennsylvania, Broomall enthusiastically joined up, primarily because "he saw that it was prepared to take stronger ground on the subject of slavery than its predecessor." He became the nominee of the Delaware County Republicans for the district's congressional seat in 1856 but withdrew in favor of the Chester County delegate. Broomall ran unsuccessfully in 1858, and was finally elected to the House in 1862. In 1860 he attended the Republican National Nominating Convention in Chicago, where despite the unit rule he opposed his own state's nominee, Simon Cameron, and cast his vote for Lincoln. He was a member of the Electoral College which made Lincoln President in 1860 and again in 1872 at the election of Grant.

Broomall served with distinction in the House of Representatives in Washington from 1862 through 1868. He was a radical Republican, a close friend and admirer of Thaddeus Stevens, who saw in the Republican Party the opportunity to bring moral principles to bear upon the affairs of a great nation. He was a vehement abolitionist and was willing to bear arms in that cause; when the war between the states began, although a Quaker, he served as a captain of a regiment of Pennsylvania emergency militia. He worked for the repeal of that clause in the Pennsylvania Constitution of 1837 which denied the suffrage to black citizens of the commonwealth, and during the war and the reconstruction period campaigned tirelessly for a federal law establishing universal suffrage. In this cause he included women as well as men, believing that "civil and political rights should be exercised by all, even without regard to sex."[25]

He worked in close concert with Thaddeus Stevens, and after Stevens's death delivered a eulogy that lauded the "great commoner" for his unremitting labors on behalf of free public education, the abolition of slavery, universal suffrage, and other populist causes. Broomall regarded himself as a radical in Stevens's own tradition and deplored "conservatism":

Too frequently in men of all stations the generous impulses and noble sentiments of youth give place, with advancing years and prosperity, to that fossil petrefaction of humanity called conservatism, which is nothing more than the want of ability to see the line of progress marked out by the hand of Omnipotence and the want of energy to follow it.[26]

He resisted vigorously the Johnson administration's efforts to ameliorate the conditions of reconstruction and favored the impeachment of the President.

But, like Stevens, he remained a radical in the capitalist evangelical tradition. Although disowned by Friends for his marriage outside the fold, he continued to attend meeting and participated in the affairs of the Society. He continued to administer the South Ward development until nearly the time of his death. He was a strong temperance advocate, and insisted on the strictest standards of financial competence and probity. He contended against government interference in business affairs (having outlived the protectionist era). Broomall represented, in a sense, the acme of evangelical success: the capture of the moral high ground from evangelical capitalism's ideological competitors.[27]

MISSIONS AND THE MILLENNIAL PASSION

The continuing improvement in the worldly situation of the people of the manufacturing districts was impressive enough in an economic sense. But in the decade of the 1850's, it took on, in the eyes of thoughtful observers, a mysterious, almost sacred quality, as though it were a sign from God. To some, the meaning of the sign was plain. The Lord was arming the Christian part of mankind for a final battle with the forces of sin and death.

This theme of conflict was not new. For centuries, Christians had perceived their own spiritual lives as a course of endless struggle against temptation to sin. The prize of victory was salvation; the price of defeat, eternal torment in Hell. Recent years had seen a great increase in the efforts of domestic and foreign missions to save unbelievers from damnation by converting them to Christianity. It would be an easy transition from simple missionary zeal to the conviction that the coming decades were the time foretold in the Book of Revelation when God's people on earth must do battle with the hosts of Hell, with tongue, pen, and sword, to conquer the world for Christ.

The Drama of Salvation and Death

In the Protestant theologies it was generally asserted that at death the body descended into the grave, there to sleep until the Second Coming of Christ, when the dead should rise and their souls be judged. Some would then be saved and enter Heaven, to enjoy endless bliss in the company of the Lord; others would be condemned to endless torment in Hell, the domain of Satan. In common metaphorical usage, however, the souls of the dead who were destined for Heaven were somehow translated there immediately, so that the dying person could be conceived as undergoing a passage directly from one life to another. Yet, much theological uncertainty surrounded the process of assignment. On the one hand, the old-school Calvinists insisted that the event had been decided from the commencement of a depraved mankind's existence by an omniscient, omnipotent, and immutable God, who in effect had condemned the vast majority of mankind to Hell in advance. The elect were saved by God's grace alone and not by good works, or love, or faith on their own part (although these were required); they were to rule the damned, and to ensure that, even though destined by Him for hellfire, these too loved God, lived moral lives, and even enjoyed the prospect of their own torture because it was part of the

Lord's divine plan. On the other hand, the Universalists insisted that God, in an equally deterministic way, had made all men basically good and had decided that all should eventually, albeit with greater or lesser speed, reach Heaven. Most American Protestant denominations in this period taught views somewhere in between, in theory preserving the theological doctrine of predestination but in practice allowing to all but a few the possibility of salvation. Those who sincerely repented and had true faith in God's mercy would be saved.

Given the uncertainties of theology as well as of personal experience, and the enormity of the issue, many sincere Christians experienced severe chronic anxiety about their fate. They continually monitored their overt behavior, private sentiments, and mood, and estimated their prospects for Heaven or Hell according to their introspections. Most highly prized of all were those peak experiences when, in the course of committing oneself unreservedly to faith in Christ the Savior, one experienced a sudden, overwhelming conviction of being loved in return by God. This awareness of the possibility of salvation, achieved during the conversion process, encouraged the believer to go on to commit himself to a life of love and charity and to march toward death with a high hope of Heaven.

Death thus was a highly interesting situation to the Christian observer. It was the final opportunity for mortal man to experience the conviction of being saved and to communicate this knowledge to family and friends. As long as a person regarded himself as dying (a condition which might be as brief as a few minutes or as protracted as several decades), he endeavored to marshal his memories and feelings so as to be able to maintain the assurance of salvation. In order to make sure his mind was clear, he refused to take any more opiates. Those around him helped by singing hymns, praying, reading religious writings aloud, and asking evocative questions to keep the moribund person's mind on his final work. It was not so much the fear, like that of the medieval practitioner of the *ars moriendi,* that he might succumb to a soul-destroying temptation of rage or pride at the last moment. Rather, it was almost a divinatory practice, encouraged by the deterministic Protestant theology, to uncover the intentions of God by observing closely the state of His creature at a time when he knew that his fate was upon him. And it was also a rite of passage designed to ensure that the dying person and his loved ones did indeed take leave of each other with an assurance of meeting again in Heaven and that he go gladly to meet his Maker.[1]

Because of its dramatic significance in the all-important process of salvation, death was a preoccupation of the more religious class of people in Rockdale. At least with those who felt themselves to be in good hope of salvation and who were intimately involved with church affairs, it was not so much a morbid as a professional interest, sometimes warmly tinged with the romantic hues of contemporary fashion, sometimes detached and analytical. As befitted his status, the Reverend Mr. (later Bishop) Lee devoted many of his public utterances to teaching the Christian way of death, and in 1856 he published a hortatory book entitled *A Life Hid with Christ; Being a Memoir of Miss Susan Allibone,* which described the twenty years of illness, and the final exemplary death, of a devout Episcopalian woman in Philadelphia. Based on her diary and letters, it described her progress in piety, the conversations with friends like Bishop Potter, her patience and faith in God's mercy during a long and painful invalidism, her occasional visits to the cemetery where she expected to be buried. There she passed many hours of delightful meditation, looking forward with joy to the period when her flesh should there rest in hope and her spirit be welcomed to its heavenly home. When she was about to die, in September 1854, she called her friends and relatives to her, and with a beautiful smile exclaimed, "I think I am going. Peace! I must go to Jesus!" These were her dying words; it was a perfect dying. As Lee observed, it was plain from the manner of her passing that "the bloodwashed soul of Susan Allibone was added to the glorious company of the spirits of the just made perfect."[2]

The correspondence of the sisterhood was filled with page after page of description of the "interesting situation." When the women knew the person who died, it was important to examine with particular care the evidences of faith and to report to friends the cheerful news that he or she remained confident of God's mercy to the very end. After Alexis du Pont was blown up in the explosion in the powder yard in the summer of 1857, he lingered in great pain for several days; his sisters attended him anxiously, watching for signs that his conversion had been effective. He held firm in faith until he died. Clementina observed, on hearing this good news, "Thank God he was a Christian."[3] A couple of years later, when the young Reverend Mr. Dudley Tyng, who had been so close to the Smiths and the Calvary congregation, died as a result of an accident with a piece of new machinery on his farm, Clementina happily compared him to Alexis:

I think with you dear Sophie that there was a striking resemblance of Christian character and zeal between dear Alexis and Mr. Tyng—and the last of their career; both so earnestly active for their Lord both so calmly meeting their sudden summons in the midst of life and manly vigours! Until a few hours before his death Mr. Tyng expected to recover and spoke of the hope of increased usefulness this trial w^d effect for him— his Father felt it his duty to tell him that he was sinking fast—He then turned to his physician and asked him if that was his opinion he said it was—then he said he had Many loved ones here but he longed to be with Jesus—and turning to his physician Dr. Ablee thanked him for his kindness which had been like a brothers and after "preaching to him Jesus" prayed that he might embrace Him as a brother in Christ. Rev. Mr. Harris said he never saw such perfect abnegation of self.[4]

Tyng's death took on an almost martyr-like quality from the circumstance that he had just been discharged as rector by the vestry at the Church of the Epiphany for condemning slavery from the pulpit as the cause of many of America's problems. His last words were "Stand up for Jesus"—a phrase that became a popular evangelical hymn.[5]

Anna Potts Smith turned to verse when she lost a loved one; and the theme of these deeply felt, if somewhat stilted, elegies was the assurance of a reunion in Heaven. When her daughter Eugenia Victorine died in 1839 at the age of seventeen (three weeks after the birth of Anna's last son and child), she mourned for a long time. She appeared to condolence callers to be properly composed and confident of Eugenia's salvation (she had been in regular attendance at Calvary Church); but next spring, the appearance of the short-lived April flowers that grew on the wooded slopes around Lenni moved her to write a painful poem:

> *Oh! bring me not the wild-flowers—those early flowers of spring!*
> *Ye little think, ye dear ones, of the painful thoughts ye bring—*
> *To you, they speak of coming joy—of sunshine—& of bloom—*
> *But they mind your Mother of the past—of death—& of the tomb.*
>
> *The earliest violets that bloomed beneath the forest trees—*
> *The wood anemonies, that bend their slight stems to the breeze—*
> *And all spring's fairy flowers she brought, when last the season smiled—*
> *And now—the flowers again are here—but oh! where is my child!*
>
> *Not that thy hand no more may cull the blossom & the flowers—*
> *Not that thou may'st no more enjoy this balmy air of ours—*
> *Oh! not for thee, these bitter tears!—In thy bright, blessed sphere,*
> *Immortal spirit! What has earth, that I should wish thee here?*
>
> *Oh! not for thee! And tho' thy death so many hopes has crushed,*
> *At thought of thy surpassing bliss e'en selfish grief is hushed.*
> *And my sad heart is comforted—no more by sorrow riven—*
> *When I think on thee, my gentle child, as an angel now in heaven!*[6]

Perhaps the polarities of an age may be reflected in the different manners of leaving it. Certainly the accounts of the passing of the deistical John

S. Phillips and the evangelical John P. Crozer illustrate the contrast between the Christian *ars moriendi* and that of the cool disciple of the Enlightenment.

After the war's end, Crozer undertook to restore the rent between the northern and southern Baptist churches and to establish philanthropies for the freed slaves. He traveled to the south on this errand of mercy and while on tour was taken gravely ill. He was brought home to Upland, where he died after a few weeks of illness. He refused opiates, which would have eased his pain, in order to remain clear-minded to the last, and he undertook to perform in classic fashion the Christian ritual of dying. Surrounded by family, clergy, and friends, his confidence maintained by the singing of hymns (he had never been known to carry a tune before), he repeatedly gave testimony to his love for Jesus and his confidence in His grace, which was (in the words of a hymn he sang) "the antidote of death." It was, for him, a peak experience, perhaps the supreme emotional experience of his life, a ritual of affirmation of faith that required, for its successful performance, the most genuine conviction. He instructed his family to carry on his work:

> The responsibilities of a large estate are upon you. You are my stewards, my almoners, to carry on the work I have so imperfectly begun; you must take it up where I have left it off, and do it for me. My children, see that you are faithful stewards.

He repeatedly burst out in ecstatic exclamations, "My God doeth all things well. Jesus is my all, he is my Saviour." He responded to questions as to his state of faith with full affirmations of assurance of salvation. When his son-in-law William Bucknell asked, "You feel the everlasting arms beneath you?" he replied, with an expression of joy, "Oh yes, underneath-underneath-underneath me. No more, let me die now."

His last intelligible utterance came when, after suffering a stroke that paralyzed his left side, his daughter inquired, "Dear father, do you still love Jesus?" He raised his right arm and emphatically said, "Yes." He died a few hours later.[7]

John S. Phillips outlived Crozer by ten years. Although he had for the most part lost contact with former associates at Rockdale and the Brandywine, he had become something of a figure in the Philadelphia artists' community. He spent much of his time assembling an extraordinary collection of 65,000 original engravings by European artists, including such masters as Cranach, Dürer, Fragonard, Hogarth, and Rembrandt; when it was bequeathed to the Pennsylvania Academy of the Fine Arts, it was considered to be the largest and most important print collection in the country. During the war he took a severely anti-southern position, going so far as "refusing his hand and even recognition to life-long friends who were disloyal to the government in its peril." In 1864, during the great Sanitary Fair in Philadelphia to raise contributions for the Sanitary Commission, which cared for the sick and wounded, he was responsible for preparing the lighting and machinery for tableau exhibitions. And he was known throughout the city as a kind of eccentric mechanical genius: the inventor of a slide-lathe that cut screws of irregular size, the head of a firm that produced the finest decorative ivory turnings in the country, and the enthusiastic friend of young mechanicians. He particularly enjoyed helping young mechanics to construct machinery for which they lacked the necessary tools—clocks, microscopes, even steam engines.[8]

The artist Cecilia Beaux, as a girl of seventeen, was introduced to Phillips by her cousin and teacher, Katherine Drinker, who painted historical and biblical pictures. She recorded a visit in his later years, when he lived with his sisters and servants in the old house on Clinton Street. Still dressed in black broadcloth, the "old gentlemen" brought them to his attic workshop, where he personally mounted his prints in looseleaf portfolios of his own design, and treated them (as he had the ladies of his youth) to long monologues on technical subjects. "I would not for the world have broken in on our host's soliloquy," Cecilia said, "and took what I could get, by way of feeling, without much mental satisfaction." At ten o'clock, a maid brought Queen's cakes and vintage Madeira. She prized the memory:

> Our old friend's hand trembled a little as he filled the delicate glasses; not from age, but from the emotion of the preceding hour, and my constrained young heart knew and was shaken also.
>
> The evening was over. He accompanied us downstairs; it was our last visit. He put an arm around each of us, bending to look into our faces. "My fine friend, my fair friend," he said.
>
> I never saw him again.[9]

Phillips was anxious to get his prints completely encased in their tamper-proof portfolios before he died and they were turned over to the Academy. And so he worked himself and his assistant Henry Whipple to exhaustion, often until after midnight. Late one Friday night, he told Whipple, "Come early on Saturday, for by Monday we may all be dead." He died before Whipple could reach him, on Saturday morning.[10]

Missionary Zeal

One of the intended functions of the death cult was to terrorize the infidel and the lukewarm Christian. The terrible contrast between the serene death of the convinced believer and the misery of the poor soul approaching the end without having genuinely accepted Christ as his personal Savior was a favorite evangelical theme. It was set before the people of Rockdale in an incessant barrage of sermons, tracts, novels, speeches, editorials, and even short stories and poetry on the front pages of the *Upland Union* and the *Delaware County Republican.* The prince of infidels, Tom Paine, was again and again described in deathbed agonies, too late recanting his deistical principles. The tract societies circulated accounts of how one or another "gentleman of infidel principles," or this or that frivolous woman, died in despair. Stark and grim was the description of the unbeliever's demise. Mrs. Archer, for instance, who succumbed to a fever "after excessive dancing," went to her death in a state of agitated depression, crying: "Torment, torment, torment, is my doom forever and ever, and ever! . . . There is no grace nor mercy for me." And young Antitheus, facing his own end, had a ghastly vision of a fellow Deist, already deceased, who told him, "alas, alas . . . we are in fatal error." Antitheus died in a delirium of fear.[11]

The somber implication of this view of death was that the larger part of mankind were doomed to a terrible eternity of punishment unless they could be saved by Christian missions. Both divine injunction and natural compassion urged that as many souls as possible should be preserved. The task of the missionary was to convince the infidel, the lukewarm Christian, and the heathen that, no matter how wise and upright and just they were in a personal sense, they would be damned forever if they did not recognize their basic human depravity and throw themselves on the mercy of God. The evangelical counterattack against the principles of the Enlightenment had merely cleared the way for an efflorescence of missionary enthusiasm. The congregations gave money to be used to support the work; the religious laymen spent time serving on committees that managed the missionary enterprise.

For Clementina, the work of missions became the central religious interest, absorbing and transcending her teaching role in the parish Sunday School. Indeed, the Calvary Sunday School became not so much a service for an evangelical community as a missionary field in itself (for missions might be both domestic and foreign).[12] Clementina's interest in the spiritual peril of the heathen was awakened in the 1830's by the perusal of a book of "missionary researches" in the Polynesian Islands. She continued her reading and began to realize "how few of the inhabitants of the globe have even the opportunity of hearing of the Christian religion."[13] Her cousin Lucy was the wife of James Beach, the federal agent to the Sac and Fox Indians of Iowa (with some of whom the United States had been lately embroiled in the Black Hawk War).[14] A house visit of the Beaches with the Smiths in Philadelphia began a lifelong interest of Clementina's in the spiritual welfare of the native Americans. Some years later, enjoying the summer season at Saratoga Springs, she was impressed by the local Indian community. At night she watched the campfires of the "poor Indians" and reflected (for Sophie's benefit), "I cannot tell you how strong the contrast suggested by the glorious objects in the Heavens and the poor degraded creatures upon whom they shine so unmindful of the blessings they might enjoy—."[15] It was not, of course, her view that the American Indians were innately any more depraved than the peoples of Oceania, India, China, Africa, or Catholic Europe, or, indeed, that they were less fitted by nature for Heaven than the Rockdalers or she herself. She subscribed to missions to them all. It was just that they, like so many of mankind, were in the degraded condition that ignorance of God inevitably entailed.

"I find," wrote Clementina to her friend, "no subject so exciting as that of foreign missions." Although she was not in circumstances that permitted her to share the work as a missionary's wife or as a missionary herself (and her charge anyway was the Sunday School), she admired women who were participants in the effort to save the "poor perishing heathen." She read the missionary literature constantly, discussed it with her friends, met missionaries returned from abroad, collected (and donated) money to support the cause. Her view was worldwide. Living with a father whose business required him to be in constant receipt of information from foreign lands, and having naval officers and diplomats as family friends, her perspective was global anyway. Now she began to look forward to the time when she might see the whole world Christian.[16]

The Smiths' erstwhile neighbor John P. Crozer had always had a general interest in missions as part of the evangelical field. But it was not until the 1850's, after he had moved to Upland, that his interest crystallized into commitment. Having made his fortune with the help of Providence, he now entered upon the exercise of his stewardship with the same "untiring industry and indomitable perseverance" with which he had addressed the manufacturing of cotton. "In success in business pursuits," he wrote in his autobiography, "I suppose I have very far outstripped any son of Delaware County." Yet he was, he felt, merely an agent of the Divine Plan.

It is safest for me to ascribe my great success to a combination of circumstances, over which I had no control, but which were kindly thrown around me by my Heavenly father for purposes which it becomes me to inquire for; and to seek to feel that I am but his steward in the fortune I have received. In this view of the case—and this I think is the true one

—I rest under a solemn and awful responsibility which no one need covet or desire.[17]

After 1850, most of Crozer's energies were directed to his philanthropic and benevolent enterprises. Every day he rose at 5:00 A.M., prayed and studied the Bible for an hour, then set forth on his errands of mercy. He devoted most of his time and income (and perhaps much of his capital as well) during the remainder of his life to various undertakings of an essentially missionary nature.[18]

One of Crozer's favorite charities was providing churches for operatives in his own and others' cotton mills. In 1851, for instance, a number of residents of the Rockdale manufacturing district, feeling that Mount Hope was too far away for the convenience of the Methodists in the community, proposed to organize a new church to be known as the Rockdale Methodist Episcopal Church. Among the leaders in this movement were John Blackburn and Archibald McDowell, the factory managers at Rockdale proper and at Penn's Grove. The congregation met for a time at Temperance Hall in Lenni; but in November, at the first meeting of their Board of Trustees in Parkmount School House, Crozer stood up to donate a building lot for a new church on Mount Road in Crozerville. Subsequently he contributed generously to the building fund. The church was completed in 1854 and was renamed Crozerville Methodist Episcopal Church in honor of its benefactor. Crozer also in 1856 reserved half a square of ground in his and Broomall's South Ward development for religious purposes; here, more than twenty years later, with the help of an additional donation from his son, a Baptist church was built.[19]

But his principal concern, in the domain of church philanthropy, was the Upland Baptist Church. Crozer was determined to build a Christian industrial village in Upland. When the Upland mills first opened, he made a rule that no work should be done in the mills or in the village (which he owned), not even emergency repairs, between midnight on Saturday and midnight on Sunday. The Baptist church was completed in 1852 and for a few months Sunday School, Sabbath services, and prayer meetings were held there without a congregation being formally organized. But religious interest was awakened in the community and there were several conversions. A congregation was then formally put together, consisting of twenty persons, twelve by dismissal from other Baptist churches and eight by baptism. (Applicants for baptism were required to describe their conversion to the congregation. If the congregation was satisfied that it was genuine, they were immersed in Crozer's millrace by the pastor, John Duncan, who had just arrived from Lowell, Massachusetts, and was used to factory towns.) Of this original congregation of twenty, nine were Crozers and Crozer in-laws, and four more were of the family of Crozer's gardener. By the end of the year, the congregation had increased to sixty-eight (forty-seven of them by baptism). The Sunday School and other services, however, were open to any person who wished to attend, so that actual exposure to the influence of the church was widespread in the town. Crozer believed firmly that it was "a positive duty of all professing Christians to give of their substance," and he accordingly established a schedule of contributions. On the first Sunday of each month a collection was taken for foreign missions; there were four other collections during the year for various other benevolent purposes, including support of the American Baptist Missionary Society, the American Bible Society, the Pennsylvania Convention, the Widows' Fund, and the Baptist Home Mission Society; and at each communion there was a collection for needy church members. The first Sabbath evening of the month was set aside for a "concert of prayer for the success of missions," and the importance of foreign missions in the minds of the congregation is attested by the fact that four times as much money was collected for this purpose as for any other.[20]

Crozer's personal power in the Upland community was of course enormous simply by reason of his ownership of the mills on which virtually every resident depended for his livelihood. But in his role as Christian steward he vastly increased that power and almost made of Upland a theocratic community. Crozer and the Crozer family selected the pastors, who were expected to avoid comment on controversial economic and political topics. As a later memorialist of the church observed:

> It has always insisted that its pastors in their pulpit ministrations confine themselves to strictly Biblical themes, and to the achievement of distinctly spiritual results. If any one of those who have had the honor of being the pastor of this church had deviated from this course to any great extent, if he had undertaken to deliver a series of sermons that were not exclusively spiritual in their aim, something in all likelihood would have happened to him. This church would not have tolerated such exploits, and he would have been obliged to cease from them or to cease from preaching here.[21]

Crozer assumed, also, a responsibility for selective care of the deserving poor, instructing the pastor: "If, in the course of your pastoral visitation, you learn of any families that are in poverty and distress, I would be obliged to you to report them to me."[22] He and his gardener were the two (and only) deacons, and Crozer personally, as deacon, visited the sick and the bereaved. He served as Sunday School superintendent. As deacon and member of the congregation he heard and judged the religious testimonials of applicants for membership, helping to decide whether the speaker was truly aware of his sinful nature and whether he sincerely loved the Heavenly Father. As deacon, he presided over the business meetings of the congregation whenever the pastor was absent. And, as deacon, he administered church discipline.

The Baptist discipline was severe. Members of the congregation were required to attend services regularly and to live moral lives, eschewing alcohol and profanity, loose sexual conduct, "inconsistency," falsehood, and a miscellany of other "disorderly" life styles, such as "separation from wife" and "refusing to live with her husband without satisfying reasons." The cases of persons accused of violating these rules were privately investigated by a committee (and the accused might if he wished testify in public). Those convicted by the congregation were suspended or expelled, in the latter case the name being "erased" from the record. The case of Benjamin Serrill will serve as an example of the process.

> Deacon J. P. Crozer made accusation against Bro. Benjamin Serrill alleging intemperance and falsehood requesting the wish of the church to be expressed as to whether he should make a statement at that time or to committee appointed for the purpose—on motion he was directed to proceed and accordingly laid before the church proofs gathered. After considerable discussion in which Bro. Serrill took part a committee of enquiry consisting of Pastor Brethren Dalton Blakely and Hart was appointed to examine into the matter and report to a special meeting called for the purpose as soon as the committee should have finished its labors.

Two weeks later the committee reported that after a "patient investigation" of the charges, they had found abundant proof that Brother Serrill had been "repeatedly guilty both of the sin of intemperance and falsehood." The sentence, by unanimous vote, was "immediate expulsion."[23]

But Crozer's eye increasingly turned to the wider field of missions. For a time he served on the board of the American Sunday School Union, before he resigned disillusioned with the poor quality of the administration of its affairs.[24] By 1853 he had become a vice-president of the Baptist Publication Society, an organization that produced, printed, and distributed books and tracts in Europe and America. In the activities of this organization he became an associate of Francis Wayland, the noted writer of textbooks on moral philosophy and president of Brown University; of William Bucknell, founder of the University of Lewisburg; and of other leading Baptist clergy and laymen. Crozer's initial role was to serve as chairman of the Committee on Accounts, to make donations, and to recruit his sons and brothers to aid in the Society's work. In 1861 he became chairman of the board.

The Baptist Publication Society fought infidelity and Catholicism in ostensibly Christian nations and was separate from the American Baptist Missionary Society and the Baptist Home Mission Society, to which he also contributed. In the field the Baptist Publication Society relied on "colporteurs"—laymen who distributed publications, formed Baptist Sunday Schools, and made "known the way of salvation to the multitudes who do not visit the Sanctuary."[25] Most of these men worked in ordinary American communities, combating Romanism and modern skepticism; some visited American Indians and some traveled abroad, particularly in Sweden, France, and Germany. The Society had two departments: a "missionary colporteur" department, which collected contributions from the benevolent to support their travels (the goal was "to place in every neighborhood a colporteur"); and a "book" department, which sustained itself "on business principles." The book department financed the preparation and publication of books and tracts to be sold to Sunday Schools and to the general reader, made grants of libraries to poor Sunday Schools and needy ministers, and provided at no charge appropriate religious publications "in all languages" (including hitherto unwritten languages like the American Indian Chippewa). The materials ranged widely over subjects of interest to Protestants young and old. Some of the titles appealed to those eager for descriptions of foreign missions: *Sketches of Life in Burmah, Sophia Brown or the Missionary's Daughter, Travels in South-Eastern Asia, Cox's History of Baptist Missions,* and *Krishna-Pal The First Hindoo Convert.* The works of John Bunyan and Andrew Fuller (the latter being one of Crozer's favorite theologians) were also featured.[26]

Crozer traveled extensively in connection with the meetings of the board, which were held in a different city each year, and he obtained a wide view of the problems of Baptist evangelism and its relation to the education of ministers (and of young men and women generally). He had contributed largely to the building of the new university at Lewisburg, of which the first president William Bucknell was his son-in-law, and in a fine ecumenical spirit had declared, "I do not particularly wish to make Baptists, but I want to make educated young men." A few years later he built an academy in Chester and then a co-educational normal school in Upland (which after his death became the Crozer Theological Seminary). But the Upland institution, constructed and liberally endowed by Crozer and administered along lines advised by the eminent Francis Wayland, was a disappointment. It was intended to provide, in a religious atmosphere and at minimal cost, "a comprehensive, thorough, and practical education for business, teaching, college, and any literal or professional pursuit . . . the dead languages not to have undue prominence." However, it proved difficult to find qualified faculty, the school was expensive to operate, many of the students came from prosperous families and did not need the financial aid Crozer had built into it, and the community was prone to epidemics of scarlet fever and smallpox.

Crozer's most personally satisfying contribution to the cause of education was probably his support of programs for the education of ministers, administered by the Pennsylvania Baptist Education Society (of which he quickly became a board member and then president in 1855). His interest was initially intrigued by the remark of one of its officers that "we had a pious and devoted ministry, but needed also men of liberal culture for prominent points of influence." Crozer caught fire at the idea. He himself was uncomfortable in public speaking, perhaps owing to his sense of the inadequacy of his own education (although in fact he read widely and judiciously and had an excellent library); and in the ideological combat with the infidels, many of whom were erudite, it was obviously important to have the defenders of the faith at least as well educated as their rivals. He was faithful in attendance at gatherings of this board, although his shyness kept him away from the annual meetings of the Society; and, among other gifts, he endowed seven scholarships of $1,500 each. Much of the board's time was spent in evaluating grant applications from needy ministerial students. Crozer was an exemplary reviewer of such requests and of progress reports. The secretary of the Society described his conduct at these meetings:

His counsel was invaluable. . . . The subject-matter was well thought out, and delivered with evident emotion and great spirituality of mind.

So intense was his interest in ministerial students, he could not rest satisfied with ordinary and general statements. He wanted details. On several occasions, after writing a full sheet, and then apologizing for its undue length, I have received the reply, "Do not fear taxing my patience by minute details. You will tax my patience much more by not giving them. I want all these incidents. They go to make up character. Please do not be sparing in letting me know how each beneficiary is advancing, both in spiritual and intellectual pursuits." From time to time he wrote such sentences as the following: "My heart is in this good work. I am glad you are succeeding as well as you are. It must be a work of time. The results will be glorious."[27]

In turning to the support of education for the ministry and to the support of missions themselves, Crozer was not merely applying his money and energies to another sector of the evangelical cause. He was also achieving at last an identification with his well-educated, much-admired, long-dead younger brother Samuel. Crozer had always had a feeling of awed respect for Samuel's Christian zeal, mechanical ingenuity, and intellectual brilliance; he called him "Doctor Crozer" and had even named his first-born son after him. Samuel Crozer had died a martyr's death on the shores of Africa as the first agent of the American Colonization Society. John P. Crozer joined the American Colonization Society in January 1856, donating $1,000 and thereby earning the title of "Life Director."[28]

Apart from his general interest in the benevolent societies of the day, and his further identification with his deceased brother, it is not clear from his biographical remains what at first motivated John Crozer. His opposition to slavery was a matter of public record: he had joined the Pennsylvania Society for Promoting the Abolition of Slavery years before, in 1837. But this did not indicate much more than a general disapproval of an outmoded institution. The Pennsylvania Society was one of the older and less militant abolition societies—founded in 1789 by Benjamin Rush, Robert Morris, Benjamin West, Lafayette, and other worthy liberals in the Enlightenment tradition—and it sought to end the institution of slavery gradually by rational persuasion. It attracted men of substance, many of them mechanicians and manufacturers, including names familiar to Crozer: Nathan Sellers, Abraham Sharpless, Joshua Gilpin, William Martin (the manufacturer's father), Samuel Painter, Matthew Carey, Joseph Trimble, James Ronaldson, the Philadelphia philanthropist and educator Roberts Vaux, Thaddeus Stevens . . .[29] Crozer does not seem to have had much sympathy for Garrison's radical abolition society, founded in Philadelphia in 1832, but the sincerity of his opposition to what he once called "the accursed traffic in human sinews" cannot be doubted.[30]

Of his attitude toward blacks, little information is available. Crozer believed that slavery was wrong but that it was legal in the states that still permitted it. He was opposed to any extension of slavery, but was not necessarily an admirer of free black people. He lived in a place and at a time when the free black population was increasingly being perceived by whites as a social problem. Blacks were being displaced from the positions as unskilled and skilled laborers and even merchants that they had been accustomed to occupy in southeastern Pennsylvania, and they made up a disproportionately large part of the inmates of poorhouses and jails. The Smiths and the Du Ponts complained about the undesirability of black domestic servants and poked fun at the outlandish antics of Philadelphia's colored people. A minister at Middletown Presbyterian Church had been dismissed because he allowed a black man to preach from his pulpit.[31] But the uncanny intensity of the local taboo against contact with blacks is perhaps most vividly conveyed in a gruesome anecdote about Dr. Gideon Humphrey, the homeopathic physician who practiced in the Rockdale district in the 1820's and 1830's. A black man had drowned in Chester Creek and Humphrey procured the body for the purpose of preparing a demonstration skeleton. He borrowed a large iron kettle from a neighbor lady. Ashmead in his county history recounted the story with some relish sixty years later; evidently it was a favorite in the community:

> In the night, while he was at work in the spring-house, a huge fire under the pot, some one passing near saw the light, went to the spring-house, and reported next day that the "Doctor had boiled a darkey's head in the pot." This coming to the ears of the owner of the article, she, when it was sent home, returned it, saying, "Tell the doctor to keep that pot to boil another nigger in. I won't have the nasty thing in my house."[32]

Seen in this context, Crozer was evidently more liberal than most of his neighbors. A biblical allusion in his address on the forty-fifth anniversary of the Pennsylvania Colonization Society is significant of a self-consciously benevolent Christian separatism. He observed that the American Colonization Society and its protégé, the new Republic of Liberia, were smiled upon by Him "who made of one blood all nations of men for to dwell on all the face of the earth, and hath determined the times before appointed and the bounds of their habitation."[33] Presumably also Crozer agreed with the remarks of the other speaker of the evening, who quoted with emphatic approval the proposition on race that allegedly justified the whole program of the American Colonization Society: "two distinct races of people so unlike that amalgamation by intermarriage is impracticable, cannot long dwell in peace on terms of political and social equality."[34]

Crozer was active in the affairs of the Pennsylvania Colonization Society, which was an auxiliary of the national organization, and had become its president. At about the same time (in 1861), perhaps *ex officio,* he became a member of the board of the American Colonization Society. He served on the Committee for Auxiliary Societies, which reviewed income from the auxiliary state organizations, and in 1861, on the eve of the Civil War, was still trying to arrange an embarkation of freedmen from Charleston, South Carolina. More importantly, he was also chairman of the Committee on Foreign Relations. At that date Liberia, although a sovereign nation, was not diplomatically recognized by the government of the United States, and the actual negotiations between the two countries were carried on through the offices of the American Colonization Society. Liberia had been organized by the thousands of freed blacks transported there over the years from the United States and by other thousands of blacks liberated by vessels of the U.S. Navy which patroled the West Coast of Africa to intercept American ships illegally carrying slaves. Crozer's committee lobbied actively and successfully in Washington to persuade Congress and the executive branch to recognize the new nation and to protect it from depredations from the British colony of Sierra Leone to the north. Liberia was recognized in 1862. Crozer also interested himself in such projects as the introduction of coffee trees into Liberia as a cash crop and the encouragement of commercial relations with the United States.[35]

The effort to solve the racial problem in the United States by persuading slaveowners to manumit their slaves and to transport the freedmen to a national home in Africa, with their own consent and at no expense to themselves (costs were met from members' subscriptions and church collections), was doomed from the start. The Colonization Society's accomplishments never even approached the rosy dreams of its members. Many distinguished people, to be sure, lent themselves to the cause: Crozer's associates in the Pennsylvania Colonization Society included such familiar figures as Bishop Potter, Judge Bell, Dr. William Darlington, and James Ronaldson. In Delaware, the names of Charles and Alexis du Pont were enrolled. Nationally, the founders included such figures as Henry Clay (who eventually became the Society's president), Andrew Jackson, Thomas Jefferson, Daniel Webster, John Marshall, James Monroe, James Madison, and Matthew Carey, and later leaders included such celebrated men as the great Lowell cotton manufacturers William Appleton and Abbot Lawrence, the Honorable Louis McLane of Delaware (Jackson's Secretary of the Treasury and erstwhile Brandywine industrialist), and dozens of bishops and university presidents. But despite the impressive array of powerful names, the program foundered. Few slaves were freed (far fewer than the nation's increase by reproduction); few free blacks wanted to go back to Africa anyway; and the effort to resolve the slavery issue by measures that offended no one attracted a withering barrage of Garrisonian accusations of complicity in the maintenance of slavery. The major result, as Crozer noted, was the establishment of the "infant Republic of Liberia" and the abolition of the slave trade along its three hundred miles of African coast. Claimed Crozer proudly:

This Republic is the offspring of the Colonization Society. It is the child of this organization and owns no other parentage. . . . I believe that the Almighty Sovereign of all, the Creator of all, inspired our forefathers to establish this society to aid in elevating the colored race to a position of freedom and equality, and to plant the colony, now the Republic of Liberia, which in the fullness of time is to serve as a beacon to the tribes and nations of Africa, and to introduce the principles of our holy religion amongst these savage people.

It was, in fact, the evangelical opportunity that most inspired Crozer:

The Republic, by its proximity to and frequent intercourse with the interior will, under God, be a great instrument in introducing Christianity into these wide wastes of heathenism and habitations of cruelty. The Christian influence of the Colonization enterprise was not, perhaps, prominent in the minds of its founders, but now its friends look to this result as of primary consequence.

The Society feels that it has a great work on hand. To send colored Christian men and women, not especially as missionaries, but as citizens, who, in cultivating the soil, or in mechanical or mercantile pursuits, will in their frequent mingling with the natives infuse the principles of the Christian religion amongst them working as leaven upon the African mind.[36]

The Millennial Transformation

To recognize oneself as sinner, to throw oneself upon the mercy of God, and to strive for the salvation of one's fellow beings had long been the threefold way of Christian living. It could be, and often was, a rather placid way, resting upon the assumption that the world was going to be pretty much the same for the next generation as it had been for the last. But by the middle of the century, it was plain that while the eternal truths of religion might remain unchanged, the material world was changing very much. People were conscious of the vast advances of machinery: the cotton factories, the railroads, the steamboats were producing a new kind of world; and along with the awareness of a new technological world was arising an awareness of the possibility of a new social world as well, a world entirely Christian. The new wealth, the new technology, made this goal seem suddenly within grasp. And it made also suddenly more real the Christian doctrine of the millennium, when (after some bloody resistance from Satan) the entire world should become Christian and Christ should return to reign for a thousand years. As the Christian nations proceeded rapidly to complete their military and economic conquest of the heathen nations around the globe, everywhere the Christian missionary penetrated. It began to seem as if the millennium were truly at hand.

Militancy in such a holy cause was justified. John P. Crozer's brother Samuel, as he set forth with the aid of the U.S. Navy to establish a beachhead of black Christians on the shores of Africa, had written to his sister explaining his motivations. He first announced his conversion, and then went on to describe his mission in language almost appropriate to a man about to set forth on a dangerous military campaign:

How long have I despised, rejected and trampled under foot the many tender mercies which God has showered on my head with a liberal and unsparing hand, how long have I spurned and crucified my blessed Redeemer. But my sins have found me out, and I have taken refuge under the shadow of the ever blessed the Prince of Peace and oh! exceeding mercy he has stretched forth his hand and rescued me from destruction.

Do not let any painful thought flit across your mind concerning me, consider the banner under which I march with Christ for my buckler. If it be the will of God that I should die in Africa consider how much I shall gain. . . . I feel exceedingly rejoiced at the prospect I have before me of being beneficial to mankind.[37]

To advance Christian missions in the wake of conquest became more explicitly an evangelical policy as the years went on. In 1857 and 1858, Sophie's husband Samuel took command of the new American frigate *Minnesota,* which carried an experimental steam engine for auxiliary power, and sailed her to China. His mission was to carry an American minister to negotiate with the Chinese in concert with the British and French. Although the United States was officially neutral in the hostilities between the Chinese government and the European powers, the overpowering military presence of the Western nations undoubtedly would give added force to American requests. The American diplomat was lawyer and politician William B. Reed of Pennsylvania, a former Anti-Masonic legislator, lately turned Democrat. He had married a daughter of the same Robert Ralston who had sent Samuel Crozer off to Africa. *Minnesota* also had on board a missionary to China. Captain Du Pont carried various charges from Bishop Lee; and, by now a convinced Christian, he studied religious tracts in his cabin on Sundays and read sermons to his crew. All in all it was as much a missionary enterprise as a diplomatic one.

Du Pont's personal observations were cool and clinical. After watching the successful European bombardment of the river ports guarding Peking (which soon after fell to the landing force), and later visiting the ruins littered with dead bodies, he was moved to comment on the poor quality control evident in the manufacture of Chinese gunpowder. He did not agree with Minister Reed's preference for force over negotiation, and hoped for "peaceful relations with China and an extended commerce with her." And he was sufficiently sophisticated to observe: "to judge of Chinese by our standards is altogether fallacious, and to get at their process of reasoning requires a long intercourse with them and a knowledge of their language."[38]

But the *Minnesota* waited patiently in Chinese waters for the European powers to force the Chinese to negotiate—and so at last they did. The upshot of the whole affair was a series of treaties signed the following summer between China and Great Britain, France, Russia, and the United States, which opened eleven more ports to Western trade, legalized the importation of opium, and permitted Christian missionaries to enter the interior of China. It also led to the alliance between British forces under Chinese Gordon and the imperial Chinese troops in prosecuting the civil war against the millennialist, Christian-influenced Taiping rebels, who had taken over much of the country. And, because of his sympathy for Oriental cultures, it resulted in Captain Du Pont's being appointed as escort to the first Japanese embassy in their travels in the United States in 1860.[39]

Observed from the quiet valley of Chester Creek, events such as these were easy to interpret in the fashion of the progressive millennialist theologians. Clementina, already deeply interested in foreign missions, now began to look forward to seeing the whole world Christian.[40] Her millennial aspirations had little in common with those of the vulgar Millerites, who were expecting a sudden apocalyptic intervention by God and were disposing of their worldly goods. She referred to such beliefs as *"crazy doctrines"* and remarked superciliously, "There is a certain class of people almost wild about them."[41] Hers was the more orthodox millennialism, which foresaw a progressive conversion of the world, a continual improvement of the material condition of mankind, perhaps a final test of arms with the forces of Antichrist, and then the Second Coming of the Christ Himself to usher in the thousand years of peace. When all of this would happen was not revealed; it might be a long time away; but now she began to feel that it was imminent. When she learned of the first transatlantic telegraph cable in 1858, like many others she interpreted the event in millennialist terms. Even the first messages reportedly sent—"Glory to God in the highest" and "Peace good will to men—" had a Christian tone. She confided hopefully to Sophie: "The signs of the times do call us to a state of expectation— sometimes I wonder if we shall see the day and coming of the Lord—or whether this is the time of preparation for that great event."[42]

The Smith family's old friend and religious associate, the Reverend Dr. Stephen Tyng, now residing in New York City, perhaps expressed their millennial views most aptly. In an address published in 1848, Tyng had seen that America's great need was to elevate "the moral, relative dignity of labor . . . as the true greatness" of the nation. He went on, in a millennial enthusiasm that combined zealousness toward the conversion of the working class with fervent anticipation of the conversion of heathen everywhere, to describe his view of America's destiny:

And when the great exalting, leveling system of Christianity gains its universal reign, mountains will be brought down, and valleys will be filled; an highway shall be made for human prosperity and peace—for the elevation and dignity, and security of man—over which no oppressor's foot shall pass; the poorest of the sons of Adam shall dwell unmolested and fearless beneath his own vine and fig tree; the united families of earth shall all compete, to acquire and encourage the arts of peace; nation shall not rise against nation, and men shall learn war no more. Let this . . . be the universal purpose of our people, and the greatness of America shall know no limited zenith, and fear no tendency to decline.[43]

Clementina's friends the Lammots, as members of the Church of the New Jerusalem, were already deeply committed to a millennialist interpretation of current history. Their form of millennialism differed, however, in some respects. The founder, Emmanuel Swedenborg, claimed that the Second Coming had already occurred, in 1757, when the proper mode of interpreting Scripture was revealed to him. Inspired by Swedenborg's writings, the members of the New Church saw their task as a missionary one too, of converting not only the heathen but also the adherents of the old Christian churches to the newly revealed theology of Swedenborg. New Church missionaries were, or soon would be in many countries, preparing the way for the world's redemption.

Baptists, too, were millennialist in their eschatology. Crozer was a careful reader of Andrew Fuller, one of the leading English nonconformist theologians and a favorite of the Baptist Publication Society. Fuller opposed the pessimistic implications of extreme Calvinism and urged an evangelical Christianity. In his essay on the *Nature and Extent of True Conversion,* Fuller also interpreted the present age as being on the brink of redemption:

The time will come when "all the kindreds of the earth" shall worship. Ethiopia, and all the unknown regions of Africa, shall stretch out their hands to God. Arabia, and Persia, and Tartary, and India, and China, with the numerous islands in the Eastern and Southern Ocean, shall bring an offering before him. Mahomedans shall drop their delusion, papists their cruel superstition, Jews shall be ashamed of their obstinacy, deists of their enmity, and merely nominal Christians of their form of godliness without the power of it. . . .

The last branch of the last of the four beasts is now in its dying

agonies. No sooner will it be proclaimed, "Babylon is fallen!" then the
marriage of the Lamb will come. There are no more tyrannical or per-
secuting powers to succeed; but "the kingdom shall be given to the
people of the saints of the Most High." All ranks of men, princes, nobles,
and people, becoming real Christians, the government of the world will
naturally be in their hands; and love, peace, and universal good shall
consequently pervade the whole earth.[44]

But the full flavor of popular millennialist thinking, in its applications
to contemporary issues, is perhaps best conveyed in the writings of the
popular author Hollis Read, an erstwhile Baptist missionary to India. In
1851 Read was in charge of the Baptist Home Mission effort in New
Mexico and Crozer met him in Philadelphia when he visited there to raise
money. He was afterward entertained by the Crozers at Upland, where he
received a "generous donation" and his wife "an expensive book which she
desired to have."[45] Read had already published a two-volume biography of
a converted Hindu named Babajee.[46] In the 1850's he rediscovered the
American Colonization Society and affiliated himself with its cause, visiting
Africa himself as a missionary and eventually (in 1864) publishing a popular
work advocating the Society's program as the solution to the "Negro problem." This work was based on the assumption of the impossibility of as-
similating the blacks into white American culture, and the consequent
desirability of transporting the freed slaves to form Christian colonies on
the dark continent. Read was articulate and persuasive in his presentation
of this view and (along with Robert Dale Owen) was appointed by Lincoln
to a commission to make recommendations on federal policy toward the
blacks of the south after emancipation.[47]

Read's views on the millennium were expressed in a series of works
beginning in 1859 and continuing at least into the 1870's. The 1859 contribution was a prize essay, published by the Seamen's Friend Society in
Philadelphia (its office was at the Bible House in the financial district),
entitled *Commerce and Christianity*. The purpose of the book was to increase
the importance of the seaman's cause in the eyes of the benevolent by
emphasizing the importance of commerce (which was the mission of the
sailor) in the progress of mankind toward the millennium. The argument
was not unsophisticated, in its way, and anticipated the mode of analysis
made popular a century later in the writings of functionalist social scientists.
Read demonstrated how international trade necessarily depended upon,
and stimulated the diffusion of, ideas or sentiments of civil liberty, honesty,
evangelical Christianity, and certain universal standards of decorum. He
proceeded from a celebration of the oceans as the binder of nations, via

commerce, to a consideration of commerce as a progressive agency, as the process by which the Anglo-Saxon "race" was acquiring worldwide ascendancy, and as a principal agency in the "great awakening." Commerce (and its operatives, the seamen), by promulgating the laws of trade and demonstrating the power of honesty, and by financing from its profits in the hands of Christian stewards the sacred work of missions, was a major instrument in the conversion of the world and the achievement of the millennium.

Read was capable, like Samuel Francis Du Pont, of some degree of cultural relativism. He criticized American false modesty in avoiding the use of the word "leg" and requiring such circumlocutions as "limb" or "lower member." The Hindu, he said, simply said "leg" and displayed it freely, with less "indelicacy in thought and imagination" than in the United States. He urged, "We must not, therefore, suppose that every deviation of the Hindu from *our* standard of propriety, is a transgression of the rules of real decorum." As an example, he described how the "cowardly" Hindu never came to blows but insulted each other instead, when angered, by obscene charges against each other's mother and dead relatives. He pointed out that no offense to these kinsmen of the opponent was really intended; it was merely the *"customary* way of abusing an adversary."[48]

Implicit in Read's functional analysis was a subtle transformation. The worth of an idea or institution was to be measured not merely on gross economic or political or even universal moral dimensions but by its contribution to the advancement of missions. In his evaluation of the commerce with Africa, he pointed out that traffic in other articles would reduce the trade in slaves; this was a peculiarly important functional consequence because the slave trade was *the great obstacle to the conversion of Africans.* In later works, urging the recolonization of Africa with black Christian freedmen from America (with the help of the American Colonization Society, of course), the argument was developed further as we have noted in *The Negro Problem Solved; or, Africa as She Was, As She Is, and As She Shall Be.* In this exposition of "romantic racialism," he saw black participation in the millennium as being neatly contained in a Christian Africa, to which the out-of-place ex-slaves from the United States had been returned as a pious leavening. Here the principle of analysis was even more plainly developed: it was the extent to which an institution or a system of ideas and values contributed to the accomplishment of the millennium that determined its worth. If it advanced the millennium, it was good and the work of God; if it held it back, it was evil and the work of Satan.[49]

The whole cosmic theme was developed to its fullest in a series of eschatological works: *The Coming Crisis of the World, The Hand of God in History, The Palace of the Great King,* and *The Foot-Prints of Satan: or, The Devil in History.* The last work is especially interesting because it so closely parallels the world-conspiracy theme of Robison and the Anti-Masons of the previous generation. Writing after the Civil War, Read blamed Satan as "the great Antagonistic Power," who had been "the instigator of the Slaveholders' Rebellion." Satan might expect a last victory or two before the millennium; but he would have only a short time of triumph, for the Second Coming of Christ was at hand. In the meantime, his vast empire, centered in the Church of Rome (and especially among the Jesuits), was an inconvenience. Satan was responsible for Owenite socialism, Fourierism, communism and the Communist Internationals, free love, the women's rights movement, infidelity and rationalism, spiritualism and rappings, Mormonism, liberal Christianity, the perversions of wealth, the infidel press ("more dangerous because more subtle men never cursed the world in the days of Paine or Voltaire"), and both the Paris Commune and the Tweed Ring in New York. Read deplored (in a not-too-subtle expression of anti-intellectualism) how Satan had subverted such "giants in intellect" as Lord Byron, Voltaire, Hume, Gibbon, Rousseau, and Thomas Paine. For Read, as for the Anti-Masons, all evil was part of one conspiracy; all good would be realized in one millennium.[50]

Read's principal work was *The Coming Crisis of the World; or, The Great Battle and the Golden Age* (1861). In an introductory note, the Reverend Dr. Stephen Tyng lauded the book as "vastly important" because it presented the prospect of "a restored earth—the future everlasting dwelling place of the redeemed of God"—of which Tyng had been convinced for many years. Such support was very significant. Known as the greatest preacher in the Episcopal Church, Tyng was the leader of the evangelical faction in the denomination. He had, like the Smiths, for many years been a devotee and founder of Sunday Schools. Tyng's theme was straightforward. The "golden age of the church" was at hand. One by one the centers of Antichrist and the iniquities of Satan's rule were being overcome. In India and China, pagan priesthoods were being overturned by Christian missionaries. In Europe, the despotism of Rome was being destroyed. In America, the slave system, "this monster of sin," the last stronghold of evil, was now being assailed and the final battle was under way. "Great Babylon is toppling to her fall."

The chapters themselves proceeded in a direct way to document, by reference to the commotions of the times, the near approach of the millennium. In particular, the financial crisis of 1857 and the subsequent revival, the Sepoy Rebellion and the "renovation" of India, the opening of the Far East and of Africa to Christian civilization, and the laying of the transatlantic cable were all cited as indications of the approaching victory of Christianity.

And the American Civil War, now just begun, was seen as one more major confrontation between the power of sin and the dominion of Christ, in which God's chosen people, the Americans, would rise up and forever abolish the satanic institution of slavery. God's people would be sorely tested but they would surely prevail in final victory and redeem the world.[51]

Such a mode of thought transformed all issues. No longer need the south be seen as deserving of opposition because it stubbornly opposed the protective tariff, threatened to outreach with slave labor a legion of white farmers in the west, and attempted to dominate the halls of Congress. The south was evil because it was a region of slaveholders. The slave power opposed the evangelizing of the blacks and the transportation of emancipated Christian blacks to Africa; the south thus was holding back the millennium by interfering with the conversion of the world.

Another purveyor of millennial imagery was Mary Gilpin's brother William, the first governor of Colorado. In his report to the U.S. Senate in 1846 (subsequently amplified in his *Mission of the North American People*), Gilpin painted America's future in imperial purple:

The untransacted destiny of the American people is to subdue the continent—to rush over this vast field to the Pacific Ocean—to animate the many hundreds of millions of its people, and to cheer them upward—to set the principle of self-government at work—to agitate these herculean masses—to establish a new order in human affairs—to set free the enslaved—to regenerate super-annuated nations—to change darkness into light—to stir up the sleep of a hundred centuries—to teach old nations a new civilization—to confirm the destiny of the human race—to carry the career of mankind to its culminating point—to cause the stagnant people to be re-born—to perfect science—to emblazon history with the conquest of peace—to shed a new and resplendent glory upon mankind —to unite the world in one social family—to dissolve the spell of tyranny and exalt charity—to absolve the curse that weighs down humanity, and to shed blessings around the world!
Divine task! Immortal mission!

A geographical and climatic determinist, but mindful of his origins along the Brandywine, he saw Denver as the commercial center of an industrial world. The gold standard and a vigorous program of public works (such as railroads and harbors) "promise to enthrone *industrial organization* as the ruling principle of nations. America leads the host of nations as they ascend to this new order of civilization . . . the industrial conquest of the world."[52]

The millennial imagery was pervasive in Delaware County. Not only did the Lammots, the Smiths, the Crozers know it well; it reached the workers too, in the labor movement as well as in the churches. During the 1850's a labor union of a new style emerged, primarily composed of the spinners, weavers, and dyers who worked the three hundred power and hand looms of the cooperative Carpet Hall Manufacturing Association, situated next door to Christ Church in Philadelphia, and the one hundred looms of the Delaware County Carpet Manufacturing Association, located on Chester Pike in Darby. The union called itself the Associated Working Women and Men, and it regularly published ten thousand copies of a newspaper entitled *The Monthly Jubilee: Published by an Association of the Daughters and the Sons of Toil.* The leaders of the organization were veterans of the constitutional struggle in Rhode Island, where in 1842 Thomas Dorr had led a brief rebellion and established a provisional government. The principal issue there had been the liberalization of archaic suffrage requirements, and although the revolutionary government was suppressed, voting privileges were extended not long afterward. General John Sidney Jones, the manager of Carpet Hall, had held a cabinet post in Dorr's provisional government, and his wife Fannie Lee Townsend, the editor of the *Monthly Jubilee,* had been an associate of Dorr's and an organizer of land and industrial congresses. The Joneses lived in Delaware County and the meeting place of the Association was in Darby.

The Association was a different kind of organization from the trades unions of the 1830's and 1840's. It did, first of all, provide a permanent organization between strikes for workers in textile factories; the trade unions had not done this. It was economically anchored in two successful factory cooperatives. It mustered a 150-man militia company commanded by General Jones. And it had an articulate and extensive social philosophy and political platform that blended somewhat more successfully into the evangelical milieu than had the older associations. The Jubilee Association did not eschew the earlier heroes of labor, to be sure. Its members celebrated the birthday of Tom Paine with speeches and public meetings, and the newspaper published sketches of the life of Fanny Wright and denounced greedy capitalists, sectarian religionists, scheming lawyers, absentee landlords, monopolistic banks, protective tariffs, and all the other *bêtes noires* of the traditional working-class propagandist. But theirs was a populist radicalism that also allowed allusions to the Divine Will and invited addresses by such conservative churchmen as Bishop Potter. And it was avowedly millennial. "Jubilee" was the millennium of labor, the working-man's Utopia, and the paper bore on its cover the progressive motto: "The ideal of the Past, is the actual of the Present; The ideal of the Present, is the actual of the Future." Harbingers of Jubilee had been Tom Paine, George Washington, Andrew Jackson, and the pro-Sunday mail (and anti-evangelical) congressional reports of Richard M. Johnson.

Fannie Lee Townsend, the prophet of the movement (or, as she called herself, the "Edita"), claimed that she was "the first human being of the age to sanction agitation of the Land and Beard question." She was impatient with traditional religious and benevolent causes, banned discussions of sectarian religion and party politics, and proscribed as a waste of time such activities as "Abolition, Temperance, Spirit Rappings, Anti-Slavery, and Women's Rights Conventions." She deplored prudery in sexual mores, favored healthy sexual activity and the reproductive role for women, advocated social equality of men and women, and urged the wearing of beards by men (a growing fashion anyway). She had several pet anti-policies: she opposed the use of petroleum for fuel; she regarded the customary failure to cover human and animal excrement in the fields as one of the causes of soil exhaustion and thus of the "Land Monopoly"; and she complained that "inordinate sexual passion or heat is frequently engendered, as the consequent of a false state of society."

But the fundamental plank in her platform was land reform. Land ownership would usher in the millennium for the workers. Like other free soilers, including such diverse partners as Horace Greeley (whom she claimed as her protégé) and the Fourierist socialists, she felt that every man had a natural right to use land without paying rent, just as he had a right to unlimited personal use of air and water without cost. Rent and the "Land Monopoly" must be brought to an end. To make good these claims, she organized an Emigrating Association which ultimately managed to send some fifty spinners, weavers, and dyers' families to free soil in Iowa and Missouri.

As the "Platform" of the Association asserted, in a working-class parallel to the "conversion of the world" theme of the manufacturing and commercial classes:

The JUBILEE will advocate not the immediate abolition of all useless LAWS, but that public attention should be diverted towards a "good time coming," when a JUBILEE will be the natural result of *public opinion,* endorsing our platform.[53]

ARMAGEDDON

In his vision recorded in the Book of Revelation, St. John witnessed the preparations for the final struggle between Satan and the Holy Redeemer.

Seven angels emptied vials, loosing terrible catastrophes upon Satan's minions on the earth. After the sixth vial was poured out, unclean spirits began in alarm to assemble the armies of the kings of the whole world, "to gather them to the battle of that great day of God Almighty . . . into a place called in the Hebrew tongue Armageddon" (Revelation XVI: 14, 16). For Protestant evangelicals in the 1860's, Armageddon meant America.

Signs and Portents

To the evangelical Protestants of the north, already schooled in the doctrine of progressive millennialism, it seemed that the deepening confrontation between the north and south, and the economic crises that developed at the same time, were the preliminary skirmishes that presaged the Second Coming of the Lord and the final battle at Armageddon.

In the fall of 1857, after a long period of material prosperity, a financial panic brought on another of the recurrent depressions. John Campbell, the Chester cotton manufacturer, failed in business and some of the mills in the Rockdale district closed down, including the mill at Old Sable. Clementina notified Sophie that it would not be difficult to find servants because "there are so many clever mill people wanting work now." She recommended to Sophie as "most qualified" to be a replacement for her departed domestic "a young man at Rockdale Hayes Griffith who used to live with us as a waiter years ago." Griffith, a loom boss, was actually thirty years old and had a wife and three small children, including a newborn baby boy, "but is now and will probably be for some time out of work. He understands the care of a horse and house work—is . . . a communicant of our church and is I believe a sincere Christian. He is as quiet . . . as Margaret Mullen."[1]

Close on the heels of the financial débâcle came an enthusiastic and protracted revival movement in the cities of the north. It had begun, in fact, before the crash, and as early as February 1857 (more than six months in advance of the bank failures) Clementina had noted an increase in devoutness among some of her acquaintances and expressed hope for "a revival of God's work in the hearts of the people of God." It fed largely on the national sense of crisis, of a sinful America about to be chastised by the Lord as the millennial point of view would predict. The vials of wrath were opening upon the continent and the people experienced a sudden urgency in their need to repent and pray for acceptance by the Redeemer. Prayer meetings were held daily in Philadelphia and other large cities, led by old friends of the Smiths, like the Reverend Kingston Goddard, formerly a reader at Calvary, now pastor of the Church of the Atonement. In the Rockdale district, there was a "a growing interest" in religion, and Clementina and Sophie remarked on a number of "amazing" conversions.[2] Later in the year came the news of the transatlantic telegraph, to which Clementina responded with her expression of hope that "we shall see the day and coming of the Lord."[3] In Upland, Crozer reported: "We have not partaken largely of the blessed revival that has extended so widely over our land but have still much cause for rejoicing that some souls around us have been born again . . . a serious Spirit now prevailing leads us to hope that a blessing is in store and will ere long descend."[4] In Philadelphia, the old patrons of Calvary Church, Bishop Potter and the Reverend Dudley Tyng, as well as the Reverend James Caughey, the revivalist who inspired the Methodists in Rockdale in the 1830's, were extremely active in stirring up the fires of revivalism, not only in Episcopal congregations but among the people of the city at large.[5]

Perhaps the most significant revival effort in Rockdale was made by Harriet Smith. In the winter of 1856–57 some of the better educated and more ambitious young working people, particularly the loom bosses in some of the weaving mills, had formed a nonreligious "literary association." Hattie, who taught the young men's Sunday School class and already knew some of the members of the new association, had exerted herself to turn it in a religious direction. Early in 1857 she organized a well-attended course of lectures by clergymen; the ubiquitous Bishop Potter was one of the speakers and addressed the group on the subject, "Washington the young man's model." Clementina cautiously opined, "I think this effort to engage the interest of the young men in mental improvement must do much good and perhaps lead the way to better things."[6] By 1859 the association had a "reading room," probably in the church, which contained no books but did provide members with some of the daily newspapers (gift subscriptions from the Smiths and other friends), including the *National Intelligencer,* the London *Times,* the *North American Review,* and the *Pennsylvania Inquirer.* Some of the young men were also members of the Delaware County Institute of Science, which had a library that contained books of radical character, and they were in the habit of bringing these borrowed volumes to the reading room.

The conflict was clear. The literary association depended upon Calvary Church and its leaders for support; but many of its members did not want religious oversight in the form of rules and regulations and censorship of the reading matter of its members. As Clementina put it, "It was not a church or even a religious association, indeed I think some of the men were very jealous of its having this character and *we* were afraid of the character of books that might find an entrance among them." Resourceful Harriet handled the problem deftly, said Clementina:

Harriet managed to have a man of good moral character and very leading mind named president and he gave the bias to all that was done. He was very much afraid of admitting any who wd. introduce books of immoral or of infidel tendency—and used great tact and wisdom in this matter— Some who were most fearful of interference of the church of religious people last year in this, are now themselves members of the church.[7]

Apparently the religious sponsors of the association were satisfied, for John P. Crozer quickly donated a building lot in Crozerville to the People's Literary Association of Rockdale and promised a gift of one-quarter the cost of the edifice, on condition that the Association find the other three-quarters.[8] The cornerstone was laid in an impressive ceremony on the Fourth of July, 1860. A band and a company of militia from West Chester arrived at the Lenni depot at 9:00 A.M., where they were met by the members of the Literary Association, and together they marched through the villages in the district until they reached the site at Crozerville. There they heard a Fourth of July oration by Robert L. Martin, the manager of Lenni Mill, attended by Mr. and Mrs. Richard S. Smith, some visiting relatives, and most of the Sunday School teachers.

The oration was followed by dinner in a tent. Then everyone repaired for the afternoon to the picnic grove in the woods where the Sunday School presented the community with its annual supper feast, prepared by Clementina, Harriet, and a few others (the company consumed 55 lbs. of beef, 400 rolls, 20 lbs. of candy, 40 lbs. of cake, 300 lemons for lemonade, and 30 quarts of ice cream).

When the parade marched past the parsonage on Mount Road on its way to the Association grounds, the Sunday School gave it a special salute:

Our school marched to meet . . . and presented to the president of the Association a very handsome wreath which Mother made, also a beautiful bouquet to another of their officers—Both these young men had been in Mother's Infant school—The children then sang the 2d. piece on the paper I enclose and gave three cheers for the literary Assn. of Rockdale. Their offering was responded to by the president in a neat and handsome speech and the band stopped and played "Yankee Doodle" for them. The children then marched back to the woods.[9]

The People's Literary Association of Rockdale was, however, forced to postpone the completion of its edifice. The collection at the time of the cornerstone ceremony was disappointing; and within the year most of the members would be in the Grand Army of the Republic. But after the war the building was completed, with library and meeting rooms on the first floor, and a large hall on the second which was used for "entertainments, lectures, and public meetings." The Association remained in a flourishing condition for many years.

As the months wore on, the sense of foreboding, of a terrible trial to be undergone, increasingly preoccupied the sensitive Christian observer. The cotton industry still languished; many people were still out of work in Rockdale. In Philadelphia, a contract for the making of soldiers' uniforms was being used by a benevolent agency at the Girard House as a relief measure, small subcontracts being let out to the unemployed. The resolute Harriet went there and secured the cloth for the making of forty-eight coats, sixteen pairs of pants, and twenty pairs of Canton flannel drawers. She and Clementina then hired fourteen women to sew up the garments at their house. The parson's sister was a "tayloress"; she instructed the two ladies, who in turn directed the women, as well as feeding them and their children. But it was all discouraging and Clemma complained, to her friend, "Alas! dearest Sophie anxiety and sorrow surround us everywhere our whole social fabric is overturned and my heart sickens with the grieff of all around us—Here there is want and sadness in most of the households and we wonder how the first is to be relieved."[10] She almost despaired of being able to help. "There is so much vice immediately about us in this place . . . I feel there is so much ought to do yet do so little."[11]

By the end of the year, after the secession of North and South Carolina and the first seizures of federal arsenals in the south, it was plain to the people in Rockdale that war was imminent. Clementina bewailed: "We know not literally what a day may bring forth—What sad times are these! We can only look to the God of Nations to relieve us from the woes that threaten. It is grievous to find the peace of families disturbed by differing political opinions."[12]

Rockdale in the Civil War

The war officially began on the morning of April 15 when, two days after the surrender of Fort Sumter in Charleston Harbor, President Lincoln declared publicly that an "insurrection" had occurred and called for three-month volunteers. There had been intense public excitement in the preceding several days, with spontaneous demonstrations against the south and much patriotic flag-waving and badge-wearing in all the mill towns. On the evening of the 15th, after Lincoln's call for volunteers, there were mass meetings in Media and Chester to organize the volunteer companies. Edward Darlington presided over the Media meeting to organize the "Delaware County Union Rifles," and John Broomall made a speech. By the end of the week the company had been mustered into the federal service as Company F, Fourth Regiment of Pennsylvania Volunteers. The same Monday evening, a company of "Union Blues" was organized at a patriotic rally in Chester, and by week's end had been mustered into the Ninth Regiment of Pennsylvania Volunteers. Within the next few weeks, home guards were organized in all the little towns of the county, commanded by scions of the existing local leadership: at Upland by John P. Crozer's son George, at Media by Edward Darlington's son George, at Glenn Mills by one of the younger Willcoxes.

In Chester, early in May, many of the Rockdale men enlisted in Company B, Twenty-sixth Regiment, First Pennsylvania Volunteers, including two of "Hattie's boys," John Newsome and Jones Bradbury, and, serving as chaplain, the Smiths' friend and former rector at Calvary Church, Charles Breck. In the Rockdale district, William Talley, a newspaper editor, was organizing the "Rockdale Rifle Guards," who marched off later in May and were mustered into the service as Company F, Thirtieth Regiment, First Pennsylvania Reserves. Among those who left with Talley was another of "Hattie's boys" from the Sunday School, Hayes P. Griffith, who enlisted as a musician. By the end of summer, most of the young men had gone.[13]

In these early days of the war, many believed that a show of strength and a brief summer's campaign would be enough to overawe the rebels, and that "the horrors of serious conflict might be averted." Enthusiasm among the civilians left at home was intense. Clementina's mother, when she learned that Major Anderson, the hero of Fort Sumter, was visiting Philadelphia, was "crazy" to see him, and dashed off, with Clementina trailing after her, into a dense throng at Independence Hall. Clementina had a close view and was shocked. "I never saw," she said, "a face in which mental conflict was so marked—It was profoundly sad and such a contrast to the frantic delight of the crowd." That night she could not sleep ("my brain was in such a commotion"). Clementina noted that those formerly cautious (like Bishop Potter) were now less reticent and were speaking their views plainly; everywhere she went, even among the young soldiers, she met a spirit of Christian dedication.[14] Inspired by the example of the young volunteers, the community leaders and the women quickly organized a system of war relief. In the crisis the mills had shut down and many families were destitute. Before the end of May, at another mass meeting in Media Courthouse, a county-wide relief organization had formed itself, headed by John P. Crozer, for the purpose of "soliciting funds to equip troops and support the families of volunteers." That very day $2,500 was collected in contributions, and in the two days afterward, in the several collection districts, another $2,700. Crozer himself invested largely in the national loan. The women were active in committee work and as seamstresses, tailoring uniforms. Harriet, as usual, was in the forefront of these relief activities.[15] It was all seen as a thrilling confrontation between a long-suffering, patient, virtuous, and invincible *national* interest and an obstinate, petulant, anarchistic minority of evil slaveholders who had merely *sectional* support. As his biographer described Crozer's attitude in this liminal period of the war: "When the nation's property was seized by force, when hostile batteries were opened upon a national fort, he felt that there was no escape—That force must be met by force, and disobedient wickedness subdued."[16]

It was the first Battle of Bull Run, at the end of July, that made it plain to almost everyone that the troops would not be home in three months. After "the stunning news . . . of the rout of our troops," Richard S. Smith, worried about his son in the service, became chronically depressed about the war; he and Robert Martin, the manager at Lenni Mill, were convinced that Washington, D.C. would soon fall to the enemy. Harriet soon became miserable too. But Clementina's letters took on a tone of hardness. On every front, in every battle, someone she knew was risking his life or his reputation to put down "this wicked rebellion." Rather than admit discouragement, she tried to cheer others up and threw herself into whatever activities she could find that would help the war effort. In August she wrote, "All the mills are stopped now, even Mr. Crozer's." She organized a brigade of women at Lenni to make army shirts and defended with ardor the good name of General Patterson (the owner of Lenni Mill), whose failure to prevent the arrival of southern reinforcements was alleged by some to have given victory to the south at Bull Run. And now that the enormity of the conflict was apparent, she began to find the millennial interpretation congenial:

> I feel more and more that the cause is God's and that He will carry it on in His own way and with what instrumentality he pleases. The folly of our people and their vain boasting and Sabbath breaking was truly punished at Manassas.[17]

Bull Run taught another lesson. The ghastly accounts of the sufferings of the maimed and dying during and after the rout, and of the unpreparedness of either side to cope with the realities of the physical and spiritual needs of the casualties, led directly to the organization of one more benevolent evangelical society. The United States Christian Commission was organized in the fall of 1861 "to promote the spiritual and temporal welfare" of the soldiers in field, camp, and hospital. John P. Crozer was one of the founders, along with John Wanamaker of Philadelphia (experienced in

Y.M.C.A. administration), Stephen Tyng of New York, and other leading evangelical laymen and clergy. The Commission, in the absence of any very effective military system for satisfying the needs of the troops outside battle (and often acting against the wishes of local commanders), took on a role that in later years would be shared by the Red Cross, the United Services Organization, the Chaplain's Office, and various entertainment centers. The goal of the Commission was to ensure that the Grand Army of the Republic was a *Christian* army, that its wounded were properly clothed and fed, that its dying had the opportunity for a Christian death. To this end the Commission, from its offices and warehouse on Bank Street in Philadelphia, equipped and sent out some five thousand "delegates" to various commands. These delegates performed an incredible service: they built 140 chapels and numberless "reading rooms"; they constructed sanitary systems and diet kitchens; they preached 58,000 sermons and wrote 92,000 letters for illiterate or crippled soldiers; they gave out 95,000 packages of food, clothing, and medical supplies; they visited numberless wounded men in hospitals; they distributed (among an army of two million men) a million and a half Bibles, a million hymn books, and eight million tracts or "knapsack books." Crozer remained active in the Commission's work as member of the executive committee, as trustee, and as financial contributor, until the end of the war. The Christian Commission finally received wide public acclaim for its assistance to the armies; President Lincoln met personally with the Commission in January 1866 to express the nation's gratitude.[18]

There was a brief spurt of hope, in the fall, that the war would soon be over, occasioned by Admiral Samuel Francis Du Pont's naval victory at Port Royal, South Carolina. Du Pont was in command of the South Atlantic Blockading Squadron, and in November his vessels, led by the flagship *Wabash,* drove off the Confederate garrison occupying the fort. The town and harbor were then occupied as one of the land bases of the effective Union blockade of the southern coast. The friends of the Du Ponts' were elated (Richard S. Smith was "in an ecstacy with it"); Clementina wrote to Sophie congratulating her on her husband's victory and describing the enthusiasm of the people of Rockdale: "I have just finished writing a letter from a mother to a son, in the army of the Potomac, in which she says, that this news has revived this neighborhood and made the people hope the war will soon be over. . . ."[19] But the war was not soon over and by Christmas news of fatal casualties (two) and men missing in action (three) began to accumulate. Clementina tried to argue herself into optimism. "Out of 200 from our neighbourhood," she said, "this is a small proportion but all feel more like making the season one of exclusively religious services."[20]

Rockdale was almost a ghost town. With the mills closed, "all that can are going away for work and our best young men are nearly all gone" (some no doubt as much motivated by need for military pay and enlistment and re-enlistment bonuses as by patriotism and millennial fervor). The rector gloomily remarked that everywhere he went he found "Ichabod is written." (Ichabod, meaning "inglorious," was the name given to her newborn son by a woman whose husband had died in Israel's great defeat by the Philistines, when the Ark of the Covenant was lost; her last words as she expired in childbirth were: "The glory is departed from Israel.") Those who remained, even the unemployed, were not actually in desperate financial circumstances, because there was "so much govt. work and so much money sent from the camps to fds. at home."[21] But in residence in Lenni, Clementina began to see the wounded limping home. One May, while she was writing to Sophie, "one of our men" who had been taken prisoner at Williamsburg "passed by our door on his way home. He was released on parole, but looks *so* sick, and said he did not feel as if he would get well." Ever cheerful, she remarked to Sophie, "Home may do more than he expects for him."[22] By fall of 1862, after the second Union defeat at Bull Run, and the bloody and inconclusive battle at Antietam, the reports of casualties and the fear of more bad news to come were casting a dark shadow over the community. The last week of September was "the bitterest in this neighbourhood in the war . . . *everything* was so sad, sighs and tears hearts burdened with dread forebodings all around us."[23] In November the rector Mr. Murphy, to allay community concern, made the round of the camps in which "Rockdalers" were stationed. On his return, after the morning sermon, the people lined the road, begging for news. In the afternoon, the custom was for the rector to come to tea at the Smiths, and while they took tea, "the people" would gather and sing hymns. The rector used this occasion to make a public statement about his visit, reassuring the community that their sons and fathers were in health and in reasonably comfortable circumstances. Much moved, Murphy broke down in tears while reading the prayer for those who had "gone out at the call of their country."[24]

As the war went on, more and more names of Rockdalers were reported on the lists of sick and wounded, killed and captured: John Newsome (wounded, captured, and released), Jones Bradbury (wounded, captured, released, and later killed), Hayes P. Griffith (discharged, sick), John Wilde (killed), Henry Odiorne (killed), James Breck (killed), John McDade (wounded) . . . And every mail brought news of the losses suffered by friends in other parts of the country. The women of the managerial class and even some of the men threw themselves into hospital work, visiting the wounded, reading to them and writing letters, teaching the illiterate to read, and bringing the solace of Christian conversation. Clementina's cousin Dan Smith served as a civilian male nurse in a hospital in Philadelphia and told Clemma the affecting story of how an acquaintance of theirs, "poor Snow," died in hope of salvation:

He said when he saw Snow could not live many hours he asked him what were his views of another life; Snow said he felt he was pardoned—Dan told him he was glad he felt he was "washed in the precious blood of the Lamb of God"—Snow nodded assent and added "write to my Mother" which Dan did the night he died—Poor Dan cried like a child when he died—[25]

Both Harriet and Clementina Smith and Eleanora Lammot spent much time in hospital activity, collecting funds, preparing wound dressings, and making visits. For a time they were busy—along with Maria Blakeley and her daughter Sophia—with the women's auxiliary at the military hospital, which was being set up in Crozer's former normal school at Upland (until, in a dispute with the military commander, the civilians were thrown out there as they had been at Dan's hospital in Philadelphia). Some of their friends, including the wife of the owner of nearby Yearsley's Mill, proposed to enlist as nurses with Miss Dorothea Dix. The Rockdale ladies also served regular schedules as visitors in the big military hospital on South Street in Philadelphia. It was not easy work, but Harriet especially was devoted to serving wounded young men and alternated days with her friend Bessie Baird. Clementina was concerned about her. "I hope she will have strength for it," she said. "I feel a little anxious for I see the depression it causes her."[26] In the summer after the battle at Gettysburg, there was a hot spell, and Clementina described the hospital as being almost "unendurable . . . —the atmosphere so affected by the wounds."[27]

The stress of war was accomplishing another change: it was achieving a final polarization of the people, so that there was no middle ground for compromise, and the two sides were seen, in the millennial interpretation, as hosts of God and Satan. Charity for the enemy was not easy to summon in this time; everyone was suspicious even of friends, finding dark plots in each military and naval reversal. "No one," cried Clementina in the summer of '63, "escapes public censure now, our excited and distressed country is unjust to its best helpers."[28] She was thinking particularly of Sophie's husband, who had recently commanded an ill-fated attack on the forts in Charleston Harbor. After extensive planning and experimentation and the assembling of the most formidable fleet of ironclad naval vessels in history, Admiral Du Pont had failed. He broke off the attack after one day's battle, in the conviction (undoubtedly correct) that continued assault on the virtually untouched land batteries "would have converted a failure into a disaster."[29] The Secretary of the Navy had relieved him of command and he was now surrounded and constantly harassed by hostile newspaper critics and investigation officers. (He was replaced by Admiral Dahlgren, the developer of the powerful guns that were eventually to pound Fort Sumter into rubble.) To be sure, as she said, "we have sinned grievously and God is very angry with us. How much better this, than for us to look to man's mistakes as the cause of our reverses."[30] But it was a difficult philosophy to maintain in the face of the blizzard of rumors, backbiting, and intrigue that filled the air. It was much easier to lay blame, and by 1864 even Clementina was bitter. Writing from Lenni, she told Sophie, "The good element is gone from our population drunken women and copperhead men are left." With evident satisfaction she gave an account of how the mother of one of her Sunday School girls, "Happy Pike," had come to an untimely end:

Her mother was a very wicked woman who did all she cd. to demoralize this place and some weeks ago went to a soldier's picnic near Chester taking her daughter with her. She left her company when the picnic was over in search of something she had lost and was killed on the R. Road and mangled in the most frightful manner.[31]

And it was with great relish that Clementina quoted at length from a letter from her own and Hattie's friend, Bessie Baird. Mrs. Baird was on the train from New York to Boston when she and her companions, a group of respectable charity women, encountered a group of twelve wounded soldiers on their way home. All during the trip they entertained the men, listening to their battle stories and opinions on the war and exchanging names and promises to write. Her daughter was the first to approach the men, who were much taken with the little girl, cut off a button from her coat and wrote down her name, and accepted her as a kind of mascot for the trip. When they began to pass around a bottle, she begged them not to drink and they actually put the whiskey away, saying, "We cannot take any more after what that child said . . . She spoke the first words of comfort we have had since we left home, and she knows as much as a man about the war." It was in the midst of this scene of romantic patriotism that Bessie suddenly encountered Dr. Lord, the well-known lecturer and advocate of compromise with the south. He sat beside Bessie and never stopped talking. Bessie was outraged and finally exploded:

We had a regular scene which ended by my saying I regret Dr. Lord that it is not in my power to apportion to you a place in Fort Lafayette as I should be delighted to do so, he got pretty red and said he was only in fun and wanted to draw me out—He never stopped talking from N.Haven to Hartford. He said my feelings amounted to religious fanaticism and asked what kind of feelings would you like *me* to have—I said oh only respectable manliness I don't ask for courage. He goes for compromise and all that stuff—32

The "religious fanaticism" to which Dr. Lord referred was of course the millennial interpretation of the war to which increasing numbers of religious people in the north subscribed. Harriet Beecher Stowe, in *Uncle Tom's Cabin,* had warned of the Second Coming, which was to be a day both of vengeance and redemption. And Julia Ward Howe, in *The Battle Hymn of the Republic,* first published in 1862, had drawn her imagery directly from Revelation, delineating the American Civil War as the final battle to which a mounted Christ in armor would bring his "terrible swift sword."33 But it was not merely a popular rhetoric, vulnerable to the charge of "fanaticism," that sounded the millennial note. This was also expressed, as we have seen, in more orthodox and measured religious language in the book by Hollis Read, published in 1861, entitled *The Coming Crisis of the World.*

Clementina began to find her chief solace in the feeling that she was playing a part in the greatest event in human history. She wrote to Sophie: "I feel more and more how insignificant this mortal condition except in its bearings upon the great universal plan, and for the *individual,* in its bearing upon Eternal life."34 After reading Lincoln's Emancipation Proclamation, she reflected on the uncertainty of its effects in a nation better prepared to grant freedom as a military necessity than out of a moral sense. And this uncomfortable train of thought was immediately followed by the expression of a millennialist hope:

May our Heavenly Father grant us His direction and deliver us from wicked men who have certainly been thrown to the surface lately—I cannot think we will be forsaken—and all I desire is that we as a people may be brought to do God's will—Perhaps *we* may be the martyr generation—if so I trust a glorious country will rise from our ashes—and we know that a heavenly one is before all those who seek it—"The time is short"—That is a comfort—35

As the end of the war neared, with the help of the rector and the Sunday School teachers Clementina was involving herself in the spreading of the millennial interpretation among all the people of Rockdale. Christmas was coming and she had been listening to the "angelic strains" of the little children practicing their Christmas carols in the church. She was moved to reflect on the pervasiveness of the theme of the Second Coming in the

Christmas services (dedicated to the birth of Jesus) and to declare her wish that everyone might know:

> What a solemn season this is dear Sophie when we have set before us the Second coming of our Lord in all our scripture readings and prayers. Oh that we all might be looking for and hasting unto that great day of the Lord when He shall come to be glorified in his Saints and to be admired in all them that believe—[36]

Hattie's Boys

Two of "Hattie's boys" from the young men's Sunday School class and the Literary Association were John Newsome and Jones Bradbury. They were both weavers and close friends, and they enlisted at the same time in the same outfit, Company B of the Twenty-sixth Regiment of the First Pennsylvania Volunteers, where for a time they were army buddies. John Newsome was a man of medium height, blond-haired and gray-eyed, twenty-six years old when the war began. He had been born in Yorkshire and had come to America in 1854, working first in a mill in New Jersey, and then coming to the Rockdale district about 1856. He lived with his parents and five of his brothers and sisters, all of whom except the youngest worked at the looms too. His mother was unable to read or write and his father, also a weaver, seems to have deferred to his oldest son, for John acted as the head of the family and just before the war had bought them a small three-room stone farmhouse at the top of the hill above Rockdale.[37]

Jones Bradbury was 6 feet tall, with blue eyes, auburn hair, and a dark complexion. Twenty-three years old when the war began, he had been born in rural Otsego County, New York. His father was a laborer, born in England; his mother a New York woman. The family had moved to Pennsylvania when Jones was two or three years old and to the Rockdale district about 1855. Now there were nine of them. Jones and his younger brother David worked as weavers in Callaghan's mill in Parkmount, and his sister Alice worked as a spooler. In April, just as the war began, his father, who was about sixty, died and Jones, earning about $7 per week, became the principal support of the family.[38]

John Newsome was a cheerful young man, who breezed through events, carrying people with him and transcending obstacles and personal disasters with a happy self-assurance. Jones Bradbury's nature was of a darker kind, moody and plagued by self-doubt, but determined to endure to the end. John Newsome was the more successful; but Jones Bradbury was Harriet's favorite.

John enlisted as a three-year man in May 1861 and was eventually promoted to first sergeant of Company B. Almost exactly two years later, during the Union defeat at Chancellorsville in Virginia, he suffered a gunshot wound of the right thigh and was captured. (Jones Bradbury wrote home to Hattie mistakenly reporting that John was killed.) He was paroled and sent back to the Union lines two weeks later, eventually reaching the South Street Hospital in Philadelphia. The wound healed slowly and he was suffering from an inguinal hernia that resulted from it, but during the summer he was given a commission as second lieutenant and furloughed to go home to be nursed back to health. He returned to Rockdale and within a couple of months had become engaged to Elizabeth Murphy, the rector's sister. He rejoined Company B in September 1863, although his wound was still suppurating and his rupture was unrepaired, and fought through Grant's Wilderness Campaign until rheumatism and exhaustion wore him down. He was furloughed in March 1864, married Elizabeth Murphy, and then again returned for more. Exhausted and sick, he was discharged in June 1864. He recalled the Wilderness Campaign clearly in the 1890's when he applied for an increase in his invalid pension:

From Bealton to Culpepper Sept. to Dec. 1863 was my first sciatic. But having my gun-shot wound & rupture & my wound still suppurating I attributed my pains to those causes, for I was an ambitious veteran with a commission but not mustered. Our Mine-Run Campaign increased my rheumatism. Nov. 26th 4 P.M. up to my armpits in the Rapahannock, then a sharp engagement and crossed another stream over knee deep, which felt cold as ice. The day we lay in front of the Rebels at Mine Run, very trying day. Feb. 6th/64 was out on the point to relieve Poulter, the streams were swollen & the ground soaked—had a bad time of it & suffered a good deal. April 9th & 10th/64 was on picket on the Rap'ck, the worst rain storm I ever saw, thoroughly drenched & all hands discouraged. May 13th/64 badly exhausted 9 P.M. our Regt. called on to relieve some 6th Corps. Pickets got lost & stood & stood knee-deep in mud till morning, all these things & more caused my rheumatism, but thank God I was ready for discharge.[39]

For a while after leaving the service John worked as a nurse for Caspar Wistar Pennock, M.D., a local physician crippled by sclerosis of the spine. Although Pennock was a distinguished man of medicine, trained in Edinburgh and Paris, and known for his research on diseases of the heart, Clementina was shocked: "John Newsome *nurse* to Dr. Pennock! We think this is a great mistake. John's time is too precious to spend in what cannot elevate or advance him."[40] But in due course John accumulated some money (borrowed, according to family tradition, from Captain Miller of Company B, whose life John had saved). Captain Miller invited John and Elizabeth to live with his family in Middletown after his discharge, and after the war he lent them money to buy a farm. In 1868 John went out west, to the end of the railroad in Iowa, and purchased a farm there, within the sound of train whistles to please his wife, who "wanted to feel she was not entirely outside the bounds of civilization." In 1869 he moved there permanently with his wife, the two children born while they had lived with the Millers, and John's parents and brothers and sisters.[41]

Jones Bradbury was a man tormented by the fear that he did not deserve salvation; and to him Harriet's compassionate nature was strongly drawn. During the summer and fall of 1858 she had taught a Sunday School class for young men, and twenty-one-year-old Jones Bradbury was one. When in January she left Rockdale for the social season in Philadelphia, she held "a sort of Entertainment" for the men at the parsonage. On Sunday evening, at the end of the last class, she saw Jones "taking a *private cry* to himself behind the stove." He pulled himself together and then unexpectedly made a short speech:

Just before they closed he said he had a few remarks to make to them & in a very manly way told them that he cd. not bear to give up their S. ev^g study of the S.S. & he wanted to propose that they should ask Mr. Murphy if there was any one in the parish who could take the class it should be continued I believe Mr. Murphy has determined to give his Sunday evenings to it—[42]

Hattie returned in the spring to her group of devoted young men; her work there, observed Clementina, was "blessed to her own heart as well as all who have been the subjects." During the summer, the family took Harriet off to a vacation in the mountains of Vermont, but she arranged for a substitute teacher, a man, who interested them "exceedingly" and brought in new recruits to the class. Jones progressed in his religious commitment and in the fall was baptized and confirmed at Calvary. Hattie spoke proudly of this and of "his simple childlike faith."

This faith was soon tested. "Poor fellow," wrote Clementina, "he has had a bitter sorrow in his early religious life." Early in January "a very dear brother of his" committed suicide. Jones was sustained, however, by his conviction that his brother could not have surrendered his hope of Heaven by taking his own life deliberately. "Jones says he thinks he should be wild with grief if he did not fully believe it was mental aberration that caused him to take his own life. A post mortem Examination proved that his brain was very much diseased."[43] A year later Jones's father died, and then the war began.

Jones went to Philadelphia with John Newsome and they enlisted together in Company B and served side by side through the first Battle of Bull Run. After Bull Run, Jones came back to Rockdale on furlough for two weeks, and Clementina declared that "his experience has made him a more earnest Christian." Jones and John were together during the subsequent actions in which the Twenty-sixth Pennsylvania was engaged: the Peninsular Campaign, the second Bull Run, and Chancellorsville, where John was wounded and captured. In August 1862, Hattie, Clementina, and Miss Davis the Sunday School teacher went to Washington and visited all over town, including the Navy Department, where they tried to call on the Secretary of the Navy, "good kind Mr. Welles," who unfortunately was not in. They also sought out the Rockdalers in service and found Jones and John: "Hattie had the satisfaction of seeing her two 'boys' John & Jones and of feeling that she could do something to bring them up from careless ways into which this unsettled condition of things has thrown them. They spent Thursday evening with us."[44]

The two men were not separated until John was wounded and captured at Chancellorsville in the spring of 1863. Jones went through the battle at Gettysburg without wounds, although the Twenty-sixth Regiment lost 213 of its 364 enlisted men and 11 of 18 officers, killed or wounded. In the fall they were reunited, with John now promoted to second lieutenant and Jones to sergeant. But their association was looser, with differences in rank and duties and quarters. In November 1863 Jones was wounded (a minnie-ball through the right foot) and hospitalized in Philadelphia. He came out of the hospital after three months with hair prematurely gray. He stayed for a while with the Smiths in their house at 1010 Clinton Street and delighted them by praising Admiral Du Pont's silence before his critics. "I am amazed," said Harriet's mother, "at Jones' improvement. If our army officers were as loyal as well acquainted with the whole condition of our country's civil war, cause to consequences—the rebels would lay down their arms."[45] He re-enlisted for another three years, this time being transferred to another regiment, the Forty-ninth Pennsylvania Volunteers, as third sergeant (and finally as first sergeant).

But Jones's time was running out. In June 1864 he was captured at Mechanicsville, Virginia, while leading his men on a skirmish line. He was sent to the notorious prisoner-of-war camp at Andersonville, Georgia, where he remained for almost six months until he was released on parole for reason of illness. After convalescing in Philadelphia, in March 1865 he returned to his regiment, then pursuing the rebels through Virginia east of Petersburg. He was shot in a small fight between pursuing units of the Ninety-ninth Pennsylvania and the retreating Confederates at Sailors

Creek, Virginia, on April 6, 1865. He lived for a couple of hours and had time to write a note to Hattie before he died. The war ended three days later with Lee's surrender at Appomattox.

Jones's letter reached Rockdale in three weeks' time and Clementina wrote the sad news to Sophie:

> We all feel very deeply Jones Bradbury's death, he was killed on the 6th April before Petersburg while leading his Comy. in a charge—He survived only two hours—A pencil note came to dear Hattie yesterday written with gt. effort when he was dying the paper was stained with his blood! We have the blessed hope that he has entered into Everlasting Life and spared the conflict with sin so dreadful to him.[46]

The Smiths did what they could for Jones's mother, who was living in Philadelphia, trying to support three of her children on the money that Jones had been sending home from his pay. A day or two after the letter arrived, Harriet went to Philadelphia and witnessed Lavinia Bradbury's application for a Mother's Army Pension, testifying that she knew that he had sent home his pay because she had read his letters to his mother. Clementina and her father supported the mother's claim. Harriet also claimed Jones's body and had it shipped to Rockdale, where she waited for it alone in the house in Lenni all through the second week in May. "She went to six trains," said Clementina, "to await the arrival of Jones body before it came and a very rough undertaker tried her sorely." Jones was buried in the cemetery behind Calvary Church.

And Clementina wrote on to Sophie (whose husband was dying), "The weariness of the road here should only make the heavenly home look brighter not lead to repinings for rest & society of those we love. My sweet little book shelf looks beautifully with its patriotic colors & has my bible & P. book in my snug little corner where I wish I had you by me."[47]

ENVOI

In the years after the war, while the grass grew green over the grave of Jones Bradbury, the mill where he had worked at Parkmount, a few hundred yards upstream, returned to normal production. Indeed, the Rockdale manufacturing district grew ever more prosperous and survived as a textile center for another hundred years; the looms at Parkmount, the last of the textile factories to close down, did not cease their clatter until 1970. And the same mills today still house light industry: Westlake Plastics, Sunroc Corporation, Container Research, a lumber mill, machine shops. The Smiths and the Riddles and the Lammots lived on too for many years, gradually dying off in their eighties and nineties as the century came to an end. But only three of the figures in this story made it into the twentieth century: Harriet Smith, who died in 1905 at the age of eighty-seven; Hayes P. Griffith, weaver, servant of the Smiths, and Civil War veteran, who reached eighty and died in 1909; and Lydia, the widow of Samuel Riddle, who died in 1915. The last of the old cohort to survive in the memories of living Rockdalers was Lydia Riddle. She used to watch the passersby as she sat on the porch of the old Leander house (now demolished as unsafe), wearing a black dress and on it a diamond brooch so bright that it flashed all up and down Pennell Road.

But already, a few years after the end of the war, the early growth of the Rockdale manufacturing district, and the lives of its people then, were becoming history even to the remaining participants. Several local histories by local residents appeared in succession, devoted to celebrating the exploits of the "men of enterprise" who had made Delaware County what it was: the first, *History of Delaware County,* in 1862, by George Smith, of the Delaware County Institute of Science; John Broomall's *History of Delaware County for the Past Century,* a product of the call for consciousness of history associated with the Centennial celebrations; then, the history of *Chester (and*

Its Vicinity) by John Hill Martin, the boy who had grown up at Lenni Mill; and, in 1884, the detailed 765-page, double-columned *History of Delaware County* by Henry Graham Ashmead of Chester, which devoted about 25 pages specifically to the Rockdale manufacturing district's mills, churches, schools, and lodges. Published genealogies began to appear, of the Riddles, the Smiths, the Darlingtons. And in Rockdale itself in 1898 William E. Griffith launched the *Rockdale Herald,* a weekly newspaper dedicated to the principles of the Democratic Party, whose first issue carried as its lead article an account, apparently derived from Ashmead, of the history of the Glen Riddle Mills—"A Short Sketch of the flourishing Textile Factory at Glen Riddle, its former management and growth." Noted men like Crozer, Smith, and Bishops Lee, Potter, and Hopkins wrote autobiographical accounts or were the subjects of biographies and memorials. Before the turn of the century, the events of this story had become history to the residents of Rockdale itself.

Today, inevitably, only a few members of the community recall much about these happenings beyond what is available in Ashmead and the *Herald.* Time has flattened out, like the optical perspective of a landscape seen through a telephoto lens, and word-of-mouth transmission of unwritten historical information has slowed to a trickle. With each death of a participant, a whole world of information dies too; for the most part only written records and physical constructions remain. And these dwindle away constantly. Records are lost, paper crumbles, old letters are thrown away, unlabeled photographs become meaningless. And the mills, dams, races, tenements, bridges—all these too are subject to constant erosion. Since beginning this study in 1969, I have seen old Parkmount successively in active use as a rug mill, abandoned, flooded, burned out in a spectacular blaze, and then partly knocked down by wrecking crews. Rotting and hazardous mansions at Lenni and Penn's Grove have been demolished; but Crozer's first mansion at West Branch is still lived in, and the Crozer mansion at Crozerville has been converted into company offices by Container Research. Glen Riddle Dam was washed away in the flood in 1971. Each year less and less information is left of a world that was once as rich and real as the one that is there today.

And yet that world lives on, in a sense, in the customs and beliefs of those who have come after. The people of Rockdale then lived in what they felt was historical time. Their lives spanned the coming of the industrial age to America; they saw themselves as participants in a grand process of development that was bringing technological progress and material prosperity to all mankind, and with it—if the observer was a Christian—salvation and even the millennium; if he was a Deist, then enlightenment and cooperative association. They communicate with us directly through their intentional literary remains; indirectly, through the legacy of beliefs transmitted without consciousness of origin, in classroom, church, political meeting, and union hall, about the social nature of the world. It was in Rockdale, and in dozens of other industrial communities like Rockdale, that an American world view developed which pervades the present—or did so until recently —with a sense of superior Christian virtue, a sense of global mission, a sense of responsibility and capability for bringing enlightenment to a dark and superstitious world, for overthrowing ancient and new tyrannies, and for making backward infidels into Christian men of enterprise.

APPENDIX

NOTES

BIBLIOGRAPHY

INDEX

Appendix X

Paradigmatic Processes
in Culture Change

The following discussion was originally published in 1972 in the *American Anthropologist*. It is reprinted here with some minor changes in wording and without the anticipatory description of the Rockdale study. I had begun the collection of material on the Rockdale manufacturing district in 1969; as the information accumulated, I realized that Rockdale was one of a number of similar villages where the Industrial Revolution began in the United States and that a standard process of cultural and social change was probably common to all of them. This essay was written as a kind of guide for organizing my thoughts about what was happening in Rockdale and deciding what kinds of data would be most relevant.

A second purpose of the essay was to direct attention to, and to delineate more thoroughly, a type of process in culture change which of late has been relatively neglected by anthropologists. Kroeber and his contemporaries over a generation ago emphasized the importance of paradigmatic regularities in historical process in their studies of the growth of culture areas and civilizations.[1] A historian of science, Thomas Kuhn, more recently has formulated in greater detail some of the essential features of the paradigmatic process in his well-known essay on the nature of scientific progress, *The Structure of Scientific Revolutions*.[2] I propose here to amplify their statements, to generalize them still further into a model of a type of culture change (which I shall call "paradigmatic"), and to outline some of the many applications of the model to the study of culture change in domains other than science itself.

Kuhn's Model of Culture Change

Thomas Kuhn argued that contrary to the belief of most scientists and of many historians of science, scientific evolution has not been a steady, continuous accumulation of data and modification of theory. It has proceeded, rather, in alternating phases of normal and revolutionary science. During the course of "normal science," an unchanging paradigm governs the work of most investigators in any given field or discipline. These paradigms are the "recurrent and quasi-standard illustrations of various theories in their conceptual, observational, and instrumental applications."[3] Explicit rules, theories, and assumptions may accompany paradigms but are not necessary for the guidance of research. The student learns the paradigm primarily by repeating as training exercises the very "illustrations" that constitute the paradigm itself, by redoing the laboratory experiments, deriving the equations, intuiting the concepts and findings which are described in the textbooks as classic and fundamental achievements. Later, his professional work as a normal scientist is to discover new applications of the same paradigm, to resolve ambiguities and apparent contradictions in the rules and theories, and to work out the as-yet-undiscovered theorems implicit in its logic. His work is problem solving within the continuously developing domain of interpretations of the paradigm itself. Thus the Greek geometers before Euclid established a paradigm for the study of plane and solid forms based upon constructions that could be accomplished by ruler and compass, by the sectioning of spheres, cones, and cylinders, and by the use of syllogistic reasoning. The formulation of axioms and theorems, and the application of Euclidean geometry to science and technology, was a problem-solving enterprise that occupied the Greek mathematical community for hundreds of years.

In the case of the Greek geometers, no new geometrical paradigm appeared in their own time; truly non-Euclidean geometries did not arrive until the nineteenth century. But inevitably, sooner or later, new paradigms directly confront and replace older ones. This confrontation occurs when the number of nagging, insoluble problems and internal inconsistencies associated with an existing paradigm has accumulated to the point where a whole new way of approaching the problem is seen as necessary by some irritated members of the scientific community. In response to the crisis, a new paradigm is devised, which is able to account for most of the phenomena explicable under the old but which is also able to solve the crucial problems refractory to it. If, after some intellectual conflict, the new paradigm is accepted, and with it a redefinition of the world view of the discipline, a "scientific revolution" may be said to have occurred. Examples of such scientific revolutions are the replacement of Ptolemaic by Galilean astronomy and the overthrow of the phlogiston theory of combustion by the oxygen theory. The development of the oxidation paradigm led directly to the complex set of principles and procedures which constituted the new atomic chemistry.

Both paradigmatic processes—normal science and revolutionary science—involve the activity of a scientific community. Such a community (or discipline, or school, or tradition, or what-have-you) is not usually a community in the ordinary sociological sense, of course, but rather a group of intercommunicating specialists, unrestricted in time or space, who jointly develop the applications of the paradigm. Kuhn does not elaborate on the nature of this community but its existence is explicitly recognized in his argument.

The General Model of Paradigmatic Processes

The paradigmatic process has five essential components: innovation, paradigmatic core development, exploitation, functional consequences, and rationalization. It is possible to think of them as overlapping stages in which each comes to the forefront of attention in due order, but the latter four "tasks" are actually continuous during the life of the paradigm.

This model attempts to embrace a far wider range of culture change processes than Kuhn's, first because Kuhn is centrally concerned with the history of science, and second because he is not attempting to deal at all with exploitation, functional consequences, or rationalization. But my model does not claim to describe *all* sequences of cultural innovations and their consequences. It applies only to those culture change sequences in which a paradigmatic core development process occurs. This restriction is essential to the application of the model.

Innovation of a new paradigm may (as Kuhn emphasizes) entail a conflict with an older one, which it may replace; in this case one may speak of a "revolution," such as the scientific revolutions of which Kuhn writes, or the cultural "revolutions" associated with the development of agriculture, urban life, and industrial technology. Whether the innovation of a new paradigm is always a revolutionary event, in the sense that it immediately challenges the adequacy of existing practice, is debatable; not all innovations basic to a new paradigm necessarily contradict an earlier paradigm, for some may initiate an entirely new line of development. But it is difficult to think of clear-cut examples of this sort of event, and for practical purposes it is probably useful to assume paradigmatic conflict to be the best evidence of fundamental innovation. A more important consideration is that not all innovations are paradigm-forming. Many can best be considered under other headings (core development, functional consequences, and rationalization). And some, perhaps, are simply not relevant to any paradigm process at all.

To qualify as paradigm-forming, an innovation need not be a complete and adequate theory or model; rather, it is an event which solves a limited problem but does so in a way which opens up a whole new line of development. It is a major "break-through." Furthermore, the paradigmatic innovation has a symbolic and charismatic quality. It is often associated with the name of a culture hero (human or divine) and it can be simply represented by some visual image or phrase or manual procedure.

In the history of American anthropology, for instance, one can find a convenient illustration in the origin of the "fieldwork" paradigm. Whether accurately or not, one thinks of Franz Boas stepping off the boat in an Eskimo village with his suitcase in hand, preparing for a long stay in residence. This image *is* the paradigm: the subsequent development of field techniques, standards of ethnographic description, ethnological theory, and training requirements for the Ph.D. stem from, and are implied by, the symbol of Boas as lone fieldworker taking up prolonged residence in a small community. This symbol is opposed in a revolutionary way to a nineteenth century tradition of library scholarship and of uncritical use of the comparative method to derive models of cultural evolution. Of course Boas was not actually the first to do fieldwork; he did not in all respects do adequate fieldwork by the standards of his own paradigm; and he did not really deny the value of library work or of studies of cultural evolution. But all that is beside the point: he did effectively establish the fieldwork paradigm for American academic anthropology.

Paradigmatic core development is the continuous elaboration of the ideas that constitute the original paradigm, according to the rules of the paradigm itself. In science, Kuhn calls this the process of "normal science." Generations of trained workers make "contributions" to the perfection of the paradigm by resolving any surviving internal ambiguities or contradictions and by demonstrating its utility in solving newly discovered problems. Doctoral dissertations, for instance, are expected to be paradigmatic contributions in their own fields. People who are working on the same paradigm tend to be visible as a profession, or a school of thought, or a tradition, and to function as a community whose reference objects are other members of the community rather than the world outside. Such paradigmatic communities in our own culture history are readily recognizable not only in science but outside science as well, in such fields as philosophy, theology, music, art and literature, and technology, and Kuhn has already recognized that humanistic scholarship traditionally assumes a paradigmatic scheme in its approaches to intellectual history and criticism.[4]

Let us briefly consider theology, art, and literature (we shall return to the technology application later in more detail). In the case of religion, almost as soon as the prophet of a revitalization movement has begun to lay down the new paradigm in the form of a code based on his revelations, his disciples begin to discuss, interpret, and apply it. Even within nonliterate or marginally literate cultures, this process of editing, interpreting, and applying the text goes on incessantly, and a body of auxiliary belief and commentary rapidly builds up within the paradigmatic community of disciples, preachers, priests, and other followers. There is a continuing process of defining and redefining the standard symbols and formulas as new historical circumstances arise. Similarly in art, once a new idea or approach has been successfully broached, a "school" is likely to develop, perhaps at first consisting of only a few disciples, who work busily at amplifying and developing their master's paradigm. And again in literature, once a classic work has been created, it provides the format for dozens or hundreds of followers who play with and explore the possibilities implicit in the original.

There is a peculiar arbitrariness in the core development process. It is often remarkably independent in its direction (though not in speed), once launched, from surrounding events, although it influences them. It is as though, once defined, the paradigm must be developed according to its own inner law; like a gyroscope, its attitude remains stable in a shifting historical frame. It is notoriously difficult to censor, suppress, or destroy a process of core development by economic, religious, or political pressures. Furthermore, within the paradigmatic community, new developments are in a sense unpredictable, for to predict the event in any detail is to have anticipated it; the event predicted occurs in the course of its own prediction. Thus, even though core development follows its own inner logic and works to realize latent implications, its course is also accompanied by a constant sense of surprised discovery.

By *exploitation* is meant the recognition and embracing of the paradigm, at some stage in its evolution, by an economic, military, religious, or political organization which sees in its application an opportunity for the protection or advancement of its own interests. The paradigmatic community can, theoretically, exploit its own paradigm, but this in all likelihood rarely happens. More commonly the exploitation is carried out by others, very often in as monopolistic a fashion as possible. The exploiting group may not only wish to apply the paradigm, and be the only applier of it; they may wish to direct in some measure the further development of the core itself, both as to direction and rate. It is in the relationship of the paradigmatic and exploitive community that some of the most interesting features of the process lie, and we shall return to them later in this essay.

By *functional consequences* are meant the new, specific problems which the exploitation of the core development process creates for society and the way in which society responds, at first by expedients, and eventually by cultural change. Recent examples in science are all too obvious: the applications of core development in normal science to the creation of new physical, chemical, and biological weaponry has threatened the survival of mankind, created new industries, developed new patterns of international relations, and so on. Ecological damage from indiscriminate waste disposal, from the incautious use of DDT and other insecticides, and from over-use of natural resources is almost as serious a threat. A result of medical research and improved methods of food production has been a vast increase in the world's population; this increase has entailed further pressure on the ecosystem; and so on *ad infinitum.* It is easy to discover examples of catastrophic problems presented by the innocent development of a core by an oblivious paradigmatic community and a ruthless exploiting group. Typically, core development will create opportunity for some; and if that opportunity is seized, functional consequences will include advantages for some and new problems for others, perhaps even eventually for the opportunist himself. And the solutions to any one problem will produce other problems and the solutions to these problems still more problems. This peculiar Pandora's box quality of the offerings of continuing core development and exploitation almost invariably generates an ambivalence, sometimes even a taboo toward the paradigmatic community by the rest of the society, with some parties interested in exploiting the new developments, others in suppressing them, and many feeling both ways at the same time.

But whether or not there is ambivalence, the problems produced by paradigmatic development are real ones and the policies which political and economic communities concoct to deal with them are an interesting field for cultural analysis, for experimental procedures tend to become policy and, when successful, to harden into conventional practice—ad hoc procedure becomes policy, and policy becomes culture.

By *rationalization* is intended the ethical, philosophical, religious, and political justifications which the paradigmatic community members offer for their participation in the core development process and which general community members offer for their relationship to the paradigm. As Garfinkel[5] and other ethnomethodologists have pointed out, people tend to act in such a way as to validate their theory of the world; but when new actions are made necessary by the challenges of functional consequences of exploiting a paradigm, a new theory must be constructed. The para-community is generally rather monotonous in its rationalizations, saying in effect that working on the paradigm is doing God's work, or that it will lead to a better world, or that basic research is a good thing in itself and will always pay off eventually. The general community has a more interesting problem. In its initial "seizure" of the paradigm for the first application, the exploiting community group may account for its action with familiar and established explanations. Indeed, as Smelser and my student Kasserman indicate, the exploiter may be an essentially conservative person who is simply trying to maintain his footing in a changing world.[6] Later on, however, as more and more expedients must be contrived to cope with spin-off problems, the rationalization must change to take account of the functional changes in the society and in their own lives.

Relations Between the Paradigmatic Community and the Rest of Society

To the historian and sociologist of science, it has long been an appealing hypothesis that the language, the customs, and the values of the general society subtly determine the ideas of supposedly objective fields. The paradigmatic notion looks at the process in another way, concentrating on the evolution of the irrelevant to the point where relevance is discovered. The discovery of relevance is the moment of exploitation. At once the paradigmatic community is confronted by organizations, up to and at times including the sovereign institutions, which make claims upon it. The interaction between these two interest groups is the subject of high drama in our own time—and even in our own profession, where the exploitation of the fieldwork paradigm by government agencies entails serious functional consequences and thus generates intense discussion of ethical issues. There are a number of dimensions along which the relations may vary and for the sake of introductory discussion let us enumerate some of them. In the case of support, the policy of the general community may range from across-the-board support of an entire para-community (e.g., of a discipline like physics) by granting unrestricted research funds and fellowships, by favorable patent and copyright laws, by establishing new research and development communities; or it may restrict support to selected aspects of the field (such as weapons research) and other purely applied projects; or it may make deliberate efforts to destroy the entire para-community (e.g., by accusing them of treason, of being witches, or whatever). In the case of communication, the general community may favor open channels (by avoiding censorship, endorsing freedom of speech, and the like) or it may impose censorship, place embargoes on immigration or emigration or even travel, or restrict foreign trade. In the case of power, the general community may eagerly include the para-community in the power structure, or exclude it from certain sorts of decision-making forums (by requiring a nonpolitical position as a condition of support), or even generally wall off the para-community into a caste-like minority group or ghetto population. In the case of control of applications, the general community may take the initiative and attempt to seduce, hire, or coerce members of the para-community into providing service, or the responsibility for exploitation may be handled jointly, or the para-community may attempt to control the nature, timing, and degree of exploitation of its paradigm, in some cases urging applications, and in others attempting to restrict or control them. And, of course, the reward system for paradigmatic work may vary from material goods, money, and power through symbolic rewards (medals, prizes, and so on) to rewards in the form of status or prestige in the para-community alone.

The development of the relationships between paradigmatic and lay communities is, in a sense, a sideplay, separate from the immediate paradigm development, functional consequence, and rationalization problems. It is, however, an important political process whose course will affect the course of the whole society.

The Industrial Revolution

The idea of formulating the theory of paradigmatic process in culture change was originally prompted by the need to develop a frame of thought for the Rockdale project. The model has indeed proved to be useful in guiding the research strategy for that project; and the Rockdale study itself has shown that the way in which the different aspects of a paradigmatic process fit together can be very clearly understood when the aspects are seen in the detail that the intensive ethno-historical study of a small community makes possible. But the paradigmatic process can be illustrated on a grander scale by one of the major events in cultural evolution: the origin of the Industrial Revolution itself. The English Industrial Revolution exemplifies the paradigmatic process very well. Let us consider it according to the five stages that were outlined above: innovation, core development, exploitation, functional consequences, and rationalization.

Innovation and Paradigmatic Core Development—Although many factors combined to create the milieu in which the Industrial Revolution occurred, the most spectacular and symbolically important innovations, by all accounts, were the inventions in the decade of the 1760's of spinning machinery by James Hargreaves and Richard Arkwright in England and of the modern steam engine by James Watt in Scotland. But it is certainly not the case that these gadgets burst unexpectedly upon a surprised world; rather, they—and a number of other innovations in pottery making, metalworking, agriculture, and transportation—represented the first exploitable products of a technological paradigm that had been established at least a century before. Thus Thomas Savery in 1698 had made a workable steam engine for the purpose of pumping ground water from Cornish mines; and Thomas Newcomen in 1708 had developed another type of steam engine for pumping out collieries. Silk-throwing machinery had been introduced from Italy in 1717, and a true factory was developed for its use; the flying shuttle had been invented by John Kay to improve weaving in 1733; and a primitive roller spinning device was produced in 1738. All of this interest in the improvement of mechanical gadgetry had roots in the efforts of millwrights, clockmakers, instrument makers, clergymen, poets, physicians, barbers, and even scientists, to solve various technical problems which had already been conventionally isolated and defined. The notion that mathematical thinking, applied to naturalistic observation and experiment, and expressed in clockwork-like machines, could lead to the solution of practical problems, had so thoroughly taken hold that by 1754 —*before* the critical inventions had been made—there had been founded a Society for the Encouragement of Arts, Manufactures, and Commerce, which offered prizes to inventors.

It is evident then that the inventions of the 1760's, which constituted the classic expressions of the industrial paradigm, were nonetheless the product of several generations of optimistic work by scientists and mechanics. Hargreaves, the millwright; Arkwright, the barber; Watt, the instrument maker, in a sense did for mechanical invention what Euclid did for Greek geometry—they codified and put in a conspicuously applicable form a body of skills and knowledge that had been accumulating for decades. The latent paradigm on which the scientists and engineers had been working was the clock, an intricate system of carefully made and mathematically articulated wheels, gears, and shafts which accepted a source of power at one end and applied it to the performance of a useful and precisely quantifiable task at the other.

Exploitation—What made the machine paradigm into an industrial revolution was its combination with an old concept: the factory. There had been factories since Roman times where large numbers of skilled artisans plied their trade under one roof and under some sort of supervision. The new factory was occupied by large numbers of clockwork-like machines, powered by an external source of energy, that performed precise manual tasks under the supervision of a group of trained operatives. This application of the paradigm, it is said, was achieved first in 1717 by Thomas Lambe in his water-driven silk works in Derby, where three hundred workmen were employed; and Lambe's model was copied by Arkwright in a water-driven cotton factory at Cranford, which by about 1772 employed approximately six hundred. Around the same time Josiah Wedgwood—without major mechanical innovations—introduced the factory method into pottery making when in 1769 he set up the Etruria works.

But before this application could be accomplished, a process of exploitation had to occur. Scientists and mechanics for generations had been producing all kinds of finely made devices which—except for the clocks themselves—were of restricted practical value. The first spinning jennies were made and sold without even the taking of a patent by their inventor, and they were adopted primarily in domestic industries, where they simply amplified the income of household spinning-and-weaving enterprises. Richard Arkwright realized the potential profitability of assembling numbers of improved spinning machines, attaching them to a water wheel as power source, and training and employing factory hands ("operatives") to guide the machines.

The initial conditions for profitable exploitation of the new machinery in England included a capitalist commercial ethic, expanding markets, demand for a higher rate of production than conventional technology could accomplish, and the availability of large sums of money which could be borrowed at relatively low interest rates or which could be attracted as investment in corporate ventures. Thus an economic milieu existed in mid-eighteenth century England which made possible the assembling of the capital required for the exploitation of technical innovations. The industrial exploiter used his capital to perform a complex task; first, to buy, or rent, or develop a mill site, including dam, races, wheel, and mill machinery, a building housing the mill, some associated housing for manager and workers, and transportation facilities; second, to buy, or have made, the desired machines, and to install them in the mill; third, to hire, train, supervise, and pay the operatives.

Functional Consequences—With the securing of capital, the commissioning of machinery, and the employment of operatives, a triad of communities was defined, whose mutual confrontations launched a still-continuing process of social and cultural change. The exploiting community consisted of the owner or owners of the mill, the banks and other lending institutions, the suppliers of raw materials, and the distributors of finished goods. They jointly risked financial loss and jointly hoped for financial gain, and their efforts to make their investment more secure and their profits higher and more certain eventually required society-wide cultural innovations in insurance, in banking, in credit relations, in measures against periodic "panics," in fire and flood control, in labor legislation, local government, and so on.

An interesting analysis of spin-off from the cotton industry's changes during the Industrial

Revolution in Great Britain has been provided by the sociologist Neil J. Smelser in his study, *Social Change in the Industrial Revolution.* He approaches the question with a Parsonian scheme that views culture change as a response to the perception that some technique or institution is not functioning adequately or that there is a bottleneck in a process (e.g., the flying shuttle enabled household weavers to supply more cloth to satisfy foreign markets; this placed a demand on spinners which was eventually met only by the adoption of the jenny). Most of his attention is directed to the families of cotton spinners. Initially, the technical innovations and the early factories merely strengthened the traditional spinner households. Their real income increased, and factory-operative spinners were able to hire and supervise their own children and other kinfolk much as they had earlier in the days of the cottage industries. Thus, despite the massive increase in the production of cotton products resulting from the development of the new machinery and the building of factories, the initial effect on the English cottage family was to confirm its traditional structure. The problem for the spinner family really began in the 1820's (fully two generations after the critical innovations), when spinning machines became so complex that a spinner had to supervise more helpers than his own family could provide and when the availability of efficient steam engines made it possible to locate factories in large towns and cities rather than at the country mill sites. Under these conditions, the authority of the father in many a family was threatened, because his children were able to enter the "free" labor market to work as spinner's helpers for other spinners and also to work as factory-employed hands in machine-weaving rooms. The dissatisfaction with the differentiation of labor within the family was in part responsible for the rise of labor unions, the introduction of factory-hour legislation, the rise of cooperative stores and savings banks, and the rapid spread of state- or industry-supported schools for factory children who could no longer be educated and socialized by their parents.

Rationalization—The initial understanding of what the new machinery and the new factories meant tended to be somewhat Utopian. There was an anticipation of wealth to be gained by merchant adventurers, inventors, and investors; there was an increase in real income among the cottage spinners and weavers; and there was an expectation that the factory system, which required high standards of punctuality and efficiency, would teach the Protestant ethic to the shiftless poor. But these interpretations of the event were made from an optimistic eighteenth-century perspective. By the 1820's the English had had enough experience with the new system to realize what some of the functional consequences of industrialization were. And so, about this time, serious efforts to rationalize the process were begun. Some sought to justify a depersonalization of man (which was implied by a national labor market responding to the prod of starvation) by anticipations of improvement in the general welfare. The Utopian scientists quickly saw both the human costs and benefits; this line of thought received a classic expression in the somewhat romantic, even nostalgic analysis by Karl Marx in *Das Kapital* in 1867. Thinking along somewhat different lines were the *laissez faire* theorists, including Adam Smith, Thomas Malthus, Ricardo, and later the Social Darwinists. Such writers as these, as Polanyi has pointed out,[7] served to make the Industrial Revolution understandable not in simple eighteenth-century "enlightenment" terms, but in terms of the kinds of decisions that industrialists, bankers, government officials and legislators, the clergy, and working people had to make in coping with the deluge of machinery suddenly let loose upon the world. Each of these lines of rationalization, furthermore, became a paradigm for further intellectual work, much as a theological tradition grows up after a new messiah formulates a religious code.

Appendix

Other Applications of the Model

The paradigmatic model is obviously closely related to the revitalization movement model; indeed, one could conceive of revitalization movements as being a special case of paradigm development. In both cases one is dealing with deliberate efforts to innovate continuously over a substantial period of time. Evidently also some of the major leaps in general evolution can be regarded as paradigmatic—not merely the Industrial Revolution, but, if we had the data, probably also the Neolithic and Urban revolutions, and conceivably even earlier processes, such as the development of stone tool traditions. The paradigm model would not, however, be useful in all acculturation studies, for in many situations one suspects that the paradigm is precisely what is *not* communicated across the interface between two cultures. The difficulty of communicating paradigms may have something to do with the problems of development in recently colonial societies and in minority communities. And finally, the paradigm model fits well with such concepts as Kroeber's culture climax and the pattern-fulfillment concepts embodied in most philosophies of history. Culture-historical analysis might be able to use such concepts too, even though the problems usually addressed are those of survival and distribution.

The examples so far cited have tended to lay emphasis largely on scientific and technological cores, with occasional reference to theology and the arts. Perhaps such "hard" domains attract attention because the problems can here be phrased in relatively formal, and therefore finite and solvable, terms. It may be that the aesthetic urge which in part prompts the process of core development is best satisfied in working with systems that permit highly structured, cumulative thinking. But paradigmatic thinking itself does not necessarily address itself to the practical problems of the world; it may appear, to those outside the paradigmatic community, that it is a domain of trivialities, a menagerie of hair-splitting pedants, cranks, and ivory-tower types whose preoccupations are irrelevant to the "real" world. Irrelevant, that is, until the paradigm has been developed to a point where one of its aspects presents a means for solving someone's practical problem. The "practical" problem, of course, may in fact be equally trivial, in comparison with the giant and enduring social and emotional problems of mankind. But it seems to be the case that the world has repeatedly been transformed by the conjunction of trivialities: specifically, by the application of new navigational gadgets to the problem of securing spices for the dining tables and beaver pelts for felt hats, by the application of mechanical rollers to the problem of making enough cotton thread to satisfy the demand for cotton cloth created by the importation of Indian cottons from recently conquered India—and so on. It remains to be seen whether paradigmatic development proceeds in as effective a way in the field of political and economic organization. Indeed, the conditions under which domains of culture become susceptible to paradigmatic change would be an interesting subject for research.

Conclusion

The purpose of this essay has been to draw attention to a pervasive, but not adequately conceptualized, process of culture change which, after Thomas Kuhn, we have called "paradigmatic." A tentative general model of such processes has been presented, delineating as stages or functions the processes of innovation and paradigmatic core development, exploitation, functional consequences, and rationalization. The English Industrial Revolution was considered as a prime example of the process, and finally some general questions were raised about the conditions under which such processes occur, and the relation of the paradigmatic process to other processes in culture change.

Notes

Part One
ROCKDALE IN 1850:
THE CLIMAX OF A WAY OF LIFE

Chapter 1: Sweet, Quiet Rockdale

1. EMHL, W9–21465, SDP to CS, Oct. 5, 1841.
2. Ashmead, 1884, p. 199.
3. *Vide* the discussion in Marx, 1964, of the idealized pastoral compromise between city and wilderness celebrated by many early nineteenth-century American authors.
4. See such advertisements *passim* in the *Upland Union.*

SLEEPY HOLLOW DAYS

1. Griffith's sketches are preserved in EMHL, Longwood MSS, Group 9, Residual, Box 1. According to the genealogical file at CCHS, he was born in 1819 and died in 1900. His later business connections with the Du Ponts on the Brandywine are recorded in the Records of E. I. du Pont de Nemours & Co. (Acc. 500), in Correspondence, Box 127, folder "Griffith, Joseph & Richard S."
2. HSP, Am. 1024, Vol. I, Journal of John Hill Martin, Sept. 24, 1856, p. 179.
3. EMHL, W9–26112, EBS to SDP, Oct. 4, 1857.
4. EMHL, W9–25288, CS to SDP, May, 17, 1838.

THE LORDS OF THE VALLEY

1. Crozer, 1861, pp. 58–60.
2. Interview with Samuel Tryens of Rockdale, July 18, 1969.
3. See Lemieux, 1976, for an extended account of the "culture of dying" in the nineteenth century, with data drawn largely from Delaware County.

THE SISTERHOOD

1. EMHL, W6–20, EBS to VB, Dec. 16, 1828.
2. EMHL, W9–25640, CS to SDP, Jan. 17, 1848.
3. EMHL, Acc. 761, Box 3, APL to MLDP, n.p., n.d.
4. *Ibid.*
5. EMHL, W10, Series E, transcripts 202 (notes on Robert Smith).
6. EMHL, W6, Series A, Box 15.
7. *Ibid.,* Folder 2.
8. EMHL, Acc. 761, Mrs. AVDP, Box 3, APL to MLDP, n.p., n.d.
9. *The Souvenir,* Vol. 2, No. 2, p. 15 (copy at PFL).
10. EMHL, W9–40380, diary of SDP, entry Nov. 28, 1832.
11. EMHL, W9–25532, CS to SDP, Nov. 4, 1845(?).
12. EMHL, W9–21612, SDP to CS, Nov. 14, 1845.
13. EMHL, W9–25580, CS to SDP, Nov. 21, 1846.
14. EMHL, W9–25825 and 25827, CS to SDP, April 8 and 19, 1852.
15. EMHL, W9–25835, CS to SDP, July 13, 1852.

16. EMHL, W9–26117, CS to SDP, Oct. 10, 1857.
17. Undated newspaper clippings from Mary Gilpin file, EMHL.
18. Karnes, 1970, p. 336.
19. The correspondence of CS and SDP at EMHL is of course the source of statements in this section not individually documented.

Chapter II: A Town of Mules and Widows

1. The demographic profile of the Rockdale manufacturing district and its constituent hamlets in 1850 is based, of course, on the manuscript schedules of the Seventh (1850) Census of population and the 1850 Census of Manufactures, both preserved in the National Archives, Washington, D.C. The district does not constitute an enumeration entity; the Delaware County schedules are organized by township, and the Rockdale district lies partly in Aston and partly in Middletown. Dissecting the Rockdale households from the rest of the schedules for these two townships proved to be a relatively simple task, however, because three other complementary bodies of data were available: the property map of Delaware County compiled by Dr. Joshua Ash (a resident of the county) and published in 1848 by Robert Smith of Philadelphia (copies at PSA, DCIS, DCHS, and CCHS); the county tax assessments for 1850 (DCCH), which list the names of workers renting tenements from Crozer and Riddle (in four of the seven hamlets); and Samuel Riddle's paybook for 1844 through March 1850 (DCHS). The boundaries of the Rockdale district were drawn by me on the Ash map (the lines being based on my own knowledge of the terrain, roads, factories, and settlement clusters, and on the ownership of land by mill owners and workers as displayed on the Ash map) and the district was divided among the seven hamlets. The census listed the occupation of males of sixteen or over, and the mill workers are thus identifiable by their designation as "factory man," "operative," "spinner" and "mule spinner," "weaver," "warper," "beamer," "machinist," "clerk," "loom boss," and "factory manager." Persons so identified are found in tight clusters separated by farmers. It is possible to identify many of the farmers on the Ash map, which shows the outlines of the real estate owned by major landowners (whose names are printed on the map). This makes it possible to follow the enumerator through the township to the boundaries of some of the hamlets. The clusters of mill workers can also be identified as occupants of particular hamlets by several other kinds of evidence: the inclusion in the census of some of the owners and manufacturers who are known to be associated with certain mills and therefore certain hamlets; the occurrence of a cluster of names both in the census schedule and also on the tax list; and the presence of a cluster of names in the census that also occur in the Riddle Pay Book for March 1850. These criteria made it possible to identify each operative and his family with a particular hamlet and usually with a particular factory.

The principal uncertainty has to do with the inclusion of farmers in the district. The boundaries of the district, as drawn on the map, include all operatives' households and a number of farms. The boundaries could, by being drawn more tightly, exclude some of these farmers, but not many—perhaps ten households in all—and I decided to draw the lines so as to include most of the farm households along the roads within the immediate watershed. Some small farmers and tradesmen whose properties lay in inter-hamlet areas within the district were sometimes difficult to assign to one hamlet or another.

The area of the district was determined by tracing the outline from the Ash map and transferring it to millimeter graph paper. The total area was then calculated by counting squares and multiplying by the scale factor.

2. See Smith's autobiographical statement in Martin, 1877, p. 460.

3. Callaghan's enterprise is described in a MS treatise of William Bagnall, edited by Victor Clark, entitled "Sketches of Manufacturing and Textile Establishments," and owned by the Baker Library at Harvard. Vol. 4 contains an account of Callaghan's textile factories and those of his sons.

THE SOCIAL STATIONS

1. The Ryedale genealogy (Ridlon, 1884) mentions "a Samuel Riddle residing at Glen-Riddle, in some way connected with the above family, but I have not the genealogy. I was introduced to him at the Family Meeting" (p. 160). The allusion to this man occurs as a footnote to the listing of the elder Samuel Riddle's children. It is no doubt this Samuel Riddle who is listed in the 1870 census as living in Middletown Township, working as a mill manager (presumably for Samuel Riddle), age forty-three, born in Ireland.

2. Richard S. Smith, 1884, pp. 119–20.

3. EMHL, Acc. 761, Box 3, APL to MLDP, n.p., n.d.

4. Martin, 1877, p. 332.

5. EMHL, Longwood MSS, AVDP Letters In, 1817–46, Box 3.

6. Martin, 1877, p. 457.

7. EMHL, Longwood MSS, Group 4, Box 5, notes "Relative to the Election for Directors held at The Columbia Ins. Office, July 2d., 1849."

8. EMHL, W9–26514, CS to SDP, Sept. 10, 1861.

9. EMHL, W9–40380, diary of SDP, Nov. 29, 1832.

10. The events surrounding the death of the wet-nurse's baby are described in EMHL, W9–26033, 26035, and 26037, CS to SDP, Jan. 17, Jan. 22, and Feb. 7, 1857.

11. Charlotte Elizabeth, 1847, p. 517.

12. EMHL, W9–25776, CS to SDP, Feb. 24, 1851. See also W9–25772, CS to SDP, Feb. 3, 1851, W9–26099, CS to SDP, Sept. 3, 1857, and entry in 1850 census for Aston Township listing the Elliot household.

13. EMHL, W9–26099, CS to SDP, Sept. 3, 1857.

14. EMHL, W9–21509, SDP to CS, July 31, 1843.

15. EMHL, W9–25526, CS to SDP, Sept. 16, 1845.

16. EMHL, W9–25910, CS to SDP, March 27, 1854.

17. EMHL, W9–25997, CS to SDP, April 7, 1856.

18. EMHL, W9–26185, CS to SDP, May 31, 1858.

19. PLTA, Letterbook Index B, Letters Rec. by Minshall Painter, 1815–64, No. 75: JPC to MP, Jan. 7, 1841.

20. The "middle class" is more difficult to document than the other two classes. The sketch here presented is based on a miscellany of sources: Ashmead, 1884, which contains a good deal of information about physicians, lawyers, schools, small farmers, and other members of the class; the U.S. census returns for 1850; and the correspondence of the Smith family at EMHL.

21. The social and economic profile of the mill workers in the period 1832–60 is drawn from NA, MS schedules of the U.S. census for Aston and Middletown townships, 1850 and 1860; and DCHS, the Parkmount Day Book, 1832–35, the Penn's Grove Pay Book, 1844–50, and the Penn's Grove Rent Book, 1847–53. Estimates of the cost of food are based on the standard calculations of the nutritional values of food substances published

by the Department of Agriculture (Watt and Merrill, 1963) and on food prices recorded by a nearby farmer, William Reynolds of Upper Chichester Township, who sold food directly to at least one family in Crozerville, and to nearby stores. Also consulted was Walker's study of *Hopewell Village* (1966), an iron-manufacturing community not far away, in the period up to 1841. Assuming a simple high-energy country diet, emphasizing pork and beef, bread and butter, hot cakes, potatoes, and coffee (providing adult males with 3,500 calories per day and adult females 3,000), the estimated daily cost is approximately $0.15 for the male and $0.13 for the female. This figure agrees with the statement that householders could profit from boarders paying $2 per week male and $1.25 per week female.

22. The Morris family's experience is recorded in detail in their letters 1829–46, published in Erickson (1972, pp. 139–74). This source contains detail on rentals and weekly boarding rates which have been used in the general discussion.

Part Two
ROCKDALE FROM 1825 TO 1835:
THE CREATING OF A WAY OF LIFE

Chapter III: The Assembling of the Industrialists

1. I am indebted to my former student David Kasserman's insights for the recognition of the conservative innovator as a type of social change agent. See his dissertation, *Conservative Innovation: Introduction of the Cotton Industry into the United States, 1789–1840.*
2. *Proceedings of the Delaware County Institute of Science,* Vol. 3 (1907), pp. 109–11.

THE FIRST ARRIVALS

1. HSP, Wm Martin Receipt Book; DCCH, Deed Book P, p. 257; Ferguson, 1965, p. 107.
2. In addition to the MS of part of his published history, and his father's receipt book, the HSP collection includes John Hill Martin's personal memoirs and journal, detailing the life of a West Point cadet and Philadelphia bachelor, various historical notes and lists, and miscellaneous personal correspondence.
3. See Porter and Livesay, 1971.
4. Martin, 1877, p. 419.
5. *Ibid.,* p. 348.
6. See the volumes of *McElroy's Philadelphia Directory* for the period 1823 to 1835; FI, Report of 1825 Exhibition, p. 30.
7. ANSP, Minutes, 1824 and 1825.
8. Bestor, 1970, p. 158.
9. FI, Report of 1825 Exhibition, p. 30.
10. The agreement is preserved at DCCH.
11. HSP, Lovering Collection, Joseph S. Lovering to Mary Lovering, July 23, 1829.
12. *Pa. Senate Journal,* 1837–38, Part 2, p. 283.
13. Walter M. Phillips and Clifford Lewis III, descendants of the two families, have very kindly allowed me to see the family records, particularly the recollections of John S. Phillips's sister Caroline Biddle of their early life in Philadelphia.
14. Crozer, 1861, p. 71.

15. *Ibid.,* p. 24.
16. Corner, 1972, p. 11.
17. Crozer, 1861, p. 87.
18. *Ibid.,* p. 161.
19. *Ibid.,* p. 53.
20. Crozer's early life is well documented in his autobiography (Crozer, 1861) and in a posthumous biography (J. Wheaton Smith, 1868).
21. Ashmead, 1884, p. 490.
22. EMHL, Pierre S. du Pont Coll., Series D, No. 29, Folder "Auctions" (broadside).
23. Boatman, MS, p. 14.
24. EMHL, Longwood MSS, Group 6, Box 2, JDC to EIDP, June 1, 1822, and June 4, 1822.
25. Boatman, MS, pp. 18–22.
26. EMHL, Acc. 1204, Folder 3 (sheriff's sale announced in the West Chester, Pa., *Village Record*).
27. Boatman, MS, p. 14.
28. EMHL, Longwood MSS, Group 6, Series B, JDC to EIDP, June 1 and 4, 1822, and EIDP to JDC, June 3, 1822.
29. Ashmead, 1884, pp. 620–1; DCCH, Tax Assessments, Middletown Township, 1823–25; Deed Book P, p. 721.
30. Ashmead, 1884, p. 620.
31. DCHS, *Upland Union,* Dec. 27, 1825.

THE FIRST CASUALTIES AND REPLACEMENTS

1. DCCH, Prothonotary's Office.
2. DCCH, Register of Deeds.
3. EMHL, E. B. du Pont Coll., File 143; *American Watchman,* July 4, 1826.
4. DCHS, *Upland Union,* Nov. 14, 1826.
5. EMHL, Acc. 500 (Records of E. I. du Pont de Nemours & Co., 1801–1902).
6. DCCH, Register of Deeds.
7. Cope, 1900.
8. *Biographical Directory of the American Congress,* 1774–1971, p. 777.
9. Ashmead, 1884, p. 249.
10. *Ibid.,* pp. 539–41.
11. *Ibid.,* p. 248.
12. DCHS, *Upland Union,* Nov. 8, 1825.
13. Martin, 1877, pp. 267–8; George E. Darlington, 1909, pp. 10–11, 70–1.
14. APS, Peale-Sellers Papers, Nathan Sellers to Coleman Sellers, n.d.
15. Information on Martin's financial difficulties is to be found in his deed of purchase in 1823 (DCCH, Deed Book P, p. 257), and the Tax Assessments for Aston and Middletown townships, reported on Nov. 17, 1828, also in DCCH; writ to the Sheriff of Delaware County, Prothonotary's Office, in the case of Peter Hill vs. William Martin, April 16, 1829; and HSP, William Martin Receipt Book, AM 1025.
16. DCCH, Prothonotary's Office, Peter Hill vs. William Martin, writ of April 16, 1829.
17. APS, Peale-Sellers Papers (B/P31/50), Coleman Sellers to Nathan Sellers, April 2, 1829.
18. APS, Peale-Sellers Papers (B/P31/50), Peter Hill to Nathan Sellers, Philadelphia, Sept. 10, 1822; Martin, 1877, pp. 141–2.
19. Martin, 1877, pp. 331–4; HSP, William Martin Receipt Books, entries 1829–32.

20. HSP, AM 1024, Vol. 1, Journal of John Hill Martin, pp. 178–9.
21. APS, Peale-Sellers Papers, DL to MLDP, May 26, 1829.
22. APS, Peale-Sellers Papers (B/P31/50), Coleman Sellers to R. C. Marsh, Dec. 29, 1829.
23. DCCH, Tax Assessments, Aston and Middletown townships, 1829–57; APS, Coleman Sellers' power of attorney to Peter Hill, Nov. 2, 1830.
24. DCCH, deed grantor and grantee lists, names of Peter Hill and George W. Hill; similarly Tax Assessments, Aston and Middletown townships, 1829–60.
25. APS, Peale-Sellers Papers, Lease of Lenni Cotton Factory, May 1, 1831; DCCH, Tax Assessments, Aston Township, under name of George W. Hill.
26. EMHL, DL to E. I. du Pont de Nemours & Co., Feb. 26, 1814.
27. Simpson, 1859, pp. 37–49.
28. EMHL, Winterthur MSS, Group 10, Series B, Box 40 (Eleuthera du Pont Smith Autobiography, Vol. 40, pp. 103–4).
29. EMHL, Letterbooks of Daniel Lammot (microfilm M-58.13), DL to Holland Weeks, July 23, 1825.
30. EMHL, Acc. 761, DL to MLDP, Nov. 15, 1824.
31. EMHL, Letterbooks of Daniel Lammot (microfilm M-58.13), DL to Holland Weeks, March 17/April 18, 1825.
32. EMHL, Longwood MSS, DL to EIDP, letters of March 16, April 6, April 9, May 7, May 10, May 17, June 6, June 10, and June 15, 1825.
33. EMHL, Group 7, Series A, Box 2 (1820–77), MLDP to Evelina du Pont, March 23, 1828.
34. EMHL, Acc. 761, Box 3, DL to MLDP, Kensington, May 26, 1829.
35. EMHL, Acc. 761, Box 3, APL to MLDP, n.p., n.d.
36. The date is confirmed by a letter of SDP to CS, Jan. 15, 1830, referring to the recent arrival of the Lammots at Lenni (EMHL, W9–21058).
37. EMHL, Acc. 761, Box 3, APL to MLDP, n.p., n.d. (different letter from note 35).
38. The family birth and baptismal records, preserved at the Swedenborgian Academy in Bryn Athyn, Pa., record no child born to Anna Potts Lammot between 1822 and Sept. 6, 1831. The condition of the roads is described in Sophie du Pont's letter cited in note 36.
39. Ridlon, 1884, p. 155.
40. Most of the information about the emigration of the Riddle family is derived from the Riddle genealogy published in 1884 by Ridlon. Biographical data, with substantially the same information, is also given in several of the biographical encyclopedias: Wiley, 1894, pp. 163–5; *Biographical Encyclopaedia of Pennsylvania in the 19th Century,* 1874; Robson, 1875, pp. 118–19.
41. The role of McDowell in managing the Springfield mill for the Riddles is detailed in the DCHS, Parkmount Day Book 1832–35, *passim.*
42. The details of the financial relations of Peter Hill and the Riddles are given in the DCHS, Parkmount Day Book, 1832–35, *passim.*
43. There is very little information about the earlier lives of Houghton and Garsed. See Ashmead, 1884, pp. 622–3, and the *Biographical Encyclopaedia of Pennsylvania in the Nineteenth Century,* 1874, pp. 289–99.

THE SMITH FAMILY

1. Martin, 1877, p. 456.
2. EMHL, Winterthur MSS (W–6), EBS to VB, October 1832.

3. The account of the Swedish episode is told in detail in Smith's autobiography of his early years (Smith, 1884).

4. See Martin, 1877, pp. 455–60, for a biographical sketch of Smith; see also his own memoirs (Smith, 1884) and the genealogy of the Smith family contained in Leach, 1912.

5. EMHL, W9–26061, RSS to SDP, July 8, 1857.

6. EMHL, W9–26112, EBS to VB [1857].

7. EMHL, W6, EBS to VB, October 1828.

8. Smith, 1884.

9. EMHL, W9–21126, SDP to CS, Jan. 15, 1830.

10. EMHL, W9–40253, obituary of E. B. Smith from *Delaware County Republican,* April 1871.

11. Elizabeth Smith's letters to Victorine Bauduy in EMHL, Winterthur MSS, W6.

12. RSS to C. E. McIlvaine, in [St. Andrew's Church], Alfred Lee, first Bishop of Delaware, 1888, p. 7.

13. CCR, Records, RSS to Missionary Society, April 1838.

14. EMHL, W9–21275, SDP to CS, March 20, 1833.

15. EMHL, W9–40351, diary of SDP, entry of Nov. 24, 1833.

16. Among Sophie du Pont's effects preserved at EMHL is an infant's knit cap labeled in her hand "My baby's cap Sept 25 1835" (Winterthur MSS, Group 9, Series F, Box 189).

17. EMHL, W9–40396, diary of SDP, entry of July 5, 1845.

18. EMHL, W9–21584, SDP to CS, Aug. 22, 1845.

19. EMHL, W9–21300, SDP to CS, May 27, 1834.

20. EMHL, W9–21584, SDP to CS, Aug. 22, 1845.

21. EMHL, W9–25194, CS to SDP, Jan. 2, 1834.

22. EMHL, W9–25369, CS to SDP, March 23, 1841.

23. EMHL, W9–25253, CS to SDP, July 22, 1836.

24. EMHL, W9–25282, CS to SDP, n.p., n.d.

25. EMHL, W9–25335, CS to SDP, March 28, 1840.

26. EMHL, W9–25232, CS to SDP, March 25, 1837 (?).

27. EMHL, W9–25640, CS to SDP, Jan. 17, 1848.

28. EMHL, W9–25231, CS to SDP, Feb. 25, [1837].

29. EMHL, W9–40355, diary of SDP, entry of April 23, 1837.

30. EMHL, W9–25488, CS to SDP, Sept. 18, 1844.

31. EMHL, W9–25642, CS to SDP, Jan. 31, 1848.

32. EMHL, W9–25332, CS to SDP, Jan. 22, 1840.

33. EMHL, W9–21606, SDP to CS, Oct. 24, 1845.

THE MECHANICAL KNOWLEDGE OF THE INDUSTRIALISTS

1. Crozer, 1861, pp. 55–7.

2. Sutcliffe, 1816. (An evaluation of Sutcliffe's career is given in Tann, 1974, pp. 80–9.)

3. For a favorable evaluation of the *Cyclopaedia,* see Harte, 1974.

4. Guest, 1823; Baines, 1835.

5. Nicholson, 1826.

6. James Montgomery, 1833, pp. i–ii.

7. Scott, 1840 (Bancroft's copy is now owned by EMHL), 1851.

8. Ure, 1835.

9. Snell, 1850; Baird, 1851.

10. Gilbert in Singer, 1958, Vol. 4, p. 427.

11. Nicholson, 1826.
12. Buchanan, 1841 (3rd edition).
13. Byrne, 1850, 1853(a), 1853(b), 1853(c).
14. EMHL, Longwood MSS, Bancroft Papers, DL to EIDP, April 9, 1825.
15. Crozer, 1861, p. 54.
16. NA, 1820 Census of Manufactures; Ashmead, 1884, p. 669.
17. EMHL, Longwood MSS, Bancroft Papers, Acc. 467, Items 986 and 987.
18. Jeremy, 1973(b), pp. 35–6.
19. Ashmead, 1884, pp. 399–400; Wiley, 1894, pp. 324–5.
20. Dennis Clark, 1972, pp. 40–9.
21. Ashmead, 1884, pp. 297, 621.

ENTERING THE COTTON MANUFACTURE IN THE 1820'S

1. Ashmead, 1884, p. 295; Sarah Trainer Smith, 1897.
2. Ashmead, 1914.
3. EMHL, Longwood MSS, Group 6, Box 2, DL to EIDP, June 15, 1825.
4. The details of the abortive negotiations are to be found in the correspondence among Daniel Lammot, E. I. du Pont, William Bryan, and Joshua Lippincott at EMHL, Longwood MSS, Group 6, Box 2, between the dates of March 16 and June 15, 1825.

Chapter IV: The Machines, Their Operatives, and the Fabrics

1. Leiper and Martin, 1826.

THE MILLS AND MILL SEATS

1. DCIS, MS map of Delaware County by John Hill, *c.* 1810; Pennsylvania State Land Office, MS map of Delaware County by John Melish, 1817.
2. Bining, 1938, p. 55.
3. General information on these early uses of the mill seats is to be found in Leiper and Martin, 1826, and Ashmead, 1884.
4. Leiper and Martin, 1826.
5. The foregoing account of the dams and races on Chester Creek is based on personal observation of the remains. No description survives (if ever one was written down) from the 1825–35 period.
6. DCHS, Parkmount Day Book, has a running account of expenses incurred in repairing the hydraulic system.
7. The description of the mills is derived in part from personal inspection (particularly of West Branch and Parkmount), in part from early photographs and sketches of mills on Chester Creek and on the Brandywine, and in part from the mill-seat survey (Leiper and Martin, 1826).
8. Data on the power transmission system within the mill must be derived from contemporary published accounts, such as Ure, 1835, and James Montgomery, 1833. The remains of the mills give little information because of subsequent changes in technology. Parkmount Day Book does however give some data corroborative of the above account.
9. See here also such early manuals as Ure, 1835, and James Montgomery, 1833.

THE SPINNING MACHINERY

1. This list of operations is based on William Martin's enumeration of his assets in machinery about 1829 (APS, Peale-Sellers Papers). It agrees in general with the contemporary descriptions in Sutcliffe, 1816, Ure, 1835, and James Montgomery, 1833, although these works described English practice. See also James Montgomery, 1840, for a somewhat later account of American practices in 1836.
2. DCHS, Parkmount Day Book, April 6, 1832.
3. DCIS, 6th Annual Exhibition (1860), list of awards.
4. Charlotte Elizabeth, 1847, pp. 537–8.
5. The account of the machines employed for spinning is derived from the usual early sources, such as Ure, 1835, and Montgomery, 1833; from information in the Parkmount Day Book; and from personal observation of early spinning and weaving machines at the Merrimac Textile Museum (which has a mule from the 1830's whose operation is recorded on film), Upper Canada Village (which has an operating mule from the 1830's spinning woolen yarn), and the National Museum of Science and Technology of the Smithsonian Institution, and of modern spinning and weaving machinery at the South Boston (Va.) Cotton Manufacturing Company, which still takes cotton in by the bale and sends it out as finished cloth.

THE WEAVING MACHINERY

1. McLane, 1833, Vol. 2, p. 200.
2. Erickson, 1972, p. 159.
3. *Ibid.*, pp. 159–61.
4. DCHS, Parkmount Day Book.
5. The description of Phillips' mill is drawn from the Leiper and Martin, 1826, mill-seat survey of Delaware County, pp. 3, 18–19. The general characteristics of power looms of this period are drawn from Batchelder, 1863, pp. 60–72; see also J. L. Bishop, 1904, Vol. 2, and English, 1969.

THE MACHINE SHOPS

1. NYHS, John Rogers Papers, John Rogers, Jr., to John Rogers, Sr., New York, Nov. 28, 1852.
2. Ferguson, 1975, pp. 160–1.
3. David H. Wallace, 1967.
4. NYHS, John Rogers, Jr., to John Rogers, Sr., Manchester, July 19, 1850.
5. Ferguson, 1975, pp. 55, 107, and the John Rogers Papers at NYHS.
6. NYHS, John Rogers, Jr., to John Rogers, Sr., Manchester, Dec. 24, 1850.
7. In this sketch of early machine shop practice, several sources have been particularly valuable: Ferguson, 1975, and APS, MS Memoirs of Nathan and Coleman Sellers; David H. Wallace, 1967; NYHS, Letters of John Rogers; Leavitt, 1969 (the Hollingsworth Letters); and HSD, the Poole letters.
8. DCHS, Parkmount Day Book, *passim.*
9. *Upland Union,* July 21, 1840, announcement of sheriff's sale.
10. DCHS, *Post Boy,* Dec. 3, 1822.

11. McLane, 1833, Vol. 2, p. 211.
12. DCHS, Parkmount Day Book.
13. *Upland Union,* "Assignees Sale," June 15, 1841.
14. *Biographical Encyclopaedia of Pennsylvania in the Nineteenth Century,* 1874, p. 298.
15. *Upland Union,* March 10, 1840.
16. The foregoing account of the Garsed power-loom factory and the associated events at the Penn's Grove mill seat has been put together from a number of sources: advertisements of sales of buildings and machinery in the *Upland Union* for Aug. 22, 1826, March 10, 1840, July 21, 1840, and June 15, 1841 (copies in DCHS), and in the West Chester *American Republican* for June 19, 1817 (copy at CCHS); the Tax Assessments for Aston and Middletown townships, DCCH, in the names of Nathan Sharpless, Peter and George W. Hill, Richard Garsed, and James Houghton; Garsed entries in the Parkmount Day Book; U.S. census schedules for Aston and Middletown townships for 1830 and 1840; the Morris letters in Erickson, 1972, pp. 158–61; the account in Ashmead, 1884, pp. 622–3; the sketch of Garsed in the *Biographical Encyclopaedia of Pennsylvania in the Nineteenth Century,* 1874, pp. 298–9; and *Journal of the Franklin Institute,* Vol. 4 (3rd series), 1847, p. 336.
17. The Hyde contract is at EMHL, Bancroft Papers (Acc. 736), Item 986–7.
18. This description of the use of local suppliers was assembled from data in DCHS, Parkmount Day Book; *McElroy's Philadelphia Directory,* 1837; HSP, William Martin's Receipt Book; *Upland Union,* June 15, 1841.
19. EMHL, Longwood MSS, Group 6, Series B, Daniel Lammot to E. I. du Pont, May 10, 1825.
20. EMHL, Bancroft Papers, Item 182: Journal of Rockford Mill 1831–32.
21. APS, Sellers Papers (B/P31), "Peter Hill Miscellaneous."
22. *Upland Union,* June 22, 1841.
23. *Ibid.*

COMMERCIAL ASPECTS OF COTTON MANUFACTURING

1. DCHS, Parkmount Day Book, is in itself an account of mill office activities. Other Riddle business records at DCHS in the 1840's and 1850's include the rent books and paybooks 1844–50. The Bancroft Papers at EMHL also provide a particularly clear picture of the business aspect of cotton manufacturing in this period.
2. McLane, 1833, Vol. 2, p. 211.
3. See Jeremy, 1971, for a discussion of yarn counts.
4. Leiper and Martin, 1826.
5. McLane, 1833, comments by Crozer (Vol. 2, p. 211), and Samuel and James Riddle (Vol. 2, pp. 225–6).
6. These are the firms from whom the Riddles bought cotton from 1832 to 1835. DCHS, Parkmount Day Book, *passim.*
7. The discussion of buying and selling practice is based on DCHS, Parkmount Day Book, *passim.*
8. McLane, 1833, Vol. 2, p. 211.
9. Erickson, 1972, p. 159.
10. *Ibid.,* p. 161.
11. *Pa. Senate Journal,* 1837–38, Part 2, p. 302.

WORKING IN PARKMOUNT MILL IN 1832

1. McLane, 1833, Vol. 2, p. 225.
2. Insurance survey of Parkmount Mill (courtesy of Aldon Rug Co.); personal inspection.
3. This arrangement, with the mules on the attic floor, the card room and preparation room on the second floor, and the other functions on the ground floor, conforms to the illustrations of English mills of the period, to contemporary description, and to my own observation of the South Boston Manufacturing Company's cotton mill on the Dan River, in southern Virginia, in the spring of 1973.
4. DCHS, Penn's Grove Rent Book (bound with Day Book).
5. The sketches of the workers' households are based on several sources of data: the U.S. censuses for 1830 through 1860 for Aston and Middletown townships, and for 1830 and 1840 for the rest of Delaware County, New Castle County, Delaware, and Philadelphia; the Parkmount Day Book, and the Penn's Grove Pay and Rent Books; Ridlon, 1884, the Ryedale genealogy for McDowell and the Maxwells; and Shaw's testimony in *Pa. Senate Journal,* 1837–38, Part 2, pp. 279–81.
6. *Pa. Senate Journal,* 1837–38, Part 2, p. 289.
7. DCHS, Parkmount Day Book, p. 128, accounting with George Horner, who in December 1833 was paid $18.94 for spinning 702 lbs. of cotton into 10,580 hanks of No. 15 yarn.
8. *Pa. Senate Journal,* 1837–38, Part 2, p. 305.
9. *Ibid.,* p. 301.
10. *Ibid.,* p. 306.
11. *Ibid.,* pp. 347–8, 292.
12. *Ibid.,* pp. 288, 313.
13. *Ibid.,* pp. 329, 280–1.

THE PRODUCT: THE FABRICS OF CHESTER CREEK

1. McLane Report, 1833, Vol. 2, p. 225.
2. DCIS, MS Correspondence, John P. Crozer to Minshall Painter, November 1845.
3. Information about the types of fabrics woven comes from three main sources: the Parkmount Day Book, 1832–35 (DCHS); the Penn's Grove Pay Book, 1844–50 (DCHS); and the 1850 Census of Manufactures (NA). The daybook includes the period when the Riddles were buying looms from the Garseds and first setting up, and gives one instance of cloth construction specifications. The pay book lists piece rates for all the types of cloth woven in the mill. The census lists the types, quantities, and values of the products of all the mills. Ashmead, 1884, gives some information about fabrics and prizes, as do the *Journals* of the Franklin Institute and the annual exhibition records of the Delaware County Institute of Science.

Chapter V: The Inventors of the Machines

1. *Pa. Senate Journal,* 1837–38, Part 2, p. 326.
2. Crozer, 1861, p. 56.
3. McLane, 1833, Vol. 2, p. 211.
4. EMHL, Acc. 761, Box 3: DL to ML, Kensington, May 26, 1829.

5. James Montgomery, 1833, pp. 56–7.
6. Erickson, 1972, p. 161.

THE MAIN SEQUENCE OF INVENTIONS

1. The most authoritative account of the mule and its history is given in Catling, 1970, and the following account is based to a large extent on this work.
2. Ure, 1835, pp. 152–5.
3. Snell, 1850, pp. vi, 184.
4. James Montgomery, 1833, p. 195; see also *Journal of the Franklin Institute*, Vol. 20 (1835), p. 356.
5. BLH, Bagnall MS; Webber, 1879, pp. 51–4.
6. EMHL, Joseph Bancroft "Machinery Account" (ledger 1831–46).
7. DCHS, Day Book, entry p. 128 re George Horner; Pay Book, Jan. 13, 1844.
8. DCIS, vault, Report of 5th Annual Exhibition, 1850.
9. EMHL, "Illustrated Catalogue of Machines Built by Alfred Jenks & Son [1853]," p. 64.
10. Webber, 1879, pp. 66–73.
11. Sandberg, 1970, pp. 120–40. General accounts of improvements in the throstle may be found in Batchelder, 1863, Bishop, 1864, and Clark, 1916.
12. Garsed's biography may be found in the *Biographical Encyclopaedia of Pennsylvania in the Nineteenth Century*, 1874, pp. 298–9.
13. Report of Franklin Institute Exhibition, 1842, pp. 4–5, and 1844, pp. 377–9.
14. *Journal of the Franklin Institute*, 3rd series, Vol. 14 (1847), pp. 170–1. See also U.S. Dept. of Commerce, Patent Office, patent no. 4645, "Looms for twilling, operating treadle cams in."
15. *Biographical Encyclopaedia of Pennsylvania in the Nineteenth Century*, 1874, p. 298.
16. See Richard Garsed's U.S. patent no. 6845.
17. General accounts of loom improvements are to be found in Jeremy, 1973(a), English, 1969, Copeland, 1912, and Lincoln, 1932 and 1933.

THE LESSER INVENTORS OF CHESTER CREEK

1. *Journal of the Franklin Institute*, Vol. 6 (1828), Part 2, p. 263.
2. Silliman, 1833, pp. 70–1.
3. See English, 1969, pp. 99–104, 195, and Jeremy, 1973(a), pp. 54–5, 60–1, 64–6, for an outline of the main sequence of inventions in warping and sizing.
4. The details on the Riddles' sizing trough are drawn from the Riddle Day Book, entries of Nov. 13 and 15, 1833, Jan. 1, 1834, July 18, 1834, and *passim* after November 1833 for purchases of coal (DCHS).
5. Dutton, 1848, pp. 17–18.
6. *Ibid.*, Preface.
7. Bigelow, 1831, p. 264.
8. The account of the Duttons is derived in part from Cope, 1871, pp. 57–9; Dutton, 1848; Ashmead, 1884, pp. 290–3 and 620; Martin, 1877, pp. 247, 251; and NA, Patent Office Records, particularly nos. 3080 (ice accumulation) and 4697 (ice manufacture).
9. Massachusetts Historical Society, Lowell Papers, Thos. Odiorne to Jos. Whipple, Exeter, June 15, 1791.

10. BLH, Boston Manufacturing Company account books.
11. CCHS, Chester and Delaware Co. *Village Record,* Jan. 9, 1811.
12. Sarah Trainer Smith, 1897.
13. Thomas Odiorne, 1792.
14. Leggett, 1874.
15. James C. Odiorne, 1875.
16. Bathe and Bathe, 1943, p. 53.
17. *Ibid.,* pp. 177–8.
18. NA, U.S. Census of Mfrs., 1820, Pennsylvania, "Henry Moore."
19. Chapin, 1860, p. 163.
20. NA, Patent Office Records, Thomas Odiorne patents of Aug. 27 and Sept. 26, 1835.
21. Ferguson, 1965, p. 92.
22. Accounts of Nathan Sellers are to be found in Ferguson, 1965, and in his grandson George Escol Sellers' "Recollections" of his grandfather, in APS, Peale-Sellers Papers.

THE INTERNATIONAL FRATERNITY OF MECHANICIANS

1. Jeremy, 1973(b); Wilkinson, 1963.
2. Ferguson, 1965, p. 112.
3. HSD, Poole Papers; Ferguson, 1965, pp. 46–61; NYHS, Letters of John Rogers, 1850–55.
4. Cantwell, 1961, pp. 143, 234.
5. See the biography of Bishop Hopkins by his son, Hopkins, 1873.
6. Bradley, 1972, p. viii.
7. APS, George Escol Sellers, "Personal Recollections of Coleman Sellers."
8. See Ferguson, 1965, *passim* for an edition of the memoirs of George Escol Sellers, which describe the mechanics' world of Philadelphia in the 1820's and 1830's.
9. See Charles Coleman Sellers, 1939, 1947, for a fine biography of Peale.
10. HSD, Poole Papers, Letters of J. Morton Poole 1830–37.
11. Ferguson, 1965, provides an intimate picture of the relations among the mechanicians.
12. Except as otherwise specified, the materials on the Philadelphia and Brandywine mechanicians are drawn from Ferguson, 1965, Wilkinson, 1963, and Jeremy, 1973(b).
13. In conversation with Eugene Ferguson, it appeared that he and the writer had independently estimated the size of the community at about the same number, in the neighborhood of three hundred.
14. See Kuhn, 1970, and Anthony F. C. Wallace, 1972, for discussions of the concept of paradigmatic community.

THE SELLERS FAMILY

1. The sources of these genealogical details are Ashmead, 1884, pp. 546–50; the biographies of Coleman and William Sellers in Allen Johnson, *et al.,* DAB, 1928–73; and the genealogy in Ferguson, 1965, pp. xiv–xix. See also McCullough, 1972, pp. 485–7.
2. Ferguson, 1965, pp. 7–8.
3. APS, Peale-Sellers Papers, "Personal Recollections of Coleman Sellers," by George Escol Sellers, pp. 1–2, 18–19.
4. *Ibid.,* pp. 24–5.
5. *Ibid.,* pp. 1–2.

6. Ashmead, 1884, p. 549.
7. Allen Johnson, *et al.*, DAB 1928–73, William Sellers; Scharf, 1888, pp. 780–2; Ashmead, 1884, pp. 548–50; HSD, Letters of John Morton Poole to Joseph Bancroft; Sinclair, 1969.
8. Wilkinson, 1963, pp. 4–5; Charles Coleman Sellers, 1947, Vol. 2, pp. 285–6.
9. Charles Coleman Sellers, 1947, Vol. 2., pp. 286–7, 295–6.
10. APS, Peale-Sellers Papers, "Personal Recollections of Coleman Sellers," by George Escol Sellers, pp. 25–7; Charles Coleman Sellers, 1947, Vol. 2, pp. 348–9.
11. Ferguson, 1965, p. 80.

THE FRANKLIN INSTITUTE

1. Ferguson, 1965, p. 38.
2. See, for example, Lyon, 1799, and Claxton, 1839.
3. The definitive study of the founding and early history of the Franklin Institute is Sinclair, 1974.
4. FI, First Annual Report, 1825.
5. Sinclair, 1974, p. 61.
6. Robison, 1822, Vol. 2, pp. vii–viii.
7. Ferguson, 1965, p. 170.
8. FI, Franklin Institute of Exhibitions, Vol. 1, 1825, pp. 8, 30.
9. See the cotton exhibit sections of the *Journal, passim.*
10. FI, Archives, MS Committee on Water Power.
11. See Burke, 1847, and Sinclair, 1974.
12. *Journal of the Franklin Institute,* Vol. 7 (March 1831), pp. 145–6. A thorough study of the history of the science and technology of water wheels is to be found in Reynolds, 1973; this source indicates that the Franklin Institute Committee was seemingly not aware of the extent of the theoretical advances in the understanding of the physics of the subject that had been made in France in the eighteenth century.
13. *Ibid,* p. 147.
14. FI, Archives, MS Committee on Water Power.
15. As noted in Sinclair, 1974, pp. 147–8.

THINKING ABOUT MACHINERY

1. See Kuhn, 1970, and Anthony F. C. Wallace, 1972.

Part Three
ROCKDALE FROM 1835 TO 1850:
THE STRUGGLE FOR CONTROL OF A WAY OF LIFE

Chapter VI: The Enlightenment's Last Campaign

THE FREETHINKERS OF CHESTER CREEK

1. John K. Zeilin's notice of the debate on Owen's system is to be found in the *Upland Union,* Jan. 17, 1826; details of his career in Ashmead, 1884, p. 250.

2. *Upland Union,* July 11, 1826.

3. The participation of John S. Phillips in the meetings of the Academy of Natural Sciences of Philadelphia is detailed in the minutes of that organization for 1824 and 1825. Information about his visits to the Brandywine, and the impression he made on the ladies there, came from EMHL, particularly the Tancopanican Chronicle, 1830–33, the diary of Sophie du Pont and her letters to Clementina Smith, and the correspondence of Elizabeth Mackie Smith (Mrs. Francis Gurney Smith) with her daughter-in-law Eleuthera (du Pont) Smith. See also Deacon, 1851, for *Warreniana.*

4. PLTA, Letterbook Index F, Minshall Painter to Ann Tyler, June 23, 1857.

5. PLTA, *Reminiscence; Gleanings and Thoughts,* No. 1 (privately printed by the Painters, 1870).

6. The museum and library of the Institute are still open to the public. DCIS, MSS in vault (membership lists, annual reports, minutes, and correspondence), provided additional information on the early activities of the Institute.

7. Smith, 1868, pp. 97–9.

8. PLTA, Letterbook Index F, Minshall Painter to Ann Tyler, June 23, 1857.

9. CCR, Records, RSS to the Missionary Society of St. James Church, Philadelphia, April 1838.

10. Erickson, 1972, pp. 157, 168.

11. HSP, William Martin's Receipt Book, *passim.*

12. Lima Methodist Church, Antiquities, Minutes by William Fox, 1870–2.

THE CONTEXT OF POST-REVOLUTIONARY RADICALISM
IN THE LOWER DELAWARE VALLEY

1. Selsam, 1971, p. 217.

2. *Ibid.,* p. 211.

3. The discussion of the 1776 constitution is based largely on Selsam, 1971, and Tinkcom, 1950. Fertig, 1926, published the texts of the several constitutions of Pennsylvania.

4. Volney, 1890 (original edition 1791), p. 17.

5. The Jefferson-Maclure-Volney-Paine connection is documented in Chinard, 1923.

6. See Marx, 1964.

7. Hardy, Jensen, and Wolfe, 1966. See also Morton, 1844, for an early appreciation of Maclure's career.

8. Neef, 1808, pp. 2–3.

9. Hagner, 1869, pp. 36–8.

10. Lowell H. Harrison, 1949, pp. 322–5.

11. Farragut, 1879, p. 49.

12. See Hackensmith, 1973, for a detailed biography of Neef.

13. Details of Mme Fretageot's school in Philadelphia are to be found in her correspondence with Maclure, published in Bestor, 1948.

14. B. G. du Pont, 1930, pp. 177–81.

15. EMHL, W9–25129, Ella DP to SDP, Nov. 25, 1823.

16. EMHL, W9–25143, Ella DP to SDP, April 18, 1825.

17. ANSP, Founding Minutes, as quoted in Mautner MS, p. 4.

18. Mautner MS, p. 9.

19. The best general account of the social reformist activities of members of the Academy in its early years is to be found in the 1973 MS of Nancy Mautner. See also APS, MS Acc.

No. 258, "A Biographical Sketch of the late Thomas Say," January 1835.

20. APS, Peale-Sellers Papers, John Wilson to Coleman Sellers, Jan. 24, 1820.
21. Bestor, 1948, p. 303.
22. *Ibid.*, p. 307.
23. WINH, New Harmony MSS, Series S, Folder 11, No. 14, John Speakman to Thomas Speakman, Pittsburgh, *c.* 1823.
24. Bestor, 1948, p. 305.
25. APS, George Ord Papers, George Ord to Charles Waterton, May 15, 1834.

PREACHING THE NEW MORAL WORLD

1. Lafayette's itinerary is given day by day in Nolan, 1934. For events in Chester, see Martin, 1877, pp. 253–9.
2. Details of Fanny Wright's association with Lafayette are given in Perkins and Wolfson, 1939, and Waterman, 1924.
3. Bestor, 1948, pp. 311–12.
4. APS, Peale-Sellers Papers, "Personal Recollections of Coleman Sellers," by George Escol Sellers, pp. 46–7.
5. Bestor, 1948, p. 314.
6. *New Harmony Gazette,* Vol. I, July 30, 1826, as quoted in Bestor, 1970, p. 222.
7. Drinnon, 1972, pp. 220–1.
8. Perkins and Wolfson, 1939, p. 171.
9. The classic study of the New Harmony experiment, cast in the context of other socialist and religious communities of the day, is of course Bestor, 1970.
10. WINH, Ella du Pont to Mme Fretageot, Feb. 10, 1826.
11. WINH, Victor du Pont to Mme Fretageot, Feb. 21, 1826.
12. EMHL, WS-3467, Rey to M. and Mme du Pont, April 14, 1826.
13. John P. Crozer, 186, p. 46.
14. Snedeker, 1942, p. 204.
15. Elizabeth Montgomery, 1851, p. 36.
16. McLane, 1833, Vol. 2, pp. 817–18. See also EMHL, Hancock MS, 1956–58.
17. See Claussen, 1970, for an account of the life of Reuben Haines.
18. Snedeker, 1942, pp. 311–13.
19. *Ibid.*
20. *Ibid.*, p. 209.
21. Bestor, 1970, p. 202; *Niles' Register,* Dec. 31, 1825.
22. HSP, Constitution of the Friendly Association, 1826.
23. WINH, Maclure to Fretageot, July 24 and July 31, 1826; CCHS, *Village Record* of West Chester, Pa., March 15, 1826; Woodman, 1922 (original edition 1850), pp. 100–2.
24. Knight, 1880, pp. 16–18.
25. Robert Dale Owen, 1874, pp. 234–6.
26. White and Taylor, 1871, p. 158; *Niles' Weekly Register,* Dec. 31, 1825.
27. WINH, Diary of William Maclure, August 25, 1825.
28. An early account of the community by a contemporary resident in the area, although not a member of the commune, is found in Woodman, 1922, pp. 100–2.
29. CCHS, *Village Record,* March 15, 1826.
30. Wendall P. Fox, 1911.
31. WINH, Maclure to Fretageot, July 31 and September 19, 1826.

32. Woodman, 1922, pp. 100–2.
33. WINH, Maclure to Fretageot, July 31, 1826.
34. Knight, 1880, pp. 16–17; White and Taylor, 1871, pp. 158–9.
35. The events in this section have been well chronicled by several labor historians in second-ary works. Of particular value is Louis H. Arky, "The Mechanics Union of Trade Associa-tions and the Formation of the Philadelphia Workingmen's Movement," 1952. See also Leonard Bernstein, "The Working People of Philadelphia from Colonial Times to the General Strike of 1835," 1950; Edward Pessen, "The Workingmen's Movement of the Jacksonian Era," 1956; Edward Pessen, *Most Uncommon Jacksonians: The Radical Leaders of the Early Labor Movement,* 1967; William A. Sullivan, *The Industrial Worker in Pennsylvania, 1800–1840,* 1955; John R. Commons (ed.), *History of Labor in the United States,* Vol. 1, 1918. Robert Owen's "Address" of June 25, 1827, at the Franklin Institute was printed in Philadelphia in 1827 and a copy is located at the APS. The HSP has an incomplete series of the *Mechanic's Free Press* from 1828 to 1831.

Chapter VII: The Evangelical Counterattack

1. The Presbyterian Historical Society in Philadelphia possesses many of Ely's publications, including his sermons and books, and his MS, *Memoirs of his own life and times.*
2. The sermon was reprinted in Philadelphia in 1828 by W. F. Geddes; a copy is held by the Presbyterian Historical Society.

CALVARY CHURCH IN ROCKDALE

1. Martin, 1877, p. 459.
2. Smith and Cole, 1935, pp. 60, 76.
3. EMHL, W9–25194, CS to SDP, Jan. 2, 1834.
4. EMHL, W9–21299, SDP to CS, Feb. 9, 1834.
5. DCHS, Parkmount Day Book.
6. Erickson, 1972, p. 159.
7. Crozer, 1861, p. 78.
8. EMHL, Genealogy of Smith Family by F. W. Leach.
9. EMHL, SDP to CS, W9–21299, Feb. 9, 1834.
10. DCCH, Register of Deeds, S496, T590.
11. CCR, Records, Letter of RSS, April 1838.
12. *Ibid.*
13. This account of the organization of the church from 1833 to 1841 is derived from a number of sources: R. S. Smith's MS letter of April 1838 in the Records of Calvary Church, in Rockdale; R. S. Smith's letter to B. P. Smith, Aug. 18, 1875, pp. 6–10, in [St. Andrew's Church], Alfred Lee, first Bishop of Delaware, 1888; Smith's account as given to John Hill Martin in Martin's, 1877, *Chester (and Its Vicinity),* pp. 459–60; and two pamphlet histories of Calvary Church published in 1933 and 1958 on the occasion of the church's 100th and 125th anniversaries.
14. Ferguson, 1965, pp. 40–2.
15. Biographies of Bishop Hopkins are found in DAB and in Hopkins, 1873.
16. This sketch of the composition of the congregation is based on several sets of records: the U.S. census schedules for Aston and Middletown townships for the years 1830–60; the MS book of records of baptisms, marriages, confirmations, and burials of Calvary

Church; the WPA listing of grave markers in Calvary Church cemetery (DCHS, WPA Project #4889, 1936–37); the list of contributors to the wardens and vestrymen. See also John K. Murphy's pamphlet, *To the Communicants and Members of the Congregation of Calvary Church, Rockdale, c.* 1861 (HSP, VoD*/.58 Vol. II).

17. Lee, 1856, pp. 8–9.
18. Lee, 1841.
19. EMHL, W9–25320, CS to SDP, Aug. 20, 1839.
20. EMHL, W9–25368, CS to SDP, March 23, 1841.
21. EMHL, W9–21451, SDP to CS, March 17, 1841.
22. Alfred Lee's life and views have been summarized in a biographical sketch published by the congregation of St. Andrew's Church in Wilmington in 1889. His early career at Rockdale is described in a series of letters from Clementina Smith to Sophie du Pont, 1839 to 1841 (Eleutherian Mills Historical Library, Winterthur Collection, W9–25308 to 25383). A number of his sermons have been published, including a Farewell Discourse to the Rockdale congregation (see Delaware County Historical Society for this); his sermons at St. Andrews in Wilmington are preserved at Eleutherian Mills Historical Library. The early Sunday School is also described in Clementina's letters from 1834 to 1841, W9–25207 to 25383, and in Sophie's letters to Clementina, also at Eleutherian Mills, W9–21301 to 21464.
23. See Potter, 1841(a).
24. CCR, Letter of RSS, April 1838; [St. Andrew's Church] a biography of Bishop Lee, 1888, p. 7 (RSS to C. E. McIlvaine, Aug. 18, 1875).
25. The Brandywine Manufacturers' Sunday School records are at EMHL; particularly valuable is the Receiving Book (Acc. 839, Box 1, Folder 3), which records the particulars of all children and their families (including the Miles and Miller families). Other data on the Miles and the Millers came from the U.S. census of 1850 and from the Penn's Grove Pay Book (DCHS). Sophie's diary contains several valuable accounts of her dealings with Maria Miles.
26. EMHL, W9–40379, diary of SDP, Nov. 18, 1832.
27. *Ibid.,* Nov. 6, 1833.
28. *Ibid.,* July 15, 1839.
29. NA, U.S. census 1850, Pennsylvania, Delaware County, Middletown Township.
30. EMHL, W9–25275, CS to SDP, Aug. 8, 1837.
31. EMHL, W9–25618, CS to SDP, July 28, 1847.
32. EMHL, W9–25523, CS to SDP, Aug. 26, 1845.
33. Govan, 1959, pp. 346–7.
34. EMHL, W9–25462, CS to SDP, March 9, 1844.
35. EMHL, W9–25526, CS to SDP, Aug. 1, 1845.
36. EMHL, W9–25480, CS to SDP, July 2, 1844.
37. EMHL, W9–25810, CS to SDP, Jan. 5, 1852.

THE BENEVOLENT WORK OF OTHER MANUFACTURERS

1. Staughton's career as briefly described in Keen, 1899, and Newman, 1898.
2. Samuel Crozer, 1902, pp. 17–18.
3. Crozer, 1861, p. 72.
4. Samuel Crozer, 1902; see also Charles W. W. Bishop, 1855.

5. Ashmead, 1884, p. 615.
6. Crozer's flirtation with Presbyterianism is revealed in Kruse's "Historical Sketch" of the Middletown Presbyterian Church (September 1920); in Ashmead, 1884, p. 615; in Kruse, 1922; and in Crozer's four letters to Robert Landis, 1833 to 1836, in the Presbyterian Historical Society, Philadelphia.
7. EMHL, W9-25231, CS to SDP. Although the letter is not dated by year, internal evidence makes 1837 the only possible date.
8. Samuel Crozer, 1902.
9. *Pa. Senate Journal*, 1837–38, Part 2, pp. 305–6.
10. The *Upland Union* regularly reported the activities of the benevolent societies in the neighborhood; see for items cited here the issues of Jan. 20, 1829, April 13 and June 1, 1841, and May 7, 1844. Martin, 1877, pp. 235–7, gives an extended account of the Bible Society and the formation of the Tract Society. For an account of the meeting at Calvary Church, see EMHL, W9-25371, CS to SDP, June 1, 1841.
11. Ridlon, 1884, Ryedale genealogy, p. 159.
12. Ashmead, 1884, pp. 300–1; "100th Anniv. Souvenir of Mt. Hope Methodist Church."
13. Ashmead, 1884, p. 300.
14. Ashmead, 1884, p. 617; "100th Anniv. of Lima M.E. Church."
15. Ridlon, 1884, Ryedale genealogy, pp. 158–9.
16. See Anthony F. C. Wallace, 1970, for an account of the early years of this mission.
17. Cope, 1871, pp. 57–9.
18. APS, Peale-Sellers Papers, Correspondence, Box, 1837–44. Peter Hill to Elizabeth Hill, March 27, 1842.
19. Humphrey's practice is commented on in EMHL, Clementina and Sophie's correspondence; his treatment of Riddle employees is remarked in the Parkmount Day Book, DCHS.
20. EMHL, Letterbooks of Daniel Lammot, Jr. (microfilm M-58.13. Acc. 801), DL to James Hargrove, Jan. 1, 1825.
21. *Ibid.*, DL to Howard Weeks, March 8, 1825.
22. EMHL, W9-40392, diary of Sophie du Pont, May 22, 1840.
23. Swedenborgian School of Religion, DL to Chas. Doughty, Penn's Grove, Dec. 28, 1843. For a general account of Philadelphia, and Swedenborgianism in the nineteenth century, see Swank, 1970.

MORAL ORDER IN THE MILLS

1. *Pa. Senate Journal*, 1837–38, Part 2, pp. 280, 302.
2. DCHS, Parkmount Day Book, *passim.*
3. *Pa. Senate Journal*, 1837–38, Part 2, pp. 280, 300, 304.
4. *Hazard's Register of Pennsylvania*, Vol. 12, p. 16 (April 19, 1834).
5. *Pa. Senate Journal*, 1837–38, Part 2, pp. 279–81, 283–5, 299–307.
6. *Ibid.*, p. 305.
7. Snedeker, 1942, p. 195.
8. *Hunt's Merchant's Magazine*, 1846, pp. 370–1.
9. *Pa. Senate Journal*, 1837–38, Part 2, pp. 301–2.
10. *Ibid.*, pp. 304–6.
11. *Pa. Senate Journal*, 1837–38, Part 1, p. 326.
12. Potter, 1841, pp. 258–9, 262–3.

THE RISE OF POLITICAL ANTI-MASONRY

1. For an excellent review of popular freethinkers and their enemies, see Post, 1974.
2. James C. Odiorne, 1830, p. 222.
3. See Post, 1974, pp. 218–19.
4. Speakman's letter to Thomas Say from Pittsburgh, undated, is to be found in the library of the Workingmen's Institute at New Harmony, Indiana.
5. Anne Royall is the subject of an excellent biography (James, 1972). Anne Royall on Ely is quoted on p. 124; the episode in Burlington is described on pp. 211–13; the harassment and trial in Washington, on pp. 250–62.
6. Information on Darlington's career in the House has been culled from a number of scattered sources: records of his speeches and votes in Gale and Seaton's *Register of Debates in Congress,* 23rd, 24th, and 25th Congresses, the *Congressional Globe* (25th Congress), and the *Journal of the House of Representatives;* his political correspondence in CCHS; and letters from his constituents in the Darlington Papers, DCHS.
7. James C. Odiorne, 1830, pp. 224–5.
8. *Ibid.,* pp. 43–44.
9. Robison, 1797 edition, pp. 138–9.
10. Barruel, 1799.

DEFEATING THE INFIDELS ON CHESTER CREEK

1. CCR, Letter of RSS, April 1838.
2. EMHL, W9–21301, 21398, 21473, SDP to CS, Sept. 3, 1834, Oct. 6, 1839, Feb. 6, 1842.
3. CCR, RSS to Alfred Lee, Aug. 1, 1838.
4. CCR, "Sequel" to RSS letter of April 1838. Written about 1843, two years after Lee's departure in 1841.

Chapter VIII: The Emergence of Christian Industrialism

THE RECESSION OF 1834 TO 1842

1. DCHS, George E. Darlington Papers, JPC to ED, April 1, 1834.
2. DCHS, Parkmount Day Book, pp. 152, 247–9.
3. Crozer, 1861, 78–9.
4. DCCH, Deed Books U, p. 263, and V, p. 630.
5. Ashmead, 1914, caption of portrait of J. P. Crozer facing p. 42.
6. Crozer, 1861, p. 80.
7. *Pa. Senate Journal,* 1837–38, Part 2, p. 302.
8. Erickson, 1972, pp. 162, 164.
9. Ashmead, 1884, pp. 621, 623; DCHS, Samuel Riddle's Rent Book (Riddle managed Houghton's estate for Farnum).
10. Ashmead, 1884, p. 296.
11. The details of Daniel Lammot's business affairs in the period 1835 to 1842 are contained in a series of letters to Alfred du Pont at EMHL, Longwood MSS, Group 5, Series A, Box 13. The accounts of the contract weaving arrangement are also at EMHL in business memoranda to E. I. du Pont de Nemours & Co., Aug. 21, 1837, to Nov. 27, 1837.

THE STRIKES OF 1836 AND 1842

1. Ashmead, 1884, p. 109; PLTA, JPC to Minshall Painter, Jan. 7, 1841; Commons, 1918, Vol. 1, p. 476.

2. *Pa. Senate Journal*, 1837–38, Part 2, pp. 279–81.

3. PHS, JPC to R. Landis, Jan. 31, 1836; DCIS, MSS, copy of Hannah Dutton's register, 6 mo 27, 1836.

4. EMHL, Longwood MSS, Group 5, Series A, Box 13, DL to AVDP, May 18, 1836.

5. EMHL, Longwood MSS, Group 4, Series A, Box 3, DL to AVDP, circa June 1836.

6. PLTA, Letterbook Index BJPC to Minshall Painter, Jan. 7, 1841.

7. *Pa. Senate Journal*, 1837–38, Part 2, pp. 280–1, 357–9.

8. *Upland Union*, open letter of Hiram McConnell, June 7, 1842.

9. J. Wheaton Smith, 1868, pp. 77–9.

10. *Upland Union*, open letter of Hiram McConnell, May 3, 1842.

11. J. Wheaton Smith, 1868, p. 78.

12. Ashmead, 1884, p. 235.

13. *Upland Union*, June 7, 1842.

14. Except as otherwise noted, the description of the events of the strike is drawn from the public press. The principal source is the paraphrase of testimony at the trial that was printed in the Philadelphia *Public Ledger*, May 30, May 31, June 1, and June 3, 1842. The *Public Ledger* also published Judge Bell's charge to the jury on July 27; the *Upland Union* published the charge on Aug. 9. The *Upland Union* printed two open letters from Hiram McConnell, May 3, and June 7, 1842, and news of the strike and its aftermath on April 5, April 12, May 31, June 21, and June 28. The *Delaware County Republican* was not sympathetic to the strikers and printed only one straight news story after the trial was over, on June 3, 1842.

15. The principles of organization in the traditional crafts are reviewed in Commons, 1910, 1918, 1926, and in Sullivan, 1955, and both authorities list the unions and strike actions in Pennsylvania in this period. See David Montgomery, 1972, for an account of the Kensington hand-loom weavers. The differing principles of the cotton workers' organization are not clearly formulated in the general surveys but become evident in the data on specific actions, like the strikes in 1836 and 1842.

16. The names of the 1842 strikers charged with conspiracy and riot are given in the records of the case in Court of Sessions, May 1842 (Delaware County Court House), and in the account of the strike in the *Public Ledger*. Dossiers on each of these men were collated from the U.S. census schedules for Aston and Middletown townships, 1790 through 1860; from the Parkmount Day Book, the Penn's Grove Rent Book, the Penn's Grove Pay Book; Delaware County Tax Assessment Records 1825 to 1860; the records of Calvary Church, Middletown Presbyterian Church, Lima Methodist Church, and Mount Hope Methodist Church; and the WPA grave marker survey for these churches.

17. *Upland Union*, June 7, 1842, April 5, 1842, and May 10, 1842 (quoting *Delaware County Republican*).

18. *Delaware County Republican*, July 8, 1842.

19. J. Wheaton Smith, 1868, pp. 80–1.

20. *Delaware County Republican*, July 1, 1842.

21. EMHL, W9–25414, CS to SDP, Rockdale, June 28, 1842.

22. Philadelphia *Public Ledger*, July 27, 1842; *Upland Union*, Aug. 9, 1842.

THE GREAT FLOOD

1. Ashmead, 1884, pp. 99–100.
2. Except as otherwise noted, the account of the flood is drawn primarily from the seventy-nine-page technical paper "The Flood of 1843," prepared in 1843 and 1844 by a committee of the Delaware County Institute of Science, composed of Dr. George Smith, John P. Crozer, and Minshall Painter. This account was republished in the *Proceedings* of the DCIS, Vol. 6, Nos. 1 and 2, 1910. Other details can be found in Ashmead, 1884, pp. 99–108, and in J. Wheaton Smith's 1868 biography of Crozer, which quotes from his letters and diaries (pp. 99–106). In September 1971 a flood occurred along Chester Creek which virtually duplicated the 1843 flood in physical characteristics, damages, and deaths and injuries. The writer's observations of this flood were of help in interpreting the 1843 accounts. The 1971 flood also destroyed the old railroad for the second time and probably permanently.
3. DCIS, "Flood of 1843," No. 1, p. 11.
4. *Ibid.,* p. 42.
5. EMHL, Acc. 801, Letterbooks of Daniel Lammot (microfilm M-58.13, No. 2, p. 3), DL to John Kiefer, Dec. 23, 1856; Swedenborg School of Religion, DL to Chas. Doughty, Penn's Grove, Sept. 20, 1843.
6. J. Wheaton Smith, 1868, pp. 101–2, 104, 107.

THE REDEFINITION OF THE COTTON MILL OPERATIVE

1. *Journal of the Franklin Institute,* Vol. 20 (1835), p. 356; see also Sandberg, 1970.
2. Ure, 1835, pp. 19–21.
3. DCCH, Tax Assessments, Aston Township, 1829.
4. The introduction of the new school system into Delaware County is described in Ashmead, 1884, pp. 95–6, 298–9, 617–19.
5. See Catling, 1970, p. 149, for an account of the conservative role of the English mule spinner. His description probably applies to America as well in this period.
6. DCHS, Parkmount Day Book and Penn's Grove Pay Book.
7. Ashmead, 1884, p. 620.
8. EMHL, W9–25828, Maria Blakely to SDP, April 23, 1852.
9. DCCH, tax lists; EMHL, W9–26153, CS to SDP, February 4, 1858.

WORKERS AS OBJECTS OF PITY: THE TEN HOURS LAW

1. EMHL, W9–26998, CS to SDP, Oct. 29, 1863.
2. *Upland Union,* April 8, 1846, July 14, 1847, Nov. 3, 1847.
3. Ashmead, 1884, pp. 108–12, gives a general account of the ten hours law in Delaware County.
4. Commons, 1910, Vol. 8, p. 200.
5. Ashmead, 1884, p. 110.
6. Commons, 1910, Vol. 8, pp. 200–5.
7. Ashmead, 1884, pp. 108–12.

THE THEORY OF CHRISTIAN CAPITALISM

1. Carey, 1852, p. 229.
2. Mayer, 1936, pp. 236–44, discusses the impact of Carey's economic philosophy on European socialist literature and particularly the pressure which, through Dühring's advocacy of it, it placed on Marx and Engels.
3. For general treatments of Carey's work, and bibliography, see Eiselen, 1932, Elder, 1880, Green, 1951, and Kaplan, 1931.

Part Four
ROCKDALE FROM 1850 TO 1865:
THE TRANSCENDING OF A WAY OF LIFE

Chapter IX. Marching to Millennium

THE ECONOMIC TAKE-OFF

1. Ashmead, 1884, p. 331.
2. Martin, 1877, pp. 313–14.
3. Samuel Crozer, 1902.
4. Ashmead, 1884, pp. 430–1; J. Wheaton Smith, 1868, pp. 120–7; *Laws of the General Assembly of the Commonwealth of Pennsylvania,* 1849, p. 577.
5. Whitehead, 1859, pp. 44–5. See also Ashmead, 1884, p. 331, and Broomall, 1876, p. 5.
6. Ashmead, 1884, pp. 332, 396–8.
7. DCIS, *Memorial of John M. Broomall,* 1894, p. 5.
8. Ashmead, 1884, p. 397.
9. Whitehead, 1859, p. 98.
10. Ashmead, 1884, p. 332.
11. EMHL, MS Group 7, Series A, Box 2, MLDP to Evelina Biderman, Oct. 14, 1838.
12. Ashmead, 1884, pp. 399–400. See also Wiley, 1894, pp. 324–5.
13. EMHL, W9–25225, Maria Miles to SDP, Sept. 6, 1835.
14. EMHL, W9–25241, Maria Miles to SDP, April 16, 1836.
15. EMHL, W9–25625, Maria Blakely to SDP, Oct. 27, 1847.
16. EMHL, W9–26705, Maria Blakely to SDP, July 11, 1862.
17. Calvary Church 100th Anniversary Memorial, 1933. See also Ashmead, 1884, pp. 294–5, 621.

THE POLITICS OF THE MANUFACTURING INTEREST

1. Martin, 1877, p. 325.
2. McLane, 1833, Vol. 2, pp. 224–6, 212.
3. Ashmead, 1884, p. 248.
4. 22nd Congress, 1st Session, House Doc. No. 171, June 25, 1832.
5. 22nd Congress, 2nd Session, House Doc. No. 134, Feb. 18, 1833.
6. EMHL, Winterthur MSS, Series C, Box 24, EDP to VB, Jan. 29, 1832.
7. DCHS, George E. Darlington Papers, Samuel and James Riddle to ED, Feb. 14, 1834.

8. *Ibid.,* JPC to ED, April 1, 1834.
9. 23rd Congress, 1st Session, House Doc. Nos. 282, 280, 287, April 7, 1834.
10. DCHS, Parkmount Day Book, June 6, 1834.
11. *Upland Union,* May 26, June 23, July 21, 1840.
12. Campbell, 1892, pp. 512–13.
13. DCHS *Proceedings,* Vol. 1, pp. 155–70.
14. The political careers of the Riddle brothers are delineated in Campbell, 1892, Ashmead, 1884, and Ridlon, 1884.
15. Martin's voting record is recorded in the *Journal* of the House of Representatives, 1827–28, located in the Pennsylvania State Library (Legislative Reference section).
16. See Martin, 1877, pp. 332–4, and *Pa. House Journal,* Jan. 18 and March 19, 1828.
17. See Ashmead, 1884, p. 248, for an account of Samuel Edwards.
18. CCHS, *Village Record,* July 26, 1828.
19. Details of Edward Darlington's political career are to be found in the regular announcements of political activities in the county in such newspapers as the *Upland Union,* the *Delaware County Republican,* and the *Village Record,* from 1825 on. Some of his political correspondence is preserved in the George E. Darlington Papers, DCHS, and in a series of letters between himself and his cousin William Darlington in CCHS. His voting record in Congress is revealed in the *Congressional Globe* and in the *Journal* of the House. See also some information in the Darlington, 1909, genealogy.
20. See the *Journal* of the House of Representatives, 23rd, 24th, and 25th Congresses, *passim.*
21. HSP, Simon Gratz Collection.
22. HSP, Henry C. Carey Papers, ED to Henry Carey, Nov. 25, 1858.
23. Darlington, 1909, p. 74. See also Zyckowski, 1937, pp. 40–2, for the connection with Stevens.
24. 25th Congress, 3rd Session, *Pa. House Journal,* Dec. 11, 1838.
25. DCIS, *Memorial of John M. Broomall,* 1894, pp. 2, 7, 8.
26. *Congressional Globe,* Dec. 17, 1868, pp. 134–5.
27. In addition to the material provided by the *Memorial of John M. Broomall* (copies of which are located at the Delaware County Institute of Science, the Friends Historical Library, the HSP, and the APS, of which he was a corresponding member), Broomall material can be found in the form of printed speeches at these same libraries, and in manuscript at the HSP, which has a file of his political correspondence amounting to some three hundred items for the years 1867 and 1868. His career has received no attention from such historians of the Republican Party as Foner, 1970, and Myers, 1940.

MISSIONS AND THE MILLENNIAL PASSION

1. See Lemieux, 1976, for a detailed study of the death cult in Delaware County during this period.
2. Lee, 1856, pp. 17, 575, 587.
3. EMHL, W9–26099, CS to SDP, Sept. 3, 1857.
4. EMHL, W9–26174, CS to SDP, April 26, 1858.
5. Francis, 1946, p. 56.
6. EMHL, Longwood MSS, Group 4, Box 10, folder "Lammott, Anna."
7. Wilder, 1866, pp. 25–30.
8. Newspaper obituary of John S. Phillips in the Pennsylvania Academy of Fine Arts.
9. Beaux, 1930, pp. 61–3.

10. Obituary notice in Pennsylvania Academy of Fine Arts. The print collection and part of Phillips' library were transferred to the Philadelphia Museum of Art in 1856. The prints have been removed from Phillips' special folders and combined with other collections.
11. See Lemieux, 1976, pp. 139–42, 246–53.
12. EMHL, W9–25810, CS to SDP, Jan. 5, 1852.
13. EMHL, W9–25263, CS to SDP, Nov. 19, 1830.
14. EMHL, W9–25288, CS to SDP, May 17, 1838.
15. EMHL, W9–25888, CS to SDP, Sept. 10, 1853.
16. EMHL, W9–25355, CS to SDP, Nov. 30, 1840.
17. Crozer, *Autobiography,* 1861, pp. 87–9.
18. Wilder, 1866, p. 22.
19. Ashmead, 1884, pp. 301, 332.
20. Upland Baptist Church, Minutes, Oct. 8, 1852, to March 1865; Samuel Crozer, 1902.
21. Williams, 1902, p. 24.
22. Wilder, 1866, p. 10.
23. Upland Baptist Church, Minutes, Nov. 27 and Dec. 11, 1858.
24. J. Wheaton Smith, 1868, p. 190.
25. *Annual Reports,* May 16, 1859.
26. *Annual Reports, passim,* 1853–66.
27. J. Wheaton Smith, 1868, pp. 141, 171–9.
28. LOC, American Colonization Society Papers, Membership Lists (Microfilm reel 299, List of life directors).
29. HSP, "Ninetieth Anniversary of the Pennsylvania Abolition Society," 1866.
30. Crozer, 1863.
31. Kruse, 1922.
32. Ashmead, 1884, p. 260.
33. Crozer, 1863.
34. Allen, 1863, p. 8.
35. LOC, American Colonization Society Papers, *Annual Reports* for 1861–65; correspondence of JPC in Records, Vols. 167–83 (Microfilm reels 93–98).
36. Crozer, 1863, p. 23.
37. LOC, American Colonization Society Papers, Series 6, Box 5, folder "Crozer, Samuel A."
38. EMHL, W9–1972, SFDP to SDP, May 21, 1858.
39. The cruise of the *Minnesota* is carefully told in "journal letters" from SFDP to SDP in EMHL, W9–1926 to 1999.
40. EMHL, W9–25355, CS to SDP, Nov. 30, 1840.
41. EMHL, W9–25430, CS to SDP, March 15, 1843.
42. EMHL, W9–26203, CS to SDP, Aug. 7, 1858.
43. Tyng, 1848, p. 23.
44. Fuller, 1845, Vol. 1, pp. 552–3.
45. J. Wheaton Smith, 1868, pp. 149–50.
46. Read, 1836.
47. Read, 1864.
48. Read, 1859, p. 219.
49. Read, 1864.
50. Read, 1874.
51. Read, 1861.
52. Gilpin, 1873, pp. 8, 124.

53. The materials describing the Associated Working Women and Men are located in the files of the *Monthly Jubilee* at PLTA.

ARMAGEDDON

1. EMHL, W9–26153, CS to SDP, Feb. 4, 1858; 1860 census, Aston Township.
2. EMHL, W9–26159, 26179, CS to SDP, March 2 and May 3, 1858.
3. EMHL, W9–26203, CS to SDP, Aug. 7, 1858.
4. Upland Baptist Church, Minutes, Sept. 25, 1858.
5. Francis, 1946.
6. EMHL, W9–26039, CS to SDP, Feb. 26, 1857.
7. EMHL, W9–26340, CS to SDP, Jan. 31, 1859.
8. Ashmead, 1884, p. 305.
9. EMHL, W9–26377, CS to SDP, July 5, 1860.
10. EMHL, W9–26360, CS to SDP, April 28, 1860.
11. EMHL, W9–26382, CS to SDP, Aug. 7, 1860.
12. EMHL, W9–26416, Dec. 31, 1860.
13. The general course of events involving Delaware County during the Civil War is provided by Ashmead, 1884; see also the newspaper accounts in the *Delaware County Republican*. Bates, 1869–71, provides valuable information on units and individual soldiers.
14. EMHL, W9–26477, CS to SDP, May 14, 1861.
15. EMHL, W9–26482, CS to SDP, June 6, 1861.
16. J. Wheaton Smith, 1868, p. 183.
17. EMHL, W9–26514, CS to SDP, Sept. 10, 1861.
18. The work of the Christian Commission is described in Moss, 1868; Crozer's participation is also described in J. Wheaton Smith, 1868, pp. 183–5.
19. EMHL, W9–26546, CS to SDP, Nov. 14, 1861.
20. EMHL, W9–26589, CS to SDP, Dec. 7, 1861.
21. EMHL, W9–26514, CS to SDP, Sept. 18, 1861.
22. EMHL, W9–26680, CS to SDP, May 24, 1862.
23. EMHL, W9–26754, CS to SDP, Sept. 30, 1862.
24. EMHL, W9–26774, CS to SDP, Nov. 12, 1862.
25. EMHL, W9–26674, CS to SDP, May 2, 1862.
26. EMHL, W9–26806, CS to SDP, Jan. 8, 1863.
27. EMHL, W9–26970, CS to SDP, Aug. 18, 1863.
28. EMHL, W9–26967, CS to SDP, Aug. 12, 1863.
29. Johnson, 1890, pp. iv–vi.
30. EMHL, W9–26715, CS to SDP, July 23, 1862.
31. EMHL, W9–27121, CS to SDP, Sept. 18, 1864.
32. EMHL, W9–26774, CS to SDP, Nov. 12, 1861.
33. In general see Tuveson, 1968, for an interpretation of the importance of millennialist thinking in popular attitudes toward the war which has greatly helped my understanding of events in the Rockdale district.
34. EMHL, W9–27164, CS to SDP, Jan. 21, 1865.
35. EMHL, W9–26812, CS to SDP, Jan. 16, 1863.
36. EMHL, W9–27147, CS to SDP, Dec. 18, 1864.
37. General information about John Newsome comes from DCCH, Tax Assessment Records, Middletown and Aston townships, 1856–61; the 1860 census, Aston Township; and his

military service record, NA. I am personally indebted to Mr. Samuel Newsome of Media, Pennsylvania, for information from family records. It happens that the writer now occupies John Newsome's house.

38. General information about Jones Bradbury comes from DCCH, Tax Assessment Records, Middletown Township, 1860–62; the 1860 census, Middletown Township; and his military service record, NA.

39. NA, service record of John Newsome, declaration for increase of invalid pension, Dec. 4, 1891.

40. EMHL, W9–27116, CS to SDP, Aug. 24, 1864.

41. An account of John Newsome's career after the war, as described in family records, was given to me in private correspondence by Samuel Newsome.

42. EMHL, W9–26239, CS to SDP, Jan. 9, 1859.

43. EMHL, W9–26340, CS to SDP, Jan. 31, 1860.

44. EMHL, W9–26732, CS to SDP, Aug. 2, 1862.

45. EMHL, W9–27040, EBS to SDP, Feb. 1, 1864.

46. EMHL, W9–27256, CS to SDP, April 28, 1865.

47. EMHL, W9–27260, CS to SDP, May 16, 1865.

APPENDIX

1. See Kroeber, 1939, 1944.

2. Kuhn, 1970.

3. *Ibid.,* 1970, p. 43.

4. *Ibid.,* 1970.

5. Garfinkel, 1967.

6. Smelser, 1959; Kasserman, 1974.

7. Polanyi, 1944.

Bibliography

The Bibliography is intended to serve several purposes: to list the manuscript repositories, and the collections therein, consulted during the research; to list the nineteenth-century newspapers and journals, some issues of which were examined; to list the published genealogies and biographical encyclopedias that yielded useful information; to provide references to the published writings of residents of the Rockdale district who figured in the text, and to other works by nineteenth-century observers, in the fields of technology and social life; and to give references to the scholarly and technical literature. The works cited in the Notes will be found here, but other sources are also listed that are not specifically mentioned yet were of value in giving background data and in stimulating scholarly interpretation. In a work such as this, which attempts to synthesize materials that are conventionally apportioned among several historical specialties—in this case, the Industrial Revolution, the Enlightenment, early nineteenth-century socialism, the history of technology, the new social history, the Jacksonian era, the Civil War, Pennsylvania history, and even economic history—the boundaries of the bibliographical task are difficult to define. In the interest of brevity, no effort is made to cite accounts of other industrial towns that would be of interest in a comparative study, or to provide a bibliography of standard secondary works for places, periods, and events.

MANUSCRIPT COLLECTIONS

Under each repository are listed the principal manuscript collections consulted there.

Academy of Natural Sciences of Philadelphia (Philadelphia, Pa.)
   John S. Phillips, misc. correspondence
   Reuben Haines, copies of papers on loan from Haverford Library
American Philosophical Society Library (Philadelphia, Pa.)
   Peale-Sellers Collection
   Minutes of Concord Monthly Meeting, 1803–28
   Minutes of the Indian Committee, Philadelphia Yearly Meeting, microfilm
   New Harmony Papers, microfilm
Baker Library, Harvard (Cambridge, Mass.)
   William Bagnall, "Sketches of Manufacturing Establishments in
      New York City and of Textile Establishments in the Eastern
      United States." Unpublished MS, 1908
   Account books of the Boston Manufacturing Co., Merrimack Manufacturing Co., Taunton
      Manufacturing Co., Isaac Pierson and Brothers
   Dun and Bradstreet Credit Ratings, Vol. 37, Delaware Co.
Calvary Church, Rockdale (Aston, Pa.)

Records of births, deaths, burials, baptisms, confirmations

Chester County Historical Society (West Chester, Pa.)

William Darlington Correspondence

Delaware County Court House (Media, Pa.)

Tax Assessment Books, Aston and Middletown townships, 1825–65

Register of Deeds

Register of Wills

Delaware County Historical Society (Chester, Pa.)

George E. Darlington Papers

Parkmount Day Book

Penn's Grove Rent Book

Penn's Grove Pay Book

William Reynolds Day Book

Anna Broomall's Notebooks

Baker Notebooks

WPA Grave Marker Surveys

Delaware County Institute of Science (Media, Pa.)

Minutes, memorials, and correspondence (kept in vault)

Eleutherian Mills Historical Library (Wilmington, Del.)

Joseph Bancroft Collection

Correspondence of Sophie du Pont and Clementina Smith

Smith Family Papers (new accession)

Tancopanican Chronicle

Francis Gurney Smith, letterbooks

Brandywine Manufacturers' Sunday School Papers

R. S. Griffith Sketches

Correspondence of a variety of Rockdale residents with members of the Du Pont family (see
   list under Abbreviations, p. 487)

Franklin Institute (Philadelphia, Pa.)

Minutes of the Committee on Water Power

Historical Society of Delaware (Wilmington, Del.)

Poole Papers

Historical Society of Pennsylvania (Philadelphia, Pa.)

John H. Martin Papers

Gilpin Collection

Delaware County Poor House Records

Willcox Papers

Joseph S. Lovering Collection

John M. Broomall Correspondence

Library of Congress (Washington, D.C.)

American Colonization Society Papers

National Archives (Washington, D.C.)

Patent Office Records

U.S. Decennial Census Schedules, Population and Manufactures

Military Service Records

New-York Historical Society (New York, N.Y.)

John Rogers Papers

Painter Library, John J. Tyler Arboretum (Middletown Township, Delaware Co., Pa.)

Minshall and Jacob Painter Correspondence
Pennsylvania Academy of Fine Arts (Philadelphia, Pa.)
  John S. Phillips Papers
Pennsylvania State Archives (Harrisburg, Pa.)
  U.S. Direct Tax, Pennsylvania, 1798 (microfilm from National Archives)
  Delaware County Election Returns
  Septennial Census
Philadelphia Free Library
  Hexamer General Surveys
Presbyterian Historical Society (Philadelphia, Pa.)
  Robert Landis Correspondence
Swedenborgian School of Religion (Newton, Mass.)
  Daniel Lammot, Jr., Correspondence
Upland Baptist Church (Chester, Pa.)
  Minutes and records of baptism
Workingmen's Institute (New Harmony, Ind.)
  Joseph Neef Papers
  William Maclure Diaries

NEWSPAPERS AND JOURNALS

African Repository (in HSP)
Hazard's Register of Pennsylvania (in DCHS)
Journal of the Franklin Institute (in FI and EMHL)
Niles' Weekly Register (in EMHL)
The Anti-Masonic Register (in PLTA)
The Delaware County Republican (in DCHS)
The Delaware Free Press (in EMHL)
The Free Enquirer (in EMHL and WINH)
The Mechanic's Free Press (in HSP)
The Monthly Jubilee (in PLTA)
The Philadelphia Inquirer (in HSP)
The Philadelphia Liberalist (in HSP)
The Rockdale Herald
The Souvenir (in HSP and PFL)
The Upland Union (in DCHS)
The Village Record, or *Chester and Delaware Federalist* (in CCHS)
The Working Man's Advocate (in HSP)

GENEALOGIES AND BIOGRAPHICAL ENCYCLOPEDIAS

Appleton's Cyclopedia of American Biography. New York: D. Appleton, 1888–1931.
Biographical and Genealogical History of the State of Delaware. Chambersburg, Pa.: Runk, 1899.
Biographical Directory of the American Congress, 1774–1971. Washington, D. C. 1971.
The Biographical Encyclopaedia of Pennsylvania in the Nineteenth Century. Philadelphia: Galaxy, 1874.
Brown, John Howard (ed.). *The Cyclopedia of American Biographies Comprising the Men and Women of the United States Who Have Been Identified with the Growth of the Nation.* Boston: Lamb, 1900.
Cope, Gilbert. *Genealogy of the Dutton Family.* West Chester, Pa., 1871.

———— (ed. & comp.). *Genealogy of the Darlington Family.* West Chester, Pa.: Committee for the Family, 1900.

———— and Henry G. Ashmead. *Historic Homes and Institutions and Genealogical and Personal Memoirs of Chester and Delaware Counties, Pennsylvania.* New York: Lewis, 1904.

Darlington, George E. *History of the Eyre and Ashmead Families Who Settled in Chester and Philadelphia, Pennsylvania.* Media, Pa., 1909.

Futhey, J. Smith, and Gilbert Cope. *History of Chester County, Pennsylvania, with Genealogical and Biographical Sketches.* Philadelphia: L. H. Everts, 1881.

Johnson, Allen, *et al.* (eds.). *Dictionary of American Biography.* New York: Charles Scribner's Sons, 1928–73. 23 vols.

Johnson, Rossiter (ed.). *The Biographical Dictionary of America.* Boston, 1906.

Jordan, John W. (ed.). *Encyclopedia of Pennsylvania Biography.* New York: Lewis, 1919.

Leach, Frank Willing. "Old Philadelphia Families (CXXI—Smith [Daniel])," *The North American,* July 28, 1912.

The National Cyclopaedia of American Biography. New York: James T. White Co., 1898–1977. 57 vols. (Vols. 1–49 republished by University Microfilms.)

Odiorne, James C. *Genealogy of the Odiorne Family.* Boston: Rand, Avery, 1875.

Painter, J. *The Gilpin Family from Richard de Goulpyn in 1206, in a Line to Joseph Gilpin.* Lima, Pa., 1870.

Ridlon, G. T. *History of the Ancient Ryedales and their Descendants in Normandy, Great Britain, Ireland, and America, From 860 to 1884. Comprising the Genealogy and Biography, for About One Thousand Years, of the Families of RIDDELL, RIDDLE, RIDLON, RIDLEY, ETC.* Manchester, N.H.: Published by the Author, 1884.

Robson, Charles. *The Manufactories and Manufacturers of Pennsylvania of the Nineteenth Century.* Philadelphia: Galaxy, 1875.

Simpson, Henry. *The Lives of Eminent Philadelphians.* Philadelphia, 1859.

Stephen, Leslie, and Sidney Lee (eds.). *The Dictionary of National Biography . . . from the Earliest Times to 1900.* London: Oxford University Press, 1949–50. 22 vols.

Townsend, Mrs. Stockton. "Phillips Bible Record," *Publications of the Genealogical Society of Pennsylvania,* Vol. 12 (1934), pp. 177–90.

Virkus, Frederick A. (ed.). *The Abridged Compendium of American Genealogy.* Chicago: Marquis, 1925.

Wiley, Samuel T. (ed.). *Biographical and Historical Cyclopaedia of Delaware County, Pennsylvania.* New York: Gresham Publishing Co., 1894.

PUBLISHED WRITINGS BY ROCKDALERS
AND OTHER NINETEENTH-CENTURY OBSERVERS

Part 1: Most Relevant to the History of Technology

Baines, Sir Edward. *History of the Cotton Manufacture in Great Britain . . .* London: Fisher, Fisher & Jackson, 1835.

Baird, Robert H. *The American Cotton Spinner and Managers' and Carders' Guide.* Philadelphia: A. Hart, 1851.

Barfoot, J.R. *The Progress of Cotton.* Helmshore: Helmshore Local History Society, 1973.

Batchelder, Samuel. *Introduction and Early Progress of the Cotton Manufacture in the United States.* Boston, 1863.

Bigelow, Jacob. *Elements of Technology.* 2nd edition, Boston: Hilliard, Gray, Little and Wilkins, 1831.

Buchanan, Robertson. *Practical Essays on Mill-Work and other Machinery, Mechanical and descriptive.* London, 1808 (3rd edition, 1841).

Burke, James. *List of Patents for Inventions and Designs Issued by the United States from 1790 to 1847.* Washington, D.C.: T. and G. S. Gideon, 1847.

Byrne, Oliver. *A dictionary of machines, mechanics, engine-work, and engineering . . .* New York and Philadelphia: Appleton, 1850.

————. *The American engineer, draftsmen, and machinists assistants . . .* Philadelphia: Brown, 1853 (a).

————. *Mechanics: Their principles and practical applications.* New York: Dewitt & Davenport, 1853 (b).

————. *The handbook for the artisan, mechanic, and engineer.* Philadelphia: Collins, 1853 (c).

Chapin, J. R. "Among the Nail-Makers," *Harpers New Monthly Magazine,* Vol. 21 (1860), pp. 145–64.

[Chester, Pa., Board of Trade]. *Chester, Pennsylvania: A History of Its Industrial Progress and Advantages for Large Manufactures. Brief Sketches of Its Representative Business Enterprises.* Chester, Pa., 1899.

Crozer, Samuel A. "The Early Manufactures and Manufacturers of Delaware County," *Proceedings of the Delaware County Historical Society, 1895–1901,* Vol. 1 (1902), pp. 130–6.

Dutton, Jonathan. *The New Planet, Containing a Degree of Novelty: Being an Effort Toward the Pleasure, Comfort, and Convenience of all Citizens.* Philadelphia, 1848.

Evans, Oliver. *The Young Mill-Wright and Miller's Guide.* Philadelphia: Lea and Blanchard, 1840.

————. *The Young Steam Engineer's Guide.* Philadelphia: H. C. Carey and I. Lea, n.d., probably 1826.

Fairbairn, Sir William, Bart. *Mills and Mill-Work.* 2 vols., 2nd edition, London, 1864–65.

Ferguson, Eugene S. (ed.). *Early Engineering Reminiscences (1815–40) of George Escol Sellers.* Washington, D.C.: Smithsonian Institution, 1965.

Francis, James B. *The Lowell Hydraulic Experiments.* New York, 1855.

Guest, Richard. *A Compendious History of the Cotton-Manufacture; with a Disproval of the Claim of Sir Richard Arkwright to the Invention of its Ingenious Machinery.* Manchester, England, 1823.

Howe, Henry. *Memoirs of the Most Eminent American Mechanics.* New York: Harper & Brothers, 1847.

Jenks, Alfred, and Son. *Illustrated Catalogue of Machines built by Alfred Jenks & Son, Manufacturers of Every variety of cotton and wool carding, spinning, and weaving machines, in all its departments. Shafting and mill gearing of the latest and most approved plans.* Bridesburg, Philadelphia Co., Pa., n.d.

Knight, Edward H. *Knight's American Mechanical Dictionary, A description of tools, instruments, machines, processes, and engineering; history of inventions; general technological vocabulary; and digest of mechanical appliances in science and the arts.* Boston: Houghton, Mifflin, 1882.

Leffel, James. *Construction of Mill Dams.* Springfield, Ohio: James Leffel & Co., 1881. Reprinted as History of Technology series, Vol. 1, Park Ridge, N.J.: Noyes Press, 1972.

Leiper, G. G., and W. Martin. *Report of the Committee of Delaware County on the Subject of Manufactories, Unimproved Mill Seats, etc. in said County, 1826.* Chester, Pa.: Lescure, 1826.

McElroy's Philadelphia Directory. 30 vols. Philadelphia. A. McElroy & Co., 1837–1867.

McLane, Louis. *Documents Relating to Manufactures in the United States.* 2 vols., Washington, D.C., 1833. (Reprinted New York: Augustus M. Kelley, 1969.)

Montgomery, James. *The Theory and Practice of Cotton Spinning: or the Carding and Spinning Master's Assistant . . .* 2nd edition, Glasgow: John Niven, 1833.

Bibliography

————. *The Cotton Manufacture of the United States of America and the State of the Cotton Manufacture of that Country Contrasted and Compared with that of Great Britain.* Glasgow: John Niven, 1840.

Nicholson, John. *The Operative Mechanic and British Machinist; being a Practical Display of the Manufactories and Mechanical Arts of the United Kingdom.* 2 vols., Philadelphia: H. C. Carey & I. Lea, 1826.

Rees, Abraham. *Cyclopaedia.* Philadelphia: Bradford, 1805–24.

Robison, John. *A System of Mechanical Philosophy With Notes By David Brewster.* 4 vols., Edinburgh: Printed for John Murray, London, 1822.

Rose, Joshua. *Modern Machine-Shop Practice.* 2 vols., 2nd edition, New York: Scribner's, 1892.

Scott, R. *The Practical Cotton Spinner and Manufacturer.* Preston, England, 1840.

————. *The Practical Cotton Spinner and Manufacturer . . .* Corrected and enlarged with plates of American machines, edited by Oliver Byrne. Philadelphia: Henry Carey Baird, 1851.

Silliman, Benjamin. *Manual on the Cultivation of the Sugar Cane, and the Fabrication and Refinement of Sugar.* Washington, D.C.: Blair, 1833.

Snell, Daniel W. *The Manager's Assistant; being a condensed treatise on Cotton Manufacturing.* Hartford, Conn., 1850.

Sutcliffe, John. *A Treatise on Canals and Reservoirs, and the best Mode of designing and Executing them . . . likewise Observations on the best Mode of Carding, Roving, Drawing, and Spinning all Kinds of Cotton Twist. . . .* Rochdale, England, 1816.

Ure, Andrew. *The Philosophy of Manufactures: or an Exposition of the Scientific, Moral, and Commercial Economy of the Factory system of Great Britain.* London: Charles Knight, 1835.

Webber, Samuel. *Manual of Power for Machines, Shafts and Belts, with the History of Cotton Manufacture in the United States.* Revised edition, New York: Appleton, 1879.

Part II: Most Relevant to Social and Cultural Matters

Allen, William H. "Address to the American Colonization Society," Oct. 25, 1863, in *African Colonization—Its Progress and Prospects,* pp. 5–21. Philadelphia: Pennsylvania Colonization Society, 1863.

[American Colonization Society]. *Annual Reports, 1818–1910.*

[Baptist Publication Society]. *The John P. Crozer Memorial.* Philadelphia: American Baptist Publication Society, 1866.

Barruel, Augustin de. *Memoirs Illustrating the History of Jacobinism.* Hartford, Conn., 1799.

Beaux, Cecilia. *Background with Figures: Autobiography of Cecilia Beaux.* Boston: Houghton Mifflin, 1930.

Bestor, Arthur E. (ed.). *Education and Reform at New Harmony: Correspondence of William Maclure and Marie Duclos Fretageot, 1820–1833.* Indianapolis: Indiana Historical Society, 1948.

Bishop, Charles W. W. *History of the Marcus Hook Baptist Church.* Philadelphia, 1855.

Broomall, John. [Eulogy of Thaddeus Stevens] *Congressional Globe,* 40th Congress, 3rd Session, 1868–69, pp. 134–5.

Broomall, Hon. John M. *History of Delaware County for the Past Century.* Read before the Delaware County Institute of Science. Media, Pa: Vernon and Cooper, Steam Power Book Printers, 1876.

Campbell, John H. *History of the Friendly Sons of St Patrick and the Hibernian Society for the Relief of Emigrants from Ireland, March 17, 1771–March 17, 1892.* Philadelphia: The Hibernian Society, 1892.

Carey, Henry C. *The Harmony of Interests, Agricultural, Manufacturing, and Commercial.* 2nd edition, New York: Finch, 1852.

Charlotte Elizabeth (Tonna, Mrs. Charlotte Elizabeth). *Helen Fleetwood* in *The Works of Charlotte Elizabeth*, Vol. 1, New York: Dodd, 1847.

Claxton, Timothy. *Memoir of a Mechanic. Being a Sketch of the Life of Timothy Claxton, Written by Himself, Together with Miscellaneous Papers.* Boston: George W. Light, 1839.

[Congressional Petitions]. "Memorial . . . For a repeal of the duty on imported raw flax, and an increase of ad valorem duty on thread and twine made from flax," by Garsed, Raines & Co. 22nd Congress, 1st Session, Senate, March 1, 1832.

————. "Resolutions passed at a Meeting of the Citizens of Delaware County, Pennsylvania, in favor of the protective system, and of rechartering the Bank of the United States." 22nd Congress, 1st Session, Senate, June 25, 1832.

————. "Pennsylvania—Delaware County Meeting—Tariff." 22nd Congress, 2nd Session, House, Doc. 134, Feb. 18, 1833.

————. "Proceedings of a Meeting in Delaware County, Against the Bank of the United States." 23rd Congress, 1st Session, House, Doc. 287, April 7, 1834.

————. "Memorial of Citizens of Delaware County, Praying a recharter of the Bank of the United States." 23rd Congress, 1st Session, House, Doc. 280, April 7, 1834.

————. "Proceedings of a Public Meeting of Citizens of Delaware County, in relation to the Bank of the United States." 23rd Congress, 1st Session, House, Doc. 282, April 7, 1834.

Crozer, John P. "Address from the Central Committee (of the Temperance Society) to the Citizens of Delaware County," in *Facts to Think About and What's the Remedy.* Chester, Pa.: Walter, 1850.

————. *Biographical Sketch of John P. Crozer, Written by Himself.* Philadelphia: Grant, Faires & Rodgers, n.d. [1861].

————. [Obituary of William Martin]. In Martin, 1877, pp. 332–4. Published in the *Delaware County Republican,* Oct. 24, 1862.

————. "Address to the American Colonization Society," Oct. 25, 1863, in *African Colonization—Its Progress and Prospects,* pp. 21–4. Philadelphia: Pennsylvania Colonization Society, 1863.

Crozer, Samuel A. "Historical Address," in *Semi-Centennial of Upland Baptist Church 1852–1902.*

Darlington, George E. *History of the Eyre and Ashmead families who Settled in Chester and Philadelphia, Pa.* Media, Pa., 1909.

————. *Recollections of the Old Borough of Chester 1834–1850.* Chester, Pa.: Delaware County Historical Society, 1917.

Deacon, William F. *Warreniana.* Boston: Ticknor, Reed, and Fields, 1851 (reprint of 1824 edition).

[Delaware County Institute of Science]. *Report of a Committee of the Delaware County Institute of Science, on the Great Rain Storm and Flood . . .* August 1843. Chester, Pa.: Walter, 1844.

————. *Memorial of John M. Broomall.* Media, Pa., n.d. [1894].

Ely, Ezra Stiles. *A Contrast Between Calvinism and Hopkinism.* New York, 1811.

————. *The Duty of Christian Freemen to Elect Christian Rulers.* Philadelphia, 1828.

————. *Visits of Mercy or the Journals of the Rev. Ezra Stiles Ely, written while he was stated preacher to the hospital and almshouse, in the city of New York.* 2 vols., Philadelphia: Bradond, 1829.

————. *A Discussion of the Conjoint Question, is the Doctrine of Endless Punishment Taught in the Bible: Or Does the Bible Teach the Doctrine of the Final Holiness and Happiness of all Mankind?* In a Series of Letters Between Ezra Stiles Ely and Abel C. Thomas. New York: P. Price, 1835.

Erickson, Charlotte (ed.). *Invisible Immigrants: The Adaptation of English and Scottish Immigrants in Nineteenth Century America.* Coral Gables, Fla.: University of Miami Press, 1972.

Farragut, Loyall (ed.). *Life of David Glasgow Farragut, First Admiral of the United States Navy. Embodying his Journal and Letters.* New York: D. Appleton & Co., 1879.

Friendly Association for Mutual Interests. *Preamble and Constitution.* Philadelphia, 1826.

Fuller, Andrew. *The Complete works . . . with a memoir of his life by Andrew Gunton Fuller, from the third London edition; revised, with additions by Joseph Belcher, D.D.* 3 vols., Philadelphia: American Baptist Publication Society, 1845.

Gardette, C. D. "Pestalozzi in America," *Galaxy,* Vol. 4 (August 1867), pp. 432–9.

Gilpin, William. *Mission of the North American People, Geographical, Social, and Political.* Philadelphia: Lippincott, 1873.

Gray, John. *A Lecture on Human Happiness . . .* Philadelphia, 1825.

Hagner, Charles V. *Early History of the Falls of Schuylkill, Manayunk, Schuylkill and Lehigh Navagation Companies.* Philadelphia: Claxton, Remsen, and Heffelfinger, 1869.

Harrison, Lowell H. (ed.). "William Duane on Education," *Pennsylvania Magazine of History and Biography,* Vol. 73 (1949), pp. 316–25.

Hawkins, Joseph. *A History of a Voyage to the Coast of Africa, and Travels into the Interior . . . and Interesting Particulars Concerning the Slave Trade.* Philadelphia, 1797.

Hemple, Charles Julius. *The True Organization of the New Church, as indicated in the Writings of Emanuel Swedenborg, and demonstrated by Charles Fourier.* New York: Radde, 1848.

Hiatt, Joel W. (ed.). *Diary of William Owen, 1824–1825.* Indianapolis: Bobbs-Merrill, 1906.

Hopkins, John Henry, Jr. *The Life of the Late Right Reverend John Henry Hopkins, first Bishop of Vermont.* New York: Huntington, 1873.

Howe, M. A. *Memoir of the Life and Services of the Rt. Rev. Alonzo Potter.* Philadelphia: Lippincott, 1871.

Hunter, John Dunn. *Memoirs of a Captivity Among the Indians of North America.* London: Longman, Hursy, Rees, Orme, Brown and Green, 1923.

Hyneman, Leon. *World's Masonic Register.* Philadelphia: Lippincott, 1860.

Jones, John R. *An Address Delivered at a Town-Meeting of the Anti-Masonic Citizens of Philadelphia, October 5th, 1830.* Philadelphia, 1830.

Knight, Jane D. *Brief Narrative of Events Touching Various Reforms.* Albany, N.Y., 1880.

Laws of the General Assembly of the Commonwealth of Pennsylvania. Harrisburg, Pa., published annually by the state printer.

Leavitt, Thomas W. (ed.). *The Hollingsworth Letters: Technical Change in the Textile Industry, 1826–1837.* Cambridge, Mass.: M.I.T. Press, 1969.

Lee, Alfred. *A Life Hid with Christ; Being a Memoir of Miss Susan Allibone.* Philadelphia: J. B. Lippincott, 1856.

_____. "A Farewell Discourse Delivered to the congregation of Calvary Church, Rockdale, Penn." Philadelphia: Joseph M. Brown, 1841.

Lyon, Patrick. *The Narrative of Patrick Lyon.* Philadelphia, 1799.

Maclure, William. "An Epitome of the Improved Pestalozzian System of Education, as practised by William Phiquepal and Madam Fretageot, Formerly in Paris, and now in Philadelphia; communicated at the request of the Editor," *American Journal of Science and Arts,* Vol. X (1826), 145–51.

_____. *Opinions on various subjects, dedicated to the Industrious Producers.* New Harmony, Ind.: School Press, 1831.

Martin, John Hill. *Chester (and Its Vicinity,) Delaware County, in Pennsylvania.* Philadelphia, 1877.

Montgomery, Elizabeth. *Reminiscences of Wilmington . . .* Philadelphia: Collins, 1851.

Morton, Samuel G. "A Memoir of William MacClure, Esq.," *American Journal of Science* (April–June 1844).

Moss, Lemuel. *Annals of the United States Christian Commission.* Philadelphia: Lippincott, 1868.

Murphy, John K. *To the Communicants and Members of the Congregation of Calvary Church, Rockdale,* c. 1861 (HSP, VoD*/.58 Vol. II).

Neef, Joseph. *Sketch of a Plan and Method of Education.* Philadelphia, 1808.

[Odd Fellows.] *Souvenir History and Program of the Seventy-fifth Anniversary of the Introduction of Odd Fellowship in Delaware County, Pa., Riddle's Grove, Rockdale, September 15, 1906.* Chester, Pa., 1906.

Odiorne, Thomas. *The Progress of Refinement.* Boston: Young and Etheridge, 1792.

Odiorne, James C. (ed.). *Opinions on Speculative Masonry, relative to its Origin, Nature, and Tendency.* Boston: Perkins & Marvin, 1830.

Owen, Robert. *A New View of Society: or Essays on the formation of the Human Character.* New York, 1825 (from 3rd London edition).

_____. "Address Delivered . . . at the Franklin Institute . . . June 25, 1827." Philadelphia, 1827.

_____. *The Book of the New Moral World.* London, 1849.

Owen, Robert Dale. *Threading My Way: Twenty-Seven Years of Autobiography.* London: Trubner, 1874.

Pendleton, J. M. *Reminiscences of a Long Life.* Louisville, Ky.: Press Baptist Book Concern, 1891.

[Pennsylvania State.] "Report of the Committee by Mr. Peltz, Feb. 7, 1838," *Pennsylvania Senate Journal,* 1837–38, Part I, pp. 322–7.

_____. "Testimony of the Witnesses, accompanying the Report of the Committee of the Senate, appointed to investigate the subject of the Employment of Children in Factories," *Pennsylvania Senate Journal,* 1837–38, Part 2, pp. 278–359.

[Pennsylvania Society for Promoting the Abolition of Slavery . . .]. "Celebration of the Nineteenth Anniversary of the Organization." Philadelphia, 1866.

Phillips, John S. "Description of Two New American Species of Helix," *Proceedings of the Academy of Natural Sciences of Philadelphia,* Vol. 1 (1841), pp. 27–8.

_____. "Effect of Conflagration on the Atmosphere," *Proceedings of the Academy of Natural Sciences of Philadelphia,* Vol. 1 (1841), p. 46.

_____. "Nomenclature of Natural Science," *Proceedings of the Academy of Natural Sciences of Philadelphia,* Vol. 1 (1841), pp. 85–90.

_____. "On Helix bidentifera, A Rectification," *Proceedings of the Academy of Natural Sciences of Philadelphia,* Vol. 1 (1841), p. 133.

_____. "Description of a new American Species of the genus Helix," *Journal of the Academy of Natural Sciences of Philadelphia,* Vol. 8 (1842), pp. 182–3.

_____. "Description of a New Fresh-water Shell and Observations on Glandina obtusa, Pfeif," *Proceedings of the Academy of Natural Sciences of Philadelphia,* Vol. 3 (1846), pp. 66–7.

Potter, Alonzo. *Political Economy.* New York: Harper, 1841(a).

_____. *The Principles of Science Applied to the Domestic and Mechanical Arts and to Manufactures and Agriculture.* New York: Harper, 1841(b).

_____. *Religious Philosophy; or, Nature, Man, and the Bible . . . Lectures Delivered Before the Lowell Institute Between the Years 1845–1853.* Philadelphia: Lippincott, 1872.

Read, Hollis. *The Christian Brahmun.* 2 vols., New York: Leavitt, Lord & Co., 1836.

_____. *Commerce and Christianity.* Philadelphia, Pa.: Seamen's Friend Society, 1859.

———. *The Coming Crisis of the World: or, The Great Battle and the Golden Age.* Columbus, Ohio: Follett, Foster and Co., 1861.

———. *The Negro Problem Solved; or, Africa as She Was, As She Is, and As She Shall Be.* New York: A. A. Constantine, 1864.

———. *The Hand of God in History; or, Divine Providence Illustrated in the Extensions and Establishment of Christianity Throughout the World.* Philadelphia: John E. Potter & Co., 1870.

———. *The Foot-Prints of Satan: or, The Devil in History.* New York: E. B. Treat, 1874.

Robison, John A. M. *Proofs of a Conspiracy against all the Religions and Governments of Europe, carried on in the Secret Meetings of Free Masons, Illuminati, and Reading Societies.* London, 1797.

Royall, Anne. *Mrs. Royall's Pennsylvania.* Washington, D.C., 1829.

[St. Andrew's Church, Wilmington]. *Alfred Lee, first Bishop of Delaware.* Wilmington, Del., 1888.

Silver, Ednah C. *Sketches of the New Church in America on a Background of Civic and Social Life.* Boston: Mass. New Church Union, 1920.

Smith, George, M.D. *History of Delaware County, Pennsylvania, From the Discovery of the Territory Included within its Limits to the Present Time.* Philadelphia: Henry B. Ashmead, 1862. (Facsimile edition published 1976 by Delaware County Institute of Science.)

Smith, J. Wheaton, D.D. *The Life of John P. Crozer.* Philadelphia: American Baptist Publication Society, 1868.

Smith, Richard S. *Reminiscences of Seven Years of Early Life.* Wilmington, Del.: Ferris Bros., 1884.

Snedeker, Carol D. (ed.). *The Diaries of Donald Macdonald, 1824–1826.* Indianapolis: Indiana Historical Society, 1942.

Stille, Charles J. *Memorial of the Great Central Fair for the U.S. Sanitary Commission, held in Philadelphia, June 1864.* Philadelphia: U.S. Sanitary Commission, 1864.

Tyng, Stephen H. *Lectures on the Law and the Gospel.* Philadelphia: Stavely and M'Calla, 1844.

———. *Twenty-first Anniversary Address before the American Institute of the City of New York, at the Tabernacle, on October 12, 1848.* New York, 1848.

———. *Forty Years' Experience in Sunday-Schools.* New York: Sheldon & Company, 1860.

Volney, C. F. *The Ruins, or, Meditation on the Revolutions of Empires: and The Law of Nature.* New York: Twentieth Century Publishing Co., 1890.

White, Anna, and Leila S. Taylor. *Shakerism: Its Meaning and Message.* Columbus, Ohio: Press of Fred J. Herr, 1871.

Whitehead, William. *Directory of the borough of Chester, for the years 1859–60 . . .* West Chester, Pa.: William Whitehead, 1859.

Wilder, Rev. William. *A Discourse, commemorative of John P. Crozer, Preached in Lewisburg, July 22nd, 1866.*

Williams, Charles L. "Address," in *Semi-Centennial of Upland Baptist Church 1852–1902.*

Windle, Mary Jane. *Life in Washington and Life Here and There.* Philadelphia: J. B. Lippincott & Co., 1859.

Woodman, Henry. *The History of Valley Forge.* Oaks, Pa., 1922.

SCHOLARLY AND TECHNICAL BOOKS AND ARTICLES

Arky, Louis H. "The Mechanics' Union of Trade Associations and the Formation of the Philadelphia Workingmen's Movement," *Pennsylvania Magazine of History and Biography,* Vol. 76 (1952), pp. 142–76.

Ashmead, Henry Graham. *Historical Sketch of Chester, on Delaware.* Chester, Pa.: The Republican Steam Printing House, 1883.

_____. *History of Delaware County, Pennsylvania.* Philadelphia: L. H. Everts, 1884. (Facsimile edition published 1968 by Concord Township Historical Society.)

_____. *History of the Delaware County National Bank.* Chester, Pa., 1914.

Ashton, T. S. *The Industrial Revolution 1760–1830.* London: Oxford University Press, 1948.

Bagnall, William R. *The Textile Industries of the United States.* Vol. 1, *1639–1810.* Cambridge: Riverside Press, 1893.

Bates, Samuel P., *History of the Pennsylvania Volunteers, 1861–1865.* 5 vols. Harrisburg, Pa., 1869–71.

Bathe, Greville and Dorothy. *Oliver Evans: A Chronicle of Early American Engineering.* Philadelphia: Historical Society of Pennsylvania, 1935.

_____. *Jacob Perkins: His Inventions, His Times, and His Contemporaries.* Philadelphia: Historical Society of Pennsylvania, 1943.

Benson, Lee. *The Concept of Jacksonian Democracy: New York as a Test Case.* New York: Atheneum, 1969.

Bernstein, Leonard. "The Working People of Philadelphia from Colonial Times to the General Strike of 1835," *Pennsylvania Magazine of History and Biography,* Vol. 74 (1950), pp. 322–39.

Bestor, Arthur E., Jr. "Patent-Office Models of the Good Society: Some Relationships Between Social Reform and Westward Expansion," *American Historical Review,* Vol. 58 (1953), pp. 505–26.

_____. "Albert Brisbane, Propagandist for Socialism in the 1840's," *New York History,* Vol. 45 (1947), pp. 128–58.

_____. "The Evolution of the Socialist Vocabulary," *Journal of the History of Ideas,* Vol. 9 (1948), pp. 259–302.

_____. *American Phalanxes, a Study of Fourierist Socialism in the United States (With Special Reference to the Movement in Western New York).* Ph.D. Thesis, University of Wisconsin, Madison, 1956.

_____. *Backwoods Utopias: The Sectarian Origins and the Owenite Phase of Communitarian Socialism in America.* 2nd enlarged edition, Philadelphia: University of Pennsylvania Press, 1970.

Billington, Ray Allen. *The Protestant Crusade, 1800–1860: A Study of the Origins of American Nativism.* New York: Macmillan, 1938.

Bining, Arthur C. *Pennsylvania Iron Manufacture in the Eighteenth Century.* Harrisburg, Pa.: Pennsylvania Historical Commission, 1938.

Bishop, J. L. *History of American Manufactures.* 3 vols., Philadelphia: Edward Young, 1861, 1864, 1868.

Blue, Frederick J. *The Free Soilers: Third Party Politics, 1848–54.* Urbana, Ill.: University of Illinois Press, 1973.

Boatman, Roy M. "The Brandywine Cotton Industry, 1795–1805," MS, 1957. Eleutherian Mills Historical Library.

Bolles, Albert S. *Industrial History of the United States.* Norwich, Conn., 1879.

Bradley, Ian. *A History of Machine Tools.* Hemel Hempstead, England: Model and Allied Publications, 1972.

Calvert, Monte. *The Mechanical Engineer in America, 1830–1910: Professional Cultures in Conflict.* Baltimore: Johns Hopkins Press, 1967.

Cantwell, Robert. *Alexander Wilson, Naturalist and Pioneer.* Philadelphia: Lippincott, 1961.

Carter, Jane Levis. *Edgmont: The Story of a Township.* Kennett Square, Pa.: KNA Press, 1976.

Catling, Harold. *The Spinning Mule.* Newton Abbot, Devon, England: David & Charles, 1970.

Chase, William H. *Five Generations of Loom Builders: A History of the Draper Corporation.* Hopedale, Mass.: Draper Corp., 1950.

Chinard, Gilbert. *Volney et l'Amérique d'après des documents inédits et sa correspondance avec Jefferson.* Baltimore: Johns Hopkins Press, 1923.

Clark, Dennis. "Kellyville. An Immigrant Enterprise," *Pennsylvania History,* Vol. 39 (1972), pp. 40–9.

Clark, V. S. *History of Manufactures in the United States, 1607–1860.* Washington, D.C., 1916.

Claussen, W. Edwards. *Wyck: The Study of a Historic House.* Philadelphia: Privately printed by Mary T. Haines, 1970.

Clifton, Ronald D. *Forms and Patterns: Room Specialization in Maryland, Massachusetts, and Pennsylvania, Family Dwellings, 1725–1834.* Ph.D. Thesis, University of Pennsylvania, 1971.

Cochrane, Thomas C., and William Miller. *The Age of Enterprise: A Social History of Industrial America.* Revised edition, New York: Harper & Row, 1961.

Coleman, John F. *The Disruption of the Pennsylvania Democracy, 1848–1860.* Harrisburg, Pa.: Pennsylvania Historical and Museum Commission, 1975.

Coleman, Peter J. *Debtors and Creditors in America: Insolvency, Imprisonment for Debt, and Bankruptcy, 1607–1900.* Madison, Wis.: State Historical Society of Wisconsin, 1974.

Commons, John R., *et al.* (eds.). *A Documentary History of American Industrial Society.* 10 vols., Cleveland, Ohio: A. H. Clark, 1900–11.

Commons, John Rogers (ed.) *History of Labor in the United States.* 4 vols., New York: The Macmillan Co., 1918–35.

Conway, Jill. "Evangelical Protestantism and Its Influence on Women in North America, 1790–1860," MS, 1972. Paper presented at meeting of American Historical Association.

Copeland, Melvin T. *The Cotton Manufacturing Industry of the United States.* Cambridge: Harvard University Press, 1912.

Corner, George W. *Doctor Kane of the Arctic Seas.* Philadelphia: Temple University Press, 1972.

Curry, Earl R. "Pennsylvania and the Republican Convention of 1860: A Critique of McClure's Thesis," *Pennsylvania Magazine of History and Biography,* Vol. 97 (1973), pp. 183–98.

Drinnon, Richard. *White Savage: The Case of John Dunn Hunter.* New York: Schocken Books, 1972.

Du Pont, B. G. *Lives of Victor and Josephine du Pont.* Wilmington, Del.: Privately printed, 1930.

Eiselen, Malcolm R. *The Rise of Pennsylvania Protectionism.* Ph.D. Thesis, University of Pennsylvania, 1932.

Elder, William. *A Memoir of Henry C. Carey.* Philadelphia, 1880.

English, Walter. *The Textile Industry: An Account of the Early Inventions of Spinning, Weaving, and Knitting Machines.* London: Longmans, 1969.

Ferguson, Eugene S. "The Mind's Eye: Nonverbal Thought in Technology," *Science* 197 (1977), pp. 827–36.

Fertig, John H. *Constitutions of Pennsylvania/Constitutions of the United States.* Harrisburg, Pa.: Legislative Reference Bureau, 1926.

Fletcher, Stevenson W. *Pennsylvania Agriculture and Country Life, 1640–1840, 1840–1940.* 2 vols., Harrisburg, Pa.: Pennsylvania Historical and Museum Commission, 1950, 1955.

Foner, Eric. *Free Soil, Free Labor, Free Men: The Ideology of the Republican Party Before the Civil War.* New York: Oxford University Press, 1970.

Foster, Charles I. *An Errand of Mercy; the Evangelical United Front, 1790–1837.* Chapel Hill,

N.C.: University of North Carolina Press, 1960.

Fox, Early Lee. *The American Colonization Society, 1817–1840.* Baltimore: Johns Hopkins Press, 1919.

Fox, Wendall P. "The Kendall Community," *Ohio Archaeological and Historical Publications,* Vol. 20 (1911), pp. 176–219.

Francis, Russell E. "The Religious Revival of 1858 in Philadelphia," *Pennsylvania Magazine of History and Biography,* Vol. 70 (January 1946), pp. 52–77.

Garfinkel, Harold. *Studies in Ethnomethodology.* Englewood Cliffs, N.J.: Prentice-Hall, 1967.

Geffen, Elizabeth M. *Philadelphia Unitarianism, 1796–1861.* Philadelphia: University of Pennsylvania Press, 1961.

———. "Philadelphia Protestantism Reacts to Social Reform Movements Before the Civil War," *Pennsylvania History,* Vol. 30 (April 1963), pp. 192–211.

Gerrity, Frank. "The Masons, the Antimasons, and the Pennsylvania Legislature, 1834–1836," *Pennsylvania Magazine of History and Biography,* Vol. 99 (April 1975), pp. 180–206.

Gerstner, Patsy. "The Academy of Natural Sciences of Philadelphia," MS, 1973. Conference on Early History of Societies for Promoting Knowledge in the United States.

Gibb, George Sweet. *The Saco-Lowell Shops: Textile Machinery Building in New England, 1813–1849.* Cambridge: Harvard University Press, 1950.

Govan, Thomas P. *Nicholas Biddle.* Chicago: University of Chicago Press, 1959.

Green, Arnold W. *Henry Charles Carey.* Philadelphia: University of Pennsylvania Press, 1951.

Griffin, Clifford S. *Their Brothers' Keepers: Moral Stewardship in the United States, 1800–1865.* New Brunswick, N.J.: Rutgers University Press, 1960.

Gutman, Herbert G. *Work, Culture, and Society in Industrializing America.* New York: Alfred A. Knopf, 1976.

Hackensmith, Charles W. *Biography of Joseph Neef, Educator in the Ohio Valley, 1809–1954.* New York: Carlton Press, 1973.

Hamy, E.-T. *The Travels of the Naturalist Charles A. Lesueur in North America 1815–1837.* Translated by Milton Haber, edited by H. F. Raup. Kent, Ohio: Kent State University Press, 1968.

Hancock, Harold. "The Industrial Worker along the Brandywine," MS, 1956–58. Eleutherian Mills Historical Library.

Hancock, Harold B., and Norman B. Wilkinson. "The Gilpins and Their Endless Papermaking Machine," *Pennsylvania Magazine of History and Biography,* Vol. 81 (October 1957), pp. 391–405.

Hardy, James D., Jr., John H. Jensen, and Martin Wolfe (eds.). *The Maclure Collection of French Revolutionary Materials.* Philadelphia: University of Pennsylvania Press, 1966.

Hareven, Tamara K. (ed.). *Anonymous Americans: Explorations in Nineteenth-Century Social History.* Englewood Cliffs, N.J.: Prentice-Hall, 1971.

Harrison, J. F. C. *Quest for the New Moral World: Robert Owen and the Owenites in Britain and America.* New York: Scribner's, 1969.

Harrison, Lowell H. "William Duane on Education: a Letter to the Kentucky Assembly, 1822." *Pennsylvania Magazine of History and Biography,* 73 (1949), pp. 316–25.

Harte, N. B. "On Rees's *Cyclopaedia* as a Source for the History of the Textile Industries in the Early Nineteenth Century," *Textile History,* Vol. 5 (1974), pp. 119–27.

Hartz, Louis. *The Liberal Tradition in America.* New York: Harcourt, Brace, 1955.

———. *Economic Policy and Democratic Thought: Pennsylvania, 1776–1860.* Cambridge: Harvard University Press, 1948.

Bibliography

Henderson, Helen W. *Pennsylvania Academy of Fine Arts and Other Collections of Philadelphia.* Boston: Page, 1911.

Hindle, Brooke. *Technology in Early America.* Chapel Hill, N.C.: University of North Carolina Press, 1960.

Hobsbawm, E. J. *Primitive Rebels: Studies in Archaic Forms of Social Movements in the Nineteenth and Twentieth Centuries.* New York: Praeger, 1963 (1959).

———. *The Age of Revolution, 1789–1848.* New York: New American Library, 1971.

———. "The Human Results of the Industrial Revolution: 1750–1850," in Y. Cohen, *Man in Adaptation. The Cultural Present.* 2nd edition, Chicago: Aldine, 1974.

Hoye, John. *Staple Cotton Fabrics: Names, Descriptions, Finishes, and Uses of Unbleached, Converted, and Mill Finished Fabrics.* New York and London: McGraw-Hill Book Co., 1942.

Hughes, Thomas P. *Changing Attitudes Toward American Technology.* New York: Harper & Row, 1975.

James, Bessie Rowland. *Anne Royall's U.S.A.* New Brunswick, N.J.: Rutgers University Press, 1972.

Jefferis, Jervas, Jr. "The Chester Mills: The History of the Industrial Development of an Area, with Emphasis upon the Years 1790–1860." M.A. thesis, Temple University, 1965.

Jeremy, David J. "British and American Yarn Count Systems: An Historical Analysis," *Business History Review,* Vol. 45 (1971), pp. 336–8.

———. "Innovation in American Textile Technology During the Early Nineteenth Century," *Technology and Culture,* Vol. 14 (1973[a]), pp. 40–76.

———. "British Textile Technology Transmission to the United States: The Philadelphia Region Experience, 1770–1820," *Business History Review,* Vol. 47 (1973[b]), pp. 24–52.

Johnson, John. *The Defence of Charleston Harbor, 1863–1865.* Charleston, N.C., 1890.

Kaplan, Abraham D. H. *Henry Charles Carey (1793–1879): A Study in American Economic Thought.* Baltimore: Johns Hopkins Press, 1931.

Karnes, Thomas L. *William Gilpin: Western Nationalist.* Austin, Tex.: University of Texas Press, 1970.

Kasserman, David. *Conservative Innovation: Introduction of the Cotton Industry into the United States, 1789–1840.* Ph.D. Thesis, University of Pennsylvania, 1974.

Keen, William W. *The Bi-Centennial Celebration of the Founding of the First Baptist Church of the City of Philadelphia, 1698–1899.* Philadelphia: American Baptist Publication Society, 1899.

Klein, Philip S. *Pennsylvania Politics, 1817–1832: A Game Without Rules.* Philadelphia: Historical Society of Pennsylvania, 1940.

———, and Ari Hoogenboom. *A History of Pennsylvania.* New York: McGraw-Hill Book Co., 1973.

Koch, G. Adolf. *Republican Religion: The American Revolution and the Cult of Reason.* New York: Henry Holt and Company, 1933.

Kranzberg, Melvin, and Carroll W. Pursell, Jr. (eds.). *Technology in Western Civilization.* 2 vols., New York: Oxford University Press, 1967.

Kranzberg, Melvin, and William H. Davenport (eds.). *Technology and Culture: An Anthology.* New York: Schocken Books, 1972.

Kroeber, A. L. *Cultural and Natural Areas of Native North America.* Berkeley, Calif.: University of California Press, 1939.

———. *Configurations of Culture Growth.* Berkeley and Los Angeles: University of California Press, 1944.

Kruse, W. T. "Historical Sketch of the Middletown Presbyterian Church." Elwyn, Pa., September 20, 1920.

———. "Curious Records of an Old Church," *Proceedings of the Delaware County Historical Society,* Vol. 2 (1922), pp. 7–17.

Kuhn, Thomas B. *The Structure of Scientific Revolutions.* 2nd edition, Chicago: University of Chicago Press, 1970.

Layton, Edwin T., Jr. (ed). *Technology and Social Change in America.* New York: Harper & Row, 1973.

Leggett, M. D. *Subject-Matter Index of Patents for Inventions Issued by the United States Patent Office from 1790–1873 Inclusive.* 3 vols., Washington, D.C.: Government Printing Office, 1874.

Lemieux, Christine M. *Living to Die: Nineteenth Century Culture of Death and Dying in Delaware County, Pennsylvania.* Ph.D. Thesis, University of Pennsylvania, 1976.

Lemon, James T. *The Best Poor Man's Country: A Geographical Study of Early Southeastern Pennsylvania.* Baltimore: Johns Hopkins Press, 1972.

Lincoln, Jonathan T. "The Cotton Textile Machine Industry," *Harvard Business Review,* Vol. 11 (October 1932), pp. 88–96.

———. "The Cotton Textile Machine Industry—American Loom Builders," *Harvard Business Review,* Vol. 12 (October 1933), pp. 94–105.

Lipson, Dorothy Ann. *Freemasonry in Connecticut, 1789–1835.* Ph.D. Thesis, University of Connecticut, 1974.

Lynd, Staughton. *Intellectual Origins of American Radicalism.* New York: Random House, 1968.

Maass, John. *The Glorious Enterprise: The Centennial Exhibition of 1876 in Philadelphia, and H. J. Schwarzmann, Architect-in-Chief.* Watkins Glen, N.Y.: American Life Foundation, 1973.

MacMurray, Robert R. *Technological Change in the American Cotton Spinning Industry, 1790–1836.* Ph. D. Thesis, University of Pennsylvania, 1970.

McCadden, Joseph J. *Education in Pennsylvania 1801–1835 and Its Debt to Roberts Vaux.* Philadelphia: University of Pennsylvania Press, 1937.

McCarthy, Charles. "The Anti-masonic Party," in *Annual Report of the American Historical Association,* Vol. 1 (1902).

McCullough, David. *The Great Bridge.* New York: Simon & Schuster, 1972.

McDonough, John E. *Idyls of the Old South Ward.* Chester, Pa: Chester Times, 1932.

McGrane, Reginald C. *The Panic of 1837: Some Financial Problems of the Jacksonian Era.* Chicago: University of Chicago Press, 1924.

McLoughlin, William G. (ed.). *The American Evangelicals, 1800–1900.* New York: Harper & Row, 1968.

Malone, Dumas. *The Public Life of Thomas Cooper, 1783–1839.* New Haven, Conn.: Yale University Press, 1926.

Mann, Julia de L. "The Textile Industry: Machinery for Cotton, Flax, Wool, 1760–1850," in *A History of Technology,* Vol. 4, edited by Charles Singer, E. J. Holmyard, A. R. Hall, and Trevor I. Williams. Oxford: Clarendon Press, 1958.

Manross, William Wilson. *A History of the American Episcopal Church.* New York: Morehouse Publishing Co., 1935.

Mantoux, Paul. *The Industrial Revolution in the Eighteenth Century.* New York: Harper & Row, 1962.

Manufacturers' Mutual Fire Insurance Co. *The Factory Mutuals 1835–1935.* Providence, R.I., 1935.

Marx, Leo. *The Machine in the Garden: Technology and the Pastoral Ideal in America.* London: Oxford University Press, 1964.

Mautner, Nancy L. "Natural Knowledge and Social Reform: A Case Study of the Academy of Natural Sciences of Philadelphia and New Harmony in 1825." Unpublished MS, 1973.

Mayer, Gustav. *Friedrich Engels: A Biography.* New York: Alfred A. Knopf, 1936.

Merrill, Gilbert, Alfred K. Macormac, and G. Herbert R. Mauersberger. *American Cotton Handbook.* New York: Textile Book Publishers, 1941, 1949.

Meyer, D. H. *The Instructed Conscience: The Shaping of the American National Ethic.* Philadelphia: University of Pennsylvania Press, 1972.

Monroe, Will S. *History of the Pestalozzian Movement in the United States.* New York: Arno Press and The New York Times, 1969.

Montgomery, David. "The Shuttle and the Cross: Weavers and Artisans in the Kensington Riots of 1844." Pp. 44–74 in Stearns and Walkowitz, 1974 (originally published in the *Journal of Social Historey* 5 [1972], pp. 411–46.

Mueller, Henry R. *The Whig Party in Pennsylvania.* Ph.D. Thesis, Columbia University, 1922.

Myers, C. Maxwell. *The Rise of the Republican Party in Pennsylvania, 1854–1860.* Ph.D. Thesis, University of Pittsburgh, 1940.

Navin, Thomas R. *The Whitin Machine Works since 1831.* Cambridge: Harvard University Press, 1950.

——. "Innovation and Management Policies in the Textile Machinery Industry: Influence of the Market on Management," *Business History Review,* Vol. 25 (1951), pp. 15–30.

Newman, Albert Henry. *A History of the Baptist Churches in the United States.* Philadelphia: American Baptist Publication Society, 1898.

Nolan, J. Bennett. *Lafayette in America Day by Day.* Baltimore: Johns Hopkins Press, 1934.

Palmer, R. R. *The Age of the Democratic Revolution.* Princeton, N.J.: Princeton University Press, 1964.

——. *The Nineteenth Century World.* New York: Mentor Books, 1963.

Perkins, Alice J., and Theresa Wolfson. *Frances Wright, Free Enquirer.* New York and London: Harper & Brothers, 1939.

Pessen, Edward. "The Ideology of Stephen Simpson, Upper-class Champion of the Early Philadelphia Workingmen's Movement," *Pennsylvania History,* Vol. 22 (1955), pp. 328–40.

——. "The Workingmen's Movement of the Jacksonian Era," *Mississippi Valley Historical Review,* Vol. 43 (1956), pp. 428–43.

——. *Most Uncommon Jacksonians: The Radical Leaders of the Early Labor Movement.* New York: State University of New York Press, 1967.

——. *Jacksonian America: Society, Personality, and Politics.* Homewood, Ill.: The Dorsey Press, 1969.

Pettyjohn, Etta M. *Nineteenth Century Protestant Episcopal Schools in Pennsylvania.* Ph.D. Thesis, University of Pennsylvania, 1951.

Polanyi, Karl. *The Great Transformation.* New York: Farrar and Rinehart, 1944.

Porter, Glenn, and Harold C. Livesay. *Merchants and Manufacturers: Studies in the Changing Structures of Nineteenth Century Marketing.* Baltimore: Johns Hopkins Press, 1971.

Post, Albert. *Popular Freethought in America, 1825–1850.* New York: Octagon Books, 1974.

Pursell, Carroll W., Jr. *Early Stationary Steam Engines in America: A Study in the Migration of a Technology.* Washington, D.C.: Smithsonian Institute Press, 1969.

Rayback, Joseph G. "The American Workingman and the Antislavery Crusade," *Journal of Economic History,* Vol. 3 (1943), pp. 152–63.

Reynolds, Terry S. *Science and the Water Wheel: The Development and Diffusion of Theoretical and*

Experimental Doctrines Relating to the Vertical Water Wheel, c. 1500–c. 1850. Ph.D. Thesis, University of Kansas, 1973.

Rezneck, Samuel. "The Rise and Early Development of Industrial Consciousness in the United States, 1760–1830," *Journal of Economic and Business History,* Vol. 4 (1932), pp. 784–811.

————. "The Social History of an American Depression, 1837–1843," *American Historical Review,* Vol. 40 (1935), pp. 662–87.

Rice, Edwin W. *The Sunday-School Movement, 1780–1917, and the American Sunday-School Union, 1817–1917.* Philadelphia: American Sunday-School Union, 1917.

Rosenberg, Charles E. *The Cholera Years: The United States in 1832, 1849, and 1866.* Chicago: University of Chicago Press, 1962.

Rostow, Walt W. *The Stages of Economic Growth: A Non-Communist Manifesto.* 2nd edition, Cambridge: Cambridge University Press, 1971.

Rothman, David J. *The Discovery of the Asylum: Social Order and Disorder in the New Republic.* Boston and Toronto: Little, Brown, 1971.

Sachse, Julius F. *Old Masonic Lodges of Pennsylvania. "Moderns" and "Ancients" 1730–1800. Which have surrendered their warrants or affiliated with other grand lodges.* Philadelphia, 1912.

[Saco-Lowell Shops]. *A Chronicle of Textile Machinery, 1824–1924. Issued to commemorate the one hundredth anniversary of the Saco-Lowell Shops.* Boston, 1924.

Sandberg, Lars G. "American Rings and English Mules: The Role of Economic Rationality," in Saul (ed.), *Technological Change,* pp. 120–40.

Sandeen, Ernest R. *The Roots of Fundamentalism: British and American Millenarianism, 1800–1930.* Chicago: University of Chicago Press, 1971.

Saul, S. B. (ed.). *Technological Change: The United States and Britain in the Nineteenth Century.* London: Methuen, 1970.

Scharf, John T. *History of Delaware, 1609–1888.* 2 vols., Philadelphia: L. J. Richards, 1888.

———— and Thompson Westcott. *History of Philadelphia: 1609–1884.* Philadelphia: L. H. Everts, 1884.

Schlesinger, Arthur M., Jr. *The Age of Jackson.* Boston: Little, Brown, 1945.

Sellers, Charles Coleman. *The Artist of the Revolution: The Early Life of Charles Willson Peale.* Hebron, Conn.: Feather and Good, 1939.

————. *Charles Willson Peale: Later Life.* Vol. 2 (1790–1827). Philadelphia: American Philosophical Society, 1947.

Selsam, J. Paul. *The Pennsylvania Constitution of 1776: A Study in Revolutionary Democracy.* New York: Octagon Books, 1971.

Sinclair, Bruce. "At the Turn of a Screw: William Sellers, the Franklin Institute and a Standard American Thread," *Technology and Culture,* Vol. 10 (1969), pp. 20–34.

————. *Philadelphia's Philosopher Mechanics.* Baltimore: Johns Hopkins Press, 1974.

Singer, Charles, E. J. Holmyard, A. R. Hall, and Trevor I. Williams (eds.). *A History of Technology.* Vols. 4 and 5, Oxford: Clarendon Press, 1958.

Smelser, Neil J. *Social Change in the Industrial Revolution.* Chicago: University of Chicago Press, 1959.

Smith, Sarah Trainer. *Sketch of Mary Brackett Willcox of Ivy Mills, Pa., 1796–1866.* Privately printed, 1897.

Smith, Timothy L. *Revivalism and Social Reform in Mid-Nineteenth Century America.* New York: Abingdon Press, 1957.

Smith, Walter B., and Arthur H. Cole. *Fluctuations in American Business, 1790–1860.* Cambridge: Harvard University Press, 1935.

Snyder, Charles McCool. *The Jacksonian Heritage: Pennsylvania Politics, 1833–1848.* Harrisburg, Pa.: Pennsylvania Historical and Museum Commission, 1958.

Staudenraus, P. J. *The African Colonization Movement 1816–1865.* New York: Columbia University Press, 1961.

Stauffer, Vernon. "New England and the Bavarian Illuminati," *Studies in History, Economics, and Public Law,* Vol. 82, No. 1. New York: Columbia University Press, 1918.

Stearns, Peter N., and Daniel J. Walkowitz (eds.). *Workers in the Industrial Revolution: Recent Studies of Labor in the United States and Europe.* Edison, N.J.: Transaction Books, 1974.

Sullivan, William A. "The Industrial Revolution and the Factory Operative in Pennsylvania," *Pennsylvania Magazine of History and Biography,* Vol. 78 (1954), pp. 476–94.

_____. *The Industrial Worker in Pennsylvania, 1800–1840.* Harrisburg, Pa.: Pennsylvania Historical and Museum Commission, 1955.

Swank, Scott T. *The Unfettered Conscience: A Study of Sectarianism, Spiritualism and Social Reform in the New Jerusalem Church, 1840–1870.* Ph.D. Thesis, University of Pennsylvania, 1970.

Tann, Jennifer. "The Textile Millwright in the Early Industrial Revolution," *Textile History,* Vol. 5 (Oct. 1974), pp. 80–9.

Taussig, Frank W. *Tariff History of the United States.* New York, 1892.

Thernstrom, Stephan, and Richard Sennett (eds.). *Nineteenth-Century Cities: Essays in the New Urban History.* New Haven, Conn.: Yale University Press, 1969.

Tiffany, Charles C. *A History of the Protestant Episcopal Church in the United States . . .* New York, 1895.

Tinkcom, Harry Marlin. *The Republicans and Federalists in Pennsylvania, 1790–1801: A Study in National Stimulus and Local Response.* Harrisburg, Pa.: Pennsylvania Historical and Museum Commission, 1950.

Tryon, R. M. *Household Manufactures in the United States: 1640–1860.* Chicago: University of Chicago Press, 1917.

Tuveson, Ernest Lee. *Redeemer Nation: The Idea of America's Millennial Role.* Chicago: University of Chicago Press, 1968.

[Upland Centennial]. *History of Upland, 1683–1969, on the One Hundredth Anniversary of the Borough Incorporation.*

Usher, A. P. *History of Mechanical Invention.* New York: McGraw-Hill Book Co., 1929.

Vedder, Henry G. *A History of the Baptists in the Middle States.* Philadelphia: American Baptist Publishing Society, 1898.

Walker, Joseph E. *Hopewell Village: A Social and Economic History of an Iron-Making Community.* Philadelphia: University of Pennsylvania Press, 1966.

Wallace, Anthony F. C. *The Death and Rebirth of the Seneca.* New York: Alfred A. Knopf, 1970.

_____. "Revitalization Movements," *American Anthropologist,* Vol. 58 (1956), pp. 264–81.

_____. *Culture and Personality.* New York: Random House, 1970.

_____. "Paradigmatic Processes in Culture Change," *American Anthropologist,* Vol. 74 (1972), pp. 467–78.

Wallace, David H. *John Rogers: The People's Sculptor.* Middletown, Conn.: Wesleyan University Press, 1967.

Wallace, Paul A. W. *Pennsylvania: Seed of a Nation.* New York: Harper & Row, 1967.

Ware, Norman. *The Industrial Worker, 1840–1860.* Boston: Houghton Mifflin, 1924.

Waterman, W. R. *Frances Wright.* Ph.D. Thesis, Columbia University, 1924.

Watson, John R. *Annals of Philadelphia and Pennsylvania, in the Olden Time.* 3 vols., Philadelphia: Stuart, 1898.

Watt, Bernice K., and Annabel L. Merrill. *Composition of Foods: Raw, Processed, Prepared.* Washington, D.C.: U.S. Department of Agriculture, 1963.

Wickersham, James P. *History of Education in Pennsylvania.* Lancaster, Pa.: Inquirer Publishing Co., 1886.

Wilkinson, Norman B. "The Education of Alfred Victor du Pont, Nineteenth Century Industrialist," *Pennsylvania History,* Vol. 28 (1961), pp. 105–20.

———. "Brandywine Borrowings from European Technology," *Technology and Culture,* Vol. 4 (1963), pp. 1–13.

Zyckowski, Stanley S. *The Antimasonic Party in Pennsylvania.* M.A. Thesis, Pennsylvania State University, 1937.

Index

A NOTE ABOUT THE AUTHOR

Anthony Wallace was born in Toronto, Canada, in 1923 and did both his undergraduate and graduate work at the University of Pennsylvania (Ph.D. 1950). He has been a Professor of Anthropology at the University of Pennsylvania since 1961. Mr. Wallace also serves as a Medical Research Scientist at the Eastern Pennsylvania Psychiatric Institute. He has written four books, King of the Delawares: Teedyuscung *(1949),* Culture and Personality *(1961),* Religion: An Anthropological View *(1966), and* The Death and Rebirth of the Seneca *(1970). He lives near Philadelphia with his wife and children.*

A NOTE ON THE TYPE

The text of this book was set, via computer-driven cathode-ray tube, in a film version of Garamond, a modern rendering of the type first cut by Claude Garamond (1510–1561). Garamond was a pupil of Geoffroy Tory and is believed to have based his letters on the Venetian models, although he introduced a number of important differences, and it is to him we owe the letter which we know as old-style. He gave to his letters a certain elegance and a feeling of movement that won for their creator an immediate reputation and the patronage of Francis I of France.

COMPOSED, PRINTED, AND BOUND
BY THE HADDON CRAFTSMEN, INC.,
SCRANTON, PENNSYLVANIA
DESIGNED BY GWEN TOWNSEND